THE CAMBRIDGE HISTORY OF LATIN AMERICA

VOLUME VI

Latin America since 1930:
Economy, society and politics

THE CAMBRIDGE HISTORY OF LATIN AMERICA

VOLUME I *Colonial Latin America*

VOLUME II *Colonial Latin America*

VOLUME III *From Independence to c. 1870*

VOLUME IV *c. 1870 to 1930*

VOLUME V *c. 1870 to 1930*

VOLUME VI *Latin America since 1930: Economy, society and politics*

VOLUME VII *Latin America since 1930: Mexico, Central America and the Caribbean*

VOLUME VIII *Latin America since 1930: Spanish South America*

VOLUME IX *Latin America since 1930: Brazil; International relations*

VOLUME X *Latin America since 1930: Ideas, culture and society*

VOLUME XI *Bibliographical essays*

THE CAMBRIDGE HISTORY OF LATIN AMERICA

VOLUME VI

Latin America since 1930
Economy, Society and Politics

Part 1 Economy and Society

---

edited by

LESLIE BETHELL

Emeritus Professor of Latin American History
University of London
and
Senior Research Fellow
St. Antony's College, Oxford

Published by the Press Syndicate of the University of Cambridge
The Pitt Building, Trumpington Street, Cambridge CB2 1RP
40 West 20th Street, New York, NY 10011-4211, USA
10 Stamford Road, Oakleigh, Melbourne 3166, Australia

First published 1994

Printed in the United States of America

Library of Congress Cataloging-in-Publication Data

Latin America since 1930. Economy, society and politics / edited by Leslie Bethell.

p. cm. – (The Cambridge history of Latin America ; v. 6)

Contents: pt. 1. Economy and society – pt. 2. Politics and society.

Includes bibliographical references and index.

ISBN 0-521-23226-0 (v. 1). – ISBN 0-521-46556-7 (v. 2)

1. Latin America – Politics and government – 20th century. 2. Latin America – Economic conditions. 3. Latin America – Social conditions. I. Bethell, Leslie. II. Series.

F1410.C1834 1984 vol. 6
[F1414]

980–dc20 93-30600
CIP

A catalog record for this book is available from the British Library.

ISBN 0-521-23226-0 hardback

CONTENTS

PART THREE. ECONOMY AND SOCIETY

PART FOUR. ECONOMIC IDEAS

PART FIVE. SCIENCE AND SOCIETY

GENERAL PREFACE

Since *The Cambridge Modern History,* edited by Lord Acton, appeared in sixteen volumes between 1902 and 1912 multi-volume Cambridge Histories, planned and edited by historians of established reputation, with individual chapters written by leading specialists in their fields, have set the highest standards of collaborative international scholarship. *The Cambridge Modern History* was followed by *The Cambridge Ancient History, The Cambridge Medieval History* and others. The *Modern History* has been replaced by *The New Cambridge Modern History* in fourteen volumes. *The Cambridge Economic History of Europe* and Cambridge Histories of Iran, of Southeast Asia and of Africa have been published; in progress are Histories of China, of Japan, of India and of Latin America.

Cambridge University Press decided the time was ripe to embark on a Cambridge History of Latin America early in the 1970s. Since the Second World War and particularly since 1960 research and writing on Latin American history had been developing, and have continued to develop, at an unprecedented rate – in the United States (by American historians in particular, but also by British, European and Latin American historians resident in the United States), in Britain and continental Europe, and increasingly in Latin America itself (where a new generation of young professional historians, many of them trained in the United States, Britain or continental Europe, had begun to emerge). Perspectives had changed as political, economic and social realities in Latin America – and Latin America's role in the world – had changed. Methodological innovations and new conceptual models drawn from the social sciences (economics, political science, historical demography, sociology, anthropology) as well as from other fields of historical research were increasingly being adopted by historians of Latin America. The Latin American Studies monograph series and the *Journal of Latin American Studies* had already been established by the Press and were beginning to publish the results of this new historical thinking and research.

Dr. Leslie Bethell, then Reader in Hispanic American and Brazilian History at University College London, accepted an invitation to edit *The Cambridge History of Latin America.* He was given responsibility for the planning, co-ordination and editing of the entire History and began work on the project in the late 1970s.

The Cambridge History of Latin America, to be published in ten volumes, is the first large-scale, authoritative survey of Latin America's unique historical experience during the five centuries since the first contacts between the native American Indians and Europeans (and the beginnings of the African slave trade) in the late fifteenth and early sixteenth centuries. (The Press will publish separately a three-volume Cambridge History of the Native Peoples of the Americas – North, Middle and South – which will give proper consideration to the evolution of the region's peoples, societies and civilizations, in isolation from the rest of the world, during the several millennia before the arrival of the Europeans, as well as a fuller treatment than will be found here of the history of the indigenous peoples of Latin America under European colonial rule and during the national period to the present day.) Latin America is taken to comprise the predominantly Spanish- and Portuguese-speaking areas of continental America south of the United States – Mexico, Central America and South America – together with the Spanish-speaking Caribbean – Cuba, Puerto Rico, the Dominican Republic – and, by convention, Haiti. (The vast territories in North America lost to the United States by treaty and by war, first by Spain, then by Mexico, during the first half of the nineteenth century are for the most part excluded. Neither the British, French and Dutch Caribbean islands nor the Guianas are included, even though Jamaica and Trinidad, for example, have early Hispanic antecedents and are now members of the Organization of American States.) The aim is to produce a high-level synthesis of existing knowledge which will provide historians of Latin America with a solid base for future research, which students of Latin American history will find useful and which will be of interest to historians of other areas of the world. It is also hoped that the *History* will contribute more generally to a deeper understanding of Latin America through its history in the United States, Europe and elsewhere and, not least, to a greater awareness of its own history in Latin America.

The volumes of *The Cambridge History of Latin America* have been published in chronological order: Volumes I and II (Colonial Latin America, with an introductory section on the native American peoples and civilizations on the eve of the European invasion) were published in 1984; Volume III (From Independence to *c.* 1870) in 1985; Volumes IV and V (*c.* 1870 to 1930) in 1986. The publication of volumes VI–X (1930 to the present) began in 1990. Each volume or set of volumes examines a period in the economic, social, political, intellectual and cultural history of Latin America. While recognizing the decisive impact on Latin America of external forces, of developments within the world system, and the fundamental importance of its economic, political and cultural ties first with Spain and Portugal, then with Britain, France and Germany and finally with the United States, *The Cambridge History of Latin America* emphasizes the evolution of internal structures. Furthermore, the emphasis is clearly on the modern period, that is to say, the period since the establishment of all but two (Cuba and Panama) of the independent Latin American states during the first decades of the nineteenth century. The eight volumes of the *History* devoted to the nineteenth and twentieth centuries consist of a mixture of general, comparative chapters built around major themes in Latin American history and chapters on the individual histories of the twenty independent Latin American countries (plus Puerto Rico).

An important feature of the *History* is the bibliographical essays which accompany each chapter. These give special emphasis to books and articles published during the past thirty years, and particularly since the publication of Charles C. Griffin (ed.), *Latin America: A Guide to the Historical Literature* (published for the Conference on Latin American History by the University of Texas Press in 1971). (Griffin's *Guide* was prepared between 1962 and 1969 and included few works published after 1966.) The essays from Volumes I – X of *The Cambridge History of Latin America* – revised, expanded and updated (to *c.* 1992) – are brought together in a single bibliographical volume, Volume XI, published in 1994.

PREFACE TO VOLUME VI

Volumes I and II of *The Cambridge History of Latin America* began with a survey of native American peoples and civilizations on the eve of the European 'discovery', conquest and settlement of the 'New World' in the late fifteenth and early sixteenth centuries, but were largely devoted to the economic, social, political, intellectual and cultural history of Latin America under Spanish and (in the case of Brazil) Portuguese colonial rule during the sixteenth, seventeenth and eighteenth centuries. Volume III examined the breakdown and overthrow of colonial rule throughout Latin America (except Cuba and Puerto Rico) at the beginning of the nineteenth century and the economic, social and political history of the independent Spanish American republics and the independent Empire of Brazil during the half century from *c.* 1820 to *c.* 1870/80. Volumes IV and V concentrated on the half century from *c.* 1870/80 to 1930. This was for most of Latin America a 'Golden Age' of predominantly export-led economic growth, as the region became more fully incorporated into the expanding international economy; material prosperity (at least for the dominant classes); significant social change, both rural and urban; political stability (with some notable exceptions, such as Mexico during the revolution); ideological consensus (at least until the 1920s); and notable achievements in intellectual and cultural life.

Volumes VI to X of *The Cambridge History of Latin America* are devoted to Latin America during the six decades from 1930 to *c.* 1990. Volume VI brings together general essays on major themes in economic, social and political history. Volume VII (already published) is a history of Mexico, Central America and the Caribbean, Volume VIII (also published) a history of the nine republics of Spanish South America, Volume IX (in progress) a history of Brazil and of Latin America's international relations (predominantly relations with Europe and the United States). Volume X (in press) is concerned with ideas, culture and society in Latin America in the twentieth century.

The Cambridge History of Latin America Volume VI, *Latin America since 1930: Economy, Society and Politics* is published in two parts. Part 1 *Economy and Society* includes chapters on demographic change (Latin America's population increased fourfold, from 110 to 450 million, during the period 1930–90); the Latin American economies – during the 1930s in the aftermath of the 1929 Depression, during and immediately after the Second World War, and during another 'Golden Age' of economic growth (1950–80), this time largely driven by ISI (import substitution industrialization), which was followed, however, by the so-called 'lost decade' of the 1980s; rapid urbanization (less than 20 percent of Latin America's population was classified as urban in 1930, almost 70 per cent in 1990) and urban social change, mainly in Argentina, Brazil, Colombia, Chile, Mexico and Peru; the transformation of agrarian structures; economic ideas and ideologies (Latin America made a major contribution to development theory in this period); and, finally, the growth and institutionalization of science and the relationship between science and society in twentieth century Latin America.

Volume VI Part 2 *Politics and Society* consists of chapters on the development of state organization from 1930 (concluding with the beginnings of 'state shrinking' in the 1980s); the advance of (as well as the setbacks suffered by) democracy in Latin America, mainly in Chile, Costa Rica, Colombia, Uruguay and Venezuela and, to a lesser extent, in Argentina, Brazil and Peru; the successes and failures of the Latin American left, both democratic and non-democratic; the military in Latin American politics: military interventions and coups, military regimes, and problems of transition to civilian rule; the urban working class and the urban labour movement, with the emphasis on its role in politics; rural mobilizations and rural violence, especially in Mexico, Central America and the Andes; changes in the role of women in the economy, society and politics of Latin America in the twentieth century; and, finally, the history of both the Catholic church, a major force in political as well as religious and social life throughout the region, and the rapidly growing Protestant churches.

This most problematical of volumes in *The Cambridge History of Latin America* – on the economic, social and political history of the region as a whole during the period from 1930 to the present – has been a long time in the writing and editing. Some chapters were commissioned a decade and a half ago. Those authors who met their original deadlines – and I am thinking in particular of Joseph Love and Thomas Merrick – have had to wait more than a decade for their work to be published. This is an unacceptably long time by any standards and I am grateful for their patience. Some authors dropped out along the way; others were dropped; one, Carlos Díaz-Alejandro, sadly died. All had to be replaced. Some authors – for example, Gabriel Palma – joined those (in this case Ricardo Ffrench-Davis and Oscar Muñoz) who had already been working on their chapters for some time. Guillermo de la Peña was persuaded to write a separate chapter on rural mobilizations which had originally been part of the chapter on agrarian structures. Arturo Valenzuela and Jonathan Hartlyn accepted an invitation to write the chapter on democracy in Latin America when the rest of the volume was already well advanced. Many of these chapters were at various times over the years extensively revised and rewritten – in some cases more than once. In the end all contributors were obliged – and here delay in publication has perhaps had some benefits – to take account of the important changes that occurred in Latin America in the 1980s.

A conference at the University of California, San Diego in February/March 1986 organized by Paul Drake, then Director of the Center for Iberian and Latin American Studies (and a contributor to Volume VIII of the *History*), and myself offered an early opportunity for a number of contributors to present preliminary drafts of their chapters to each other and to a group of distinguished non-contributors. The conference was generously funded by the Tinker Foundation. Two workshops were also held at the Institute of Latin American Studies of the University of London – in 1990 and 1991 – during my term as Director of the Institute, with financial support from the Institute and from Cambridge University Press.

Many of the contributors to this volume – eight Latin American (one resident in the United States, one in the United Kingdom), seven British (two resident in the United States), six North American (one resident in France) and one French – commented on the chapters of their colleagues. I am especially grateful in this respect to Alan Angell, Victor Bulmer-Thomas, Ian Roxborough and Laurence Whitehead. James Dunkerley, who served as an associate editor on Volumes VII and VIII of the *History*, offered support and encouragement at various key stages in the editing of Volume VI. Christopher Abel, besides generously agreeing to help in the editing of Enrique Dussel's chapter on the Catholic church, contributed the bibliographical essay which accompanies that chapter. Stephen Suffern took on the task of reviewing and revising a less than satisfactory translation from the French of Alain Rouquié's chapter on the military in Latin American politics and added a final section on demilitarization in the 1980s. Varun Sahni contributed the bibliographical essay on the Latin American military.

Tom Passananti and Tim Girven, graduate students in Latin American history at the University of Chicago and the University of London respectively, were research assistants in the final stages of the editing of this volume during 1993. Secretarial assistance was provided by Hazel Aitken at the Institute of Latin American Studies, University of London (in the period 1987–92) and Linnea Cameron at the Department of History, University of Chicago (in 1992–93).

Part One

POPULATION

1

THE POPULATION OF LATIN AMERICA, 1930–1990

In the sixty years from 1930 to 1990 the population of Latin America more than quadrupled – from approximately 110 million to almost 450 million. Population growth was higher in Latin America than in any other region of the world except, marginally, Africa (see Table 1.1). Though average population density in Latin America remained low in comparison with other areas, this was misleading because of the way in which population was distributed. The bulk of population increase after 1930 occurred in cities. While export-led economic growth in the period 1870–1930 had stimulated the growth of a few cities, principally ports and administrative centres, Latin America was still in 1930 predominantly rural. About 17 per cent of the population resided in cities with 20,000 or more people. During the following half century city populations increased more than tenfold, accounting for two-thirds of total population growth. Internal migration (fed by a high natural increase in the population of rural areas) was responsible for most of the difference between rural and urban population growth and was a major demographic feature of the inward reorientation of the region's economy, which experienced a decline in the share of agriculture and an increase in the share of urban based manufacturing and service activities in total production and employment.

Population trends after 1930 contrasted in several important respects with those of the period before 1930. Immigration had had a significant impact on population increase between 1870 and 1930, although it was concentrated in a few areas: Argentina, southern Brazil, Chile, Cuba and Uruguay. Population growth rates elsewhere were generally lower. After 1930, growth rates accelerated in most countries of the region as a result of higher rates of natural increase. Even before the Second World War, mortality was declining in response to improved living standards and health interventions. Declines came earliest in countries which had experi-

Table 1.1. *Population of the world's main regions, 1930–90*

	1930	1990[a]	1990/1930
World	2,008	5,292	2.64
Latin America[b]	110	448	4.07
North America	134	276	2.06
Europe[c]	540	813	1.51
Africa	155	642	4.14
Asia	1,069	3,113	2.91

Notes: [a] 1990 estimates based on United Nation's assumed growth rates during 1980s.
[b] Latin America includes the Caribbean.
[c] Europe here includes U.S.S.R. and Oceania.
Sources: 1930: United Nations, *The Determinants and Consequences of Population Trends* (New York, 1953) table 2; 1990: United Nations, *World Population Prospects 1990* (New York, 1991) table 31.

enced large immigration flows before 1930. After the Second World War, mortality decline spread quickly to most of the region, so that by the late 1950s death rates were less than half of what they had been before 1930. At the same time, birth rates remained high except in countries that had experienced immigration; in Argentina, Uruguay, Cuba, Chile, and southern Brazil birth rates were already declining by 1950. It was the mid-1960s before fertility decline spread to other countries, and rates were still high in some Central American countries and the Caribbean even in the early 1980s.

The surge in population that resulted from the lag between declines in birth and death rates raises a number of questions about the interrelationship between population and socio-economic change. Theories about fertility and mortality declines based on the demographic transition in Europe link those declines to social, economic and cultural factors, particularly urbanization and increased education. In Latin America and other developing regions, public health interventions accelerated mortality decline at a comparatively early stage of social and economic change, raising the issue of whether interventions to reduce birth rates would be needed to bring birth and death rates back into balance. In the neo-Malthusian view of the question, such interventions are required for countries to escape from a situation in which rapid population growth has an adverse impact on the achievement of levels of social and economic development needed to trigger fertility decline. Both the rapidity of population increase and the youthful age structure associated with high birth rates figure heavily in the neo-Malthusian assessment of the effects of rapid population growth on economic and social development.

The issues of the adverse effect of population growth on economic development and the measures required to bring about fertility decline have been highly controversial in Latin America. Though a number of Latin American governments have established publicly supported family planning programmes or have adopted permissive policies relating to the activities of international family planning agencies, few have accepted the logic of population control as the basis of those actions. Critics of the neo-Malthusian perspective argue that many of the problems attributed to population growth are really manifestations of the particular social and economic structure that Latin America inherited from its history of political and economic colonialism, exacerbated by the import substituting industrialization strategy of the period after 1950. Much of the emphasis of their critique is on the unequal distribution of wealth and income associated with that structure. Once birth rates started to decline, the debate expanded to the question of the relative roles of family planning interventions and socio-economic change in triggering the decline.

Whatever the balance of the argument on the social and economic causes and consequences of high birth and low death rates, their demographic impact is manifest, particularly in the youthful age structure of the region. During the 1930s about 4.5 million children were born annually in Latin America. By the 1970s, this number had doubled. Besides its immediate impact on resource needs in education, there were two important longer term effects of the increased size of younger age cohorts. One was increased fertility; while birth *rates* declined in the 1970s and 1980s, the number of births continued to increase, because the number of women in early childbearing ages continued to increase as an echo of the high birth rates of earlier decades. Demographic change is a slow process. Another effect was the growing demand for jobs. The ages at which individuals typically seek their first regular job, start a family, need additional housing units, and so on, are those of young adulthood (ages fifteen to twenty-four). In 1950, there were about 17 million people in these age categories. By 1975, this number had increased to 31 million, and by 1990 to an estimated 36 million. (Fifteen to twenty-four year-olds in 1990 were born between 1965 and 1975.)

Employment was one of the key economic and demographic issues facing Latin America in the 1980s. One manifestation of the problem was the increased flow of international migration within the western hemisphere. The growing imbalance between the supply and demand for jobs within national economies contributed to an increased internationalization of labour markets in the region.

The remainder of this chapter is dedicated to more detailed discussion of the questions raised here. It begins with an overview of population growth trends, followed by consideration of the components of population growth: fertility and mortality, and their determinants. Several key population characteristics are then examined (nuptiality, rural-urban residence, ethnicity, educational attainment, labour force participation), before returning to the issue of the relationship between population change and socio-economic development in the region.

DEMOGRAPHIC TRENDS

The 1930s closed an era during which immigration contributed most to Latin American population growth and ushered in a period of rising natural increase, which accelerated sharply after the Second World War. From 107 million in 1930, the population of Latin America (including the Caribbean) grew to 166 million in 1950, then surged to 448 million in 1990 (Table 1.2). The average annual population growth rate, which had been 2.17 per cent during 1930s and 1940s, jumped sharply to 2.72 per cent between 1950 and 1970 and then declined moderately to 2.25 per cent a year between 1970 and 1990.

Growth rates (also shown in Table 1.2) in eleven of the region's twenty countries followed this overall pattern (increase, followed by decrease in growth rates). In four countries (Argentina, Cuba, Panama and Uruguay) as well as in the Caribbean, growth rates declined from 1930–50 to 1950–70, while rates continued to rise from 1950–70 to 1970–90 in five others: Bolivia, Haiti, Honduras, Nicaragua and Paraguay. Even in countries where growth rates declined after 1970, their levels remained high: more than 3 per cent a year in Venezuela, for example.

Variation in growth rates had little effect on the rank ordering of Latin American countries by population size. The five largest in 1930 were Brazil, Mexico, Argentina, Colombia and Peru. This order was virtually the same in 1990, except that Colombia had narrowly overtaken Argentina in third place from 1970. The greatest absolute increase between

Table 1.2. *Latin America: total population and population growth rates by country, 1930–90*

	In thousands				Average annual growth rate		
	1930	1950	1970	1990[a]	1930–50	1950–70	1970–90
Total	107,408	165,880	285,695	448,076	2.17	2.72	2.25
Argentina	11,896	17,150	23,962	32,322	1.83	1.67	1.50
Bolivia	2,153	2,766	4,325	7,314	1.25	2.24	2.63
Brazil	33,568	53,444	95,847	150,368	2.33	2.92	2.25
Chile	4,424	6,082	9,504	13,173	1.59	2.23	1.63
Colombia	7,350	11,946	21,360	32,978	2.43	2.91	2.17
Costa Rica	499	862	1,731	3,015	2.73	3.49	2.77
Cuba	3,837	5,850	8,520	10,608	2.11	1.88	1.10
Dominican Republic	1,400	2,353	4,423	7,170	2.60	3.16	2.42
Ecuador	2,160	3,310	6,051	10,587	2.13	3.02	2.80
El Salvador	1,443	1,940	3,588	5,252	1.48	3.07	1.91
Guatemala	1,771	2,969	5,246	9,197	2.58	2.85	2.81
Haiti	2,422	3,261	4,535	6,513	1.49	1.65	1.81
Honduras	948	1,401	2,627	5,138	1.95	3.14	3.35
Mexico	16,589	28,012	52,771	88,598	2.62	3.17	2.59
Nicaragua	742	1,098	2,053	3,871	1.96	3.13	3.17
Panama	502	893	1,531	2,418	2.88	2.70	2.29
Paraguay	880	1,351	2,351	4,277	2.14	2.77	2.99
Peru	5,651	7,632	13,193	21,550	1.50	2.74	2.45
Uruguay	1,704	2,239	2,808	3,094	1.37	1.13	0.48
Venezuela	2,950	5,009	10,604	19,735	2.65	3.75	3.11
Others[b]	4,519	6,312	8,665	10,898	1.67	1.58	1.15

Notes: [a] 1990 estimates are based on the United Nations' assumed growth rates during 1980s and may vary from 1990 census figures.
b Includes English, French and Dutch-speaking Caribbean countries and territories not listed individually in table.
Sources: 1930: CELADE, *Boletín Demográfico,* No. 13, 1974. table 1; 1950–90: United Nations, *World Population Prospects 1990* (New York, 1991), table 31.

1930 and 1990, nearly 117 million, came in Brazil because of its large population base. Mexico, Costa Rica, and the Dominican Republic led in relative growth, with five- to sixfold expansions in population size since 1930.

Declines in death rates that brought the acceleration of population increase were already under way in some countries during the 1930s, but in most they came after the Second World War. Table 1.3 presents crude birth and death rates for four benchmark periods, beginning with the early 1930s and ending in the early 1980s. Death rates were already comparatively low during the 1930s in Argentina, Cuba, Uruguay, and Panama. For the rest of the region, death rates remained in the twenty to thirty per thousand range until after the Second World War. Some decline is suggested in the years immediately after the war by data for 1945–9, but the big declines came between then and the early 1960s. Data for 1960–5 show that death rates fell during that interval to the low teens or lower in ten more countries (Brazil, Chile, Colombia, Costa Rica, the Dominican Republic, Ecuador, El Salvador, Mexico, Paraguay and Venezuela). Countries that lagged behind were Bolivia and Peru in South America as well Haiti and the republics of Central America. By the 1980s, only Bolivia and Haiti had crude death rates that were substantially above ten per thousand.

Generally, birth rates remained very high until the 1960s. In most countries, rates then ranged upwards from forty-five per thousand. There is evidence that birth rates actually increased in several countries between the 1930s and the 1950s, a trend reinforced by increased marriage rates and declining mortality. With death rates in the low teens, this produced rates of population growth that exceeded 3 per cent a year. Again, the exceptions were Argentina, Cuba and Uruguay, which already had relatively low birth rates by 1950, and Chile and Panama, whose rates were below the regional average during the 1950s, though apparently were not declining. Cuba is another exception, because its birth rate increased from 1945–9 to 1960–5. Several other countries also had increasing birth rates during the 1950s, probably an effect of declining mortality on their age structures. However, Cuba's increase from thirty to thirty-five per thousand has been interpreted as a post-revolution 'baby boom'.[1]

After 1960, birth rates started to decline in a number of Latin American countries. Cuba led, with an nineteen-point decline in the crude rate (from thirty-five to sixteen per thousand) between the early 1960s and the early 1980s. Chile and Costa Rica also experienced early declines during the 1960s. By the late 1960s declines were occurring in Brazil, Colombia, Panama and Venezuela, with the Dominican Republic, Ecuador, Mexico,

[1] Sergio Díaz-Briquets and Lisandro Pérez, 'Cuba: the demography of revolution', *Population Bulletin*, 36, 1 (Washington, D.C., 1981).

Table 1.3. *Latin America: Crude birth (CB) and death (DR) rates for selected five-year intervals, 1930–85*

	(Births, deaths per 1000 population)							
	1930–5		1945–9		1960–5		1980–5	
	BR	DR	BR	DR	BR	DR	BR	DR
Argentina	28.9	11.6	25.2	9.6	23.2	8.8	23.0	8.7
Bolivia	–	–	*47.1	24.1	46.1	21.5	44.0	15.9
Brazil	–	–	*44.6	15.1	42.1	12.3	30.6	8.4
Chile	40.2	24.5	37.0	17.5	31.6	12.1	24.2	6.3
Colombia	43.3	22.5	43.4	20.8	41.6	11.5	29.2	6.3
Costa Rica	44.6	21.5	42.7	13.2	45.3	9.2	30.2	4.1
Cuba	31.3	13.3	30.0	8.7	35.1	8.9	16.0	6.3
Dominican Republic	–	–	*50.5	20.3	49.4	14.8	33.6	7.5
Ecuador	48.5	25.7	45.9	20.0	45.6	14.3	35.4	8.0
El Salvador	46.5	32.7	44.8	22.8	47.8	14.8	38.0	11.1
Guatemala	46.2	31.7	49.1	26.5	47.8	18.3	42.3	10.5
Haiti	–	–	*43.5	27.5	41.9	22.2	36.6	14.5
Honduras	42.0	21.7	44.5	10.0	51.2	18.1	42.3	9.0
Mexico	44.1	26.7	44.5	17.8	45.5	11.3	31.7	6.3
Nicaragua	–	–	*54.1	22.7	50.3	17.1	44.2	9.7
Panama	37.4	15.1	38.3	10.8	40.8	9.6	28.0	5.4
Paraguay	–	–	*47.3	9.3	42.3	8.1	35.8	6.7
Peru	–	–	*47.1	21.6	46.3	17.6	34.2	10.5
Uruguay	22.3	11.6	19.7	9.1	21.9	9.6	18.3	10.0
Venezuela	39.9	21.9	43.6	16.1	44.2	9.1	33.0	5.5

Sources: 1930–35: Andrew Collver, *Birth Rates in Latin America* (Berkeley, Cal., 1965); 1945–49 from Collver, except for countries with (*), these are from United Nations, *World Population Prospects 1990*, (New York, 1991); figures for 1950–5, 1960–65 and 1980–85 also from United Nations, *World Population Prospects 1990*.

Paraguay and Peru following suit during the 1970s. A few countries that lagged in mortality decline (Bolivia, Haiti and much of Central America) also had lesser declines in birth rates.

In addition to generating very high rates of population growth, a major demographic impact of Latin America's high birth rates was its youthful age structure. Demographic theory tells us that the age structure of a population bears the imprint of the demographic forces that drive its growth. This is borne out in age data for Latin America, which are summarized in Table 1.4. In 1960 the proportion of population under the age of fifteen was 40 per cent or more in all Latin American countries

Table 1.4. *Population under age 15 and age-dependency ratio: 1960 and 1985*

	Per cent of population under age 15		Age-dependency Ratio* (per cent)	
	1960	1985	1960	1985
TOTAL	42.5	37.6	85.3	72.7
Argentina	30.8	30.5	57.0	64.1
Bolivia	42.9	43.8	85.3	88.5
Brazil	43.6	36.4	86.9	68.7
Chile	39.4	31.5	79.0	59.5
Colombia	46.4	37.8	98.4	71.4
Costa Rica	47.4	36.8	102.4	68.7
Cuba	34.2	26.2	64.8	52.7
Dominican Republic	46.7	39.7	98.8	75.2
Ecuador	44.8	41.4	95.4	82.2
El Salvador	45.5	46.0	92.5	97.7
Guatemala	46.0	45.9	94.9	95.5
Haiti	39.4	40.5	80.0	80.9
Honduras	45.1	46.3	90.3	98.5
Mexico	45.4	40.9	94.8	80.2
Nicaragua	47.9	46.8	101.3	97.1
Panama	43.5	37.6	90.5	72.5
Paraguay	47.6	41.0	103.9	80.1
Peru	43.3	39.9	87.8	76.9
Uruguay	27.9	26.8	56.2	60.7
Venezuela	46.1	39.5	94.4	75.1

Note: *Sum of the population under 15 and over 64 divided by the population aged 15–64.
Source: United Nations, *World Population Prospects 1990*, (New York, 1991), country tables.

except Argentina, Cuba and Uruguay, and over 45 per cent in areas with higher birth rates – Mexico and Central America, for example. Declining birth rates reduced this proportion, in some cases very substantially. In Costa Rica, the per cent under the age of fifteen dropped from 47 per cent in the 1960 to 37 per cent in 1985.

Age structure is one of the principal ties between demographic processes and socio-economic changes. One measure of the potential economic and social impact of age structure is the age-dependency ratio, which is a rough approximation of the ratio of consumers in an economy (those under the age of fifteen and aged sixty-five and over) to those who both produce and consume (individuals in ages between fifteen and sixty-five), usually expressed in percentage terms. In theories about the effect of rapid population growth on economic development, a high dependency ratio is viewed as a threat to economic growth because it drains resources away from productive investment and puts pressures on social services used by younger and older people (education and health services being two that are often cited).

In 1960, dependency ratios were 80 to 90 per cent in most Latin American countries, and in come cases (Costa Rica, Nicaragua, Paraguay) they were over 100 per cent. This compares to a recent estimate of 60 per cent for the United States. (The U.S. ratio has been rising since the 1970s because of increases in the proportion of the population over the age of sixty-five.) Declining birth rates in Latin America brought reductions in the dependency ratio. Costa Rica provides a dramatic illustration, with the ratio falling from 102 in 1960 to 69 in 1985. Significant declines also occurred in other countries, but rates were rising in some, including those where emigration of individuals in the young adult ages had an offsetting effect, as in several Central American countries. For Latin America's lower fertility countries (Argentina and Uruguay), population dynamics were producing an aging population, so that their dependency ratios were rising in response to increases in the proportion of population aged sixty-five and over. In Cuba, the aging effect was offset partially when the 1960s 'baby boom' cohorts reached working ages. Other Latin American countries will eventually experience this aging effect. Adequate assessment of the impact of dependency requires separation of the youth and old age component; as the experience of Europe and North America show, the needs of the two groups are distinct, and are often in competition for scarce public service resources.

Summing up the main features of Latin American population growth over the past six decades, three sub-regional patterns emerge from the data. The *first* pattern reflects the experience of countries with earlier and more gradual declines in birth and death rates, and generally lower overall rates of population increase. This group includes Argentina, Cuba and Uruguay, with Chile and Panama as borderline cases. The *second* group consists of countries whose death rates declined rapidly during the 1950s, and which also experienced declining birth rates after 1960. Brazil, Colombia, Costa Rica, the Dominican Republic, Mexico, Paraguay and Venezuela fit here. Peru and Ecuador are borderline cases because of their delayed declines in mortality, but appear to be catching up with fertility decline. On the whole, the second group experienced two decades of very rapid population growth after the Second World War, but shows definitely slower growth during the 1970s and 1980s. The *third* group consists of Bolivia, Haiti and four Central American countries (El Salvador, Guatemala, Honduras and Nicaragua), all late starters in mortality decline and still well behind the rest of the region in fertility declines. These countries have experienced the highest and most sustained population increase in the region in the post-war period.[2]

MORTALITY DECLINE

In 1930, with death rates still generally high, life expectancy was low for Latin American populations compared to Europe and North America. In most countries for which data are available, life expectancy at birth was around thirty-five years, a level attained by north west Europe before 1850 and by the rest of Europe around 1900. There was also considerable variation within the region. Life expectancy in Argentina and Uruguay more closely approximated levels in Southern Europe at the time. Costa Rica and Cuba were also above average, with life expectancies over age forty, while much of the rest of Central America and the Dominican Republic lagged behind with life expectancies below age thirty.

After 1930, gains in life expectancy accelerated and intraregional differences narrowed. Underlying both trends was a weakening of the link between living conditions and mortality brought about by the spread of public health measures and new means of prevention and treatment of infectious diseases. The main demographic consequence of these changes was an acceleration in the rate of population growth, because death rates were declining while birth rates remained high. As noted earlier, birth rates increased slightly as a consequence of mortality decline because of increased survival of mothers-to-be from birth to the end of the childbearing ages.

Differences in living conditions accounted for most of the variation in life expectancy in Latin America before 1930. Countries which had experienced rising living standards during the export-led growth period and

[2] Sergio Díaz-Briquets, *Conflict in Central America: The Demographic Dimension,* Population Trends in Public Policy Paper No. 10 (Washington, D.C., 1986).

invested their export earnings in improving environmental conditions experienced earlier mortality decline. In most instances, these improvements were limited to capital cities and/or principal port cities, many of which had been ravaged by epidemics of cholera and yellow fever during the middle decades of the nineteenth century. The political outcry of both the *criollo* (creole) elites and resident Europeans led to the building of water and sanitation systems and to the drainage of mosquitoe-infested swamps and marshes surrounding those cities. Europeans were especially vulnerable during epidemics because they lacked the natural immunity acquired by natives who had been exposed earlier in life and survived. Smallpox vaccine was also introduced during this period. Although these measures could be regarded as public health interventions, they depended for the most part on the prosperity that the export boom generated among urban elites. They had little impact on the rural masses who provided labour for the production of agricultural exports.

Immigration was another factor. Mortality was generally lower in the Latin American countries to which immigration contributed to population growth during this period. Immigrants were generally healthier on average than other groups, particularly the indigenous, slave and former slave populations. At the very least, immigrants had survived to young adult ages, during which most made their moves to the New World; they were also better educated and had better living conditions than other groups, except the urban elite. The abolition of slavery in Brazil and Cuba may also have contributed to lower mortality during the 1890s.

After 1930, and particularly in the period immediately after the end of the Second World War, private and public international assistance agencies introduced new methods for treatment of infectious diseases and contributed to the spread of public health measures designed to control disease vectors. Malaria was endemic to much of tropical Latin America, particularly the Caribbean, Central America and Mexico. During the 1940s, international agencies, including the Pan American Sanitary Bureau (later the Pan America Health Organization), mounted a major effort to eradicate malaria-bearing mosquitoes by spraying swamps and marshlands with DDT, which in combination with treatment of those already infected, led to dramatic declines in malaria deaths. The introduction of sulfa drugs and penicillin to treat other infectious diseases reduced mortality rates from tuberculosis, pneumonia and influenza. Vaccines were introduced to immunize populations against measles, diphtheria, tetanus and typhoid.

The result was a dramatic increase in life expectancy between 1950 and

1980, along with a narrowing of some of the differentials that previously had been associated with differences in living conditions (see Table 1.5). By the early 1980s, most Latin American countries had life expectancies at birth of sixty-five years or higher, though Bolivia and Haiti were still far below average and several Central American countries lagged. Compared to 1950, gains of ten to fifteen years of life expectancy occurred in most countries. Improvements since then have been much slower, mainly because due to causes other than infectious diseases account for a larger proportion of the total and these are less likely to be averted using the types of interventions that are effective against infections.

The largest absolute declines in mortality occurred among young children and adults over forty, while greater proportional declines occurred among older children and young adults. For the latter, mortality rates were low to begin with compared to the former, so that larger percentage mortality declines resulted in absolute cuts in rates that were a fraction of the decline in rates for infants and older age groups. Among young adults, females experienced somewhat greater decline in mortality than males. Arriaga suggests that continued higher male mortality due to accidents and violence rather than reductions in female deaths resulting from complications of pregnancy account for the difference.[3]

While reductions in identifiable serious infectious diseases – tuberculosis, typhoid, typhus, cholera, measles, diphtheria, whooping cough, malaria – are often regarded as the main contributors to increased life expectancy, declines in the respiratory disease category (influenza, pneumonia, bronchitis) and diarrhoeal diseases contributed significantly to proportional reduction in deaths. Palloni estimated that declines in deaths from infectious diseases accounted for 21 per cent of the decline in mortality between 1950 and 1973 in Latin American countries reporting deaths by cause, with another 11 per cent attributed to reductions in respiratory diseases and 10 per cent to diarrhoea.[4]

The slowing of mortality declines in Latin America since the late 1960s has stirred renewed interest in the effect of living conditions on mortality differentials, particularly those associated with income-class differences within Latin American countries. Aggregate statistics suggest that the

[3] Eduardo E. Arriaga, *Mortality Decline and its Demographic Effects on Latin America* (Berkeley, Cal., 1970).

[4] Alberto Palloni, 'Mortality in Latin America: Emerging Patterns', *Population and Development Review*, 7, 4 (1981): 623–49. See also Arriaga, *Mortality Decline* and Samuel H. Preston, *Mortality Decline in National Populations* (New York, 1976) for similar findings.

Table 1.5. *Life expectancy and infant mortality, 1950–5 and 1980–5*

	Life expectancy[a]		Infant mortality[b]	
	1950–5	1980–5	1950–5	1980–5
Total	51.9	66.7	126	61
Argentina	62.5	69.7	64	32
Bolivia	40.4	53.1	176	110
Brazil	51.0	64.9	135	63
Chile	53.8	71.5	126	20
Colombia	50.7	68.3	123	40
Costa Rica	57.3	74.7	94	18
Cuba	59.4	75.2	82	15
Dominican Republic	46.0	65.8	149	65
Ecuador	48.4	65.4	150	63
El Salvador	45.3	62.2	175	64
Guatemala	42.1	62.0	141	59
Haiti	37.6	54.8	220	97
Honduras	42.3	63.9	169	69
Mexico	50.8	68.9	114	43
Nicaragua	42.3	63.3	167	62
Panama	55.3	72.0	93	23
Paraguay	62.7	66.9	106	42
Peru	43.9	61.4	159	88
Uruguay	66.1	72.0	57	24
Venezuela	55.2	69.6	106	36

Notes: [a]At birth, number of years; [b]deaths per 1000 live births.
Source: United Nations, *World Population Prospects 1990*, (New York, 1991), tables 44 and 45.

link between mortality and living conditions (as measured by per capita income) was weaker in 1960 than in 1930, but the persistence of mortality differences between high and low income groups within countries suggests that interventions and innovations have benefited the rich more than the poor.[5]

Infants and young children are more susceptible than other age groups to infectious diseases associated with malnutrition and unsanitary living conditions and, because of their low body weights, they are more likely to

[5] Preston, *Mortality Decline;* Ruth R. Puffer and Wynne G. Griffith, 'The Inter-American Investigation of Mortality', in *United Nations World Population Conference 1965*, Vol. 2 (New York, 1967).

die from these infections without prompt medical attention than people at other ages. In fact, infant and child mortality rates are more sensitive to income and living conditions; they are often used as indicators of socio-economic development. Latin American infant mortality rates fell by 30 to 50 per cent between 1950 and 1980, but the current average rate for the region, sixty-one deaths under age one for every 1,000 live births, is still about six times the level of developed countries, and the rates range from as low as fifteen in Cuba to ninety-seven in Haiti and over 100 in Bolivia.

Persistent gaps between the rich and poor are major obstacles to lowering infant mortality, as indicated by studies that show wide disparities in rates between income and education groups. Education of mothers is strongly related to the health and survival of young children, both because a woman with some schooling knows more about sanitation and medical care and because she is more likely than an uneducated woman to be in a high income group enjoying a healthier life style and to live in an urban area where medical services are more accessible. In a study of seven Latin American countries in the 1970s, Behm showed that children of mothers with no schooling were three to five times more likely to die before their second birthday than those born to mothers with at least ten years of schooling.[6]

The majority of children in many Latin American countries are born into the higher-risk, lower-income and education groups. This is partly because these groups represent the largest share of total population, but also because low-income women tend to have higher fertility and produce a disproportionate share to annual births. High fertility contributes to high infant mortality because births are so closely spaced. Research has shown that children born less than two years apart have higher risk of birth defects and of death in infancy or early childhood. Data for Costa Rica and Peru show that children born within a year of a sibling were five or six times more likely to die before age one than those born after a three- or four-year interval.

Infant mortality in Costa Rica has fallen dramatically in all income groups, largely because of government policies to expand medical services throughout the country and to provide safe drinking water. In the late 1960s, infant mortality was four to five times higher among the 'working classes' than those who were more privileged. This differential

[6] Hugo Behm, 'Socio-economic Determinants of Mortality in Latin America', *Population Bulletin,* 13 (New York, 1980): 1–15.

then narrowed, bringing a dramatic decline in the average infant mortality rate from sixty-seven to twenty deaths per 1,000 live births between 1970 and 1980.

Thus, while mortality in Latin America is low compared to other developing regions, major health problems persist. Crude death rates are low in part because of the broad-based age structure associated with high fertility. Even aggregate levels of life expectancy are comparatively high. The problems appear when class differences and causes of death affecting different class are taken into account. Future gains in life expectancy are likely to depend not so much on the introduction of new health technology as on increasing the access of low-income groups to health services and on improvement of adverse living conditions accounting for poor health and higher mortality among low income groups.

FERTILITY DIFFERENTIALS

In most Latin America countries, fertility rates remained high until at least the mid-1960s. As late as the early 1970s there was considerable doubt about whether and when Latin America would experience the transition to lower fertility. During Europe's demographic transition in the nineteenth century, there was a lag of about one generation (two to three decades) between the decline of mortality and the onset of fertility decline. According to demographic transition theory, the same social and economic changes that led to lower mortality brought subsequent reductions in fertility. Sceptics of the theory's applicability to Latin America pointed out that public health measures reduced mortality at a stage at which social and economic development was lower than it had been in Europe and argued that the region's birth rates were thus not likely to fall without deliberate and strenuous publicly supported efforts to reduce them.

Early defenders of demographic transition theory were more optimistic about prospects for fertility decline in Latin America, calling attention to wide variations in the timing of mortality and fertility in Europe, to similar variations in Latin America, and to the rapid social and economic changes, including urbanization, rising income, and increased educational levels, that were occurring in Latin America during the decades after the Second World War. During the early 1970s, two studies, one by Beaver and the other by Oechsli and Kirk surveyed links between fertility levels in the 1960s and a variety of social and economic indicators.[7] They found strong ties between fertility levels and socio-economic variables as well as signs that fertility declines would not be long in coming. Oechsli and Kirk argued that a number of Latin American countries had experienced social and economic changes that put them on the threshold of rapid fertility decline, and Beaver predicted that once fertility decline was established, it would be at least as rapid as the region's recent decline in mortality.

Fertility trends during the 1970s supported their views. In 1950–5, the total fertility rate (a more refined measure that indicates the total number of children born to women during their childbearing years) was usually over six children per woman, and over seven in many instances (see columns one to three of Table 1.6). As noted earlier, Argentina, Uruguay, Chile, and Cuba were special cases. Argentina and Uruguay already had fertility closer to three children per woman in the 1950s, and Cuba and Chile also had lower than average fertility rates at that time. Cuba's fertility rate then increased during the 'baby boom' that came after the revolution of 1959. After 1965, fertility decline spread to other Latin American countries. In some instances declines were precipitous. Although there was little or no change in total fertility rates between 1950–5 and 1960–5, declines of 25 per cent were common between 1960–5 and 1980–5 (see columns four and five of Table 1.6). The greatest percentage declines occurred in Cuba, Costa Rica, Chile and Colombia with Cuba reaching the lowest total fertility rate (1.9 children per woman) in Latin America in the early 1980s. Little change occurred in Argentina and Uruguay, which already had low fertility, and declines were also very limited in Bolivia, Guatemala, Haiti, Honduras and Nicaragua. With the exception of Costa Rica and Panama, declines were more limited in Central America than in other parts of Latin America.

While social and economic changes played a major role in fertility decline, it is necessary to recognize that the reproductive behaviour of individual couples is what drives aggregative rates, and that biological and demographic factors as well as broader socio-economic forces influence this behaviour. Marriage patterns and fertility control practices are examples of the former; demographers have labelled them 'intermediate' variables affecting

[7] Steven E. Beaver, *Demographic Transition Theory Reinterpreted: An Application to Recent Natality Trends in Latin America* (Lexington, Mass., 1975); Frank W. Oechsli and Dudley Kirk, 'Modernization and the Demographic Transition in Latin America', *Economic Development and Cultural Change,* 23, 3 (1975): 391–419.

Table 1.6. *Total fertility rates, 1950–5, 1960–5, and 1980–5*

	Births per woman 15–49			Ratio of columns	
	1950–5 (1)	1960–5 (2)	1980–5 (3)	(2)/(1)	(3)/(2)
Total	5.8	6.0	3.9	1.03	0.65
Argentina	3.2	3.1	3.1	0.97	1.00
Bolivia	6.8	6.6	6.3	0.97	0.95
Brazil	6.2	6.2	3.8	1.00	0.61
Chile	5.1	5.3	2.8	1.04	0.53
Colombia	6.8	6.8	3.5	1.00	0.51
Costa Rica	6.7	7.1	3.5	1.06	0.49
Cuba	4.1	4.7	1.9	1.15	0.40
Dominican Republic	7.4	7.3	4.2	0.99	0.58
Ecuador	6.9	6.9	4.8	1.00	0.70
El Salvador	6.5	6.9	5.2	1.06	0.75
Guatemala	7.1	7.0	6.1	0.99	0.87
Haiti	6.3	6.3	5.2	1.00	0.83
Honduras	7.1	7.4	6.2	1.04	0.84
Mexico	6.8	6.8	4.2	1.00	0.62
Nicaragua	7.3	7.3	5.9	1.00	0.81
Panama	5.7	5.9	3.5	1.04	0.59
Paraguay	6.8	6.8	4.8	1.00	0.71
Peru	6.9	6.9	4.7	1.00	0.68
Uruguay	2.7	2.9	2.6	1.07	0.90
Venezuela	6.5	6.5	4.1	1.00	0.63

Source: United Nations, *World Population Prospects 1990*, (New York, 1991), Table 41.

fertility behaviour. It is through such variables that broader social and economic changes influence fertility rates. For example, educational attainment influences age at marriage and contraceptive use, with these two variables in turn affecting the number of children a woman actually bears.

John Bongaarts has identified four key intermediate variables that he has labelled 'proximate determinants' because they explain most of these biological differences in fertility levels: they are (1) age at marriage and the proportion of women who ever marry, (2) the duration of breastfeeding, (3) abortion and (4) contraception.[8] Census and survey data provide a consis-

[8] John Bongaarts, 'Intermediate Variables and Marital Fertility', *Population Studies*, 30, 2 (July 1976): 227–41 and 'A Framework for Analyzing the Proximate Determinants of Fertility', *Population and Development Review*, 4, 1 (March 1978): 105–32.

tent, though fragmentary account of the proximate determinants of recent fertility declines in Latin America. Marriage patterns and duration of breastfeeding have had little impact. The next section examines marriage patterns in greater detail and finds little evidence of change after 1960, indicating that fertility declines resulted more from decreases in births within unions than from changes in the proportion of women in unions.

Prolonged breastfeeding of fifteen to twenty months, common in Africa and Asia, can lengthen the time between births and ultimately lower overall fertility by extending the period of women's natural infertility after childbirth. During the 1970s, survey data for several Latin American countries revealed average durations of breastfeeding of less than ten months, which were too short to have much effect in reducing fertility rates. In some instances, the duration of breastfeeding was declining and offset the effect of rising contraceptive use. This delayed the onset of fertility decline. However, recent emphasis on the health benefits of breastfeeding appears to have motivated a modest revival in breastfeeding.

The effect of abortion is difficult to estimate. Known to be widespread, abortion is illegal in all Latin American countries except Cuba and therefore unrecorded. Because women do not give reliable responses on abortion in survey interviews, hospital records of women treated for complications of abortion are the principal source of information on its frequency. Estimates for 1974 based on such records indicated a regional ratio of 300 abortions per 1,000 pregnancies. At this level, abortion would lower fertility rates by around 20 per cent. Other authors have estimated that abortion accounted for as much as 25 per cent of fertility declines in Latin America.[9]

Increases in contraceptive use and shifts from traditional to more effective modern methods such as the pill and surgical sterilization account for most declines in fertility that can be attributed to intermediate variables. Bongaarts' index of contraception, which scales the level of fertility in a country in accord with its current contraceptive mix (accounting for both effectiveness and prevalence) relative to what it would be with no contraception (so that a level close to one indicates low contraceptive effect and values below one a higher impact), shows values in the early 1980s ranging from 0.39 in Costa Rica to 0.54 in Colombia and 0.53 in Mexico. In

[9] Christopher Tietze, *Induced Abortion: A World Review,* 5th edn (New York, 1983) p. 21; see also Tomas Frejka and Lucille C. Adkin, 'The Role of Induced Abortion in the Fertility Transition of Latin America', IUSSP/CELADE/CENEP Seminar on the Fertility Transition in Latin America, Buenos Aires, 1989.

Haiti, where only 7 per cent of women in unions were practicing contraception in 1983, the index was 0.94.[10]

Available data indicate that few Latin American women used modern contraceptives before 1965, but by the mid-1980s, 50–65 per cent of women who were married (including those in consensual unions) were using some form of contraception in a number of countries. A number of important changes brought the increased contraceptive use that reduced marital fertility. Increased access to contraception, through family planning programmes supported by governments and other agencies as well as increased commercial distribution, played a major direct role. Underlying social and economic changes increased motivation to control fertility, either to delay childbearing or to attain smaller completed family size, usually a combination of both.

Even before the onset of rapid fertility declines, important social and economic differentials were marked within Latin American countries. Total fertility rates were two to three children higher in rural areas than in the cities, and fertility rates among the urban middle- and upper-income classes were often more comparable to those of southern European countries than the high rates typical of developing countries. Educational attainment is perhaps the strongest socio-economic variable associated with fertility differentials, with women having a completed primary education showing lower fertility than those with no education, while fertility was lower among women with secondary and higher education. Educational differentials in fertility are linked to and therefore paralleled in differentials by income class and rural-urban residence.[11]

Because of this, it is difficult to assign a specific causal role to any one variable, since all are closely related. Most of them influence fertility through a variety of causal paths. Education is a good example. More educated women typically are aware of a wider range of contraceptive methods, and are more open to the idea of controlling fertility. Education is also an important factor in motivation to control fertility, since a higher proportion of more educated women work and earn more, both factors that raise the opportunity cost of time spent in rearing children. These costs have been offset to some extent in Latin America by the

10 Based on data in Kathy A. London et al., 'Fertility and Family Planning Surveys: an update', *Population Reports,* Series M, No. 8 (Baltimore, Md: Population Information Program, Johns Hopkins University, 1985).

11 Raul Urzua, 'Social Science Research on Population and Development in Latin America', *Report of International Review Group on Social Science Research on Population and Development* (Mexico D.F., 1978), appendix 11.

availability of servants to provide child care for upper-income working women.

Recent changes have worked in a variety of ways to increase motivation to control fertility. Women who were in primary school in 1960 reached their early childbearing years during the 1970s. A higher proportion of women were working in paying jobs in the 1970s than before (see section on labour force, employment and education below). More importantly, these changes affected higher fertility social and economic groups. Whether the shifts represented upward economic mobility is open to question, since they took place during a period when Latin America's persistent income inequality showed little signs of being ameliorated. A plausible, though not thoroughly tested, hypothesis is that the combination of increased aspirations associated with higher educational attainment and exposure to urban amenities, increased economic pressures associated with inflation and income inequality, and increased availability of contraceptives was responsible for the spread of lower fertility rates to lower income classes, without whose participation the rapid declines in fertility would not have occurred.

The completion of Latin America's fertility transition is dependent on several factors. One is the spread of lower fertility norms to rural areas. Although the share of rural population has declined, so that rural fertility has less impact on national average rates, social and economic conditions conducive to high rural fertility continue in many Latin American countries. Land tenure systems that provide little opportunity to own or bequest land to succeeding generations among the rural masses, or which require a given number of family members in order to maintain control of the land that is allotted, are examples of institutional forces inhibiting changes in reproductive attitudes. Added to this is the higher economic value of children who labour as family members on subsistence plots. One institutional change that has contributed to lower rural fertility is the recent shift from owner or tenant status of members of farm families to wage labour in rural areas arising from the consolidation of land for commercial agriculture. This process has increased the likelihood of rural women working outside the home, while at the same time decreasing opportunities for work at home by younger children.

Age structure also affects the pace of decline of birth rates. Although total fertility per woman has declined, the number of women entering childbearing age has increased as the very large age cohorts born during the period of high population growth rates in the late 1950s and early

1960s reached their mid-1920s. Another uncertainty relates to income inequality. A high proportion of middle- and upper-income class women in Latin American countries have relied on commercial outlets and private physicians for birth control, whereas lower income women depend on government or private agency supported clinics. As budget crises force cutbacks in spending on social projects, the spread of these services may be jeopardized at precisely the moment at which the need is greatest.

Too little is known about the incipient spread of fertility control to lower income groups in Latin America to predict that the trend to lower fertility is permanent. It could be that economic pressures that motivated more women to delay or terminate pregnancies during the 1970s might ease and that the desire for additional children persists and will be realized when families can afford them. Not to be forgotten are the 'baby booms' that occurred in the United States and several other industrialized countries after many observers had concluded that fertility decline was irreversible once started.

MARRIAGE AND FAMILY STRUCTURE

The prevalence of consensual and other types of informal unions in Latin America complicates the use of 'marriage' as a measure of the extent to which women are exposed to the risk of pregnancy. Though the average age at marriage has been higher in Latin America than Asian countries in which early marriage is very common, it may not be a reliable indicator of the age at which exposure to pregnancy and childbearing begins because of the variety of union types that exist, the way in which they are recorded, and the ages at which different types predominate. Consensual unions account for a significant proportion of unions in many Latin American countries, and visiting or non-cohabitational unions are common in the Caribbean.

One way to measure early marriage is to examine the per cent of females aged fifteen to nineteen reported as married. International comparisons based on recent data show that the figure for Latin America is only 17 per cent. This is higher than the 2 per cent for East Asia, but much lower than the 58 per cent average for South Asia, the 55 per cent for Africa, and the 34 per cent for the Middle East.[12] Zulma Camisa

[12] Carmen Arretx, 'Nuptiality in Latin America', in *International Union for the Scientific Study of Population, International Population Conference: London 1969*, Vol. 3 (Liege, Belgium, 1971),

surveyed census data from 1950 through 1970 for several Latin America countries and found three basic patterns.[13] Central American countries, with the exception of Costa Rica and Panama, had the lowest average at marriage and the highest proportion of women of childbearing age in unions. Argentina, Uruguay and Chile had later average marriage ages and higher proportions of women who never married, while Andean countries and Brazil showed intermediate rates. Countries with the lowest age of entry into unions also showed the highest proportion of consensual unions. Latin American nuptiality patterns fit neither the 'European' model, in which later marriage and a high proportion of women who never marry is common, nor the non-European pattern of very early and nearly universal marriage.

Data for tracking trends in Latin American marriage patterns before 1950 are limited, but available evidence suggests that marriage rates increased in the period immediately after the Second World War. Carmen Arretx cites data from censuses taken around 1950 and again in 1960 showing increases in the proportion of women aged twenty to forty-five reported as 'married' in a number of Latin American countries.[14] Some of the increases represent increased legal recognition of unions, others in decreased reporting of widowhood (a reflection of declining mortality of spouses), and fewer women were reported as 'single'. Increases in the prevalence of marriage in the post-war period has been cited as a contributing factor in the rise of birth rates that occurred in many Latin American countries at that time.

A further reason for caution in using marriage prevalence as an indicator of the risk of conception is that pregnancy itself may be a reason for establishing or formalizing a union. The proportion of consensual unions is higher among younger women. Civil or religious formalization of unions may be selective of women who become mothers, since documentation is required for the child's schooling and other purposes. The cost involved may also lead to differential degrees of formalization among different social and economic classes, with lower income groups, the less educated, and rural couples being less able and less anxious to secure a marriage certificate. Higher incidence of non-formal union types among indigenous groups and people of African heritage in Latin America may reflect their lower level of integration into the social and legal structure

[13] Zulma C. Camisa, *La Nupcialidad de las Mujeres Solteras en America Latina* (San José, Costa Rica, 1977).

[14] Arretx, 'Nuptiality in Latin America'.

of their societies as well as the cultural factors to which it is often attributed.

Social, cultural and economic forces play a role in the relation between union type and fertility. In contrast with the English-speaking Caribbean, where there is some evidence of higher fertility among women in legal unions, studies of Latin American women have revealed higher fertility among women in consensual unions, possibly because these women were less effective in practicing contraception, or because pregnancy was viewed as a way of stabilizing the relationship. Conclusions about links between union type and fertility need to be viewed cautiously because the causal links between them run in both directions and affect reporting attitudes and practice as well. This is also true of statistics on divorce and separation in Latin America, which frequently are under-reported in situations where legal divorce is not recognized or difficult.

Family composition is another dimension of the relation between union types and fertility. The nuclear family has been found to be the most common type in Latin America, though the importance of non-residential extended family relationships and *compadrio* (ritual kinship, described by one observer as 'an elaborate form of godparenthood') is also stressed.[15] In spite of its wide acceptance, the generalization that women in extended families have higher fertility than those in nuclear families is not supported by empirical evidence from Latin America.[16]

While nuclear families are the most common type, not all consist of formalized unions of couples with children. An important sub-group, and one that is over-represented among the poor, consists of less stable family units, particularly those headed by women in informal unions or who are single mothers, divorced, separated or widowed. Cultural biases in reporting of family headship has led to systematic under-reporting of female headship. One in five households in Latin America was estimated in 1983 to have a woman as the de facto head in terms of carrying the primary burden of providing the basic needs of dependent members.[17] Women-headed households are particularly disadvantaged because often they have

[15] Francesca M. Cancian, Louis M. Goodman and Peter H. Smith, 'Capitalism, Industrialization, and Kinship in Latin America', *Journal of Family History,* 3, 4 (Winter 1978): 322.

[16] Thomas K. Burch, and Murray Gendell, 'Extended Family Structure and Fertility: some conceptual issues', *Journal of Marriage and the Family,* 9, 2 (1970): 227–36.

[17] Nadia H. Youssef, and Carol B. Hetler, 'Establishing the Economic Condition of Woman-headed Households in the Third World: a new approach', in Mayra Buvinic, Margaret A. Lycette, and William P. McGreevey (eds), *Women and Poverty in the Third World* (Baltimore, Md, 1983), pp. 216–43.

been abandoned by working-age males, because the female head has to provide both income and home care for dependent children, and because basic institutional supports such as access to credit and social services are orientated to 'normal' family units with a male head and based on a formalized union. The legal structure of many Latin American countries recognizes women's rights and entitlements (in many instances even to their children) only for those who are legally married.

Household and family dynamics have played an increasingly important role in the analytical frameworks guiding research on linkages between demographic changes and social and economic processes in Latin America. Demographic events (migration, birth, death) typically relates to and are measured in terms of individuals. But explanations of behaviour that leads to and follows from specific demographic events need to take account of both societal and individual level processes. Households and families provide a key mediating link in explaining major demographic changes such as the rapid decline of fertility described in the previous section of this chapter and in relating them to changes in women's role (particularly through increased education and labour force participation), internal and international migration.

Analysts in the region have focussed attention on ways in which household and family units adapt and respond to changing economic conditions. One approach has conceptualized these responses in terms of 'household survival strategies', seeking explanations of migration, reproductive patterns, work and other demographic household behaviour among different strata of society in relation to the economic, social and political institutions that define and limit the options and choices available to each.[18] The approach resembles microeconomic approaches to household demographic behaviour, which focus on the individual level choices involved in demographic events in terms of their costs relative to those of other goods and available resources. An important difference is that microeconomists generally view constraints as a given and pay only limited attention to the way in which institutional forces impinge on individual behaviour. In the survival strategy and similar frameworks, institutional forces are seen as critical, with intra-household/family ties and conflicts playing a powerful mediating role in determining how individuals act in response to them. Explanations of recent declines in fertility in Latin America as responses to

[18] Marianne Schmink, 'Household Economic Strategies: review and research agenda', *Latin American Research Review*, 19, 3 (1984): 35–56.

increasing pressures arising from inflation and other economic trends on household resources (available time and money) by delaying or curtailing childbearing so that married women can work or so that families can more adequately feed children already born illustrate this approach.

ETHNICITY AND NATIONAL ORIGIN

Latin America is rich in ethnic and cultural diversity, with a history of assimilation and mixing of racial and ethnic groups in many of its populations. There is a great deal of ambivalence about race and ethnicity in Latin America, with many of the differentials associated with race being attributed instead to social and economic class. Statistically, racial and ethnic categories are elusive and difficult to measure both because of the blurring of the lines between categories that mixing and assimilation have caused and because their association with class leads to ambiguous reporting, particularly when it is based on declaration by the individual for whom the report is being made or by enumerators who themselves think of race in class terms. For that reason, there is little comprehensive information on racial and ethnic differences in demographic statistics on Latin America.

By 1930, four major groups had contributed to the region's racial and ethnic stock. Its indigenous Indian population included groups that had developed organized agriculture and urban systems in pre-Columbian Middle America and the Andean region. Their numbers were comparatively large in the fifteenth century, but conquest, disease and harsh living conditions drastically reduced their numbers during first two centuries of Spanish colonial rule. However, these populations had been growing since the eighteenth century, and represented important components of the populations of Mexico, Central America, and Andean countries. A second group were the creoles (*criollos* in Spanish), consisting of natives of Latin America who traced their bloodlines to the original Spanish and Portugese conquerors, and who by the end of the colonial era controlled the wealth and political power of the region. The third group consisted of descendants of African slaves, who had been imported during the seventeenth to nineteenth centuries to labour on the plantations, particularly those of Brazil and the Caribbean, and constituted an important share of their populations. The last to arrive were the migrants, mainly southern and eastern Europeans, but also including eastern and southern Asians, who came in response the demand for labour generated by the export expansion that occurred in the region after 1850. Their descendants constitute an important component of the populations of Argentina, Uruguay, Cuba and southern Brazil, and to a lesser extent those of Chile, Venezuela, Costa Rica and a number of Caribbean countries.

Latin American censuses taken around 1950 reported the largest number of foreign born in Argentina (2.4 million) and Brazil (1.2 million), though the share was much higher in the former (15 per cent) that the latter (2 per cent) owing to its smaller population base. Other countries reporting 4 per cent or more of their population as foreign born in 1950 were Costa Rica, Panama, Paraguay and Venezuela. Cuba was just under 4 per cent. In most instances these proportions understated the significance of immigrant groups because by 1950 they were represented by the second or third generation of those who had arrived during the peak decades of immigration just before the First World War rather than the more limited flows that came during the inter-war period.[19]

Census estimates of the shares of populations of Indian and African descent are complicated by the effects of racial mixing and assimilation on reporting. In Guatemala, for example, John Early has tracked the proportion of the Mayan Indian population through several censuses and found it as low as 49 per cent in the 1964 census and as high as 57 per cent in the 1973 census.[20] While the higher birth rate of the Indians could account for part of the increase, he also found evidence of under-reporting of Indian groups. The reason given for this is that the statistical system was run by and orientated towards the politically and economically dominant *ladino* groups, and that Indians who adopted *ladino* dress, life styles and language were often classified as *ladino*.

In a number of Latin American countries with large indigenous groups, language may be the only census variable that provides an indication of their size. This is true of Mexico, which has the second largest (after Peru) Indian population in the region, and where the census reported 11 per cent of its population as speakers of an indigenous language in 1950, with a decline to 8 per cent in 1970. The 1972 census of Peru enumerated 32 per cent of its population with a language other than Spanish (mainly Quechua and Aymara) as the first language spoken, though estimates of the percentage of Indians in the total population run as high as 47 per

19 Giorgio Mortara, *Characteristics of the Demographic Structure of the American Countries* (Washington, D.C., 1964).

20 John D. Early, *The Demographic Structure and Evolution of a Peasant System: The Guatemalan Population*, (Boca Raton, Fla., 19812), p. 176.

cent.[21] Other Latin American countries in which indigenous groups represent a large share of the population include Bolivia (63 per cent) and Ecuador (30 per cent). In all instances, the indigenous groups are mainly rural and are the poorest and least educated groups in their countries. They also have higher fertility and mortality that the general population.

Reporting of race is equally problematic in Latin American censuses. Brazil's 1950 census reported 11 per cent as Black and 26.5 per cent as mixed or *parda*. Since race is self-declared, the categories are very ambiguous. Brazilian Portuguese has a plethora of terms to describe the variety of racial mixes in its population, and there is a complex relationship between race and status in Brazilian society. Brazilian census authorities abandoned race as a census category in 1970, but reinstated it in 1980, when only 6 per cent reported as Black and 38 per cent as *parda*). The increase in the mixed as well as the decline of the Black and White categories (White dropped from 62 per cent to 55 per cent) may reflect reporting as much a differential population increase between groups. Other countries in the region with a significant Black population include Haiti, with the highest proportion in the region, as well as the Dominican Republic and Cuba. Cuba's 1953 census lists 12.4 per cent as Black and 14.5 per cent in a category labelled 'mixed racial ancestry', a category in which mulattoes predominated.[22]

Ethnicity and race play an important though secondary role in fertility and mortality differentials, though it is generally difficult to separate the causal effect of either from the generally low levels of education and income of the Black and Indian populations of the region. Indian populations have higher fertility and mortality, as well as earlier entry into unions and a higher proportion of consensual unions. Higher proportions of non-formal union types are also found in the Black population, though the effect on fertility varies. Intermarriage between groups has contributed to even further diversification of the ethnicity and culture of countries in the region.

URBAN AND RURAL POPULATIONS

Latin America is by far the most urbanized of the world's developing regions. By the 1980s, two-thirds of its population resided in localities that were classified as 'urban' according to official definitions (see Table

21 Kenneth Ruddle and Kathleen Barrows, *Statistical Abstract of Latin America 1972* (Los Angeles, Cal., 1974), table 41.

22 Díaz-Briquets and Pérez, 'Cuba: the demography of revolution', p. 32.

1.7). This contrasts with 30 per cent in Africa and 24 per cent in South Asia, and is more comparable to levels found in Europe (73 per cent) and North America (74 per cent). Since 1950, the average annual rate of growth of Latin America's urban population has been 4.1 per cent, compared to about 1 per cent for the rural population. Rural populations have declined in absolute as well as relative terms recently in several countries. This has accentuated already large differences between the region's urban population growth rates and overall population growth rates.

Historically, Latin America has a strong urban tradition. During the colonial era, highland centres, many of which had been built on the sites of pre-Columbian cities, were focal points of Spanish political control and economic exploitation of indigenous population groups, while coastal cities functioned as ports and administrative centres for both Spanish and Portuguese colonial traders. During the nineteenth century, cities that had emerged as political and economic centres grew in size and wealth with the boom in exports, and many – like Mexico City, Rio de Janeiro and Lima – became 'primate' cities commanding a disproportionate shares of their country's urban population and amenities.

Comparatively few Latin Americans lived in cities at the beginning of this century, when exporting of primary products was the backbone of most economies. But those who did tended to concentrate in single large city, typically the capital or main seaport. Concern about urban primacy, as the process came to be labelled, stemmed from the accompanying centralization of political and economic power in these centres, usually to the detriment of development in other parts of the country. With the region's post-Second World War population surge, there were added concerns that migration to these centres would lead to further concentration, exacerbating difficulties in providing jobs and urban services. Mexico City, with an estimated 1985 population of 15 million (five to six times that of the Mexico's second largest city, Guadalajara) and expected to grow to over 20 million by the end of the century, is an often-cited example of high urban concentration.

In fact, urban concentration in Mexico is actually lower than in some other Latin American countries. A simple measure of urban primacy is the ratio of population size for the largest city to the combined population sizes of the next ranking three cities. These ratios were high in a number of Latin American countries before the Second World War: 4.2 in Peru, 2.4 in Mexico, and 1.8 in Chile, compared to less than one in the United States (and also in Brazil and Colombia).

Table 1.7. *Urban population in Latin America, 1930–80*

	1930[a]	1950[a]	1950[b]	1980[b]	Urban growth rate 1950–80
Total	17	26	41	65	4.1
Argentina	38	50	65	83	2.5
Bolivia	14	19	38	44	2.9
Brazil	14	20	36	66	4.8
Chile	32	43	58	81	3.1
Colombia	10	23	37	64	4.5
Costa Rica	20	18	34	43	4.1
Cuba	26	36	49	68	2.7
Dominican Republic	7	11	24	51	5.5
Ecuador	14	18	28	47	4.7
El Salvador	7	13	37	42	3.3
Guatemala	11	11	30	37	3.6
Haiti	4	5	12	24	3.9
Honduras	n.a.	7	18	36	5.6
Mexico	14	24	43	66	4.5
Nicaragua	14	15	35	53	4.5
Panama	27	22	36	50	3.7
Paraguay	11	15	35	42	3.4
Peru	11	18	36	65	4.7
Uruguay	35	53	78	84	1.1
Venezuela	14	31	53	83	5.2

Notes: a Per cent in cities with 20,000 or more residents, 1930 and 50. *b* Per cent in areas officially defined as urban, 1950 and 1980.
Source: 1930–50: United Nations, *Growth of the World's Urban and Rural Population, 1920–2000* (New York, 1969); 1950–80: United Nations, *World Population Prospects 1990*, (New York, 1991) country tables.

Post-war industrialization did not lead to increased primacy in all instances. Harley Browning found that while primate cities increased in absolute size, the primacy ratio was stable or declined from 1940 to 1960 in Brazil and Colombia, increased a little (to 5) in Mexico, and grew more in Chile (2.5 in 1960), Peru (5) and Venezuela (1.2 in 1940 to 1.6 in 1960).[23] In Brazil, Colombia and Mexico, industrial expansion took place in cities (São Paulo, Medellín, and Monterrey) other than the capital. In Brazil, a bi-polar primacy pattern combining Rio de Janeiro and São Paulo

[23] Harley L. Browning, 'Primacy Variation in Latin America during the Twentieth Century', in Instituto de Estudios Peruanos, *Urbanización y Processo Social en América Latina* (Lima, 1972): 55–78.

had emerged even before the Second World War. After 1960, São Paulo surpassed Rio as Brazil's largest city, and is expected to be the world's second largest (after Mexico City) by 2000.[24]

Browning predicted further declines in primacy as industrialization continued for three reasons. First, sheer size would eventually slow large city growth; spatial limitations increase the time required for the doubling of a city of 10 million compared to a city of 5 million, and the number of potential rural-urban migrants in a population dwindles as rural populations stabilize or decline. Diseconomies of large scale are a second consideration. The marginal costs of providing adequate intra-urban transportation and communication, water and sewage disposal as well as other urban services become proportionally greater with the distances involved as well as increased land values. Third, as industrial development passed from import substitution to development of internal markets, companies were more inclined to locate factories closer to regional markets and sources of raw materials. Though national policies to control population concentration directly are difficult to design, attention to the indirect effects of programmes that affect employment and investment opportunities can influence population distribution patterns. During the 1970s, primacy patterns remained fairly stable in Brazil, Colombia and Venezuela, increased in Chile and Mexico, and declined in Peru. It remains to be seen whether Mexico City's disastrous 1985 earthquake, which came in the wake of already serious problems of air pollution and an inadequate water supply, has spurred decentralization in Mexico.

Despite the growth of primate cities, the region was still predominantly rural before the Second World War; most countries did not even classify the population as 'urban' or 'rural' before 1950. Dramatic shifts in rural-urban population balances came after the war. However, tracking these shifts using country definitions of urban areas can be misleading, because some countries use administrative criteria, whereas others have size thresholds; cross-country comparisons as well as time trends are affected. To achieve comparability, United Nations' statisticians have compiled data for populations residing in localities of 20,000 inhabitants or more, for 1930 and 1950. This is more restrictive than the official definitions of urban areas of most countries in the region used after 1950. For compari-

[24] United Nations, *Estimates and Projections of Urban, Rural and City Populations, 1950–2025: the 1982 Assessment* (New York, 1985), pp. 146–7.

son, both the '20,000-and-over' and officially defined urban populations for 1950 are shown in Table 1.7.

According to these data, 17 per cent of the population of the region was urban in 1930 compared to 26 per cent in 1950. Using official definitions for 1950, the percentage rises to 41 per cent, reflecting the incorporation of many smaller towns and cities that qualified as 'urban' under the administrative definition that was widely used. By 1980 this percentage had risen to 65 per cent, when 236 million of Latin America's 363 million population lived in urban areas. Examining the data in Table 1.7, we see that in 1930 only Argentina, Chile and Uruguay had more than 30 per cent of their population in urban areas. After 1950, however, several countries experienced substantial increases in the urban share of their population and many countries experienced urban population growth rates that exceeded 4 per cent per annum between 1950 and 1980. The Dominican Republic and Honduras led with rates in excess of 5 per cent. Except for Bolivia, only countries that already had comparatively high urban shares in 1950 (Argentina, Cuba and Uruguay) experienced urban growth rates that were lower than 3 per cent a year during those decades.

Problems associated with Latin America's rapid urban growth – unemployment, urban poverty, slum housing, stress on urban services as well as the political unrest that they may generate – are among the most pressing issues that the region faced in the final decades of the twentieth century. There was strong consensus that these problems were aggravated by the extreme concentration of population and wealth in a few large cities. Very large cities often drain resources from smaller cities and rural areas where investments might have been more effective in raising living standards. Latin America's largest and still rapidly growing metropolises (São Paulo and Mexico City) are expected to pass the 20 million mark by the year 2000, making them two of the largest urban agglomerations in the world. Several other major Latin American cities (Rio de Janeiro, Buenos Aires and Lima) also are also projected to rank among the world's largest cities.

Fuelling the post-war urban population surge were both the region's high overall rate of population growth and the restructuring of economies from export-orientated agricultural to more regionally orientated industrial economies. On the demographic side, both natural increase and internal migration played roles in the shifting rural-urban distribution of population. United Nations' estimates for nine countries in the region attribute an average of 64 per cent of urban growth during the 1950s and

1960s to natural increase (births minus deaths) and 36 percent to internal migration and reclassification of localities.[25]

INTERNAL MIGRATION

Massive internal migration is a conspicuous feature of post-war social and economic changes in Latin America. Rural-urban shifts have dominated the flows; however, intercity movements, migrants returning from metropolises to small towns and rural areas, and settlement of agricultural frontier areas have also reshaped population distribution patterns. Policy-makers and research analysts have been concerned with a variety of questions about internal migration and its relation to socio-economic changes. One set relates to the causes of population movements, Another concerns the issue of who moves, that is to say, migrant selectivity. A third focusses on geographic patterns of movements, the direction and distances involved in flows. A final group of questions concerns the economic, social and political consequences of migration in both sending and receiving regions, and on policies to deal with problems created by large-scale population movements.

Individuals move. Their motives are important for understanding why migration occurs, but societal forces are equally important if not more so because they shape the contexts in which migration decisions are made. A move may be motivated by marriage, for example, or the desire to join family members who have moved earlier. However, economic considerations usually carry most weight and these are largely determined by broad social forces.

A basic explanation for the rural exodus in Latin America is that economic opportunities have not kept pace with population increase; entrenched economic and social institutions have limited the capacity of rural areas to absorb additional population. Foremost among these is the extreme inequality of land tenure. From the colonial period through to the twentieth century, most of the region's land and other agricultural resources, such as credit and new technology, have been controlled by a small minority of large land owners, while the majority of the rural population worked small plots that provided only a margin of subsistence or remained landless labourers who worked on large estates. Despite efforts at land reform, consolidation of holdings has continued or increased in many countries during the post-war period.

[25] United Nations, *Patterns of Urban and Rural Population Growth* (New York, 1980), p. 24.

Rising rates of natural increase aggravated the economic stress created by economic inequality. Most of rural Latin America did not have the system of social control over resources and reproduction that enabled peasant populations in Europe to balance population and productive resources – a system that encouraged couples to delay or abstain from marriage until land was available to support the formation of a new family unit. Instead, post-war population increase accelerated the fragmentation of small-holdings. Migration played an important role in their attempt to maintain living standards through temporary or permanent relocation of one or more members in the wage economy.

Another contributing cause of migration was the so-called 'urban bias' of post-war industrialization strategies adopted by many Latin American countries. Investments in productive and social infrastructure were concentrated in urban centres, often the capital or major metropolis. Policies to contain food prices and channel availability credit to industry short-changed the rural economy. The few incentives that did reach the rural sector favoured large landowners and commercial producers. *Campesino* households faced constrained and shrinking economic possibilities at the same time that their numbers were increasing.

On the other side of the coin is the growing lure of the city, which not only held out the promise of jobs and other earnings opportunities, but also offered better access to public services, particularly health and education. Cheaper transport and increased communication networks also figured in migrants' assessments of whether they could increase their living standards more by moving to the city than by staying in the countryside.

Also driving the flight from the land have been manmade calamities and natural disasters to which Latin America is prone: violent struggle to control land, civil war in Central America, worsened environmental conditions, particularly soil erosion, and adverse climate and natural catastrophes such as the periodic droughts that have ravaged northeastern Brazil and southern Peru, as well as floods and frosts. Such factors have often proved to be the final impetus for population movements after longer-standing economic and institutional factors and population pressures weakened the resilience of rural populations.

The stereotypical image of migrants in the developing world is of the rural peasant arriving at the bus station of a nation's largest city with all of his or her worldly belongings in a bag. In statistical terms, net rural-urban migration flows have indeed had the greatest overall impact on population distribution in Latin America. But underlying these net flows are a complex of migration streams which reveal a much richer pattern of individual moves than are revealed by summary data.

Studies of migration to large cities in Latin America show that most rural moves are directed to towns and smaller cities and that moves to larger cities come from smaller cities and towns rather than directly from rural areas, but this is not always true. While nearly 70 per cent of migrants to Brazil's metropolitan areas came from other urban places, studies of Mexico City and Monterrey, Mexico showed that migrants from rural origins represented a larger share of the total. When origins were classified in terms of distance from the destination, regions surrounding the destination had a higher proportional representation. When length of stay was controlled, the data suggested that migration flows start with shorter moves with a larger share of individuals from urban origins, but shifts to longer distances and rural origins with time.[26]

A serious limitation of most studies of migration is that they identify movers at a particular place (usually the most recent destination) and time, and miss those who came earlier and left. This exaggerates the volume of migration to a particular destination by not taking account of individuals who moved on or returned to their origins. Return and temporary migration flows are statistically more elusive, but play an important role in the economic strategies of individuals and family units in many Latin American countries.

Movements to rural destinations have also been a feature of the region's post-war migration patterns. Most of these moves originate in other rural areas, but some come from small towns and cities in economically depressed, highly populated areas. These flows generally have been linked to agricultural colonization schemes and/or settlement of agricultural frontiers, the most recent being movements to the Amazon basin frontiers of Brazil, Peru, Colombia and Venezuela. Rural settlement schemes have been linked to irrigation and road-building projects, such as the Trans-Amazon Highway in Brazil, and to the growth of rural hinterlands around new cities such as Brasilia and Ciudad Guyana.

One of the most widely accepted generalizations about migration is that it is highly selective with respect to age, sex and other population characteristics. Numerous studies of migrants in Latin America report age selectivity patterns that conform to the expectation of that young adults –

[26] Jorge Balán, Harley L. Browning and Elizabeth Jelín, *Men in a Developing Society: Geographic and Social Mobility in Monterrey* (Austin, Tex., 1973).

aged from the mid-teens to the mid-thirties – account for the largest share of migrants. The majority of urban migrants were unmarried, while migration of family units was common in flows to rural areas.

In most urban centres in Latin America, female migrants outnumber males, with high proportions of younger female migrants being attracted to the rapidly growing service sector in larger cities – domestic service, in particular, as well as clerical, commercial and teaching positions. Variation in sex selectivity is related to the nature of origins and destinations. In Brazil, the proportion of males was higher among migrants to industrially orientated São Paulo than to Rio de Janeiro, which is service orientated. Males have out-numbered females during the early stages of frontier migration, but the gender balance shifted with increased arrivals of family members later on.

Latin American migrants are characterized by higher educational attainment and a more highly skilled occupational than the general population of sending areas. More educated, highly skilled migrants tend to be the 'pioneer' movers, and are followed by individuals with more average education and skill levels. By removing younger, better educated and more skilled workers from the human resource base of sending areas, migration may slow productivity increases and act as a stimulus to further exodus of individuals who want to get ahead. It also increases the demographic dependency burden of these areas because age selectivity reduces the proportion of people of working age relative to children and older people. On the other hand, if age and sex selectivity of out-migration favours younger women, there is a compensating demographic effect resulting from reduced births in origin areas. It has also been speculated that out-migration reduced chances for political reforms, since individuals with frustrated aspirations have left rather than stayed work for such changes.

At destinations, migrants tend to be less educated and less skilled on average than natives. These differentials increase as migration dips further into the skill and educational resource pool of sending areas. Though migrants appear to be at a disadvantage compared to natives in destination areas, research on the adaptation of migrants in Latin American cities has largely invalidated an earlier expectation that the migration process would generate marginalized, alienated and politically explosive urban masses. Efforts to track the social and economic mobility of migrants suggest that they have done at least as well as natives in succeeding economically and socially. In a review of forty studies of migrant assimilation in Latin America, Cornelius concluded that urban migration did 'not necessarily result in severe frustration of expectations for socioeconomic improvement or widespread personal and social disorganization'.[27] Although individual migrants may indeed find the easier access to schooling for their children and health services that attracts many of them to cities, the net effect of these moves is to put added stress on the capacity of cities to provide services. Migration also adds to the demand for housing and urban infrastructure such as water, sanitation, streets and public transport systems.

In analysing these stresses, it is important to distinguish between the experiences of individual migrants and the impact of migration on the society in which they live. Rapid increase in housing demand caused by migration-fed urban population growth has indeed contributed to the spread of urban shanty-towns in many Latin American cities. Yet studies of the characteristics of shanty-town populations reveal that migrant status is only one of a number of social, economic and demographic characteristics determining who resides in them. A particular problem for urban administrators is that the tax base of a city with a large informal sector, with many informal workers living in shanty-towns, is limited, so that revenues do not keep up with the demand for urban services. Their problems have been exacerbated further by the fiscal constraints under structural adjustment regimes imposed by international lenders as a condition for debt relief.

With rapid overall population increase, the social and economic problems associated with city-ward migration are generally issues that a society would have had to confront regardless of whether migration occurred. What migration does is concentrate demand for services and other problems in the large cities. Such concentration makes them more visible. It may also ease them to the extent that economies of scale can be realized, provided that urban growth has not already reached proportions at which large-scale increases rather than decreases the costs and difficulty of providing services.

LABOUR FORCE, EMPLOYMENT AND EDUCATION

Post-war urbanization was accompanied by dramatic changes in the structure of Latin America's economically active population. In 1950, agriculture accounted for half or more of the labour force in all but five countries in the region (Argentina, Chile, Cuba, Uruguay and Venezuela), and two-

[27] Wayne A. Cornelius, Jr., 'The Political Economy of Cityward Migration in Latin America: toward empirical theory', in Francine F. Rabinowitz and Felicity M. Trueblood (eds), *Latin American Urban Research,* Vol. 1 (Beverly Hills, Cal., 1971), p. 103.

thirds or more in the Dominican Republic, Haiti and several countries in Central America. By 1980, only three countries (Guatemala, Honduras and Haiti) remained with half or more of the labour force in agriculture (see Table 1.8).

Though import-substituting industrialization was one of the forces contributing to rapid urban growth, declines in the share of the labour force in agriculture were generally not matched by proportional increases in employment in manufacturing and other industries. In Brazil, for example, the labour force in agriculture declined by 29 percentage points between 1950 and 1980, but the share of industry increased by only 10 points. Similar patterns are observed in Colombia, Costa Rica, Mexico and Venezuela. The demand that drove the post-Second World War expansion of manufacturing in Latin America was concentrated in product lines (consumer durable goods such as television sets and refrigerators, and in transportation equipment, petrochemicals, and so on) that required more complex and capital intensive technologies than labour in order to be competitive with imports from other industrial economies.

Job-seekers sought employment elsewhere, particularly in construction and services. Many of these jobs were generated in the so-called urban 'informal' sector, which encompasses a range of activities from street sellers and odd-job handymen to small-scale construction and repair shops, all operating without the institutional umbrella of wage contracts, tax payments and bank credit found in the formal sector. The informal sector has played a crucial role in the absorption of migrants as well as younger native workers in Latin American cities. Before the economic crisis of the 1980s affected employment so adversely in the region's formal sector industries, informal employment contributed to the low measured unemployment reported by many countries at levels of 2 to 3 per cent.

A major issue is whether informal employment is really disguised unemployment or underemployment. On the positive side, having the informal sector available to absorb labour has enabled the formal sector to utilize more advanced technologies. On the negative side, productivity and earnings are clearly lower in the informal sector. The wage gap between the two sectors has contributed to a worsening of measured income inequality in urban areas and increased adverse economic pressure on low income workers.

In the case of services, productivity is difficult to measure because workers' earnings provide the main basis for determining the service share of national income accounts. The earnings capacity of service workers has

Table 1.8. *Sectoral distribution of labour force 1950–1980; secondary school enrolment rates, 1960–1981*

	Percent of labour force by sector				Secondary school enrolment rate*	
	1950		1980			
	Agriculture	Industry	Agriculture	Industry	1960	1981
Total	53.4	19.5	31.8	25.9	n.a.	n.a.
Argentina	25.2	31.8	13.1	33.8	23	59
Bolivia	61.4	20.0	46.5	19.7	12	34
Brazil	59.8	16.6	31.2	26.6	11	32
Chile	34.3	30.2	16.5	25.2	24	57
Colombia	57.2	19.7	34.3	23.5	12	48
Costa Rica	57.6	16.7	30.8	23.2	21	48
Cuba	42.7	20.5	23.8	28.5	14	75
Dominican Republic	72.8	11.2	45.7	15.5	7	41
Ecuador	65.4	15.4	38.6	19.9	12	40
El Salvador	65.4	15.5	43.2	19.4	13	20
Guatemala	68.4	13.8	56.9	26.1	7	16
Haiti	85.6	5.7	70.0	8.3	4	13
Honduras	72.3	8.9	60.5	16.2	8	30
Mexico	60.4	16.8	36.6	29.0	11	51
Nicaragua	67.9	15.2	46.6	15.8	7	41
Panama	56.4	13.6	31.8	18.2	29	65
Paraguay	56.0	20.0	48.6	20.6	11	26
Peru	57.7	18.3	40.1	18.3	15	57
Uruguay	24.4	28.0	15.8	29.2	37	70
Venezuela	42.9	21.4	16.1	28.4	21	40

Note: *Enrolment rate is population aged 12–17 divided by number enrolled; data for c. 1960 and 1981.

Source: Labour force, International Labour Office, *Economically Active Population, Estimates 1950–1980*, Vol. III (Geneva, 1986), table 3; Secondary enrolment, World Bank, *World Development Report 1984*, table 25.

been hampered by low skills, lack of access to credit and policies that have been detrimental to artisan workers. Excessive reliance on government employment has been another troublesome aspect of the expansion of services, particularly in primate cities. Increases in the numbers of teachers, public health professionals and other urban service workers have helped meet the increased demands for these services by growing urban

Figure 1.1. *Labour Force Participation Rates, 1950–1980*

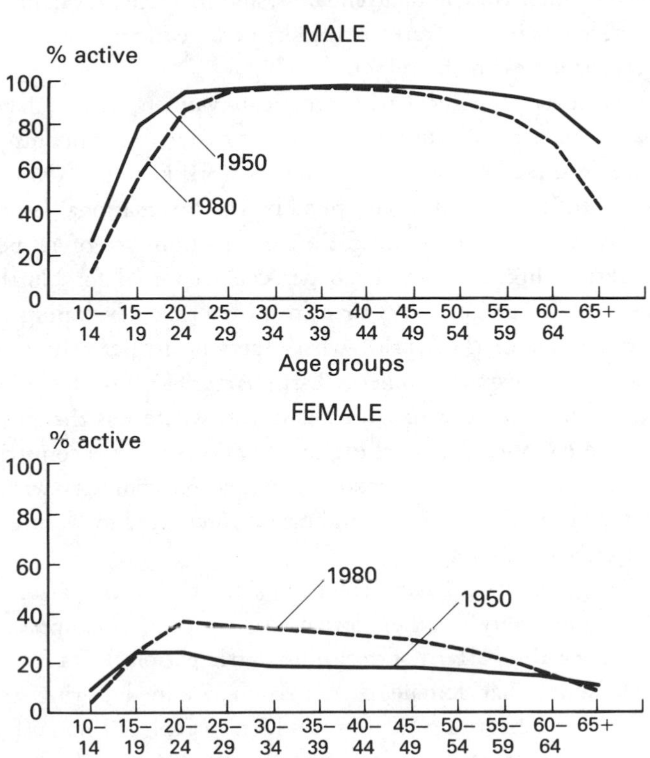

Source: International Labour Office, *Economically Active Population, 1950–2025* (Geneva, 1986)

---

population; however, they have also added to the strain of large payrolls on government budgets, to concentration of services in a few centres, and to the bureaucratic inefficiencies and potential for corruption that ensue when the government becomes the employer of last resort.

Urbanization and industrialization have also brought changes in the age and sex composition of the labour force. According to an important study by Durand, Latin American males traditionally entered the work force at a young age and left at a comparatively late age, with high participation rates in middle years.[28] The profile of age specific rates for the region resemble the inverted 'u' common in most countries (Figure 1.1). With urbanization, increase school attendance, and increase prevalence of formal retirement, participation rates have declined, reducing overall participation levels for males in the region.

The reverse is true for Latin American women, whose labour force participation patterns are also more difficult to document because of inconsistencies and under-reporting of women's work in census data. This was still true in 1980, when data complied by the International Labour Office reveal an average female labour force participation rate of 18 per cent in Latin America, higher than the 8 per cent reported for North African countries, but lower generally than in most other developing as well as developed regions of the world, where rates of 40 per cent or more are common.[29] This disparity reflects Latin America's low recorded female participation rates for the agricultural sector, where less than 15 per cent of women were reported as working in all Latin American countries except Bolivia. The age pattern of female participation contrasts with that for males (see Figure 1.1), with the highest rates reported for younger women and lower ones at older ages.

Outside agriculture, Latin American's female participation rates are generally higher than in other developing regions. This appears to be a reversal of an earlier pattern of declining participation. Data for Argentina and Brazil show that female participation declined during the initial stages of industrialization. Factory production replaced home-based artisan activities, reducing opportunities for women to combine productive and reproductive roles.

Increases in female activity rates are linked to the rise of service employment. The largest increase in female activity has occurred in rates for single women aged twenty to twenty-nine. As noted earlier, women have also been figured prominently in rural-urban migration flows, with large numbers employed as domestic servants in the cities. Cultural factors play a role in these patterns, first because of generally permissive attitudes about migration of unmarried women and second because of the high incidence of consensual unions that afford little economic security to women in them. Participation rates for women in formal unions have been lower, but they too have increased recently. Latin America still has not

[28] John D. Durand, *The Labor Force in Economic Development* (Princeton, N.J., 1975).

[29] International Labour Office, *Economically Active Population 1950–2025, Vol. V, World Summary* (Geneva, 1986).

experienced the large overall increases in female labour force participation observed in Europe and North America.

Increased educational attainment has also influenced both the age pattern and occupational structure of female employment. Increased school attendance has delayed labour force entry for females, though not so markedly as for males. It also contributed to increases in earnings and occupational differentials among working women, with those who delay labour force entry to attend school entering the labour force later and moving up the income and occupational scales more rapidly than those who entered at a earlier age with less education.

The post-war period brought remarkable increases in the educational attainment of both males and females in Latin America. Two basic indicators are the level of educational attainment and enrolment at a given level as a per cent of the population in the relevant age categories. Both need to be interpreted with caution because of difference in how countries define them. With reference to the first measure, United Nations Education and Social Organization (UNESCO) has compiled data on the proportion of adults age twenty-five and over with no schooling.[30] The proportion range from a high of 94 per cent in Guatemala in 1973 to lows of 4 per cent in Cuba in 1981 and 6 per cent in Argentina in 1980, with percentages generally higher in Central America (except for Panama and Costa Rica) and lower in South American countries.

Age-specific enrolment ratios provide another measure of progress in education. School enrolment ratios in Latin America increased significantly during post-war period. In 1960, the first year for which UNESCO reports an overall average for the region, the enrolment ratio for primary school ages six to eleven was 58 per cent; by 1985 it was 84 per cent. An even more telling indicator of increases in enrolment at the secondary level. Efforts to expand access to secondary education were mounted in a number of Latin American countries during the 1960s and 1970s. Around 1960, enrolment rates ranged from a low of 4 per cent in Haiti to 37 per cent in Uruguay, with most countries falling in the 10–20 per cent range; by the early 1980s most countries had rates in the 30–50 per cent range.

Gender differences in education are much less in Latin America than other developing regions, where average female enrolment ratios are typically two-thirds to three-quarters those of males. In Latin America, enrolment ratios for primary school-age girls were only one percentage

[30] UNESCO, *Statistical Yearbook 1985* (Paris, 1985), table 1.4.

point lower than those for males in both 1960 and 1985. At ages twelve to seventeen, the 5 percentage point gap in 1960 (39 per cent vs. 34 per cent) narrowed to just one percentage point in 1985. Even at ages eighteen to twenty-three, when many reported students are probably attending university, the marked male advantage in 1960 (7 per cent vs. 4 per cent) dropped significantly by 1985 (to 26 per cent vs. 23 per cent).[31]

Educational attainment and labour force participation are highly correlated, and both have contributed to changes in the roles of women in Latin America. As noted earlier, they have also contributed to fertility declines that have been occurring in many countries since the late 1960s and are related to a variety of other important individual and household level social and economic changes, including migration, improved health and consumption patterns. It would not be an exaggeration to say that increased education of both males and females is one of the major forces behind the often dramatic shifts in demographic patterns that Latin America has experienced in the post-war period.

INTERNATIONAL MIGRATION

Before 1930, international migration flows to Latin America consisted mainly of trans-Atlantic movements from Europe to Argentina, Brazil and Uruguay, and to a lesser extent, Chile and Cuba, Spain, Portugal and Italy were the principal countries of origin, though there were also Eastern European and Asian immigrants, including a significant number of Japanese immigrants to Brazil. Immigration slowed during the economic crisis of the 1930s, when many countries restricted immigration on grounds that immigrants were competing with natives for scarce jobs. The volume of migration increased again after the Second World War, with Venezuela emerging as the principal destination for migrants of European origin.

Immigration from origins outside the western hemisphere has continued since 1950, but at substantially lower levels. Meanwhile, two new international migration patterns within the hemisphere have taken on important economic, political and demographic significance. One consists of emigration of better educated, highly skilled workers to industrialized countries outside the region, particularly the United States, and from less to more developed countries within the region. Though limited in terms of its overall volume, the 'brain drain' has attracted much attention from researchers and policy-makers because it represents a loss of human capital for sending

[31] UNESCO, *Statistical Yearbook 1985*, table 2.11.

countries. These flows are also fairly well documented, because most are legal migration and recorded in administrative reporting systems. The out-migration of skilled workers and professionals appears to have accelerated during the economic crisis of the 1980s, which affected occupations that hitherto had been relatively more insulated from economic slowdowns.

The second main international migration current to emerge within the hemisphere since the 1950s is less well documented. This one consists of massive movements of unskilled and semi-skilled workers, joined in the 1970s by refugees fleeing civil strife in Central America. A significant fraction of this migration is illegal and therefore undocumented. It also involves temporary and seasonal moves, which further complicate efforts to measure flows. These flows are grossly underestimated in conventional data, including reports of the number of foreign-born tallied in periodic censuses.

Venezuela, Argentina and the United States have been the main destination countries for both legal and undocumented migration flows. Other important intra-regional streams involve moves among Central American countries, between Central America and Mexico, and movements among countries in the Caribbean region. Net flows for Central America, Mexico and the Caribbean underestimate the total volume of migration, since these areas are both the source of major flows and destinations for sub-regional moves.

Although legal immigration into Venezuela was highly restricted between 1959 and 1973, undocumented migration increased steadily. Sassen-Koob estimated that there were a million entries during the 1960s, though the net accumulation by the early 1970s amounted to only half a million because a significant proportion of the migrants were seasonal or temporary movers.[32] Venezuela attracted the majority of undocumented migrants from Colombia, though outflows from that country have also been directed to the United States, Ecuador and Panama. In 1973, with an economic boom underway because of rising oil prices, Venezuela attempted to gain control of the migration process by adopting a selective but more open immigration policy. By late 1977, the total number of foreign born with residence permits numbered 1.2 million out of a total population of 13 million. Migrants from Spain were the largest single group, followed by Italy, Colombia and Portugal. Estimates of the number of migrants (documented and undocumented) suggest that by 1979 there were at least a million Colombians, 200,000 from Ecuador and

[32] Saskia Sassen-Koob, 'Economic Growth and Immigration in Venezuela', *International Migration Review,* 13, 3 (1979): 455–74.

Peru, and 150,000 migrants from the Dominican Republic in Venezuela.[33] Economic conditions in Venezuela deteriorated after 1979, but the large return migration flows that had been anticipated did not materialize.

Argentina also attracted migrants from neighboring countries after the Second World War, mainly from Bolivia, Chile and Paraguay, with Uruguay and Brazil also contributing. In contrast to Venezuela, the volume of movement was greater during the 1950s than later. Buenos Aires was the principal pole of attraction for international migrants. Unskilled and semi-skilled migrants sought employment in construction and the service sector; the city also attracted skilled workers and professionals, including many whose moves were politically motivated. After 1976, there was significant emigration of professionals and skilled workers as a consequence of the political and economic crisis.

The United States was the principal destination of international migration flows from Mexico and attracted significant numbers from Central America, Colombia and Caribbean countries. Total legal migration, including refugees, increased from less than 330,000 a year during the early 1960s, to 450,000 per year during the 1970s, and 600,000 during the 1980s. Latin Americans accounted for about 40 per cent of this total during both the 1970s and the 1980s. They were the largest group during the 1970s, but fell to second place during the 1980s when Asians, represented 44 per cent of the total.[34] Mexicans remained the largest single national group among those legally admitted to the United States. Reliable data on the number of undocumented migrants do not exist, and estimates vary widely. Research based on the 1980 census suggested a figure of between 2.5 and 3.5 million illegal aliens, though data from other sources are consistent with estimates than run as high as 3.5 million, and estimates for 1986 suggest an increase in the number to between 3 and 5 million. After passage of the Immigration Reform and Control Act of 1986, which granted amnesty to 2.5 million formerly illegal aliens, the estimates drop to about 1.8 to 3 million. Mexicans accounted for nearly 60 per cent of the estimated number of illegal aliens.[35]

[33] Sergio Díaz-Briquets, *International Migration Within Latin America and the Caribbean: An Overview* (New York, 1983).

[34] Michael and Jeffrey S. Passel, 'The Door Remains Open: recent immigration to the United States and a preliminary examination of the Immigration Act of 1990', mimeo, The Urban Institute, Washington, D.C., 1991.

[35] Karen A. Woodrow, Jeffrey S. Passel, and Robert Warren, 'Preliminary Estimates of Undocumented Immigration to the United States, 1980–1986', *Proceedings of the Social Statistics Section of the American Statistical Association: 1987* (Washington, D.C., 1987).

Mexican immigrants to the United States are concentrated in the southwest, mainly Texas and California. California has also attracted significant numbers of Central Americans. Florida was the prime destination of Cuban migrants during the 1960s and again during the 1980 Mariel 'boatlift' period. New York City and nearby New Jersey, along with a few metropolitan areas in the Northeast and Midwest have also atracted immigrants from Latin America. The 1990 U.S. census enumerated 22.4 million individuals who claimed Hispanic origin. This is an increase of of nearly 8 million over the 1980 figure of 14.6 million. California accounted for 7.7 million of this total, followed by Texas, with 4.3 million. Los Angeles County, with a total 1990 population of 8.9 million, had 3.4 million people of Hispanic origin, a very high proportion of whom were Mexicans. California's Hispanic population increased by 3.1 million during the 1980s.

There is also evidence that the character of immigration from Mexico to the United States has changed. Before 1980, a high proportion of migrants were young males who were uneducated and working in agriculture while residing temporarily in the United States in a predominantly Spanish-speaking enclave and who could be characterized as 'cyclical sojourners' supporting a family left behind in Mexico. New evidence suggests that while the educational gap between natives and Mexican-born immigrants remains, migrants are more diverse in terms of their occupational characteristics and more likely to be permanent residents with families. Changes in U.S. immigration law have made it possible for Mexicans to immigrate as families.

Although Central Americans have contributed to international migration streams to Mexico and the United States, intra-regional flows have also been important in Central America, particularly when measured against the total populations of the countries involved. During the 1960s, tens of thousands of Salvadorans migrated to Honduras. Tensions created by these movements led to the 1969 war between the two countries, after which most Salvadorans left Honduras, many of them then settling in Guatemala. Costa Rica has been a main destination for Nicaraguans, and more recently Salvadorans. Panama has also attracted migrants from Central American, as well as from Colombia. Increased levels of hostility added impetus to intra-regional flows created by pre-existing stressful economic conditions. Another important set of sub-regional flows are those within the Caribbean region, including movement of Haitians to the Dominican Republic and other Caribbean islands, and of Dominicans to Puerto Rico. The Bahamas and Jamaica represent other important destinations for Caribbean migrants.

International migration occurs for many of the same reasons that motivate internal migration. Many observers have urged that internal and international population movements within the western hemisphere be considered as part of the same overall process, giving more attention given to the international scope of regional labour markets. Unequal distribution of land, limited employment and earnings opportunities in sending areas, along with high rates of natural increase in the population, have generated pressures that increasingly spilled over international borders. They also created political tensions that frequently erupted in violence, which further propelled international movements. Increased availability of low cost transportation and communications (even direct-dial long-distance telephone service) also facilitated moves.

International migration has important social, economic, and political consequences for sending as well as receiving areas. Migrants have supplied labour to occupations in receiving areas for which demand has exceeded local supply in terms of the number of individuals willing to work at a given wage level. Migrants earn less on average than local natives, but more than they would have earned doing the same work in their home country. Remittances of earnings by migrants have mounted up to significant shares of income in origin communities. At the same time, it has been shown that a significant proportion of migrants pay taxes and contribute to social insurance programmes in destinations countries.

Like internal migrants, international migrants are generally younger, better educated and more highly skilled individuals than non-migrants. Males tend to dominate streams orientated to agriculture and construction, whereas females are better represented in flows to destinations with employment opportunities in services and light industry. Selective migration tends to drain human resources from the sending region's labour pool, with detrimental effects on local productivity. The labour transfer process is often a complex overlaying of successive migration streams. The construction industry in Mexico City draws on migrant labour from Guatemala to fill jobs left by Mexicans seeking better opportunities in the southwestern United States.

POPULATION GROWTH AND ECONOMIC DEVELOPMENT

The acceleration of population growth rates in Latin America after 1950 aroused much concern that rapid population increase would adversely affect its economic development. Much of this concern was expressed in so-called 'neo-Malthusian' views of the relation between population and economic growth. The logic of neo-Malthusian theory rests on three sets of relationships between economic and demographic variables. The first is a straightforward accounting relationship: as the rate of population growth increases, so does the rate of growth in income required to achieve or maintain a given level of growth in income per capita. With higher population growth, investment that might have increased per capita income must go instead to maintain income per capita at the level it was when population growth was lower.

The second focus is on the relation between age structure and investment. When a population's growth rate is increasing as a result of high fertility and declining mortality (rather, for example, than because of immigration), its age structure is heavily weighted with children, which means that there are fewer producers per consumer than in a population with a low birth rate. Neo-Malthusians argue that this makes it more difficult to raise the percentage of investment required to achieve an increase in per capita income and, conversely, that a population with a lower birth rate will be able to achieve a higher level of income per capita over the long run. Timing is the key to this strand of the argument. Eventually, a large population will have higher total output because there are more workers, but the lag between birth and entry into the labour force – typically 15–20 years – will give the population with a lower birth rate an edge in building up per-worker capital, so that its output per worker will be greater over the long run. Economists refer to this process as 'capital deepening'.

The third set of relationships involves the determinants of demographic change. Neo-Malthusians doubted the applicability of demographic transition theory in Latin America. They pointed out that mortality decline depended on the introduction of exogenous medical technology, which weakened the link between mortality and living standards in developing countries, and went on to argue that high rates of population growth would prevent those countries from reaching the higher living standards needed to bring about a fertility transition. Developing countries would be caught in a 'Malthusian trap', in which high birth rates inhibit economic development. Without economic development, birth rates will not decline. The main policy conclusion of neo-Malthusian theory is that interventions to reduce birth rates are needed for countries to escape this trap.

As late as the 1960s most Latin American countries fitted the neo-Malthusian profile of rapid population growth, high levels of age dependency and low savings rates. Yet Latin American social scientists and economic planners treated the theory with a great deal of scepticism. They criticized it for overlooking fundamental institutional obstacles to development and were suspicious of the motives of outside agencies who appeared to be using the theory to push family planning rather than deal with these more fundamental issues.

This critique is rooted in the Latin American intellectual tradition that came to be labeled as the 'structural' approach to economic development.[36] Structuralists viewed the unequal distribution of wealth, particularly land and other productive resources, and of political power as the fundamental obstacles to development, and traced these problems to the region's colonial experience (including the economic colonialism of the export phase) and to industrialization policies that aggravated rather than alleviated inequality in more recent decades.

Structuralists challenged the neo-Malthusian suggestion that population was the root cause of under-development, which neo-Malthusians tried to demonstrate by using economic-demographic models to show that per capita income would be higher with lower birth rates. Structuralists also question the age dependency/savings link on the grounds that income inequality kept the incomes of the masses of the population so low that the added consumption expenditures that they might have incurred with larger families were not likely to have had much effect on aggregate savings and investment.

Following the structuralist line, Latin Americans played a major role in promoting the rallying cry that 'development is the best contraceptive' at the 1974 World Population Conference at Bucharest. This was not meant to imply that individuals could control their fertility without using some form of contraception but, in a challenge to neo-Malthusian views, to assert that if fertility rates were to decline, individuals had to see some personal benefit to reduced fertility, and that much of this benefit, or the perception of it, depended on their being able to raise their living standards. With great income inequality, poor couples may not perceive much benefit in having fewer children, even if the national economy grows more rapidly. The extreme variant of this view held that putting resources into family planning programmes rather than rather than basic social development was counter-productive. At a minimum, family planning efforts would only succeed to the extent that they took account of the social and economic context in which they are being promoted.

[36] See Joseph L. Love, 'Economic Ideas and Ideologies in Latin America since 1930', Chapter 7 in this volume.

The polarization between neo-Malthusians and their critics that surfaced at the Bucharest Conference softened during the 1980s. A middle view emerged, based on recent experiences in Latin America and other developing countries, which demonstrated how both socio-economic changes as well as family planning programmes contributed to fertility declines, their effects being mutually reinforcing rather than conflicting. Family planning agencies in Latin America sought to broaden the scope of services that they delivered, integrating them with general maternal and child health care as well as nutrition programmes, while agencies that had been reluctant to include family planning in the past began to recognize it as an important element in efforts to improve the welfare of the poor.[37]

Though die-hard pessimists and optimists continued their debate on the effects of population on development, adherents of the broader view came to recognize both the fundamental institutional obstacles to development as well as the problems that rapid population increase created for dealing with such obstacles. Rapid population growth did not prevent a number of Latin American countries from achieving high rates of growth in per capita product during the post-war period. However, the broad-based age structures they inherited from periods of high birth rates before 1965 did not made it any easier to cope with problems of providing adequate employment opportunities, housing and other services needed to raise the living standards of the poor masses.

Ansley Coale came to similar conclusions when he was invited to visit Mexico twenty years after his study (co-authored with E. M. Hoover) on *Population Growth and Economic Development in Low Income Countries* to discuss how actual experience had measured up to the projections he had made in 1956.[38] What Coale found was not atypical of the experience of a number of Latin American countries: Mexican *population* had followed the high birth rate path projected in the Coale–Hoover model (there was only a fraction of a percentage point difference between his earlier projections and later population estimates for 1976), but the Mexican *economy* grew at a rate that generated growth of per capita income that was closer to what was projected in the low birth rate path. Moreover, despite urbanization, increased education, and lower mortality, birth rates had not declined

[37] Thomas W. Merrick, 'World Population in Transition', *Population Bulletin,* 41, 2 (Washington, D.C., 1986).

[38] Ansley J. Coale, and E. M. Hoover, *Population Growth and Economic Development in Low Income Countries* (Princeton, N.J., 1958) and Ansley J. Coale, 'Population Growth and Economic Development: the case of Mexico', *Foreign Affairs,* 56, 2 (1978): 415–29.

between 1955 and 1975, as suggested by those who held the optimistic view that fertility decline would follow economic and social progress.

Mexico's experience appeared paradoxical to pessimists who held that rapid population growth inhibits economic growth as well as for optimists who were sure that social progress would reduce birth rates. The experience is much less paradoxical when one looks at the distribution of income rather than average levels of income. That much of Mexico's population did not share in the high overall average rate of growth in income is evident in income distribution figures; in 1977 the bottom 20 per cent of households received only 3 per cent of income, while the top 20 per cent received 58 per cent and the top 10 per cent 41 per cent.[39] An economy that produced high rates of growth in average output per capita was also one that employed relatively few workers in the high-income, modernized sectors. This, combined with the large numbers in the young adult age cohorts produced by the continuation of high birth rates between 1950 and 1975, meant that Mexico faced a severe problem of providing productive employment for those cohorts. The potential political repercussions were also serious, because urbanization, increased education and media exposure raised expectations that have proved difficult to realize in the face of increasingly limited economic opportunities.

Starting in the mid-1970s, Mexico's birth rate declined. It may or may not be coincidental that in 1973 Mexico changed its official population policy from a pronatalist position to one supporting family planning programmes in order to reduce its birth rate. Neo-Malthusians could interpret this as vindication of their argument that intervention was needed to bring down birth rates; structuralists may see it as supporting their view that socio-economic change led to fertility decline. What the Mexican experience and similar stories in other countries reveal is that a combination of increased availability of family planning and of economic and social pressures arising from the gap between the aspirations of young adults and their capacity to realize them was being manifested in the acceleration of fertility declines that occurred in Latin America after 1975.[40]

POPULATION POLICY

One of the mechanisms promoted by international development assistance agencies to elicit developing country responses to the problem of rapid

[39] World Bank, *World Development Report 1985* (New York: 1985), table 28, p. 229.

[40] Francisco Alba, and Joseph E. Potter, 'Population and Development in Mexico since 1940: an interpretation', *Population and Development Review*, 12, 1 (1986): 44–75.

population growth was the establishment of official population policies, usually in the form of targeted reductions in population growth rates and explicit incorporation of development plans, or at least official support of family planning programmes even if for purposes other than the slowing of population growth rates. This was a major goal of the 1974 World Population Conference at Bucharest, which sought adoption of a World Population Plan of Action by representatives of developing countries.

Latin Americans were generally cool, and in some cases openly hostile to the Plan as originally drafted, charging that it represented an attempt by neo-Malthusians in the industrialized countries to create an anti-natalist 'bandwagon' that served their own interests rather than those of the developing countries. Argentina and Cuba played lead roles in reorientating the Plan toward the 'development as the best contraceptive' philosophy that characterized the document as finally adopted. The Bucharest experience revealed the political sensitivity among Latin Americans and other developing country representatives on the population question at that time, particularly to what they perceived to be overly aggressive interference in what was essentially an internal affair.[41]

Latin American attitudes on population reflect at least three major intellectual, political and cultural currents. Intellectually, Latin American thinking on the relation between population and economic development was strongly influenced by the structuralist school, whose criticisms of neo-Malthusian theory were outlined in the previous section. Two other currents are represented: the first by the nationalistic orientated military who, directly or indirectly, played a major political role in the region during the post-war period, and second, by the Catholic Church. Sovereignty and national security have been recurrent themes in nationalistic thought. These ideas can be traced to concerns about the need to establish settlements in insecure frontier areas to prevent others from doing so first. Although not exclusively the domain of the military, such concerns were often at the root of resistance by military governments in Latin America to demographic interventions by outsiders.

In assessing the influence of the Catholic Church, to which the majority of Latin Americans are at least nominally affiliated, it is important to distinguish the role of the Church in popular culture from the Church hierarchy, its teaching and its political influence. The rapid rise in contraceptive prevalence in many Latin American countries is a reflection of the relatively limited influence of the official ban on artificial birth control at

[41] Thomas G. Sanders, 'Latin Americans at Bucharest', *American Universities Field Staff Reports*, East Coast South America Series, 18 (1974).

the popular level. Still, the conservative wing of the hierarchy has stood firmly behind the Church's 1968 prohibition of artificial birth control and shows little sign of liberalizing its stance on the question, particularly after visits to Latin America by Pope John-Paul II. Even more liberal bishops, who often challenged right-wing military regimes on human rights issues, remained conservative on family planning, adopting a view (under the rubric of 'liberation theology') that came close to structuralist theories on development issues in general.

At times the Latin American Church hierarchy used or attempted to use its political influence to alter block implementation of organized family planning programmes. Its impact was limited. Family planning organizations were quick to learn that a non-confrontational approach was the most effective way to deal with the Church. They learned quickly that it was better to act cautiously rather than try to push openly for public consensus through processes that might force the Church's hand by having it appear either as opposed to measures that were being promoted in the public interest or as abrogating its theological stance on birth control.

Despite the uproar about population policy created by the Bucharest Conference, Latin America's two largest countries, Brazil and Mexico, adopted population policies in 1974. President Echeverría announced a major shift away from Mexico's pronatalist position in his September 1972 'State of the Nation' report, which was incorporated in a 1974 population law that called for stabilization of population growth. Mexico later established a National Population Council, set a target for population growth rate at 1 per cent per annum by the year 2000, and implemented a broad-based national family planning programme. Brazil also articulated an official policy on population in its 1974 national development plan, but did not follow Mexico in seeking population stabilization. Rather it sought a rate of population increase that was consistent with overall development objectives, gave tacit approval to widespread family planning efforts by private organizations, and even permitted private physicians to perform (and be remunerated for) sterilizations in publicly owned hospitals.

Brazil's more cautious approach is more typical of most Latin American countries. For over a decade, Dorothy Nortman compiled data on national population policies in developing countries.[42] She classified policies in

[42] Dorothy L. Nortman, *Population and Family Planning Programs: A Compendium of Data Through 1983*, 12th edn (New York, 1985), table 6.

three groups: (a) those with specific goals to reduce population growth rates through family planning programmes; (b) those which did not overtly seek to reduce growth rates, but supported family planning for other purposes; and (c) those with no explicit policy or which had adopted explicitly pro-natalist positions. Only five Latin American countries were classified in group (a) in the most recent (1985) compilation. In addition to Mexico, these included Colombia, the Dominican Republic, El Salvador and Guatemala (along with Barbados, Jamaica and Puerto Rico). Only two, Bolivia and Chile, were classed in group (c), though Argentina and Uruguay, which were not included in Nortman's survey, should also be considered in this class. Chile's inclusion represented a major shift away from an earlier anti-natalist position; indeed, it was one of the pioneer (1966) Latin American members of group (a) until the military government adopted a pronatalist policy in 1979.

Most (eleven of twenty) Latin American countries belonged to Nortman's category (b), which covers a wide range of policies as well as family planning implementation. There was Costa Rica, which did not have a specific policy about population growth reduction, but mounted what was once one of the hemisphere's most effective family planning programmes. Brazil and Peru, in contrast, had official policies to seek growth rates that were consistent with development objectives, but did not view their rapid population growth rates to be inconsistent with those goals. Nor did they implement vigorous national family planning programmes.

Clearly, there is no single answer to the question of how important the establishment of an official population policy was for the reduction of population growth rates in Latin America. Mexico exemplifies how a policy shift that was introduced with substantial ceremony and publicity created broad political support for family planning at a time when increased access to these services contributed to a very substantial decline in fertility. Colombia, on the other hand, was much more circumspect about official policy pronouncements, but moved early and vigorously to establish private-sector family planning programmes that contributed to a fertility decline that began several years earlier than Mexico's. Brazil, in contrast, had neither strong policy statements nor national level financial support of family planning, but nevertheless experienced a fertility decline that was similar in most respects to the ones observed in Mexico and Colombia.[43]

[43] Thomas W. Merrick, 'The Evolution and Impact of Policies on Fertility and Family Planning: Brazil, Colombia, and Mexico', in Godfrey Roberts (ed), *Population Policy: Contemporary Issues* (New York, 1990), pp. 147–66.

Although population growth and fertility rates have been the principal topics the population policy debate in Latin America, other issues have also surfaced. Internal population distribution and urbanization, particularly the problems associated with the concentration of population in the largest cities, have been long-standing concerns to Latin American governments. Sporadic resettlement efforts have been mounted, but because the process of population redistribution and its links to other social and economic changes are so complex, governments have found it very difficult to articulate policies and establish programmes to shape distribution patterns.

Increased international migration flows have generated similar concerns. This question surfaced as one of the major policy issues at a conference of parliamentarians concerned with interrelations between population and development held in Brasília in late 1982 and again at the 1984 International Population Conference in Mexico D.F. Several countries in the region have tightened or are considering revisions of their policies and laws regulating international migration in response to the increased volume of movement in the hemisphere. Sparking a lot of debate was 1986 legislation restricting migration flows in the United States, largely aimed at stemming the flow of undocumented immigration along the U.S. southern border. Some Latin Americans questioned the length to which national governments ought to go in restricting the access of migrants from poorer areas to economic opportunities in destination regions that are richer by comparison, notwithstanding possible displacement of natives at the destination and other social problems that these flows would create. One of the more controversial political issues raised by U.S. migration was the question of migrants' access to social benefits, their children's access to public schooling and other entitlements.

POPULATION IN RETROSPECT AND PROSPECT

Looking back a half century from the 1980s to the 1930s, there are many parallels within the two decades that bracket the period reviewed in this chapter. During the 1930s Latin America was forced to adjust to a world economic crisis that undermined the export based economic system on which it had relied since the colonial era. In the 1980s the region experienced another major economic crisis, this one brought by major recessions in Europe and North America, staggering debts and fluctuations in energy prices. Both crises were triggered by external shocks, but their severity and responses to them at the national level were strongly influenced by the internal economic and social structures that had emerged in preceding decades.

Many of the quandaries that confronted Latin American countries in the 1980s crisis are rooted in the structural shifts that accompanied the region's response to the crisis of the 1930s and the subsequent re-alignment of the world economy that followed the Second World War. The inward-looking refocussing of Latin American economies on import substituting industrialization during the 1950s and 1960s brought with it profound changes, including the demographic and social trends described in this chapter: increased life expectancy, smaller families, a near-quadrupling of total population, most of it concentrated in cities because of the rapid urbanization that occurred. These changes generated new pressures on national political-economic systems, pressures which increased the vulnerability of those systems to shocks in the world economy.

When fluctuations in energy prices during the 1970s threatened to slow the expansions that the industrialization process had started or (for the region's oil exporters) provided what appeared to be opportunities for further expansion, many Latin American countries borrowed heavily on world financial markets anxious to channel newly available funds into the region's then promising economic environment. This strategy backfired when rising interest rates and the serious major world recession in the early 1980s created a debt-servicing nightmare for borrowing nations, forcing many even deeper into debt in order to pay the interest on existing debt.

Fiscal and monetary policy adjustments demanded by international financial institutions in return for continued lending and rescheduling of debts clashed with demands created by the demographic and social changes of the last five decades. Not only was Latin America's population almost four times larger and much more urbanized than it was in 1930, it was also a youthful, better educated population with higher expectations about living standards. Because the post-war economic expansion failed to generate sufficient employment and earnings opportunities to incorporate large segments of that population, many of these expectations have yet to be realized. Rubens Vaz da Costa, a prominent Brazilian economist, has termed this the region's 'social debt' in an analogy to the large financial debts plaguing so many countries.[44]

However desirable it would have been for Latin America to move back the historical clock and substitute a more equitable and labour-absorbing economic structure for the one that actually evolved, the shifts were for the most part irreversible. The same is true of demographic trends, which raised a number of challenges with which countries have had to cope in dealing with their economic crises. One of these was population growth itself. While population growth rates were slower by 1980, Latin American was still faced with the potential for substantial absolute increases in population size before population stabilization would be achieved.

These large prospective increases are rooted in the nature of post-war demographic trends. Even after some fertility declines, the region's birth rates remained high by international and historical comparisons. There was a very large population base that accumulated over several decades of rapid growth. While rates were lower, the volume of increase remained large because of the large base. Demographers have compared this phenomenon to the momentum of massive physical objects – large populations take about a generation to slow to zero growth after fertility reaches the replacement level (where couples have about two children, on average) because of 'demographic momentum'. During this braking period, a population may well double in size.[45]

International organizations as well as government statistical agencies have been making projections of the population of Latin American over the past several decades. A 1951 United Nations document projected a population of 321 million for the region in 1980, which is about 12 per cent below the most recent estimate for 1980, which puts the total at 363 million. The 1951 projection underestimated the impact of mortality decline on population increase. A later (1970) projection took account of mortality decline, but it failed to anticipate the dramatic decline in fertility that occurred during the 1970s, so that it was about 4 per cent higher than recent 1980 estimates.[46]

Recently revised CELADE (Centro Latinoamericano de Demografía)/United Nations' projections take fertility declines into account and project

[44] Rubens Vaz da Costa, 'Introductory remarks', in International Planned Parenthood Federation, Western Hemisphere Region, *Population and Development* (New York, 1981), p. 2.

[45] See Merrick, 'World Population in Transition,' p. 6.

[46] See Thomas Frejka, *World Population Projections: A Concise History,* Center for Policy Studies Working Paper No. 66 (New York, 1981).

a total population of 538 million for the region by the end of the century. Those projections continue to the year 2025, and show a total population of 757 million by that date.[47] The projections assume that there will be declines in growth rates during the next several decades, but that population stabilization is still a long way off.

When the regional totals are disaggregated, the numbers implied for specific countries and sub-regional groups are awesome: Brazil growing from 121 million in 1980 to 246 million in 2025; Mexico from 70 million to 150 million in the same period; the combined populations of Central American countries increase from 23 million to 63 million. Whether these countries can support the continuation of population growth to levels that are more than two times their present size depends on social, political and economic changes that are themselves conditioned by demographic pressures. It is hard to envision how populations of such magnitude could be supported without profound changes in existing institutions, or how such changes, when brought about by population pressures, would not themselves slow population increase more quickly than anyone now imagines. At this point one leaves the realm of demographic projections and enters that of imagining scenarios which need to take account of the human potential for adaptation and technical advance as well as the risk of the demographic catastrophes which have plagued humanity in past epochs.

While many questions remain to be answered about the long-run course of demographic change in Latin America, over the short run (the next decade or two) the impact of the very rapid increase during 1955–75 will be felt in a number of ways. Employment will be a central problem. The labour market entrants of the 1980s and 1990s were born between 1960 and 1980. Even with declining birth *rates* during the 1970s, the pressures for job opportunities will continue until well into the 1990s because the *number* of births did not decline in proportion to the decline in the birth rate, again because of the large population base that accumulated. According to projections, the region's 'youth' population (ages fifteen to twenty-four) is estimated to increase by 29 million between in the twenty years between 1980 and 2000 (from 73 to 102 million), and will further increase to 122 million in the year 2025 unless birth rate declines much more rapidly in the 1980s than during the 1970s.

Urban growth is another major demographic feature of the 1980s and

[47] United Nations, *World Population Prospects 1990* (New York, 1991).

1990s. It is almost certain that towns and cities will absorb the natural population increase in Latin America during the coming several decades, plus spillover from rural areas through migration. The staggering projections of population size for the region's major metropolitan regions have already been noted. Even in secondary cities the projections exceed the size of most primate cities in the 1960s: over 5 million, for example, in Guadalajara and Belo Horizonte. The projections suggest that there will be more than fifty cities with populations of over a million by the end of the century. Projections of this magnitude suggest that even if planners succeed in dampening the growth of the very largest cities, their problems in coping with large city populations will only spread to other localities rather than disappear.

Latin America's cities will bear the main brunt of the employment problem. The labour-saving bias of post-war industrialization has already created an imbalance between the supply and demand for jobs, and demographic factors increase rather than decrease that demand in coming decades. Other needs generated by rapid urban growth – housing, public transportation, water and sanitation, schools, hospitals and health facilities – are also feeling the pinch of tighter government budgets and the unwillingness of foreign banks to further extend themselves in what they view to be very risky situations.

Another demographic trend that is likely to continue at least in the short run is international migration within the western hemisphere. Economic and demographic pressures brought a substantial increase in international population movements during the 1970s, and there is little sign that these pressures abated during the 1980s. For the United States, the proximity of Mexico and Central America and their limited capacity to provide productive employment for youth pose a special challenge. They account for nearly 10 million of Latin America's projected 29 million increase in its youth population between 1980 and 2000. Improved transportation and communication have contributed to the internationalization of the region's labour markets. These flows are difficult (therefore expensive) to measure and control, despite increasing national sentiment in some of the receiving areas to protect their own natives from having to compete for jobs against migrants who are willing to accept lower pay and poorer working conditions which, to them, appear to be better than having no job in the place that they came from. Because of international migration, population pressure and the problems that it generates are increasingly regional rather than national in scope, which means that even those countries that have had slower growth during the post-war period are likely to share during the next few years in the consequences of the rapid growth experienced by their neighbours.

Part Two

ECONOMY

2

THE LATIN AMERICAN ECONOMIES, 1929–1939

The Depression of 1929 has usually been portrayed as a turning-point in Latin America's transition from outward-looking (export-led) economic growth to inward-looking development based on import substituting industrialization (ISI). This analysis has been shared equally by the 'structuralists', who generally view the shift favourably, and by 'neo-conservatives', who regard the 1930s as the decade in which Latin America 'lost its way'. There is no doubt that the decade saw the emergence in many countries of new economic, social and political forces, which would ultimately provide a very different shape to the Latin American model of economic development. However, although traditional export-led growth became very difficult in the 1930s, a residual commitment to primary products and outward-looking development survived throughout the region and foreign trade played an important role in the recovery from depression. It was not until the 1940s and 1950s that a number of Latin American countries explicitly rejected export-led growth and even then there were many (smaller) countries that remained committed to a version of outward-looking development.

FROM THE FIRST WORLD WAR TO THE 1929 DEPRESSION

The export-led growth model had been changing long before 1929. By the beginning of the twentieth century, the stimulus from export growth given to non-export sectors, such as manufacturing, had already reached the point where a group of countries (in particular Argentina, Brazil, Chile and Mexico) could meet a relatively high proportion of domestic demand with local rather than imported goods. This virtuous circle, under which productivity gains in the export sector were transferred to the non-export economy, did not always work smoothly (e.g., Peru) and in some cases hardly at all (e.g., Cuba), but the rudiments of a more sophisticated, and more balanced, export-led growth model were clearly apparent by the beginning of the twentieth century. Thus, export-led growth in some countries was quite consistent with the growth of manufacturing geared to the home market and replacing imports of consumer goods.

The model, however, depended on relatively free access to world commodity and factor markets and this was placed in jeopardy as early as the First World War. When war broke out in Europe on 2 August 1914, it was not just the international balance of power that was shattered; the global trade and payments system, which had slowly evolved since the end of the Napoleonic wars, was also thrown into disarray. With the signing of the armistice in 1919, a brave face was put on attempts to reconstruct the pre-war system; yet the old international economic order had perished and the new one established in the 1920s was dangerously unstable. This instability was scarcely perceived at the time, leaving peripheral regions – such as Latin America – extremely vulnerable to the collapse of international trade and capital flows at the end of the 1920s.

The main feature of the old order had been the existence of relatively unrestricted international trade – a reflection of the interests of the dominant economic power (Great Britain) in the nineteenth century; the limited restrictions in force generally took the form of tariffs, which had the advantage for all concerned of being transparent. Both capital and labour were free to move across international boundaries and passports were the exception rather than the rule. The gold standard, adopted first by Britain, had spread to all the main industrial countries by the end of the century and provided a well-established mechanism for balance-of-payments adjustment. Internal equilibrium (full employment and zero inflation) was regarded as less important than external equilibrium so that the burden of adjustment to adverse shocks was usually achieved through price deflation and underemployment.

Latin American countries had slotted into this scheme relatively easily on the basis of primary product exports, capital inflows and – in the case of Argentina, Brazil and Uruguay in particular – international migration. Balance-of-payments adjustment was never very smooth and capital flows were usually procyclical, falling at just the moment when they were most needed, but these disruptions with rare exceptions (e.g., the Baring crisis) had little impact on the dynamics of world economic growth. Internal adjustment was cushioned by the existence of a large non-export agricultural sector with low productivity to which many workers could withdraw in the event of a fall in the demand for labour.

At the apex of the pre-war international economic system stood Great Britain. Although its dominant position in manufactured exports and its leadership in science and technology were under threat by the end of the nineteenth century, Britain was still the financial powerhouse of the world, a source of capital for the periphery and a major importer of primary products. British financial pre-eminence reinforced the rules of the international system and its navy stood ready to block all attempts at restricting the freedom of trade and capital movements.

The first casualty of the Great War was the gold standard and the movement of capital. Currency convertibility was suspended by the belligerent countries, new capital issues were cancelled and old loans recalled to shore up the balance sheet of financial institutions in Europe. Latin American republics heavily dependent for balance-of-payments finance on the European market, such as Argentina and Brazil, were particularly badly hit as European-owned banks called in loans and provoked a domestic financial crisis.

The hostilities in Europe also brought to an end the inflows of direct foreign investment from the Old World. The United States, neutral in the Great War until 1917, increased its direct investment in Latin America sharply, particularly in the extraction of strategic raw materials, but was not in a position to increase portfolio lending until the 1920s. U.S. banks, however, prevented until 1914 by law from investing in foreign subsidiaries, began to set up branch operations in Latin America: by 1919 National City Bank, the first U.S. multinational bank, had forty-two branches in nine Latin American republics.[1]

The upheavals in the capital market were mirrored in the disruption of commodity markets, but here the short-run impact was very different from the long-run. Shortages of shipping at the start of war, coupled with the absence of trade credit, disrupted normal supplies, but demand fell even faster and drove down prices in many markets. The fall in short-run export earnings, together with the decline in new capital inflows, reduced the demand for imports (the supply of which was in any case also disrupted by shipping shortages). The fall in imports was so sharp that Latin America as a whole was estimated to be running a current account surplus by

[1] See Barbara Stallings, *Banker to the Third World: U.S. Portfolio Investment in Latin America, 1900–1986* (Berkeley, Cal., 1987), p. 66.

1915, but this rapid short-run adjustment to external disequilibrium brought a big decline in real government income – dependent as it was on import tariffs. In Chile, for example, government revenue fell by one-third between 1913 and 1915 and this was a major contributor towards political instability at that time.

The short-run impact of commodity market disruption was soon overwhelmed by the shift towards a war economy in the main industrial countries. The demand for strategic raw materials (e.g., copper, petroleum) soared and shipping space was made available by the allied powers. The prices of strategic materials rose sharply and countries exporting a high proportion of strategic materials – for example, Mexico (oil), Peru (copper), Bolivia (tin) and Chile (nitrates) – even enjoyed an improvement in the net barter terms of trade despite the rise in import prices. However, although the capacity to import rose sharply, the volume of imports remained restricted in many cases. The consequent rise in import prices, coupled with trade surpluses and budget deficits, provoked domestic inflation. The impact of this inflation on urban real wages was a contributory factor in the political upheavals in a number of Latin American countries during and immediately after the First World War.

Countries exporting non-strategic raw materials (e.g., coffee) were not so favoured. Prices rose, but the terms of trade deteriorated and shipping remained a serious constraint on the volume of exports. Brazil, for example, heavily dependent on the export of coffee, was unable to sustain its first coffee valorization scheme and saw its barter terms of trade fall by 50 per cent between 1914 and 1918, while the quantum of exports was unchanged.[2] Small countries in Central America and the Caribbean were protected to some extent by their proximity to the United States, although banana exports suffered badly from a shortage of shipping until towards the end of the war.

The outbreak of hostilities in Europe did not lead to the total loss of traditional markets. Britain remained heavily dependent on food imports (e.g., meat, sugar) and strenuous efforts were made to maintain supplies of Latin American exports. However, almost equally strenuous efforts were made by the allied powers to prevent German access to Latin American raw materials. Although the major countries in the region (except Brazil) were neutral throughout the war, trade with Germany became increasingly difficult and both the United States and Britain employed a

[2] See Bill Albert, *South America and the First World War* (Cambridge, 1988), pp. 56–7.

blacklist of firms in Latin America believed to be under the control of German nationals. The result was a sharp squeeze on the share of Latin American exports and imports accounted for by Germany.

The principal beneficiary of this squeeze was the United States. Already the main supplier for Mexico, Central America and the Caribbean, the United States during the war became the most important market for most Latin American countries while its share of imports reached a quarter in South America and nearly 80 per cent in the Caribbean basin (including Mexico). The fortuitous timing of the opening of the Panama Canal at the beginning of the war, when transatlantic trade was becoming dangerous and difficult, allowed exports from the United States to penetrate markets in South America which had previously been supplied from Europe in general and Germany in particular. The network of U.S. branch banks which followed this trade, coupled with an aggressive diplomatic effort in support of U.S. business, ensured that the outbreak of peace would still leave the United States in a hegemonic position in the northern republics and a strong position elsewhere.

The eclipse of Germany as a trading partner not only contributed to the rise in importance of the United States, but also softened the decline in importance of Great Britain. British dominance was retained only in trade with Argentina, but this was still by far the largest market in Latin America and Argentina remained the region's most important exporter. However, Argentine exports to Britain substantially exceeded its imports from the same source and this trade surplus was roughly matched by a trade deficit with the United States. This triangularity of foreign trade – observed in reverse in the case of Brazil – could only work in a world system of convertible currencies and multilateral payments so that the external trade of the major Latin American republics became vulnerable in the 1920s to any departure from gold standard orthodoxy.

The restoration of the gold standard was indeed a priority after the Treaty of Versailles, but it took some years to achieve and – in the case of Great Britain – involved great hardship as a result of the adoption of an over-valued parity for the pound sterling. The slow growth of the UK economy in the 1920s was a blow for those Latin American countries which had traditionally looked to Britain as a market for exports and the emergence of the United States as the dominant economic power was little consolation for those republics selling goods in competition with U.S. farmers. Between 1913 and 1929, U.S. imports from Latin America rose by 110 per cent (far more rapidly than British imports which increased by only 45 per cent), but US exports to the region rose by 161 per cent outpacing imports from the region by a considerable margin. Thus, Latin America, which had run a substantial trade surplus with the United States before and during the war, was by the end of the 1920s in the reverse position. Exports to the United States in 1929 represented 34 per cent of all exports while U.S. suppliers took nearly 40 per cent of all imports.

The surplus enjoyed by the United States in its commodity and service trade with Latin America reflected its emergence as a capital exporter. New York replaced London after the war as the leading international financial centre and Latin American republics increasingly turned to the United States for the issue of bonds, public sector loans and direct foreign investment. At first supported by U.S. government efforts in favour of dollar diplomacy, the flow of capital soon acquired a momentum of its own; foreign investment (direct and indirect) poured into Latin America and the proportion of the stock controlled by U.S. investors steadily rose at the expense of European countries. Britain and France continued to invest in parts of Latin America, but the new investments were modest and commensurate with the weak balance-of-payments position of the two countries.

The emergence of the United States in the 1920s as a major source of foreign capital was a mixed blessing for Latin America. The appearance of dynamic new capital markets in the western hemisphere was clearly of great importance in view of the shrinking capital surplus available from traditional European markets, but the new borrowing was only achieved at a price. In the smaller republics, the new lending was intertwined with U.S. foreign policy objectives and many countries found themselves obliged to submit to U.S. control of the customs house or even national railways to ensure prompt debt payment. In some of the larger republics, the new lending reached such epidemic proportions that it became known as 'the dance of the millions'. Little effort was made to ensure that the funds were invested productively in projects that could guarantee repayment in foreign exchange[3] and the scale of corruption in a few cases reached massive proportions. U.S. officials might occupy the customs house in pursuit of fiscal rectitude, but they had little or no control over U.S. bankers issuing bonds to cover widening public sector deficits.

[3] It has been estimated that only 36 per cent of all U.S. loans to Latin America in the 1920s were for infrastructure projects. The rest were for 'refinancing, general purposes or purposes unknown'. See Stallings, *Banker to the Third World*, p. 131.

The changing international balance of power and the shifts in the international capital market were not the only problems in the 1920s with which Latin America had to grapple. Even more serious were changes in commodity markets and the increase in commodity price and earnings instability. The unstable conditions during and after the war led to sudden shifts in demand curves which could play havoc with commodity prices. The world recession in 1920/1 was a case in point. Prices for many commodities (notably sugar) collapsed as stocks held for strategic purposes were unwound. The abolition of wartime price controls, enforced by civil servants with draconian powers in the major countries, led to an initial price surge, a dynamic supply response and a subsequent price collapse in many markets.

The 1920/1 world depression was short-lived, but the problem of commodity over-supply was to last much longer. While the long-run growth of demand for primary product exports in the centre was slowing down – as a result of demographic change, falling income elasticities of demand and the creation of synthetic substitutes – the long-run rate of growth of supply was speeding up as a result of technological progress, new investments in social infrastructure (including transport) and the protection of agriculture in many parts of Europe.

These demand and supply shifts produced changes in long-run equilibrium prices which should have acted as signals for a change in resource allocation in Latin America. For many countries, the net barter terms of trade deteriorated between 1913 and 1929. However, a number of factors distorted the information provided by price signals, while the uncertainty created by war and its aftermath made it difficult for private entrepreneurs and public sector officials in Latin America to draw appropriate conclusions. As a result Latin America not only failed to adjust its external sector to the new international conditions in the 1920s, but even increased its dependence on primary product exports quite markedly.

The first problem was the short-run instability of commodity prices which concealed long-run trends. This had been a problem for Latin American primary product exporters before the war, but was much greater in the 1920s; in Chile, for example, export price instability was double what it had been before 1914 and export value instability was nearly five times higher.[4] Even in Argentina, with its much more diversified exports,

[4] See Gabriel Palma, 'From an Export-led to an Import-substituting Economy: Chile 1914–39', in Rosemary Thorp (ed.), *Latin America in the 1930s* (London, 1984), p. 55.

export instability was greater in the 1920s than at any other time in the republic's history.[5]

The second problem was the continuation of 'strategic' demand for minerals for a number of years after the war. The need to control supplies of petroleum, copper, tin, and so forth, led to official encouragement of U.S. firms to invest heavily in Latin America; with European powers doing the same in colonies and dominions, there was a real danger of world over-supply of certain minerals. Furthermore, as these new investments came on stream in the second half of the 1920s, strategic demand had in many cases abated and stocks began to increase. When world interest rates rose in the wake of the stock market boom in 1928, the costs of holding stock rose sharply and discouraged additional purchases.

The third problem was the manipulation of prices in a number of key markets. The Brazilian coffee valorization scheme, revived in the 1920s, reduced Brazilian supplies reaching the world market and raised prices. However, other coffee exporters (e.g., Colombia) responded to higher world prices by increasing plantings; this increased production hit the market a few years later and the coffee market was saturated as early as 1926. Brazil attempted to repeat the experiment with rubber, but its share of the world market was by now too small to have a significant impact on prices.

The final problem was the weakness of the non-export sector in so many Latin American countries. The idea that resources would shift smoothly out of primary product exports in response to falling long-run equilibrium prices assumed not only that the long-run prices were observable, but also that the resources could find alternative employment. In those republics where industrialization had made a promising beginning, this was a legitimate assumption; however, most of the Latin American republics had taken only a modest step towards industrialization by the 1920s so that only a massive drop in the long-run equilibrium price – such as happened in the 1929 depression – was likely to induce the required shift in resources. Small declines in the long-run equilibrium price – even if they were observable – could always be offset by exchange rate depreciation, export tax reductions or more favourable credit terms. Indeed, some of the smaller republics were prepared to resort to such policies even in the 1930s rather than promote a wholesale shift of resources from the export sector.

[5] See Arturo O'Connell, 'Argentina Into the Depression: problems of an open economy', in Thorp (ed.), *Latin America in the 1930s*, p. 213.

By the end of the 1920s, the industrial sector had indeed taken root in a number of republics. These were either the largest countries (Argentina, Brazil, Chile, Colombia, Mexico and Peru) or sufficiently prosperous to have built a vigorous domestic market (Uruguay). Even before the First World War export-led growth had generated an internal market in most of these seven republics large enough to justify modern manufacturing establishments. These factories produced mainly non-durable consumer goods (e.g., textiles, processed food and beverages) which could compete with imports thanks to the tariffs which already had a protectionist element. The First World War gave a further boost to manufacturing in a few countries (notably Brazil) as imports became scarce, but the main stimulus to industry came from the growth of domestic consumption and the latter was still firmly linked – even in the 1920s – to the fortunes of the export sector. In no republic was the manufacturing sector sufficiently large to act as the engine of growth, although it was beginning to acquire a certain dynamism of its own in Argentina and Chile – the two republics where industrialization had proceeded furthest by the 1920s. Brazilian manufacturing, despite its huge textile industry, was still dwarfed by the country's backward agricultural sector, which accounted for over 50 per cent of the labour force, and much the same was true of Mexico.

The first decade after the First World War brought about some resource shifts in the major Latin American economies in the direction of structural change, industrialization and diversification of the non-export economy. Without exception, however, all republics continued to follow a version of export-led growth; by the end of the 1920s (see Table 2.1), exports still accounted for a high proportion of the gross domestic product (GDP) and the openness of the economy – measured by the ratio of the sum of exports and imports to GDP – varied from below 40 per cent in Brazil to over 100 per cent in Costa Rica and Venezuela.[6]

Structural change in the 1920s did not bring diversification within the export sector. On the contrary, the composition of exports by the end of the decade was very similar to what it had been on the eve of the First World War with a high degree of concentration. The leading three export products accounted for at least 50 per cent of foreign exchange earnings in

[6] There are GDP data (of varying quality) for fourteen of the twenty republics in the 1930s (Argentina, Brazil, Chile, Colombia, Cuba, Mexico, Peru, Uruguay, Venezuela and the five Central American countries). The Cuban source, however (see note 13), does not provide data on real imports so that for the purposes of Table 2.1 only thirteen countries can be used. At 1929 prices the trade ratios are on average lower – significantly so in the case of Mexico. See Angus Maddison, *Two Crises: Latin America and Asia 1929–38 and 1973–83* (Paris, 1985), table 6.

Table 2.1. *The external sector in Latin America: trade ratios (1970 prices)*

	Exports as % of GDP 1928	Exports as % of GDP 1938	(Exports + imports) as % of GDP 1928	(Exports + imports) as % of GDP 1938
Argentina	29.8	15.7	59.7	35.7
Brazil	17.0	21.2	38.8	33.3
Chile	[a]35.1	32.7	[a]57.2	44.9
Colombia	24.8	24.1	62.8	43.5
Costa Rica	56.5	47.3	109.6	80.7
El Salvador	48.7	45.9	81.0	62.4
Guatemala	22.7	17.5	51.2	29.5
Honduras	52.1	22.1	69.8	39.5
Mexico	31.4	13.9	47.7	25.5
Nicaragua	25.1	23.9	54.9	42.3
Peru	[a]33.6	28.3	[a]53.2	42.6
Uruguay	[b]18.0	18.2	[b]38.0	37.1
Venezuela	37.7	29.0	120.4	55.7

Notes: [a] 1929 [b] 1930

Sources: Comisión Económica para América Latina (CEPAL), *Series Históricas del Crecimiento de América Latina* (Santiago, 1978); CEPAL, *América Latina: Relación de Precios del Intercambio* (Santiago, 1976); V. Bulmer-Thomas, *The Political Economy of Central America since 1920* (Cambridge, 1987); G. Palma, 'From an Export-led to an Import-substituting Economy: Chile 1914–39', in R. Thorp (ed.), *Latin America in the 1930s* (London, 1984); D. Rangel, *Capital y Desarrollo. El Rey Petróleo* (Caracas, 1970); J. Millot, C. Silva and L. Silva, *El Desarrollo Industrial del Uruguay,* (Montevideo, 1973); H. Finch, *A Political Economy of Uruguay since 1870* (London, 1981); A. Maddison, 'Economic and Social Conditions in Latin America, 1913–1950', in M. Urrutia, (ed.), *Long-term Trends in Latin American Economic Development* (Washington, D.C., 1991). Data have been converted to a 1970 price basis where necessary and official exchange rates have been used throughout.

all republics and one product accounted for more than 50 per cent of exports in ten countries (Bolivia, Brazil, Colombia, Cuba, Dominican Republic, El Salvador, Honduras, Guatemala, Nicaragua and Venezuela). Virtually all export earnings came from primary products and nearly 70 per cent of external trade was conducted with only four countries (United States, Britain, France and Germany).

Thus, on the eve of the Depression of 1929, the Latin American economies continued to follow a development model which left them highly vulnerable to adverse conditions in the world markets for primary products. Even Argentina, by far the most advanced Latin American economy in the late 1920s with a gross domestic product (GDP) per head twice the regional average and four times higher than Brazil, had been unable to break the link whereby a decline in export earnings would undermine imports and government revenue, leading to expenditure cuts and a decline in internal demand.

THE 1929 DEPRESSION

The onset of the Depression of 1929 is usually associated with the stock-market crash on Wall Street in New York in October 1929. For Latin America, however, some of the warning signals came earlier. Commodity prices in many cases peaked before 1929, as supply (restored after wartime disruption) tended to outstrip demand. The price of Argentine wheat reached its maximum in May 1927, Cuban sugar in March 1928 and Brazilian coffee in March 1929. The boom in stock markets before the Wall Street crash led to excess demand for credit and a rise in world interest rates, raising the cost of holding inventories and reducing demand for many of the primary products exported by Latin America. The rise in interest rates – the discount on New York commercial paper jumped by 50 per cent in the 18 months before the stock market crash – put additional pressure on Latin America through the capital market. Flight capital – attracted by higher rates of interest outside the region – increased, while capital inflows declined as foreign investors took advantage of the more attractive rates of return offered in London, Paris and New York.

The stock-market crash in October set in motion a chain of events in the main markets supplied by Latin America; the fall in the value of financial assets reduced consumer demand through the so-called wealth effect; loan defaults led to a squeeze on new credit and monetary contraction and the whole of the financial system came under severe pressure; interest rates started to fall in the fourth quarter of 1929, but importers were unable or unwilling to rebuild stocks of primary products in the face of credit restrictions and falling demand.

The subsequent fall in primary product prices was truly dramatic. Not a single Latin American country was unaffected. Between 1928 and 1932 (see Table 2.2), the unit value of exports fell by more than 50 per cent in ten of the countries for which data are available and the only countries with a modest fall in unit values were those where the prices of primary products were administered by foreign companies and did not reflect market forces accurately (e.g., Honduras and Venezuela).

Prices of imports also fell, as the decline in world demand and the fall in costs produced a double squeeze on the unit value of goods sold to Latin America. However, import prices did not in general fall as fast or as far as export prices and the net barter terms of trade (see Table 2.2) declined sharply for all but two Latin American countries between 1928 and 1932. The exceptions are Venezuela, where the unit value of oil exports fell by 'only' 18.5 per cent (roughly in line with the fall in import prices), and Honduras where the export 'price' of bananas was set by the fruit companies simply to cover their local currency costs and was reduced between those years by 9 per cent.[7]

While all republics faced a fall in price for their primary product exports, the volume of their export sales differed sharply. Worst affected were those republics (see Table 2.2) with a severe drop in the price and volume of exports. This group included Bolivia, Chile and Mexico; significantly, the exports of all three countries were dominated by minerals as firms in importing countries reacted to the depression by running down existing inventories rather than placing new orders. Not surprisingly, these countries experienced the steepest decline (see Table 2.2) in the purchasing power of exports (i.e., the net barter terms of trade adjusted for changes in the volume of exports). In the Chilean case, the 83 per cent fall in the purchasing power of exports was the largest ever recorded in Latin America in such a short period of time and was one of the most severe in the world.

Cuba, although not mentioned in Table 2.2 through lack of comparable data, should also be included in this first group. Exports, dominated by sugar, fell rapidly after 1929 as the island suffered the consequences of its specialization in sugar and heavy dependence on the United States. A committee led by Thomas Chadbourne, a New York lawyer with Cuban sugar interests, shared out the U.S. market in 1930 in a way that implied a steep reduction in Cuban sugar exports and the next year an International Sugar Agreement was signed between the main producers and consumers which imposed further limits on Cuban exports.

[7] Administered export prices were used for bananas until 1947 for balance-of-payments purposes. The fruit companies calculated their domestic costs in local currency and set a dollar price for exports which, at the official exchange rate, would meet their domestic obligations.

Table 2.2. *Price and quantity changes for exports, net barter terms of trade and export purchasing power in 1932 (1928 = 100)*

Country	Export prices	Export volumes	Net barter terms of trade	purchasing power of exports
Argentina	37	88	68	60
Bolivia	79[a]	48[a]	n.a.	n.a.
Brazil	43	86	65	56
Chile	47	31	57	17
Colombia	48	102	63	65
Costa Rica	54	81	78	65
Dominican Republic	55[b]	106[b]	81[b]	87[b]
Ecuador	51	83	74	60
El Salvador	30	75	52	38
Guatemala	37	101	54	55
Haiti	49[b]	104[b]	n.a.	n.a.
Honduras	91	101	130	133
Mexico	49	58	64	37
Nicaragua	50	78	71	59
Peru	39	76	62	43
Venezuela	81	100	101	100
Latin America	36	78	56	43

Notes: a = 1929 *b* = 1930
Sources: CEPAL, *América Latina: Relación de Precios del Intercambio* (Santiago, 1976); V. Bulmer-Thomas, *Political Economy of Central America since 1920* (Cambridge, 1987); R. L. Ground, 'The Genesis of Import Substitution in Latin America', *Cepal Review*, 36, (December, 1988).

A second, more numerous, group of countries experienced a modest decline (less than 25 per cent) in the volume of exports. This group – Argentina, Brazil, Ecuador, Peru and all Central America – produced a range of foodstuffs and agricultural raw materials where demand could not be so easily satisfied from existing stocks;[8] the United Kingdom, for example, held port stocks of imported wheat in August 1929 equivalent to only 2 per cent of annual wheat imports.[9] Similarly, the steep fall in price was in some cases sufficient to sustain consumer demand despite the

[8] Peru's main exports were minerals, but the most important was oil, the price of which suffered less than other minerals in the Depression.

[9] See League of Nations, International Institute of Agriculture, *International Yearbook of Agricultural Statistics 1932/3* (Rome, 1933), p. 577.

fall in real income in importing countries; the volume of world coffee imports, for example, was still at its 1929 level in 1932.

A third group of countries (see Table 2.2) experienced a very small (less than 10 per cent) decline in the volume of exports between 1928 and 1932; Colombia, exploiting the confusion caused by the collapse of Brazil's coffee valorization scheme,[10] managed a small increase in the volume of coffee exports; Venezuela suffered a decline in the volume of oil exports after 1929, but this merely offset the huge increase between 1928 and 1929. Exports from the Dominican Republic, dominated by sugar, steadily increased during the worst years of the Depression as sugar exporters took advantage of the restraints on Cuba imposed first by the Chadbourne Committee and later by the 1931 International Sugar Agreement which was not signed by the Dominican Republic (or Brazil).[11]

The combination of falling export prices for all countries and falling export volumes for most countries produced a sharp decline in the purchasing power of exports over the worst years of the Depression (see Table 2.2). Only Venezuela, protected by oil, and Honduras, helped by a decision of the fruit companies to concentrate global production on their low-cost Honduran plantations, escaped. Elsewhere, the impact of the Depression on the purchasing power of exports was severe, affecting mineral producers (e.g., Mexico), temperate foodstuff producers (e.g., Argentina) and tropical foodstuff exporters (e.g., El Salvador).

While export and import prices were falling after 1929, one 'price' remained the same; this was the fixed nominal interest rate on public and private foreign debt. As other prices fell, the real interest rate on this debt (mainly government bonds) rose, increasing the fiscal and balance-of-payments burden for those governments anxious to preserve their credentials in the international capital market through prompt payment of debt service.

The rise in the real burden of the debt meant that an increasing share of (declining) total exports had to be allocated to debt service payments. Argentina, for example, devoted 91.2 million pesos to foreign debt service payments in 1929 against total exports of 2,168 million pesos. By 1932 exports had dropped to 1,288 million pesos, while foreign debt service payments remained at 93.6 million pesos implying a virtual doubling of the real debt burden.

[10] The Brazilian coffee *defesa* collapsed in 1929. See W. Fritsch, *External Constraints on Economic Policy in Brazil* (London, 1988), pp. 152–3.

[11] See B. C. Swerling, *International Control of Sugar, 1918–41* (Stanford, Cal., 1949).

The combination of unchanged debt service payments and falling export receipts exerted a strong squeeze on imports. As the volume and value of imports fell, governments had to come to terms with a new problem caused by the heavy dependence of fiscal revenue on external trade taxes. The principal source of government revenue, the tariff on imports, could not be maintained in the wake of an import collapse; Brazil, for example, collected 42.4 per cent of total government revenue from taxes on imports in 1928. By 1930, import tax collection had been cut by one-third and government revenue by one-quarter. Those countries which also depended heavily on export taxes (e.g., Chile) experienced a particularly severe cut in government revenue.

The rise in the real burden of debt service affected the fiscal position in much the same way as it affected the balance of payments. The combination of falling government revenue and debt service payments fixed in nominal terms put intense pressure on government expenditure. Efforts were made at creative accounting (Honduran civil servants, for example, were paid in postage stamps for a time), but this could not conceal the underlying crisis. Most Latin American republics witnessed a change of government during the worst years of the depression with the swing of the pendulum favouring the parties or individuals out of government at the time of the Wall Street crash. The most important exceptions were Venezuela where the autocratic government of Juan Vicente Gómez, in power since 1908, survived until the dictator's death in 1935, and Mexico where the recently formed Partido Nacional Revolucionario presided over a country exhausted by revolutionary upheaval and civil war.

In a less crisis-ridden international environment, a Latin American government might have hoped to borrow its way out of its difficulties with the help of international loans. However, the flow of new lending to Latin America – already in decline even before the Wall Street crash – had ground to a halt by 1931. In that year, repayment of U.S. portfolio capital exceeded new U.S. portfolio investment for the first time since 1920 and the net flow remained negative (with the minor exception of 1938) until 1954.[12] Even Argentina, which by any standards had the highest credit rating in Latin America, was unable to obtain significant new loans during the first years of the depression.

No Latin American country escaped the depression of the 1930s, but for some countries the impact was much worse than for others. The most

[12] See Stallings, *Banker to the Third World*, appendix I.

disastrous combination was a very high degree of openness, a large fall in the price of exports and a steep decline in the volume of exports. It is no surprise, therefore, that the republics most seriously affected were Chile and Cuba where the external shock was strongest. Indeed, estimates of Cuban national income in the inter-war years have been constructed and show a drop of one third in real national income per head between 1928 and 1932,[13] while the decline in Chilean real GDP between 1929 and 1932 has been estimated at 35.7 per cent.[14]

The impact of external shock could be mitigated, but not avoided, only under exceptional circumstances. Thus, the Dominican Republic – dependent on sugar exports – was able to exploit its position as a non-signatory of the post-1929 sugar agreements; Venezuela took advantage of its position as the oil producer with lowest unit costs in all the Americas; countries with exports dominated by foreign companies (e.g., Peru) saw some of the burden transferred to the outside world through a reduction in profit remittances and an increase in returned value as a proportion of total exports. Generally, however, the external shock was very severe and the introduction of stabilization measures to restore external and internal equilibrium could not be long delayed.

SHORT-TERM STABILIZATION

The external shocks associated with the Depression of the 1930s created two disequilibria which policy-makers in each republic had to address as a matter of urgency. The first was the external imbalance created by the collapse of earnings from exports and the decline in capital inflows; the second was the internal imbalance caused by the decline in government revenue, which gave rise to budget deficits that could no longer be financed from abroad.

During the 1920s, the republics of Latin America had either adopted the gold exchange standard for the first time (e.g., Bolivia) or had returned to it (e.g., Argentina). Under the gold exchange standard, adjustment to external disequilibrium was supposed to be automatic – indeed, this was one of its principal attractions. As exports fell, gold or foreign exchange would be drained out of a country, lowering the money supply,

[13] See C. Brundenius, *Revolutionary Cuba: the Challenge of Economic Growth with Equity* (Boulder, Colo., 1984) table A 2.1. The primary source is J. Alienes, *Características Fundamentales de la Economía Cubana* (Havana, 1950).

[14] See Palma, 'From an Export-led to an Import-substituting Economy', table 3.5.

credit and the demand for imports; at the same time monetary contraction would lower the price level, making exports more competitive and imports more expensive. Thus, imports would fall both through expenditure reduction and through expenditure switching and the process would continue until external equilibrium was restored.

The decline in the value of exports, however, was so severe after 1929 that it was by no means clear if external equilibrium could be restored automatically; furthermore, the decline in capital inflows and the initial determination to service the foreign debt meant that the drop in imports needed to be particularly steep to eliminate a balance of payments deficit. Argentina, for example, saw the value of its exports drop from US$1,537 million in 1929 to US$561 million in 1932 and this was by no means the most severe case; with imports in 1929 valued at US$1,388 million, Argentina needed to cut foreign purchases by 70 per cent if it wished to maintain debt service payments in 1932 on the same terms as in 1929.

Those countries that did try to play by the rules of the gold exchange standard saw their holdings of gold and foreign exchange reserves fall very rapidly. Colombia, for example, struggled on until four days after the British suspension of the gold standard (on 21 September 1931), by which time the republic had seen its international reserves fall by 65 per cent. Most countries, however, either abandoned the system formally (e.g., Argentina in December 1929) or limited outflows of gold and foreign exchange through a variety of banking and other restrictions (e.g., Costa Rica). This did not avoid the need for stabilization policies to reduce imports and reestablish external disequilibrium, but it did mean that the process would no longer be automatic.

Three countries (Argentina, Mexico and Uruguay) suspended the gold standard before the British decision to stop selling gold and foreign exchange on demand, although Peru – alone in Latin America – twice introduced a new gold parity. Most countries, however, adopted exchange control in one form or another and created a rationing system for imports. This included all the most important republics; indeed, the only countries that did not make use of exchange controls were the small Caribbean Basin republics using the U.S. dollar as means of payment officially (Panama and the Dominican Republic) or unofficially (Cuba and Honduras).

The desire to stick by the international rules of the game meant that devaluation – currency depreciation – was at first used sparingly. No one expected the depression to be as severe as it turned out to be. The last world depression (1920/1) had passed quickly without a permanent disruption to the international financial system. Furthermore, prompted in some cases by the missions led by E. W. Kemmerer, many Latin American republics had overhauled their financial systems in the 1920s, returned to exchange rate orthodoxy and the gold standard, created Central Banks and struggled for monetary discipline; the 1929 depression was seen as the first real test of the institutions and there was a natural reluctance to admit failure through currency depreciation.

By the end of 1930, only five countries (Argentina, Brazil, Paraguay, Peru and Uruguay) had seen their currencies depreciate by more than 5 per cent against the U.S. dollar since the end of the previous year. Peru, however, had changed its gold parity and the Paraguayan peso, officially pegged to the Argentine gold peso, also depreciated against the U.S. dollar as an unintended consequence of exchange rate policy. The British suspension of the gold standard and the subsequent depreciation of the pound sterling meant that those Latin American currencies with a sterling link – Argentina, Bolivia, Paraguay (via the Argentine peso) and Uruguay – fell sharply against the U.S. dollar after September 1931 until the U.S. suspension of the gold standard in April 1933 produced an equally abrupt appreciation.

The decision by Britain and the United States to abandon the gold standard finally forced all the republics to address the problem of exchange rate management. Six small republics (Cuba, the Dominican Republic, Guatemala, Haiti, Honduras and Panama) all pegged their currencies to the U.S. dollar throughout the 1930s; three others (Costa Rica, El Salvador and Nicaragua) tried to do the same, but were eventually forced to devalue; even in South America, among the larger republics, there were many attempts to peg currencies to the pound sterling or U.S. dollar, while Paraguay persisted with its policy (albeit with little success) of tracking the Argentine peso; Argentina (with some success) and Bolivia (with none) tried to link their currencies to the pound sterling after January 1934 and January 1935 respectively, while Brazil (December 1937), Chile (September 1936), Colombia (March 1935), Ecuador (May 1932) and Mexico (July 1933) all tried to link their currencies to the U.S. dollar.

Examples of genuinely floating currencies were rare. The Venezuelan bolívar was floated and promptly appreciated by 50 per cent against the U.S. dollar between the end of 1932 and the end of 1937. Several of the South American countries (Argentina, Bolivia, Brazil, Chile, Ecuador and Uruguay) adopted a dual exchange rate system after the suspension of the gold standard by the United States with the non-official rate allowed to fluctuate freely; this free rate was used for a variety of transactions, including capital exports, profit remittances, non-traditional exports and non-essential imports. This experience – a source in many cases of exchange rate profits for the public sector – was to prove invaluable for exchange rate management after the Second World War.

In view of the reluctance to adopt genuinely freely floating exchange rate regimes, the majority of republics were forced to rely on other techniques for achieving external equilibrium. The most popular was exchange control and a non-price rationing system for imports; this technique was not limited to the larger republics with several small countries (Costa Rica, Bolivia, Ecuador, Honduras, Nicaragua, Paraguay and Uruguay) adopting the system aggressively. In most countries, tariff rates were raised at a time when the price of imports (inclusive of international transport costs) was falling; this raised the real cost of imports sharply and encouraged a switch in expenditure towards domestic substitutes. Even in those cases where tariff rates were not formally raised, the real cost of imports tended to increase as a result of the widespread use of specific tariffs.

In a few cases external equilibrium was achieved without exchange control and non-price import rationing; this occurred through a gold standard type mechanism, in which current account deficits were financed through an outflow of international reserves which reduced the money supply so sharply that nominal demand fell in line with the required reduction in nominal imports; the clearest cases of this automatic adjustment to external equilibrium can be found in Cuba, the Dominican Republican, Haiti and Panama. Mexico, however, also experienced a sharp decline in its nominal money supply in the first years of the depression as a result of its peculiar monetary system in which silver and gold coins made up most of the money in circulation.[15]

By the end of 1932, external equilibrium had been restored in virtually all republics at a much lower level of nominal exports and imports and a slightly lower level of nominal debt service payments. A balance of trade surplus for Latin America in 1929 of US$570 million had increased to US$609 million by 1932 despite a two-thirds fall in nominal exports from US$4,683 million to US$1,663 million. The eight countries that had

[15] See E. Cárdenas, 'The Great Depression and Industrialisation: the case of Mexico', in Thorp (ed.), *Latin America in the 1930s*, pp. 224–5.

recorded a balance of trade deficit in 1929 had been reduced to six by 1930, five by 1931 and four by 1932. These four (Cuba, the Dominican Republic, Haiti and Panama) were, however, the exceptions which proved the rule; all were economies in which the dollar circulated freely without exchange control so that a trade deficit and foreign exchange outflow was the mechanism by which nominal demand was brought into line with the purchasing power of exports.

The achievement of external equilibrium, however painful, was inevitable. Most of the republics could not pay for imports in their own currency so that the supply of foreign exchange set a limit on available imports once international reserves were exhausted. Internal equilibrium was different, however, since a government could always issue its own currency to finance a budget deficit. Only in countries such as Panama, where the dollar circulated freely and where there was no Central Bank, could one be certain that the achievement of external equilibrium also implied internal equilibrium.

In most republics suspension of the gold standard and the adoption of exchange control drove a wedge between external and internal adjustment. Where budget deficits persisted and were financed domestically, the supply of nominal money would not fall in line with the decrease in nominal imports. This would cause the ratio of domestic credit to imports to rise, creating an excess supply of money which in turn would stimulate domestic expenditure in nominal terms. Whether the increase in nominal expenditure was reflected in price or quantity increases would be crucial in determining how quickly and how successfully a country escaped from the depression.

The idea of a monetary overhang finds empirical support in many countries. While the United States experienced a nearly 40 per cent drop in nominal commercial bank deposits in the period 1929 to 1933, some Latin American republics (e.g., Bolivia, Brazil, Ecuador and Uruguay) saw the nominal value of commercial bank deposits rise while others (e.g., Argentina, Chile, Colombia) experienced only a modest fall (see Table 2.3). In real terms, i.e. adjusted for the change in the price level, the performance is even more remarkable since prices fell between 1929 and 1933 in all the Latin American republics (except Chile) for which price data exist.

There are several reasons for the relative buoyancy of the nominal money supply. First, the decision to impose exchange control in many republics restricted the outflow of gold and foreign exchange and therefore limited

Table 2.3. *The money supply: commercial bank time and demand deposits. Current prices (1929 = 100)*

	1930	1931	1932	1933	1934	1935	1936
Argentina	101	90	90	89	88	86	94
Bolivia	84	78	133	144	322	520	547
Brazil	97	101	115	109	125	131	141
Chile	84	68	82	96	110	124	143
Colombia	87	78	90	94	102	110	120
Ecuador	98	59	92	145	187	187	215
El Salvador[a]	74	68	64	57	42	44	37
Mexico[b]	111	67	74	107	108	136	143
Paraguay	[c]100	76	64	72	125	191	170
Peru	69	63	62	78	100	116	137
Uruguay	114	115	126	114	116	124	139
Venezuela	49	68	69	76	85	106	89
United States	101	92	71	63	72	81	92

Notes: [a] Includes dollar deposits.

[b] The data were compiled on a different basis in 1932 and 1935 so that the series is not consistent.

[c] 1930 = 100.

Source: League of Nations, *Statistical Yearbook* (Geneva, various years).

the reduction in the supply of money of external origin. Uruguay, one of the first countries to impose exchange control, suffered only a modest drop in international reserves while Mexico – with no exchange controls – was drained of the gold and silver *specie* which constituted such a high proportion of its monetary stock.

Second, budget deficits persisted despite enormous efforts to increase revenue and cut expenditure. Brazil, for example, managed to increase the yield from direct taxes on income by 24 per cent between 1929 and 1932 despite the contraction in real GDP, but the overwhelming importance of external trade taxes forced down fiscal revenue in line with the collapse in imports and exports. Furthermore, the initial determination to service the public debt (internal and external) and the difficulties associated with sharp cuts in nominal wages and salaries for public employees made it virtually impossible to cut expenditure by enough to eliminate budget deficits. In the absence of new external loans, the deficits had to be financed through the banking system with an expansionary effect on the money supply.

Third, the decline of private domestic credit was by no means as sharp as might have been expected in view of the close links between the banking system and the export sector. The small number of banks – Mexico, for example, had only eleven – and their high public profile created a powerful incentive to avoid bank failure; the close relationship between bankers and exporters (sometimes the same individuals) allowed for greater flexibility in debt rescheduling than would have been permitted in a more competitive environment; banks also tended to operate in the 1920s with cash reserves well above the legal minimum, leaving a certain cushion available for the difficult times after 1929. Foreign banks, unable to remit profits after exchange control, had additional resources to sustain themselves through the depression years.

Thus, monetary policy in the depth of the Depression was relatively slack in many republics so that internal equilibrium – unlike external equilibrium – had not been restored by the end of 1932. Efforts to raise taxes, including tariffs, had proved insufficient and further increases promised to be self-defeating. Cuts in the public sector wage and salary bill were made more difficult by the turbulent political circumstances at the start of the 1930s so that policies for reducing the budget deficit came increasingly to focus on debt service payments.

Debt default was nothing new in Latin American economic history; indeed, the customs houses of some small republics (e.g., Nicaragua) were still full of U.S. officials appointed to collect external trade taxes and avoid a repetition of past debt defaults. Strenuous efforts, however, were at first made by all the republics to maintain debt service payments in the hope that this would preserve access to international capital markets. Here, however, there was an intriguing dilemma; the main creditor in terms of the stock of international bonds remained Great Britain, where stock exchange rules made it impossible for countries in default to float new bond issues; meanwhile, the annual flow of new capital to Latin America had become increasingly dependent on the United States where the penalties for default were less clear. As it became apparent that Latin America could not in general expect additional finance from Britain, the temptation to default became almost overwhelming.

Mexico, still caught up in the aftermath of its revolution, had suspended debt service payments as early as 1928; generally, however, suspension began in 1931 and gathered pace in the next few years. Default was unilateral, but no countries repudiated their external debts and not all issues were treated equally; Brazil, for example, established seven grades of bonds in 1934 with treatment varying from full service to complete default on interest and principal.[16] Thus, the impact on government expenditure varied substantially even among defaulting countries, although the resources committed to debt service tended to decline everywhere as the decade advanced.

Not all countries defaulted on the external debt and default on the external debt did not necessarily imply default on the internal debt (nor vice versa). Venezuela, under Gómez, completed the redemption of its external debt – begun fifteen years earlier – in 1930; Honduras defaulted on its internal debt, but serviced its external debt in full (along with the Dominican Republic and Haiti). Of the major countries (apart from Venezuela), only Argentina serviced its internal and external debt in full for reasons which are still controversial. Its special relationship with Britain, the close trading links and the prospect of continuing loans were some of the factors which persuaded Argentine policy-makers to service the debt, the bulk of which was owed to Britain; in addition, the financial orthodoxy of the conservative Argentine administrations in the 1930s provided a strong bias in favour of debt repayment.

Debt default eased the pressure on the budget deficit in most countries and (in the case of the external debt) released foreign exchange which could be spent for other purposes. The decline of debt service payments, however, took some of the pressure off fiscal policy because it avoided the need for further tax increases or expenditure cuts. Budget deficits, therefore, remained common and internal equilibrium a distant goal in most republics. The tension between external equilibrium and internal disequilibrium did produce serious financial and economic instability in some republics (e.g., Bolivia), but it could also contribute to economic recovery at a faster pace than was found in countries where tight fiscal and monetary policies left the non-export sector with insufficient demand and unable to respond to the new vector of relative prices.

RECOVERY FROM DEPRESSION

The policies adopted to stabilize each economy in response to the depression were intended to restore internal and external equilibrium in the short-term; inevitably, however, they also had longer-term implications

[16] See B. Eichengreen and R. Portes, 'Settling Defaults in the Era of Bond Finance', Birkbeck College, University of London, Discussion Paper in Economics, No. 8, 1988.

in those countries where they affected relative prices in a permanent fashion.

The collapse after 1929 of export prices, the deterioration in the net barter terms of trade and the rise in nominal tariffs favoured the non-export sector (both non-tradeables and importables) over the export sector in terms of relative prices. In those countries where real devaluation occurred (i.e., nominal devaluation faster than the difference between home and foreign prices), both exportables and importables received a price advantage relative to non-traded goods. Thus, the price of the import-competing sector improved relative to both exportables and non-traded goods in every case, whereas the non-traded sector increased its price relative to the export sector unless real devaluation occurred (in which case the result was indeterminate).

Whether these short-term shifts in relative prices persisted depended to a large extent on the movement in export and import prices. For Latin America as a whole, export prices fell steadily until 1934; at that point a new cycle began, which produced a sharp recovery in prices in 1936 and 1937 followed by two years of export price falls. Import prices remained very weak, however, so that the net barter terms of trade improved from 1933 to 1937 and even in 1939 were still 36 per cent above the 1933 level and equal to the 1930 level. Thus, for the region as a whole a permanent improvement in the relative price of the import-competing sector depended less on movements in the net barter terms of trade and more on increases in tariff rates and real devaluation.

The import-competing sector consisted of all activities capable of substituting for imports. It has conventionally been identified with import-substituting industrialization (ISI) in view of the importance of manufactures in the import bill. However, many countries in the 1920s were importing substantial quantities of agricultural goods which could in principal be produced by domestic activities. Thus, it is also necessary to consider import-substituting agriculture (ISA) as part of the import-competing sector.

The change in relative prices encouraged resource shifts and acted as a mechanism of recovery from the depression. However, this was only part of the story; a fall in the output of the export sector, for example, and a rise in the output of the import-competing sector would not necessarily produce a recovery in real GDP, although it would produce structural change. Recovery was only assured if the import-competing sector expanded without a fall in the export sector or if the import-competing sector grew so rapidly that it could compensate for export decline; the first possibility points to the importance of export sector performance in the 1930s – a much neglected topic – while the second requires consideration of the growth of nominal demand.

It was argued above that stabilization programmes after 1929 had been very successful at restoring external equilibrium in almost all republics by 1932; however, many countries had had less success in eliminating budget deficits. The persistence of deficits in some republics, even after the reduction in debt service payments through default, provided a stimulus to nominal demand which under certain circumstances could be expected to have real (that is, Keynesian) effects; these conditions included the existence of spare capacity and a price elastic supply response in the import-competing sector together with a financial system capable of supplying finance for working capital at low real rates of interest. Where these conditions did not exist (e.g., Bolivia), the consequence of fiscal deficits and the growth of nominal demand was simply inflation and a collapse of the nominal exchange rate; where they did exist (e.g. Brazil), loose fiscal and monetary policies could contribute to recovery. Thus, for some republics the consequences of incomplete stabilization measures in pursuit of internal equilibrium after 1929 were by no means unfavourable; by contrast, some 'virtuous' republics (e.g., Argentina) faced the paradox that orthodox fiscal and monetary policies in pursuit of balanced budgets may have lowered the rate of economic growth in the 1930s.

Recovery from the Depression, in terms of real GDP, began after 1931/2 with only two minor exceptions (Honduras and Nicaragua). In the remainder of the 1930s, all republics for which data are available achieved positive growth and all surpassed the pre-Depression peak in real GDP with the same two exceptions; the speed of recovery, however, varied considerably and so did the recovery mechanisms. In particular, almost no countries relied exclusively on ISI for their recovery and some simply depended on the return of more favourable conditions in export markets.

Following Chenery,[17] we can explore recovery in the 1930s in Latin America through a growth accounting equation in which the change in real GDP is decomposed into the sum of:

1. the change in the volume of agricultural exports;
2. the change in the volume of mineral exports;

[17] See H. Chenery, 'Patterns of Industrial Growth', *American Economic Review*, 50, 1960: 624–54. See also M. Syrquin, 'Patterns of Structural Change', in H. Chenery and T. Srinivasan (eds), *Handbook of Development Economics*, Vol. 1 (Amsterdam, 1988).

3. the change in home final demand for agriculture without ISA;
4. the change in agriculture's share of home final demand due to ISA;
5. the change in home final demand for industry without ISI;
6. the change in industry's share of home final demand due to ISI;
7. the change in home final demand for non-traded services.

The first two terms in the growth accounting equation draw attention to the role of the export sector in economic recovery; the fourth and sixth terms reflect the role of import substitution; the third and fifth terms are affected by the growth of nominal demand, income redistribution and income elasticities; the final term is affected by relative prices, nominal demand and income elasticity affects.

It is not possible to estimate this growth accounting equation empirically for any Latin American republic in the 1930s. However, it is possible to identify a number of recovery mechanisms that correspond loosely to the entries in the growth accounting equation. This is done in Table 2.4, where the fourteen republics for which GDP data exist have been grouped into three categories: rapid, medium and slow recovery.

The rapid recovery group contains the eight republics where real GDP had risen by more than 50 per cent between the trough year (1931 or 1932) and 1939. Two countries (Brazil and Mexico) can be considered large, four (Chile, Cuba, Peru and Venezuela) medium-sized and two (Costa Rica and Guatemala) as small. Thus, there is no correlation between size and speed of recovery. ISI is an important recovery mechanism in most of the group, but not in Cuba, Guatemala and Venezuela; indeed, Cuban recovery was due mainly to better prices for sugar, which contributed to a doubling of the value of exports between 1932 and 1939; Venezuelan recovery was due primarily to the growth of oil production and Guatemalan recovery depended heavily on ISA.

The medium recovery group contains the republics where real GDP rose by more than 20 per cent between the trough year and 1939. Only three republics (Argentina, Colombia and El Salvador) can be placed with certainty in this group, although some other republics (Bolivia, Ecuador, the Dominican Republic and Haiti), for which national accounts in this period do not exist, all registered a significant increase in the volume of exports after 1932 and are likely to have experienced a rise in GDP that would place them in the second category. ISI was very important as a recovery mechanism in Argentina and Colombia, but export growth was not significant.

Table 2.4. *Qualitative analysis of sources of growth in 1930s*

	ISI	ISA	Export growth
(A) RAPID RECOVERY COUNTRIES			
Brazil	●		□
Chile	●		□
Costa Rica	●	■	
Cuba		■	□
Guatemala		■	
Mexico	●	■	
Peru	●		□
Venezuela			□
(B) MEDIUM RECOVERY COUNTRIES			
Argentina	●	■	
Colombia	●		
El Salvador		■	□
(C) SLOW RECOVERY COUNTRIES			
Honduras		■	
Nicaragua		■	
Uruguay	●		

Notes: Fast recovery countries assumed to increase real GDP from trough year to 1939 by more than 50 per cent; medium recovery countries by more than 20 per cent and less than 50 per cent; low recovery countries by less than 20 per cent.

●: ratio of manufacturing net output to GDP assumed to increase significantly

■: ratio of domestic use agriculture (DUA) to GDP assumed to increase significantly
□: ratio of exports to GDP assumed to increase significantly in either nominal or real terms.
Sources: see Table 2.1.

The final group includes the republics with the least successful performance. Only three (Honduras, Nicaragua and Uruguay) are listed in Table 2.4, but the disastrous export performances of Paraguay and Panama (for which national accounts data are not available) suggest that they should also be included. All five were small economies with little possibility (with the exception of Uruguay) of offsetting a weak export performance through an increase in import-competing activities. Uruguay did at least experience a rise in industrial output and ISI was important, but this was not sufficient to compensate for the stagnation of the crucial livestock industry. In the case of Panama, where service exports are so important, the decline in world trade volumes produced a drop in the number of ships using the canal in the 1930s and this had an adverse impact on overall economic performance. Paraguay, although the victor in the Chaco War with Bolivia (1932–5), suffered terrible losses and the nominal value of exports continued to fall until 1940.

If we limit ourselves to the period 1932 to 1939, when the recovery was at its strongest in Latin America, there are twelve countries – all those except Uruguay in Table 2.1 – providing sufficient national accounting data to produce a limited version of a growth accounting equation in which the change in real GDP is broken down into the proportion due to the growth in home final demand (with no change in import co-efficients), the proportion due to the change in import co-efficients and the proportion due to export recovery (see Table 2.5). By far the most important contribution in all cases is the recovery of home final demand, followed by export promotion, whereas the contribution due to changes in import co-efficients is generally negative as import co-efficients tended to rise rather than fall after 1932.

If a year in the 1920s rather than 1932 is used as the starting point, the picture changes considerably (see Table 2.5) as import co-efficients in 1939 were invariably lower than a decade earlier. Nevertheless, export promotion was still a positive source of growth in most cases, while the contribution of home final demand (assuming an unchanged import co-efficient) was more important than import substitution in all the major countries except Argentina. These results do no mean that import substitution in industry was not important, since the sources of growth equation applied to the manufacturing sector alone can yield a different outcome. Yet, using a longer period (1929–50), the contribution of import substitution to industrial growth in the larger countries (Argentina, Brazil, Chile, Colombia and Mexico) has been estimated at a weighted average of 39 per cent – implying that the growth of home final demand (the contribution of industrial exports can be ignored) was very important for the manufacturing sector as well.[18]

The recovery of home final demand was a reflection of the loose fiscal and monetary policies referred to above. Budget deficits were common and – in the absence of foreign sources of loans – were usually financed

[18] See J. Grunwald and P. Musgrove, *Natural Resources in Latin American Development* (Baltimore, Md., 1970), table A.4, pp. 16–17.

Table 2.5. *Quantitative analysis of sources of growth (%)*

	1932–9			1929–39		
Country	(1)	(2)	(3)	(1)	(2)	(3)
Argentina	+102	+6	−8	+51	+84	−36
Brazil	+74	−11	+37	+39	+31	+31
Chile	+71	−24	+53	[a]+67	+28	+5
Colombia	+117	−35	+18	+61	+24	+15
Costa Rica	+96	−21	+25	+36	+64	0
El Salvador	+39	−4	+65	[b]+31	+11	+58
Guatemala	+92	+2	+6	+64	+30	+6
Honduras		[c]		[b]+55	+17	+28
Mexico	+108	1	−9	+113	+61	−74
Nicaragua	+98	−1	+3	[d]+64	+47	−11
Peru	+85	−2	+17	+68	+30	+2
Venezuela	+80	−1	+21	+19	+67	+14

Notes: (1) Percentage contribution to increase in real GDP of home final demand assuming no change in import co-efficient.
(2) Percentage contribution to increase in real GDP of change in import co-efficient.
(3) Percentage contribution to increase in real GDP of export promotion.
[a] 1925–39; [b] 1920–39; [c] sources of growth equation cannot be applied as home final demand fell between 1932 and 1939;
[d] 1926–39.
Source: Author's calculations using data from same sources as in Table 2.1.

through the banking system with an expansionary effect on the money supply. Financial institutions, strengthened by the creation of Central Banks in several countries (e.g., Argentina and El Salvador) or underpinned by the monetary reforms of the 1920s, were able to compensate losses on loans to the export sector with this new and profitable source of lending. Given the depths to which capacity utilization had fallen, the growth in the money supply was only mildly inflationary and had real as well as price effects.

Home final demand consists not just of government expenditure, but also of investment and private consumption. Public investment, sharply cut between 1929 and 1932, was stimulated by road-building programmes in virtually all republics as governments seized on a form of investment expenditure with a low import content. The growth of the road network was truly impressive in some republics and contributed indirectly to the growth of both manufacturing and agriculture for the home market. Even private investment, despite its high import content, was able to recover after 1932 as the balance-of-payments constraint began to be relaxed.

The increase in private consumption – the most important element in home final demand – was a necessary condition for industrial growth in the 1930s. Private consumption was promoted both by the recovery of the export sector and by loose fiscal and monetary policies. As home demand recovered, domestic firms were provided with an excellent opportunity to satisfy a market in which the relative price of imports had increased. Few financial institutions – even those newly established in the 1930s – were primarily concerned with providing consumer credit so that demand for expensive consumer durables (e.g., motor cars) was still very modest; non-durable consumption, however, such as beverages and textiles, experienced substantial growth.

There has been some speculation that the growth of consumer demand in the 1930s may have been fuelled by shifts in the functional distribution of income. The data do not exist to confirm or deny this hypothesis, but it is clear that within certain sectors there were important changes in the return to labour relative to capital. In the export sector, for example, the impact of the depression fell most heavily on the owners of capital with real rates of return falling more sharply than real wages; recovery of the sector after 1932 helped to rebuild profit margins, but it is unlikely that the rate of return on capital was restored to its pre-1929 level. Thus, in the export sector it is realistic to talk of a shift in the functional distribution of income in favour of labour.

In the import-competing sector, on the other hand, the opposite is more likely to have occurred. The growth of the sector on the back of depreciated exchange rates and higher nominal tariff rates created a relative price shift from which the owners of capital would have been the primary beneficiaries. At the same time, nominal wages were slow to respond to the gentle rise in prices in countries with depreciating currencies and a further shift towards profits may well have taken place. In the non-traded sector both the Depression and the subsequent recovery are likely to have left the functional distribution largely unchanged so that the aggregate change in the functional distribution of income cannot have been very large. Thus, it is improbable that the growth of consumer demand in the 1930s can be attributed to sharp changes in income distribution.

THE INTERNATIONAL ENVIRONMENT AND THE EXPORT SECTOR

The recovery of the export sector, both in terms of volume and price, contributed to the increase in import capacity after 1932 and the restoration of positive rates of economic growth. Yet this export recovery was not simply a return to the world trading system in force before 1929. On the contrary, the international economic environment in the 1930s underwent a series of changes that had an important bearing on the fortunes of individual republics.

The main change in the world trading system was the growth of protectionism. The notorious Smoot–Hawley tariff in 1930 raised the barriers faced by Latin American exporters in the U.S. market while a specific tariff imposed on U.S. copper imports in 1932 hit Chile particularly hard; Britain's retreat behind a system of imperial preference at the Ottawa conference in 1932 left Latin America facing discriminatory tariffs in its second largest market; the rise of Hitler in Germany produced the askimark – an inconvertible currency paid to Latin American exporters which could only be used to buy German imports; some staples (notably sugar) were subject to international agreement which set export quotas for the main producers (e.g., Cuba), while Bolivian tin was regulated by the International Tin Agreement.

Despite the retreat into protectionism, world trade in dollar terms grew steadily after 1932 – at least until a new U.S. depression drove down U.S. imports and world trade in 1938. The imports of the major industrialized countries reached a turning point between 1932 and 1934 (only in France was recovery delayed until after 1935). In the crucial U.S. market, imports recovered by 137 per cent between 1932 and 1937 – stimulated in part by the efforts of Secretary of State Cordell Hull to dilute the impact of Smoot–Hawley through bilateral trade treaties involving reciprocal tariff cuts.

For Latin America as a whole, the export performance after 1932 appears at first glance undistinguished. In the seven years before the outbreak of the Second World War, exports in value terms were virtually unchanged, whereas the volume of exports rose by a modest 19.6 per cent. This, however, is very misleading since the figures are heavily influenced by the poor performance of Argentina – by far the most important exporter from Latin America with almost 30 per cent of the regional total.

Excluding Argentina, the volume of exports rose by 36 per cent between 1932 and 1939. Furthermore, if Mexico is also excluded, the volume of exports of the remaining eighteen republics rose by 53 per cent over the same period – an annual rate of 6.3 per cent. Mexico's exports, which in fact grew rapidly from 1932 to 1937, fell by 58 per cent between 1937 and 1939. Higher prices for gold and silver after the collapse of the gold standard could not compensate for the trade embargo imposed in retaliation against the expropriation of the foreign oil companies in 1938.

Argentine exports have been the subject of much analysis. In volume terms there was a steady decline after 1932 which was not reversed until 1952. The trend, however, was obscured by the favourable prices and net barter terms of trade (NBTT) which Argentina enjoyed for much of the 1930s – between 1933 and 1937, for example, the NBTT improved by 71 per cent in response to a series of bad harvests in North America which drove up the prices of grain and meat. The dependence of Argentina, however, on the British market was a major obstacle to export expansion. The Roca–Runciman Treaty of 1933 may have given Argentina a quota in the British market for exports of its main primary products, but the best that could be hoped for under this arrangement was the preservation of import market share; British farmers, on the other hand, now had a price incentive provided by discriminatory tariffs to increase production at the expense of imports. Thus, even the preservation of import market share could not prevent a small decline in Argentine exports to Great Britain. Argentine exports were also undermined by real exchange rate movements. Although traditional exports in many Latin American republics enjoyed long-run real depreciation, Argentine exporters faced a real exchange rate which tended to appreciate in the 1930s. For example, with British wholesale prices falling by 20 per cent in the decade after 1929 and Argentine wholesale prices rising by 12 per cent, the nominal devaluation of the peso against the pound sterling needed to keep Argentine exports to Britain competitive was at least 32 per cent. This was far more than the actual depreciation of the official exchange rate over the decade, although there were marked year-to-year fluctuations which did little to bolster confidence in the export sector. By contrast, Brazilian exporters over the same period enjoyed a 49 per cent real devaluation based on the official exchange rate and an 80 per cent real depreciation based on the free market rate.

In the rest of Latin America, export performance after 1932 was surprisingly robust (see Table 2.6). Of the seventeen countries providing data on

Table 2.6. *Annual average rates of growth from 1932 to 1939 (%)*

Country	GDP	Export volume	Import volume	Net barter terms of trade
Argentina	+4.4	−1.4	+4.6	+2.1
Bolivia		+2.4		
Brazil	+4.8	+10.2	+9.4	−5.6
Chile	+6.5	+6.5	+18.4	+18.6
Colombia	+4.8	+3.8	+16.1	+1.6
Costa Rica	+6.4	+3.4	+14.0	−5.4
Cuba	+7.2			
Dominican Republic		+3.0	+4.4	+15.2
Ecuador		+4.4	+9.7	0
El Salvador	+4.7	+6.7	+4.2	+1.9
Guatemala	+10.9	+3.4	+11.2	+2.0
Haiti		+4.9		
Honduras	−1.2	−9.4	+0.8	−0.3
Mexico	+6.2	−3.1	+7.8	+5.7
Nicaragua	+3.7	+0.1	+5.6	+5.5
Peru	+4.9[a]	+5.4	+5.0	+7.2
Uruguay	+0.1[a]	+3.5	+3.0	+1.4
Venezuela	+5.9[a]	+6.2	+10.4	−3.4

Notes: [a] 1930–9
Sources: see Table 2.1 and note 13.

the volume of exports, only Honduras – in addition to Argentina and Mexico – saw a decline between 1932 and 1939. Furthermore, if 1929 is taken as the base, half of the reporting countries experienced an increase in the volume of exports despite the exceptionally difficult circumstances prevailing throughout the following decade.

Three factors accounted for the relatively strong performance of exports. The first was the commitment of the authorities to the preservation of the traditional export sector – the engine of growth in the export-led model – through a network of policies from real exchange rate depreciation to debt moratoria. The second was the movement in the net barter terms of trade after 1932. The third was the commodity lottery, which produced a number of winners from within the Latin American menu of exports in the 1930s.

Few, if any, republics in the early 1930s could afford to ignore the traditional export sector. This was particularly true of the smaller republics, where the sector remained the major source of employment, capital accumulation and political power. Even in the larger republics, a decline in the export sector threatened to undermine the non-export sector as a result of the direct and indirect linkages between the two. Significantly, all but one of the thirteen countries with real GDP and export data for the 1930s recorded an increase in real exports and real GDP at the same time; the exception was Argentina, where – as we have already seen – the quantum of exports failed to recover.

Argentina, however, was the exception which proved the rule. The richest country by far in Latin America in the early 1930s (its only rival in terms of income per head was Uruguay), it had the most diversified economic structure and the strongest industrial base. The non-export sector was sufficiently robust to become the new engine of growth in the 1930s so that real GDP and real exports moved in opposite directions. At the same time, it must be remembered that the NBTT improved significantly in Argentina, which gave a boost to home final demand and private consumption after 1932. Thus, even Argentina could not entirely escape from its inherited dependence on the export sector.

Measures to sustain and promote the export sector in Latin America were varied, complex and often unorthodox. Only six of the twenty republics (Cuba, the Dominican Republic, Guatemala, Haiti, Honduras and Panama) eschewed all forms of exchange rate management, preferring instead to preserve their pre-1929 peg to the U.S. dollar. Elsewhere, nominal devaluation was frequent and multiple exchange rates common. As the example of Argentina has shown, nominal devaluation did not necessarily mean real depreciation, but domestic price increases were generally modest and only Bolivia collapsed into a vicious circle of high domestic inflation and exchange rate devaluation – a victim of the chaotic financial conditions created by the Chaco War and its aftermath.

The decline of credit for the export sector after 1929, from both domestic and foreign sources, threatened many firms with foreclosure by banks. Overwhelmingly, governments intervened with debt moratoria to prevent the erosion of the export base; in some cases, new financial institutions were set up with state support or government participation to channel additional resources to the export sector. Pressure groups representing the export interests were strengthened or set up for the first time and export taxes were frequently revised downwards.

The improvement in the NBTT after 1932 was a further boost to the export sector. Out of fifteen reporting countries (see Table 2.6), only four recorded a deterioration in the period from 1932 to 1939. Two of these (Costa Rica and Honduras) were major banana exporters and suffered from the downward revision in the administered prices for bananas used by the giant fruit companies in their global operations; since these prices were highly artificial, the deterioration in the NBTT was not very serious in practice. The same is true of Venezuela, where world oil prices remained weak and caused the fall in the NBTT; however, Venezuela began to squeeze a higher returned value from the foreign oil companies after the fall of Gómez through the revision of contracts and an increase in tax revenue, so that the purchasing power of exports steadily increased.[19]

The only other country to experience a fall in the NBTT was Brazil. The collapse of coffee prices after 1929 hit Brazil hard. A new coffee support scheme, financed in part by a tax on coffee exports and in part by government credits,[20] provided the funds to destroy some of the crop; this reduced the supply reaching the world market and allowed Brazil to sell at higher dollar prices than would otherwise have been possible. At the same time, devaluation raised the local currency price of coffee exports so that the fall in coffee income was much less severe than implied by the NBTT deterioration. However, no amount of tinkering with the instruments available could conceal the fact that the coffee sector was in deep crisis. With the price of cotton relative to coffee rising in the 1930s, there was a reallocation of resources so that Brazilian cotton production and exports soared. From 1932 to 1939 the area planted to cotton increased nearly fourfold, production nearly sixfold, while exports rose so rapidly that Brazilian exports in volume terms grew faster than in any other republic (see Table 2.6). Brazilian dollar earnings from exports may have remained weak, but the growth in volumes and in domestic currency terms was much more impressive.

The commodity lottery produced a series of winners and losers in Latin America. The main loser was Argentina, its traditional exports hurt by their dependence on the British market. Cuban tobacco exports, including

[19] See J. McBeth, *Juan Vicente Gómez and the Oil Companies in Venezuela, 1908–1935* (Cambridge, 1983), ch. 5.

[20] The macroeconomic impact of this funding scheme has been the subject of much debate. See, for example, Celso Furtado, *The Economic Growth of Brazil* (Berkeley, Cal., 1963) and C. Peláez, *História da Industrialização Brasileira* (Rio de Janeiro, 1972). There is an excellent survey of the debate, generally favouring Furtado's interpretation of the scheme as expansionary, in A. Fishlow, 'Origins and Consequences of Import Substitution in Brazil', in L. Di Marco (ed.), *International Economics and Development* (New York, 1972).

cigars, also lost and suffered severely from the protectionist measures adopted in the U.S. market. The main winners were exporters of gold and silver as prices rose steeply in the 1930s. This windfall from the lottery benefited Colombia and Nicaragua in the case of gold and Mexico in the case of silver. Bolivia benefited from the price increases for tin achieved by the International Tin Committee after 1931 and a further boost to tin prices came from rearmament in the late 1930s. Chile too, having suffered the most severe drop in export prices in the worst years of the depression, saw its NBTT increase by an average 18.6 per cent a year between 1932 and 1939 as rearmament fed its way through to copper prices. Finally, the Dominican Republic exploited its position outside the International Sugar Agreement to enjoy higher prices and increased volumes from sugar sales.

The recovery of the traditional export sector was the main reason for the growth of export volumes after 1932. Export diversification (with the exception of cotton in Brazil) was of limited importance with only a few sporadic efforts such as cotton in El Salvador and Nicaragua and cacao in Costa Rica (on abandoned banana plantations). The rise of Nazi Germany, however, and its aggressive trade policy based on the aski-mark meant that the geographical composition of foreign trade changed quite sharply. By 1938, the last year not affected by war, Germany was taking 10.3 per cent of all Latin American exports and supplying 17.1 per cent of all imports compared with 7.7 per cent and 10.9 per cent respectively in 1930. The main loser from the increased German share was Britain, although the United States also declined as a market for Latin American exports (from 33.4 per cent in 1930 to 31.5 per cent in 1938).

The rise in importance of the German market owed a great deal to the commercial policy of the Third Reich. The carrot to induce countries to accept the inconvertible aski-mark was the offer of higher prices for their traditional exports; Brazil, Colombia and Costa Rica, for example, all searching for new markets for coffee, saw a steep rise in the importance of the German market – the loss of which was to cause serious problems following the outbreak of war. Uruguay, facing problems of access to the British market, saw exports to Germany rise to 23.5 per cent of the total by 1938. By contrast, the reciprocal trade treaties promoted by Cordell Hull failed to achieve an increase in U.S. market shares, although they did contribute towards the increase in the absolute value of trade until the 1938 depression.

The export sector by the end of the decade still had not fully recovered its earlier importance, but it had contributed in no small part to the recovery of real GDP after 1932. Comparing 1928 with 1938 (see Table 2.1), most reporting countries experienced a drop in the ratio of real exports to real GDP; yet only in Mexico, Honduras and Argentina – the special cases already examined – was there a major decline and Brazil even experienced an increase.

The recovery of the export quantum in most Latin American republics helps to explain the steep increase in the volume of imports after 1932 (see Table 2.6). It is not the whole story, however, as the quantum of imports recovered in every reporting case – including the three where the volume of exports fell. The additional explanations for the movement in imports are provided by changes in the net barter terms of trade and reductions in factor payments due to debt default, exchange control and the fall in profit remittances. Thus, even in Argentina – where the external debt was serviced punctually and the volume of exports fell – favourable movements in the NBTT and a reduction in profit remittances made possible an annual increase in the volume of imports of 4.6 per cent between 1932 and 1939.

The growth in the quantum of imports for every republic after 1932 is so striking that it is worth examining the correlation between changes in real imports and real GDP. For the twelve republics for which data are available – that is to say, all those except Uruguay in Table 2.1 – this is positive with a least squares correlation co-efficient of 0.75 – significant at the 1 per cent level. Considering the standard view of the 1930s as a period of economic recovery based on import substituting industrialization and import compression, this result is a salutary reminder of the overwhelming importance of the external sector and foreign trade even after the 1929 depression.

It is worth exploring this point further since the standard view is so firmly established. Import substitution in industry was indeed important, as we shall see in the next section, and over the decade 1928 to 1938 the ratio of real imports to real GDP did fall. However, import compression was most severe in the worst years of the depression (1930–2) and led to an intense squeeze on consumer imports. After 1932, industrial growth was able to satisfy much of the demand for consumer goods previously met by imports, but at the same time real imports rose faster than real GDP in virtually all cases as the marginal propensity to import remained extremely high. The composition of imports shifted away from consumer goods – particularly non-durable consumer goods – but economic performance was still highly sensitive to and dependent on the growth of imports. Without export recovery, or at least an improvement in the NBTT, it would have been much more difficult for Latin America in the 1930s to carry out successful ISI.

RECOVERY OF THE NON-EXPORT ECONOMY

The recovery of the export sector, either in terms of volumes or prices or in many cases both, contributed to the growth of the Latin American economies in the 1930s. The resurgence of the export sector, coupled with loose monetary and fiscal policies, brought about an expansion of nominal home final demand. With price increases kept to very modest levels in most republics, this corresponded to an increase in real home final demand which permitted the non-export sector in some cases to expand rapidly. The major beneficiary was manufacturing, although domestic use agriculture (DUA) also increased and there was significant growth in some non-traded activities such as construction and transport.

Argentina was the only country where the recovery of real GDP is not associated with the recovery of the export sector. On the contrary, the nominal and real value of exports continued to fall in Argentina for several years after real GDP reached its trough in 1932. Argentina, however, had the largest and most sophisticated industrial structure (with the exception of textiles) of any republic by the end of the 1920s and this industrial maturity allowed manufacturing to lead the Argentine economy out of recession in response to the abrupt change in the relative price of home and foreign goods brought about by the depression.

The change in relative prices – which affected all importables and not just manufactured goods – came about for three reasons. First, the widespread use of specific tariffs in Latin America meant that tariff rates started to rise as import prices fell; specific tariffs – a serious disadvantage in times of rising prices – brought increasing protection in times of falling prices even without state action; however, most republics responded to the depression by raising tariffs, thus giving a further twist to nominal protection. These increases were often designed primarily to raise government revenue, but – as usual – they also acted as a protective barrier against imports. Venezuela, for example, saw the average tariff rate rise from 25 per cent in the late 1920s to over 40 per cent by the late 1930s.[21]

The second reason for the change in relative prices was exchange rate

[21] See W. Karlsson, *Manufacturing in Venezuela* (Stockholm, 1975), p. 220.

depreciation. In the early 1930s, when prices were falling almost everywhere, a nominal exchange rate depreciation was a reasonable guarantee of real devaluation. By the middle 1930s, with modest price increases in some countries, real devaluation was only assured if the nominal depreciation exceeded the difference between domestic and foreign price changes. Many countries, particularly the larger ones, met these conditions and exchange rate policy became a powerful tool for shifting relative prices in favour of home goods competing with imports. In those republics using multiple exchange rates (most of South America), a further opportunity was provided for raising the domestic currency cost of those consumer good imports that local firms were best placed to produce.

Exchange control provided the third reason for the change in relative prices. The rationing of foreign exchange for non-essential imports effectively drove up their local currency cost even without devaluation. Thus, some of the republics which pegged their exchange rate to the U.S. dollar still enjoyed a de facto devaluation as a result of exchange control. The outstanding exception is Venezuela, where the bolívar appreciated sharply against the dollar and wiped out much of the advantage offered by the increase in tariff rates.

The change in relative prices, coupled with exchange control in many cases, provided an excellent opportunity for manufacturers in those countries where industry had already taken root. Even better placed were those countries where the manufacturing sector had developed spare capacity before 1929; in such countries, production could respond immediately to the recovery of internal demand and the change in relative prices without the need for expensive investments dependent on imported capital goods.

A number of Latin American countries did, indeed, meet these conditions. Argentina has already been mentioned. Brazil, although much poorer than Argentina, had been steadily developing its industrial base and had taken advantage of favourable circumstances in the 1920s to expand its manufacturing capacity. Mexico had seen a wave of industrial investments during the Porfiriato and, following the upheavals of the revolution, had begun to invest again on a modest scale. Among the medium-sized countries, Chile had succeeded in building a relatively sophisticated industrial base even before the First World War and Peru had enjoyed a boom in industrial investment in the 1890s which was subsequently sustained only during periods of favourable relative prices. Colombia, its industrial progress delayed by the failure to build a strong internal market in the nineteenth century, had finally begun to build an important industrial base in the 1920s. Among the small republics, only Uruguay could be said to have established modern manufacturing with firms attracted by the concentration of population and high incomes in the capital Montevideo.

These seven republics were best placed to take advantage of the exceptional conditions facing the manufacturing sector after domestic demand began to recover. Indeed, the annual rate of growth of manufacturing net output exceeded 10 per cent in a few cases (see Table 2.7). Although spare capacity was used at first to meet the increase in demand, this had begun to be exhausted by the middle of the decade. In Mexico, the giant iron and steel works at Monterrey – unprofitable for most of the century – was finally able to pay healthy dividends as capacity utilization reached 80 per cent in 1936.[22] Thereafter demand could only be satisfied through new investments involving the purchase of imported capital goods. Thus, industrialization began to change the structure of imports with a declining share accounted for by consumer goods and an increasing share by intermediate and capital goods.

Argentina remained the most industrialized republic, both in terms of the share of manufacturing in GDP and in terms of net manufacturing output per head (see Table 2.7). However, the Brazilian manufacturing sector made considerable progress in the 1930s. Despite the decline in world coffee prices, local currency income derived from coffee fell much more modestly as a result of the coffee support programme and cotton exports provided a new dynamic source of earnings. At the same time, the combination of real depreciation, tariff increases and exchange controls gave consumers a strong incentive to switch from imported commodities to local products. This stimulus was at work in other countries, but capacity constraints often prevented firms from responding more positively. In Brazil, however, manufacturing capacity had been significantly enlarged by the high level of imported capital equipment made possible during the 1920s. Thus, Brazilian firms were poised to meet demand not only in traditional industries, such as textiles, shoes and hats, but also in new industries producing consumer durables and intermediate goods.

Even the Brazilian capital goods industry advanced in the 1930s. However, its share of value added was still only 4.9 per cent in 1939.[23]

[22] See S. Haber, *Industry and Underdevelopment: the Industrialization of Mexico, 1890–1940* (Stanford, Cal., 1989), p. 177.

[23] See Fishlow, 'Origins and Consequences of Import Substitution in Brazil', table VII.

Table 2.7. *Industrial sector indicators*

	(1)	(2)	(3)	(4)
Argentina	7.3	22.7	122	12.7
Brazil	7.6	14.5	24	20.2
Chile	7.7	[c]18.0	79	25.1
Colombia	11.8	9.1	17	32.1
Mexico	11.9	16.0	39	20.1
Peru	[a]6.4	[d]10.0	29	n.a.
Uruguay	[b]5.3	15.9	84	7.0

Notes: [a] 1933–38; [b] 1930–39; [c] 1940; [d] 1938.
(1) Annual rate of growth of manufacturing net output, 1932–9.
(2) Ratio (%) of manufacturing to GDP in 1939 (1970 prices).
(3) Net manufacturing output per head of population (in 1970 dollars converted at official exchange rate) c.1939.
(4) Number of workers per establishment c.1939.
Sources: see Table 2.1; also G. Wythe, *Industry in Latin America,* (New York, 1945); C. Boloña, 'Tariff Policies in Peru, 1880–1980', unpublished D.Phil. dissertation (Oxford University, 1981).

Brazilian industrialization therefore remained heavily dependent on imported capital goods so that capacity constraints in several branches began to reassert themselves in the late 1930s. In common with other large Latin American countries, these capacity constraints encouraged labour-intensive operations and the substitution of labour for capital wherever possible. Manufacturing employment growth in Brazil was rapid, favouring São Paulo in particular where the rate of increase was over 10 per cent per year after 1932. Indeed, labour inputs 'explain' most of the growth in Brazilian industry in the 1930s so that productivity increases were modest. The efficiency of this industrialization and the ability of firms to compete internationally can therefore be questioned.

The industrialization of the 1930s brought about an important shift in the composition of industrial output in the major Latin American countries. Although food-processing and textiles remained the most important branches of manufacturing, several new sectors began to acquire importance for the first time; these included consumer durables, chemicals (including pharmaceuticals), metals and papers. The market for industrial goods also became more diversified; although the majority of firms continued to sell consumer goods (durable and non-durable) to households, inter-industry relations were now more complex with a number of establishments providing inputs needed by other industries which were previously purchased from abroad.

These changes were significant, but they should not be exaggerated. By the end of the 1930s, for example, industry's share of GDP was still modest (see Table 2.7). Only in Argentina did the share exceed 20 per cent and even there agriculture was still more important. Despite its late industrial spurt, the manufacturing sector in Colombia accounted for less than 10 per cent of real GDP in 1939. Brazil and Mexico had made important progress towards industrialization, but the net output of manufactures in both countries per head of population was still far below the levels in Argentina, Chile and Uruguay (see Table 2.7).

There were other problems faced by the industrial sector in the 1930s. Attracted by the highly protected internal market, it had no incentive to overcome its many inefficiencies and to start to compete in export markets. By the end of the 1930s, the sector was still very small scale with the average number of employees per establishment ranging from 7.0 in Uruguay to 32.1 in Colombia (see Table 2.7). The productivity of the labour force was also low with value added per worker even in Argentina only one-quarter of the U.S. level, and in most republics over half the workforce was employed in food products and textiles.

The problems of low productivity in the industrial sector could be traced to shortages of electric power, lack of skilled labour, restricted access to credit and use of antiquated machinery. By the end of the 1930s, the governments of several republics had accepted the need for indirect state intervention on behalf of the industrial sector and had set up state agencies to promote the formation of new manufacturing activities with economies of scale and modern machinery. A notable example was the Chilean Corporación de Fomento de la Producción (CORFO), with similar development corporations being formed in Argentina, Brazil, Mexico, Bolivia, Peru, Colombia and Venezuela. Most of these corporations came too late to have much impact on industrial developments in the 1930s – CORFO, for example, was formed in 1939 – so that their influence was felt more in the 1940s.

In a few cases, state intervention was direct rather than indirect. The nationalization of the oil industry in Mexico in 1938 brought the oil refineries into public ownership; state ownership in social democratic Uruguay was extended into meat-packing and cement manufacture. Generally, however, industry was controlled by private domestic interests with a vital role played by recently arrived immigrants from Spain, Italy and Germany. Only in Argentina, Brazil and Mexico were foreign-owned subsidiaries of overseas companies important and even in those countries their contribution to total industrial output was modest.

The change in relative prices of home and foreign goods favoured import substitution in agriculture (ISA) as well as ISI. The export-led model before 1929 had brought specialization to the point where imports of many foodstuffs and raw materials were required to meet home demand. The change in relative prices provided an opportunity to reverse this and encouraged production of domestic use agriculture (DUA).

The expansion of agriculture for the home market was particularly impressive in the Caribbean Basin. These small republics, lacking a significant industrial base, found in ISA an easy way of compensating for the lack of opportunities in ISI. Export specialization and the existence of numerous foreign-owned enclaves had created by the end of the 1920s a hugh demand for imported foodstuffs to feed the rural proletariat and the growing populations of the urban centres; with surplus land and labour, together with the incentives provided by the change in relative prices, it was a relatively simple matter to expand domestic production at the expense of imports.

Although ISA was most important in the smaller republics of Central America and the Caribbean, it affected South America as well. A clear pattern can be discerned for many agricultural staples with imports falling sharply in the Depression in line with the collapse of purchasing power and then failing to recover their pre-Depression peak as domestic production of food and raw materials expanded. The main exceptions (e.g., cotton, hemp) were all raw materials required by the rapidly expanding industrial sector so that imports remained important.

The change in the relative prices of home and foreign goods was an important explanation for the expansion of DUA and industry. Non-traded goods and services also advanced, however, in line with the growth of the real economy and the recovery of home final demand. The shift of resources towards the industrial sector and the related increase in urbanization drove up the demand for energy, for example, and stimulated new investments in electricity supply (including hydroelectric dams), oil exploration and petroleum refineries. The gap between supply and demand remained a problem throughout much of the 1930s, but the existence of excess demand was a powerful stimulus for the growth both of public utilities and of the construction industry.

The construction industry was also a beneficiary of new investments in the transport system. By the 1930s, Latin America's railway boom was over, but the region had barely begun to develop the road system needed to cope with the demand for trucks, buses and cars. The construction of roads – overwhelmingly financed by the state – had the great merit of using labour and local raw materials rather than being heavily dependent on complementary imports. Throughout Latin America, there was an expansion of the road system in the 1930s with a particularly impressive increase in Argentina and this expansion provided an opportunity to absorb unemployed labour in many rural areas.

The expansion of the road system required an increase in government expenditure which put further pressure on the limited fiscal resources of the state. Some authoritarian governments, notably Ubico's regime in Guatemala, relied on coercion to obtain the labour inputs needed for expansion of the road system. Once built, however, the network of roads permitted isolated regions to market an agricultural surplus and contributed to the growth of DUA. This has been clearly demonstrated in the case of Brazil.[24]

The air transport system also expanded rapidly in the 1930s, although it started from such a low base that its ability to carry passengers and freight was strictly limited by the end of the decade. Nevertheless, in countries where geography made travel by train impossible and by road difficult, the creation of an air transport system was an important step towards modernization and national integration. In Honduras, for example, where President Carías granted a monopoly to a New Zealand entrepreneur as a reward for his role in converting civilian planes into bombers during the 1932 civil war, the newly formed Transportes Aereos Centroamericanos (TACA) played an important part in linking the country's isolated eastern provinces to the capital city.

Finally, whereas the depression in Europe and North America cut a swathe through the financial system of the developed countries, with runs on deposits and bank collapse a common experience, Latin America came through the worst years of the depression with only modest damage to its financial system. Furthermore, the 1930s witnessed the creation of new central banks, the expansion of the insurance industry and the growth of secondary banking (including state-owned development corporations).

[24] See N. Leff, *Underdevelopment and Development in Brazil,* Vol. I (London, 1982), p. 181.

The stability of the financial system was all the more remarkable in view of the close relationship between many banks and the export sector. As the value of export earnings collapsed after 1929, many exporters could not meet their financial commitments and the position was made even worse for the banks when a number of governments declared a moratorium on foreclosures. The wholesale financial reforms in the 1920s (spurred on in many cases by Professor Kemmerer) had, however, led to the creation of a much stronger financial system in Latin America with clearly defined rules by the time of the depression. The novelty of the system meant that in many countries cash reserve ratios were far above the legal limits so that it was easier to absorb the inevitable decline in deposits. A second explanation for the survival of the banking system was provided by exchange control. The close links between banks in Latin America and foreign financial institutions had led to a high degree of dependence on foreign funds; the existence of exchange control rescued a number of banks from having to make payments of interest or principal to foreign creditors which might otherwise have bankrupted the institutions. Yet perhaps the most important reason was the role of the banking system in funding budget deficits in the 1930s. Banks contributed handsomely to domestic bond issues by governments and were rewarded with a steady stream of interest payments; bank funding of the deficit may have contributed to the rise in prices in Latin America after the early 1930s, but inflation remained modest and for the banks the interest receipts became a useful source of income. Furthermore, as the export sector began to recover, the banks were able to return to a more normal relationship with many of their traditional clients and some began to exploit the new opportunities opening up outside the export sector.

Economic recovery in Latin America in the 1930s was rapid (see Table 2.6). Real GDP in Colombia, where the depression was relatively mild, surpassed its pre-Depression peak as early as 1932. Brazil achieved this in 1933, Mexico in 1934 and Argentina, El Salvador and Guatemala in 1935. Chile and Cuba, where the depression had been particularly severe, had to wait until 1937, while the luckless Honduras – overwhelmingly dependent on the export of bananas – had to wait until 1945. With the population growing at around 2 per cent a year, most republics had recovered the pre-Depression levels of real GDP per head by the late 1930s. The most serious exceptions were Honduras and Nicaragua.

CONCLUSION

The world depression, which began at the end of the 1920s, was transmitted to Latin America through the external sector. In almost all cases, the recovery from the depression was also associated with the recovery of the external sector. The growth of exports, coupled with debt default, a reduction in profit remittances and an improvement in the NBTT, permitted a substantial growth in the volume of imports with which the growth of real GDP in the 1930s is highly correlated. Loose fiscal and monetary policies, the change in relative prices in favour of domestic production competing with imports and the availability of complementary imports through the relaxation of the balance-of-payments constraint combined to produce significant structural change in the 1930s, which particularly favoured the manufacturing sector in the larger countries and domestic use agriculture in the smaller republics.

The performance of the Latin American economies in the 1930s should not therefore be seen as marking a 'turning-point', as has so often been claimed, although the decade did mark an important milestone in the transition from traditional export-led growth to ISI. It is true that the industrial sector was particularly dynamic, growing faster than real GDP in almost all countries. But this had also been true in the 1920s. Only in Argentina, where the manufacturing sector led the recovery out of depression in the early 1930s, could it be claimed that the economy had reached by the beginning of the decade a sufficiently advanced level for performance not to be seriously affected by the decline in the volume of exports. Elsewhere, there is no evidence that larger countries with a broader industrial base performed better than the small republics with virtually no modern manufacturing; in both cases, performance was highly dependent on the recovery of import capacity and even in Argentina performance was not insensitive to the sharp improvement in the NBTT after 1933.

By the end of the decade, however, it could be argued that industrial growth had produced a qualitative as well as quantitative change in the structure of the economies of the larger republics. In the 1940s and 1950s, these changes matured to the point where industry and real GDP in many republics were capable of moving in the opposite direction to primary product exports so that the export-led growth model had ceased to be an accurate description of their performance. Thus, changes in the 1930s can be seen as laying the foundations for a transition towards the pure import-substitution model, which reached its most extreme form in the 1950s and 1960s. This was certainly true of Brazil, Chile and Mexico which had joined Argentina by the end of the 1930s as the only countries to have pushed industrialization and structural change to the point where internal demand was no longer primarily determined by the export sector.

The most important change in the 1930s involved the switch from self-regulating economic policies to policy instruments which had to be manipulated by the authorities. By the end of the 1920s, attachment to the gold standard had left most Latin American republics without an independent exchange rate policy; the operation of the gold standard also meant that monetary policy was largely passive, with inflows and outflows of gold underpinning movements in the money supply to bring about automatic adjustment to external and internal equilibrium. Even fiscal policy had lost much of its importance; in the smaller republics, dollar diplomacy and high conditionality had produced in many cases foreign control of external trade taxes – the major source of government revenue – and in the larger countries the 'dance of the millions' had made it much easier to finance expenditure by foreign borrowing than by fiscal reform.

The collapse of the gold standard forced all republics to address the question of exchange rate policy. A few (smaller) republics preferred to peg to the U.S. dollar, thereby abandoning the exchange rate as an active instrument. Most republics, including some of the smaller ones, opted for a managed exchange rate. In highly open economies, the exchange rate has an immediate and powerful effect on the prices of many goods so that it is the single most important determinant of relative prices and the allocation of resources; an independent exchange rate policy also encourages the formation of pressure groups to lobby the authorities in support of exchange rate changes to favour their interests. Not surprisingly, many republics in Latin America in the 1930s opted for a multiple exchange rate system as a way of resolving these competing pressures. That is one reason why in 1945, after the Bretton Woods Conference, the newly formed International Monetary Fund found that thirteen out of the fourteen countries operating multiple exchange rate systems throughout the world were in Latin America.

The balance-of-payments constraint in the 1930s, coupled with exchange control, meant that movements in international reserves – money of external origin – ceased to be a major determinant of the money supply. Instead, base money was driven more by government budget deficits and the rediscount policy of the Central Bank, while the money multiplier was affected by changes in reserve ratios. Thus, changes in the money supply were due more to changes in money of internal origin and this implied the adoption of a more active monetary policy in almost all republics. The main exceptions were those countries, such as Cuba and Panama, which lacked a Central Bank and were therefore unable to influence the money supply through changes in the monetary base.

The recovery of the export sector and import capacity did not necessarily imply an increase in the value of external trade. Thus, government revenue from taxes on trade was seriously affected and the reduction was not fully compensated by the need to spend less on public external debt service as a result of default; the crisis provoked fiscal reform and a more active fiscal policy in all republics. A prime candidate was upward revision of tariff rates, but a further modest shift towards direct taxes – income and property – can be detected in the 1930s as well as the introduction of a variety of indirect taxes aimed at home consumption. By the end of the decade, the correlation between the value of external trade and government revenue had been loosened, thereby undermining a crucial link in the operation of the export-led growth model.

The adoption of more aggressive exchange rate, monetary and fiscal policies was so widespread that it is difficult to sustain the thesis that Latin American republics can be divided into larger countries adopting 'active' policies and smaller countries following 'passive' policies. While all the larger republics did indeed follow active policies, so did many of the smaller countries including Bolivia, Costa Rica, Ecuador, El Salvador, Nicaragua and Uruguay. The most obvious examples of passive countries (Cuba, Haiti, Honduras and Panama) were all semi-colonies of the United States in the 1930s, but not all semi-colonies (e.g., Nicaragua) could be described as passive.

These changes in the management of key instruments of economic policy did not amount to an intellectual revolution. On the contrary, the theory of inward-looking development was still inchoate, the export sector was still dominant and its supporters still politically powerful. Yet the choices forced on the authorities in the 1930s in the fields of exchange rate, monetary and fiscal policy do mark an important steppingstone on the way to the intellectual revolution associated with the U.N. Economic Commission for Latin America (ECLA) after the Second World War and the explicit development of the import-substitution model. Policy management in the 1930s showed the sensitivity of resource allocation to relative prices and the response of the manufacturing sector in the larger republics was a salutary reminder of how efficacious economic policy could be.

The management of economic policy in the 1930s was, indeed, quite successful and compared favourably with the post-war experience. What the authorities lacked in experience was compensated in a number of ways. First, the officials in charge of fiscal and monetary policy (e.g. Rául Prebisch at the Argentine Central Bank) were often very competent technocrats who benefited from public ignorance of economic science and were able to take decisions in a relatively apolitical environment. Second, perfect foresight and perfect information – the two conditions required for the rational expectations conclusion on the impotence of government policy – were clearly absent in the 1930s, so that there was much less danger that the intended thrust of a change in economic policy would be thwarted by the omniscience of the private sector. Third, the scourge of economic policy in the post-war period – the acceleration of inflation – was much less of a problem in the 1930s. Money illusion (based in part on the absence of price statistics), falling prices in the world economy and spare capacity in the domestic economy meant that expansionary economic policies were less likely to collapse in a vicious circle of budget deficits and inflation.

Loose fiscal and monetary policies in the 1930s underpinned the growth of home final demand. As Table 2.5 has shown, this was of enormous importance in pulling the republics out of depression and providing the stimulus needed for the growth of importables and non-traded goods and services. Associated with this growth was an increase in urbanization so that a number of republics could be described as primarily urban by the end of the 1930s and all republics saw a big fall in the proportion of the population classified as rural.

While economic performance in the 1930s – at least after 1932 – was generally satisfactory, there were a number of deviations from the regional pattern. Some republics – the 'low recovery' countries in Table 2.4 – were marked by stagnation or even decline in economic activity. The basic problem was the export sector which remained depressed throughout most of the 1930s for reasons beyond the control of the authorities; in Honduras, for example, banana exports collapsed after 1931 as a result of the spread of disease on the banana plantations and the real value of exports did not recover its 1931 peak until 1965. With depressed exports, the best hope for recovery lay in the import-competing sector (ISA and ISI), but the small size of the market made it difficult to compensate for the decline in the export sector.

The 'medium recovery' countries based their recovery from the depression mainly on the export sector with the important exceptions of Argentina and Colombia. Economic growth in the 1930s did not therefore imply significant structural change and there was little alteration in the composition of exports. Recovery in Bolivia depended crucially on the formation of the International Tin Cartel in 1931, which brought higher prices for tin exporters and therefore higher revenue for the government from export taxes. The export sector did expand in Colombia, but its growth was overshadowed by the spectacular rise of the manufacturing sector where the increase in textile production was particularly impressive. In Argentina, however, the export sector stagnated in real terms so that the recovery depended crucially on the non-export sector. The performance of this sector, whether in industry, transport, construction or finance, was generally satisfactory so that it is difficult to conclude that the long-run decline of the Argentine economy dates from the 1930s.

The 'fast recovery' countries include republics where the impact of the depression was relatively minor (e.g., Brazil) and countries where it was very severe (e.g., Chile and Cuba). Fast growth in the second group of countries therefore consisted primarily of a 'recovery' of real output lost in the worst years of the Depression, although Chile also enjoyed a considerable amount of new ISI. In Brazil, on the other hand, fast growth primarily involved additions to real output; although export recovery was important in Brazil, the structure of the economy began to shift in favour of industry. Brazil remained desperately poor, however, with a real GDP per head in 1939 only one-quarter of that in Argentina and 60 per cent of the Latin American average. Mexico also enjoyed significant structural change; land reform under President Cárdenas (1934–40) strengthened non-export agriculture, the state became a major source of investment and many firms in the industrial and construction sectors began to be reliant on public sector contracts.

The 1930s in Latin America may not have represented a sharp break with the past, but the decade did not represent a lost opportunity either. In the face of a generally hostile external environment, most republics did well to rebuild their export sectors; where it was feasible, republics with only a few exceptions expanded the production of importables and increased the supply of non-traded goods and services. These changes provided the basis for a significant growth in intra-regional trade in the early 1940s when access to imports from the rest of the world was cut off. Changes in economic policy in the 1930s were also generally rational; a wholesale retreat from the export sector and the construction of a semi-closed economy would have involved a massive increase in inefficiency; a slavish commitment to the export-led model of growth would have locked the region into an allocation of resources no longer consistent with long-run dynamic comparative advantage. Economic historians searching for the period in the twentieth century when Latin American economic policy and performance go seriously wrong need to look beyond the 1930s.

3

THE LATIN AMERICAN ECONOMIES, 1939–c. 1950

This chapter examines trends in Latin American economic performance and Latin American economic policy during and immediately after the Second World War. The emphasis is principally on the interaction of the Latin American economies with the international economy. In the 1930s, as the previous chapter has shown, Latin American economic performance as a whole was still driven by the export of primary products, although in most countries industry grew faster than real gross domestic product (GDP). Economic policy achieved the unusual feat of stimulating primary exports and industrial development at the same time. This was an important achievement, since primary exports were the main source of foreign exchange for the import of intermediate and capital goods. By the 1950s, however, Latin America was deeply entrenched in import-substituting industrialization (ISI). Its key characteristics were a strong discrimination against exports combined with an increased need for foreign exchange. Thus it discriminated against the sector which was crucial to its functioning. We need to understand, therefore, how and why policy evolved from the relative consistency of the 1930s to the contradictions of the 1950s. This chapter will explore first, the impact of the Second World War on the Latin American economies, and second, the evolution of economic policies – and economic performance – in the immediate aftermath of the war. The analysis will necessarily have to touch on the 1950s, since our conclusion is that the explicit rejection of the old export-led growth model and the consolidation of the new inward-looking ISI model of economic growth and development occurred, in the larger countries at least, between the late forties and the middle of the following decade.

THE SECOND WORLD WAR

Arthur Lewis has described the years 1913 to 1939 as 'an age of dislocation and an age of experiment' in the world economy.[1] The First World War acted as a catalyst in opening cracks and exposing shifting structures: by 1918 the old system centred on London and the gold standard was in disarray, and the dominance of the United States in trade and capital flows was apparent. Yet in a real sense the system was not ready to change: contemporary thinking could only seek to reinstate the old forms, returning to the gold standard and even to inappropriate currency parities. The extent to which the old system had depended for its success not only on an underlying equilibrium but also on a single centre, London, was ignored. Since there was now more than one financial centre, and a much larger supply of volatile short-term funds, the system became dangerously unstable. The United States which at the end of the war had a long-term credit balance of US$3.3 billion (equivalent to more than 40 per cent of its annual merchandise exports)[2], did not adopt the behaviour of a 'wise creditor', importing goods to permit debtors to pay and lending prudently to projects which would foster payments capacity. Instead, it adopted protectionist policies and much of the capital that was exported took the form of loans by inexperienced private bankers, funding many extravagant and unwise projects. The crash of 1929 highlighted the fundamental weaknesses of the system. Subsequently, during the 1930s most governments pursued purely defensive policies dominated by increasing protectionism and exchange controls that permitted only slow growth of world trade. There was little foreign investment during that period; indeed the main capital flow was toward the United States which once more became a net debtor.

While profoundly affected by the disruption of the international system during the First World War and more especially during the 1929 Depression, the period 1913–1939 was not for Latin America primarily one of depression. On the contrary, particularly in the 1930s, significant growth was achieved. Import-substituting industry emerged as the leading sector in most of the larger countries and agriculture for domestic use in some of the smaller countries. In several notable cases like Brazil and Colombia, economic recovery occurred before exports returned to the levels of the

[1] W.A. Lewis, *Economic Survey 1919–1939* (London, 1949), p. 12.

[2] Barbara Stallings, *Banker to the Third World, U.S. Portfolio Investment in Latin America, 1900–1986* (Berkeley and Los Angeles, Cal., 1987), p. 345.

1920s, and owed much to unorthodox policy management: trade, exchange and capital controls and counter-cyclical government spending. With industrialization and the expansion of state intervention the preconditions for a new model of economic growth different from the export-led growth model were beginning to take shape. As the preceding chapter has shown, however, in the decade of the 1930s while reliance on primary exports was becoming more and more obviously an uncertain path these policies were still combined with active promotion of traditional exports, using exchange rate depreciation and other measures, and aided by a recovery in the terms of trade. This policy was necessary given the political and economic weight of the primary sectors in the Latin American economies. The only country that pursued a different line was Argentina, an exception which proves the rule, since economic diversification had already in this case reduced the weight of the primary sector.

With the outbreak of war in 1939, the Latin American republics were presented not only with common legal and political problems but also with common economic problems in that their sources of supply, export markets, shipping services and credit facilities were all threatened.[3] The British blockaded Germany after September 1939 but the effects of the blockade took time to make themselves felt. By the summer of 1940, however, when Italy entered the war and Germany controlled much of the coast of Europe, Latin America had lost not only the German but most of the European market, which had absorbed some 30 per cent of Latin American exports, and had provided a rather larger proportion of imports. British purchases continued but were more and more confined to essential supplies – sugar and oil, but not tobacco for example. Chilean copper was replaced by imperial supplies, but large quantities of foodstuffs and raw materials were purchased from the other countries on the eastern seaboard of Latin America. As a result the value of British imports from Latin America increased in 1939 and 1940. But, in order to conserve Britain's gold and hard currency reserves, these imports had to be paid for, as far as possible, in special account sterling which could only be used to finance purchases from Britain or the Empire and for payments to British creditors. A mission was sent to South America in October 1940 to explain the British position, and her wish to damage the South American economies as little as possible, but by the time it had sailed, the British Cabinet had

[3] The following description of the effect of the Second World War on Latin America draws heavily on the outstanding secondary source for this period: R.A. Humphreys, *Latin America and the Second World War,* Vol. I: *1939–1942,* and Vol. II: *1942–45* (London, 1981 and 1982).

decided that it would be necessary to limit the amounts bought from non-Commonwealth and imperial sources.

At the same time, Britain had less and less to export. British exports to Latin America began to fall in 1941 and continued to do so. Rising freight rates and rising prices contributed to the decline. The major economic problem for Latin America began to be the accumulation of huge export surpluses – wheat, maize, linseed, coffee, cacao, sugar and bananas, whose prices inevitably fell, and surpluses also of hides, wool, cotton, nitrates and metals, for which, however, the war was creating an increasing demand. The countries most seriously affected were those with stronger trading connections with Europe than with the United States. In Brazil, the fall in coffee exports had at first been counterbalanced by British meat purchases, but it now lost a third of its former markets. In Argentina, 40 per cent of normal export trade was cut off. In Chile there were surpluses of agricultural products, wool and timber as well as nitrates. In June, Peru had sold only one-third of its cotton crop.

One non-European country, Japan, attempted to take advantage of the European blockade to ensure its own safe supplies of essential raw materials. In 1940 a barter deal was completed with Argentina, a trade pact ratified with Uruguay, an oil agreement signed with Mexico and purchases of Chilean minerals and Peruvian and Brazilian cotton increased. But Japan was unable to supply the goods that Latin America wanted and that Europe had previously supplied, and in addition there was strong anti-Japanese feeling. The Japanese trade drive continued in 1941, but was increasingly hampered by agreements between the United States and various Latin American countries for the acquisition of their critical raw materials, and the closing of the Panama Canal to Japanese shipping. Trade relations came to an end with the Japanese attack on Pearl Harbor.

The United States was well aware of the dangers to Pan-American solidarity posed by Latin America's economic difficulties. At the Conference of American Foreign Ministers held in Panama in September 1939 primarily to discuss neutrality in the war and the protection of peace in the western hemisphere, economic co-operation was also discussed and the decision was taken to establish the Inter-American Financial and Economic Advisory Committee (IAFEAC). The IAFEAC in turn created an Inter-American Development Commission to stimulate the increase of non-competitive imports to the United States, intra-Latin American trade and the development of Latin American industry. It drafted a charter for an Inter-American Bank to assist in the stabilization of currencies and economic development, but this idea was not well received and the Bank was not established at this time. In June 1940 Roosevelt put forward the idea of a gigantic cartel to control the trade of the western hemisphere, inspired by fears of a Europe controlled by the Axis, but this met with little support. However, a Rubber Reserve Company and a Metals Reserve Company were set up to acquire and stockpile supplies of strategic raw materials used to produce weapons and munitions, from Latin America and elsewhere. The Export-Import Bank was strengthened with an injection of new capital and became a major instrument of US control of raw material sources in the region. The Havana Conference of Foreign Ministers in July 1940 asked the IAFEAC to try to develop commodity arrangements. As a result, it drafted the Inter-American Coffee Convention which came into effect in April 1941, and set basic export quotas for the coffee-producing countries. Purchases of agricultural commodities were motivated partly by a desire to keep supplies out of Axis hands and partly by a general perception that economic survival was an important component of hemispheric solidarity.

In September 1940 the Export-Import Bank had concluded an agreement with Brazil for a credit of US$20 million to construct a steel plant at Volta Redonda, which the German firm of Krupps had been offering to assist. In November, the Metals Reserve Company contracted to buy for five years almost the entire output of Bolivian tin other than that of the Patiño mining companies (much the largest producers), which was sold to Britain. The United States also bought Chilean copper and nitrates on a considerable scale. Meanwhile, trade between the United States and Latin America increased. As compared with 1938 exports from the United States to Latin America rose by 45 per cent in 1940 and imports from Latin America by 37 per cent.[4] Another significant trend was an increase in intra-Latin American trade and efforts to enhance it. Argentina, for example, signed agreements with Brazil, Bolivia, Colombia and Cuba and ratified a pact with Chile.

Thus it was well understood by the United States that hemispheric defence rested as much on economic as on political and military foundations. Various expedients had been proposed to deal with export surpluses and declining prices and to strengthen the Latin American economies, and

[4] Humphreys, *Latin America and the Second World War*, I, p. 57.

some practical steps had been taken. But though exports from Latin America to the United States had increased, there had been a far greater increase in exports from the United States to Latin America. By the end of 1940, Latin America was left with a large negative balance of trade with the United States.

As the United States was drawn more heavily into the war, declaring war not only on Japan but also on Germany and Italy in December 1941, following the attack on Pearl Harbor, so Latin America was more sharply affected. First, commitment to the Allied cause was demanded by the United States. Second, in return for its solidarity and support and in response to sharply increased strategic needs, so the possibilities of increased levels of economic aid opened up. At the Conference of American Foreign Ministers in Rio de Janeiro in January 1942 the decision was taken to sever diplomatic and commercial relations with the Axis powers: only the Southern Cone countries stood apart from this. Mexico's stand changed radically in the course of 1941 in favour of strong collaboration with the United States. Mexico and most of the Central American and Caribbean states declared war immediately after Pearl Harbor. In August 1942 Brazil was the first South American country to make a formal declaration of war. It was followed by Bolivia in April 1943 and Colombia in January 1944.

The benefits followed swiftly. The earlier agreement to purchase Bolivian tin was followed by a series of agreements for the purchase of strategic materials from Mexico, Brazil, Chile, Peru and Argentina. As a result the demand for some products, formerly in surplus, threatened to exceed supply, and for others, including a number of agricultural and forest products, it was greatly enlarged. The Export-Import Bank now made credits available for the building of roads, notably the Pan-American highway, for the acquisition of transport equipment and machinery, and for development projects. In Brazil, the United States gave special priority to orders for steel, machinery and other equipment for Volta Redonda, and it undertook to facilitate generally the shipment of materials needed for Brazilian industry. The Cooke mission to Brazil (1942) was one of the numerous U.S. trade and technical co-operation missions to Latin America. In Peru U.S. money and exports helped set up the Corporación Peruana del Santa (iron and steel). Currency stabilization agreements were concluded with several countries, including Brazil and Mexico. U.S. investment in Latin America, public and private, began to rise, particularly in the crucial fields of transport and communications. By 1943 these sectors accounted for 31 per cent of total foreign direct investment to Latin America compared to 15 per cent in 1924.[5]

Not surprisingly, some of the strongest effects were felt in Mexico, where on 15 July 1941, a commercial agreement was concluded under which the United States undertook to buy the entire surplus output of eleven Mexican strategic materials and to provide the greatest possible facilities for the export of those products most needed for Mexican industry. On 19 November, after months of patient negotiation (and mounting exasperation in the State Department at the intransigence of the oil companies), a comprehensive settlement of all outstanding problems in regard to the nationalization of the oil industry was reached, finally placing the relations between the two governments on a firm basis of friendship and co-operation. By a series of agreements the United States promised financial assistance to stabilize the Mexican peso, to buy Mexican silver in large quantities, to furnish loans and credits for the completion of the Mexican portion of the Pan-American Highway, and to negotiate a trade treaty. Mexico undertook to pay US$40 million to American citizens. As for the oil dispute, a joint commission of two experts was to be set up to value the expropriated properties and recommend the amount and method of compensation. The experts' recommendations were made, and accepted on 19 April 1942, much to the anger of the companies. Some slight modifications followed, but, with the settlement, a long and difficult chapter in United States-Mexican relations was closed.

In July 1943 the Mexican-American Commission for Economic Cooperation produced a report which considered both the short and long-range problems of the Mexican economy, taking as a guiding principle the industrialization of Mexico at as rapid a pace as was consistent with the necessary restrictions on the use of materials and equipment during the war. One result of the report was the setting up of an industrial commission which outlined a so-called minimum economic programme for 1944, involving twenty projects, including developments in the steel, textile, cement, paper and chemical industries and costing some US$24 million, approved a number of long-range projects, and was responsible for the creation in June 1944 of a Mexican-United States Agricultural Commission.

The exceptions to this flow of US benefits were those Southern Cone countries unwilling to a greater or lesser extent to throw in their lot with the United States. Argentina, however, benefited from the British need

[5] United Nations, *Foreign Capital in Latin America* (New York, 1955), pp. 155 and 160.

for meat, and to a lesser extent hides, linseed oil and wheat. The United Kingdom needed meat both for its civilian population and for the fighting forces; and, with some reason, it had no confidence that adequate replacements for Argentine beef could be supplied from the United States or elsewhere. This made the United Kingdom an unwilling partner in the U.S. campaign to exert pressure on Argentina. Then in June 1943 came the coup which three years later led to the first Peronist government. Despite strong disapproval of the new regime, the British Ministry of Food concluded a new contract to run until October 1944 for the purchase of Argentine meat by Britain on behalf of the United Nations and another for eggs. The State Department was anxious that the British government should issue a statement to dispel all possible suspicion that the signing of the meat contract implied in any way British approval of Argentine neutrality, and the Foreign Office chose the signing of the egg contract as an appropriate moment to issue such a statement.

In December 1943 the Bolivian government was overthrown by a nationalist coup, and Cordell Hull, the virulently anti-Argentine U.S. Secretary of State, wanted to impose sanctions against Argentina for its alleged support. The Foreign Office urged that no precipitate action should be taken. It pointed out that in 1944 Argentina would be providing 14 per cent of the wheat, 70 per cent of the linseed, 40 per cent of the carcass meat, 29 per cent of the canned meat, and 35 per cent of the hides imported into Britain.[6] It believed that the British meat ration could not be cut. The British Chiefs of Staff feared that military operations in 1944 could not continue as planned unless the civilian meat ration were severely curtailed, that a reduction in the leather supply would have a serious effect on military operational capacity towards the end of the year and that a shortage of linseed would affect maintenance of material and the production of essential camouflage.

Only when Argentina finally declared war on Japan and Germany in March 1945 did the United States lift restrictions on sales to and from Argentina. Britain renewed negotiations for a long-term meat contract, suspended at the wishes of the United States the previous November, the State Department now showing itself all compliance, though reservations were to be raised later on the ground that the contract would offend against the principles of multilateral, non-discriminatory trade.

[6] Humphreys, *Latin America and the Second World War,* II, p. 155.

Chile also was unwilling to break with the Axis powers. The Chilean press argued that the United States could afford no protection to Chile, and that Chile, which was supplying copper and other strategic minerals to the United States – an agreement had been signed with the Metals Reserve Company on 29 January 1942 – could contribute more to hemisphere defence by not breaking with the Axis than by doing so. Axis propaganda fuelled the ideas that the United States was attempting to exert improper pressure on Chile, and that Peru, and for that matter Bolivia, were being favoured over Chile. Products imported from the United States were very scarce – petrol rationing had begun in April – and this scarcity was wrongly attributed to economic discrimination. The Chilean government also failed to institute the economic and financial controls recommended by the Rio conference over 'undesirable' business enterprises, to ensure full governmental control over telecommunications with Axis and Axis-occupied countries, and to prevent the continuance of commercial and financial relations with them.

A United States note presented to the Chilean government in October 1942 declared that so long as effective controls were not exercised locally over the firms of countries inimical to the Allies, it would be difficult for the United States to furnish goods and materials which might eventually find their way into the hands of enemy concerns and individuals whose activities were undermining hemisphere defence. Britain and the United States intended to give priority to countries where they could be sure that supplies would not indirectly benefit Axis interests. The Chilean position gradually shifted; the United States promised that a Lend Lease agreement would be signed when a breach with the Axis powers was achieved. In January 1943 relations were severed, and in March the long-delayed Lend Lease agreement was signed.

What then was the significance of the Second World War for the process of economic transition? Above all, following the First World War and the 1929 Depression, it represented yet another shock to the export-led model, this time exposing its vulnerability to the availability of imports and of shipping and to the instability of primary products markets in the face of world political disturbance. Shocks need to be seen as cumulative: as a result of this latest shock the larger countries of the continent were at last prepared to act to respond to the growing sense of a need for an endogenous source of dynamism.

What was paradoxical about this external shock, however, and helps to account for the ambiguity of the subsequent evolution of policy, is that it did not increase Latin American autonomy: on the contrary, as we have seen, it was accompanied by an overwhelmingly strong increase in US influence, as the United States sought to safeguard existing supplies and to push for the development of new essential resources. In Mexico, for example, the transformation of U.S.-Mexican relations was so total that as early as 1942 the Mexican foreign minister described the frontier as 'a uniting not a dividing line'. Remarks like these were astonishing in the light of the bitter clash over oil between the two countries only four years earlier.[7] During this period economic links between Brazil and the United States were considerably reinforced and helped to strengthen the growing links between Brazilian industry and the military. Of the larger economies, only Argentina resisted the growth of U.S. presence and influence.

Among the striking paradoxes of the war years, and one of the major consequences of the war itself, was the growing economic involvement of the United States in Latin America alongside the expanding role of national governments, including the use of direct controls. Over much of Latin America, private sector interests were becoming more closely tied to government in much the same way that in the United States business leaders were co-opted by the government to plan and execute a whole range of new projects. These two developments were to be fundamental to the new model of growth in the post-war period.

The immediate and most marked specific economic effect of the war was the growth of exports (see Table 3.1) in response to the increased demand for primary products. Practically every country experienced export growth at constant prices of over 4 per cent a year. However, a country's ability to benefit from this varied widely. In the case of minerals, price controls and delayed payments meant little extra revenue received. This explains the relatively limited growth of export revenues of mineral exporters like Chile, Bolivia and Peru. But even where revenues were available there was little to spend them on: there was thus substantial accumulation of reserves although again to a variable extent. Brazil's foreign reserves increased by 635 per cent between 1940 and 1945, Colombia's by 540 per cent, Mexico's by 400 per cent, Chile's by 214 per cent, Argentina's by 156 per cent and Peru's by 55 per cent.[8]

Contradictory forces operated on industry. Scarcity of imports certainly encouraged new efforts at substitution, but these same efforts were limited

[7] See Stephen R. Niblo, *The Impact of War: Mexico and World War II,* La Trobe University Institute of Latin American Studies, Occasional Paper No. 10 (Melbourne, 1988), p. 7ff.

[8] See R. A. Ferrero, *La política fiscal y la economía nacional* (Lima, 1946), p. 39.

Table 3.1. *Latin American economic indicators, 1940–45*

	Exports[a]	GDP, per capita[b]	Industry as % of GDP 1940	Industry as % of GDP 1945	Cost of living, 1945 (1939 = 100)
Argentina	4.0	1.2	23	25	133
Bolivia	2.4	n.a.	n.a.	n.a.	320
Brazil	12.1	0.3	15	17	247
Chile	1.5	2.4	18	23	233
Colombia	6.6	0.4	8	11	161
Costa Rica	0.9	−1.5	13	12	189
Cuba	15	n.a.	n.a.	26[c]	205
Dominican Republic	n.a.	n.a.	n.a.	n.a.	n.a.
Ecuador	18.9	2.0	16	18	n.a.
El Salvador	12.8	−0.3	10	11	191
Guatemala	5.5	−7.3	7	13	191
Haiti	19	n.a.	n.a.	7	n.a.
Honduras	2.7	0.8	7	7	146
Mexico	4.6	4.6	17	19	200
Nicaragua	−1.1	0.5	11	11	433
Panama	−2.5	n.a.	n.a.	6	n.a.
Paraguay	20.9	−0.1	14	16	233
Peru	4.5	n.a.	n.a.	13	183
Uruguay	5.4	1.3	17	18	133
Venezuela	9.7	2.6	14	15	134

Notes: [a]Compound annual growth rates of commodity exports in constant dollars.
[b] Annual growth rates of real GDP at 1970 prices.
[c] Non-sugar manufacturing as per cent of total production, i.e., the total is less than GDP.
Sources: Exports: James W. Wilkie, *Statistics and National Policy,* Supplement 3, UCLA, (Los Angeles, Cal., 1974). Data deflated by US Export Price Index: 1930 = 100, 1940 = 1.07 and 1945 = 1.52.
GDP: United Nations Economic Commission for Latin America (ECLA), *Series Historicas de Crecimiento de América Latina* (Santiago, 1978); V. Bulmer-Thomas, *The Political Economy of Central America since 1920* (Cambridge, 1987).
Industry: ECLA, *Series Historicas,* Bulmer-Thomas, *The Politicial Economy of Central America;* Cuba: C. Brundenius, *Revolutionary Cuba. The Challenge of Economic Growth with Equity* (London, 1984), p. 146.
Cost of Living: James W. Wilkie, *Statistics and National Policy.*

in turn by scarcity of crucial capital goods imports. The net result was a continuation of the industrial growth already experienced during the 1930s, but with a new bias towards capital goods and basic inputs. A number of the firms later to be important in the Brazilian capital goods industry, for example, evolved from workshop to factory in this period.[9] The emphasis of the foreign missions and advisers on iron and steel and other basic inputs contributed to pushing the pattern of industrialization in a direction which would later be swamped by a renewed emphasis on consumer goods. In addition, exports of manufactures began within the continent: Brazilian and Mexican textile exports rose from virtually zero in the late 1930s to 20 per cent of exports by 1945. In the case of Brazil, most of these sales were to other Latin American countries; Mexico also sold outside the region.[10] The results in terms of growth of per capita income are shown in Table 3.1. As the table shows, there is no correlation between GDP and real exports. This is intelligible in terms of the factors we have noted: the variable extent to which export revenues actually accrued to the producing countries, and the limits on using foreign exchange in conditions of war. In many cases, the demand impetus coming from exports and the import supply difficulties inevitably meant inflation, over and above that originating in rising world prices. But the pressures were worsened by the push to increase export supplies, as land was diverted from production for the home market. Accumulation of large export balances worsened the problem. Table 3.1 shows the behaviour of prices. Only Colombia appears to have put in place rather sophisticated monetary instruments to control domestic demand pressures.[11]

One serious consequence of these inflationary pressures was the overvaluation of the exchange rate. Many countries could perceive no short-run gains from devaluing, since their exports were being sold at fixed prices in direct purchase agreements with the United States. The resulting strong deviations from a 'reasonable' exchange rate were to prove one of the most disastrous aspects of the wartime period, as we shall see.

A more positive effect of rising reserves was that the defaulted foreign debt of the 1930s could now be paid. By 1943 several countries, for

[9] See Bishnupriya Gupta, 'Import Substitution in Capital Goods: the case of Brazil, 1929–1979', unpublished D. Phil. thesis (Oxford, 1989).

[10] UN-ECLA, *Study of Inter-Latin American Trade* (New York, 1957), p. 25.

[11] On this we have an unusual testimony. Robert Triffin, celebrated U.S. economist and expert in monetary matters, visited Colombia in 1944, and wrote a brief history of Colombian banking which was published as a supplement to the *Revista del Banco de la República*. In it he detailed the measures taken to sterilize the effect of the inflow of foreign exchange from 1941 to 1943, all directed at increasing savings. They were a combinaton of increased direct taxation and forced savings through various kinds of bond issues, to be forcibly taken up by banks, the Federación Nacional de Cafeteros de Colombia and importers of capital. Further, 20 per cent of profits of all enterprises had to be invested in new certificates, non-negotiable, of two years life with interest at 3 or 4 per cent. See R. Triffin, 'La moneda y las instituciones bancarias en Colombia', *Revista Banco de la República* (supplement), June, 1944, pp. 23–7.

example Mexico and Brazil, had totally settled their outstanding debt, thus clearing the way for their renewed integration with international capital markets which was to be an important element of the post-war model of growth.

THE AFTERMATH OF THE WAR

Whereas in the inter-war decades the signals pointing to the need for change in the international system were there but were weak and conflicting, in the years following the Second World War the international system was clearly perceived to have broken down, and to require major institutional change. One country, the United States, was clearly centre stage of the world economy. Its productive capacity had increased 50 per cent during the war and in 1945 it produced more than half the world-wide total of manufactured goods. Still more significant, the United States owned half the world supply of shipping (compared with only 14 per cent in 1939) and supplied one-third of world exports while taking only one-tenth of world imports.[12] Furthermore, the United States was fully prepared to act deliberately and positively to generate institutional change and to provide funds to aid recovery. At the end of the war U.S. policy-makers had a relatively clear idea of the changes that were necessary to reconstruct the international economy. First, there had to be a complete dismantling of the controls established during the 1930s and necessarily much increased in wartime. This implied both a reversal of the protectionism in evidence before the war, and an ending of the many types of intervention that had proliferated with war. Second, inflation, an unavoidable wartime evil, now had to be conquered.

Under the Bretton Woods agreement of 1944 the goal was a return to a system of stable exchange rates and to an assured supply of long-term capital going to productive purposes. The creation of the International Monetary Fund (IMF) and the World Bank at Bretton Woods was designed to achieve both purposes. A 'gold-exchange' standard was restored: one where convertible currencies (in practice the dollar) were accepted as part of exchange reserves. For the next two decades this measure established the dollar as the reserve currency. Both the IMF and the World Bank were committed to press for liberalization of trade and capital accounts.

Initially, it was hoped that after the inevitable emergency aid of the

[12] W. Ashworth, *A Short History of the World Economy Since 1850* (London, 1975), p. 268.

immediate post-war period, these new institutions would facilitate enough private flow of funds to ease the functioning of the system. In fact, the problems caused by the U.S. trade surplus and the resulting dollar shortage, and the urgent need of Europe for funds, were not so easily solved. As a result in 1947 the 'Marshall Aid' initiative was launched, in the form of a four-year recovery programme for Europe, with Europe committed in return to raising productivity, and lowering trade barriers and inflation. By 1953 the foreign grants of the United States since the war totalled US$33 billion, of which US$23 billion went to Europe. By that time European recovery was well and truly launched, and world trade in manufactures began to rise sharply. In 1951, however, Latin America was the one area not under a U.S. aid programme. Belgium and Luxembourg together received more aid 1945–51 than all of Latin America.[13]

Unlike the aftermath of the First World War when such steps were regarded as threatening the interest of home industries, the United States was no longer opposed to its firms directly investing abroad in manufacturing. Economic growth now came to be seen as the best protection for democracy. U.S. business was interested in third world industrialization at this time, since such a development would provide markets for U.S. products and opportunities for U.S. investment.[14] But although U.S. investment in Latin America did rise during the late 1940s, it was relatively low compared with elsewhere, and with what was to develop later. Total capital inflow to Latin America was positive in 1946–50, but negative once Venezuela (oil) and Cuba (sugar) are excluded.[15] Only with the Korean War, as the United States sought to extend its grip over strategic mineral supplies in Latin America, were significant quantities of U.S. private capital invested in, for example, iron ore in Brazil and Venezuela, copper and lead in Mexico and Peru, and bauxite in the Caribbean.

For the United States Latin America was neither in economic nor political terms a major focus of interest. Once Communist movements had been banned in a number of countries such as Brazil and Chile, it was seen as an area relatively safe from the communist threat. Reversing the focus, however, and considering Latin America's perception of its

[13] Stephen G. Rabe, 'The Elusive Conference: United States' economic relations with Latin America, 1945–1952', *Diplomatic History,* 2, 3 (1978), p. 288.

[14] See Sylvia Maxfield and James H. Nolt, 'Protectionism and the Internalization of Capital: U.S. sponsorship of import-substitution industrialization in the Philippines, Turkey and Argentina', *International Studies Quarterly,* 34 (1990): 49–81.

[15] United Nations, *The Economic Development of Latin America in the Post-war Period* (New York, 1964), p. 3.

dependence on the United States, we find that the war had brought much more sharply into focus the extent of U.S. power and influence in Latin America both in economic and political terms. The new dominance of the United States following the war was reflected in both trade and investment flows.

The changes in the trade patterns of Argentina, Brazil, Mexico and Chile during and after the war are shown in Table 3.2. In every case, the share of Europe in the country's exports falls at least 20 percentage points between 1938 and 1950, while the share of the United States and Canada rises, most notably in the case of Mexico. Intra-regional trade fell back after the war, although not to its previous low level, except for Mexico; but the tables make clear the continuing essential marginality of intra-regional trade. The wartime interest in regional trade agreements swiftly died away – in Argentina, for instance, there had been considerable war-time interest in a Southern Cone free trade area.[16]

Although, compared with Europe, Latin America did not receive much U.S. investment after the war, there continued to be very little investment from Europe either and the new trend set in the 1920s continued. Whereas in the 1920s still slightly more investment income was returned to Europe than to the United States, by 1949 the United States was receiving ten times more income from Latin America than the income flowing from Latin America to the rest of the world (see Table 3.3). Of the increment in the book value of investment from the United States in Latin America between 1936 and 1950, 42 per cent was in Venezuelan oil, followed by 23 per cent in Brazil and 17 per cent in Panama.[17]

Having promoted state intervention strongly for war purposes, the United States by 1945 was anxious to take a vigorous step back. U.S. representatives set out an 'Economic Charter of the Americas' at the Inter-American Conference on Problems of War and Peace, at Chapultepec, Mexico D.F., in February/March 1945. The United States not only asked for a blanket commitment from Latin America to reduce tariffs and welcome foreign capital, but also condemned economic nationalism and proposed the discouragement of state enterprise. The Latin American participants asked whether the first steps should not come from the United States

[16] D. Rock, *Argentina 1516–1987. From Spanish Colonization to Alfonsín,* (Berkeley and Los Angeles, Cal., 1987), p. 249.

[17] United Nations, *Foreign Capital in Latin America* (New York, 1955), p. 159.

Table 3.2 *Latin American export markets 1938 and 1950 (%)*

		Exports to US and Canada	Exports to Europe	Exports to Latin America
Argentina	1938	9.0	72.0	8.7
	1950	20.4	51.4	11.1
Brazil	1938	34.6	49.1	4.8
	1950	55.9	29.7	8.0
Chile	1938	15.9	52.4	2.5
	1950	54.1	24.7	17.5
Mexico	1938	67.4	27.4	6.7
	1950	93.5	4.9	3.4

Source: United Nations, *Yearbook of International Trade Statistics* (New York, 1954)

or the United Kingdom: what evidence did they have that the United States would now welcome imports from the South? The final document contained no commitment at all on tariffs, and accepted freedom of investment except when it would be 'contrary to the fundamental principles of public interest'.[18] It condemned only 'excesses' of economic nationalism, and dropped the reference to state enterprises. In Latin America sentiments in favour of protectionism were becoming stronger. As a Mexican entrepreneur was subsequently to remark: 'What we need is protection on the model of the United States.'[19]

The years 1945–8 were characterized by continued hope on the Latin American side that substantial U.S. aid would be forthcoming, and continued foot-dragging on the U.S. side, partly resulting from the hope that under the threat of losing U.S. aid, other Latin American countries would successfully pressure Argentina to abandon fascist sympathies and interventionist policies.[20] Various conferences were postponed, and finally at the Ninth Conference of American States held in Bogotá in March–April 1948 it became clear that the United States had no intention of offering a Marshall Plan for Latin America.[21] Meanwhile the United Nations' conferences leading up to Havana (November

18 S. Mosk, *Industrial Revolution in Mexico* (Berkeley, Cal., 1950), pp. 17–19.

19 Ibid., p. 38.

20 Rabe, 'The Elusive Conference'; C. A. Macdonald, 'The U.S., the Cold War and Perón', in C. Abel and C. M. Lewis (eds), *Latin America: Economic Imperialism and the State* (London, 1985) pp. 411–2.

21 Rabe, 'The Elusive Conference,' p. 286–7.

Table 3.3. *Balance of payments of Latin America, 1925–29, 1949 and 1950 (US$ millions)*

		Exports (f.o.b.)	Imports (f.o.b.)	Investment income (net)[a]	Long-term capital (net)[b]
1925–29 (annual average):					
United States		990	840	300	200
Europe		1,460	910	−360	30
	Total	2,450	1,750	−600	230
1949:					
United States		2,503	2,624	−550	588
Rest of world		2,592	1,845	−47	−104
	Total	5,095	4,469	−597	484
1950:					
United States		3,090	2,658	−748	194
Rest of world		3,020	1,837	−7	−161
	Total	6,110	4,495	−755	33

Notes:
[a] Including non-monetary gold.
[b] Including reinvested earnings of subsidiaries together with amortization and repurchase of foreign long-term debt and transactions with the International Bank of Reconstruction and Development; excluding government grants.
Source: United Nations, Economic Commission for Latin America (UN, ECLA), *Foreign Capital in Latin America* (New York, 1955), p. 163.

1947–March 1948), convened to consider the formation of an International Trade Organization, had little time for the Latin American proposals in favour of protectionism, though limited success was achieved inasmuch as the Latin American group defeated early proposals which would have forced less developed countries to enter negotiations to reduce tariffs.[22]

The United Nations Economic Commission for Latin America (ECLA), which came into existence in 1948, soon presented a major challenge to the orthodox thinking of the time. The new organization had to prove itself in a short space of time if it was to stay alive at all, and the group of young economists gathered together had to show that there was a valid 'Latin American viewpoint'. Out of this came, by 1949, the

[22] K. Kock, *International Trade Policy and the GATT, 1947–67* (Stockholm, 1969), pp. 41–2. Throughout this period, there were conflicting interests within US policy as well, as 'internationalist' business interests pushed for investment opportunities overseas behind tariff barriers. See Maxfield and Nolt, 'Protectionism', pp. 52–3.

'Prebisch thesis':[23] initially lacking in coherence, its basic argument was that the productivity gains from technical progress in industry at the centre are not reflected in lower prices but retained there, while at the periphery productivity gains in the primary sector are less significant, and wages are held down by surplus labour. Later versions emphasized more strongly the demand side of the model: the asymmetry of the development of income elasticities of demand for imports in the centre and periphery, with consequent implications for the behaviour of the terms of trade. At the core of this approach was the analysis of why Latin American economies would not respond 'automatically' to the price signal of the terms of trade: the reason was 'structural rigidities' – market imperfections rooted in infrastructural deficiencies and in institutions and social and political systems and values. The Latin American economies therefore required deliberate government promotion of industrialization. Foreign capital inflows were helpful to ease the overcoming of rigidities, but the ECLA of the 1950s envisaged such inflows as representing largely public capital. Industrialization was to provide independence from unstable and undynamic primary exports. No contradiction was seen in using foreign capital to achieve this, channelled through government, and issues such as external constraints on policy options were not directly tackled.

More was required than the rationalization provided by ECLA, however: for the pattern of development based on ISI to settle into place in a stable manner an evolution of two political factors was needed. The first concerned the necessary preconditions for the required flow of foreign finance. As we have stressed, the original ECLA version emphasized the role of *public* foreign capital, and this was consistent with the latter's role during the Second World War and with the hopes entertained of new money as the United States looked toward post-war reconstruction in Europe, and, it was hoped, would look elsewhere. However, with hindsight we now know that the model as it actually developed depended crucially not on public money but on direct foreign investment. For this to come about, a further development of the delicate relations between state, domestic and foreign capital was required: only when this was more fully resolved than in 1945 would a

[23] The key original document is United Nations Economic Commission for Latin America (ECLA), *Economic Survey of Latin America*, 1949. See chapter by Joseph L. Love, 'Economic Ideas and Ideologies in Latin America since 1930' in this volume for a full discussion and bibliography and for an account of ECLA's early history. See also E. V. K. Fitzgerald, 'ECLA and the Formation of Latin American Economic Doctrine', in D. Rock (ed.), *Latin America in the 1940s: War and Postwar Transitions* (Berkeley, Cal., 1994).

clear commitment to industrialization become evident. The second element is a consequence of the first: if private foreign capital was to enter Latin America in quantity and feel secure, then the position of labour had to be established. The militant tendencies emerging during and immediately after the war had to be 'controlled' for adequate business confidence.

The conflict over private foreign investment can be studied in the case where it was most developed (and has been most fully documented): Brazil. Already at its inception, ECLA thinking found its echo in Brazil's industrial bourgeoisie. ECLA articulated the views of the group of industrialists led by Roberto Simonsen.[24] There was a strong and complete coincidence of ideas, even as to the role of public foreign capital rather than private. Initial differences of emphasis quickly vanished: for example the ambition of industrialists immediately after the war was focussed on maintaining and expanding export markets. At least in Brazil, the experience of the General Agreement on Tariffs and Trade (GATT) negotiations of 1947 showed them all too vividly how unwilling the centre countries were going to be to allow any market penetration at all; the way was thus prepared to accept the ECLA emphasis on the domestic market.

But during the 1940s, this was not yet a 'hegemonic' project, even in Brazil, and *a fortiori* in other smaller countries. The lack of consensus is seen most vividly over the issue of the role of interventionist policies. The swing away from wartime controls, which was strong in the United States, was certainly also responding to internal forces in Latin America. This was sharply evidenced in Brazil by the famous polemic between Roberto Simonsen and Eugenio Gudin at the end of the War.[25] Gudin headed a strong neo-liberal faction which, while not opposed to industrialization per se, was firmly opposed to protection, and indeed to state intervention of any kind. The strength of the liberal faction was evidenced by the fact that it was the basis for Brazil's first post-war administration, the presidency of Eurico Dutra (1946–50). The complexity of the reality underscores the point we are here making about the contradictory elements in play. While the rhetoric and some of the actions were liberal in fact strong elements of interventionism and authoritarianism were retained.[26] The brief experiment with

[24] M. A. P. Leopoldi, 'Industrial Associations and Politics in Contemporary Brazil', unpublished D. Phil. thesis (Oxford, 1984) pp. 138–40.

[25] See Instituto de Planejamento Econômico e Social (IPEA), A Controvérsia de Planejamento na Economia Brasileira: Coletânea da Polêmica Simonsen x Gudin (Rio de Janeiro, 1978) pp. 21–40.

[26] See, in particular, Sonia Draibe, *Rumos e Metamorfoses: Estado e Industrialização no Brasil: 1930–1960* (Rio de Janeiro, 1985), pp. 138–76. She is arguing against the interpretation of O. Ianni, *Estado e Planejamento Econômico no Brasil 1930–1970* (Rio de Janeiro, 1971).

tariff reductions had to end by 1947, when import controls were reintroduced, owing to the size of the deficit. But the forces behind Gudin were strong enough that industrialists in Brazil seem to have realized that to pin all their hopes on a major tariff reform thereafter was unrealistic. Instead, they secured piecemeal but substantial protection via import controls (and later via multiple exchange rates). Only in 1957 was the first ever systematic new tariff introduced and ratified by Congress.

Elsewhere in Latin America the role of tariffs was more readily accepted. But the issue that was not so clearly accepted was that of the direct entrepreneurial role of the state. In Brazil Petrobras faced constant opposition as it emerged in the early 1950s. In Mexico, a curious paradox was the proposal emanating from the Mexican-American Commission for Economic Co-operation, for a 'Comisión Federal de Fomento Industrial', to expand industry with direct state ownership. Even though the state role was intended to be temporary, it aroused deep concern and opposition in the business community, and failed to get acceptance.[27] In Chile, as in all the economies with a very high productivity mining sector, state intervention was particularly essential, since without it the exchange rate would be at a level at which new (or indeed other) exports were unprofitable. Of course, this still meant conflict – in Chile's case focussed round the role of Corporación de Fomento de la Producción (CORFO), the state industrial development agency, founded in 1939. The industrial sector welcomed CORFO, but more for its provision of subsidized credit than for its direct entrepreneurial role, which they naturally feared. Nevertheless, this role accounted for the greater part of CORFO's resources in its early years.[28]

The acceptance of protection and the proliferation of controls in the immediate post-war years led to a great growth in all the industrializing economies of Latin America of state-business 'clientelistic' relations, as the obvious way to reconcile the need for and fear of the state. In Mexico, for example, it is clear that 'the system' grew by leaps and bounds during the war and the years immediately after. The links were mostly due to business initiative, but often with considerable encouragement from government.[29] The delicacy of the relationship has been well described by Sanford Mosk: 'Businessmen assign the government a prominent role, it is

[27] Mosk, *Industrial Revolution in Mexico*, pp. 95–7.

[28] Ortega, L., et al., *CORFO: 50 años de realizaciones 1939–1989*, (Universidad de Chile, Santiago, 1989), pp. 112.

[29] See Shafer, *Mexican Business Organizations*, p. 126.

true, but they want the government to arrive at its decisions on the basis of information and advice supplied by the interested industrialist groups. What they propose is business intervention in government rather than government intervention in business.'[30]

The same expansion of the web of interconnections can be traced elsewhere,[31] partly in legislated participation in boards and other institutions, partly in informal contacts. The system was clearly one where often the best way to increase profits was to operate at the political level rather than on the conventional technical variables determining productivity. In Brazil by the mid-1950s, the echoes of the Simonsen–Gudin debate had died away and the new role of the state was so well accommodated and accepted that Juscelino Kubitschek's 'Plano de Metas' (1956) aroused no opposition.

Conflicting forces were at work also in the 1950s in relation to the role of foreign capital. Again, the Simonsen–Gudin debate is representative. Simonsen wanted 'selective' access for foreign capital, and saw public capital as the major solution. He was one of those who argued subsequently for a 'Marshall Plan' for Latin America. Gudin wanted, of course, total liberalization. However, as protection encouraged the entry of foreign capital into the Brazilian manufacturing sector so the relative weight of different interests shifted. The industrial bourgeoisie became more fragmented. New groups emerged in the late 1940s and early 1950s increasingly associated with foreign capital, thus nullifying potential resistance to the eventual legislation embodied in the Superintendência da Moeda e do Crédito (SUMOC) instruction 113 of 1955, which effectively gave preferential treatment to foreign capital.[32] The issue was further confused by the 'carrot and stick' policy pursued by successive governments, offering bonuses for exporting, favourable exchange rates and eventually the tariff reform. The paradox involved in the evolution of a successful industrialization model which was to lead to rapid growth in the coming decade, based on a triple alliance between state, multinationals and domestic bourgeoisie where the latter was definitely the junior partner, is summed up in a quote from one of the

30 Mosk, *Industrial Revolution in Mexico*, p. 29. He is here writing of the 'New Group' of industrialists which emerged with the War, whose importance later writers claim he exaggerated. But they would agree that the description fits the general attitude which was now to develop widely across Latin America.

31 For example, in Chile – see O. Muñoz, *Chile y su industrialización: pasado, crisis y opciones* (Santiago, 1986), p. 210; Brazil – see Leopoldi, 'Industrial Associations and Politics', pp. 245–92.

32 SUMOC, the Superintendency of Money and Credit, was created in 1945 with a view to gradually developing a genuine central bank.

members of the group: 'In the end we won but we did not take the prize.'[33]

Gradually, country by country, the main features of economic policy for the post-war decades were consolidated. This typically comprised measures which settled the issue of foreign capital, achieved some reduction in the use of direct controls, particularly import and foreign exchange controls, and attempted a reduction in the degree of over-valuation of the exchange rate, usually combined with a simplification of the previous multiple exchange rate system.

This consolidation was assisted, and indeed sometimes promoted, by the growing strength from 1949 of the lobby within U.S. policy-making which favoured Third World industrialization, and saw tariffs as providing opportunities for U.S. multinational investment. This pressure, strong during the Second World War, was weakened during the post-war attention to European reconstruction. But by 1949 the issue was again on the agenda. The Executive Committee on Economic Foreign Policy, a U.S. inter-departmental government committee, began to push with renewed vigour for third world industrialization from this point on, with increasing acceptance of the need for protection.[34]

In Brazil the new focus was embodied in the foreign exchange law of 1953 and the SUMOC instruction 113 in 1955. In Chile the crucial legislation on foreign capital also came in 1955, though Chile was further ahead in the process of consolidating the attitudes and institutions needed for ISI to flourish, given its early start and the strength and breadth of state involvement. By the early 1950s, inflation and balance-of-payments problems were already generating a fear that import substituting industrialization had its limit, and the reorientation of 1955 was more fundamental than elsewhere, involving a major stabilization effort and a commitment to more market-oriented policies.[35] In Argentina, 1955 was the critical year once again, when the trigger for the fall of Perón was precisely the issue of foreign capital. However, a fuller move to a pro-foreign capital and non-interventionist stance did not occur until Frondizi assumed power in 1958.

During the war, in 1944, in an attempt to control foreign investment an executive decree was passed in Mexico, which limited

[33] João Paulo de Almeida Magalhães, interviewed in 1981 by M. A. Leopoldi (Leopoldi, 'Industrial Associations and Politics', p. 337).

[34] Maxfield and Nolt, 'Protectionism', p. 58.

[35] Ortega, *CORFO*, pp. 132–8.; Muñoz, *Chile y su industrialización*, pp. 125–45.

foreign ownership in firms to 49 per cent. 'Strategic' industries were to be wholly owned by Mexicans. However, the decree failed to define which these strategic industries were, a confusion which was not cleared up until 1945 when it was decided that fifteen industries were strategic. It was also decided that foreigners could be allowed to own more than 49 per cent of other 'non-strategic' industries, each case to be left to the discretion of the Minister of Economy. After the war enormous pressure was put on the Mexican government to relax its foreign investment laws. In 1946 the Ley de Industrias Nuevas y Necesarias gave in to these pressures, while enabling the government to save face publicly. The law was intended to provide a stimulus to infant industries. However, it stipulated that all benefits could be provided to foreign, as well as Mexican investors, thus giving an equal stimulus to both.

Chile, as we have seen, was unusually advanced in its level of industrialization. The exclusive nature of the dominance of foreign capital in Chilean copper, and the dominance of copper in Chile's exports, forced local elite groups to look elsewhere and in particular to industry for profit opportunities at a relatively early date. The effect of buoyant copper revenues on the exchange rate was such that other tradeables could only survive by means of fairly strong state action. Chile had developed mechanisms of intervention in favour of industry in the 1920s and 1930s to a degree unusual for that size of country,[36] culminating in the creation of CORFO. By contrast, Colombia's leading export sector, coffee, was locally owned, and very special institutional developments meant that even the commercialization of coffee stayed in local hands: the strength of the Federación Nacional de Cafeteros Colombianos was such that foreign trading houses preferred other easier terrain. In addition, the link between coffee and industry was harmonious and natural: regionally diffuse coffee activity led to local processing and related industrialization, and the surplus from the coffee trade needed an outlet.[37] There was a relatively low level of industrialization by the 1940s, due to a very late start, but the reconciling of diverse interests was not a problem. The need to 'resolve' the issue of foreign capital was not a relevant problem either: Colombia maintained its consistently subtle but discouraging attitude to a substantial penetration of direct foreign invest-

[36] Muñoz, *Chile y su industrialización*, p. 101; Ortega, *CORFO*, pp. 33–64.

[37] R. Thorp, *Economic Development and Economic Management in Peru and Colombia* (London, 1991), pp. 6–11.

ment, and certainly enacted no law parallel to those we have noted in all other economies of any size.

We have described the evolution of the political economy of important instruments in implementing ISI policies, namely tariffs, exchange rates and foreign capital legislation. There is a further potential instrument that has not been mentioned: taxation (other than taxation implicit in the above policies). The omission reflects the fact that tax reforms were conspicuous by their absence in this period. The single taxation policy that did evolve was taxation of exporting multinationals: in both Chile and Venezuela this appeared an obvious way in which to finance industrialization.[38]

If the first half of the 1940s revealed several characteristics important to the 'shift in model' which was clearly due to come – industry was stimulated and even basic and capital goods sectors grew, the role of the State was extended, a beginning was made in intra-regional trade, and the insecurity of a strongly trade-dependent model was once again confirmed – in a sense the rest of the decade was to prove a step backward, even in the larger economies. For example, we have seen external pressures moving strongly to reduce the degree of State involvement once again: this, while it stimulated an attempt to rationalize somewhat the wartime distortions, also weakened the forces behind the push to develop basic industries. At the same time the move to reduce distortions achieved little: the key distortion was the over-valued exchange rate in most countries, and fear of the inflationary consequences of devaluation led, if anything, to increased dependence on import controls, and not less, as the import boom gathered momentum in the immediate post-war years. Foreign investors felt the distortions and controls of most Latin American countries to be a relatively unfriendly environment. Meanwhile, as Table 3.4 shows, primary export growth was generally vigorous in the years immediately following the Second World War, responding first to post-war recovery and then to the Korean War, despite exchange rate over-valuation, indeed permitting over-valuation. Table 3.5 shows the annual movement of the terms of trade. Oil and minerals experienced the strongest price rises, reflected in the buoyant export revenues of Venezuela and Mexico. Coffee also experienced a strong demand in these years, as did temperate products satisfying the wartime food shortages. With buoyant exports and renewed import sup-

[38] J. Behrman, *Foreign Trade Regimes and Economic Development: Chile* (New York, 1976), p. 105; Stephen G. Rabe, *The Road to OPEC: United States' Relations with Venezuela 1919–1976* (Austin, Tex., 1982), pp. 80–93.

Table 3.4. *Latin American economic indicators, 1945–55*[a]

	GDP in 1970 dollars[a]	Commodity exports annual growth rates at constant prices %		Annual growth of real GDP per capita		Industry as % GDP			Cost of living (1945 = 100)	
	1950	1945–50	1950–5	1945–50	1950–5	1945	1950	1955	1950	1955
Argentina	14018	5.0	−8.8	1.6	1.0	25	24	25	255	585
Mexico	12926	11.7	3.3	3.0	2.7	19	19	19	148	248
Brazil	12309	8.1	−3.3	3.3	3.4	17	21	23	173	384
Colombia	4325	17.5	4.0	1.8	2.0	11	14	15	193	242
Chile	3499	2.2	6.1	1.0	1.5	23	23	23	252	1438
Venezuela	3360	23.1	5.3	6.9	5.2	15	11	13	122	130
Peru	2518	8.8	2.6	2.4	3.9	13	14	15	236	333
Cuba	n.a.	10.0	−1.0	1.0	1.0	26[b]	26[b]	30[b]	118	118
Uruguay	1867	10.7	−10.4	4.1	2.4	18	20	23	129	220
Guatemala	885	16.1	1.7	−0.9	−0.3	13	11	11	156	166
Ecuador	796	17.0	4.3	6.9	2.3	18	16	15	n.a.	n.a.
Bolivia	698	−1.2	−2.7	0.0	−0.8	n.a.	12	15	188	2,525
Dominican Republic	533	n.a.	n.a.	5.0	3.0	n.a.	12	12	116	125
El Salvador	512	21.7	4.1	6.7	2.0	12	13	14	130	167
Paraguay	410	3.1	−2.6	0.0	−0.9	16	16	16	229	2,057
Honduras	323	22.4	−5.4	1.7	−0.2	7	9	12	115	144
Costa Rica	298	30.1	3.0	4.2	4.3	12	12	12	133	125
Nicaragua	239	16.8	23.1	4.1	5.2	11	11	11	95	165
Panama	217	29.8	4.6	−2.5	1.1	6	8	10	110	113

Notes:

[a] Ranked by size of 1950 GDP. Cuba ranked on basis of current price 1950 figures, since no estimate exists at 1970 prices.

[b] Non-sugar manufacturing as per cent of total material production, i.e. the total is less than GDP.

Sources: Economic Commission for Latin America (ECLA), *Estadísticas Históricas* (Santiago, 1978); James W. Wilkie, *Statistics and National Policy*, Supplement 3, UCLA (Los Angeles, Cal. 1974); V. Bulmer-Thomas, *The Political Economy of Central America since 1920* (London, 1987); C. Brundenius, *Revolutionary Cuba: The Challenge of Economic Growth with Equity* (London, 1984)

plies, aggregate growth rates were quite impressive as Table 3.4 shows. Industrialization, however, did not continue at its wartime pace. The share of industry in GDP actually fell in Argentina, Venezuela, Ecuador and Guatemala, and generally rose little.

In Argentina industry's share of GDP fell one point between 1945 and 1950. Growth in income per capita was rather slow, and slower in the early 1950s than in the immediate post-war years. Inflation was much higher than during the war. These events reflect the contradictions in Argentina's economic policy as well as the external environment, contradictions which were an exaggerated form of what was happening elsewhere.

The Argentine context is dominated by the conflicts with the United States which predated the war but which became considerably worse with the war and the emergence of Peronism. In the 1930s the focus was trade: the United States refused any concessions to farm producers like Argentina's whose goods duplicated those of its own heavily depressed rural sector.[39] Argentina in return used discriminatory exchange rates to induce a fall in imports from the United States. Argentina's refusal to support the Allied forces meant it received nothing under Lend Lease, and the rise of the Peronist movement was rapidly identified by the United States as one of the strongest threats in the continent to a return to 'sane and manageable' market capitalism.

Faced with the U.S. trade policy, with the problem of the inconvertibility of much of the country's foreign exchange reserves, and with the need to favour its internal political base in the urban labour movement, the new government of Juan Perón opted for a strong policy of promotion of the industrial sector for the internal market. He combined the elements common to many of his neighbours, an over-valued exchange rate and the use of import controls and tariffs to protect industry, with the creation in 1946 of a state purchasing board, Instituto Argentino para la Promoción del Intercambio (IAPI), which proceeded to pay exporters less than half the international price. In addition, he gave ample and cheap credit to the industrial sector. The policy rapidly became self-defeating. Wartime manufacturing exports would have ceased anyway, as they did throughout the continent. By 1947–9 their value was less than a third of that in 1945–6.[40] But grain and meat exports also did poorly: between the mid-1930s and 1948–52 Argentina's share of the world wheat market feel

[39] Rock, *Argentina*, p. 225.
[40] Rock, *Argentina*, p. 269.

Table 3.5. *Latin America: terms of trade, 1939–55 (1939 = 100)*

	Terms of trade
1939	100.0
1940	95.3
1941	97.0
1942	98.2
1943	98.2
1944	93.9
1945	97.3
1946	127.7
1947	138.4
1948	133.8
1949	134.7
1950	161.2
1951	161.0
1952	146.0
1953	156.6
1954	164.2
1955	152.0

Source: United Nations, Economic Commission for Latin America, (ECLA), *Economic Survey of Latin America 1949* (New York, 1950), p. 17. UN ECLA (1962), *Boletín Económico de América Latina,* Vols V–VII, p. 46.

from 23 per cent to only 9 per cent, the share for corn from 64 per cent to only 24 per cent. With rising urban wages, domestic consumption rose strongly: over the same period domestic consumption of meat and grain rose one-third while export volume fell two-thirds.[41] Thus foreign exchange rapidly came to be in short supply, the problem being complicated by the issue of convertibility. Needing imports from the United States but unable to sell grain or meat, Argentina amassed inconvertible funds on its trade with Europe which it could not use in the United States. In early 1948 the United States further decided that Marshall Plan dollars could not be used to purchase Argentine goods.

The poor performance both of industry and of the whole economy in

[41] Ibid.

Argentina is thus readily understandable. It was aggravated by infrastructure bottlenecks, as investment failed to take place in traditional sectors or in the newly purchased railways and other assets bought from the British with blocked sterling balances. By 1949 Perón had realized that squeezing agriculture was a self-defeating policy – but as we shall see each attempt to reverse the relative price policy brought inflation rather than a supply response.

The complexity of Brazil's political economy during the aftermath of war has already been indicated. A straightforward interpretation of the economic data is difficult. First, however, it is clear that exports grew strongly (Table 3.4) and that this growth was based on coffee. This permitted the maintenance of an over-valued exchange rate, which remained unchanged between 1939 and 1952, despite a rise in internal prices of several hundred per cent in that period. The rise in coffee prices was so strong that investment flowed into coffee despite the exchange rate[42] but minor exports suffered, and in particular the new exports of the wartime period collapsed abruptly.

The extent to which the liberal government of Dutra neglected industry is most controversial. The main priority was intially clearly the fight against inflation, and the fixed exchange rate plus *liberalization* of imports were the main initial policy tools, in addition to conservative monetary and fiscal policies. This policy choice was based on initial optimism as to the supply of foreign exchange, based on expectations of an inflow of resources from the United States[43] as well as coffee price prospects. At the same time the rhetoric was that of pulling back the role of the State, and indeed the only specific initiative in terms of State action was the Plano Salte (Saude, Alimentacao, Transporte, Energia), only approved by Congress in 1950 and abandoned in 1951.

However, as we have seen[44] even in the early years considerable intervention was present, while the easing of imports allowed replenishment of capital goods.[45] On the other hand, the liberalization of imports ended by 1947 when controls were reintroduced since the inflow of capital did not come up to expectations. It is thus easy to understand how the exchange rate policy has been seen as shifting resources strongly from exports to

[42] Sérgio Besserman Vianna, 'Política econômica externa e industralização: 1946–1951', in Marcelo de P. Abreu (ed.), *A Ordem do Progresso* (Rio de Janeiro, 1990), pp. 115–16.

[43] Abreu (ed.), *A Ordem do Progresso*, pp. 107–8.

[44] See Draibe, *Rumos e Metamorfoses*, p. 138.

[45] Abreu, *A Ordem do Progresso*, p. 108.

industry, and exactly the opposite.[46] The fact is, however, that Brazil did not actually experience a fall in the share of industry in the post-war years, as did many Latin American countries (see Table 3.4).

Industrialization was made the central feature of Mexican economic policy by Avila Camacho when he took office in December 1940, and President Alemán carried forward the same policy line in the immediate post-war years (1946–52). Alemán's first Minister of Economy, Antonio Ruiz Galindo was a prominent industrialist and an aggressive advocate of Mexican industrialization. In February 1946, a new Industrial Development Law increased tax concessions to industry and gave the President freedom to make tariff changes without consulting Congress. Protection was much increased in these years. As elsewhere, however, the rate of increase of wartime industrial production could not be maintained: the rise of two percentage points in the share of industry 1940 to 1945 moderated to a maintaining of its share in a rapidly growing gross domestic product (GDP), as exports boomed 1945–50 (see Table 3.4) and GDP per capita grew almost as fast as Brazil's, with similar rapid rates of population growth.

Mexican policies followed the general pattern, with an over-valued exchange rate and direct controls as well as tariffs, and a post-war flood of imports leading to deficits by 1947–8. In 1947 and 1948 tariff protection increased further. The devaluation which elsewhere was delayed until the 1950s, came in Mexico in 1949.

A great deal of emphasis has been placed in the literature – more than in other countries – on the inflationary funding of Mexico's industrial growth. However, as Table 3.4 shows, Mexican inflation was actually the most moderate of the largest economies. Industrial producers faced import, foreign exchange, legal, administrative and other bottlenecks.[47] The most serious constraint on production was the slow rate at which machinery and equipment could be imported after the starvation of the war years. There was, moreover, enthusiasm for industrialization, but no true planning, no comprehensive programme of national economic development.[48]

Chile is the only case among the five largest whose exports grew quite modestly in real terms after the war. This was a product of U.S. price

46 Pedro S. Malan, Regis Bonelli, Marcelo de P. Abreu and José Eduardo de C. Pereira, *Política Econômica Externa e Industrialização no Brasil* (1939/52) (Rio de Janeiro, 1977), p. 78.

47 C. W. Reynolds, *The Mexican Economy, Twentieth Century Structure and Growth* (New Haven, Conn., 1970), p. 39.

48 Mosk, *Industrial Revolution in Mexico,* p. 308.

controls on copper, and also of the Chilean government's conscious decision to increase taxation on the copper sector to fund industrial development through CORFO. The economy was relatively advanced in its level of industrialization, as we have seen. The remarkable institutional development accompanying and promoting this was the key to maintaining industrial growth in the face of a relatively slow and difficult period of general growth. But the cost was clearly inflation. Hirschman's classic explanation of inflation in Chile in this period is that it was the preferred escape valve for social tensions. He claims that in any one year in the period we are analysing several of the following were likely to be operating: 'fiscal deficits, monetization of balance of payments surpluses, massive [nominal] wage and salary increases . . . , bank credit expansion, war-induced international price booms, Central Bank credit to state sponsored development agencies': 'perhaps the only common thread running through all the successive stages was the extreme weakness of anything we would today call meaningful anti-inflationary action'.[49]

Colombia enjoyed booming coffee exports, yet grew quite slowly. The principal reason was that the institutions to moderate the effects of a coffee boom were already in place and policy was governed by a desire for prudence and resistance to possibly inflationary expansion. As we have seen, Colombia ended the war with an exceptionally low level of industrialization: given the room for catching up it is hardly surprising that its industry's share of GDP should rise more than in any other Latin American country. What is most interesting about the economic management behind this is a point we come to later when we discuss agriculture: Colombia, alone among the countries discussed here, implemented a rather moderate protectionist policy and one which sought to avoid the discrimination against agriculture and exports implicit in every other case. The concept in Colombia was one of integral protection based on stimulating both agriculture and industry.

Uruguay is a curious and exceptional case. At first glance it appears to fit the policy pattern of the larger economies, since there was a substantial devaluation in 1955 followed by the extensive policy switch represented by the Exchange and Monetary Reform Law of 1959, eliminating many internal and external controls. In fact, as with Peru, the appearance of fit

[49] A. Hirschman, *Journeys Toward Progress: Studies of Economic Policy-Making in Latin America* (New York, 1963), p. 183.

is superficial, for the 1959 Law represented not the blossoming of full ISI, but its virtual end. Uruguay, of course, was already highly industrialized for its size in 1945, with 18 per cent of GDP in industry, a figure characteristic of Brazil and Mexico with GDP of six times the size. This was a product of the protectionist policies of the Battlista state. The growth of industry 1945–55 was over 6 per cent a year, based on high protection. The issue of controls which deterred foreign capital elsewhere was not a problem: there was little foreign investment, but in the short-term surplus was available from protected profits and from the rural sector, benefiting from the Korean War boom. Underneath, however, the situation was anything but healthy: the long-run stagnation of the rural sector continued, with no growth at all in export volume during these years. This stagnation is clearly related to lack of investment in the sector, the explanation of which is the key controversy in Uruguayan economic history, and a debate which goes far beyond our period. The growth of industry was a product of trade and exchange controls, and elements of a long-run development policy were lacking. As Henry Finch has written 'The structure of domestic production was in fact reshaped fundamentally by policy weapons operating on the external sector, rather than by domestic fiscal instruments, integrated industrial credit policies or an industrial development bank'.[50] By the mid-1950s, industrial growth had slowed right down, as rural stagnation brought problems of raw material and foreign exchange supplies and as the market limitation began to be reached. Uruguay thus reached prematurely the point of 'exhaustion' which elsewhere would only be perceived as a problem in the 1960s.

Venezuela, Ecuador, Peru, Bolivia and Paraguay were less prepared for industrialization in the immediate post-war period in terms of their prior base. But whereas in Central America the strength of export-elite interests and the success of exports dictated a relatively clear-cut continued adherence to the old primary export model, the developments in these medium-sized economies are less simple, since there was already a relatively greater internal differentiation of interest groups. In each case the share of imports in GDP rose, usually with a rise in the share of consumer goods, indicating little progress in industrialization (see Table 3.6). But this was associated with extreme differences in export performances, as Table 3.4 showed. Bolivia and Paraguay lost ground radically, while Venezuela and Ecuador, and, to a lesser degree, Peru appear as transparent cases of strong

[50] M. H. J. Finch, *A Political Economy of Uruguay since 1870* (London, 1981), p. 177.

Table 3.6. *Imports as a percentage of GDP, consumer goods as a percentage of imports, 1945–49/1955–61*

	Imports as percentage of GDP		Change in share of consumer goods imports in total imports
	1945–49	Change in share 1945–49/1955–61	1945–49/1955–61
GROUP I: declining import coefficients			
Argentina	12	−2	−1
Brazil	10	−2	−9
Chile	20	−3	+7
Colombia	13	−2	−10
Mexico	14	−3	−1
GROUP II: rising import coefficients			
Ecuador	15	+5	−2
Bolivia	41	+1	+8
Peru	19	+2	−3
Venezuela	21	+0	+3

Source: United Nations, *The Economic Development of Latin America in the Post War Period* (New York, 1964).

primary export growth permitting and pushing a fresh commitment to old-style export-led growth.

Table 3.1 showed the share of industry in GDP in Venezuela as a mere 14 per cent in 1940, despite its ranking as Latin America's sixth largest economy. The answer is obvious: the oil boom began in the 1920s and generated the serious distortions associated with such favourable shocks. Other tradables suffered severely, particularly coffee, given the appreciation of the exchange rate, and the only industry which did not suffer was that related to construction, related industries such as cement, and certain naturally protected sectors such as beer and bottled drinks.[51] There was no question of needing to resolve 'tensions in the model' over the role of foreign capital or the relation of the national bourgeoisie with the State, since the welcome given to foreign capital was total and national groups identified completely with the State.[52] The concentration of resources in the hands of government via petroleum revenues led to a

[51] M. Ignacio Purroy, *Estado e Industrialización en Venezuela* (Caracas, 1982), p. 51.

[52] H. Silva M., 'Proceso y crisis de la economía nacional, 1960 – 1973', *Nueva Ciencia,* 1 (1975); Purroy, *Estado e Industrialización en Venezuela,* p. 207.

perception that 'development comes through the state' which was unrivalled elsewhere. The centrality of government as controller of the rent from petroleum also led the political elite to press for acceptance of its views on economic policies in a more forceful fashion than elsewhere. The concentration on oil was expressed in, and reinforced by, the treaty of 1939 with the United States which reduced tariffs on nearly two hundred goods in return for a 50 per cent cut on the tariff on Venezuelan oil in the US market.[53] In the immediate post-war period, Romulo Betancourt's first administration began a development policy which aided industry, by increasing taxes on oil and creating the Corporación Venezolana de Fomento in 1946, which began the development of a metal refining sector and promoted agri-based industry with the participation of foreign capital (e.g., Nestlé).[54] With the establishment of the Pérez Jiménez dictatorship in 1948, the relationship was positive but less close: a statute was passed, for example, eliminating the obligation to have a representative of Fedecameras, the umbrella entrepreneurs' association, on the Board of the Corporación Venezolana de Fomento.[55] In this sense, Venezuela was there early: it anticipated some of its neighbours in developing the interventionist role of the State. However, strong classic protectionist policies had to await the more populist government of Romulo Betancourt's second turn in office in 1959.[56]

Ecuador shared some of Venezuela's strong export success. The economy had grown relatively slowly since the collapse of cocoa in the 1920s. Now the banana sector began to grow rapidly, rising from 2 per cent of exports in the 1930s and 6 per cent in 1948 to 42 per cent by 1955. Not surprisingly, therefore, it was a time of reversion to the agro-export model, with bananas, coffee and cocoa accounting for 90 per cent of exports in 1955. As always in Ecuador, the regional implications were crucial. The economy had survived the Depression by the incorporation of unused resources, by the expansion of industry and new export crops: the heart of the expansion process had occurred in the Sierra. It had given rise to much social change, but not yet to the consolidation of anything approaching an industrial bourgeoisie. The new wealth was centred in the coastal lowlands; it was therefore not surprising that industry fell from 16

[53] Purry, *Estado e Industrialización en Venezuela,* pp. 49–50.

[54] D. Melcher, 'Renta petrolera e industrialización en Venezuela', paper submitted to workshop in Industrialisation of Latin America, International Economic History Congress (Louvain 1990), p. 14.

[55] M. Betancourt, *Venezuela, Política y Petróleo* (Caracas, 1967), p. 718.

[56] Purroy, *Estado e Industrialización en Venezuela,* p. 219.

per cent of GDP in the 1940s, to 15 per cent by 1955 (Table 3.4), while imports rose as a percentage of GDP (Table 3.6) and exports of panama hats fell from 9 per cent of exports in 1948 to 1 per cent by 1955. With this, the process of building a political economy that might sustain an alternative path was directly undermined. The element of fragmentation was emphasized by the continued growth of autonomous public enterprises, many reflecting regional interests, which received a remarkable 50 per cent of public sector revenue in 1951.[57]

Peru's immediate post-war experience was superficially rather similar to that of the larger economies, since a period of controls and intervention 1945–8 was followed by strongly favourable foreign capital legislation in 1949. But the similarity was more apparent than real. Peru's diverse and rich resource base had led to several decades of strong export growth, with a substantial presence of foreign capital, but, unlike Chile, always with room for an associated and profitable role for domestic elites, who therefore had never had the incentive to push for protection of industry. The State had a considerable presence in the economy, employing large numbers of people, but was weak in experience of interventionist policies. The brief period of populist government (1945–8) led to such chaos in the use of interventionist policies, as a result of inexperience and an incoherent political base, that they were deplored even by the industrialists whom the policies were meant to favour. The unfavourable attitude to intervention generated by this experience, plus the strong growth of mineral exports, led, with the right-wing coup of Odría in 1948, to an early swing back to market orientated policies and to primary exports. Industry grew in the early 1950s but the dynamic sectors were strongly related to exports. Export processing industry grew from 18 per cent of industrial production in 1950 to 26 per cent by 1960.[58] Only with the 1960s did the more classic ISI policies develop as unemployment and rural unrest became preoccupations.

The explanation of Bolivia's relative stagnation is related both to the international tin market, and to the internal political economy of tin. The Bolivian economy was centred on tin from the first decades of the century, with the sector dominated by the 'rosca', the three major mine owners, Patiño, Hochschild and Aramayo. Between 1900 and 1929, tin exports increased fivefold, and Bolivia's share of world production more than

[57] L. Cuera Silva, *Finanzas Públicas del Ecuador* (Quito, 1960), p. 207.
[58] Thorp, *Economic Development*, p. 49.

doubled, accounting for approximately a quarter of total world production from 1918 to 1929.[59] Most of this was in the hands of Patiño. The economic and political power of the 'rosca' was inversely matched by the weakness of the state. This meant that the capacity for administration and tax collection was underdeveloped even by Latin American standards.[60] The rest of the economy suffered from lack of investment as the power of the tin industry to act as an engine for growth was not harnessed, so that debt was used as a substitute for extracting revenue from the tin industry. Borrowing allowed the government to keep on good terms with the mining elite and to use money borrowed to pay off interest on previous loans and on railroad construction.

The Depression severely affected the tin sector, but allowed the 'rosca' to consolidate power. The 1940s were dominated by the confrontation between the old guard and new nationalist groups led by the Movimiento Nacional Revolucionario (MNR) wanting incorporation, wider distribution of the gains from tin and an end to the power of the 'rosca'. Bolivia was set apart by the dominance of tin, the strength of the elite group dominating tin, and the strength and relative coherence of the corresponding political reaction.

Following the war, various elements crucial to Bolivia's survival were strongly modified. The United States now dominated the tin market, so that the 'rosca's' former ability to play U.K. and U.S. interests off against each other was weakened. Demand fell heavily, and Far Eastern producers returned to the market, while Bolivian costs were rising (there had been no new investment during the war).

Faced with falling profits, the 'rosca' resorted to more repression and violence. The political reaction was only temporarily softened by the Korean War boom. The MNR took power again in the revolution of 1952 intending to use the nationalized tin sector for 'national autonomous development', but found they had taken over assets in poor condition, faced international recession following the Korean War and needed to pay off their political debts to the mine workers. The resulting hyper-inflation led in 1956 to drastic stabilization and a shift to the right.

Paraguay was dominated until the dictatorship of Stroessner in 1954 by

59 Manuel E. Contreras, 'Debt, Taxes and War: the political economy of Bolivia, c.1920–1935', *Journal of Latin American Studies*, 22, 2 (1990), p. 265.

60 Contreras, 'Debt, Taxes and War'. The ability to rely on foreign borrowing is seen as one of the major reasons for the lack of fiscal efficiency of the Bolivian state. This improved during the 1930s giving credence to this interpretation, as during this period taxation was improved to fund the war effort and money was not forthcoming from abroad (p. 267).

a small number of families closely tied to the primary export sectors (meat and tobacco), and with a strong presence of foreign capital in land and infrastructure. The one attempt at more broadly based policies, in the 1930s, is described as having failed precisely because of the absence of the social forces which industrialization would have produced.[61] So, as with Central America, the 1940s simply saw a strengthening of the traditional model, but after a brief wartime boom in meat exports the result is far less successful than in Central America.

The geographically isolated and rather closed nature of the Paraguayan economy meant an absence of the 'discipline of openness' much in evidence in Central America. Yet there was no internal base to create something out of the possibility of autonomy which isolation offered.

Bolivia, Ecuador and Paraguay all had GDPs comparable to the classic 'small economies' of the region, the Central American economies. But the latter remained in a far more clear-cut fashion within the export-economy model in the immediate post-war period. There was simply no question of extending controls or other interventionist policies to permit the emergence of a more autonomous or nationalist model. The only partial exception to this was Guatemala, where the Arévalo government (1944–50) introduced a progressive constitution modelled on the Mexican 1917 charter, supported the labour movement and attempted educational and other reforms. But even here there was no break with traditional export-led growth.

This was a product of related phenomena: the strength of the elite and export-dominated political model in each country, relative good fortune in the commodity lottery, and the continued existence of at least some spare capacity to permit the expansion of crops in response to buoyant conditions. A natural accompaniment of the model was the tying of currencies to the U.S. dollar. With abundant foreign exchange, easy importing soon led to the abating of the wartime inflationary pressures and remarkable exchange rate stability ensued.

The rapid growth of Central American exports is shown in Table 3.4. Coffee was particularly buoyant, and, being locally controlled, potentially provided a surplus for reinvestment elsewhere in the economy. Banana exports recovered quickly after the war, although there were severe problems with disease. The losses from disease were offset by improved prices

[61] R. A. Nickson, 'The Overthrow of the Stroessner Regime', *Bulletin of Latin American Research,* 8, 2 (1989), p. 188.

in the immediate post-war period. This period also saw some shift in the balance of power between the fruit companies and host governments, in favour of the latter. The most striking characteristic of this period was the increase in the state's share of net benefits from banana production. This led to a shift in the role of the state, and gradually to a shift in the balance of power between the state and foreign companies. Outside of banana production, however, most foreign-owned companies remained largely untaxed.

The most important example of export diversification in this period was the expansion of cotton production. This was of major importance in El Salvador, Guatemala and Nicaragua. It was a highly concentrated industry and cotton growers began to form a distinct social class and pressure group comparable to coffee growers (both coffee and cotton were largely in national hands). Their combined influence was strong enough to distort the fiscal system in their favour and to deny the state an equitable share in the expansion of the two industries.[62]

The share of bananas and coffee in total exports remained extremely high in the ten years after 1944. However, the very high coffee prices concealed the fact that there was some degree of agricultural diversification both in exports and in output for the domestic market. By the early 1950s, however, the export of abacá (Manila hemp) had fallen off as production from the Far East recovered. Rubber exports also virtually ended, while in 1946 Central American vegetables and fruits ceased to be supplied by contract to the Panama Canal Zone.

The issue of policy reform, so important elsewhere in Latin America, was simply not an issue here: the economic model was solidly 'open' and pro primary exports. Only in the 1960s would Cepalista influence promote the idea of more deliberate industrialization within the context of a Central American Common Market.

One economy of intermediate size behaved so totally within the Central American pattern that discussion of it has been left to the end. Cuba remained within the extreme export-dependent mode of development which had characterized the economy from the 1920s. Sugar was still able to provide satisfactory growth based on strong international prices; the rate of growth of per capita income was 2.4 per cent 1946–52, though there was little development of activities other than sugar. Non-sugar

[62] See V. Bulmer-Thomas, *The Political Economy of Central America since 1920* (Cambridge, 1987), p. 106.

manufacturing is estimated to have grown at 6 per cent a year 1946–52, but from an extremely low base.[63] The problems of obsolete machinery and low productivity in the sugar industry which were to be a serious source of stagnation in the 1950s were eased in the 1940s by good prices.

We have mentioned several times in this discussion of the post-war political economy in Latin America the discrimination against agriculture implicit in ISI policies. The two extreme and dramatic cases of such discrimination are Mexico and Argentina. In both, agricultural development constituted a vital political issue, for extremely different reasons. In Mexico, the agrarian base of the Revolution, and the socialist and co-operative tendencies of elements within that Revolution, ensured that the issue of how to develop agriculture was always top of the political agenda. In 1940 an anti-Cárdenas and elitist group achieved office, determined to strengthen modern capitalist elements in the rural sector. The coming of the Rockefeller Institute in 1941 and the remarkable research effort which followed have been thoroughly documented.[64] The introduction of high-yielding varieties in wheat led to a surge in productivity. But the research was effectively accessible only to relatively large irrigated enterprises. Even in their case, as, for example, Sonora shows, substantial infrastructure investments and guaranteed prices were required from the government before large land owners would go ahead. Furthermore, the research most benefited wheat, an export crop, while the gains for maize, grown by small farmers for domestic consumption, were very slight. There is no doubt, however, that rapid agricultural development took place, aided also by the expansion of irrigated land as a result of investments in the 1930s. This had important beneficial consequences for the process of industrialization.

The case of Argentina forms a complete contrast. Perón's industrialization policy was based for political and economic reasons on extracting a surplus from the meat and wheat producers, which he did by a state purchasing agency, IAPI. The unprofitable prices rapidly began to kill the goose the significance of whose golden eggs Perón somehow never seemed to grasp. In this case agriculture for export and for domestic use were identical, and both suffered, resulting in inflation, a foreign exchange bottleneck and by 1955 an extreme version of 'estrangulamiento externo'.

[63] Claes Brundenius and Mats Lundhal (eds), *Development Strategies and Basic Needs in Latin America. Challenges for the 1980s* (Boulder, Col., 1982), p. 18.

[64] C. Hewitt de Alcantara, *Modernising Mexican Agriculture* (Geneva, 1976), pp. 20–45. See also Niblo, 'The Impact of War', p. 7, on the role of the United States.

Although early in the 1950s Perón began to attempt to reverse his policies, farmers did not trust the improved prices, and the inflationary impact led rapidly to the justification of their distrust.[65] The disinvestment in agriculture throughout this period was severe.[66]

In the majority of countries, where policies were less extreme, agriculture for the domestic market continued to suffer from the neglect which it had always endured and export agriculture suffered from the discrimination implicit in the protectionist policies being widely and incoherently followed, a situation only partially remedied by the devaluations of the early and mid-fifties. It remained the case that the agriculture sector was being taxed by all policies that forced it to sell at below world prices. Growth rates varied – but the fast growth rates were due to good world market conditions and the possibility of expanding area under production, rather than major increases in yield.

The one exception to the pattern of discrimination against agriculture appears to be Colombia, perhaps because of the fact that coffee producers were also often food producers, and because of the unique influence of coffee producers in policy management. There was an unusually clear perception in this one case that the problems with protection was that it tended to damage agriculture. The concept pushed by the Ospina government (1946–9) was 'integral protection': protection which stimulated *both* agriculture and industry. Purchasing local materials was, needless to say, unpopular with industry – but a solution was worked out: in 1948 import quotas began to be allocated *conditional* on purchase of local raw materials, and other measures of support to agriculture. Meanwhile, for example, the government strengthened the Instituto de Fomento Algodonero, itself an initiative of Antioqueño textile producers. The Minister of Economy, Hernán Jaramillo Ocampo, on introducing more severe import restrictions in 1949, tells how he went himself to Medellín to reassure producers that there was actually ample exchange available for their real needs and 'took the opportunity' to remind them of the virtues of purchasing local raw materials.[67]

This last point has been recounted in some detail precisely because it is

[65] C. Díaz-Alejandro, *Essays on the Economic History of the Argentine Republic* (New Haven, Conn., 1970), pp. 126ff., 364ff., 384; E. Eshag and R. Thorp, 'Economic and Social Consequences of Orthodox Economic Policies in Argentina in the Post-War Years', *Bulletin of the Oxford University Institute of Economics and Statistics,* 27, 1 (1965), pp. 3–44.

[66] See the calculations in ECLA, *El Desarrollo Económico de la Argentina* (Mexico D.F., 1959) Part I, pp. 32, 65.

[67] H. Jaramillo Ocampo, *1946–1950; de la Unidad Nacional a la Hegemonía Conservadora* (Bogotá, 1980), p. 270.

so exceptional. Elsewhere, while the new 'model' began to function rather well for the purposes of capital accumulation, it nevertheless contained contradictions and malevolent side-effects which were not perceived and in no way allowed for. The chief of these lay in the biases against exporting and against agriculture, as well as in the excessive dependence both upon imports and foreign technology.

It would be desirable to conclude the analysis of performance by reflecting on the record in regard to income distribution. It will be no surprise that systematic data are simply lacking. Full documentation exists only for Mexico[68] where the worsening distribution is consistent with the unequal access to gains from greater agricultural productivity described above. Arguing from rising wage earnings under Perón's management, it is clear, and again no surprise, that in Argentina there was redistribution towards labour.

We can, however, argue negatively with some confidence: for income distribution to improve, either the labour market must significantly tighten or there must be significantly increased access to the means of production, usually through ownership reform or education. The period we are dealing with here is one where population growth is still accelerating, industry is replacing the artisan sector and creating little net new demand for labour, and land and tax reform are conspicuous by their absence, at least until the Bolivian revolution (1952), which was to be an unhappy demonstration of how not to use land reforms to achieve equality. It is therefore quite improbable that there was any improvement in distribution, and with the continued and growing discrimination against agriculture for the domestic market (typically the province of small farmers), and the repression of urban labour, every reason to expect a worsening.

CONCLUSION

The 1930s had been a period of growth for Latin America after the initial disaster of the Depression of 1929. The greater degree of policy autonomy than at the time of the First World War had allowed an escape from the corset of the gold standard, and policies stimulating internal demand and raising tariffs had permitted growth of non-tradables and of import-competing tradables. At the same time real depreciation plus recovering

[68] I. M. de Navarrete, *La Distribución del Ingreso y el Desarrollo Económico de México* (Mexico, D. F., 1960), pp. 43–93.

terms of trade had allowed traditional exports to grow – an elusive and unusual combination. The State had begun to move into new areas of activity, sometimes directly undertaking industrial activity, and new industrial interests were becoming sizeable.

The Second World War, we have argued, brought both positive and negative effects. It helped export receipts, but there was little to spend them on, and the result tended to be over-valued exchange rates and internal inflation fed by the expansionary effect of accumulated reserves. The growing role of the United States was paradoxical: it clearly increased its influence on the region, with foreign advisers and missions appearing everywhere. Yet it also stimulated the developmental role of the State and the development of basic industries. As the State's role increased, so did the intensity of the relationship with the private sector, and the latter's growing involvement with the policy-making process was one of the most interesting results of the war.

In terms of our central preoccupation, the tension between the continuing need for a dynamic source of foreign exchange and the need to diversify the economy, reduce dependence and develop internal sources of dynamism, the war left a peculiarly unfortunate situation of over-valued exchange rates and accelerated inflationary pressures. The fear of inflation and of the inflationary effects of devaluation in the immediate post-war period led, first to the disbursement of accumulated foreign exchange on imports and then to the use of import controls to restrict imports in a rather unco-ordinated fashion. Unfortunately, this situation occurred just as all the largest economies had moved through to a point where in terms both of the macro functioning of the economy and of the weight of political interest, it appeared (for the first time except in the case of Argentina) possible to neglect and even penalize the traditional export sector. As the policy became embedded, so the costs of changing it mounted, in terms of the inflation threat. By the late 1940s major policy adjustments were badly needed.

We have seen that two models were in play to guide reform. On the one hand, the emerging structuralist view wanted state-induced industrialization, using modest and efficiently managed protection and relying on inflows of public foreign money to ease bottlenecks and facilitate the process. This view relied on a somewhat naive view of the capacity and coherence of the public sector, and on loans being available from abroad. The second view responded to U.S. interests and to more conservative interests within Latin America, and wanted a radical reversion to market forces with low protection and a pro-private foreign capital stance. As it became clear that public foreign capital was not forthcoming in substantial quantities, and that the dividends from pleasing the United States by a free trade position were negligible, so policy consolidated around an unhappy mix of the two positions. Private foreign capital became strongly sought after, being lured by a protected domestic market as well as by favourable legislation. Any early sensitivity to the desirability of exporting the new manufactured goods rapidly disappeared, and efficiency came a very poor second to the need to create significant short-term profit opportunities. The wartime emphasis on basic industries disappeared in the face of a surge of interest in the local production of consumer durables. Policy makers tended to neglect the extent to which 'substituting for imports' was producing growing bills for imported inappropriate technology and high import needs. The implicit bias against agriculture as well as exports also went largely unnoticed and unprotested, while growth was good and new opportunities were constantly opening up. The day of reckoning would come later.

There were important incipient contradictions and tensions in the new model. We have observed the growing role of the State and the growing demands of new groups within society, with the acceleration of population growth and urbanization and even with industrialization itself. We have seen how the ambiguous feelings of the private sector towards the State were resolved into an amplified 'clientelistic' relationship. We have seen the interesting wartime trends of stimulus to intra-regional trade and to basic industry disappear almost completely in the post-war scene. We have watched public foreign capital fail to materialize in adequate quantities. We have noted the incipient balance-of-payments implications of mismanaged ISI, of unmonitored foreign investment, of the growing sectoral imbalance between agriculture and industry, and the fragility of an accumulation model dependent on an often tenuous trust between state and private sector. We have seen that some at least of these tensions appeared to reach resolution by the end of our period, with some rationalization and reduction in complex trade controls, a reduction in the bias against exporting, and a whole-hearted acceptance of and welcome for private foreign capital. How far all this was no real resolution would, in fact, be covered up through the buoyant 1960s, with the growth of world trade, and even into the 1970s with the growth of the supply of foreign lending. Eventually, however, in various ways the tensions were to become overwhelming, as the fiscal and balance-of-payments implications of the underlying model became exposed.

4

THE LATIN AMERICAN ECONOMIES, 1950–1990*

An important feature of Latin American economic development historically has been the interaction between external and domestic economic structures. Links between the Latin American economies and the world markets increased in importance during the international trade boom towards the end of the nineteenth century when a production structure based on raw materials for export (and imports of manufactures) was consolidated. After the end of the Second World War, the region's development efforts were directed to transforming the structure of production and reducing external dependence. Import substitution industrialization (ISI) produced some positive results. The regional economy expanded rapidly. From 1950 to 1981 gross domestic product (GDP) increased at an average annual rate of 5.3 per cent. However, while average income per capita increased at an annual rate of 2.6 per cent, vast inequalities in the distribution of the benefits of economic growth persisted throughout the region – between social groups, between urban and rural areas, between regions within countries and between countries. At the same time, new forms of dependency on the international economy emerged. ISI and the diversification of consumption patterns in the 1950s and 1960s gave rise to the adoption of increasingly complex imported technologies, capital intensive as well as highly dependent upon imported inputs. Also, the 1960s saw a significant inflow of direct foreign investment concentrated in the produc-

* We are very grateful to the Editor, to O. Altimir, V. Bulmer-Thomas, H.J Chang, F. Fajnzylber, G. Harcourt, A. Hofman, J. Pincus, O. Sunkel, I. Sodre, A. Singh, V. Tokman and to the other contributors to this volume for their comments, and to M. Cabezas, D. Hahn, K. Lewis and A. Repetto for research assistance. The ideas of Carlos Díaz-Alejandro and Fernando Fajnzylber strongly influenced some sections of this chapter. We also are indebted to CIEPLAN and Cambridge University where most of this chapter was prepared and to the Ford Foundation and the Instituto de Cooperación Iberoamericana (ICI) of Spain for their financial support. The Division of Statistics of ECLAC kindly provided access to its data bank.

tion of manufactured import substitutes, benefiting from high levels of effective protection. Given the sizeable import content of these industries and high profit rates, the net savings of foreign currency were sometimes negligible or even negative.

Nevertheless, the international trade boom of the 1960s encouraged diversification of Latin America's exports and promoted dynamic growth of manufactured exports in those countries where the industrialization process was more firmly established. This was especially the case in the region's largest countries, Brazil, Mexico and Argentina (whose sales of manufactures reached over one-third of total exports), but it also occurred in smaller countries such as Chile and Uruguay and in some Central American and Caribbean nations.

In the 1970s most Latin American countries enjoyed easy access to cheap external capital, at a time when foreign exchange requirements were particularly pressing because of the oil shocks of 1973 and 1979. Although borrowing did relax the foreign exchange constraint, it also linked Latin American economies tighter to international financial markets and to the fiscal and monetary policies of the developed market economies (DMEs) than at any time since the 1930s. Because of the large external debt accumulated from 1973 to 1982 and the requirements of debt servicing, the region became highly vulnerable to the availability of new loans and changes in interest rates. The pervasive foreign exchange shortages that ensued were at the core of the crisis faced by the region during the 1980s, when the annual rate of growth fell to one-quarter of the level achieved during the previous period and when average income per capita *decreased* by 0.8 per cent per annum. Income inequality worsened and poverty increased significantly.

THE WORLD ECONOMY

The quarter century following post-war reconstruction was a period of unprecedented prosperity and expansion in Europe, Japan and the United States. Between 1950 and 1973, output in the DMEs grew at nearly 5 per cent per annum and in per capita terms rose 3.8 per cent annually. Thus, in just twenty-three years, GDP increased more than threefold and income per capita by a factor of 2.4. This rate of economic growth was twice as fast as in any period since 1820. Labour productivity, in turn, grew two and a half times faster than in the period 1913 to 1950, while the rapid growth in non-residential capital stock represented an investment boom which in its dimensions and continuity were unparalleled in the economic history of the DMEs (see Table 4.1). As a result, the average ratio of investment to GDP during this period also doubled that of any previous period since 1820.

Growth in the volume of exports was even faster than that of output, expanding at 9 per cent per annum between 1950 and 1973; this rate was nearly twice as fast as that achieved during any previous period. As a result, the DMEs' average export share of GDP grew from 10 per cent to 16 per cent during this period, with the average for the European DMEs reaching 26 per cent in 1973. Trade in manufactures was the most dynamic component (particularly trade among DMEs), with imports growing at an average rate of 8 per cent per annum for the whole period – and 12 per cent per annum between 1960 and 1973. As a consequence, the DMEs' imports of manufactures grew sixfold between 1950 and the early 1970s.

The period was not only characterized by rapid economic growth, but also by a significant improvement in economic stability. Fluctuations in GDP and export growth were much smaller than in previous periods. Unemployment rates were substantially lower as well. Rates of inflation, however, were higher and showed more fluctuations than in previous periods.

Although all DMEs enjoyed prosperity and stability from 1950 to 1973 we should not lose sight of the significant differences in economic performance among these countries. On the one hand, growth of output, capital stock and productivity accelerated more slowly in the United States and the United Kingdom than in other DMEs; on the other, Germany, Japan and France attained remarkable rates of expansion of productivity capacity and income. As a result, the latter countries managed to improve considerably their position vis-à-vis the United Kingdom, and to reduce substantially the income and productivity gap with the United States.

This 'Golden Age' began to show some signs of weakening in the late 1960s, and came to a halt in the early 1970s. There was as a result a surge of interest in the study of the key economic factors that had produced sustained growth for a period of more than twenty years (twice as fast as in any earlier period), and the longest ever period of full employment. At the same time, there was interest in the forces that undermined the Golden Age.

The rise (and later fall) of the 'Golden Age', was shaped by four key economic arrangements of the post-war period. The first was the set of

Table 4.1. *Growth and structural characteristics of different phases of DMEs' economic development, 1870–1990 (annual average compound growth rates)*

	1870–1913	1913–50	1950–73	1973–90
GDP	2.5	2.0	4.8	2.6
GDP per capita	1.4	1.2	3.8	2.1
Volume of exports	3.9	1.0	8.6	4.7
Non-residential gross fixed capital stock	3.4[a]	2.0	5.8	4.2[b]
Productivity				
Labour	1.7	1.9	4.5	2.3
Capital	n.a.	0.5	0.7	−1.6
Joint Factor productivity	n.a.	1.3	3.6	0.4
Employment structure (%)	1870	1900	1950	1990
Agriculture	49	38	25	5
Industry	27	31	36	30
Services	24	31	39	65

Note: [a] refers to 1890–1913 [b] refers to 1973–87
Source: Angus Maddison, *The World Economy in the 20th Century* (OECD, Paris, 1989), *Dynamic Forces in Capitalist Development* (Oxford, 1991) and 'Explaining the Economic Performance of Nations 1820–1989', in W. J. Baumol, R. R. Nelson and E. N. Wolff (eds), *International Convergence of Productivity* (Oxford, forthcoming); the data have been, if not otherwise indicated, updated to 1990 using the same sources as Maddison. All figures here are simple averages of the countries included in each item.

Keynesian macroeconomic mechanisms for managing the overall level of domestic economic performance – output, employment and growth. The second was the new 'international order' organized around the new 'Pax-Americana' that emerged after the war and that facilitated the rapid development of international trade and the end of the United States' traditional isolationism as symbolized by the Marshall Plan. The new international order also provided the context for the post-war regime of international trade and finance, usually called the 'Bretton Woods system'. The third was the development of institutions shaping capital-labour relations, mainly the organization of work within factories together with the standardization of work practices, and the intensive use of machinery, the organization of firms as large corporations, and their internationalization. The final economic arrangement was the 'rules of coordination' by which the actions of economic agents (individuals, firms and states) were brought into line with one another as well as with the demands of macroeconomic policies and labour relations.

The new economic arrangements of the post-war period worked smoothly at first. Internally, the welfare state, increases in real wages, and adequate demand management combined to maintain high levels of effective demand, consistent high expectations of growth, high capacity utilization and stable profits. At an international level, U.S. hegemony guaranteed the fluidity of international trade, both in manufactures and in raw materials. Within the DMEs, the excess demand for dollars and the willingness of the United States to recycle trade surpluses removed the threat of foreign exchange bottlenecks.

Nevertheless, serious problems began to emerge in the mid-1960s. An important stumbling block was the progressive imbalance between productivity growth and wage growth.[1] This phenomenon took place first and foremost significantly in the United States, but also appeared later in Europe and finally, though to a lesser extent, in Japan. The coincidence of slower productivity growth and continued real-wage increases resulted in a progressive decline in the profit rates. This eventually had important repercussions for both the demand for investment and the supply of savings which, in turn, affected the levels of effective demand.

An important characteristic of this 'full-employment profit squeeze' was that it was in operation well before the oil shock of 1973 and was probably the result of the long period of sustained growth, diminishing 'animal spirits', high levels of employment and increasing security for workers. As a consequence of lower productivity growth and rising wages, increments in production and employment increasingly became associated with higher rates of inflation. The oil shocks of the 1970s exacerbated these problems and contradictions but were not the original cause; in fact, even without the oil shocks non-inflationary growth would have been extremely difficult to sustain.

Because the process described above appeared first and most markedly in the United States, its previous international leadership position was challenged. Combined with the political and economic effects of the Vietnam War the relative decline of the U.S. economy shook the foundations of the

[1] The balance between the growth of productivity and real wages between 1950 and the mid-1960s not only ensured a strong profit rate, but also allowed consumption to grow roughly in line with production. It is important to note that the rate of growth of productivity began to fall in many DMEs in the second half of the 1960s, despite a strong rate of investment; in fact, the rate of growth of non-residential fixed capital stock rose from about 4 per cent per annum in the 1950s to 6 per cent per annum in the 1960s.

'Bretton Woods system' based on U.S. hegemony. The dollar was transformed in the 1960s from an under-valued to an over-valued currency, and faced with this external constraint, the United States could no longer play the same leadership role in the management of global aggregate demand. The first step away from the old system was the rescinding of full convertibility of the dollar into gold. Then, in 1971, the U.S. unilaterally abandoned the Bretton Woods system of fixed parities when its trade balance sustained the first major deficit in this century (US$2.3 billion).

The new system of floating exchange rates that emerged was not subject to hegemonic control by any country, nor did it have a cooperative leadership which could replace U.S. leadership. In an increasing interdependent and unstable world economy, the new system was incapable of resolving global financial disequilibria in a way that would ensure full-employment and an appropriate distribution of aggregate demand among countries. In the absence of an effective international co-ordinating mechanism, imbalances in the international economy were inevitable, due to the close relationship between balance of payments disequilibria, exchange rate fluctuations, inflation, and output.

In the 1970s, the United States attempted to induce a domestic expansion by stimulating aggregate demand (particularly in 1977 and 1978). However, by then, the rest of the world was no longer willing to accept an increased supply of dollars. The United States posted large trade deficits in 1977, 1978 and 1979, equivalent to about one-quarter to one-fifth of its exports. The resulting fall in the value of the dollar, in combination with the rising domestic inflation in the United States, set the stage for a sharp monetarist reaction under the leadership of the Federal Reserve.[2]

Therefore, the retreat from Keynesian policies of demand management was based on domestic as well as on international considerations; prominent among the former were the acceleration of inflation and the increase in the conflict over wages and profits; and among the latter, the end of the original arrangements of the Bretton Woods system, international financial instability, and the oil shocks.

The Golden Age not only provided the DMEs with unprecedented prosperity and growth, but also stimulated a similar phenomenon in most less developed countries (LDCs). In fact, as Table 4.2 shows (in relative terms to their respective economic histories) the LDCs achieved during this

[2] One of the first measures of the Federal Reserve, after a new chairman, Paul Volker, took office in 1979, was to increase drastically U.S. interest rates, which was to have dramatic consequences for the LDCs' foreign debt.

period levels of expansion which were on average even higher than those of the DMEs. However, there was large – and increasing – diversity in the performance of LDCs.

Output growth per capita of LDCs in the period 1950–73 was nearly three times faster than their best performances in previous periods. As a result of this dynamic growth total output trebled. Despite the notably more rapid increase in population, the LDCs managed a much faster increase in income per capita growth relative to the level achieved between 1913 and 1950, nearly doubling income per capita in twenty-five years. Latin America produced the best performance, followed by China, the rest of Asia and then Africa. However, the Asian newly industrializing countries (NICs) had the fastest rates of growth when figures for these countries are taken as a sub-group. The LDCs' performance was particularly good during this period in terms of growth of manufactured output, achieving an average growth of 7 per cent per annum.

Although the volume of exports increased by 6 per cent per annum, the LDCs' share of total world exports fell by one-third due to the fast growth of DMEs' exports. Furthermore, there were substantial variations within LDCs. Countries exporting manufactures faced rapidly expanding demand from the DMEs, and were therefore able to link their export sectors (and their economies) in a more dynamic way to the expansion of DMEs. As Table 4.1 and Figure 4.2 (below) show, DMEs' imports of manufactures consistently surpassed those of primary commodities. This was the case both in periods of expansion and in periods of slow growth in the DMEs. Thus, while imports of manufactures by DMEs grew at 8 per cent per annum between 1950 and 1973, their imports of primary commodities increased by only 6 per cent. The difference is even greater if we consider the more dynamic growth years 1960–73, when DMEs' imports of manufactures grew at 12 per cent per annum, compared with 7 per cent for primary commodities. Imports of manufactures by DMEs continued to expand even during the post-1973 period, while their imports of primary commodities after 1973 stagnated. This phenomenon became more pronounced after the second oil shock and the beginning of the Reagan–Thatcher monetarist experiments: during the 1980s, DMEs' imports of manufactures grew at 11 per cent per annum, while those of primary commodities expanded at less than 2 per cent.

When compared with other LDCs and the DMEs, Latin America's performance in terms of exports of primary commodities (which accounted for more than 90 per cent of total exports at the beginning of the period) was particularly disappointing, growing at less than 3 per

Table 4.2. *Growth and structural characteristics of different phases of LDCs' economic development, 1870–1990 (annual average compound growth rates)*

	1870–1913	1913–50	1950–73	1973–90
GDP	2.1	2.6	5.2	3.9
Latin America (unweighted)	2.9	3.2	5.1	2.7
Latin America (weighted)	n.a.	n.a.	5.3	2.8
GDP per capita	0.9	0.8	2.6	1.5
Latin America (unweighted)	1.1	1.4	2.5	0.6
Latin America (weighted)	n.a.	n.a.	2.6	0.5
Africa	n.a.	1.2	1.9	−0.3
China	0.3	−0.5	3.7	5.7
NICs[a]	n.a.	0.1	5.7	6.3
Rest of Asia	0.4	−0.3	1.6	3.3
Volume of exports				
Latin America	4.6	1.8	3.6	5.9
Productivity				
Latin America				
Labour	n.a.	n.a.	3.4	0.3
Capital	n.a.	n.a.	−0.6	−1.4
Joint factor productivity	n.a.	n.a.	1.3	−1.1
NICs[a]				
Labour	n.a.	n.a.	4.3	5.1
Capital	n.a.	n.a.	2.2	−1.0
Joint factor productivity	n.a.	n.a.	2.4	1.4
Employment structure (%)	1950	1973	1980	1990
Latin America				
Agriculture	50	32	29	24
Industry	24	30	26	28
Services	26	38	45	48

Note: [a] Refers to South Korea and Taiwan only.

Source: Same as Table 4.1 and Latin American and NIC's productivity from André A. Hofman, 'Economic Development in Latin America in the 20th Century – a Comparative Perspective', in A. Szirmai, B. van Ark and D. Pilat (eds), *Explaining Economic Growth. Essays in Honour of Angus Maddison* (North-Holland, 1993).

cent per annum. Exports of primary commodities during this period compares unfavourably with Latin America's previous record and overall economic performance during 1950–73. Thus, despite strong growth in exports of manufactures, Latin America lost half its share in total world exports. As Figure 4.1 (below) shows, the share of exports in GDP also fell by half. Latin America's ISI was carried to such an extreme that it absorbed most of the region's scarce resources; the export sector and particularly agricultural production were the main casualties of these policies.

In terms of LDCs' investment efforts, there was a remarkable boom of capital formation in the NICs, where the ratio of investment to GDP more than doubled. In the case of Latin America, this ratio increased from 16 per cent to 19 per cent; this was an important achievement that contributed to expand productive capacity.

Finally, the process of rapid industrialization not only produced a substantial change in the sectoral composition of output, but also in the structure of employment; there was a substantial transfer of labour from agriculture to industry and then to services. This phenomenon was particularly marked in the NICs, but was also significant in Latin America.

Relative to their own economic history, the LDCs experienced between 1950 and 1973 an unprecedented period of growth. This economic expansion in the LDCs was for the first time since the 1820s similar to that of DMEs. However, since the LDCs had a much faster rate of population growth, different attempts at measuring the income differential between the LDCs and the DMEs show that (except for the NICs and some Latin American countries, like Brazil and Mexico) income per capita continued to increase more rapidly in the DMEs. In fact, it was only in the decade *after* 1973 that the LDCs reduced the income gap between them and the DMEs for the first time since 1820. This reflects the fact that LDCs achieved a rate of growth of output that was more than double that of the DMEs (4.4 per cent and 2 per cent, respectively). However, as the World Bank data shows, there was a marked difference in performance between the low income and the middle income LDCs; in fact, it was only the middle income LDCs, including Latin America, that managed to reduce their income differential with the DMEs between the oil shock of 1973 and the debt crisis of 1982.[3]

The strong performance of a large number of LDCs (including many oil-

[3] See P. Bairoch, in P. Bairoch and M. Lévy-Leboyer (eds), *Disparities in Economic Development Since the Industrial Revolution* (London, 1981); A. Maddison, 'A Comparison of the Levels of GDP Per Capita in Developed and Developing Countries, 1700–1980', *Journal of Economic History,* XLIII (1983); World Bank, *World Tables* (1990).

importing LDCs) relative to the DMEs is probably the most significant feature of the period 1973–81. This trend was particularly noticeable in terms of growth of manufactures (6 per cent in LDCs and 3 per cent in DMEs), and of manufactured exports (12 per cent and 5 per cent, respectively). As a result, the LDCs' share of world manufacturing production increased from 7 per cent in the early 1970s to 10 per cent in 1981; and their share in world exports of manufactures rose from 5 per cent in the early 1970s to 9 per cent in 1981.[4]

The LDCs' economic performance during the inter shock period is remarkable in view of the non-oil LDCs' substantial balance-of-payments deficits which resulted from the oil price increase of 1973. The current account deficit of the average middle income oil-importing country increased from 1 per cent of GDP in 1973 to 5 per cent in 1975, and that of the average low income country from 2.4 per cent to 3.9 per cent.

It is important to emphasize that this improved relative performance of the middle income LDCs was mainly due to the fact that they were able to continue to grow during 1973–81 at rates similar to those prior to the oil shock of 1973, while the DMEs experienced a significant slowdown in terms of output, exports and manufacturing production, reducing their rate of growth by about half.

This apparent 'immunity' of Middle Income LDCs to the mounting problems of the inter-shock period was no doubt helped (as we shall see below) by their increasingly easy access to foreign borrowing. In fact, these countries were able to borrow in such quantities that the abundance of foreign exchange over-valued their currencies, leading many LDCs to adjust in the opposite direction than the one required by developments in the real side of the international economy. In the NICs and some Latin American countries, the rapid increase in exports was an additional factor in their relatively rapid economic growth, as was the sharp increase in the price of oil in the OPEC countries.

One of the most crucial issues regarding LDCs' foreign borrowing

[4] The rapid increase in DMEs imports from Middle Income LDCs during this period of low growth and rising unemployment, led to anxieties about de-industrialization and calls for protectionism. Nevertheless, several studies have shown that LDCs' exports did not cause de-industrialization in that period to any significant extent, that the LDCs also had a high rate of growth of imports of manufactures from the DMEs, and that the Middle Income LDCs still had a substantial trade deficit in manufactures with the DMEs. See, for example, A. Singh, 'Third World Industrialization and the Structure of the World Economy', in D. Curry (ed.), *Microeconomic Analysis: Essays in Microeconomics and Development* (London, 1981), and 'Third World Competition and De-industrialization in Advanced Countries', in T. Lawson, J. G. Palma and J. Sender (eds), *Kaldor's Political Economy* (London, 1989).

during this period is that it was consistent with international financial market signals: when deflated by the price index of Latin America's non-oil exports, the London Inter-Bank Offer Rate (LIBOR) for operations in U.S. dollars (three months) was actually negative in seven of nine years between 1972 and 1980 (with an average value of −5.3 per cent).

Therefore, superficially at least, the floating exchange-rate regime (that followed the breakdown in 1971 of the Bretton Woods' relatively fixed parities) and the world financial system were able to accommodate the financial disequilibria following the 1973–4 oil shock. OPEC's surplus was recycled to the balance-of-payments constrained non-oil LDCs, enabling them to maintain growth momentum to the benefit of the world economy through support of world aggregate demand. However, the economic and financial disruptions even before the second oil shock of 1979 were a great burden on the DMEs, as were the high costs paid by many LDCs after the 1982 debt crisis.[5]

After 1981 the economic performance of the Asian LDCs (including China, India and the NICs) diverged sharply from that of Africa and Latin America. Asia as a whole more than doubled its previous growth rate, with China, India and the NICs showing particularly strong growth. On the other hand, Africa and Latin America experienced a decline in per capita income. Thus the income differential between Latin America and Asia declined for the first time since 1820; and in the case of the NICs (which had already overtaken Latin America's income per capita in the early 1970s), having reached in 1981 a level of income per capita one-third higher than Latin America, by the end of the 1980s achieved levels two and a half times those of Latin America.

In Latin America, the long period of sustained growth since 1950 came to an abrupt end in 1980–81. For three decades the GDP of Latin America had grown at an average rate of 5.5 per cent per annum, while output per capita rose 2.8 per cent. However, during the 1980s the region achieved a rate of growth of output of only 1.2 per cent per annum, while income per capita declined at nearly the same rate. Almost every indicator reflects this overall picture of stagnation and decline. Manufacturing output, for example, which grew at a rate of 6.5 per cent per annum between

[5] See A. Hughes and A. Singh, 'The World Economic Slowdown and the Asian and Latin American Economies: a comparative analysis of economic structure, policy and performance', and A. Fishlow, 'Some Reflections on Comparative Latin American Economic Performance and Policy,' in T. Banuri (ed.) *Economic Liberalisation: no panacea* (Oxford, 1991). In fact, 1982 was the first year since the Second World War when the average per capita GDP in the LDCs actually fell.

1950 and 1981, rose only 1.1 per cent between 1981 and 1990.[6] Gross domestic investment per capita decreased from US$500 in 1980 to US$330 in 1988 (both measured in 1980 prices). A negative transfer of resources abroad of US$25 billion per year took place between 1982 and 1990 (US$221 billion in all); urban rates of unemployment at times stood at over 20 per cent in several countries; many countries, including Brazil, Mexico and Argentina, experienced three, four and even five digit rates of inflation.

Thus, at the end of the 1980s the LDCs were a heterogeneous group: several countries in Asia continued to exhibit dynamic economic growth, whilst most countries in Africa and Latin America were suffering their worst economic crises since the 1930s.[7]

LATIN AMERICA AND THE WORLD ECONOMY

Latin America interacted with the world economy mainly through the international goods and financial markets. With regard to international trade, demand-side factors consisted of: (a) the level of the international demand for the region's exportables; (b) the stability of that demand; (c) the degree of access of Latin American producers to various international markets; and (d) the terms of trade, that is, the prices of Latin America's exports relative to those of its imports. Supply-side factors relating to the international goods markets centred on the region's capacity to respond to international demand, that is, the capacity to mobilize factors of production (physical, human and financial).

Latin America's linkages to the international financial market depended, as it always had, primarily on supply-side factors: (a) the level of international liquidity; (b) interest rates for both commercial and conces-

[6] The most significant exception to this rule of stagnation and decline was the behavior of exports, particularly the volume of manufactures, for which the rate of growth increased from 7.3 per cent to 16.2 per cent, respectively. This is primarily (though by no means exclusively) a reflection of developments in the larger countries (particularly Brazil and Mexico). It is a remarkable phenomenon which is discussed in more detail below.

[7] The heterogeneity of the LDCs' performance during the 1980s can be seen from the fact that while in the 1960s and 1970s the yearly output growth rates of LDCs had tended to cluster around 5–6 per cent, in the 1980s fluctuations grew larger. For example, during the 1980s the average yearly growth rate of 'high performers' (LDCs with per capita yearly growth rates of 2 per cent or more *and* above-trend levels of investment) was more than *five times faster* than the average of 'poor performers' (LDCs that failed both tests); the first group of LDCs contained fourteen countries and the second forty-five (including most of Sub-Saharan Africa and Latin American countries). There was a third group of LDCs that performed poorly on only one of the two criteria.

sional loans; (c) credit rationing; (d) the type of conditionality attached to foreign loans; and (e) the level of capital flight, which depends, among other things, on access to foreign tax havens.[8]

The chronology of Latin America's relationship with the external environment (and its effects on the region's economy and policy-making) can be divided into four phases: first, the 1950s; second, the following years until 1973; third, the decade between the first oil shock and the financial crisis of the early 1980s; and finally, the subsequent years of recessive adjustment.

The 1950s

The main characteristics of this period were the (justifiable but exaggerated) pessimism with which the region viewed the prospects for exports of traditional primary commodities and its access to international financial markets, and the (also justifiable but exaggerated) optimism regarding the prospects for ISI. As a result, the period is characterized by a progressive delinking from the international economy and the implementation of ambitious industrialization programmes.

Latin America's scepticism about the possibility for sustained access to international financial markets can be traced back to the Depression of the 1930s (and, in some cases back to the First World War). The collapse in the DMEs' demand for primary products (which made a large contribution to the region's output, public revenue, employment, investment and savings) and sudden halt in the flow of new lending to Latin America in 1929 plunged the region into a period of economic hardship that persisted for more than a decade.

During the 1950s the DMEs' demand for a primary products grew slowly, particularly during the first half of the decade, when it averaged less than 2 per cent per annum. Moreover, the positive effect on export prices associated with the Korean War was short-lived; export prices fluctuated considerably during this decade. And the terms of trade fell by more than 20 per cent. At the same time, Latin American countries continued to have difficulties penetrating many DMEs' markets, particularly for

[8] Latin America's foreign borrowing has been basically supply-determined. Latin American countries seem prepared to borrow as much as they are allowed by the international financial markets, often irrespective of the prevailing interest rates. Thus, the four periods of large increases in foreign borrowing which have taken place since independence – the late 1810s and early 1820s, the 1860s and early 1870s, the 1920s and the 1970s – have all been made possible by particularly high levels of international liquidity. See C. Kindleberger, *Manias, Panics and Crashes: a History of Financial Crises* (London, 1978).

more processed primary products. Latin America could not look to the financial markets to relieve pressure on the economy caused by the foreign exchange constraint. The defaults of the 1930s continued to complicate efforts to obtain new loans throughout the 1950s. At end of the 1940s, 53 per cent of outstanding publicly offered or guaranteed dollar bonds were still in default (interest and sinking fund), 45 per cent were receiving an 'adjusted' debt service, and only 2 per cent were being serviced in full.[9] Even if Latin America had had normal access to international financial markets, the cost of new loans would have made this expensive. During the 1950s real interest (deflated by changes in non-oil export prices) rose rapidly, reaching an annual peak of 14 per cent in 1958.[10]

The region's pessimistic view of the international goods and financial markets at the beginning of the 1950s is therefore understandable. However, the reaction against primary commodities exports was so disproportionate that the share of these exports in GDP halved during the 1950s (down from 17.2 per cent to 8.9 per cent). This neglect of the export sector was carried to such an extent that, when the international markets for primary products did eventually pick up towards the end of the 1950s, Latin America had little capacity to respond (see Figure 4.3 below). Thus, when the yearly rate of growth of DMEs' imports of primary products increased from 1.9 per cent (first half of the 1950s) to 6 per cent (mid-1950s to 1972), Latin America's export of primary commodities only increased its rate of growth from 1.7 per cent to 3.3 per cent.

The combination of slow growth in the volume of exports and rapidly declining terms of trade meant that Latin America's capacity to import remained stagnant during the 1950s.[11] As a result, while the output of the region was growing at 5.1 per cent per year, the actual purchasing power

[9] See Foreign Bond Holders Protective Council, *Annual Report for the Years 1946–49* (New York, 1950), and R. Dornbusch, 'World Economic Issues of Interest to Latin America', in R. E. Feinberg and R. Ffrench-Davis (eds), *Development and External Debt in Latin America* (Notre Dame, Indiana, 1988).

[10] This happened despite the fact that nominal interest rates reached only 5 per cent. To obtain real interest rates from the point of view of Latin America, we have deflated nominal interest rates of international financial markets by the export price index of Latin America's non-oil exporting countries. We have chosen this deflator rather than the price index that includes oil-exporting countries, because the non-oil index reflects more closely the situation of the large majority of Latin American countries; in any case, the indices of both groups of countries remained very similar until the oil shock of 1973. See Figure 4.4 for sources and methodology.

[11] Latin America's capacity to import corresponds to the volume of exports multiplied by the terms of trade (from 1973 onwards, by the non-oil exporters terms of trade); it reflects the amount of imports that can be purchased by Latin America's exports (non-oil exports from 1973).

of the region's exports in 1960 was still stuck at the 1950 level (see Figure 4.2 below).

The poor performance of the export sector during the 1950s was reflected in a decline in the region's trade surplus, which fell from 3.9 per cent of GDP in 1950 to only 0.7 per cent in 1959 (both figures are three-year averages; see Figure 4.5 below). As the trade surplus vanished, the deficit in current account increased from US$ 1.4 billion in 1950 to US$3 billion in 1959 (both figures in 1980 prices and three-year averages). Although this represented only a modest 1–2 per cent of GDP, the Latin American countries found themselves unable to borrow to any significant extent on the international financial markets. As a consequence, an external constraint began progressively to obstruct the growth of output, fiscal revenues, employment, investment and savings.

Many Latin American countries (particularly in South America) tried to use deficit financing to limit the adverse effects of this emerging external constraint and also to finance an ambitious programme of infrastructural investment. The combined public sector borrowing requirements of Latin American countries grew (in real terms) at a rate of 12 per cent per annum during this period and in several countries (particularly in Argentina, Brazil and Chile) excessive public sector borrowing generated inflationary pressures. Thus, to the emerging external disequilibrium most Latin American countries added a damaging domestic imbalance.

High rates of inflation prompted the first stabilization plans of the post-war period, for which external financing had to be sought under the supervision of the International Monetary Fund (IMF). Attached to this source of finance was the condition that inflation-ridden Latin American countries adopt a set of monetarist macroeconomic policies which disregarded the structural sources of inflation. These monetarist stabilization plans were the subject of great controversy in Latin America and were strongly criticized by the United Nations' Economic Commission for Latin America (ECLA).[12]

One of the main concerns of the structuralist economists associated with ECLA was that orthodox stabilization policies would only work at the cost of slowing down the process of industrialization, together with the growth of investment and employment. The monetarists' emphasis on the reduction of domestic absorption would mean that control of inflation would

[12] See, for example, J. Noyola 'El desarrollo económico y la inflación en México y otros paises Latinoamericanos', *Investigación Económica,* 4th quarter, 1956; O. Sunkel, 'Inflation in Chile: an unorthodox approach', 1958, reprinted in 1960 in *International Economic papers,* 10; and A. Pinto, 'Ni Estabilidad ni Desarrollo – la política del FMI' (Santiago, 1958).

come at the expense of investment, an unsavoury trade-off for countries engaged in concerted industrialization efforts. Thus, from a structuralist point of view, these policies created a false dilemma between price stabilization and growth.

The structuralist approach, on the other hand, sought to reduce inflationary pressures not by 'repressing' inflation, but by attacking the root causes of inflation which they saw mainly as shortages of key products which constrained domestic production growth. Thus the modernization of agriculture, particularly land tenure systems and the fostering of ISI were considered to be as important in the struggle against inflation as the control of monetary aggregates.

Under the pressure of these external and internal disequilibria and also motivated by political and ideological considerations, most Latin American countries attempted to diversify their economies away from traditional output structures. In this sense, trade policies during this period were not primarily about trade, but about production incentives to foster structural change and the financial requirements of these changes. Under the intellectual influence of ECLA – in particular that of Raúl Prebisch – they tried to accelerate economic growth by switching the engine of growth from primary commodities to the manufacturing sector. The effects of this policy are all too evident in Figure 4.1.

Thus, the trade and industrialization policies of the 1950s have to be judged against the background of the developments in the international economy during the 1940s and 1950s, and of the changes in the intellectual and political paradigms of the region. The 'collective memory' of the 1930s and the restrictions of external supply of goods and finance during the war reduced the availability of imported manufactures, fostered the domestic production of import substitutes and strengthened the political clout of both the industrial entrepreneurs and the more progressive intelligentsia. This new climate was reinforced by the fact that when foreign supply was normalized after the war, Latin America still faced obstacles to expanding and diversifying their exports and to being able to have access to international finance.

However, ISI suffered greatly from the fact that trade and industrialization policies were executed through unsophisticated, unnecessarily obscure, and often particularly inefficient controls. There arose a great variety of tariff and quantitative import restrictions, widely fluctuating multiple exchange-rates, and varied administrative obstacles to primary commodity exports; these controls were not only unnecessarily complicated and often

Figure 4.1. *Latin America: Shares of manufactures, exports and exports of primary commodities in GDP, 1950–90 (%)*

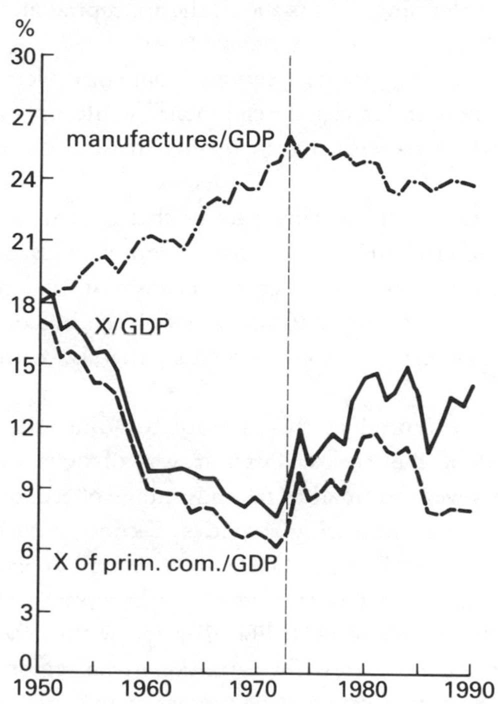

Sources: Share of manufactures (at constant 1980 prices) from ECLAC Statistical Division; share of exports (at current prices) from John Wells, *Latin America at the Cross-roads* (Santiago, 1988) updated with ECLAC statistics.[13]

unpredictable, but also, in some cases, subject to bureaucratic manipulation. As Nicholas Kaldor commented in an article discussing Chile's economic policies of the 1950s: 'The Chilean Governments have . . . pursued a policy of intervention with a multiplicity of detailed and complicated controls . . . without any clear overall view of either the basic objectives which these instruments were intended to serve, or of any overall attempt

[13] There are some important discrepancies between different sources regarding the actual share of exports in GDP (but not regarding its trend). The data for the years 1950–60 is taken from ECLA, *External Financing in Latin America* (New York, 1965), and for 1960–90 from IMF, *International Financial Statistics Yearbook* (Washington, D.C., various issues). The data from the latter source is similar to that of ECLA's *Preliminary Overview of the Latin American Economy* (Santiago, various issues), and differs from that found in the United Nations, *Monthly Bulletin of Statistics* (New York, various issues). Although this statistical discrepancy is important, both series present a similar tendency for the export sector during this period. For a discussion of this problem, see Wells, *Latin America at the Cross-roads*, p. 22.

to assess their efficacy in relation to such objectives. . . . All this is not intended as a defense of the free market or of *laissez faire* or as an argument against economic planning – (it is about) the appropriateness of the instruments chosen.'[14]

By the end of the 1950s, various countries were experiencing problems with their industrial development, while unemployment and poverty persisted, thus creating increasing frustration in wide social sectors.

As this frustration with the slow pace of change arose across a range of groups, a series of criticisms against the design of industrial policies was developed. The main focus of such criticisms – in which ECLA had a crucial influence – was the difficulties involved in continuing Latin America's ISI in 'watertight compartments', that is, within each country's frontiers.

Two things were crucial in this attempt to adjust the process of ISI towards the end of the 1950s. First, it was obvious that the size of domestic markets was too small to take advantage of economies of scale in a large number of manufacturing activities. Second, after the normalization of economic life in Europe, DMEs were setting an example of trade integration through the establishment of the European Common Market and the successive rounds of tariff liberalization within the framework of GATT. Support therefore grew for Latin American regional integration, particularly as a way to accelerate the process of industrialization. At the beginning of the 1960s groups of countries were giving shape to LAFTA (the Latin American Free Trade Association) and the Central American integration scheme, which were followed by the Andean Pact in the late 1960s. These initiatives achieved some important results, though they were modest compared with original expectations (see the section on Latin American Economic Integration in this chapter).

As in the case of the export pessimism of the period, the industrialization optimism of the 1950s seems to have been justified, but exaggerated. Latin America did manage a convincing yearly rate of growth of manufactures during the 1950s (6.6 per cent) – with the production of steel growing at a rate of 13 per cent per annum, cellulose and derivatives of oil at 11 per cent each, and manufactured exports (during the second half of the 1950s) at 7 per cent. As a result, the share of manufactures in GDP grew from 18 per cent to 21 per cent. Manufacturing was also an effective

[14] Nicholas Kaldor, 'Economic Problems of Chile', *El Trimestre Económico,* (April–June, 1959), p. 12.

engine of growth for the whole of the economy, with gross domestic investment expanding at a yearly rate of 7.8 per cent and GDP at 5.1 per cent. However, practically the whole orientation of economic policy and an inordinate amount of new resources were directed towards ISI, with the consequent neglect of traditional export activities and agriculture for the domestic market; in turn, ISI was constantly under threat of a foreign exchange constraint produced by the slow growth of exports. At the same time, many of the social and political problems that industrialization was supposed to solve remained unresolved.

As is now obvious with the benefit of hindsight, policy-makers of the 1950s were excessively pessimistic regarding the economic potential of the primary commodity sector and unreasonably optimistic about the long-term effectiveness of their new engine of growth. Ironically, something similar occurred at the end of the 1980s, when pessimism about ISI stood alongside exaggerated expectations regarding the new engine of growth, the primary commodity export sector. This excessive reliance on the economic dynamism of one particular economic activity has often led to highly unbalanced economic structures under which the engine itself was likely to lose its power. The increasing awareness of these shortcomings encouraged a relaxation of the anti-export bias during the 1960s.

1960–1973

As we have seen, the period from 1960 to 1973 constituted the most dynamic phase ever in the economic history of DMEs and LDCs alike. Reciprocal trade liberalization among DMEs was one of the central features of the international economy during this period and the driving force behind both the rapid technological change and the intra-industry specialization that took place. DMEs' imports of manufactures grew at a rate of 12 per cent per annum and their exports at 8 per cent per annum during this period; as a result, the ratio of exports to GDP in DMEs increased from 10 per cent in 1950 to 13 per cent in 1960 and 16 per cent in 1973. The increasing importance of transnational corporations was also conducive to more dynamic trade growth. This latter development, however, presented both opportunities and obstacles for LDCs; while these corporations contributed to productivity growth, in many cases they controlled marketing channels and used them to limit market access of new competitors from LDCs.

Among LDCs, the best performance was posted by the NICs and some Latin American countries (particularly Brazil, Mexico and Colombia). The first group of countries benefited enormously from the DMEs' rapidly growing demand for imported manufactured goods, which, as Figure 4.2 shows, grew almost twice as fast as their demand for primary commodities during this period.

From this point of view, Latin America made two mistakes: it continued to rely heavily on exports of primary commodities that faced slower and unstable demand growth (instead of making a special effort to direct new industries towards export markets), while being unable to increase export volumes even in step with the growth of demand (due to the anti-export bias of their trade policy). As a result, its capacity to import grew even slower than its exports (particularly in the first half of the 1960s). Therefore, the growth of the region had to continue struggling against a balance-of-payments constraint.

During this period, two major regional circuits emerged: one within Europe and between Europe and the United States, and the other formed by the East Asian countries under Japan's leadership, including the NICs and other Asian countries. The main characteristic of these circuits was the positive effects of the growth of manufactured exports on the industrialization process. In the case of the more advanced DMEs, the principal instruments were the reduction of tariffs and other trade barriers, and the transnationalization of capital (which also encouraged the transfer of technology from the United States to Europe). In the East Asian countries the most important instrument in terms of industrial policy was the active role played by the State in defining priority sectors in which these countries launched major drives to accelerate technological learning. On the tariff front, rather than across-the-board import liberalization, this second group of countries used protection in a more flexible and effective way than Latin American countries. They tended to grant similar effective protection to producers for domestic and for foreign markets, but with large variations among products.

The experiences of the NICs exerted some positive influence over the orientation of Latin America's industrial policies. Latin America's initial exclusive reliance on ISI as a route to industrialization was reaching its limit at the end of the 1950s, as import ratios declined to their minimum and the share of primary commodities exports in GDP fell by half. Thus, by the beginning of the 1960s this model had outlived some of its useful-

Figure 4.2. *DMEs: imports of manufactures and primary commodities. Latin America: exports and capacity to import, 1950–90*

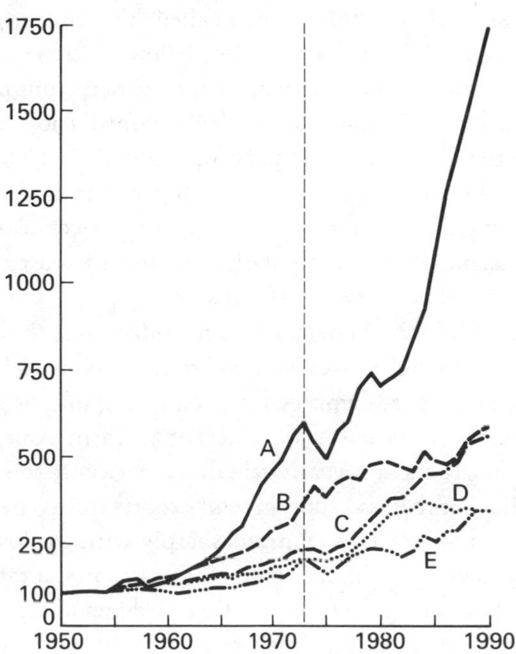

Notes: 1950 = 100. All figures are in constant US$ terms (quantum).
A: DMEs' imports of manufactured goods. B: DMEs' imports of primary commodities. C: Latin America's exports. D: Latin America's exports of primary commodities. E: Latin America's capacity to import.
Sources: OECD, *Historical Statistics* and *National Accounts,* various years, OECD and World Bank databases, ECLAC Statistical Division and John Wells, *Latin America at the Crossroads* (Santiago, 1988).

ness as evidenced by the growing internal and external imbalances which characterized Latin American economies. These problems and the success of the NICs led many Latin American countries to try to complement their pattern of industrialization with many forms of export promotion (subsidies, dual exchange rates, export processing zones, regional integration, and so on), but export markets were not viewed, as they were in the case of the NICs, as their main engine for growth in the manufacturing sector.

Another policy tool that was used in this attempt at integrating both dimensions of trade policy (creating incentives for a more selective ISI as well as for exports) was the exchange-rate reform that took place first in Chile (in 1965), followed by Colombia (in 1967) and Brazil (in 1968). These nations started to follow the so-called 'crawling-peg' policy that represented a major policy innovation (see below, p. 204).

Despite the expansion of the demand for primary commodities, Latin America's terms of trade continued to decline until 1967, at which time they had fallen to a level nearly 30 per cent below that of 1950. There was a small recovery between 1967 and 1972 (6 per cent) and then, with the oil shock of 1973 and its repercussions on the prices of other primary commodities, Latin America temporarily recovered in just two years from the decline in its terms of trade suffered since 1950.

The rapid growth in world demand for manufactures, the easier access to DMEs' markets for manufactures, and the stronger industrial base of several Latin American countries, combined to produce significant growth in manufactured exports. Between 1960 and 1973, Latin America expanded exports of manufactures at a yearly rate of 11 per cent; this rapid growth increased the share of manufactures in total exports from 9 per cent in 1960 to 21 per cent in 1973.[15] This contrasts sharply with the low 3.3 per cent annual rate of growth of primary commodities exports, a rate which is *less than half* the 7 per cent growth of the DMEs' demand for these products during this period. As a result, the share of primary commodity exports in GDP dropped to an even lower level, down from 9 per cent in 1960 to 6 per cent in 1972, or just one-third of the 1950 level of 17 per cent.

As Figure 4.3 shows, this decline in the share of exports to GDP in Latin America contrast sharply with the experience of other LDCs and DMEs during this period of rapid expansion in world trade.

The slow growth of primary commodity exports (which still accounted for some 80 per cent of exports) had a negative effect on Latin America's trade balance, which was reversed from a small surplus equal to 0.8 per cent of GDP in 1960 to a deficit of 1.1 per cent in 1971 (both figures are three-year averages, see Figure 4.5 below). As the trade balance deteriorated, the deficit in current account grew from US$2.9 billion in 1960 to US$8.6 billion in 1971 (both figures in 1980 prices and three-year averages).

[15] The positive contribution of Latin American economic integration to the process of industrialization in the region is illustrated by the annual rate of growth of nearly 15 per cent recorded by intraregional exports of manufactures during this period.

Figure 4.3. *Latin America, Asia, OECD and World: Long term trends of the ratio of merchandise exports to GDP, 1900–90 (%)*

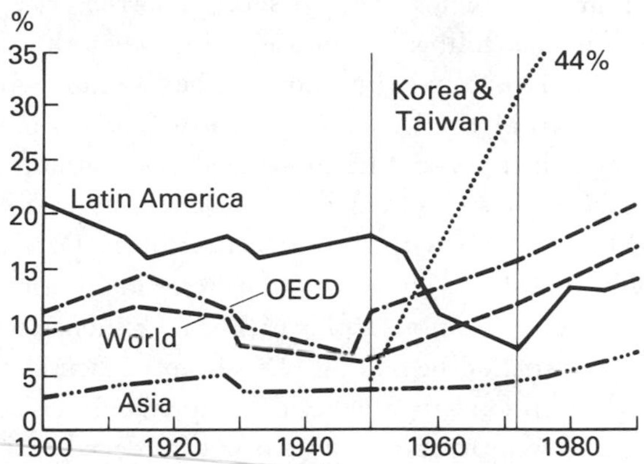

Sources: As Table 4.1 and World Bank, *World Development Report* (Washington, D.C., 1991).

Overall, except for primary commodities exports and agriculture for the domestic market (which had a rate of growth of 3.3 per cent per annum in both cases anyhow), the 1960–73 period, from an economic point of view, was the most dynamic in Latin America's history. Manufacturing production grew at a yearly rate of 6.8 per cent and its shares of GDP rose from 21 per cent to 26 per cent. Gross domestic investment expanded 9 per cent per annum (that is, the level of investment in 1973 more than tripled that in 1960). GDP grew at a yearly rate of 5.9 per cent, which meant that output doubled during this period; and, given the 2.7 per cent annual growth of population, income per capita increased 3.2 per cent per annum. The abrupt end to the 'Golden Age' in DMEs, the limits of ISI (as it was being implemented in Latin America), the oil shocks of 1973 and 1979, and the negative consequences of financial liberalization after 1973 (with the excessive borrowing and its often inefficient use), were radically to change most of this rapid development process in Latin America.

1973–81

The most significant economic event in the 1970s was the four-fold increase in the price of oil in 1973–4, after several years of decline in real terms. The timing of this unexpected price rise was (economically and politically) extremely inconvenient for the DMEs, as it came on top of mounting economic problems. The oil shock (and the price increases in other commodities that followed) came at a time when the 'Golden Age' was showing clear signs of winding down. The 'Bretton Woods regime' had been undermined by the U.S. unilateral abandonment of the convertibility of the dollar in 1971 and its subsequent devaluation. By 1973 the new floating exchange-rate system was not yet firmly established. This new system had to struggle with abrupt changes in the DMEs' and LDCs' balance of payments; in just one year, the increase in oil prices turned the DMEs' current account from a surplus of US$10 billion into a deficit of US$15 billion, and that of the non-oil LDCs from a deficit of US$9 billion into one of US$21 billion. Together with the private international financial markets, the new floating-rate system was burdened with the largest ever trade-related transfer of resources from the DMEs to a group of LDCs (OPEC), as well as recycling a large share of these resources back from initially low-absorbing OPEC to the DMEs and non-oil exporting LDCs.

In terms of economic growth, most LDCs were able to adjust to the 1973–4 shock better than the DMEs. However, LDCs were more adversely affected by the twin oil and financial shocks of 1979 and 1982, with the exception of some Asian countries. Thus, while the average yearly growth rate of DMEs fell from nearly 5 per cent in the years 1960–73 to 2.8 per cent in the years between the two oil shocks, the LDCs' growth declined only marginally from about 6 per cent to 5.2 per cent. However, as we shall see below, after 1982 many LDCs, particularly those in Africa and Latin America, experienced a sharp decline in their levels of economic activity from which many had still not recovered at the beginning of the 1990s.

The 1973–4 oil shock obviously had a different effect on the oil-exporting and oil-importing LDCs. In the case of Latin America, net oil exports rose (in 1981 prices) from US$7 billion in 1973 to US$23 billion in 1981. However, as Figure 4.4 shows, the oil shocks of the 1970s affected the terms of trade of oil exporters and those of oil importers of the region in opposite ways.

Among Latin America's oil exporters, Venezuela, Ecuador and later Mexico were the main beneficiaries of the oil shocks. Peru also became an oil exporter, but expectations of windfall gains were frustrated when actual reserves turned out to be less than previous estimates. Most other

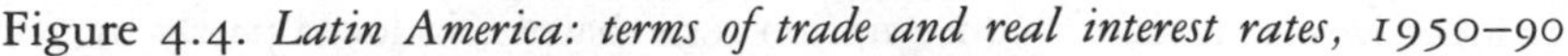

Figure 4.4. *Latin America: terms of trade and real interest rates, 1950–90*

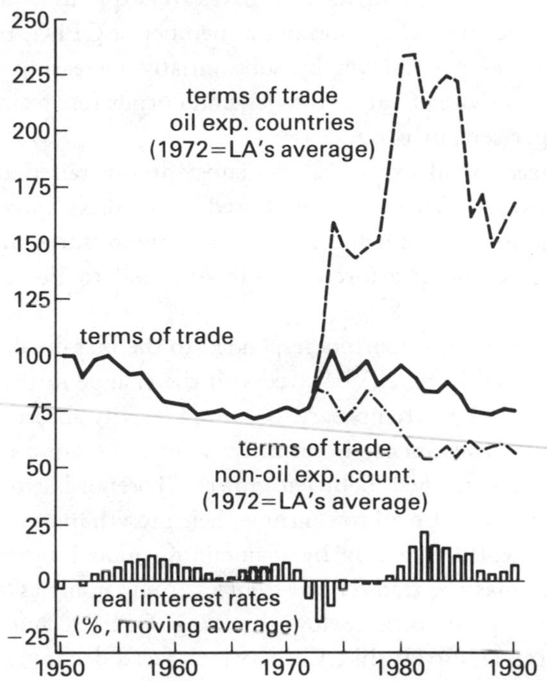

Sources: ECLAC Statistical Division and World Bank, *World Tables* (Washington, D.C., 1991).

countries were net importers, with Brazil's oil bill reaching 54 per cent of the country's total imports in 1983.

Venezuela, then the principal Latin American producer of oil, experienced a major increase in exports earnings and domestic disposable income. Exports rose from US$3.1 billion in 1972 to US$11.3 billion in 1974, with real income increasing by one-quarter due to the terms of trade effect alone. However, Venezuela followed OPEC's policy of reducing output in order to support prices; as a result, its exports fell by 20 per cent in 1975 and did not recover their 1974 nominal value until the new round of price increases in 1979. Paradoxically, GDP at constant prices (including constant terms of trade) did not increase after the oil shock. The non-oil sector grew but this was counter-balanced by the fall in oil output. A similar phenomenon was found in Ecuador where the production of oil was reduced while domestic consumption rose sharply, induced partly by low domestic prices for oil and its derivatives. The picture was different in Mexico; this country, which was not a member of OPEC, benefited from the discovery of new reserves by substantially increasing output. As a result, Mexico's share of Latin America's oil output rose from 9 per cent in 1973 to 44 per cent in 1982.

Latin American oil exporters also substantially raised their levels of foreign borrowing. Their improved creditworthiness encouraged overly liquid international bank lenders to exert strong pressures on Latin American countries to increase foreign borrowing and to liberalize domestic capital markets.

Latin American oil importers responded to the first oil shock in various ways. Some, notably Brazil, behaved as if the change in the international relative price of oil was temporary, borrowed heavily abroad and sustained a high level of investment, in an attempt to maintain a dynamic GDP growth. This was termed 'debt-led growth'. Foreign borrowing not only helped countries like Brazil to continue their growth momentum, but also benefited the world economy by maintaining global aggregate demand following the massive transfer of resources from countries with high absorption capacity to initially low-absorbing OPEC countries. In other Latin American countries, like Chile, which faced declining export prices and restricted access to international financing, a more orthodox adjustment to the new structure of relative prices was implemented by abruptly reducing economic activity.

After the 1979 oil shock, Brazil, having already accumulated a large debt and having some difficulty in refinancing amortization, chose to reduce its level of economic activity. However, Southern Cone and oil-importing countries like Chile, which since 1976 had gained increasingly easy access to bank financing, increased their foreign borrowing heavily until the sudden cessation of voluntary lending by commercial banks in 1982 (see External Financing and Domestic Adjustment in this chapter).

Most countries were thus confronted with an over-supply of cheap foreign funds. The standard reaction in response to an excess supply of foreign currency was a growing appreciation of exchange-rates in relation to their purchasing power parities. Exchange-rate appreciations and easy access to financing were reinforced by import liberalization policies implemented by several Latin American countries. This process was more intense in countries launching neo-conservative experiments such as Argentina and Chile, and in new oil-exporting countries like Mexico, whose foreign currency availability increased dramatically with both foreign loans and rapidly growing oil export proceeds. As a result, between 1973 and 1981 Latin America's imports of goods increased in real terms (1980 prices) from US$44 billion to US$93 billion, and its current account deficit from US$10 billion to US$40 billion.

Closer financial links between Latin American countries and the international financial markets further tied the economic fortunes of the region to the economic policies and performance of the DMEs. Traditionally, the links between the two had worked mainly through trade-flows, with the DMEs' level of demand for primary commodities being the crucial factor. Under the new conditions, a strong and unstable financial link was added, characterized by floating interest rates and large amounts of loans with short term maturities.

Within this framework, the inability of DMEs stabilization policies to curb inflationary pressures and reactivate growth in the second half of the 1970s contributed to the Latin American countries' external imbalances. The turning point for Latin American countries was associated with three shocks: first the unprecedented rise of interest rates, partly associated with the second oil shock; second, the 14 per cent deterioration in Latin America's terms of trade between 1980 and 1982 (18 per cent for non-oil exporters); and third, the sudden cessation of foreign lending. As has happened often in the past during times of crisis, DMEs transferred part of the cost of their adjustment to the periphery via the combination of high nominal interest rates (this time on a floating interest rate debt), a halt to their lending, contraction of imports, and low prices for primary commodities' imports (see External Financing and Domestic Adjustment in this chapter).

Paradoxically, notwithstanding the negative and unstable external environment and the problems created by the neo-conservative experiments in the Southern Cone countries (which exhibited a rather poor record), Latin America's growth performance between 1973 and the early 1980s was still competent, particularly in comparison with that of the DMEs (see Table 4.3 below). Exports of primary commodities exhibited a weak performance; some oil exporters reduced sharply the production of oil in order to support the increased world price. This was reflected in the fact that the volume of total exports of oil-exporting nations reached in 1980 a level similar to that in 1970. However, exports of manufacturers of all the region achieved a vigorous growth, with their volume averaging a 12 per cent annual rise in the 1970s, a figure similar to the 1960s. Gross domestic investment (partly financed by the growing foreign debt) increased by one-third (in real terms), with the share of investment in GDP rising from 19 per cent in the 1960s to 24 per cent in the second half of the 1970s. In turn, GDP grew at an annual average rate of 5.2 per cent in 1973–80 although falling to nearly zero in 1981, due to the early arrival of the recession in Argentina and Brazil. Since the DMEs only achieved an annual rate of GDP growth of 2 per cent in this period, income differentials between Latin America and DMEs were reduced during the 1970s: according to World Bank estimates, the ratio of Latin America's income per capita to that of the High Income OECD members rose from 17 per cent in 1973 to 19 per cent in 1981.

However, the mounting internal and external deficits could not be financed by foreign and domestic debt forever. The sudden halt in foreign loans in mid-1982 meant that Latin American countries had to start paying the service of foreign debt from export revenues and not from additional borrowing. Thus, Latin America was forced to stop its 'debt-led' growth and implement a drastic adjustment process so as to reverse the growing domestic and external imbalances. A recessive adjustment put an end to the longest period of sustained economic growth ever experienced by the region.

The 1980s

The region faced a deep crisis during the 1980s arising from both the large debt accumulated during the 1970s and the recessive effects of the worst external environment since the 1930s, both in the goods and the financial markets. During this decade, the region was confronted with the combined shock of the massive increase in real LIBOR (London Inter-bank Offer Rate) from −2.5 per cent in 1979 to 22 per cent in 1981, a complete cessation of voluntary lending by the international financial markets, stagnation of DMEs' demand for primary commodities (which grew at a yearly rate of only 0.3 per cent between 1980 and 1987), and a 23 per cent drop in the terms of trade between 1980 and 1990 (19 per cent in non-oil countries). As a consequence of the suspension of voluntary lending, the increase in interest payments, and the reduction of foreign investment, capital outflows from Latin America exceeded capital inflows into the region (see External Financing and Domestic Adjustment in this chapter).

The enormous task required to generate the foreign exchange needed to service Latin America's foreign debt was made more difficult by the sharp fall in the prices received for its exports. Thus, for instance, despite an increase in the volume of Latin American exports by 30 per cent between 1980 and 1986 (helped by substantial devaluations of domestic currencies), the actual value of exports dropped by 12 per cent.

However, there was a significant difference between the performance of the primary commodities export sector and that of manufactured goods. Output of primary goods (excluded oil) reacted better and faster to the domestic recession. For instance, agriculture, forestry and fishing increased its share of GDP (at constant prices) from 9.6 per cent in 1980 to 10.8 per cent in 1985, and thereafter fluctuated around that share. On the other hand, manufacturing dropped from 26 per cent of GDP in 1980 to 24 per cent in 1990, with the level of its value-added almost stagnant in both years. The volume of agriculture and mineral exports increased moderately, though faster than DMEs' demand for these goods, with a depressing effect on international prices. However, exports of manufactures rose strongly, notwithstanding the stagnated domestic sectoral output. In fact, the volume of manufactured exports averaged a 9 per cent annual growth during the 1980s. There was a significant opening of the sector to trade, strengthening the trend inaugurated in the mid-sixties. As a result, the share of manufactures in total exports doubled during this period reaching nearly 40 per cent (see also Figure 4.7 below).

The slow growth of total export revenue as a consequence of declining relative prices meant that Latin America had to generate foreign exchange – both to close the gap in its balance of trade and to achieve enough surplus to service its foreign debt – mainly through a reduction in imports. Thus, in order to convert the 1981 trade deficit of US$14 billion into a surplus of US$36 billion in 1984, the region had to reduce imports of goods and services from US$127 billion to US$78 billion, almost a 40 per cent reduction. To achieve this, policy-makers by and large opted for a combination of devaluation and massive reductions in absorption. The cost pressures of devaluation proved to be notably stronger on domestic prices than the depressive effect of repressed demand.

Inflationary pressures (partly because of the rapid increase in public sector deficits due to the service of the public debt and mounting subsidies to private debtors) brought the annual increases in the level of consumer prices to three, four or even five digits in many Latin American countries: 12,250 per cent in Nicaragua (1988), 11,750 per cent in Bolivia (1985), 672 per cent in Argentina (1985), 667 per cent in Peru (1988), 586 per cent in Brazil (1988) and 132 per cent in Mexico (1987). In brief, for several years in the 1980s, many Latin American countries experienced hyper-stagflation.

ISI-LED GROWTH AND STRUCTURAL CHANGE

This section focusses on the process of ISI and its effects on the rest of Latin America's economic structure. Although, to a certain extent, each country has attempted to follow its own industrialization path, most Latin American countries from the 1950s to the 1980s have in common the basic feature of relying upon the manufacturing sectors as their main engine of growth. It is therefore possible to speak of a common Latin American development experience of ISI during this period, although the policy instruments, timing, intensity and achievements of their industrialization processes may differ.

As we have seen, from 1950 to the early 1980s, Latin America experienced a long phase of sustained economic growth, which had no precedent in its economic history. Latin America's average yearly growth rate between 1950 and 1981 was one-quarter faster than that of the DMEs (5.3 and 4.2 per cent per annum, respectively). Latin America's relative growth performance was particularly strong during the inter-shock period (1973–80). However, this dynamic Latin American average performance masks a great difference between countries.

As Table 4.3 shows, the most striking disparity is found between the three largest economies, Argentina, Brazil and Mexico. In 1950, at the beginning of this period, Argentina's was the largest economy in the region, accounting for one-quarter of combined GDP; it had a level of output 10 per cent larger than that of Brazil and 25 per cent larger than that of Mexico. Due to its poor relative performance between 1950 and the early 1980s, Argentina's GDP only grew by a factor of 2.7, while Brazil recorded a sevenfold increase. By the end of the period Brazilian GDP had reached nearly three-quarters of U.K. GDP. Mexico achieved a similar high growth during the period. By 1990 Brazil and Mexico together accounted for nearly three-fifths of Latin American GDP. In that year, Argentine output corresponded to only about one-third of the Brazilian and one-half of the Mexican output.

If we compare the performances of Brazil and Mexico with that of the Asian countries, we find that their record between 1950 and 1981 was

Table 4.3. *Latin America: growth of gross domestic product (GDP), 1950–90*[a] (annual average compound growth rates)

	1950–60	1960–73	1973–81	1950–81	1981–90	1950–90
Argentina	2.8	4.0	1.2	2.9	−0.6	2.1
Brazil	6.8	7.5	5.5	6.8	2.3	5.8
Chile	4.0	3.4	3.6	3.6	2.5	3.4
Colombia	4.6	5.6	4.5	5.0	3.9	4.8
Mexico	6.1	7.0	6.6	6.6	0.8	5.3
Peru	5.5	4.8	3.8	4.8	−1.7	3.3
Venezuela	7.6	4.7	−0.1	4.4	0.6	3.5
Small countries[b]	3.6	5.4	4.3	4.5	1.2	3.8
LATIN AMERICA	5.1	5.9	4.5	5.3	1.3	4.4
Oil exporters[c]	6.1	6.1	4.8	5.8	0.4	4.6
Oil importers	4.2	5.8	4.2	5.0	2.1	4.3

Notes:

[a] Figures for the 1950s and 1960s are measured in US$ 1970, and from 1970 to 1990 in US$ 1980.

[b] Includes twelve countries, [c] Includes five countries.

Source: Data from ECLAC, Statistical Division.

much better than either that of China or India, but not quite as good as that of the NICs. According to World Bank methodology, the income per capita differential between Brazil and Mexico on the one hand, and the NICs on the other, was reversed during this period, from the former having a 22 per cent advantage in 1950 to the latter having achieved a 16 per cent edge in 1981. However, most of this change is due to Brazil and Mexico having had a faster population growth (3 per cent and just less than 2 per cent, respectively); in fact if the NICs had had the same rate of population growth, other things being equal, the per capita income differential between these two groups of countries would hardly have been reduced in these three decades (from 22 per cent to 17 per cent in favour of Brazil and Mexico).

During the 1980s, however, these two Latin American countries performed much worse than all the Asian countries. Thus, the income per capita differential between Brazil–Mexico and China–India, having increased from being 5.3 times larger in the former in 1950 to 7.8 times in 1981, fell to just 4.6 times larger in 1990. Between the two Latin American countries and the NICs, the income per capita differential that was 22 per cent higher in the former in 1950 had become a massive 2.3 times higher in the NICs in 1990.[16]

Brazil and Mexico's performance between 1950 and 1981 is also impressive relative to that of the DMEs. During this period, the two Latin American countries grew at an average yearly rate approximately 50 per cent higher than the rate of the DMEs; thus, despite their much faster population growth, they managed to increase their income per capita relative to that of the high income OECD countries from 16 per cent to 21 per cent. This phenomenon was more marked if the comparison is made with the United States alone; during this period, Brazil and Mexico reduced their income per capita differential with the United States from a factor of approximately 8 to one of 5. However, between 1981 and 1990, this change was partially reversed.

Latin America's economic growth between 1950 and 1981, and the rapid transformation of its productive structure, was made possible by a remarkable process of capital accumulation. Gross domestic investment grew at a yearly rate of 7.4 per cent (that is, the level of investment in 1981 was, in real terms, about 9 times higher than that of 1950), and investment in machinery and equipment grew even faster, at a yearly rate of 8 per cent.[17]

This accumulation resulted from the productive use of both domestic and foreign investable resources, encouraged by institutional changes in the public sector and in capital markets. As Table 4.4 shows, investment grew faster than GDP during this period, increasing from 18.4 per cent of GDP in the 1950s to 22.2 per cent in 1973–81. Thereafter capital formation slowed down sharply with Latin America's gross domestic investment in 1990 about one-fifth lower than its 1981 value (and the 1982–90 average ratio of investment in GDP one-quarter lower than the value for 1973–81). This was due to the recessionary adjustments implemented after the debt crisis of 1982, and to the shortage of funds resulting from the negative transfer of financial resources from the region.

It is difficult to compare the investment performances of individual countries because of the different ways in which they are measured.[18]

[16] With the same population growth in both groups of countries by 1990 the difference in favour of the NICs would have been only 64 per cent.

[17] The latter figure corresponds to the period 1960–81, because there are no reliable figures for the 1950s.

[18] Also, there are differences between the investment ratios expressed by 1970 dollars and those in 1980 dollars. This is due to sharp changes in relative prices.

However, the available data indicates the obvious fact that the countries with the best growth performance, like Brazil and Mexico, were those with higher rates of capital accumulation. While these two countries had a combined yearly growth rate in gross fixed capital formation of 8 per cent between 1960 and 1981, in Argentina it only reached 2.9 per cent. Furthermore, Brazil's and Mexico's performances contrast sharply not only with that of Argentina, but also with that of other Latin American countries which followed neo-conservative experiments from the early 1970s. In every one of the sixteen years of the Pinochet dictatorship, for example, Chile's gross fixed capital formation was below the average ratio of the 1960s. That is one of the most important factors explaining why average growth of GDP dropped from a rate of 4.6 per cent per annum between 1961 and 1971 to 2.6 per cent between 1974 and 1989.

According to World Bank data (which only covers the 1968–88 period), Brazil increased its gross domestic investment per capita in real terms from US$170 in 1968 to US$420 in 1978. This indicator fell back to US$330 in 1988 (all figures in 1980 prices). Mexico's figure rose from US$350 to US$550, then declining to US$420, while Argentina only increased gross domestic investment per capita from US$300 in 1968 to US$380 in 1978, falling back to US$200 in 1988. In 1988 Chile had still not recovered the 1968 level of US$420, having dropped to US$320 in 1978 and to a low of US$170 in 1983.

In the 1950s capital accumulation had to be financed mainly out of domestic savings due to the Latin American countries' lack of access to international financial markets. However, as external finance became more freely available, its share began to rise, reaching nearly one quarter of domestic investment in 1981.

One crucial aspect of investment is the origin of capital goods. As a rule, the higher the proportion of capital goods supplied by domestic producers, the more endogenous the growth process; that is, the greater the multiplier effects of investment on output. In most small- and medium-sized Latin American countries, despite the rapid growth rates of ISI, this proportion was still very low at the end of the period studied here. Therefore, increases in investment tended to be associated with rapid growth of imports, exerting pressure on the balance of payments. This was also the case for other inputs associated either directly or indirectly with the investment process. For this reason, governments have frequently concentrated investment efforts in public works and construction, which

Table 4.4. *Latin America: gross fixed capital formation as a percentage of GDP, 1950–90*[a]

	1950–59	1960–72	1973–81	1982–90
Argentina	15.1	19.0	20.8	12.2
Brazil	21.9	19.6	23.6	17.2
Chile	20.6	18.5	14.6	15.7
Mexico	16.7	18.8	22.7	17.8
LATIN AMERICA	18.4	17.9	22.2	16.7

Note: [a] See Table 4.3, note [a].
Source: Data from ECLAC's Statistical Division.

are intensive in domestic inputs. Large countries, like Argentina, Brazil and Mexico, on the other hand, were able to develop important capital goods industries. Brazil, for example, had reduced the imported content of investment to 11 per cent in 1973, while in Argentina the share of imports was below 7 per cent. For Latin America as a whole, the share of imported capital goods in total capital formation fell from 28 per cent in 1950 to 15 per cent in 1973.

After the first oil shock, the imported content of investment rose again, mainly due to the swift increase in imports among the oil exporting countries of the region, the greater availability of foreign credits, and new import liberalization policies in many Latin American countries. Even in Brazil, the country with by far the most advanced domestic capital goods industry, the share of imported capital goods in total imports rose from 19 per cent in 1980 to 29 per cent in 1988.

Another important aspect of the growth process was the transformation of the productive structure. In Latin America, as in other developing areas, rapid economic growth led to a significant drop in the share of agriculture in GDP, falling from nearly 18 per cent in 1950 to 12 per cent in 1973 and 11 per cent in 1981 (a share that remained constant during the 1980s). Parallel to this, there was a rise in the manufacturing sector's share from 18 per cent of GDP in 1950 to 27 per cent in 1973 (see Figure 4.1 above).

These changes in Latin America's productive structure were more marked in fast-growing countries like Brazil and Mexico than in smaller, less developed ones, like those of Central America, where the share of agriculture in GDP only fell from about a third to a quarter during the same period.

With the rapid increase in income per capita which took place during this period, a change in the productive structure in this direction was to be expected from the domestic demand point of view. However, the speed of the change had also to do with the way in which ISI was carried out. From the point of view of comparative advantage, the rapid reduction in the relative size of the agricultural sector in countries such as Argentina and Uruguay (where it was down to 11 per cent of GDP in the 1980s), is difficult to justify. These countries have strong comparative advantages in food crop and livestock farming and are successful exporters of these products. As in the case of other primary export products, a common feature of the development policies of most Latin American countries during this period was a bias against agriculture, particularly through discriminatory exchange-rate policies and declining domestic terms of trade vis-à-vis manufacturing industry. This contrasts sharply with the massive subsidization of agriculture in Europe, the United States and Asia at the time, which narrowed the market for Latin American agricultural exports even further.

Latin American agriculture was extremely heterogeneous.[19] Large modern estates, where technological change and capital accumulation contributed to the raising of productivity levels, co-existed side by side with peasant holdings barely providing minimum subsistence for those who worked on them. While capitalist relations of production transformed commercial farms and plantations into modern enterprises, often the source of substantial foreign exchange revenue, a large share of the rural population still either worked small, self-subsistence plots or were landless seasonal labourers.

Some changes took place during the 1960s and 1970s in at least some Latin American countries that altered the traditional 'latifundia-minifundia' pattern. Some countries undertook radical land reforms that either diminished the importance of or nearly eliminated the old *latifundia* system. This was particularly true in Chile (both under the Frei and Allende governments), Ecuador and Peru. As a result, a new form of

[19] For further discussion of agrarian structures, see chapter 6 by Norman Long and Bryan Roberts in this volume.

small and medium-sized agricultural capitalism emerged, exhibiting a more entrepreneurial approach to management, a stronger interest in technological innovation and investment, and a greater concern for the selection of more appropriate crops. An example of this was the introduction of modern crops like fruit production in the Central Valley of Chile.

Important as they were as an instrument of structural change, land reforms were often limited in scope as far as the agricultural population was concerned. Large groups of peasants did not benefit, because they were not employed on the large estates that were expropriated. For those who were employed on these estates, the possibility of their development as peasant producers was dependent on their access to credit, technological assistance and marketing. Therefore, their success depended critically on whether the new land settlements could be organized into co-operatives, and whether the state was willing and able to adapt public institutions for agricultural development.

There were also land reform reversals as neo-conservative ideologies swept in with authoritarian regimes. The most clear example of this turnabout was in Chile after the 1973 coup. The new government either returned a significant portion of the expropriated land to previous owners, or, when this was not possible, withdrew government support from the peasant settlers and abruptly re-established free-market arrangements. As a result, most of them lost their land.

Agricultural output in Latin America expanded at a slightly higher rate than world agricultural output. The annual average growth between 1960 and 1973 was 3.5 per cent, rising to 3.9 per cent in 1973–81, and then dropping to 1.7 per cent in 1981–90. According to the Food and Agriculture Organisation (FAO), the increase in area of land under cultivation, rather than productivity growth, seems to have been the main factor in raising output. The area cultivated grew from 53 million hectares in the first half of the 1950s to 96 million in 1977 and 111 million in 1987 – an increase of 2.5 per cent and 1.3 per cent per annum, respectively. This increase was concentrated in the Amazonian basin, and, to a lesser extent, in some areas of the Andes. However, irrigated area also increased rapidly at a rate of 3 per cent per annum between the early 1960s and 1980. At the same time land became more intensively used, and productivity on the traditionally fertile lands in temperate zones increased with the introduction of modern technology – both mechanization and the more intensive use of fertilizers and other inputs.

It has been estimated that three-fifths of output growth in the 1970s was due to the increased area under cultivation, and only two-fifths to higher yields. Most of the latter was concentrated in large estates and plantations. As plantations became more capital-intensive and more productive, the productivity gap between plantations and peasant agriculture increased. Productivity growth also slowed down after the 1982 crisis, as a result of lower levels of investment and reduced use of fertilizers.

Notwithstanding the anti-agriculture bias of trade policies, the agricultural sector has played an important (though diminishing) role in Latin America's foreign trade, representing, on average, about one-third of total exports and one-tenth of imports. In several small Latin American countries, agriculture contributed to over half of exports.

Although Latin America has traditionally been a net exporter of agricultural goods, as Table 4.5 shows, imports grew faster than exports until the 1982 debt crisis; from 1961 to 1982 imports grew at a yearly rate of 6.6 per cent while exports did so at only 3.7 per cent. The rapid growth of agricultural imports was mainly caused by rising domestic income, exchange-rate appreciation, import liberalization of farm products, and cheap (subsidized) DMEs' exports. This trend was reversed after the 1982 external financial shock, since imports of agricultural products diminished, while exports grew more rapidly.

There have also been significant changes in the composition of agricultural exports. Soya beans, for example, which in 1969 represented only 1 per cent of agricultural exports, accounted for 16 per cent in 1984, while the relative weights of maize, sugar and cotton dropped. By and large, these variations can be explained by changes in the structure of relative prices and governments' export incentives.

The share of Latin America's exports in the world trade of agricultural products rose from 36 per cent in 1975 to 46 per cent in 1984, and using the three digit International Standard Trade Classification (ISTC) of Latin America's exports, the region supplied between 10 per cent and 59 per cent of world exports in eleven product groups.[20]

Industrialization in Latin America started early in the three larger countries (Argentina, Brazil and Mexico) and in some smaller countries. In

[20] See IDB, *Economic and Social Progress in Latin America* (Washington, D.C., 1986), ch. 9. This source does not provide information prior to 1975.

Table 4.5. *Latin America: foreign trade in agricultural products, 1953 and 1961–88*[a] (at 1980 constant US$ million)

	Imports	Exports	Balance	Imports/exports
(1953)[b]	(3269)	(14795)	(11526)	(0.22)
1961	3293	12716	9423	0.26
1973	8784	26131	17346	0.34
1982	12682	27295	14613	0.47
1988	10723	30295	19572	0.35

Notes:
[a] Includes farm products, livestock, fishing and forestry.
[b] Figures for 1953 are not strictly comparable with those of 1961–88 because they were obtained from a different source and by different methodology.
Sources: 1953, from sources of Table 4.2; 1961–88, from ECLAC. Statistical Division (elaborated by the Joint ECLA-FAO Agricultural Division based on FAO data). Nominal figures were deflated by the wholesale prices index of industrial countries.

Chile, the origins of industrial development can be traced to the second half of the nineteenth century. Later, the disruption of international trade caused by the First World War and the Depression of 1929 gave further stimulus to manufacturing in these countries and encouraged moves towards ISI. Other Latin American countries, on the other hand, did not diversify their domestic economic structure to any significant extent during the nineteenth century, and faced the external disruptions of the 1910s and 1930s with 'passive' orthodox policies.[21] After the Second World War, some medium-sized countries such as Colombia, Peru and Venezuela also moved fully into ISI, achieving high growth rates of manufactures during the 1950s. In the Central American countries, the main stimulus of industrialization was the integration agreement of the 1960s.

Typically, ISI in Latin America started with the production of light consumer goods, then moved to intermediate goods, consumer durables and capital goods. Economies of scale, specialization and the size of the domestic market became increasingly important, and technology grew more complex as ISI progressed towards more advanced stages. Some countries that had begun their ISI earlier, like Argentina and Chile, soon began to encounter difficulties mainly due to the inability to exploit

[21] See, for example, C. Díaz-Alejandro, 'Latin America in the 1930s', in R. Thorp (ed.), *Latin America in the 1930s* (London, 1984); this author focusses particular attention on the difference between 'reactive' and 'passive' countries.

economies of scale given their limited exports of manufactures. These obstacles were reflected in lower growth rates.

As Table 4.6 shows, Latin America obtained high rates of growth of manufactures between 1950 and 1981, with output increasing more than sixfold during the period. This growth rate was faster than the overall growth rate for world manufacturing production (5.7 per cent), which meant that Latin America increased its share in world output during these three decades.

Despite many similarities, there were important differences in performance that should not be overlooked. While Brazil and Mexico achieved nearly a tenfold increase in industrial output, Argentina and Chile could only achieve a threefold increase. Some latecomers to ISI also grew fast: Venezuela was able to reach a yearly growth rate of 7.6 per cent between 1950 and 1973, before falling to 2.4 per cent between 1973 and 1981 (in part due to the 'Dutch disease' emanating from the rise in oil income). Meanwhile, Colombia maintained a stable rate of growth, with an average of 5.9 per cent between 1950 and 1973. Among the smaller countries, the five members of the Central American Common Market also expanded rapidly during this period.

By the end of the 1970s, Latin American countries had reached very different levels of industrialization as measured by the share of manufactures in GDP. In the large countries, between 22 per cent and 32 per cent of GDP came from the manufacturing sector, while in Venezuela and in most of the smaller countries this figure was less than 19 per cent (see Table 4.7). As a rule, this share tended systematically to increase during this period; the exceptions were the countries of the Southern Cone in which the neo-conservative experiments of the mid-1970s brought about a process of de-industrialization. The share of manufacturing in Argentina's GDP was reduced from a peak of 29 per cent to 25 per cent, while in Chile the share declined from 26 per cent in the early 1970s to 21 per cent in 1980.

Notwithstanding the satisfactory performance of the region as a whole between 1950 and 1981 (in relation both to its previous performance and to that of the rest of the world), Latin America's industrialization suffered from a series of problems that frustrated some of the initial expectations. For example, it has been argued that the region was unable to develop an 'endogenous core' of manufacturing activities that might have succeeded in stimulating other sectors of the economy.[22] This was

[22] See for example, F. Fajnzylber, *La Industrialización Trunca* (Mexico, D.F., 1983).

Table 4.6. *Latin America: growth of manufacturing output, 1950–90 (annual average compound growth rates)*

	1950–60	1960–73	1973–81	1950–81	1981–90
Argentina	4.1	5.4	−1.8	3.1	−1.1
Brazil	9.1	8.5	4.5	7.6	1.1
Chile	4.7	4.6	0.9	3.7	2.5
Colombia	6.5	6.7	3.7	5.9	3.5
Mexico	6.2	8.8	6.6	7.4	1.3
Peru	8.0	5.5	2.4	5.5	−2.3
Venezuela	10.0	5.8	1.0	5.9	2.1
Central America[a]	5.7	8.2	3.3	6.1	0.8
Other small countries[b]	3.6	4.4	5.1	4.4	−0.2
LATIN AMERICA	6.6	7.3	3.7	6.1	0.3
Oil exporters	7.1	7.7	5.3	6.9	1.1
Oil importers	6.5	7.1	2.9	5.8	0.1

Notes:
[a] Includes the five countries of the Central American Common Market. [b] Includes seven countries.
Source: Data from ECLAC, Statistical Division.

due partly to domestic policies, such as extreme forms of protectionism and overvalued exchange-rates, and partly to the weaknesses of local entrepreneurs who have been characterized for lacking innovation, 'animal spirits' and a long-run approach to risk-taking. Others have cited the instability of domestic policies that biased investment efforts towards short-run objectives, and the high propensity to consume especially among high-income groups, stimulated by the unequal income distribution of the region and the premature diversification of consumption patterns.[23]

One consequence of these deficiencies has been the weakness of the local technological base for industrial growth. Many technologies used in Latin America were obsolete versions of those used in advanced industrial countries, with indigenous technological adaptation and change concentrated in the largest countries (but even in these countries technological policy did not receive sufficient attention).

In the 1980s, the recession (both at home and abroad) and the debt

[23] See, for example, J. G. Palma and M. Marcel, 'Kaldor on the "Discreet Charm" of the Chilean Bourgeoisie', *Cambridge Journal of Economics*, 13, 1 (1989): 245–72.

Table 4.7. *Latin America: share of the manufacturing sector in GDP, 1950–90 (percentages)*

	1950	1960	1970	1980	1990
Argentina	21.4	24.2	27.5	25.0	21.6
Brazil	23.2	28.6	32.2	33.1	27.9
Chile	20.6	22.1	24.5	21.4	21.7
Colombia	17.2	20.5	22.1	23.3	22.1
Mexico	17.3	17.5	21.2	22.1	22.8
Peru	15.7	19.9	21.4	20.2	18.4
Venezuela	10.2	12.7	17.5	18.8	20.3
Central America[a]	11.5	12.9	15.5	16.5	16.2
LATIN AMERICA	18.4	21.3	24.0	25.4	23.4

Notes:
[a] Includes the five countries of the Central American Common Market.
Sources: ECLAC, *Statistical Yearbook for Latin America and the Caribbean* (Santiago, 1991) and data from ECLAC's Statistical Division. Figures for 1950, 1960 and 1970 in 1970 prices; those for 1980 and 1990 in 1980 prices.

crisis revealed these long-term structural problems in a dramatic fashion, and the sustained industrial growth that the region had exhibited until 1980 came to a sudden halt. In Brazil, for example, manufacturing output fell by nearly 16 per cent between 1980 and 1983, and in the region as a whole it fell by more than 11 per cent. In 1983 only Colombia, Ecuador and the Dominican Republic had a level of manufacturing output larger than that already achieved before the crisis. For most countries the recovery started in 1984 but it was not until 1986 that the region as a whole recovered the level of manufacturing output reached in 1980.

Although the 1980s crisis affected all countries of the region regardless of their previous economic policies, in some cases, such as Argentina and Chile, problems arose much earlier. In these countries, restrictive monetary policies, the high cost of domestic credit, over-valued real exchange rates and drastic reductions in tariff protection in the 1970s caused a sharp decline in output in several branches of the manufacturing sector that was not compensated for by the expansion of other activities. In fact, in per capita terms, in Chile value added in manufactures was by 1981 one-sixth lower than in 1974.

The post-1984 recovery in manufacturing output across the region was stimulated by the expenditure-switching policies (particularly the large exchange-rate depreciations) implemented after the initial 1982–3 expenditure-reducing shock. This initial shock brought about a drastic reduction in imports of manufactured goods; in fact, in 1983–4 the trade deficit in manufactured goods of the eleven member countries of LAIA (the Latin American Integration Agreement) fell below US$10 billion as compared to US$45 billion in 1980–81 (both figures in 1983–4 prices). This was a reversal of the second half of the 1970s' trend, when the trade deficit in manufacturing was rising fast. The post-1984 adjustment favoured the substitution of imported manufactured goods for domestic production and stimulated exports. Notwithstanding the recovery of output and the significant growth of exports, the unstable political and macroeconomic environment, frequent foreign-exchange crises and inflationary bursts kept the level of investment in the manufacturing sector throughout the 1980s below the pre-crisis level.

Industrialization in Latin America has been closely linked to developments in the balance of payments. Events such as the First and Second World Wars and the Depression of the 1930s provided strong incentives for local production of manufactures as the supply of imported manufactured goods was either interrupted or prohibited. However, as domestic production increased and Latin America moved into ISI, the volume and the composition of trade in manufactures was transformed. First, ISI reduced the trade deficit in manufactures (as a percentage of GDP). Second, with ISI domestic production became increasingly dependent on the imports of intermediate and capital goods.

As Figure 4.5 shows, the trade balance in manufactures dropped from a deficit of about 8 per cent of GDP in the early 1950s to around 5 per cent in the late 1960s. Then, after an increase during the first oil shock, the deficit remained relatively stable at around 5–6 per cent of GDP until 1982, when – as a result of the debt crisis – the figure dropped to around 2–3 per cent. In 1953–4 manufactured exports represented 14 per cent of manufactured imports; this figure had increased to 20 per cent in 1965–66, 27 per cent in 1972–3 and over 50 per cent in the mid-1980s.

At the same time, however, ISI increased the dependence of domestic production on imports of intermediate and capital goods. Before ISI, the direct effects of cyclical fluctuations of international demand for primary commodities exported by Latin America were transmitted to the domestic economy mainly through changes in the level of effective demand (both

Figure 4.5. *Latin America: trade balances as a percentage of GDP, 1950–90 (current prices, moving averages)*

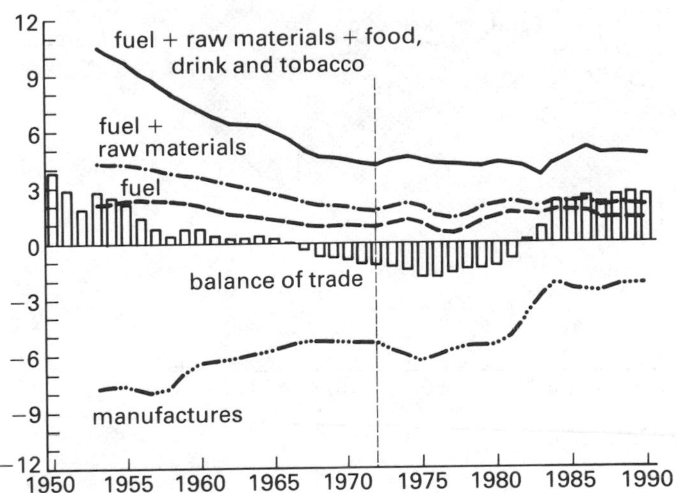

Sources: J. Wells, *Latin America at the Crossroads* (Santiago, 1988) and Table 4.2.

public and private). Later, with ISI, there was a new supply-side connection as the production of manufactures required large amounts of imported intermediate and capital goods. It became increasingly difficult to accommodate external recessive cycles without directly affecting domestic production of manufactures. The development of 'import-intensive' ISI (mainly of inputs without domestic substitutes) brought about a growing rigidity in the demand for imports as reflected by reduced price elasticity of these goods.

The effect of ISI on the demand for imports was strengthened by the structure of protection, which gave low (and often negative) effective protection for the production of intermediate and capital goods. This policy was a disincentive to the domestic production of these goods and encouraged the use of capital intensive technologies.

One effect of the high import requirements of ISI was the fact that despite fast growth in the production of manufactures and a reduction of the trade deficit in these products, imports of manufactures remained at around 70 per cent of total imports until the 1973 oil shock. In the following years, the increased value of oil imports seems to have been balanced by a reduction in the imports of manufactures (see Figure 4.6).

Figure 4.6. *Latin America: structure of imports, 1953–90 (current prices)*

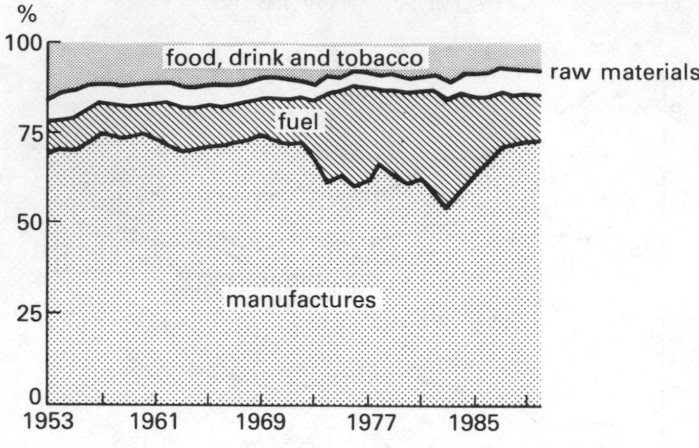

Sources: as in Figure 4.5.

In some countries ISI also led to an increase in imports of food. Wages therefore became more sensitive to the exchange rate and the price of imported food. In part this was a consequence of the structure of protectionism itself, which resulted in a deterioration of the agricultural terms of trade (vis-à-vis the manufacturing sector), a reallocation of investment resources to urban sectors, and a slower growth of agriculture. Slow agricultural growth became an obstacle to industrial development as the trade surplus of this sector decreased rapidly during the 1950s and 1960s.

Another mechanism linking ISI to balance-of-payments problems was the anti-export bias of related trade policies. A pessimistic perception of the possibilities of expanding and diversifying exports (particularly of primary commodities) led to an underestimation of the capacity of exports to serve as a dynamic source for economic growth. With hindsight, it seems clear that Latin American countries were slow to perceive the changes which were gradually taking place in the world economy, as well as in predicting the exhaustion of ISI (as it was being applied in Latin America). The fact is that the emphasis placed by development policies on domestic markets was maintained far too long. Without export subsidies to compensate for price distortions associated with ISI, export activities were in many cases exposed to negative effective protection. This discouraged investment and the diversification of exports which, despite the rapid growth of manufactured exports in the larger countries, remained excessively dependent on a few primary commodities.

Therefore ISI, as applied in Latin American countries during this period, led to a reduced share of the foreign sector in GDP – with a faster fall in the share of exports than of imports, and a growing rigidity in the demand for imports. The result was a structural trend towards larger deficits in the trade balance until the oil shock of 1973–4. Thus, the trade balance changed from a surplus of around 3 per cent in the early 1950s, to a deficit of nearly 2 per cent in 1972 (see Figure 4.5 above).

As a net oil exporter, Latin America as a whole benefited from the price rises of 1973–4 and 1979–80. Moreover, oil-importing countries attempted to increase and diversify exports, particularly into manufactures (see Figure 4.7 below). These two phenomena in association with the recession induced by the debt crisis transformed a trade deficit of around 2 per cent of GDP in the first half of the 1970s into a surplus of around 3 per cent in the second half of the 1980s (with a peak of 4 per cent in 1985).

During the 1960s, there was growing awareness that ISI, despite some important achievements, was not succeeding either in making Latin American economies less vulnerable to external shocks or in reducing their foreign exchange constraints. In fact, in many countries it was absorbing such a large proportion of new investment that many traditional export sectors were relatively stagnant, and manufactured exports were not growing fast enough to compensate for this. As a result, a new consensus began to emerge that ISI needed a greater balance in its trade structure, that it should be more selective and that it was essential rapidly to expand and diversify exports.

At the same time, ECLA actively promoted the creation of a regional Latin American market, convinced that ISI could not effectively progress much further in what it called 'watertight compartments'. Apart from Brazil, Mexico and Argentina, the domestic markets of the Latin American countries were too small to take advantage of economies of scale under modern technologies. Therefore, as we have seen, a process of progressive integration was proposed in which the first steps were the setting up of the Latin American Free Trade Association (LAFTA) and the Central American Common Market (CACM), followed by the Cartagena Agreement. This process of integration made a significant contribution to the growth of manufactured exports in the 1960s and 1970s (see below, section on Latin American Economic Integration).

The international trade boom of the 1960s and the success of the Asian NICs, were also influential factors in the attempt at diversifying Latin American exports. The Latin American countries which had already progressed more in their ISI process were more successful in increasing their manufactured exports. This was particularly the case for Brazil and Mexico, but it also extended to other countries such as Argentina and Colombia. All of them, to different degrees, diversified their exports of manufactured goods within the Latin American markets, as well as outside them. This was the result of the changes that occurred in the Latin American and international markets, as well as of trade policy reforms implemented by some Latin American countries.

Of the policy reforms aimed at encouraging non-traditional exports, the most important were those directed at the real exchange rate, tariffs and export incentives. In relation to exchange rates, the main purpose was to avoid currency appreciation in periods of high inflation and the need for abrupt and unpredictable nominal devaluations. The new policy aimed at greater stability in the real exchange rate via continuous adjustment of nominal values so as to reflect domestic and external inflation and changes in international competitiveness. Different forms of 'crawling-pegs' were established, starting with Chile in 1965. The policy consisted of small and regular rate adjustments to avoid the accumulation of imbalances; this would favour the real side of the economies and discourage the speculative fluctuations that affect the foreign-exchange markets when rates are maintained either fixed in nominal terms or are allowed to fluctuate freely.[24] The new exchange rate policy contributed to stabilizing price relations between domestic and foreign products, and encouraged non-traditional exports which are more sensitive to the level and stability of real exchange rates. This policy was also considered to be a factor contributing to a reduction in 'redundant' protection, which had been used as a buffer against recurrent artificial appreciation in inflation-prone countries.

The tariff reforms were another policy change, tending to replace quantitative restrictions on imports with *ad valorem* tariffs, and to reduce the list of prohibited imports. The quantitative restrictions used in the 1950s had

[24] For a comparative analysis, see John Williamson (ed.), *The Crawling Peg: Past Performance and Future Prospects* (London, 1981).

a series of allocative, distributive and administrative problems. For this reason reforms began to replace or complement those import restrictions with tariffs considered to be more effective, easier to manage and more useful in providing larger public revenues to the government. Tariff reforms, which began to be implemented during the 1960s, also attempted to change the anti-export bias derived from negative effective protection prevailing for many export activities. A third group of economic policies aimed at export promotion consisted of increased public investments in export infrastructure, subsidies and easier access to finance for exporters.

As can be seen in Figure 4.7 and Table 4.8, the results of these policy reforms were very significant. Exports of manufactures, which had been growing at a rate of 3.8 per cent per annum during the 1950s, grew 11.3 per cent per annum between 1960 and 1973, and (after four years of stagnation following the first oil shock) about 15 per cent per annum between 1977 and 1990; that is, Latin America's exports of manufactures in 1990 were 25 *times larger* than those of the early 1950s and exports of semi-manufactures five and a half times larger. As a result, the share of manufactures and semi-manufactures in Latin America's exports rose from 9 per cent in 1952–55 to 12 per cent in 1960, 15 per cent in 1970, one-third in 1980 and nearly 40 per cent in the early 1990s. The country that diversified its exports most was Brazil, with sales from the automobile sector overtaking those of coffee in the 1980s, and manufactures representing over half (52 per cent) of exports in 1990. However, the enlarged role of manufactures was generalized across the region. For instance, in the combined exports of Colombia, Peru, Uruguay and Venezuela the share of manufactures in total exports rose from 1 per cent in 1960 to 10 per cent in 1980 and 17 per cent in 1990.

The main components of agro-industrial exports were in the late seventies canned fruits and fruit juices, coffee extracts and essences, canned meat and chocolate and other foods containing cocoa. Other manufactured exports included clothing (18 per cent), telecommunications equipment (8 per cent), iron and steel products (7 per cent), chemical products (7 per cent), electrical machinery (6 per cent), leather and paper manufactures (5 per cent), footwear (5 percent), vehicles (5 per cent) and motors (5 per cent).[25] As in many other LDCs, in Latin America the growth of manufac-

[25] The percentages correspond to 1978 and refer to the shares in manufactured exports excluding agro-industrial exports. See M. Movarec, 'Exports of Manufactured Goods to the Centres: importance and significance', *CEPAL Review,* 17 (1982): 47–77.

Figure 4.7. *Latin America: structure of exports, 1953–90 (current prices)*

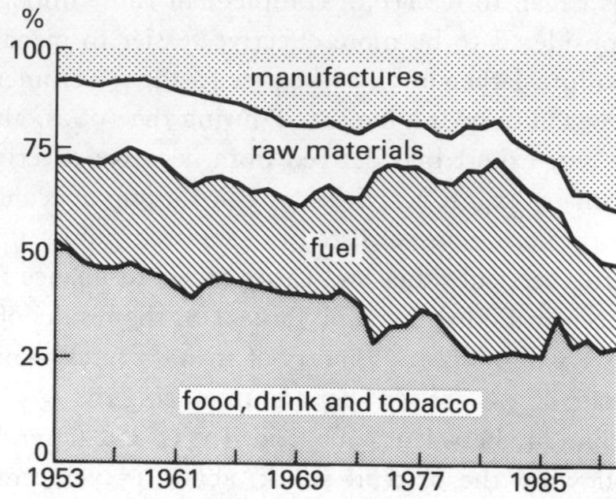

Sources: as in Figure 4.5.

tured exports was also greatly supported by the domestic industrial base generated by the ISI.

One peculiar export sector in Latin America is that of 'maquila' (assembly plant) exports, to be found especially in Mexico and in some Caribbean countries. The contribution of these exports to industrial development of the host country tends to be low, but they provide a significant amount of employment.

The principal DMEs' markets for Latin America's manufactured exports were the United States and some of the European Community countries. LAFTA's share in OECD imports of manufactures practically doubled (from 1.3 per cent to 2.5 per cent) in the period 1971–88. LAFTA's exports of machinery and transport equipment grew particularly fast.

It is important to emphasize that these exports grew fast despite the fact that they encountered an upsurge of protectionism in DMEs during this period. This protectionism, called 'new protectionism' because of its emphasis on non-tariff restrictions, created serious problems for some products. These restrictive practices became widespread with respect to textiles, clothing, footwear and some processed agricultural products in which exports from LDCs were substituting domestic production in DMEs. The irony was that in several Latin American countries, the policy

Table 4.8. *Latin America: composition of exports, 1965–90 (at constant 1991 prices, in US$ billion, and %)*

	1965		1970		1975		1980		1985		1990	
	Value	%	Value	%	Value	%	Value	%	Value	%	Value	%
Primary products	12.53	24.2	13.86	22.9	13.29	27.4	16.38	25.2	22.41	24.9	23.08	22.2
Crude oil	28.43	54.9	31.40	51.9	14.09	29.1	18.22	28.0	21.37	23.7	25.13	24.2
Semi-manufactured products	8.79	17.0	11.12	18.4	13.13	27.1	16.70	25.7	22.23	24.7	24.01	23.1
Manufactured products	1.88	3.6	3.93	6.5	7.60	15.7	13.32	20.5	23.64	26.2	30.66	29.5
Other	0.11	0.2	0.23	0.4	0.34	0.7	0.42	0.7	0.47	0.5	1.11	1.1
TOTAL	51.74	100.0	60.54	100.0	48.45	100.0	65.05	100.0	90.11	100.0	103.99	100.0
Purchasing power of crude oil exports[a]	12.0		10.1		17.2		35.8		43.3		30.6	

Notes: With the exception of the last row, all figures are deflated by their respective price indices, thus reflecting the evolution of the quantum of exports.

[a] Current exports of crude oil, deflated by the price index of DMEs' manufactured exports.

Sources: Data from ECLAC's Economic Development Division.

orientation was precisely the reverse, with quantitative restrictions and other non-tariff mechanisms being gradually removed during these years.

This trade liberalization and the increased share of exports in GDP after 1973, together with financial relaxation, left Latin American economies more vulnerable to (positive and negative) external developments, a phenomenon that became evident in the 1980s. The importance of external instability differed from one country to another, being stronger in countries such as Argentina, Chile and Uruguay (which implemented free trade policies) than in countries with more moderate, 'mixed' policies. As a matter of fact, in 1975 and 1982 Chile was the Latin American country exhibiting the sharpest recession associated to negative external shocks. And yet, in the late 1980s it was the Latin American country with the fastest growth in GDP associated with an improved external environment (increasing export prices and decreasing oil price and external interest rates).

We can conclude this section by pointing out three main characteristics of Latin America's export diversification experience.[26] First, large countries were the most successful ones in this respect; these countries were the ones that followed the most effective ISI and had a more developed industrial base. This phenomenon is similar to the experience of some East Asian countries in their transition from import substitution to export promotion. In the smaller countries favourable exchange rates and other incentives towards export diversification were not as effective as in large, more industrialized economies. It is clear that larger domestic markets helped ISI to take advantage of economies of scale in a wider range of activities. Second, the more successful countries in terms of export diversification were those in which the State intervened actively with measures aimed at export promotion. In other words, as in the case of the NICs, the opening up of ISI was generally carried out by the reorientation of many instruments of direct promotion, such as public investment, subsidies, public financing and tax exemptions, together with the correction of some harmful distortions such as negative effective protection and an artificially appreciated exchange rate. Finally, regional economic integration was another factor that had a significant impact on export promotion and diversification.

[26] See Carlos Díaz-Alejandro, 'Some Characteristics of Recent Export Expansion in Latin America', *Yale Economic Growth Center Papers*, 209 (1974).

LATIN AMERICAN ECONOMIC INTEGRATION

During the 1960s, ambitious attempts were launched in Latin America to reinforce the process of ISI through the integration of regional markets. These processes of integration were the result of a growing awareness that ISI, particularly in the medium-sized and small countries, was beginning to be seriously constrained by the size of domestic markets. From a political and ideological point of view, economic integration was also envisaged as a defence against U.S. economic superiority.

The need for economic integration was from the very beginning an essential component of proposals for Latin American industrialization. As is well known, for ECLA the main lesson from the First World War, the instability of the 1920s, the Depression of the 1930s and the Second World War was the urgent need for the region to industrialize. However, for Prebisch, development from within through ISI was clearly development from *within Latin America as a whole:*

> As progress is made in this direction [ISI], increasingly complex activities will have to be undertaken in which the size of the market is of paramount importance from the point of view of productivity. Thus, if production continues to take place in twenty watertight compartments, as under the present system [of ISI], the return on new capital investments . . . will continue to be lower from that achieved in the great industrial centres with larger markets at their disposal. . . . [As ISI progresses] towards products that can be produced efficiently only in large markets, the necessity to develop intra-Latin American trade asserts itself.[27]

Prebisch was convinced that by progressively opening up domestic markets *within the region* the newly emerging industries would benefit from both larger markets and competition with their regional peers – competition that would restore the discipline of the market into ISI.[28]

The process of economic integration in Latin America passed through three distinct stages. The first (the 1960s and early 1970s) was characterized by extensive state intervention, and timetables for both the gradual

[27] R. Prebisch, *The Latin American Common Market* (New York, 1959), pp. 18 and 378.

[28] For Prebisch regional integration had this dual purpose, to enlarge the market to a viable size and to restore a minimum degree of 'healthy' competition with ISI. For example, as early as 1959 he strongly criticized the excessively high levels of tariffs operating in most countries of the region: 'The return to the use of tariffs as a flexible instrument of protection [that is, not simply as an instrument to indiscriminately exclude imports], the lowering of intra-regional duties in some cases, and their abolition in others, would do much to restore the spirit of competition, to the great advantage of industrialization' (Prebisch, *The Latin American Common Market,* p. 8).

elimination of intra-regional trade barriers and movements towards the establishment of common external tariffs. Subsequently, by the late-1970s, frustration with the growing gap between the high initial expectations and the actual achievements of the first phase of integration brought on a period of reaction and consolidation. During this second stage, Latin American countries abandoned their earlier targets and adopted a more cautious approach, based primarily on bilateral trade agreements with a partial scope. The onset of the third stage of integration, the new wave of regional integration in the late 1980s and early 1990s was concurrent with the transformation of trade and industrialization policies. It was no longer viewed as a stimulus for ISI and as an instrument of 'collective defence' of Latin American markets from foreign competition; instead, closer cooperation was seen as a lever on world markets to boost the market shares of Latin American exports, particularly in the industrialized nations.

The first stage of integration policy consisted of three separate attempts in Latin America and one in the Caribbean at forming regional trade organizations. These organizations together included most Latin American countries and 95 per cent of the region's population, GDP and international trade. In 1960 the Central American Common Market (CACM) agreement was signed; it eventually included Costa Rica, El Salvador, Guatemala, Honduras and Nicaragua. In the same year, the Latin American Free Trade Association (LAFTA) was formed; this was the largest of the region's groupings and came to include all Hispanic South America, Brazil and Mexico. In 1969, Bolivia, Colombia, Chile, Ecuador and Peru (with Venezuela joining four years later) established the Andean Common Market (ANCOM), the most ambitious attempt at economic integration; its members retained their links with LAFTA. In turn, the Caribbean countries formed the Caribbean Free Trade Area (CARIFTA), later replaced by the more ambitious Caribbean Community (CARICOM). Table 4.9 shows the relative importance in terms of population, GDP and trade of each of these groupings.

The momentum gained by the initial surge of activity in the 1960s was weakened subsequently by domestic political setbacks and the economic shocks of the 1970s. Military coups in Brazil and Argentina disturbed the progress of LAFTA; similarly, the violent military takeover in Chile in 1973 placed serious obstacles in the path of the Andean group. On the economic front, the 1973 oil shock drove a wedge between oil exporters – such as Ecuador, Mexico and Venezuela – and most of their common market partners. Oil exporters, facing an abundance of foreign exchange and a contraction of their non-oil tradable sector (the so-called 'Dutch disease'), found it increasingly difficult to produce non-oil exports for their regional partners. At the same time, all countries in the region took advantage of easy access to cheap foreign loans during the second half of the 1970s, thereby reducing the need to earn foreign exchange through exports. The 1982 debt crisis also worked against the expansion of regional trade, as countries set up import restrictions to conserve foreign exchange, prompting retaliation by their neighbours.

Despite these problems, economic interdependence has in fact grown substantially since the 1950s. Economic integration arrangements have had a positive effect on regional trade in manufactured goods and trade financing.

The Latin American Free Trade Association (LAFTA)

Efforts in the 1950s to establish a regional trade organization as intra-Latin American trade actually declined (from 11 per cent of the region's trade in 1953–5 to 6 per cent in 1961) culminated in the Treaty of Montevideo in 1960. Signed by seven Latin American countries (despite strong U.S. reservations), the treaty called for the creation of a Latin American free trade area within twelve years. LAFTA members were gradually to eliminate tariffs and other trade restrictions in annual rounds of negotiations, working within the general rules regulating economic integration agreements for members of the General Agreement on Tariffs and Trade (GATT).

Considerable progress was made towards the elimination of trade barriers over the course of the first three annual rounds of negotiations. By the mid-1960s, levels of intra-LAFTA trade had already regained their post-war high. Following this brief period of success, however, negotiations stalled. The stalemate was attributable to three main features: (a) shortcomings within the Treaty of Montevideo itself; (b) a lack of political will among several key member countries; and (c) antagonism to trade liberalization by import substituters seeking to maintain monopoly control over key domestic markets.

The Treaty of Montevideo itself contained several major problems. First was the failure to include effective mechanisms to bring about common

Table 4.9. *Latin American and Caribbean common markets: Population, GDP, GDP per capita and Imports, 1960–90*

	Population (millions)				Gross domestic product (at 1980 constant US$ billions)			
	1960	1970	1980	1990	1960	1970	1980	1990
1. Latin American Free Trade Association (LAFTA)[a]	184.4	242.8	308.9	380.4	222.4	384.4	678.5	760.4
2. Andean Group[b]	41.2	55.5	71.8	92.0	52.6	90.9	119.7	147.4
3. Central American Common Market (CACM)[c]	11.2	15.2	20.2	26.2	7.1	12.0	18.4	20.1
4. Caribbean Community (CARICOM)[d]	3.3	3.8	4.4	4.8	n.a.	7.4	9.8	9.1
5. Others[f]	8.0	10.4	13.1	16.1	3.7	6.2	11.3	12.8
TOTAL[g]	203.6	268.4	342.2	422.7	233.2	402.6	708.2	793.4

	GDP per capita (at 1980 constant US$)				Imports[b] (at 1980 constant US$ millions)			
	1960	1970	1980	1990	1960	1970	1980	1990
1. Latin American Free Trade Association (LAFTA) [a]	1206	1583	2196	1999	24388	38503	80123	76872
2. Andean Group [b]	1277	1636	1667	1602	6869	10752	21066	16552
3. Central American Common Market (CACM) [c]	637	789	913	767	1753	3372	7542	7812
4. Caribbean Community (CARICOM) [d]	n.a.	1971	2245	1902	440	1799	3695	3400[e]
5. Others [f]	462	594	862	797	876	2330	4833	4958
TOTAL [g]	1145	1500	2070	1877	27017	44205	92499	89642

Note:

[a] Argentina, Brazil, Chile, Mexico, Paraguay, Uruguay and the Andean countries (in 1980 LAFTA became LAIA, Latin American Integration Area)

[b] Bolivia, Colombia, Ecuador, Peru and Venezuela.

[c] Costa Rica, El Salvador, Guatemala, Honduras and Nicaragua.

[d] Barbados, Guyana, Jamaica and Trinidad and Tobago.

[e] Approximate value.

[f] Includes only Dominican Republic, Haiti and Panama.

[g] Because of lack of comparable data, it excludes Cuba and the Caribbean community.

[h] Includes both imports from group partners and from the rest of the world.

Sources: ECLAC, *Statistical Yearbook for Latin America,* various issues, and ECLAC's database.

external tariffs. Second, the Treaty lacked adequate measures to achieve an equitable distribution of benefits among member countries. Finally, insufficient attention was paid to the need to harmonize economic policies among participants.[29]

The original treaty was modified in 1968 with the signing of the Protocol of Caracas (Venezuela having joined LAFTA in 1966). The protocol extended the target for complete trade liberalization to 1980. Like the Resolution of 1964, however, the protocol was never put into practice.

However, innovative financial arrangements and the so-called 'Complementary Agreements' did allow significant progress in financial and trade agreements from the mid-1960s onwards. The 'Agreement on Multilateral Settlements and Reciprocal Credit', including all LAFTA countries and the Dominican Republic, was promoted by the Central Banks of member countries. It aimed to foster a direct relationship between Latin American commercial banks, in order to avoid having to use external financial intermediaries in their reciprocal dealings; it also intended to improve credit availability for reciprocal trade in countries with balance of payments problems. Initially, two-thirds of reciprocal trade was settled under this multilateral payment system, a figure which reached over 80 per cent by 1980. In all, more than US$60 billion were channelled through this system between 1965 and 1985.

The main mechanism by which this system worked was that the Central Banks of those countries with positive balance in reciprocal trade would grant credits to those countries with a deficit. Every four months debtor countries would settle their debts. An important result of this financial mechanism was the growing interconnection among local banks and the encouragement to reciprocal trade resulting from credit availability.

In the 'Complementary Agreements', two or more member countries could agree to liberalize the trade of a specific group of commodities and establish other mechanisms to foster reciprocal trade. The 'Complementary Agreements' took place mainly in sectors in which output was diversified within the firms, making intra-firm specialization feasible. Frequently, agreements were reached between subsidiaries of foreign multinationals, most of which had such subsidiaries in more than one country. After 1964 most of the limited additional liberalization that took place was implemented via new 'Complementary Agreements'. By

[29] Non-reciprocal tariff preferences were established in favour of Bolivia, Ecuador, Paraguay, and Uruguay, but they proved to be insufficient in achieving a fair distribution of the benefits of integration among member countries. Uruguay used these preferences more actively.

1970 eighteen Agreements had been subscribed, all relating to manufactured goods.

Despite the loss of momentum after 1964, LAFTA persevered, even managing some additional tariff reductions at annual negotiation rounds. Indeed, despite all the problems, the share of intra-LAFTA trade in total trade of LAFTA members doubled between 1962–4 (10 per cent) and 1979–81 (20 per cent).

The increase in intra-LAFTA trade can be traced to four factors. First, there was a lag of a few years between the adoption of tariff preferences and their use by exporting countries, as market channels needed to be established, product designs adjusted, production bottlenecks overcome and information made available on regional trade opportunities. Second, financial arrangements initiated in 1966 facilitated an increase in trade among member countries. Third, the improvements in access to information, marketing and financial channels benefited all intra-LAFTA trade, including products not covered by tariff agreements. Fourth, trade between members of the Andean Pact grew particularly quickly after the creation of this group in 1969.

As shown in Table 4.10, an important feature of the growth of intra-LAFTA trade was the rapid increase of manufactures – from 10.6 per cent of total regional trade in 1960 to 46.1 per cent in 1980. The growth of manufactured exports to LAFTA partners was particularly strong in Argentina, Brazil and Mexico.[30] In Brazil, for example, exports of manufactures to LAFTA countries comprised 80 per cent of its total intra-LAFTA exports in 1980, more than double the share of manufactures in total Brazilian exports.[31]

Between 1965 and 1980 exports of basic foodstuffs and raw materials fell from 41 to 25 per cent of total intra-Latin American exports, while the share of manufactures rose from 27 to 52 per cent. This shift towards manufactures took place despite the fact that food and raw material exports increased at a rate of 5.2 per cent per annum from 1965 to 1980.

To sum up, although LAFTA's achievements fell far short of the goals set out in the original Montevideo Treaty, the agreement did in fact contribute significantly to the expansion of intra-regional trade. The most

30 The figure for Mexico decreases after the large increase in the share of oil in its total exports towards the end of the 1970s.

31 In 1980, Brazilian exports of manufactures to the rest of Latin America were five times larger than its corresponding imports. One reason for this is that Brazil is a more closed economy than the LAFTA average; in that year, total exports of goods represented only 8 per cent of Brazilian GDP while the figure was 15 per cent for the rest of LAFTA.

Table 4.10. *LAFTA (LAIA) and CACM: shares of manufactures in total and intra-regional trade, 1960–90 (percentages calculated on the basis of current US$)*

	1960		1970		1980		1982		1985		1990	
	Total Mfg exp./ Total Exports (1)	Intra-reg. Mfg exp./ Intra-reg. Exports (2)	Total Mfg exp./ Total Exports (3)	Intra-reg. Mfg exp./ Intra-reg. Exports (4)	Total Mfg exp./ Total Exports (5)	Intra-reg. Mfg exp./ Intra-reg. Exports (6)	Total Mfg exp./ Total Exports (7)	Intra-reg. Mfg exp./ Intra-reg. Exports (8)	Total Mfg exp./ Total Exports (9)	Intra-reg. Mfg exp./ Intra-reg. Exports (10)	Total Mfg exp./ Total Exports (11)	Intra-reg. Mfg exp./ Intra-reg. Exports (12)
LAFTA (LAIA)	3.4	10.6	9.8	33.4	17.3	46.1	10.4	26.6	24.8	45.8	33.0	51.3
Argentina	4.1	6.6	14.2	33.0	23.2	43.7	24.2	42.1	21.4	36.8	29.3	45.3
Brazil	2.2	8.4	13.2	47.3	37.2	79.9	38.3	71.7	43.7	77.4	51.8	82.9
Mexico	15.7	65.6	32.5	75.4	11.9	50.2	9.4	28.4	27.1	37.0	43.7	75.9
CACM	3.7	26.3	21.2	74.5	23.8	77.2	22.1	76.1	17.5	76.3	23.1	69.8
LATIN AMERICA[a]	3.4	12.6	10.7	40.5	17.7	47.3	11.5	33.4	24.4	48.2	26.7	52.6

Note: [a] Excludes Cuba and the Caribbean countries

Sources: Column 1 ECLA, *Statistical Yearbook for Latin America,* Santiago de Chile, various issues.
Column 2 ECLA, *Dirección y Estructura del Comercio Latinoamericano* (Santiago, 1984).
Columns 3 to 12, United Nations Statistical Information System, COMTRADE databank.

outstanding gains were scored in the manufacturing sector, as LAFTA aided some regional producers in their efforts to secure markets and increase capacity utilization.

The Andean Pact

The Cartagena Agreement establishing the Andean Pact was signed in 1969 by Bolivia, Chile, Colombia, Ecuador and Peru, with Venezuela joining the group four years later. As in LAFTA, an initial period of optimism was soon overtaken by events. The most significant setback was the 1973 coup d'état in Chile. Although the latter withdrew completely from the Pact in 1976, the remaining members never regained the group's early momentum.

The Andean Pact was designed to work within LAFTA, rather than supersede it. In terms of levels of economic development, the Andean countries were relatively homogenous compared to the larger grouping: the multiple of largest to smallest country GDP among Andean countries was nineteen in 1980, as opposed to nearly fifty among LAFTA members. By negotiating trade and tariff agreements with Argentina, Brazil and Mexico as a single economic unit, Andean countries hoped to make greater progress towards regional integration.

Moreover, with the LAFTA experience behind them, participants in the Cartagena Agreement were able to incorporate institutional arrangements which they considered superior to those established under the Treaty of Montevideo. First, provision was made for an executive body (Junta del Acuerdo de Cartagena – JUNAC) with substantive powers. Second, the new treaty set out a clear schedule for trade liberalization including the gradual establishment of common external tariffs. Third, a system was designed to achieve an equitable distribution of benefits, comprising both sectoral programmes for industrial development and tariff preferences for the least developed members, Bolivia and Ecuador. Finally, the agreement sought to harmonize economic policies, beginning with rules pertaining to foreign direct investment.

Intra-Andean trade was to be liberalized based on four categories, with separate tariff-reduction mechanisms for each category. Tariffs were abolished on goods not produced within the Pact, and on goods included within the first tranche of the LAFTA Common List. At the same time, some 30 per cent of all products were reserved for 'Sectoral Programmes for Industrial Development', and each of these programmes included a separate set of liberalization guidelines. Trade restrictions on all remaining goods (nearly two-thirds of all items) were to be gradually reduced from 1971 onwards, with the proviso that each country could postpone the commencement of liberalization for up to 5 per cent of products (about 250 items).

The Cartagena Agreement established that internal tariffs of the latter group of products were to be reduced by 10 per cent per year, and phased out altogether by 1981. However, this schedule was repeatedly revised. None the less, by 1979 the maximum tariff applied by Colombia, Peru and Venezuela to reciprocal trade of this large group of items was 32 per cent, while the average tariff was 14 per cent (only one-third of the 1969 value).

The Pact's Common External Tariff (CET), implemented gradually from 1971 in 1976, set a so-called 'minimum common external tariff' covering all tradable products. Under the minimum CET, members could not charge duties on imports from outside the region lower than the agreed rates; however, higher duties were permissible for a limited period.

Industrial planning was to be facilitated by the 'Sectoral Programmes for Industrial Development' (SPID). Under these schemes, the production of selected goods was assigned to member countries along with a guarantee that the regional market would be free from internal import restrictions and would be covered by a common external tariff on extra-regional imports. Products covered by the SPID were to be selected based on economic and technological criteria (including scale economies).

Implementation of SPID did not live up to initial ambitious expectations, largely due to the changing policy environment of the 1970s. The availability of cheap foreign funding encouraged exchange-rate appreciation and weakened efforts to promote the production of local tradables and to rationalize existing ISI activities. At the same time, while policy on direct investment by transnational corporations (TNCs) had been framed with the understanding that regional integration offers substantial benefits to TNCs in improved access to enlarged markets, concern that benefits from direct investment accrued mostly to TNCs at the expense of host countries led to changes in foreign investment policy. The adoption of the landmark 'Decision 24' established strict, uniform regulations for foreign direct investment in member countries markets.

Nevertheless, the overall trade impact of the ANCOM agreements was largely positive during the 1970s. Intra-Pact exports of manufactures

Table 4.11. *Andean Pact: Total and intra-Andean exports, 1970–86 (at 1980 constant US$ million, annual average compound growth rates, and %)*

	1970	1980	1986	1970–80 (%)	1980–86 (%)
Total Exports					
All products	16911	30082	14578	5.9	−7.0
Manufactures	1662	3235	2013	6.9	−4.6
Intra-Andean Exports					
All products	1406	4640	1654	12.7	−9.8
Manufactures	248	1161	618	16.7	−6.1
Share of Intra-Andean Exports in Total Exports (%)					
All products	8.3	15.4	20.8	–	–
Manufactures	14.9	35.9	36.7	–	–

Source: ECLAC's International Trade Division; oil excluded. Current dollar figures were deflated by the export price index of Latin America's non-oil exporting countries.

increased at an annual rate of 24 per cent, while manufactured exports to non-Pact countries grew by a respectable 14.2 per cent. By 1980 the Andean market absorbed 36 per cent of all manufactured exports by member countries (see Table 4.11).

The Central American Common Market (CACM)

The formation of the Central American Common Market (CACM) can be traced back to 1951 with the creation of the Central American Economic Cooperation Committee and the efforts to bring about a convergence of several bilateral free trade agreements. This committee drew up the Multilateral Treaty on Free Trade and Economic Integration, signed in 1958. This was followed by a more ambitious agreement between El Salvador, Guatemala, Honduras and Nicaragua, the General Treaty for Central American Integration, which took effect from 1960 and formed the basis of the Central American Common Market, which Costa Rica joined in 1963.

The General Treaty of 1960 agreed on free trade in 95 per cent of all goods considered, and called for the removal of remaining tariff barriers by 1966 and an agreement on a common external tariff. The Treaty also included the 'Agreement on Integration Industries', which in the end had a very limited impact. It sought to achieve economies of scale in certain key industries by limiting entry and freeing trade among members. Tax incentives and external tariff protection were to be granted to these industries, which were to be distributed equally among member countries. The agreement also provided for the harmonization of fiscal incentives to industry; incentives would be given to firms using raw materials of domestic origin or those making a substantial contribution to the regional balance of payments. The Common Market also included provisions for Central American Monetary Union, initially intended for co-ordinating regional foreign exchange and monetary policy. Success on this front, however, has been limited to co-ordination of multilateral payments.

Table 4.12 shows that the CACM achieved important successes during the 1960s, with the share of intra-CACM exports reaching 28 per cent of total exports and 96 per cent of total manufactured exports in 1970.[32] Progress in trade was much more significant in the CACM than in the Latin American Integration Agreement (LAIA). Since industrialization took place for the most part simultaneously with the integration process, vested interests grew as a force in favour of intra-regional trade. It was a case of integration-led ISI. Contrary-wise, in LAIA, the efforts to foster intra-regional trade in many cases were defeated by the vested interests built during the earlier national phase of ISI between the 1930s and 1950s.

The CACM achieved a broad liberalization of reciprocal trade and a common external tariff. However, it faced mounting problems towards the end of the 1970s. Both export growth and investment were distributed unequally among members, with Guatemala, Costa Rica and El Salvador benefiting the most; some differences also remained in tariff protection and fiscal incentives for local industries. Moreover, competing interpretations of the agreement on 'integrated industries' and strong opposition from the U.S. private sector to this investment scheme resulted in its abandonment early on with only two firms having been created.

At the end of the 1970s, Honduras became the first country to reimpose tariffs on imports from Central American partners, responding to a large imbalance in its intra-CACM trade. It was, however, the debt crisis of the early 1980s which brought the shares of all intra-CACM trade in total

[32] Figures from ECLA's International Trade Division.

exports down from 28 per cent in 1980 to 14 per cent in 1986, and that of manufactures from 85 per cent in 1980 to 69 per cent in 1986. In this sense, Central America faced in the 1980s a similar type of problem to the rest of Latin America. The sharp recession discouraged reciprocal trade more intensively than that with extraregional markets. Given the large share that manufactures had captured in intraregional exports, the manufacturing sector suffered a significant impact with the drop of reciprocal trade.

The negative effect of the economic crisis was reinforced by political events. In fact, particularly due to Honduras and El Salvador's support to the 'contras' in Nicaragua, the CACM came close to a final breaking-point at the end of the 1980s. Nevertheless the process of integration survived the turmoil. After the change of regime in Nicaragua, the CACM countries launched a new integration agreement in 1990, the 'Comunidad Económica Centroamericana'.

The 1980s

By the 1970s it had become apparent that economic integration, despite significant achievements, had failed to fulfill its early promise; in particular, it had not been allowed to provide the strong stimuli and challenge required by economies in advanced stages of ISI, especially in the small and medium-sized countries; in fact, it was proving to be ISI's 'weakest link'. Conflicts of interests, economic policy instability within the countries of the region, external pressures (particularly from the U.S. private sector and government), and shortsighted domestic industrial groups (which often preferred the monopolistic control of their own small national markets than ISI's long-term viability and the discipline of a regional market), had all been growing obstacles to the process of integration. Furthermore, for governments embarking on the neo-liberal experiments of the 1970s and 1980s, particularly in the Southern Cone, integration came to be seen as another form of protectionism, and was therefore rejected from an ideological point of view.

Intra-regional trade declined sharply during the 1980s. Although total and intra-regional exports continued to rise until 1981, the debt shock of 1982 led to a drastic fall in trade among Latin American countries. For example, in real terms, the 1985–6 level of intra-Latin American exports was less than two-thirds of the 1981 level (US$7.5 billion and US$11.9 billion, respectively).

Table 4.12. *CACM: Total and intra-CACM exports, 1970–86 (at 1980 constant US$ million, annual average compound growth rates, and %)*

	1970	1980	1986	1970–80 (%)	1980–86 (%)
Total Exports					
All products	3437	4390	3074	2.5	−3.5
Manufactures	740	1151	447	4.5	−9.0
Intra-CACM exports					
All products	964	1240	439	2.6	−9.9
Manufactures	708	974	310	3.2	−10.8
Share of Intra-CACM Exports in Total Exports (%)					
All products	28.0	28.2	14.3	--	--
Manufactures	95.7	84.6	69.3	--	--

Source: ECLAC's International Trade Division. Current dollar figures were deflated by the export price index of Latin America's non-oil exporting countries.

Also, in 1986 both intra-Andean and intra-CACM exports were just over one-third the 1980 level (with non-oil intra-regional trade falling by 56 per cent in 1983 alone). Overall, the ratio of regional to total exports returned to levels similar to those of the late 1960s.

A major factor in the decrease in regional exports was the steep decline in import capacity throughout the region. Contraction of domestic demand associated with orthodox adjustment policies caused a generalized reduction of imports. Import restrictions, including goods from regional trading partners, were reintroduced as a means of conserving scarce foreign exchange. In addition, large-scale currency devaluations discouraged imports. Although simultaneous devaluations in most Latin American countries meant that relative prices among them remained broadly stable, exchange rate realignment with the industrial countries reduced the relative costs of Latin American exports outside the region, contributing to an increase in the volume of extra-regional exports.[33]

During the economic downturn of the 1970s in the DMEs, regional trade was an anti-cyclical adjustment mechanism, as exports were redirected to Latin American trading partners. In the 1980s, however, Latin

[33] In nominal terms, manufactured exports to non-Latin American countries rose by 66 per cent between 1980 and 1985, while those to the region fell by 38 per cent during the same period.

American countries endeavoured to reduce imports from all sources. This must be viewed as a missed opportunity, since intra-regional trade could have provided expanded export outlets and made available essential imports; this could have permitted higher levels of capacity utilization, particularly in manufactures, thus reducing the heavy costs of adjustment in the 1980s.

This period also saw a reassessment of the entire integration project. Fixed targets, regional planning and coordination of direct foreign investment policies were rejected in favour of a more 'informal' approach to integration, expressed in bilateral agreements with a partial scope. The new Montevideo Treaty of 1980 (in which LAFTA was transformed into LAIA, the Latin American Integration Agreement) reflected this atmosphere. In this respect, it is significant that this change occurred *before* the 1982 debt crisis, that is, because of pessimism regarding the role and potentialities of economic integration, and of drastic changes in economic ideology rather than as a result of the debt crisis. In turn, in 1987, the former Andean Pact countries joined in the 'Protocolo de Quito' which revised the group's integration schedule. In Central America, although continued political tension between the Sandinista government in Nicaragua and the U.S.-supported regimes in Honduras and El Salvador made it particularly difficult to produce a new CACM treaty, a presidential summit in 1990 launched a new integration agreement, the Comunidad Económica Centroamericana. The main objectives of this new scheme were to preserve earlier gains and to proceed via bilateral agreements.

The 1980 Montevideo Treaty was also an attempt to salvage some of the gains of integration on the basis of bilateral agreements. Of the US$2.2 billion of intra-regional imports covered by trade preferences by 1984, 84 per cent were carried out under bilateral agreements. Another feature of the new LAIA grouping was the endorsement of bilateral agreements with countries from outside the region. Mexico, for example, signed bilateral accords (including non-reciprocal tariff and non-tariff preferences) with Costa Rica, Cuba, Nicaragua and Panama. Argentina, Colombia and Venezuela entered similar agreements with several Central American countries.

Despite the decline in Andean Pact trade, some aspects of the liberalization programme were continued. Colombia and Peru eliminated all internal tariffs, although some non-tariff barriers were increased. Another sign of progress (albeit largely symbolic) within the Pact was the debut in 1985 of the use of the 'peso andino' – a six-month note tied to the LIBOR and issued by the Andean Reserve Fund – to settle imbalances among Andean countries within LAIA.

In Central America, the increase in political tensions posed obstacles to the CACM process. However, it was the debt crisis that was the main factor discouraging regional trade. In addition, low international prices for the region's commodity exports (coffee, sugar, cotton), and the general overvaluation of CACM currencies, generated increased pressures for protection. During the 1980s import barriers were raised and bilateral agreements replaced CACM mechanisms.

The most outstanding bilateral agreement of the 1980s was the 'Argentina-Brazil' accord of July 1986, covering issues as varied as the renegotiation of tariff preferences, binational firms, investment funds, bio-technology, economic research and nuclear coordination. Of the 'sixteen protocols' signed, the most significant was 'Protocol Number One' that dealt with the production, trade and technological development of capital goods. The stated goal of this measure was to establish a customs union covering half of all capital goods.

Another experiment in economic integration was the Caribbean Basin Initiative, conceived by the Reagan administration as a further way of isolating Nicaragua and Cuba. It consisted of Costa Rica, Honduras, El Salvador, Guatemala, Panama and the Caribbean region (except Guyana and Cuba). This agreement provided for duty-free access to the American market (excluding textiles, garments, footwear, leather apparel, work gloves, canned tuna, petroleum products, watches and watch parts) for twelve years. Sugar, however, a major commodity export from the Caribbean, remained subject to import quotas. To qualify, goods must be exported directly to the U.S. and have a minimum domestic value added of 35 per cent. However, since 80 per cent of the region's exports were already covered by special agreements, the new facility increased the list by only 15 per cent. Costa Rica and the Dominican Republic benefited most from investments encouraged by the new scheme, as capital moved into the electronics, fisheries, wood and furniture industries, as well as some non-traditional agricultural products such as strawberries, melons and cut flowers.

A more ambitious proposal was put forward by the Bush administration in 1990. Presented as the U.S. President's 'Initiative of the Americas', the stated objective of the plan was the creation of a free-trade zone stretching 'from the Port of Anchorage to Pantagonia'. The first step was envisaged as a free trade zone including Canada, the U.S. and Mexico – the North

American Free Trade Agreement, NAFTA, with ambitions to encompass all Latin America at some unspecified future date.[34]

The irony of the Bush administration's proposal was that it represented a complete reversal of the initial motivation for integration in the 1950s. Economic integration was then envisaged both as an essential stimulus to ISI and as a creative defense against U.S. economic superiority and expansionism, and was therefore opposed by that country (with the exception of the Alliance for Progress period). Could it be that the most successful regional economic integration scheme would be developed at the behest of a U.S. president?

Over a period of three decades Latin American countries had launched a range of initiatives to achieve economic integration. These initiatives have taken a variety of forms. Most achieved some degree of initial success, but stalled in the later stages of negotiations when they moved into areas where conflicts of interest were more pronounced. With the benefit of hindsight, it is apparent that many of the goals set out in the original agreements were overly ambitious and in some cases economically and politically naive. The inability of the various groupings to meet standard objectives undoubtedly damaged the credibility of the entire integration project, and generated frustrations which hampered attempts to achieve more practical goals.

Another major problem was the inability or unwillingness of the larger, more developed countries to take a leadership role in the integration process. Moreover, these countries did not do enough to dispel doubts among the smaller and poorer countries that the benefits of increased regional trade would be shared by all country members. Domestic political and economic obstacles were also important. In many countries, domestic producers were reluctant to surrender monopoly control over local markets. Thus, they were prepared to relinquish the long-term viability of ISI for short-term gains.

The lack of commercial, financial and infrastructural ties prior to these efforts did not augur well for the kind of rapid, comprehensive integration sought under the various agreements. In addition, the emphasis on tariff reduction as the principal mechanism of integration was

[34] A free trade zone between the United States, Canada and Mexico would be the largest in the world; in 1990 these three countries had a US$6.2 trillion combined GDP and US$720 billion combined exports. The U.S.'s main interest for a free trade zone with Mexico seems to follow Samuelson's old hypothesis that free trade in commodities is a perfect substitute for factor mobility; in other words, the more commodities 'migrate' across the U.S.-Mexico border, the less Mexican workers will want to do the same.

misplaced when non-tariff obstacles accounted for a large share of trade barriers.

Despite these problems, some important gains were made. Until the 1980s crisis, intra-regional exports had doubled as a share of total Latin American exports. Achievements were more substantial in the CACM than in the Andean Pact and LAFTA; but even in the latter, intra-regional trade expanded significantly, allowing for some specialization and increasing rates of capacity utilization. Furthermore, the more dynamic export activities in terms of intra-regional trade were those with larger domestic value added. However, its main setback was not to be able to provide ISI, particularly in the smaller and medium-sized countries, with the essential 'critical mass' market and degree of competition required for it to succeed in the long run.

In the last analysis the main obstacles to regional economic integration were the same that constrained economic development in general in Latin America during this period, namely lack of continuity in economic policies, abrupt political and economic changes, short-sightedness of most entrepreneurial groups, over-ambitious expectations, external shocks and the foreign debt crisis.

EXTERNAL FINANCING AND DOMESTIC ADJUSTMENT

The size and composition of capital flows into Latin America changed substantially during the four decades from 1950 to 1990. As Table 4.13 shows, direct foreign investment represented nearly 60 per cent of all capital movements during the 1950s, while in the 1960s the focus shifted to official lending. Net capital flows (which, except for errors and omissions, should be equal to the deficit in current account) were low in both decades, fluctuating between 1 and 2 per cent of GDP. Bank lending was limited mostly to trade credit, but with an upsurge of loans by the late 1960s. Net financial transfers (total net capital flows minus profit and interest payments) were also small in the 1950s and 1960s.

During the 1970s vigorous recycling of OPEC surpluses and a generalized increase in international liquidity encouraged lending by private transnational banks. Net capital movements to Latin America rose rapidly: in real terms, the annual average for 1974–81 was four times that of 1966–70. New loans were for the most part provided without conditionality. Although this phenomenon of easy access to bank loans was common to all developing regions, in Latin America the inflow of foreign capital was more marked, and as a result it had a greater impact on domestic policies and national development.

At the beginning of the 1980s Latin America had the largest stock of debt in the Third World. It also had accommodated more of its consumption and production patterns to the abundance of foreign credit (as if this were to be a permanent state of affairs). This placed Latin America in a vulnerable position vis-à-vis developments in the international economy. As a consequence, during the international financial crisis of the 1980s, Latin America paid a high price for allowing, in Kindleberger's terminology, the cycle of 'manias, panics and crashes' to take its course freely.

Domestic politics, economic structures, policy stances and ideology combined to shape the effects of changes in the external environment on Latin America's domestic markets. The same factors also resulted in the unequal distribution of the benefits and costs of massive external borrowing.

The evolution of external financing varied to a certain extent from country to country. Differences in economic strategies and policies (particularly the timing and degree of financial and trade liberalization and exchange-rate policies), economic structures, the availability of oil and the level of development all influenced the evolution of external financial relations. However, there were important similarities as well in the trend, volume and composition of external finances, with the larger nations taking the leading role in adopting changes that were to characterize these four decades.

Latin America had accumulated large reserves of foreign currency and a substantial surplus in its trade account during the Second World War. After the war, the volume and prices of Latin American imports increased rapidly, and by the mid-1950s most of these reserves and half of the trade surplus had already been lost. In the second half of the decade, Latin American countries were faced with a generalized scarcity of foreign currency and large fluctuations in its terms of trade, forcing reductions in imports and public revenues, and weakening levels of output, investment and employment.

As shown in Figure 4.5 above, the region's trade surplus was equivalent to 4 per cent of GDP in 1950. In the years that followed this figure declined rapidly, falling to 2 per cent in 1955 and just 0.8 per cent of

Table 4.13. *Latin America: composition of capital movements, 1950–89 (annual averages at 1980 US$ millions)*

	Direct foreign investment (1)	Net loans (2)	Official unrequited transfers (3)	Net capital movements (4)	Payments of interest and profits (5)	Net transfers (6)*	Change in reserves (7)*
Average 1950–60	2,067	1,451	231	3,673	3,562	111	(75)
Average 1961–65	1,131	1,861	480	3,370	4,860	(1,480)	(101)
Average 1966–70	2,283	5,460	524	6,900	7,369	(469)	(1,367)
Average 1971–73	3,418	11,757	498	9,100	8,371	729	(6,572)
Average 1974–77	3,495	20,355	348	25,048	10,237	14,811	(6,394)
Average 1978–81	5,940	29,233	575	38,048	19,535	18,513	(5,243)
Average 1982–89	4,599	5,549	1,428	14,513	35,863	(21,350)	3,327

Notes:
*Column (4) is the sum of (1) to (3) plus errors and omissions. In column (6), equal to (4)–(5), parenthesis indicate a negative transfer; in column (7) an increase.
Sources: Based on data for 19 countries from ECLAC Statistical Division and United Nations, *Monthly Bulletin of Statistics,* several issues.
Figures in current US$ were deflated by the unit value index of DMEs' exports of manufactures.

GDP in 1960. Moreover, a growing negative balance in services (financial and non-financial, including tourism) created a deficit in the current account during this period for almost all countries in the region. Direct foreign investment, four-fifths of which was from the United States, had an impact on all three components of the external account – trade, services and capital movements. Profit remittances accounted for nearly 90 per cent of net financial services, the remainder of which was taken up by interest payments.

The deficit in current account was partially financed by new direct foreign investment, but on the whole this amount was smaller than total profit remittances. In many countries, direct foreign investment played a significant role in the production of primary commodities for export. However, what appeared as increased exports and surpluses on the trade account in some cases never materialized as increased availability of foreign exchange. This was due to the low 'returned value' – the amount of foreign exchange that was actually returned to the region by foreign investors (to pay for domestic inputs, wages, taxes, etc.) – in many primary commodity export activities.

During the 1960s direct foreign investment began to move into manufactures. This was the result of a new world trend of multinational corporations, changes in the structure of DMEs' demand for imports (see Figure 4.2 above), improved productive and technological capacity in the region as a by-product of ISI, and growing political pressure in many countries for the nationalization of foreign companies engaged in primary commodity exports.

This decade also saw a rapid increase in long-term official loans. The 'Alliance for Progress' launched by the Kennedy government brought with it significant increases in official lending. U.S. bilateral loans were soon followed by European and Japanese credits, and the creation of the Inter-American Development Bank also contributed to the growth of multilateral funding.

Net official loans (consisting of approximately two-thirds bilateral and one-third multilateral lending) grew in importance, clearly exceeding net flows of direct foreign investment. Interest rates were fixed at levels far lower than the average return on direct foreign investment (between one-half and one-third of the latter). Furthermore, interest payment did not fluctuate with the terms of trade as did profit remittances, though this difference lost importance since the decade exhibited a significant lessening of international price instability.

The main component of debt with private lenders continued to be suppliers credit, although bank trade credit grew and financial loans started to arrive in the second half of the 1960s. The net flow of funds of direct foreign investment continued to be negative, particularly in oil-rich Venezuela. Profits by foreign investors became increasingly associated with production for the highly protected domestic markets of host countries. The negative sign of net transfers was reinforced by several nationalizations with compensation which took place during the decade, though nationalizations allowed several countries to increase sharply the share of economic rents they were able to capture. This benefit was notably significant for Venezuela and Chile.

Bilateral loans were commonly tied to imports from creditor countries, while multilateral loans came with various forms of conditionality attached, usually related to economic policy. These were often criticized by debtor countries. The expansion of non-conditional bank loans towards the end of the decade was therefore welcomed by debtor countries as an alternative to the restrictions attached to official loans.

Private banks quickly became the main creditors of the region during the 1970s. Thus, while direct foreign investment and official credits had accounted for three-quarters of net capital flows in the 1960s, these sources had fallen to one-third by 1980. Meanwhile, the share of private bank credit in the region's outstanding foreign debt climbed to 80 per cent in the early 1980s.

After three difficult decades, international financial markets began to expand rapidly during the 1960s. This created an unusual situation as LDC access to external financing had been limited and subject to stringent terms since the end of the 1920s. From 1973–4 to the 1982 debt crisis, LDCs' foreign bank debt expanded at an average annual rate close to 30 per cent (in nominal terms). This was roughly one-half faster than the yearly growth of international financial market operations during the same period. Non-guaranteed private debt grew particularly fast, reaching 40 per cent of the total Latin American debt in 1980. This debt had on average less than one-half the maturity period and twice the normal interest rates of the rest of the region's foreign debt.

The rapid expansion of world financial markets during this period differed in important ways from the previous period of increased international liquidity half a century earlier. Owing to the unprecedented availability of funds, little attention was paid to the fact that interest rates on these loans were 'floating' and that a large share of new lending carried maturities notably shorter than those of offical loans. One reason for the tendency to ignore the short maturities attached to these loans was the fact that they were almost automatically refinanced. On the other hand, in a context of excess supply of finance and high inflation in DMEs during the 1970s, real interest rates declined rapidly and were actually negative during most of this period: when deflated by the export price index of Latin America's non-oil exporting countries, the London Inter-Bank Offer Rate (LIBOR) for operations in U.S. dollars (three months) was negative in seven out of the nine years between 1972 and 1980, with an average value of −5.3 per cent. By way of contrast, the average value for 1950–71 was 5 per cent, and for 1981–7 was 14.6 per cent.[35]

The main characteristic of this period is that three phenomena of transitory nature converged at the same time: the rapid expansion of an 'infant' international market, and a growing share of LDCs in this market that provided large net inflows to borrowers, and an 'abnormally' low real interest rate that made borrowing extremely profitable in the short run. The transitory nature of these phenomena was missed by the majority of financial specialists, governments and private agents.

LDCs' foreign borrowing during this period was therefore totally in line with international financial market signals: that is, due to negative real interest rates, Latin American countries were in fact encouraged to borrow. The countries of the region did not, of course, have to follow these risky short-term price signals passively. None the less, market signals had made borrowing extremely profitable in the short-run, with large spreads between domestic and international interest rates. Consequently, borrowing rose fast.[36]

Latin American countries actually borrowed in excess of their capacity to use foreign currency. As a consequence, the abundance of foreign exchange

[35] See Figure 4.4 above and sources. This negative average real interest rate for 1972–81, of course, is even lower if nominal LIBOR is deflated by the export price index of all Latin American countries, including oil exporters.

[36] For additional background on the Latin American foreign debt, see R. Devlin, 'External Finance and Commercial Banks, the Role in Latin America's Capacity to Import between 1951 and 1975', *Cepal Review*, 5 (1978); E. Bacha and C. Díaz-Alejandro, 'Los mercados financieros; una visión desde la semi-periferia', and country case studies of Argentina, Brazil, Colombia, Chile and Mexico in R. Ffrench-Davis (ed.), *Las relaciones financieras externas: su efecto en la economía latinoamericana* (Mexico, D.F., 1983); R. Ffrench-Davis, 'External Debt and Balance of Payments: recent trends and prospects in Latin America', in IDB, *Economic and Social Progress in Latin America 1982* (Washington, D.C., 1982). A comparison of fourteen LDCs in all regions is made in R. Ffrench-Davis, 'International Private Lending and Borrowing Strategies of Developing Countries', *Journal of Development Planning*, 14 (1984).

led to accumulation of international reserves in the Central Banks of the region and to over-valuation of their currencies, generating maladjustments. Adjustment in the late 1970s, under the stimulus of exchange-rate appreciation, operated in a direction that was inconsistent with sustainable development, given the trends in the real national and international economies. Current accounts deteriorated rapidly, reaching in 1980 a combined deficit of US$ 40 billion for the region as a whole, as the second oil shock, world financial imbalances and stagnation of commodity markets delivered a gloomy international economic environment.

While foreign borrowing across Latin America followed a common course, in fact the pace differed from case to case. There was diversity in the volume of borrowing and in the use made of it. By 1973 some Latin American countries already had large stocks of foreign debt relative to GDP, and high debt service ratios relative to exports. These countries, notably Brazil and Mexico, had achieved significant access to private financial markets during the 1960s and early 1970s, and foreign borrowing expanded rapidly after 1973. As a result, the median debt/GNP ratio before the 1973 oil crisis was already equal to 17 per cent, and the debt service ratio had reached nearly one-quarter of all exports.[37] In contrast, Asian countries (although they had a similar level of foreign debt in relation to GNP) posted debt service ratios which were only approximately half as high as Latin American levels.

Several other countries in the region, such as Argentina, Bolivia, Peru, Chile, Colombia and Venezuela also became important recipients of foreign loans. By the end of the decade almost all countries of the region had easy access to the world financial markets. This, added to fast rising deficit on the current account and the relatively low levels of exports (in relation to their GNP), resulted in the region's rapidly growing and eventually unsustainable debt service ratios. By 1980 the debt/GNP ratio had nearly doubled to 42 per cent and by 1983 it had increased to 61 per cent – twice the level in Asia. Of the region's 13 major debtor countries Colombia had the lowest foreign bank debt/GDP ratio (23 per cent in 1982). This was the result of a deliberate policy (followed until 1980) of safeguarding domestic economic stability by controlling inflows of private foreign capital.

In 1982, bank debt exceeded 45 per cent of annual GDP in four countries of the region. Two of these, Venezuela and Ecuador, were oil

[37] See Fishlow, 'Some Reflections', and World Bank, 1992, op.cit.

exporters, while Argentina and Chile followed monetarist experiments. In Chile and Venezuela bank debt/GDP ratios were well over 60 per cent that year. The only countries which did not increase bank debt rapidly were those which had been denied access to foreign borrowing from private international financial institutions for political reasons, and the deliberate policy-induced case of Colombia. In the case of Peru, access to external finances was severely restricted after 1976, while borrowing by Nicaragua was sharply curtailed during the Sandinista government.

The rapid growth of foreign borrowing left annually a large net balance of foreign exchange (after amortization and interest payments) in most countries up to 1981. It has been estimated that the yearly average of these positive transfers between 1977 and 1981 was equivalent to approximately 16 per cent of the total stock of debt with private banks.

By and large, foreign borrowing was used to pay for oil imports, to expand other imports (of consumers and investment goods and military equipment) and to finance capital flight out of the region. Capital flight was particularly pronounced in Argentina, Mexico and Venezuela – the result of a combination of tax heavens abroad and the absence of foreign controls in the domestic markets. But in the majority of countries, most of the loans were used to increase imports. Imports of military equipment were substantial in several countries of the region ruled by military dictatorships; Argentina, Chile, Mexico and Venezuela headed the group of countries whose imports of consumer goods rose sharply; and financing of productive investment was significant in Brazil, Colombia and Mexico.[38]

Export volumes of primary commodities and manufactures expanded during this period. Nevertheless, the rate of growth of exports did not keep pace with that of imports and interest payments. The result was a rapid increase in current account deficits, from 2 per cent of GDP in 1973 to 6 per cent in 1981. Since Brazil had already made a downward adjustment in 1981, it was able to reduce its deficit below 5 per cent of GDP, while Chile's deficit climbed to 18 per cent.

Adjustment to the plentiful supply of foreign exchange generally meant that both output and consumption structures became more import-intensive, and foreign exchange assets and liabilities came to dominate financial portfolios. Negative international real interest rates for most of

[38] See S. Griffith-Jones and E. Rodriguez (eds), *Cross-conditionality, Banking Regulations and Third-World Debt* (London, 1992), M. Wionczek (ed.), *Politics and Economics of Latin American Debt Crisis* (Boulder, Colo., 1985), and R. Ffrench-Davis (ed.), *Las relaciones financieras externas*.

the 1973–81 period not only encouraged indebtedness, but were also widely used as an argument in favour of further liberalization of capital movements, especially in the Southern Cone.

Most countries in the region behaved as if the practically unlimited supply of foreign credit was to last forever. Monetarist policies gained ground, as reflected by permissive attitudes towards the enormous volume of foreign credit and the introduction of domestic financial reforms which relaxed regulations concerning interest rates, portfolio composition, maturity terms and the use of funds. The financial liberalization process was particularly extreme in Chile, Argentina and Uruguay, although most countries adopted policies that were influenced, to a greater or lesser degree, by the orthodox approach to international trade and finance. Even Colombia, the most cautious borrower during the 1970s, introduced similar though moderated reforms in 1980.

The access to private capital markets in the 1970s at first increased the autonomy of debtor countries. They gradually freed themselves from balance-of-payments constraints, some increased their imports of capital goods, raised their capital formation and accumulated reserves of foreign exchanges. However, as borrowing continued to increase and imports expanded at high rates, the economies of the region began to accommodate their expenditure patterns, production structures and expectations as if the pressure of large capital inflows were to be permanent. As a consequence, they became increasingly dependent upon the continuation of these flows.

The financial situation of Latin America economies thus grew more vulnerable in two fundamental respects. First, the 'confidence' of external creditors became increasingly important to ensure continued access to international financial markets. Indeed, attention to the attitudes of creditors was a major factor in the conversion of many policy-makers to monetarism. Second, the more the domestic economies had accommodated to international financial flows, the greater was their vulnerability vis-à-vis sudden changes in the international financial market. Events after 1982 were to demonstrate just how precarious the position of Latin American countries had become.

In short, the region made intensive use of external financial resources, adjusting economic structures to the seemingly unlimited supply of foreign funds. The process took place under the influence of negative international real interest rates and pressure from lender banks to liberalize capital movements. The 'rationale' of the approach was provided by the advocates of global monetarism, with the active participation of institutions such as the IMF, DMEs governments and international commercial banks. They succeeded, as far as Latin America was concerned, in convincing governments and public opinion that debt to private lenders was a private affair (and therefore not really different from any other private transaction), and that the abundance of international liquidity, and willingness of international banks to lend to the region, was a permanent condition.

A growing share of external loans after 1973 originated from private instead of official financial institutions: by 1980, 80 per cent of the region's foreign debt was held by private banks. As a result, maturity periods were shortened, and the cost of credit increased (in 1980, bank credit posted interest rates that more than doubled those from official sources). Furthermore, nominal interest rates on commercial loans were very unstable during the 1970s, at times changing by as much as 50 per cent over short periods of time. Since bank loans were taken mostly with floating rates, this led to large fluctuations in debt service.

The shortening of credit maturity terms also implied the need to obtain larger volumes of gross credit in order to maintain a given net flow. This would be of no major importance if the international financial markets were competitive and stable and if borrowers enjoyed unrestricted access. In practice, however, shorter maturities would represent an additional source of external instability in the face of a change of mood of the market.

While capital flows contributed to softening the effects of unexpected changes in foreign trade (like the oil shocks of 1973 and 1979), they also introduced external instability into the domestic economy by sudden changes in the availability of funds and interest rates. Reassessments by lenders of the 'creditworthiness' of specific debtor countries also contributed to domestic uncertainty.

At the macroeconomic level, external instability in trade and finance was transmitted into domestic economies through the balance of payments, the fiscal budget and money markets. At the microeconomic level, changes in relative prices and the availability of funds to producers and consumers added an element of unpredictability to domestic markets.

Changes in export and import prices, access to external markets, international interest rates, and the supply of foreign funds affected directly different components of the balance of payments. But from there it significantly affected the rest of the domestic economy. The severity of the effects of external shocks on the domestic economy largely depended both on the nature of the shocks and of domestic policies adopted as a response.

In the 1950s, the response to external shocks was mainly via changes in import restrictions (import deposits and quantitative restrictions were the preferred policy instruments). Because in several Latin American countries imports of consumer goods had been reduced drastically by ISI policies, any additional import restrictions fell principally on capital and intermediate goods. This may help to explain the significant role played by foreign exchange shortages in capital formation.[39]

The influence of external shocks on the exchange rate was more passive. In periods in which shocks improved the availability of foreign exchange (for example via above 'normal' export prices), it contributed to the freezing of nominal exchange-rates whose purchasing power was eroded by high domestic inflation. During the 1950s and early 1960s the compensating mechanism of foreign-exchange reserves adjustments played a secondary role. In this way, external shocks were transmitted from the balance of payments to the domestic economy mainly via changing restrictions on imports and passive appreciation of real exchange-rates and subsequent abrupt devaluations.

In the mid-1960s, as we have seen, several South American countries adopted crawling-peg policies which drastically reduced exchange-rate instability. Greater predictability in exchange-rate movements enabled some countries to remove many quantitative import restrictions and allowed them to have more stable import policies. Carlos Díaz-Alejandro has argued[40] that reduced real exchange-rate instability also fostered non-traditional exports, particularly of manufactured goods. The greater stability of exchange rate policy was associated as well with the adoption of an active policy of accumulating foreign reserves. Countries increased their stock of reserves, thus raising their capability to soften the impact of external shocks.

A strong feature of the 1970s was the relaxation of restrictions on capital movements and a rapid increase in the inflow of private funds. Although a large proportion of funds was absorbed by import liberalization and capital flight, foreign-exchange reserves accumulated rapidly too,

[39] See C. Díaz-Alejandro, *Foreign Trade Regimes and Economic Development: Colombia* (New York, 1976).
[40] Díaz-Alejandro, 'Some Characteristics of Recent Export Expansion'.

with a corresponding impact on money supply and exchange-rate appreciation. Since changes in the money supply were generally larger than targets set by monetary authorities, domestic credit and public expenditure were restricted so as to sterilize some of the increase in the money supply created by the mounting foreign exchange reserves.

Despite the large inflow of foreign capital, and the liberalization of capital movements and domestic capital markets, segmentation in financial markets persisted for several years. One of the consequences of this segmentation was a large spread between the domestic and foreign interest rates, which had significant allocative and distributive effects within the domestic markets.[41]

By the beginning of the 1980s, Latin American countries had 'adjusted' to the easy availability of foreign funds to such degree that the region had a combined current account deficit in 1981 equivalent to nearly 6 per cent of GDP and 44 per cent of exports. The scene was thus set for the 1982 debt crisis.

The debt crisis of the 1980s

When Mexico suspended the service on its foreign debt in August 1982, the international financial markets awakened to the fact that Latin American countries had borrowed far more than was sustainable, and international banks had lent well beyond a reasonable level of exposure. In 1982, the loans/capital ratio of the nine largest U.S. banks with respect to Latin America was 180 per cent; of this figure, exposure to Mexico accounted for 50 percentage points, Brazil 46, Venezuela 26, Argentina 21 and Chile 12. British banks lending to the region followed a similar pattern.[42]

There is little evidence that DME governments or international institutions like the IMF and the World Bank were aware of the explosiveness of this situation, despite the fact that debt-service ratios were rising fast in many Third World countries, especially in Latin America, and the banks' portfolios were loaded with Third World debt. As late as October 1981, only months before Mexico's moratorium, Geoffrey Howe, then Margaret Thatcher's Chancellor of the Exchequer, was still extolling the benefits of

[41] See R. Ffrench-Davis, (ed.), *Las relaciones financieras externas*.

[42] See R. Devlin, *Debt and Crisis: the Supply Side of the Story* (Princeton, N.J., 1989); R. Ffrench-Davis and R. Devlin, 'Diez años de crisis de la deuda latinoamericana', *Comercio Exterior,* 43 (1993); and M. Marcel and J. G. Palma, 'Third World Debt and its Effects on the British Economy: a southern view on economic mismanagement in the North', *Cambridge Journal of Economics,* 12, 3 (1988): 361–400.

the recycling process: 'The private markets have . . . served us well in the continued success of the recycling process. The international capital market has continued to function in a practical and pragmatic way. . . . It is the free market system that has recycled the surpluses and continued to deliver some growth worldwide.'[43]

European politicians were not alone in their optimism. Across the Atlantic, in March 1980 Paul Volcker, the chairman of the Federal Reserve, remarked that: 'The impression I get from the data that I have reviewed is that the recycling process has not yet pushed exposure of either the borrowers or lenders to an unreasonable or unsustainable point in the aggregate, especially for (North) American banks [. . .]'[44]

Volcker's confidence was echoed by Walter Robichek, then Director of the Western Hemisphere Department of the IMF, who argued in a speech given in Chile in 1980, that: (a) there was no real difference between domestic and foreign debt in LDCs; (b) LDCs had presumably taken into account exchange-rates and other risks in their foreign borrowing; and (c) private businesses in LDCs were very unlikely to over-borrow.[45] As Robichek spoke, Chile's per capita foreign debt was among the highest in the Third World. Moreover, non-guaranteed private sector debt accounted for two-thirds of the national total. Ironically, shortly after the publication of this speech in 1981, the IMF was back in Chile to discuss the country's mounting arrears in debt payments, focussed on non-guaranteed private borrowing.

It is possible to distinguish four phases in the management of the debt crisis which began with Mexico's suspension of debt service. This first spanned the period between August 1982 and September 1985, i.e. between Mexico's moratorium and the beginning of the 'Baker Plan'. The two most important characteristics of this initial phase of the debt crisis were the massive economic adjustments imposed upon LDCs, and the effective co-ordination of creditor banks in their negotiations with debtors. As all LDC governments rejected open default, adjustment was necessary not only to reverse the large deficits in LDCs trade accounts but also to generate the foreign exchange needed to service interest payments on

[43] Speech at the 1981 annual IMF World Bank meeting, in IMF, 'Summary Proceedings', Annual Meeting 1981 (Washington, D.C., 1981).

[44] Quoted in C. Díaz-Alejandro, 'Latin American Debt: I don't think we are in Kansas anymore', *Brookings Papers on Economic Activity,* 2, 1984.

[45] See W. Robichek, 'Alternativas de políticas financieras en economías pequeñas y abiertas al exterior', *Estudios Monetarios* VII, Banco Central de Chile, 1981, pp. 171–2.

their foreign debt. The mobilization of the creditor banks 'cartel', in turn, enabled the international banks to negotiate from a position of strength which, given their levels of exposure to Third World debt, was not justified by their precarious financial situation. This attitude of creditor banks contrasted sharply with the lack of co-ordination among the anonymous bond holders of the 1930s.

The banks insisted on a 'case by case' approach so as to discourage the formation of a debtor's cartel, and were able to impose small steering committees generally representing the banks with the highest exposure to the country in question. The steering committees conducted all the negotiations that restructured maturities and considered new loans in order to service some of the interest payments due. These negotiations were backed up by the DME governments and the IMF, which applied heavy pressure on creditor banks unwilling to follow the recommendations of the most highly exposed banks represented in the committees.

Despite their great efforts to achieve trade surpluses, Latin American countries could not repay their foreign debt in full. This was mainly the result of high interest rates, the large amortization quotas due each year, and weak demand in the international markets for Latin American primary commodity exports.

A common feature of debt renegotiations during this period was the requirement that governments provide an ex-post guarantee on non-guaranteed private debt. This was a particularly arbitrary measure imposed on the governments of the region by creditor banks, and governments of DMEs, with the support or acceptance of international agencies. It did not appear to matter that banks had willingly given these loans without government guarantees, and had charged premiums for the additional risks involved.

The second phase corresponds to the period of the 'Baker Plan' from September 1985 to September 1987. The Baker Plan attempted to reverse the most recessive effects of the first phase of the debt crisis, calling for 'structural adjustment with growth'. The core of the new strategy was a commitment by James Baker, the U.S. Secretary of the Treasury, to obtain US$29 billion of new loans in a period of three years, consisting of US$20 billion in private lending and the rest from international agencies. The new money could help LDCs to cushion the effects of adjustment. Also, the plan brought the World Bank into the process of management of the debt crisis for the first time.

Mexico was the first country to join the Baker Plan, followed by Argentina, Brazil, Chile, Uruguay and Venezuela. A gross total of US$176 billion in debt was restructured during this period. The Baker Plan also included softer conditionality for new loans, longer maturities, lower spreads and no commissions for debt renegotiations.

The third phase, usually referred to as 'Baker Plan B' took place between September 1987 and March 1989, and added a new feature: debt reduction in the form of discounted debt buy-backs, 'exit bonds' with low interest rates, and debt swaps. For the first time it was openly admitted that the real value of LDCs debt was lower than its face value. However, it was also made clear that options for debt reduction were *voluntary* for creditor banks, and that DMEs' tax payers would not have (directly) to foot the bill.

The fourth and last phase of debt renegotiations during the 1980s was launched in March 1989 with the 'Brady Plan'. It included important new instruments for debt renegotiation. The most important of these was the priority given to debt reduction, particularly the commitment of US$30 billion for this purpose (US$12 billion each from the IMF and the World Bank and US$6 billion from Japan). These funds could be used to finance debt buy-back by LDCs, or its conversion into bonds at a discount. There were also tax advantages for creditor banks and a policy to de-link debt renegotiation from IMF programmes. This meant that a country could reach a normal agreement with the IMF even though it was behind in its debt repayments.

Mexico, Venezuela, Costa Rica and Uruguay were the first to renegotiate foreign debt under this plan. These countries reduced their debt by US$8 billion and converted US$34 billion into long-term bonds with *fixed* rates of interest. Argentina and Brazil also reached agreement in principle to restructure foreign debt along similar lines. Bolivia and Guyana, followed by Honduras, El Salvador, Nicaragua and Panama successfully renegotiated part of their debt in the Paris Club, obtaining substantial reductions in debt service.

The recessive adjustment of the 1980s

All Third World regions were confronted by similar external conditions during the period, including restricted access to new borrowing, soaring

Table 4.14. *Latin America: debt indicators, 1978–90*

	1978	1980	1981	1982	1984	1987	1990
Total debt (US$ billions)	153	228	285	328	368	420	432
Debt as % of GDP in current US$	31	28	32	44	56	58	44
Debt as % of total exports	253	215	249	322	329	399	292
Interest payments as % of total exports	16	20	28	41	37	30	25
Net transfers of funds (US$ billion)[a]	16	13	11	−19	−27	−16	−14

Note: [a] Net capital inflows minus net interest and profits paid. A positive figure represents a positive transfer. Includes eighteen countries, excluding Panama.
Source: Data for nineteen countries from ECLAC, Statistical Division.

real interest rates on their foreign debt, generally declining terms of trade and stagnant demand in the North for primary commodities. Most Latin American countries, however, were more vulnerable to these negative shocks and therefore less able to achieve an efficient adjustment during the 1980s.

Table 4.14 shows how fast debt indicators can change. In fact they experienced a drastic worsening between 1980 and 1982, with the interest to exports ratio, for example, jumping from 20 to 41 per cent, and the net transfers shifting from plus US$13 billion to minus US$27 billion. There was a massive and generalized worsening of economic and social indicators.

It is interesting, however, to note that net transfers usually remained positive in Central American nations and Paraguay, as a consequence of large loans from official sources. In the rest of Latin America, the increase of public lending, basically provided by multilateral institutions, represented a minor compensation of the negative transfers delivered by the region to creditor banks. Among large debtors, Chile was the country that received proportionally larger net financing from the IMF, the Inter-American Development Bank (IDB) and the World Bank: net transfers from them were equivalent to 2 per cent of GNP in 1985–8, with transfers from Chile to private banks of the order of 6 per cent.[46] Multilateral financing played a crucial role for the capacity of debtor countries to pay interest to private banks, and this support was notably more significant for Chile.

Latin America's combined trade deficit totalled US$14 billion in 1981, while the corresponding figure for the current account was US$42 billion, financed by capital inflows. In 1982, however, the surplus in the capital account dropped by half, and by 1983 it had fallen to a mere US$3 billion; the fall in net financing was a consequence both of a sharp reduction in formal inflows (net loans and direct foreign investment) and a significant rise in capital flight as measured by errors and omissions in the balance of payments. As a result of the abrupt drop in financing and the rapid increase in interest rates, Latin American countries had to reduce abruptly the deficit in their trade accounts, generating a surplus of US$27 billion in 1983 and US$36 billion in 1984. The surpluses were used to cover interest and profit remittances abroad.

Despite efforts to increase exports, Latin America's revenues grew slowly during this period due to falling export prices (see Figure 4.4 above). As a result, the region had to rely heavily on import reductions to generate the trade surplus and the corresponding foreign exchange required to close the large gap in its balance of payments.

On the one hand, inflationary pressures soared, because of worsened expectations, sharp exchange-rate devaluations and rapid increases in public sector deficits due to the service of the foreign public debt (including subsidies to interest payments on private debt for which governments had provided transfers or ex-post guarantees).[47] On the other hand, domestic output, employment and investment all suffered a substantial drop. GDP fell by 4 per cent between 1981 and 1983 and then recovered slowly, with real gross national disposable income (which had grown at a rate of 6.2 per cent per annum during the intershock years) only recovering its 1980

[46] Figures based on data of the World Bank, *World Debt Tables*. See R. Ffrench-Davis, 'Adjustment and conditionality in Chile, 1982–88', in Griffith-Jones and Rodriguez (eds), *Cross-conditionality*. In 1982 two-thirds of Chile's foreign debt were private and with no government guarantee. In 1987, after several rescheduling rounds and new borrowing by the Central Bank to save several private banks and domestic debtors from bankruptcy, this proportion fell to 15 per cent. The most striking feature of this 'nationalization' of private liabilities is that the country obtained from banks few or no concessions in exchange, but a generous flow from multilateral institutions (IMF, IDB and the World Bank).

[47] In 1987–8 public sector foreign debt was equal to 170 per cent of total current public revenue. As LIBOR plus average spread reached 8 per cent in these years, almost 15 per cent of current public revenue had to be used to service the public foreign debt.

Table 4.15. *Latin America: poverty, income, education, and health, 1980–90*

		1980	1986	1990
1. Poor population (%) of total population)	Latin America[c]	41	43	46
2. Indigent population (% of total)	Latin America[c]	19	21	22
3. Poor population (urban areas)	Latin America[c]	30	36	39
4. Poor population (rural areas)	Latin America[c]	60	60	61
5. Poverty gap[a] (% of GDP)	Latin America[c]	2.4	3.7	(1989) 4.1
6. Wages (% of GDP)	Latin America[d]	34	28	(1989) 28
7. Illiteracy[b]	Latin America and the Caribbean[e]	23.0		15.3
8. School enrolment rate ages 6 to 11	Latin America and the Caribbean[e]	82.3		87.3
9. Secondary school enrolment rate	Latin America and the Caribbean[e]	47.4	54.9	
10. Life expectancy (years)	Latin America and the Caribbean[e]	65.2		68.0
11. Infant mortality (per thousand born alive)	Latin America and the Caribbean[e]	70.9		54.6

Notes:

[a] The poverty gap measures the transfer of economic resources to poor households needed in order to bring them up to the poverty line.

[b] Percentage of the population 15 years of age and older.

[c] Except Cuba

[d] Brazil, Chile, Colombia, Costa Rica and Peru.

[e] Latin America except Cuba, plus Barbados, Cuba, Guyana, Haiti, Jamaica, Suriname and Trinidad and Tobago.

Sources: ECLAC, *Notas sobre el desarrollo social en América Latina* (LC/G.1665/Rev. 1), (Santiago, February 1992) for indicators 1–4 and 7–11; O. Altimir, 'Income Distribution and Poverty through Crisis and Adjustment', in G. Bird and A. Helwege (eds), *Latin American Recovery* (New York, forthcoming) for indicators 1–4 (1990); and R. Infante and V. Tokman, 'Monitoring Poverty and Employment Trends: an index for social debt', *Documentos de trabajo,* no. 365 (Santiago: PREALC, August 1992) for indicators 5 and 6.

value during 1987. Gross fixed capital formation in 1990 was still one-quarter below the 1980 figure.

Social indicators reflected the unequal way in which the effects of economic contraction were distributed among the population during this period. There was a substantial drop in real wages (with minimum wages in 1990 still being one-third below their 1980 level), a rapid increase in 'open' urban unemployment to 8 per cent and 'under-employment' to a further one-third of the labour force in 1990, and public social expenditures per capita were severely curtailed in most countries (particularly weakening the quality of health and education). By the early 1990s, 46 per cent of the population of the region, or 200 million Latin Americans, were living below the poverty line, a figure that was nearly 50 per cent higher than that of 1980 (see Table 4.15). As in the past, people in rural areas continued to be proportionally poorer. However, during the 1980s the increase in poverty was concentrated in the urban areas. In part this was because agriculture was capable of responding better to the crisis; it was the manufacturing sector that bore the brunt of the recession.

Notwithstanding the worsening of so many socioeconomic indicators – average wages, employment, social expenditure – there were several indicators that continued to show some improvement during the 1980s. As Table 4.15 shows, literacy, years at school, life expectancy and infant mortality, for example, improved in most countries.

The domestic and external macroeconomic indicators presented in Table 4.16 illustrate in more detail the severe economic consequences of the recessive adjustment in Latin America, following the onset of the debt crisis. In 1990, GDP per capita was still 8 per cent lower than in the base period (the average of 1980–81). This was in sharp contrast to previous decades, when GDP per capita grew about 30 per cent per decade. Adjustment had an even greater negative impact on capital formation and imports of capital goods: gross fixed capital formation per capita decreased by one-third between 1980–81 and 1983–90 (see Table 4.16, line 4). This was to have evidently negative consequences for productive capacity and employment. However, the decline in investment was not associated with a drop in domestic savings, which remained more or less stable (see Table 4.16, line 5). It was 'national' savings that diminished sharply, because both the private and public sectors had to devote a sizable amount of savings to service the foreign debt. In fact, net transfers of funds from the region averaged the equivalent of between one-half and two-thirds of net fixed capital formation in 1983–90.[48] The region's declining terms of

[48] During the 1970s foreign resources did, to a certain extent, contribute to capital formation. There were, however, important differences among Latin American countries. For example, those nations (such as Chile and Uruguay) that liberalized capital inflows, domestic financial markets and

4.16. *Latin America: macroeconomic indicators, 1979–90 (percentages of per capita average GDP in 1980–81)*

	1979	1980	1981	1982	1983	1984	1985	1986	1987	1988	1989	1990	Average 1980–81	Average 1983–90
1. GDP	97.5	101.0	99.0	95.7	91.4	92.3	92.7	94.6	95.7	94.5	93.5	92.0	100.0	93.3
2. Domestic expenditure	97.9	102.7	100.0	93.4	85.2	85.5	85.9	88.6	88.9	87.5	86.0	84.6	101.4	86.5
3. Consumption	75.0	77.8	76.2	73.9	70.2	70.4	69.9	72.5	71.9	70.9	70.5	70.5	77.0	70.8
4. Gross fixed capital formation	22.7	23.7	22.9	19.8	15.8	15.4	15.4	16.4	16.6	16.3	15.3	14.8	23.3	15.7
5. Domestic saving[a]	22.6	23.2	22.7	21.8	21.2	21.9	22.8	22.0	23.9	23.7	23.1	21.5	23.0	22.5
6. Trade balance[b]	(0.4)	(1.7)	(1.0)	2.2	6.2	6.8	6.7	6.0	6.8	7.0	7.5	7.3	(1.4)	6.8
a) Exports of goods and services	14.3	14.5	15.1	15.2	15.9	16.8	16.5	16.2	17.3	18.2	18.8	19.4	14.8	17.4
b) Imports of goods and services	(14.7)	(16.1)	(16.2)	(13.0)	(9.7)	(10.0)	(9.8)	(10.2)	(10.5)	(11.2)	(11.2)	(12.0)	(16.2)	(10.6)
7. Terms of trade effect	(0.7)	0.0	(0.8)	(2.4)	(2.6)	(2.2)	(2.8)	(4.3)	(4.6)	(4.7)	(4.7)	(5.0)	(0.4)	(3.9)
8. Net transfers of funds (c–d)	1.1	1.7	1.8	0.2	(3.6)	(4.6)	(3.9)	(1.8)	(2.2)	(2.3)	(2.9)	(2.3)	1.7	(2.9)
a) Capital movements[b]	4.7	4.5	5.1	2.5	0.4	1.4	0.5	1.4	2.0	0.8	1.4	2.5	4.8	1.3
b) Factor services	(2.3)	(2.6)	(3.6)	(4.9)	(4.5)	(4.8)	(4.5)	(4.2)	(3.7)	(3.7)	(3.9)	(3.4)	(3.1)	(4.1)
c) subtotal	2.4	1.8	1.5	(2.3)	(4.2)	(3.4)	(4.0)	(2.7)	(1.7)	(2.9)	(2.5)	(0.9)	1.7	(2.8)
d) Change in international reserves	1.3	0.2	(0.4)	(2.5)	(0.5)	1.2	(0.1)	(1.0)	0.6	(0.6)	0.4	1.4	(0.1)	0.2

Notes: [a] Calculated as the difference between GDP and expenditure on consumption.
[b] Unrequited net transfers are included in capital movements.
Source: Calculations based on ECLAC, Statistical Division, covering nineteen countries.

trade reduced even further the availability of funds for investment. The worsening of the terms of trade were equivalent to 4 per cent of GDP between the averages of 1980–81 and 1983–90 (see Table 4.16, line 7). At the same time, capital inflows per capita diminished in 1983–90 to almost one-fourth of the 1980–81 levels (see Table 4.16, line 8a), while interest payments and profit remittances per capita increased by one-third (see Table 4.16, line 8b). Trade and financial shocks, of roughly similar magnitudes, resulted in a decline in available resources, between 1980–81 and 1983–90, equivalent to 9 per cent of GDP.

It is revealing that, during the 1980s, many LDCs, particularly in Latin America, made larger transfers as a proportion of GDP than those made by Germany after the First World War. Most crucially, the effects of the LDC's debt crisis were not limited to the financial sector of the DMEs with high exposure in the Third World: their exports – particularly of manufactures – to heavily indebted LDCs were damaged by the crisis, resulting in losses in output, employment and market shares. Evidence suggests that a reduction in interest flows from LDCs to DMEs' banks would have been almost offset by increases in DMEs' exports. A contradiction existed between the self-interest of creditor banks and the real side of both debtor and creditor countries, and it was the former that ultimately prevailed.

In brief, the combined effects of the trade and financial external shocks caused a 7 per cent decline in average GDP per capita between 1980–81 and 1983–90, and a 15 per cent decline in domestic absorption. This contrasts markedly with the dynamism of the 1970s, when annual average GDP growth was 5.6 per cent, consumption grew by 6.1 per cent, and investment increased by 7.3 per cent per annum, vis-à-vis a 2.4 percent rise in population.

Since governments of the region carried the burden of financing the bulk of the net transfers of resources abroad (about 70 per cent in all), the whole process depended crucially on the autonomy of public revenues. Therefore, governments which owned export activities, such as Chile, Mexico and Venezuela – and as a consequence did not have to depend so

imports across-the-board, tended to show both lower investment and reduced national savings during this period. On the other hand, a better performance was attained during that period by countries (such as Brazil and Colombia) that reformed their trade and financial policies in a moderate and selective manner. After 1982, investment became constrained not only by the abrupt halt to foreign borrowing and the recession, but also by a shortage of domestic investable resources; both the private and public sectors had to channel a sizeable proportion of their savings into interest payments on their foreign debt.

much on domestic taxes – were able to transfer these resources more effectively. In contrast, governments that had to rely on domestic taxes to finance their debt service, such as Argentina, Brazil, Peru and Uruguay, ended up with large fiscal deficits and mounting inflation.

The Third World debt crisis of the 1980s was a global problem. The deficits of non-oil developing countries absorbed a significant part of OPEC surpluses, thus helping DMEs to soften their recession in the 1970s. Since 1982, the burden of debt repayment imposed massive costs on LDC economies, particularly in Latin America. However, this adjustment also negatively affected DMEs' exports to LDCs, and therefore output, public revenues, investment and employment in the industrialized countries. The debt crisis also contributed to instability in world financial markets. Given the existence of a growing interdependence in the world economy, a better-timed and more balanced treatment of the debt crisis would have left both developing and developed nations better off.

CONCLUSION

The stagnation of the 1980s obscured the comparatively strong economic performance achieved by the Latin American countries during the previous three decades. In this period of ISI-led growth, Latin American GDP multiplied fivefold, resulting in significant economic and social progress. With hindsight, ISI can be seen to have been consistent with conditions prevailing in international trade and international financial markets after the Second World War; also, it was consistent with the economic development thinking predominant at the time and with the political demands arising from newly emerging groups in Latin American societies.

There were inconsistencies in the form in which ISI was implemented, lack of continuity in economic policy-making, a broad and often arbitrary pattern of effective protection, and disregard for exports. Excessive protectionism, combined with overappreciated exchange-rates, frequently discouraged both primary and manufactured exports. Nevertheless, overall, the ISI strategy was a positive factor contributing to the growth of GDP and general economic development during the 1950s, the 1960s and, to a lesser extent, the 1970s.

As opportunities opened up in world markets for exports of commodities and manufactures, and as the domestic economies developed new productive capacities, the Latin American countries – in contrast to those of East Asia – were hesitant and slow to adapt the ISI strategy to changing conditions. However, some policy changes were implemented from the 1960s which enhanced the role of exports, principally of manufactures. And some latecomers to ISI, for example, the Central American nations, were successful in the use of economic integration as a means to improve the efficiency of ISI. Annual growth of manufactured exports averaged 13 per cent in 1962–70, with growth particularly strong in exports to Latin American markets.

During most of the 1970s ISI in Latin America continued to shift toward export promotion. However, external events such as the oil shocks and increasing international lending created strong incentives for borrowing abroad on a massive scale, which tended in the end to discourage the export drive during the second half of the decade. Capital flows had a determinant influence on the economic performance of Latin American countries in the second half of the 1970s and subsequently during the 1980s. The entire region experienced 'positive' financial shocks, but policy responses varied. In particular, there was great diversity in the degree of openness to inflows and in the use made of new funds. The net balance was an increase of capital formation ratios during the 1970s and early 1980s, and significant exchange-rate appreciations in the latter part of that period with large domestic and external disequilibria.

The easy and (in the short term) inexpensive access to international bank lending, which was wrongly assumed to be permanent, stimulated aggregate demand beyond domestic output. Necessary tax reforms were delayed, and controls on fiscal budget deficits were largely absent in many countries, most notably Argentina, Mexico and Venezuela. In some cases, such as Chile, the private sector also over-borrowed. Only a few nations, notably Colombia, attempted to implement effective policies to avoid macroeconomic imbalances induced by the growing supply of capital inflows during this period.

During the 1980s, the region was forced rapidly to adjust aggregate demand to spending capacity. In fact, the downward macroeconomic adjustment went beyond the limits posed by domestic productive capacity, since the region faced the need to make substantial net transfers abroad. As a result, a significant share of domestic savings was diverted from the financing of national investment.

There were other debt-induced changes taking place. The intensity of the crisis led policy-makers to give priority to short-term targets, to the neglect of long-term development. As the nature of the crisis was associated with financial flows, the leading role in the adjustment was played by financial agents and mechanisms at the expense of the real economy. Together with deep financial reforms of a neo-liberal orientation implemented in several Latin American countries went low real investment, meager GDP growth, and worsening income distribution. The costs of the adjustment were unequally distributed among the various income strata of the population, resulting in an overall deterioration of the already highly skewed distribution of opportunity, income and wealth in Latin American societies and a sharp increase in the number of those living below the poverty line.

Following a decade of stagnation several Latin American economies began to show signs of recovery in the early 1990s. The revival of economic growth was associated with the first positive net inflow of financial resources from the rest of the world since 1981 – the result of both improved access to private external financing and a sharp decline in real interest rates in the U.S. market. Here was evidence of the continuing sensitivity of the Latin American economies to external factors. At the same time, the pace of neo-liberal structural reform accelerated. Broad liberalization of markets and privatization of public enterprises spread throughout the region contributing to a deep curtailment of the role of the state. From an active intervention in resource allocation and direct productive activities up to the 1970s, the state was left to focus on macroeconomic policy, the building of infrastructure and social programmes. However, in the process of reform and adjustment, the capacity of the state to fulfill even its new, more limited, role was severely weakened. As a consequence, there emerged an inconsistency between the reformed state's capacity and the need, imposed in large measure by the depth of the 'social crisis' and by the transition to and consolidation of democratic governments throughout the region, to pursue development-with-equity strategies. It is here that the major challenges of the 1990s are to be found.

Part Three

ECONOMY AND SOCIETY

5

URBAN GROWTH AND URBAN SOCIAL STRUCTURE IN LATIN AMERICA, 1930–1990

This chapter analyses the changes in urban social structure, and especially the changes in occupation structure, in Latin America from the 1930s to the 1980s that resulted from the coming together of three processes: rapid urbanization; industrialization in its different stages; and the growing importance in the Latin American economies of the service sector, both traditional services and modern services linked to the growth of government bureaucracy and to twentieth-century business practices (technical, financial, administrative). In developed countries similar processes produced a convergence of social structures: the expansion of the middle classes, the consolidation of an industrial working-class, and improvements in the general welfare of the population. In the case of Latin America, there has been a greater heterogeneity in patterns of stratification. The dependence of the region on foreign technology and, increasingly, on external finance, combined with its role in the world economy as a supplier of primary and, hence, rurally based commodities, resulted in an uneven modernization, both between countries and between regions of the same country. This chapter will emphasize these differences and the need to pay attention to the specific situation of each country.

In terms of social stratification, there was in Latin America a contradictory relationship between urban growth, economic development and modernization. The cities multiplied and concentrated economic resources. Industrial growth stimulated the increase in levels of education, the proletarianization of the labour force and also the expansion of the non-manual sectors. On the other hand, this same urban growth brought with it a marked polarization of the social structure, both in terms of income and in labour conditions as shown by the persistence of non-waged forms of labour (self-employed workers, unpaid family workers) and highly skewed income distributions. The cities of Latin America at the end of the twentieth century, just as those at the beginning of the century, were scenes of extreme social inequality. Opulence co-existed with the poverty of important sectors of the population.

The socio-economic and political changes in the region drastically modified urban social stratification. Some social actors – for example, professionals and craftsmen – became less important. Others became stronger, such as the working-class in industry and services. New actors came on stage, for example, the salaried middle class dependent on the state and on private enterprise. With these changes, the bases for the formation of collective identities altered, as did the social roots of urban politics.

To capture the heterogeneity of these changes in Latin America, we mainly use data from six countries – Argentina, Brazil, Colombia, Chile, Mexico and Peru – which, in 1980, made up 85 per cent of the Latin American population. We emphasize the contrast in the patterns of urbanization. looking at the difference between their middle and working classes, showing how womens' roles in the labour market have changed, and seeing the implications of these processes for social mobility and inequality.

To emphasize the transformations in urban organization from 1930 to 1990, we periodize the trends in three stages, though, in reality, this was a period of relatively continuous change. Moreover, the three stages overlap, and the countries of Latin America differ in the timing of the stages and in the extent to which they were affected by the dominant trends of the period. The first, which began in the 1930s and had come to an end by the beginning of the 1960s was that of the expansion and consolidation of industrial centres. In this period there was a strong surge of industrial growth based on import substitution of basic consumer goods – textiles, food and drink, shoes. There were high levels of urban growth and an intense rural-urban migration. The industrial activities that expanded made an intensive use of labour.

The second period began at the end of the 1950s. It was characterized by a marked internationalization of the urban economies and a new stage of industrialization, (as well as the modernization of agriculture and the stagnation of the peasant sector). The phase of import-substitution of basic consumer goods began to exhaust itself, and investments concentrated in intermediate and capital goods industries. The technology needed by these industries was expensive and often could only be obtained through association with foreign companies. This new stage of industrialization was more capital than labour intensive, leading to linkages with multinational companies. This shift in emphasis was in part produced by changes in the organization of the world economy, in which multinational companies integrated hitherto fragmented national markets and, in developing countries, sought new markets for their products.

Finally, the period from the 1970s to the 1990s saw the Latin American economies become highly dependent on external financing, increasingly reliant on modern services for employment generation and revenue, and oriented to the production of industrial goods for export. In addition, the 1980s were years of economic crisis for Latin America that resulted in an abrupt halt to the modernization of certain sectors of the urban economies. The crisis had negative consequences for per capita incomes and employment. Together with high rates of inflation and the inadequacy of social security, these contributed to a marked decline in the standards of living of the region's population. The crisis manifested itself as an urban crisis. The withdrawal of urban subsidies of various kinds and a general reduction in government expenditures led to a deterioration in urban infrastructure and services, and increasing environmental problems. Also social problems became more evident. Many of the cities of Latin America were unquiet places in the 1980s with high rates of urban violence, frequent protests against price rises and outbursts of looting. Social and economic exclusion was visible – from street beggars to street sellers. Apart from these immediate consequences, the crisis marked the relative failure of the social mobility that was apparent in the 1960s and 1970s, based on improvements in consumption and in style of life resulting from economic growth, and high rates of occupational mobility from agricultural to non-agricultural and from manual to non-manual jobs.[1]

URBAN GROWTH

In 1930, Latin America was still a predominantly rural region in terms of where its population lived and in terms of economic activity. The important cities depended, with few exceptions, on their links to the agricultural sector. Some of them, such as Buenos Aires, São Paulo or Medellín, prospered through the commercial and transportation activities associated with agricultural exports. Others were mainly regional administrative and commercial centres in which landowners had their main residences and

[1] See J. Durston 'Transición estructural, movilidad ocupacional y crisis social en América Latina, 1960–1983,' Documento de Trabajo, LC/R.547. Reproduced in CEPAL, *Transformación Ocupacional y Crisis Social en América Latina* (Santiago, 1989).

whose economic activities chiefly served the rural economy and population. National differences in urban systems were important since countries differed considerably in area, population and level of economic development. These differences, combined with the nature of their external trade, had already produced sharp contrasts between, for example, Buenos Aires or São Paulo, bustling with European migrants and the wealth brought by the export economy, Lima or Mexico City, whose period of rapid population growth was only just beginning and was to be based on internal migration, and the much smaller capitals of the Central American countries, all of which were below 100,000 in population in 1930.

The 1930s and 1940s saw the beginnings of fundamental changes in the spatial distribution of population in the region. Latin America was still linked to the world economy, though now more insecurely, through the export of raw materials and the import of manufactured goods. The Depression of 1929 and the Second World War stimulated import-substitution industrialization. Combining with the modernization of agriculture, this industrialization gave rise to rapid urbanization based on the rural-urban migration that began, on a large scale, in the 1940s.

Urban growth in Latin America was more rapid than that of the advanced industrial world in its comparable period of growth. For example, England in the nineteenth century experienced an urban 'explosion'. Yet in no decade of that century did the rate of urban growth exceed 2.5 per cent, whereas in Latin America the rates of urban growth were almost double that figure throughout the period 1940–60, reaching their highest levels in the 1950s (4.6 per cent) (see Appendix 1).[2] In 1940, only 37.7 per cent of the population of the six countries we are considering lived in urban areas, and many of these were little more than villages that served as administrative centres of a rural area. In contrast, the figure had risen to 69.4 per cent by 1980. In 1940, the urban structure was highly polarized: small and medium-sized towns had 53.5 per cent of the urban population, whereas the metropolitan centers contained 35 per cent of the urban population. By 1980, the distribution of the urban population had diversified: the relative weight of intermediate cities increased at the expense of smaller places, though metropolitan concentration continued, and the urban system of Latin American remained highly unbalanced.[3]

[2] Metropolitan population concentration was at its high point at the beginning of the 1950s, reaching 40.6 per cent of the urban population in 1950, 39.5 per cent in 1960 and 39.4 per cent in 1970.

[3] Internal migration and reclassification of rural places as urban contributed between 30 and 50 per cent of urban growth in the period 1950 to 1975 according to United Nations figures for various

Table 5.1. *Distribution of population and its growth in Latin America, 1940–80 (based on six countries)*

Size of place	Distribution of population in 1940 %	Distribution of population in 1980 %	Annual rate of growth 1940–80 %
Rural	62.6	30.5	0.08
Urban[a]	37.4	69.5	4.1
In towns[b]	20.0	23.3	3.0
In intermediate cities[c]	4.3	19.0	6.3
In metropolises[d]	13.1	27.2	4.4
Total %	100.0	100.0	
Total population	(95.7)	(268.3)	2.6

Notes:[a] Urban follows the census definition of each country, usually administrative centers and places of more than 2,000 population.
[b] Towns are urban places of less than 100,000.
[c] Intermediate cities are between 100,000 and metropolis.
[d] Metropolis is defined as those cities with more than 2 million inhabitants in 1985.
Source: Estimated from the relevant Population Censuses of Argentina, Brazil, Chile, Colombia, Mexico and Peru listed in Appendix 1, this chapter.

The growth of towns (see Table 5.1) was slower than that of cities throughout the period, and little different from the overall rate of population increase, suggesting that much rural-urban migration bypassed the smaller urban places to move directly to the cities. The cities that were classed as metropolitan centres by the mid-1980s grew rapidly between 1940 and 1980. Until the 1970–80 decade, their rate of growth was higher than that of the urban population. By the end of the 1980s, however, there was a reduction in urban primacy in these countries.[4]

Intermediate cities had the highest rates of increase throughout the period, growing much faster than both the small towns and the large

Latin American countries: United Nations, *Patterns of Urban and Rural Population Growth* (New York, 1980), table 11. The reclassification of places from rural to urban is likely to have make a limited contribution to growth in urban areas as defined by national censuses because this urban definition includes administrative, and not simply size of population requirements.

4 See Alejandro Portes, 'Latin American Urbanization During the Years of the Crisis', *Latin American Research Review,* 24, 3 (1989): 7–49. Urban primacy is usually measured by the ratio of the population of the largest city in an urban system to the next largest or next two largest. Urban systems have high primacy if the largest city is two or more times larger than the next largest. The preliminary 1990 figures from Mexico indicate that Mexico, D.F. was five times larger than Guadalajara, the second city, as compared with six times larger in 1980.

metropolitan centres. The high rates of growth of intermediate cities was due in part, however, to increases in the number of such cities as smaller towns grew and passed into the intermediate category.[5] The rate of increase of individual intermediate cities was, at times, lower than that of the metropolitan centres. In Mexico, cities that had more than 100,000 inhabitants in 1980 grew at a 4.1 per cent rate of annual growth between 1940 and 1950, 4.2 per cent between 1950 and 1960, 4.6 per cent between 1960 and 1970 and 4.1 per cent between 1970–80. In contrast the metropolitan centres (Mexico City, Guadalajara, Monterrey) grew at 5.2, 5.3, 5.2 and 4.3 per cent in the respective years.[6] The higher growth rates of the largest Mexican cities appears not to have been sustained in the 1980–90 period since preliminary data from the 1990 census showed the metropolitan centres growing at a lower rate than many intermediate cities.

The growth of intermediate cities became associated with greater urban specialization accompanying new phases of industrialization. In the 1970s the increasing complexity of the industrial structure, with the production of intermediate and capital goods, resulted in the location of new plants outside the large cities. For example, the big steel plants of Brazil and Mexico were located in secondary cities. The automobile industry and heavy engineering was also located outside the metropolitan centres: Córdoba in Argentina; Puebla, Toluca and Saltillo in Mexico.

Two further tendencies reinforced this dispersion of industrial activities. First, the separation of administrative functions from those of production occurred in Latin America just as in the advanced industrial world. Administrative offices were located in the large cities where modern services were found, whereas manufacturing facilities were placed where land was cheap, infrastructure adequate and subsidies provided. The increased emphasis in the 1980s on export manufacturing in certain countries contributed further to the dispersion since plants producing for export had little incentive to locate near the major internal markets. This tendency was also due to the policies of multinational companies to locate plants in low-cost areas. The automobile and autoparts industry of Mexico began to transfer

[5] The United Nations estimates that 15 per cent of the growth of cities with over 250,000 population was due to graduation from a smaller size class between 1970–75: United Nations, *Patterns,* table 21.

[6] Gustavo Garza y Departamento del Distrito Federal, *Atlas de la Ciudad de México* (Mexico, D.F., 1987), table 4.2. United Nations' estimates for the 1960–70 period indicate that when the same cities are compared between census points, the larger cities in the region (above 250,000) grew faster than the intermediate ones (100,000–250,000): United Nations, *Patterns,* table 17.

its operations to the northern border region, and became closely integrated with US automobile production.

This change from the concentration of economic activities in a few urban places towards a more diversified, and specialized, urban system took place throughout the region. It did not occur to the same extent in each country, nor follow the same pattern, producing contrasts between and within urban systems. There were 'successes' in terms of cities that, industrializing early and on the basis of protected markets, soon resembled in their economic and social organization cities of the advanced industrial countries. Some of these cities, for example, São Paulo, were to retain their importance in face of the lowering of tariffs on industrial products and increasing economic integration on a world scale. In the case of other cities, such as Buenos Aires, early success did not guarantee a smooth transition to becoming leading regional and international industrial and service centres. There were also the relative 'failures', provincial centres and some national capitals which neither industrialized in the early phases nor captured, at later phases, specialized economic functions demanded by the new economic order.

Comparing the six countries between 1940 and 1980 shows significant differences between them in the levels of urbanization and in the rates of urban growth (see Appendix 1). The most important contrasts are between those countries which, starting with high levels of urbanization, had relatively low rates of urban growth over the four decades, and those which beginning with a low level of urbanization subsequently had high rates of urban growth. Among the first group are Argentina and Chile, which in the 1940s were the most urbanized, with 61.2 and 52 per cent of their population living in urban areas. The rates of urban growth of these two countries between 1940–80 were the lowest of the six. Chile experienced a more rapid rate of urban growth than Argentina in the 1950s, had rates above 3 per cent in the 1960s and lower rates in the 1970s, reaching Argentina's level of urbanization by 1980, when both had more than 80 per cent of their population in urban areas.

Brazil, Colombia, Mexico and Peru had the highest rates of urban growth between 1940 and 1980. In 1940 they had between 30 and 35 per cent of their population living in urban areas. By 1980, this proportion had increased to around 65 per cent. The period of most rapid urban growth varied, however, from country to country: Mexico experienced it in the 1940s; Colombia and Brazil in the 1950s and Peru in the 1960s.

Though these differences in timing were important, equally strong were the contrasts between the urban systems of each country. The contribution to urban growth of the metropolitan centres, of intermediate cities, and of towns showed marked contrasts from one country to another. Geography and population size were factors accounting for why Brazil and Mexico were the only countries to have more than one city above two and half million population by 1985. The proliferation of large cities was, however, a common feature in most countries of Latin America. In Argentina, the intermediate cities grew faster than Buenos Aires during the four decades, and Buenos Aires was the only metropolis in the region that lost in relative importance between 1940 and 1980. The predominance of Lima continued in Peru, but this must be set against the increasing significance of the intermediate city. In the 1940s, Peru had no intermediate city, while by 1980, eight cities had more than 100,000 population. The growth of intermediate cities such as Arequipa, Trujillo, Chiclayo, Chimbote and Huancayo, was marked, and occurred at the expense of the towns. Colombia, where intermediate cities already had a substantial presence in 1940, showed the strongest decline in the weight of the towns. There, intermediate cities, such as Medellin, Cali and Barranquilla, concentrated most of the urban population by 1980 despite the rapid growth of Bogotá. In Mexico intermediate cities also grew rapidly, proliferating in these years: there were seven in 1940 and fifty in 1980 containing 30 per cent of the urban population.

Chile and Brazil had the most polarized urban systems by 1980, but for different reasons. The sparse population of most regions of Chile was an insufficient base for the growth of intermediate cities that could counter population concentration in the central valley, in Santiago and the port of Valparaíso. In Brazil, intermediate cities grew rapidly, but this growth was not sufficient to offset early population concentration in towns and the strong growth of its six metropolitan centers – São Paulo, Rio de Janeiro, Belo Horizonte, Porto Alegre, Salvador and Recife.

These contrasts were based on differences in regional organization in each country, and in the pattern of agricultural modernization. Colombia and Peru – the countries in which the relative decline of the town was most marked – had, in the 1940s, a predominantly peasant agrarian structure. The majority even of the urban population in these countries lived in towns closely linked to agriculture and to craft production. The stagnation of the peasant economies of these countries, together with the weakness of the local economy, resulted in large-scale migrations to regional urban centres, without needing the pull of urban economic development. The continuing polarization of Brazil's urban system was due to a heterogeneous regional structure: in the northeast, the decline of agricultural production (both plantation and peasant) stimulated migration to the cities of the south and concentrated the regional population in local centres that reached metropolitan size, such as Recife, Salvador and Forteleza. In contrast, in the centre-south and south of the country – Minas Gerais, São Paulo, Paraná, and Rio Grande do Sul – an economically dynamic agriculture and small-scale commerce was integrated through a local transport and trading network. This pattern of regional development, which included continuing industrialization, sustained an urban system based on towns, intermediate-size cities and metropolis.

The growth and modernization of regional economies appeared more clearly in the case of Argentina, in face of the declining importance of Buenos Aires. It was also apparent in Chile which, though highly centralized in Santiago, contained a number of dynamic local economies in which the agricultural labour force lived, at times, in towns, as in the case of the valley of Putuendo. Mexico showed a combination of all these tendencies: zones in which the peasant population was expelled to Mexico City, to other regional centres or to the United States; zones in which commercial agriculture combined with new industries such as tourism, automobile production and micro-technology to sustain the growth of intermediate cities – as in the case of the north (Hermosillo), the centre (Aguascalientes, Quertetaro) and some urban areas of the south and southeast (Mérida and Villa Hermosa).

A large part of urban population growth in Latin America between 1930 and 1990 was due to migration, and here, too, patterns differed between countries. The difference between the rate of increase of the total population and the rate of increase of the urban population provides a crude estimate of the weight of migration in urban growth. Using this measure, Table 5.1 indicates the broad changes in the role of migration during the period. In the 1950s, when urban growth was at its peak, a considerable part of that growth (approximately 44 per cent) was due to migration from the rural areas. In the following decades, the contribution of rural-urban migration declined relatively. This process was most marked in the case of the metropolitan centres. There migration contributed more than half their growth in the 1940s, whilst by the 1970s, its contribution had declined to a third.

At the apogee of urbanization in Latin America migration became the salient issue in public policy discussion and in social science research. This research concentrated on issues such as the differences between migrants and natives, migrant assimilation to urban life and the contribution of migrants to the urban labour markets. From the 1970s, rural-urban migration became a less important issue in urban development, while inter-urban, intra-urban, and international movements became more significant themes. This tendency was clearest in those countries that had high levels of urbanization and in which the rural population had declined in absolute numbers.

The impact of migration was different between countries (see Appendix 1).[7] The contribution of migration to urban growth was greatest throughout most of the period in Brazil, followed by Chile and Colombia. It was less important in Mexico, in Peru except from 1960 to 1970, and in Argentina except from 1950 to 1960. Only in Argentina was rural-urban migration a relatively insignificant factor in metropolitan growth, accounting for about 20 per cent of the growth of Buenos Aires between 1940 and 1980. In Mexico, migration, though more important to metropolitan growth than in Argentina, was never the principal component, mainly because of the high rates of natural increase of the population. In contrast, migration, not natural increase, contributed half or more to metropolitan growth in Brazil and Peru in two of the periods between 1940 and 1970, and in Colombia throughout this period.

International migration also became significant in the region, and, again, its importance differed according to country. In Mexico, the permanent or temporary migration of rural inhabitants to the United States probably helped diminish the flow of migrants to the Mexican cities. In Argentina, the role of international migration has been a different one, increasing the contribution of rural migration to urban growth: in Buenos Aires, a large part of the foreign migrants reported in 1970 were from Bolivia and Paraguay, and probably from the rural areas of those countries; in contrast, internal migration to Buenos Aires in the same year principally came from urban areas.

Urban land use patterns in Latin America between 1930 and 1990 were rarely neatly ordered by such market factors as urban land rent gradients

[7] For alternative estimates of the contribution of migration and reclassification to urban growth, see United Nations, *Patterns*, table 11. Migration was most important to urban growth in Argentina from 1947 to 1960 (50.8 per cent), followed by Brazil (49.6 per cent from 1950 to 1960 and 44.9 per cent from 1960–70), Peru (41.6 per cent from 1961–72), Chile (36.6 and 37.4 per cent from 1952–60 and 1960–70 respectively), Colombia (36.6 per cent from 1951–64), and Mexico (31.7 from 1960–70).

tied to the costs and benefits of central location.[8] The Latin American city became, if anything, more heterogeneous in its residential and economic land use patterns than it had been in the beginning of the period. Spatial organization, and the changes therein, provided only a loose framework channelling social and economic interaction. In 1930, the normal pattern for towns and cities, in Spanish America at least, was to be organized around a central square, near to, or around which were found the major government offices, the principal religious edifices, the mansions of the elite, and the major commercial establishments. Distance from this centre meant, on the whole, declining social importance, with respectable urban crafts-people inhabiting the next ring of buildings which provided both shelter and a placc of business. On the outskirts of the city were found the poorest urban inhabitants who worked as day labourers, street sellers, or by offering a variety of personal services. The proximity to the countryside meant that the urban outskirts merged economically as well as spatially with the rural world, with inhabitants cultivating kitchen gardens or working as paid labourers in agriculture.

This account was truer for the older and less dynamic cities than for those that were industrializing in the 1920s and 1930s. Already, the elites of cities, such as Buenos Aires and Mexico City (and in Brazil, São Paulo), had begun to move out from the centre to neighbourhoods that were free of the noise and pollution. The 'frontier' cities of the 1930s were already spatially heterogeneous with industry, business and housing sharing space, and rich and poor living in close proximity.

Housing was rarely purpose built for the working classes. Even in the few cities where such housing appeared – Buenos Aires, São Paulo, Monterrey – it covered only a fraction of the population. The working classes found what housing they could – through the subdivision of the abandoned mansions of the rich as in some of the *vecindades* of Mexico, D.F. or through the intensive occupation of other central spaces.[9]

Increasingly, they sought out alternative forms of cheap shelter, such as self-construction after invading land or semi-legal purchases from property speculators. This land occupation was not spatially ordered since though most unoccupied space was on the urban periphery, its availability de-

[8] See discussion in Oscar Yujnovsky, 'Urban Spatial Configuration and Land Use Policies in Latin America', in Alejandro Portes and Harley L. Browning (eds), *Current Perspectives in Latin American Research* (Austin, Tex., 1976), pp. 17–42.

[9] For an account of these processes, including illegal settlement, see Peter Ward, *Mexico City: the Production and Reproduction of an Urban Environment* (London, 1990).

pended on political factors such as whether it was public or private, the strength of popular organization, and the speculative intentions of its owners – what has been described as the 'logic of disorder'.[10] Moreover, some of the unoccupied spaces were in the centre of the city, as in the case of the hillsides of Rio de Janeiro or the ravines of Guatemala City. Despite self-construction, renting continued to be the major means of access that the poor had to shelter, with its incidence probably increasing towards the 1990s as even squatter settlements became a 'normal' part of the city, and the original owners rented out space as a means of supplementing their incomes.[11]

The flight of the middle and upper classes from the centre of cities was tempered by poor communications and inadequate infrastructure in prospective suburban areas. Also, the proximity of squatter settlements to most middle-class suburbs diminished their social exclusivity. Further complications were created by the economic heterogeneity of the cities. The persisting importance of informal economic activities, to be discussed later, meant that small-scale industrial and commercial establishments were to be found throughout the city, in middle-class as well as in working-class neighbourhoods, as entrepreneurs saved the cost of renting space by using part of their family residence to conduct their business.

By the 1980s and 1990s, conflicting tendencies were apparent in urban spatial organization. In Santiago, there was a 'qualitative leap' in class polarization as a result of the land market and urban administrative policies of the military government.[12] In contrast, though patterns of residential segregation according to occupation and income, had clearly emerged by the 1970s in Montevideo and Bogota, they were partially reversed in the 1980s as economic crisis led most classes to seek affordable shelter irrespective of location. In other cities, such as Rio de Janeiro and São Paulo, the occupation of space had become more socially and economically heterogeneous as high-rise middle-class housing was built in poor areas. Poor squatters were expelled to make way for new middle-class suburbs,

[10] See Lucio Kowarick, 'The Logic of Disorder: capitalist expansion in the metropolitan area of greater São Paulo', Discussion Paper (Institute of Development Studies, University of Sussex, 1977), and *Espoliação Urbana* (Rio de Janeiro, 1979).

[11] See Alan Gilbert and Peter Ward, *Housing, the State and the Poor: Policy and Practice in Three Latin American Cities* (Cambridge, 1985) and Alan Gilbert and Ann Varley, 'Renting a Home in a Third World City: choice or constraint?', *International Journal of Urban and Regional Research,* 14, 1(1990): 89–108.

[12] The phrase is from Alejandro Portes when he contrasts the patterns of spatial polarization in Santiago with Bogotá and Montevideo: 'Latin American Urbanization During the Years of the Crisis', *Latin American Research Review,* 24, 3 (1989), p. 22.

while the poor sought whatever niche they could find within established residential neighbourhoods.[13] Though substantial progress had been made up to 1980 in the provision of basic urban services, such as water, electricity and sewage disposal, access remained inadequate for a substantial part of the urban population in most of the major Latin American cities.[14]

SOCIAL STRATIFICATION, 1930–1960

In 1930, the urban class structure of Latin America was already diverse because of the differences in size and economic complexity between the large metropolitan centres, which were often national capitals, the administrative and commercial centres of provincial regions, and the smaller urban places that served as market centers and transport nodes for the farming population. In the largest cities were to be found the highest concentrations of the landed or commercial elite, clergy, liberal professionals, foreign migrants, and the classes that worked for them and constructed the infrastructure of the great cities: domestic servants of various kinds and labourers.

Latin American cities had a heterogeneous social structure in which the worker-employer relation was not the dominant class relation. Deriving their income mainly from agriculture and the import-export trade, most elites were not large-scale employers of urban labour, and were of diverse ethnic origins, especially in countries, such as Argentina and Brazil, which experienced large-scale overseas immigration. Even in the most industrialized cities, factory owners rarely constituted a homogeneous elite with common origins and business practices. Many of the early industrialists were immigrants from Europe and the Middle East, such as the São Paulo industrialist, Francisco Matarazzo or Juan Yarur, the Palestinian who became Santiago's leading textile manufacturer. Only in a few cities, such as Monterrey, Medellín and São Paulo, had industrialists of national origin begun to acquire considerable political and economic power by the 1930s. Whether the entrepreneur was immigrant or native-born, family ties and paternalist management practices were the usual means of running an enterprise. The large-scale industry of this period was basically a

[13] See Raquel Rolnik, 'El Brasil urbano de los años 80: un retrato', in M. Lombardi and D. Veiga (eds), *Las Cuidades en Conflicto* (Montevideo, 1989).

[14] See the articles in Matthew Edel and Ronald G. Hellman (eds) *Cities in Crisis: the Urban Challenge in the Americas* (New York, 1989), especially those of Vilmar Faria and Elizabeth Jelín. For an analysis of Mexico, D.F., see Ward, *Mexico City,* 138–77. Much of the progress was due to popular movements, and their pressure on urban and national governments.

family firm so that even the industrial combines were managed and controlled in terms of kinship relations, with sons, brothers and other kin taking charge of different parts of the enterprise.[15]

The middle classes in most towns and cities were relatively numerous compared not only to the urban elite but to the working classes. They were chiefly made up of those who worked independently, at times with the help of family members, or who were owners of small businesses with a few employees. They included white collar workers in government or private employment. Towards the upper end of this 'middle class' were the liberal professionals such as lawyers and doctors, and towards the lower end were the self-employed craftspeople or owners of small neighbourhood stores.

In the Latin American economies of the 1930s and 1940s, still predominantly based on agriculture, the middle class of small-scale entrepreneurs and independent craft-workers were widespread. Internal trade routes needed a host of small-scale entrepreneurs to distribute and transport the goods. Local craft-workers repaired and produced many of the basic goods and implements both for the populations of large cities and for the needs of a scattered rural population. Rio Cuarto, a town of about 40,000 people in the 1940s, located in the Pampas region of Argentina, exemplified this type of social structure. The town had no factories or other enterprises employing a sizeable working class. The middle classes were estimated to make up some 53 per cent of the population: owners of small commercial and industrial enterprises, white-collar employees of the bigger commercial establishments, teachers, professionals, and medium-scale farmers who preferred to live in the town.[16]

In the cities, the wealth of the elite and the demands of government required more professional and administrative services than was the case in smaller places, and the clientele of trades-people and crafts-people was a more differentiated one. Yet, no matter the size or importance of the town or city, working independently or in a white-collar job seems to have brought a sense of status that differentiated these people from those who worked manually and at the behest of others.[17]

[15] Examples are the Garza Sada enterprises in Monterrey which included glass, iron and steel and beer enterprises, and the family-based industrial empire of the Gómez which controlled a considerable part of the textile production of Mexico. See Larissa Lomnitz and Mariso Pérez Lizuar, *A Mexican Elite Family; 1820–1980: Kinship, Class and Culture* (Princeton, N.J., 1987).

[16] See J. L. Imaz, 'Estructura social de una ciudad pampeana', *Cuaderno de Sociología,* 1–2(1965): 91–169.

[17] Elizabeth Jelín questions the usefulness of classing the self-employed with the middle strata: 'Trabajadores por su cuenta propia y asalariados: distinción vertical u horizontal?', *Revista Latino-*

A sense of the importance of these status considerations is given by a study of the small (100,000) Argentine city of Paraná.[18] The study took place in the early 1960s, but the situation described is unlikely to have changed significantly since the 1930s. Paraná had few industries and served, as it had done since the beginning of the century, as an administrative and market center for a prosperous zone of small-scale farming. Informants in Paraná had little difficulty in distinguishing three urban classes in terms of life style and aspirations. The upper class consisted of traditionally important families and of members of more recently arrived economic and professional elites. The middle classes – the respectable classes – appear to have been almost as numerous as the lower class, and were subdivided into levels ranging from professionals and entrepreneurs, to white-collar workers, small-scale entrepreneurs, and independent crafts-people. Finally, there was the lower class, or *clase humilde* made up mainly of rural migrants and holding unskilled jobs as labourers, service workers and domestic servants.

Informants in the middle strata differentiated themselves both from the elite and from the poor who were viewed as not respectable because they did not command a steady income and could not provide adequately for their family's needs. Among these needs was education to secondary or university level for their children. An evident problem in Paraná was the growth of a middle-class population with secondary education, but with few local career opportunities.

The most important numerical sectors of the working classes were domestic servants, street sellers and labourers. An industrial proletariat was only to be found in the textile and food industries and then mainly in a few cities – Buenos Aires, São Paulo, and, to some extent, Lima and Mexico City. In 1910, the two manufacturing sectors in Buenos Aires with most workers were textiles and shoes. At that date, there were nineteen non-specialized textile factories with a total of 3,151 manual workers, an average of 166 workers per factory. In contrast, the shoe sector had 3,214 workers and an average of forty-five workers per factory. These workers were only a small minority (6.2 per cent) within the manufacturing sector of Buenos Aires, where the overall average number of workers

americana de Sociología (1967) pp. 388–410. Yet, compared to the situation which we will describe for the 1980s, the self-employed in the period 1930 to 1950 were much more likely to be seen by themselves and others as middle class, and much less likely to be seen as, essentially, a disguised proletariat.

18 See Ruben Reina, *Paraná: Social Boundaries in an Argentine City* (Austin, Tex., 1973).

per firm was only eleven.[19] In 1931, Lima had 2,504 men and women working in textiles and twenty-one factories registered. These workers, like their counterparts in Argentina, constituted a small fraction (7 per cent) of the industrial labor force.[20] In Santiago, Chile, the most important textile sector had, in 1930, 1,618 workers and 233 owners, or an average of only seven workers per owner.[21]

The 1940s and 1950s witnessed substantial growth in the Latin American economies, and in employment opportunities mainly for men. There appears to have been a rise in real incomes that benefited urban workers. Despite rates of growth of the urban economically active population averaging 5 per cent in these years, there was considerable growth in formal urban employment. There was a substantial decline in the proportions of employers, independent professionals and self-employed. Also, traditional services, such as sales and domestic service, as sources of employment decreased in importance in these years, to be replaced by social, business and administrative services (office workers, teachers, health workers, other salaried professionals and technicians), and by other modern urban services, such as car repairing (see Table 5.2).

This change marked the relative decline in importance of the 'old' middle classes – small-scale entrepreneurs, independent crafts-people – of the smaller provincial cities, towns and villages. In 1940, most non-agricultural self-employment and small-scale entrepreneurship was found in these places since it was there that most of the urban population lived. The classes that increased, in importance, were those associated with the large cities which, in this period and subsequently, were acquiring a greater weight within the urban population: among the non-manual strata it was the professionals, managers and office workers who grew fastest in numbers; among the manual strata it was workers in construction and the service industries, such as the repair services, the restaurant and hotel trade, and janitorial services.

A 'new' urban middle class emerged consisting of office workers, managers and professionals employed in government and business organizations, and needing educational qualifications to do so. The increasing importance of education to social mobility was one of the major modifications that the economic changes of the period 1940–60 made to patterns of

[19] *Censo General de la Ciudad de Buenos Aires, 1910* (Buenos Aires), Tomo I.

[20] *Censo de las Provincias de Lima y Callao, 1931* (Lima), tables 80 and 103.

[21] Dirección General de Estadistica, X *Censo de la Población, 1930* (Santiago, 1931), Vol. III, p. 69.

Table 5.2. *Urban occupational stratification in Latin America: 1940–80*

Non-agricultural population	(%) 1940	1950	1960	1970	1980
Higher non-manual strata	6.6	9.4	10.1	12.7	15.9
Employers, independent professionals	4.4	5.2	1.9	2.6	2.4
Managers, employed profs., and technical personnel	2.2	4.2	8.2	10.1	13.5
Lower non-manual strata	15.2	16.0	16.9	18.5	19.0
Office workers	8.4	10.0	11.1	11.7	13.2
Sales clerks	6.8	6.0	5.8	6.8	5.8
Small-scale entrepreneurs	0.8	2.5	2.6	2.5	2.5
Commerce	0.8	2.3	1.5	1.2	1.3
Other (manufacturing, services)	0.0	.2	1.1	1.3	1.2
Self-Employed	28.5	19.8	20.5	17.4	18.6
Commerce	9.5	7.1	7.5	6.6	5.8
Other	19.0	12.7	13.0	10.8	12.8
Wage workers	35.9	41.3	40.4	39.4	36.4
Transport	6.1	3.8	4.5	3.7	2.7
Construction	5.4	7.0	7.1	7.8	7.1
Industry	20.1	19.2	19.1	16.3	16.5
Services	4.3	11.3	9.7	11.6	10.1
Domestic servants	13.0	11.0	9.5	9.5	7.6
TOTAL	100.0	100.0	100.0	100.0	100.0
AGRICULTURE (% of the active population)	61.6	52.5	46.7	39.5	30.6

Source: Calculations taken from the national censuses of Argentina, Brazil, Chile, Colombia, Mexico and Peru. The years are approximate: 1940 includes figures from the 1914 Argentine Census; the figures for 1980 do not include Colombia.

urban stratification, both creating opportunities and, at times, frustrating them when the newly entering cohorts were 'over-educated' for the available jobs.[22]

Industrialization (as well as the consolidation of the export economy) brought another major modification with the formation of a substantial industrial proletariat in certain of the largest cities (as well as in mining and plantation towns). As new regions became the focus of economic development, and as rural and small town craft industries were displaced with improved communications and competition from factory-made products from both home and abroad, some places prospered, others stagnated.

There was also a change in the nature of manufacturing employment that is partly concealed in the aggregated figures in Table 5.2. In the 1940s, many 'manufacturing' workers were self-employed craft-workers or employed in small-scale workshops in which there was often little differentiation between producing and repairing. By 1950, most censuses made a distinction between, for example, shoemakers who repaired shoes and those who worked as manufacturing workers in a shoe factory. This change in classification reflected a real trend: the gradual decline of craft-type production and an economic differentiation resulting in larger proportions of the manufacturing working class being employed in factories, and in the emergence of a specialized service sector of repairs.

Manufacturing industry was labour intensive in this period of industrialization relative to later periods, using imported technology which changed little from year to year. Factory workers gained in importance as a sector of the working class, as did workers in the railways and ports. Nevertheless, the skills demanded by these jobs were still basically craft skills, and did not mark a sharp break with previous working-class traditions. In the 1940s and 1950s, factory workers reached the peak of their relative importance as manufacturing began to expand to include capital goods production, employing more factory workers in large and medium-scale enterprises, while craft workers were displaced by factory competition. It is likely that the classic proletariat – industrial wage-workers employed in large-scale enterprises – was more consolidated in 1960 than in 1940. By 1960, a greater proportion of workers in manufacturing were employed in medium

[22] Torcuato Di Tella contrasts Argentina and Chile in the 1950s: 'Estratificación social e inestabilidad politíca en Argentina y Chile', *Sixth Conference of the Instituto de Desarrollo Económico y Social* (Buenos Aires, 1962). Argentina had enough middle class positions to meet the aspirations of the increasing numbers with secondary and higher levels of education; the Chilean population, in contrast, was 'over-educated' for the more limited number of middle-class positions available.

and large-scale rather than in small enterprises. Factory employment in enterprises of 100 or more people covered, by 1960, half or more of the total industrial labour force in countries such as Brazil, Colombia and Chile.[23]

Little is known about women's paid work in Latin America before the 1950s. The absence of information and analysis indicates the lack of interest in the theme. In the 1930s and 1940s, women's participation in the urban labour market was undoubtedly low due to the lack of diversification of these markets. Female labour was mainly concentrated in the rural areas and engaged in domestic production. As such it was rarely captured by the censuses, which under-registered female work in the household production units of rural areas.[24]

The references to female work in Brazil between 1920 and 1940 indicate that, as in the case of males, most of the female economically active population worked in agriculture. Urban female workers were usually seamstresses or domestic servants.[25] The available data for 1950 show that for the region as a whole women's economic participation rates were still very low (18.2 per cent).[26] The countries with the highest levels of urbanization at this time – Argentina and Chile – had higher female participation rates than did Brazil, Colombia and Mexico. However, Peru had higher rates of recorded female economic participation than these last three countries, despite its modest economic development. Numerous comparative studies show that both countries with high levels of economic development and those with low levels are likely to have high female participation rates. High rates of economic participation at polar extremes is based, however, on very different economic realities, and affect different age groups and social classes.

In the decade 1950–60 there was only a very small increase in female paid work in the region. Only in five of twenty countries were there slight increases, though these included the region's largest countries, Brazil and Mexico.[27] In Argentina and Colombia female participation rates remained constant, while they declined in Chile in this period.

23 F. H. Cardoso and J. L. Reyna, 'Industrialización, estructura ocupacional y estratificación social en América Latina', F. H. Cardoso (ed.) *Cuestiones de Sociología del Desarrollo de América Latina* (Santiago, 1968).

24 See Catalina Wainerman and Zulma Recchini de Lattes, *El trabajo feminino en el banquillo de los acusados: la medición censal en América Latina* (Mexico, D. F., 1981).

25 F. R. Madeira and P. Singer, 'Estructura do emprego e trabalho feminino no Brasil: 1920–1970', *Cuaderno 13* (São Paulo, 1973).

26 PREALC, *Mercado de trabajo en cifras 1950–1980* (Santiago, 1982), table 1.

27 Edith Pantelides, *Estudios de la población feminina económicamente activa en América Latina, 1950–1970* (Santiago, 1976).

These variations in the pattern of economic growth, and its unevenness, brought a sharpening of differences in the class structure of the urban population within and among countries. Using examples from Argentina, Di Tella outlines four basic types of urban stratification in Latin America by the 1950s, based on the degree of concentration of the working class and on the possibilities of social mobility.[28] First, there were the large, industrializing cities in which the class pyramid broadened at its base through the increasing numbers of manual workers. The decline in the relative importance of the middle strata was offset, and education-linked mobility opportunities created, by the emergence of a 'new' middle class of professionals and office workers needed to meet the demands of administration and of more complex business organization. Examples of this type were the cities of the littoral of Argentina, above all Buenos Aires. Second, were the plantation or mining towns, such as those of the sugar producing areas of Argentina, dominated by a mass of workers, with few intermediate occupations and few opportunities for upward mobility. Third, were the towns and cities in regions that historically had been economically important but that had declined or stagnated. Towns in the northeast of Argentina, for example, had, relative to other regions, a substantial middle class in 1950, but its members had limited local prospects of retaining their relative status. Last, was the pattern of stratification found in dynamic agricultural regions, such as that of Santa Fe, where small towns servicing the farm economy provide multiple opportunities for economic mobility mainly through small-scale entrepreneurship.

These types of urban situation were found throughout Latin America in this period. Most Latin American countries, excepting Central America, began to industrialize in the 1930s and 1940s, and had at least one city with a high concentration of manual workers working in large-scale enterprises such as factories, transport (mainly ports or railroads) or construction. The concentration of workers in isolated localities was found in the mining camps of Bolivia, Peru, Chile and Mexico; and concentrations of plantation workers had appeared in northern Peru by the 1930s. Many countries had agricultural frontiers where the expansion of farming had stimulated a flourishing small town economy – the state of Paraná in Brazil; Sonora in northwest Mexico; the coffee region of Antioquia in Colombia. Improved communications intensifying the exchange of agricul-

[28] See Torcuato Di Tella, *La Teoría del Primer Impacto del Crecimiento Económico* (Santa Fe, Argentina, n.d. [c. 1965]), pp. 163–7.

tural and industrial products also changed the character of towns lying in established agricultural areas. Zamora, Michoacan in Mexico is a good example.[29] There, as a result of the partial application of the agrarian reform and increasing trade with the major cities, medium-scale, entrepreneurial farming, commerce and the services replaced large-scale landowning and craft industry as the basis of the town and region's social and economic structure in the 1930s and 1940s.

The by-passing of previously important regions by new patterns of economic growth was also common. Examples are the Los Altos region of Jalisco in Mexico with its numerous towns whose prosperity had been based on trade with the north and on cattle raising; the towns of northeastern Brazil tied to a declining sugar economy or the 'gold' towns of Minas Gerais; or Popayán, whose dominant families had played a significant role in Colombian history, but which had become economically isolated by the 1930s, though retaining a substantial upper and middle class.[30]

The industrialization and economic growth of the period from 1930 had, consequently, diverse consequences for stratification. It resulted, in most countries, in marked regional differences in the nature of class organization. Since working-class concentration and the relative weight of the middle-class differed between countries, broad national contrasts also appeared in overall patterns of stratification contributing to differences in political regimes between the Latin American nations. A further factor in this period was the importance of the rural population in the formation of the working class, and, to some extent, of the middle class. In most countries, the urban classes were in an early stage of consolidation since their links with the large rural population still remained strong.

For the period up to 1960, Argentina can be identified as having on the one hand, a relatively small agricultural population, and on the other, a strong middle class, and a consolidated urban proletariat, both often of European origin and with a long urban tradition. By 1947, the agricultural population was 25.2 per cent of the total economically active population, the urban middle class approximately 19 per cent and the proletar-

[29] See Gustavo Verduzco's accounts of the social history of Zamora from the late nineteenth century to the 1980s: 'Trayectoria histórica del dearrollo urbano y regional en una zona del occidental de México', *Estudios Demograficos y Urbanos* 1, 3 (September–December 1986): 333–50; 'Economía informal y empleo: una visión hacia la provincia Mexicana', *México en el umbral del milenio* (Mexico, D.F., 1990), pp. 375–96; *Zamora* (Mexico, D.F., 1992).

[30] See Andrew Hunter Whiteford, *Two Cities of Latin America: a Comparative Description of Social Classes* (Garden City, N.Y., 1964), and *An Andean City at Mid-century: a Traditional Urban Society* (East Lansing, Mich., 1977).

iat, 34 per cent of the nonagricultural population.[31] Chile had a relatively small agricultural population, a strong middle class, but its manual workers were mainly concentrated in isolated mining or plantation towns. The Chilean agricultural population was 34.3 per cent of the population in 1952. Among those not working in agriculture the middle class made up 12.4 per cent, and salaried manual workers, 25.2 per cent. Both the middle classes and the manual workers were relatively consolidated, and their importance was enhanced by their concentration in Santiago, Valparaiso and, in the case of the workers, the mining towns of the north.[32]

Brazil and Mexico had large agricultural populations in 1950 – 59.8 and 58.1 percent of the total population respectively. The weight of the agricultural population diminished the relative importance and urban character of both proletariat and middle classes. Both countries had important proletarian concentrations in certain cities, and this stratum made up 26 per cent of non-agricultural employment in Brazil and 24 per cent in Mexico. This urban working class was less consolidated than in the Argentine or even Chilean case since many of them were recent recruits from rural areas. In the case of Brazil, however, European migrants to the south had created a strong working-class tradition in certain cities, such as São Paulo. Likewise, the urban middle class in both countries was less well-established, and more dispersed with many middle-class occupations based on servicing the rural population. The middle classes contributed 9.6 per cent to nonagricultural employment in Brazil and 11.4 percent in Mexico. Finally, there were those countries that had large agricultural populations, and neither a strong middle class nor a consolidated urban working class, neither in cities nor in mining or plantation towns: Colombia, Ecuador, Paraguay and the Central American countries, except Costa Rica. Colombia's agricultural population was 50.2 per cent of the total population, whereas the urban middle class was 10 per cent, and a further 19 per cent were urban manual wage workers. The data for Peru show a

[31] These figures are based on the percentages in Appendix 2, taking account of the agricultural population, and defining urban middle class by a strict definition as the total of the higher non-manual strata and office-workers. The urban proletariat is the total of manual employees (excluding domestic servants). The basis of calculation is the same for other countries from the tables.

[32] Chile had the highest levels of education among the six countries in 1960, with almost 25 per cent of its economically active population having seven or more years of education (Table 5.4). There were more people in Chile with 'middle-class' levels of education than there were suitable occupational positions. The reverse was true for Argentina. Torcuato Di Tella also discusses the type represented by the cases of Costa Rica and Uruguay, which in contrast to the other types had strong urban middle classes, but few industrial workers: *Clases sociales y estructuras políticas* (Buenos Aires, 1974).

higher agricultural population than Colombia – 57.7 per cent of the total – while the figures for the middle and working classes were similar, 10.3 and 18.3 per cent respectively. There was an important difference, however, between the pattern of stratification in Peru, and that of the type represented by Colombia. Peru, like Venezuela and Bolivia, which also had a relatively small urban middle class, had concentrations of industrial workers in isolated mining, plantation or oil industry towns. In Peru, as in Bolivia, these industrial workers were 'peasant workers', retaining rights to land in their villages of origin, and returning there to farm after a period of industrial work.[33]

The differences in the consolidation of an urban working class can be seen in relation to the relative importance of the self-employed craft-worker (shoemaker, weaver, carpenter).[34] In Argentina and Chile, wage workers were three to four times more important than self-employed craft workers by the 1940s. In Brazil and Mexico, wage workers were about twice as important as self-employed craft-workers by this date; whereas in Peru and Colombia self-employed craft-workers were as numerous as non-agricultural wage workers. The relative decline by 1960 of manufacturing employment (which included craft work) among wage workers in Argentina, Brazil and Chile, and the slight growth in Mexico, reflected the consolidation of that employment in urban factories and the disappearance of craft-work as a category of manufacturing. Manufacturing became differentiated from craft-work, with a consequent expansion of service employment in the various branches of repair work and other personal services. Regional inequalities in Brazil, and to some extent in Mexico, made this process an uneven one, with self-employed craft-workers concentrated in the poorer regions. Peru and Colombia maintained relatively low proportions of manufacturing wage workers throughout this period. Though there was a decline in the relative weight of self-employed craft-workers, the proportions remained high, probably reflecting the continuing importance of the independent crafts-people of villages and small towns.

Migration added to the social heterogeneity of the urban population throughout Latin America. Differences in dress, accent and other aspects of culture made migrants a highly visible group. Since most migration

[33] See Julian Laite, *Industrial Development and Migrant labor in Latin America* (Austin, Tex., 1981) and Adrian W. De Wind, 'Peasants Become Miners: The Evolution of Industrial Mining Systems in Peru', unpublished Ph. D. thesis (Columbia University, 1977).

[34] See Appendixes 2–7. Self-employed craft-workers are the 'Self-employed, Other' category in the tables.

was concentrated among the economically active younger age groups, their impact on the labour market was a dramatic one. These factors served to create the impression of the Latin American city as containing an extensive socially marginal population. Some commentators emphasized the 'over-tertiarization' of Latin American cities in the 1960s, seeing it as resulting in permanent under-employment in marginal service activities such as street vending or domestic and other personal services. Case studies of urban poverty carried out in Mexico and Puerto Rico in the 1950s and early 1960s reinforced this view. The term 'culture of poverty' was used to describe the vicious circle which trapped many of the urban poor.[35] The case studies of families, most of whom were rural migrants, described the difficulties they faced in obtaining steady and adequately paid work, forcing most members of the household, children as well as adults, to find some legal or illegal income opportunities. Constantly at the edge of extreme poverty, these urban poor were depicted as having a fatalistic orientation to life that, combined with lack of education, reinforced their disadvantage and passed it on from generation to generation.

The available evidence does not confirm this pessimistic picture of a sharply segmented urban labour market in which rural migrants were a socially marginal under-class. Studies in such cities as Lima, Ciudad Guayana, Rio de Janeiro, Santiago, Chile, Guatemala City and Mexico City, carried out in the late 1950s and 1960s, showed that the urban poor whether city natives or rural migrants were effective in organizing to obtain what resources were available.[36] Through kin and friendship networks, they both obtained jobs and, over time, improved their job opportunities. Families placed considerable importance on education for their children, and educational levels rose sharply in these years. Also, these studies report an overall feeling that families had improved their situation when compared with their parents, and, in the case of migrants, with the opportunities available in the village or small town from which they had

[35] See, in particular, Oscar Lewis, *The Children of Sanchez: an Autobiography of a Mexican Family* (New York, 1961) and *La Vida* (New York, 1968), pp. xliii–liii.

[36] For an overview of these studies see R. Morse, 'Trends and Issues in Latin American Urban Research', *Latin American Research Review*, 6, 1–2, (1971) pp. 3–52, 19–75, and D. Butterworth and J. K. Chance, *Latin American Urbanization* (Cambridge, 1981). See also W. Mangin, 'Latin American Squatter Settlements: A Problem and a Solution', *Latin American Research Review*, 2,3 (1967): 65–98; J. Matos Mar, *Urbanización y Barriadas en América del Sur* (Lima, 1968); Lisa Peattie, *The View from the Barrio* (Ann Arbor, Mich., 1968); Alejandro Portes, 'Rationality in the Slum', *Comparative Studies in Society and History*, 14,3 (1972): 268–86; Anthony Leeds, 'The Significant Variables Determining the Character of Squatter Settlements', *América Latina*, 12, 3 (1969): 44–86; Bryan R. Roberts, *Organizing Strangers: Poor Families in Guatemala City*, (Austin, Tex., 1973); Larissa Lomnitz, *Networks and Marginality in a Mexican Shantytown* (New York, 1977).

come. Studies in some cities showed that migrants had a higher occupational attainment than natives.[37] In other cities, the natives had somewhat higher occupational status than migrants, but the differences were small and diminished with length of stay in the city.[38]

Existing housing was inadequate to cater for the rise in urban population, and squatter settlements became in this period a familiar feature of the city landscape of Latin America. Even these settlements, usually located on the outskirts of the cities, were not repositories of recently arrived rural migrants. All city inhabitants, native as well as migrant, used squatting and self-construction of housing as a means to obtain cheap shelter, and to escape the crowded tenements of the city centres.

Economic change and industrialization also began to alter the composition of urban elites. Foreign direct investment brought a managerial group of expatriates, mainly North American, but also European. These were counted among the elite, although their period of residence in any one place was usually only a few years and although their social contacts were mainly confined to the circles of their own nationality.[39] The size and complexity of the urban economies, increasingly externally linked through investment and technology, made the family type enterprise of the 1930s difficult to sustain. The business elites adopted more impersonal styles of management and obtained technical training either through the private technological institutes that developed apace in many parts of Latin America or by going abroad.[40] These trends, along with the growing importance of the state to business through contracts, subsidies, licences to

[37] W. Bock and S. Iutaka review data from Buenos Aires, São Paulo, Rio de Janeiro and Santiago to reach this conclusion: 'Rural-urban Migration and Social Mobility: the controversy on Latin America', *Rural Sociology*, 34, 3, (1969).

[38] As reported in the late 1960s in studies of Monterrey, Mexico, D.F. and Guatemala City. See, respectively, Jorge Balán, Harley L. Browning and Elizabeth Jelin, *Men in a Developing Society: Geographic and Social Mobility in Monterrey* (Austin, Tex., 1973), pp. 201–8; Humberto Muñoz, Orlandina de Oliveira and Claudio Stern, *Migración y desigualdad social en la ciudad de México* (Mexico, D. F., 1977), table 5.5; and Bryan R. Roberts, *Organizing Strangers*, pp. 29, 123–43.

[39] For an account of the expatriate business elite in Argentina, often not speaking Spanish, living in segregated neighbourhoods and using the schools and clubs of their nationality, see J. L. Imaz, *Los que Mandan* (Buenos Aires, 1964), pp. 145–7.

[40] Peter Winn reports this as happening in the Yarur textile enterprise after 1954: *Weavers of Revolution: Yarur Workers and the Chilean Road to Socialism* (New York, 1986), pp. 21–4. For a detailed account of this change as it affected the Gomez industrial empire, with the tension between maintaining a family-based enterprise and the need to develop social relations with government officials, and the limits placed on the Gomez enterprises by the refusal of the patriarch to forgo his particularistic style of control, see Lomnitz and Pérez Lizuar, *A Mexican Elite Family: 1820–1980*. For the case of Monterrey, see Humberto Muñoz and Herlinda Suarez, *Educación y Empleo: Ciudad de México, Guadalajara y Monterrey* (Cuernavaca, 1989).

import new technology and labour regulation, undermined family and paternalism as the basis of elite ideology and practice. Business elites increasingly sought alliances on a class basis, and extended these to include government officials and the military.[41] The economic power of the state meant that a career in government service became a means of entry into the urban elites, and an increasingly acceptable career for children of traditional elite families.

The trends in the nature of urban elites can be summarized in three broad tendencies. First, urban elites became more interconnected in their interests and social networks. Family ceased to be the main basis of economic as well as social power. Access to credit, to technology, usually externally based, and to political and economic information became more important to the success of an enterprise irrespective of the sector of the economy. In this context, the use of personal relationships as a means of furthering economic and political interests remained as salient as in the past, but, especially in the most dynamic urban economies, social networks began to include a wider ragne of elite positions than hitherto. The media, politics, bureaucracy, finance and professional services acquired a new salience for the maintenance and furthering of elite careers. Second, the importance of the state as economic entrepreneur as well as manager, and the relative weakness of the private entrepreneurial sector, made high government officials coequal members of urban elites. Third, the increase in the foreign economic presence, whether through multinationals or technology transfer, attenuated the national character and independence of urban elites.

These trends were most evident in the largest metropolitan centres, and especially in those which were also national capitals. Because of their lesser political and economic centrality and their particular histories, the elites of other cities were less exposed to these trends. The result was a degree of regional diversity in elite characteristics and ideologies which can be illustrated by reference to the elites of Monterrey and Guadalajara in Mexico, and to those of Medellín and Cali in Colombia.[42] In Monterrey,

41 In interviews with Argentine and Brazilian industrialists in the 1960s, Fernando Henrique Cardoso documents the importance for them of intra-and inter-class alliances to achieve economic development, including landowners, bankers, military, politicians and workers. Brazilian industrialists were less likely than their Argentine counterparts to place importance on alliances with workers. Also, in both countries, the industrialists with the highest external dependence were those most likely to discount the need to innclude workers in such alliances. See F. H. Cardoso, *Ideologías de la Burguesía Industrial en Sociedades Dependientes* (Mexico, D. F., 1971).

42 For an analysis of elite organization in these four cities based on extensive interviews with elite members, see John Walton, *Elites and economic Development: Comparative Studies on the Political Economy of Latin American Cities* (Austin, Tex., 1977).

the nature of the region, agriculturally poor but close to the United States and rich in minerals, was one factor in the consolidation of industrialization from the 1940s onwards through large-scale industrial combines, employing a large sector of the labour force. Monterrey's elite was small in numbers, cohesive, and retained considerable independence and power of negotiation both with respect to foreign capital and to central government and its local officials.[43] In contrast, Guadalajara, developing on the basis of a rich agricultural region and control over important trade routes, had by the 1960s an elite that was much more fragmented than that of Monterrey, and based on medium-scale enterprises in commerce and basic goods industries. Government officials were seen by informants as key members of the elite with power much greater than that attributed to them in Monterrey. External capital, whether foreign, or based in Monterrey, or in Mexico City, was highly influential. Local elites had less of a sense of controlling their environment than did their counterparts in Monterrey. The contrast between Medellín and Cali illustrates other factors of variation. Cali, of the four cities, showed most elite factionalism. The city's rapid but uneven economic development, had resulted in differences between a 'traditional' local elite, newcomers from other regions of Colombia, and a powerful foreign presence. Medellín, like Monterrey, had an industrially based and cohesive elite that retained considerable power of negotiation with central government or foreign capital. Unlike the Monterrey elite, but like that of Guadalajara, the Medellín elite was relatively numerous, based on medium-scale enterprise, and committed to projects of civic betterment.

OCCUPATIONAL STRUCTURES, 1960–1980

The period from the late 1950s to the mid-1970s was the nearest that the Latin American countries came between 1930 and 1990 to consolidating their urban occupational structures through clearly differentiated strata of wage earners. An increasing sector of non-manual workers coexisted with a still large sector of wage-earning manual workers, and with a declining sector of self-employed workers. There was also the emergence of an elite based on modern business enterprises. The nature of work also changed. The independent professionals and small-scale

[43] See, also, Balán et al., *Men in a Developing Society,* and Menno Vellinga, *Economic Development and the Dynamics of Class: Industrialization, Power, and Control in Monterrey, Mexico* (Assen, 1979).

entrepreneurs gave way to waged work in large-scale enterprises, whether public or private. Social relations lost their predominantly clientelistic character as they became transformed into work relations which, in the main, were contractual ones.

Between 1950 and 1980, modern non-agricultural sector employment grew at a 4.1 per cent per annum; the manufacturing sector grew at a lower rate (3.5 per cent) leading to a continuing decline in the relative importance of manufacturing employment with respect the rest of non-agricultural employment.[44] Though manufacturing industry began to be a less dynamic source of job opportunities for manual workers, manufacturing employment grew faster than that in the services (excluding commerce, transport and electricity) in several countries of the region from 1960 to 1970.[45] Noteworthy was the dynamism of industrial employment in Brazil, Chile and Mexico.[46] Although the new technologically based industry was not labour intensive, the fact that it produced new products diversified and expanded manufacturing employment.

Despite these variations, there were similarities in the changing composition of the proletariat from 1960–80 in the six countries under consideration. Non-domestic service workers increased, except in Argentina and Peru, and the relative weight of domestic service in the occupational structure diminished in all six cases. With the exception of Brazil, the relative importance of workers in manufacturing industry declined. However, this change had a different significance in each country: in Argentina, Chile and Peru it reflected the marked deterioration of manufacturing, whereas in Brazil and Mexico it reflected, in part, the shift in the composition of industrial work – from manual to non-manual. In Chile, jobs in manufacturing declined absolutely from 1970 to 1982. In industrial cities, such as Concepción, this negative growth reached rates of 3.2 per cent annually.[47] In Peru, the manual working class was, throughout the period, of less importance than elsewhere. The Peruvian figures for 1981 show that state employment, together with personal services and commerce, absorbed about 55 per cent of the labour power in four major cities – Lima,

[44] PREALC, 'Desarticulación social en la periferia latinoamericana', Documento de Trabajo (Santiago, 1987).

[45] Henry Kirsch, 'El empleo y el aprovechamiento de los recursos humanos en América Latina', *Boletín Económico de América Latina,* Vol. XVIII, 1 and 2 (1973).

[46] See Humberto Muñoz and Orlandina de Oliveira, 'Algunas controversias sobre la fuerza de trabajo en América Latina', in R. Katzman and J. Reyna (eds), *Fuerza de trabajo y movimientos laborales en América Latina* (Mexico, D.F., 1979).

[47] Instituto Nacional de Estadistica (Chile), Censos 1970–1982.

Arequipa, Trujillo and Huancayo.[48] In none of these cities, did the industrial labour force make up more than 20 per cent of total employment, and the predominant type of industrial employment was small-scale.

The continuing importance of small-scale enterprise was shown by employment trends. Only in Mexico and Chile was there a marked increase by 1980 in the relative importance among the working class of workers employed in enterprises of five or more people.[49] In Mexico, these workers increased from 51.9 to 60.4 per cent of the urban labour force, and in Chile, where levels of unemployment in 1980 were 20 per cent, they rose from 52.7 to 63.2. In Peru and Brazil, the relative weight of this class of worker remained constant in the same period, but at very different levels: 58.7 per cent in Brazil and close to 43 per cent in Peru. In Argentina, there was a marked reduction in the proportion of workers in enterprises of over five people, from 73.4 to 57.1 per cent.

One explanation for continuing high levels of small-scale employment in Brazil until 1980, despite economic growth, was the sharp social inequalities of that country and the heterogeneity of its urban system. For example, there was a marked contrast between São Paulo which was highly industrialized and had over 70 per cent of its work force formally employed in 1980, and Fortaleza and Recife in which approximately 40 per cent of the labour force was informally employed.[50] It is important to remember, also, that the dynamism of the modern sector of the economy did, under certain circumstances, sustain informal activities through, for instance, sub-contracting.[51]

In all the six countries, except Argentina, economic modernization in the 1960s and 1970s continued to reduce the importance of the self-employed. The decline was least marked in Peru, followed by Colombia. Peru began the period with the highest level of urban self-employment – 30.1

[48] Instituto Nacional de Estadistica (Peru), *Perú: Algunas Características de la Población: Resultados Provisionales del Censo del 12 de Julio de 1981* Boletín Especial No. 6 (Lima, 1981).

[49] See PRELEAC, *Mercado de trabajo en cifras 1950–1980* (Santiago, 1982).

[50] E. Telles, 'The Consequences of Employment Structure in Brazil: earnings, soci-demographic characteristics and metropolitan differences', unpublished Ph.D. dissertation (University of Texas, Austin, 1988), table 2.4.

[51] See Francisco Oliveira, 'O terciario e a divisão social do trabalho', *Estudios CEBRAP* 24, (Petropolis, n.d.); Brígida García, *Desarrollo Económico y Absorción de Fuerza de Trabajo en México: 1950–1980* (Mexico, D.F., 1988); Marta Roldan and Lourdes Benería, *The Crossroads of Class and Gender* (Chicago, Ill., 1987). Some 11 per cent of formal industrial enterprises in Mexico's second most important state, Jalisco, subcontracted work to workshops or domestic workers in 1982 – before the crisis: Bryan R. Roberts, 'Employment Structure, Life Cycle and Life Changes: formal and informal sectors in Guadalajara', in A. Portes, M. Castells and L. Benton (eds), *The informal economy in comparative perspective* (Baltimore, Md., 1989).

percent – and by 1972, this still stood at 28.9 per cent. Peru and Colombia were partial exceptions because of their comparative failure to industrialize in this period.

A large part of the increase in employment in the services was due to the increase in business services (financial, technical, and so on) and in social and administrative services. These modern services were linked to the expansion of the state and to a capital intensive manufacturing sector. They became the most dynamic source of employment in the service sector in the 1960s and 1970s. The numbers and proportions of owners, managers, professionals, technicians and clerical workers increased continuously between 1960 and 1980 (see Table 5.2). Commerce and transport also modernized through supermarket chains and large transport companies and reduced their relative weight in employment over the two decades. The traditional services – petty commerce and personal services – and construction continued to be points of entry into the labour market for new cohorts of unskilled workers. It was in these activities, and in manufacturing workshops and unskilled and casual work in modern industry, that informal employment and low salaries became concentrated.

These trends came earlier in some countries than in others (see Appendix 2 to 7). Argentina already had a non-manual sector that amounted to close to 30 per cent of the urban labour force in 1914, and in this case, the most dramatic changes had occurred from 1914 to 1960 when managers, professional and technical personnel gained at the expense of liberal professionals and employers, and office workers at the expense of shop assistants. In the decade 1970–80, the increase in managerial, professional and technical occupations was marked, as was the decrease in waged employment in the services. The decline in self-employment and in the importance of small business had reached its zenith in the period 1930–60 and it was from 1960 to 1980 that the importance of independent work increased again. Self-employment in Argentina was different from that of other countries: in many cases, it was quite formal and modern, involving relatively high levels of capital investment in stores or workshops.[52]

In Brazil and, to a lesser extent, in Mexico, the increase in the non-manual strata was mainly among its top ranks – managers, professionals and technical workers. Both countries industrialized rapidly in these years and also experienced a rapid growth in the services linked to industrialization. The changes in the structure of industrial labour in-

[52] Durston, Transición estructural', p. 76.

cluded the expansion of non-manual employment: technological change not only replaced manual workers by machines but also brought more technical and administrative workers. In Mexico, for instance, managerial, technical and administrative workers grew from some 11 per cent of those employed in industrial firms in 1940 to 24 per cent in 1980.[53] And the 1940 figure gives a false impression of the size of the white-collar work force of that year since it mostly consisted of employers in small-scale enterprises.

In the decade 1970–80, in Brazil, the most dynamic sectors in terms of creating employment were business services (11.6 per cent annual rate of growth), electricity and water (14.3 per cent) and manufacturing industry (7.5 per cent).[54] This last rate of growth contrasted with the slight increase in manual employment in this sector and suggests the importance of manufacturing in creating non-manual employment as we have seen to be the case in Mexico. In contrast, personal services and commerce in Brazil expanded at much lower rates (4.8 and 6.0 per cent respectively).

In Peru, the main non-manual expansion came mainly from the lower strata but higher white-collar strata also increased. The relative expansion of office workers was the highest of any of the six countries and was based on the expansion of employment in the state sector rather than in the private sector. The manufacturing sector in Peru, contrasting with the case of Brazil, was a less important source of employment than commerce and services. In Chile and to a somewhat lesser extent in Colombia, both high level and low level non-manual occupations expanded but the increase in the latter was more marked from 1960 to 1980.

The urban reality of Latin America was extremely heterogeneous within countries as well as between countries. To pursue the analysis of how economic, demographic and political processes combined to produce diverse patterns of urban occupational structure, we would need to consider the different types of urban context. Though such a detailed analysis is beyond the scope of this chapter, we will give some examples.

In those countries which grew economically most rapidly in the 1960s and 1970s, there were sharp contrasts between cities in the structure of employment. In Brazil in 1980, for example, 34 per cent of employment in São Paulo was in the manufacturing sector; in Rio de Janeiro, employment in manufacturing was only 19 per cent, with 22 per cent in modern

[53] Censos Industriales de México, 1940 and 1980.

[54] The subsequent figures are calculated from the Censo Demográfico do Brasil, 1970 and 1980.

services and 34 per cent in traditional services; in Salvador (Bahia) traditional services were the most important in absorbing labour (38 per cent), and employment in construction was as important as that in manufacturing industry (15 per cent each).[55] Mexico showed similar contrasts between its metropolitan areas: Monterrey was the home of large-scale industry, Guadalajara of small and medium-scale firms, and Mexico City was highly diversified, but with a high concentration of modern services. Some of the smaller cities, such as Zamora, had become highly specialized in commerce and the services, without any significant manufacturing presence. Of Zamora's 3,563 enterprises, just 7 per cent were industrial, and these were almost entirely workshops since the average number of workers per enterprise in the industrial sector was 9.7.[56] A similar process had occurred in Huancayo, a city of some 150,000 in Peru, where large-scale industry had practically disappeared by 1972, and the industrial sector was mainly composed of family-based workshops, bakeries or butchers' establishments.[57]

By 1980, the State had become increasingly important both in generating, and in regulating employment. Most Latin American governments had begun by the 1960s to pursue substantial centrally directed economic development programmes aimed at modernizing agriculture, raising educational levels, providing health care, renovating and extending economic infrastructure, and improving the fiscal capacity of the State. On a world level, the 1960s was a 'development' decade with the advanced industrial countries providing funds and technical assistance through international or bilateral agencies to assist Latin American governments in their development programmes. The end result of the internal and external pressures to modernize was a substantial increase in State employment in administration, in State financed development agencies, in public enterprises, and in social services, such as health and education.

Unfortunately, comparable series are not available for the whole period, and the data that follow are partial illustrating the quantitative importance of public employment to the formal employment sector. In Argentina, Brazil, Colombia and Peru, public employment represented higher proportions of urban formal employment than of total employ-

[55] Censo Demográfico do Brasil, 1980.

[56] Verduzco, 'Trayectoria histórica', 'Economia informal y empleo'; *Zamora* (see note 29).

[57] Norman Long and Bryan R. Roberts, *Miners, Peasants, and Entrepreneurs: Regional Development in the Central Highlands of Peru* (Cambridge, 1984), pp. 140–68.

ment and of non-agricultural employment. In Argentina in 1980, public employment represented 33.8 per cent of formal urban employment; comparable figures were 29.3 per cent in Brazil, 21.2 per cent in Colombia in 1982, and 49.1 per cent in Peru in 1981. Irrespective of the measures used, Colombia had a lower level of public employment than either Argentina or Peru.[58]

The increase in public employment was particularly significant in the non-manual strata in all countries of the region. In some countries, public employment became the major source of non-manual employment. By 1981, the public sector employed 57 per cent of non-manual workers in Peru, and 52 per cent of non-manual workers in Argentina.[59] Between 1978 and 1981, the rate of increase of public employment in Peru was 7.2 per cent annually, whereas the non-agricultural economically active population grew by 4.9 per cent annually. Public employment in Chile grew between 1964 and 1973 at an annual rate above 7 per cent, but from 1973, the economic policy of the Pinochet government brought a sharp contraction in government administration and in public enterprises.[60] The growth of public employment in Mexico appears to have been dramatic: central government employment in Mexico grew 12.5 per cent annually between 1970 and 1980. Whereas it was just over a million persons in 1970, by 1980 it was 3.2 million, or 17 per cent of total employment. In Mexico, public enterprises, such as the state oil monopoly PEMEX, accounted for about 24 per cent of public employment, administration 33 per cent and health and educational services, 43 per cent.[61]

This government employment was concentrated in the major cities, especially the capital cities, but it was significant in smaller cities and towns also. In Zamora, Mexico, a town of 100,000 by 1980, it was estimated that there were 1,000 State employees in the Ministry of Agriculture and the Rural Bank alone, and that schools, health and social services accounted for the major part of non-manual wage employment.[62] In Mexico, political considerations, such as the proximity of presidential

[58] Rafael Echeverría, *Empleo Público en América Latina* Colección sobre Empleo, num. 26 (Santiago, 1985).

[59] Censo de Población de Peru, 1981, Resultados Definitivos, Vol. A, Tomo II, Cuadro 28; Censo Nacional de Población de Argentina, 1980, Serie D: Población Total de País, Cuadro A. 10, p. 59.

[60] Echeverría, *Empleo Público en America Latina* indicates that this creates a large sector of 'marginal' public employment.

[61] See M. Blanco Sanchez, 'Empleo en México: evolución y tendencias', unpublished PhD thesis, El Colegio de México, 1990, and Teresa Rendón and Carlos Salas, 'Evolución del empleo en México: 1895–1980', *Estudios Demográficos y Urbanos,* 2,2 (Mexico, D.F., 1987), pp. 189–230.

[62] Verduzco, *Zamora.*

elections and clientelism, were contributing factors to fluctuations in the growth of public employment.[63]

In Brazil, jobs in public administration grew at an annual rate of 5.8 per cent between 1978 and 1985, whereas formal employment grew at only 0.9, per cent making public employment perhaps the major new source of formal jobs in the country. By 1973, public administrative employees in Brazil numbered 3.4 million persons, with 40 per cent of these working in decentralized agencies such as regional development agencies or public enterprises. By 1980, public employment exceeded five million people, or 11.4 per cent of total employment, with 43 per cent of public employees working in decentralized agencies.[64] In Brazil, there was an inverse relation between economic dynamism and the demand for employment in public administration, with the growth of public employment serving to ameliorate the negative social impact of the economic crises of the 1970s.[65]

The increase in state employment had both direct and indirect consequences for the status of both non-manual and manual urban employment. Latin American governments became active agents in stablizing and formalizing urban labour markets, creating clear-cut categories of worker with different entitlement and contracts. Social security benefits, such as health care and pension rights, were extended first to state employees, and mainly to white-collar employees. Key manual worker groups, such as railroad workers or workers in the energy sectors, who were often state employees, received such benefits next.[66] In the 1950s and 1960s, such benefits were extended to many sectors of the urban working class, especially those working in large-scale formal enterprises. There was also a growing regulation of the labour market, resulting in labour codes that gave some security of employment, established minimum wages and set up health and safety

[63] See F. Zapata, 'El empleo estatal en México', in Adriana Marshall (ed.) *El Empleo Público frente a la Crisis: Estudios sobre América Latina* (Geneva, 1990).

[64] On the growth of central state involvement in local agencies in Brazil and the growing importance of the state's entrepreneurial functions during the period of military rule in Brazil, see Antonio Medeiros, *Politics and Intergovernmental Relations in Brazil, 1964–1982* (New York, 1986), table 3.

[65] See Jaime Gatica, *Características y Ajuste del Empleo Formal: Brasil, 1985–1987,* Textos para Discussão, núm. 7 (Brasília, 1988). S. Cutolo dos Santos and C. A. Ramos argue that expanding public employment was a deliberate policy aimed at weakening public protest during economic crisis: *Mercados de Trabalho no Setor Público Federal: Subsídios para o Debate,* Textos para Discussão, núm. 9 (Brasília, 1988).

[66] See Carmelo Mesa-Lago, *Social Security in Latina America: Pressure Groups, Stratification and Inequality* (Pittsburgh, Penn., 1978); 'Social Security and and Extreme Poverty in Latin America', *Journal of Development Economics,* 12 (1983): 38–110; 'Social Security and Development in Latin America', *CEPAL Review,* 28 (1986): 135–50.

requirements. These labour codes were often not enforced, but they did create a distinction between formal and informal employment that was to become an increasingly significant feature of urban class structure in the 1970s and 1980s. Moreover, social security benefits and employment protection made non-manual employees – administrators, professionals, technical staff and office workers – a distinct urban class, a 'new' middle class that contrasted with the 'old' middle class of independent professionals and small-scale entrepreneurs.

In the 1960s and 1970s, state non-manual employment was not only among the fastest growing sectors of employment, it was also among the most secure and better paid, if non-wage benefits were taken into account. Access to government loans, specially built housing, and government-owned subsidized stores were among the attractions of state employment throughout Latin America. They made possible a distinctive style of life, based on comfortable single-family housing often located in purpose-built housing estates. It included cars and well-equipped houses, domestic servants, and, increasingly, private education for the children, who, in growing numbers, were going on to university. Whereas for the generation of the parents, secondary education was sufficient for middle-class status, by the 1970s university education was becoming the norm for their children.

The rise of wage-employment among women was one of the most important changes in the urban occupational structures of Latin America after the 1950s. Of all developing countries, Latin America showed the highest female economic participation rates in the 1970s. This rate was low, however, when compared with the developed world.

The modifications, in different historical periods, of female work outside the home resulted from, and contributed to, a set of economic, social, demographic and cultural changes in the region. The transformations in women's paid work were shaped by the inter- and intra-national differences that we have already noted, and by differences in time. The 1960–80 period shows, in contrast to previous decades, a general increase in female paid work.[67] Female participation in Latin American labour mar-

[67] For the participation trends on which the following review is based see Durston, 'Transición estructural' and CEPAL, *Transformación Ocupacional y Crisis Social en América Latina* (Santiago, 1989); for Argentina Zulma Recchini de Lattes, *Dinámica de la Fuerza de Trabajo Feminina en la Argentina* (Paris, 1983); and for Mexico Orlandina de Oliveira and Brigida García, 'Expansión del trabajo feminino y transformación social en México: 1950–1987' mimeo (Mexico, D.F., 1988).

kets increased in fifteen of the twenty countries analysed, though with differences in the timing of the increase and in the levels of participation. In Argentina, the increase was greatest in the 1960s. In Mexico and Brazil, it occurred most markedly in the 1970s.

Although female participation increased from 1960 to 1980, masculine economic participation declined. In Argentina and Chile, where there was a small increase in female participation, there was a sharp drop in male participation rates. In the countries of rapid economic modernization – Brazil and Mexico – the increase in female participation was high, while the drop in male participation was small. In Peru, the country of weakest economic development, female participation remained constant while male participation dropped sharply. Part of the reduction in male economic participation was due to the expansion of education among younger age groups and retirement among older urban residents. However, in the case of some countries – Argentina, Chile and Peru, for example – the decline in male participation was due also to economic stagnation.

In Argentina and Peru, the increases in female participation rates occurred among women of twenty-five years and more, whereas those younger than twenty participated less. In contrast, Brazil and Mexico showed increases in female participation in all the age groups, and the increases among young women (fifteen to nineteen) was marked.

The increase in female participation rates was due to changes in the supply of labour and to modifications in the social and spatial division of labour. Increase in educational levels delayed the age of entry into the labour force, but also increased female participation. Highly educated women became more likely to seek work outside the household. Lower levels of fertility, already evident in Argentina and Chile and being rapidly reached in Brazil and Mexico, also encouraged the growing labour force participation of women.

Rapid urbanization was perhaps the most important factor affecting both the demand and supply of female labour. Female participation rates were highest in the large metropolitan areas, which grew markedly, as we have seen, through natural increase and rural-urban migration. The occupational structures of these metropolitan areas were particularly open to female employment: in domestic service and other personal services, in commerce and in the expanding ranks of office workers. Female employment became part of the increasing polarization of the urban occupational structures. Women had more job opportunities than in the first half of the twentieth century in 'middle'-class occupations, for example as teachers or skilled secretaries, but they also entered informal employment, in increasing numbers, as personal service workers or as domestic out-workers. The concentration of women in certain types of work had little effect on the gender division of labour. Women remained segregated in the labour market, despite the changes in occupational structures. Opportunities for women were restricted not as a result of competition in the labour market, but by factors such as the possibility of combining domestic and extra-domestic work and by social norms which fixed which occupations were accepted as suitable for women.

There were clear differences between countries between 1960 and 1980, in the economic sectors and occupations in which women worked. CEPAL estimates show that the relative proportions of women in the personal services remained the same in Argentina, diminished markedly in Chile and increased in Brazil.[68] In all three countries, the proportion of males working in the services increased. In all countries, the relative importance of women workers increased in nonmanual jobs due to the expansion of technical, professional and clerical occupations linked to the growth of public administration and health and educational services. In Brazil and Chile, the increase in the relative proportions of males in non-manual occupations was high, but less than that for women. In Argentina, the proportion of male non-manual employment declined.

It needs to be emphasized that the expansion of the service sector in Latin America resulted not only in an increase in informal employment (low-paid workers in personal services, street sellers, and so on) but also created middle-class occupations in the public and private sector, a significant part of which were held by women. Peru was an exception in that the expansion of female employment in the services occurred basically through personal services.

Female employment in commerce and in finance increased sharply in several Latin American countries. The percentage of females working in commerce almost doubled in Argentina, and more than doubled in Chile and Brazil. In Mexico, too, in the 1970s, the relative proportions of women working in commerce almost doubled, and the rise in self-employment in this sector was equally marked.[69]

Women's employment in manufacturing industry did not increase to the same extent as it did in the services, and differed between countries. In

[68] Durston, 'Transición estructural'.

[69] CEPAL, *América Latina: las mujeres y los cambios socio-ocupacionales 1960–1980* Documento LC/R.504 (1986); Oliveira and García, 'Expansión del trabajo'.

Argentina, Chile, Brazil and Peru, women's employment in industry declined between 1960 and 1980, mainly due to the decline in craft industry.[70] Female manufacturing employment increased in Mexico from 1950 to 1970 due to the expansion of assembly operations by multinational companies, the persistence of industries (such as the garment industry) that traditionally were heavy users of female labour, and the spread of domestic out-work. Brazil showed a slight expansion of female manufacturing workers and craft-workers between 1970 and 1980, due probably to the expansion of industrial activities that made heavy use of female labour. The expansion of female employment in production activities also occurred in other developing countries, such as Puerto Rico, the Dominican Republic and Honduras in Latin America, and Sri Lanka, Thailand, Singapore, South Korea, Hong Kong and the Philippines in Asia. In all these countries, export zones were created that attracted industries manufacturing products such as electronics, garments, shoes, toys, which made intensive use of low-paid female labour.[71]

Underlying the complex changes in the urban occupational structure, there was a pattern that helps us understand the link between the transformation of the social structure up to 1980, and the differences between countries in economic development and in employment policies. The general tendency for non-manual activities to expand had a specific significance in each country. Despite the regional inequalities in Brazil and Mexico, the expansion of non-manual activities was based on the relative dynamism of their economies, of the industrial sector in particular, and of state activities. In Peru, this expansion was due to the weakness of the economy and to the willingness of the state to generate non-manual employment. In contrast, in Chile, the reluctance of the state to expand its own employment was offset by the increasing importance of financial and commercial services. In Argentina, both factors appeared to be present: the dynamism of modern services, and the increase in state employment.

By 1980, the urban occupational structures of Argentina, Chile, Brazil

[70] CEPAL, *América Latina.*

[71] See Guy Standing, *Global Feminisation through Flexible Labour,* Labour Market Analysis and Employment Planning Working Paper no. 31 (Geneva, 1989); UNCTAD, *Export processing free zones in developing countries: implication for trade and industrialization policies,* Documento TD/B/C.2/211 (1983); Richard Anker and Catherine Hein, 'Empleo de la mujer fuera de la agricultura en países del tercer mundo: panorama general de las estadísticas ocupacionales', en *Desigualdades Entre Hombres y Mujeres en los Mercados de Trabajo Urbano del Tercer Mundo* (Geneva, 1987).

and Mexico had become more alike. The levels of self-employment were relatively low and approximately the same in each country. The employed middle classes had become as numerous as the working classes. These similarities were produced, however, by a different pattern of economic development. Brazil and Mexico had industrialized rapidly, and this had been an important factor in the expansion of employment in the modern services. In Argentina and Chile, the expansion of the service sector was not based on continuing industrialization. The major divergence occurred in the case of Peru. Though Peru expanded its non-manual strata rapidly, this was heavily based on the expansion of state employment. Peru became the only country in which the levels of self-employment were as high as those of manual wage work. Colombia's occupational structures began to approximate those of the other four countries in this period, but the lack of data for 1980 makes comparison difficult.

Economic, demographic and social changes resulted by the mid-1970s in an urban class structure that in certain crucial respects had become increasingly similar throughout Latin America. The most salient divisions within this class structure can be identified in terms of four criteria: the degree of control over the means of production, control over labour power, type of remuneration, and the difference between manual and non-manual work.[72]

This class division includes, first, a proportionately small dominant class, based largely on ownership of large-scale enterprises mainly in the service and manufacturing sectors. Below that had emerged a clearly defined bureaucratic-technical stratum with high levels of education, and employed in managerial and administrative positions in both public and private sectors. Both classes probably have been more concentrated in metropolitan centers and large urban areas.[73] These classes correspond to the occupational categories of higher non-manual workers used in Table 5.3 which, by 1980, made up approximately 13 per cent of the urban population.

The basis for making class distinctions among the rest of the urban population is complicated by the importance to life chances of whether the economic activity and employment is formally regulated by the state or

[72] See Alejandro Portes' discussion of the first three of these criteria as means to characterize the Latin American class structure: 'Latin American Class Structures', *Latin American Research Review*, XX, 3 (1985): 7–39. We have added the manual/non-manual distinction.

[73] Portes, 'Latin American Class Structures', Table 2 estimates that the dominant class and the bureaucratic technical class make up about 8 per cent of the economically active population.

not. By the 1970s, the informal/formal distinction had become an important factor in the stratification of the urban populations of Latin America. Both informal workers and informal employers had a different set of interests, and different levels of income than their formal counterparts. The partial extension of social security coverage to the Latin American population created two classes of wage-workers – those who received a range of benefits including contractual security and those who did not. These benefits constituted a premium for workers who were further benefited through higher wages resulting from trade union negotiations and collective contracts.

Likewise, the partial extension of state regulation of economic activity and the uneven development of urban economies created two classes of entrepreneurs. One group – mainly large-scale operators – were increasingly enmeshed in sophisticated credit, marketing and supply networks that necessitated their having legal status and made it more difficult to avoid fiscal and social security obligations. A second group of mainly small-scale entrepreneurs worked so close to the margins of profitability, often in markets that experienced sharp fluctuations, that savings on overheads, such as their fiscal and social security obligations, became an important part of their survival strategies.[74] The small size of the enterprise, the low level of technology and precarious market position compared to larger and better endowed enterprises were also factors in giving this group of entrepreneurs an especial class position.[75]

Both the informal petty bourgeoisie and the informal proletariat were likely to have been concentrated in the smaller cities and towns, whereas the formal working class represented a more important share of the urban economically active population in the large cities.[76]

[74] Victor Tokman points out that this distinction was a continuum rather than a sharp break: 'The Informal Sector in Latin America: from underground to legality', in Guy Standing and Victor Tokman (eds), *Towards Social Adjustment: Labor Market Issues in Structural Adjustment* (Geneva, 1991), pp. 141–57. Most enterprises observed one or more of their legal obligations, though only a minority observed all of them.

[75] The PREALC studies of the 1970s tended to emphasize size, low levels of capital endowment, and market – and not state regulation – as the main factors in distinguishing informal and formal sectors.

[76] See Rafael Menjívar and J.P. Pérez Sainz (eds), *Informalidad Urbana en Centroamérica: Entre la Acumulación y la Subsistencia* (San José, 1991); E. Telles, 'The Consequences of Employment Structure in Brazil: earnings, socio-demographic characteristics and metropolitan differences', unpublished Ph.D. dissertation (University of Texas, Austin, 1988) table 2.4; Bryan R. Roberts, 'The Changing Nature of Informal Employment: the case of Mexico', in Standing and Tokman *Towards Social Adjustment,* pp. 115–40; and Secretaría de Programación y Presupuesto (SPP), *La Ocupación Informal en Areas Urbanas* (Mexico, D.F., 1979) for large cities. Carlos Briones shows that the smaller urban places of El Salvador have higher proportions of both the informal bourgeoisis and the

A further stratum of lower non-manual workers needs to be added to this description of the urban class structure.[77] This lower middle class included semi-professionals, such as teachers, nurses and other health workers, secretaries, bank clerks, and sales clerks. Evidence from Mexico suggests that in the 1960s, this stratum of the urban population earned more than a skilled industrial worker, but that the differential had decreased or been eliminated by the 1970s.[78] In Brazil, by 1980, the mean income and prestige scores of those in semi-professional occupations were higher than those of most manual workers in industry, construction and the personal services.[79]

Though the differences were small between the incomes of this lower middle-class group and that of the skilled, formal working class, several factors make it important to include this group as one of the six urban strata. Average levels of education of this class were higher than for the manual working class, with formal education being essential not only for carrying out the job but for reaching the better-paid positions. Conditions of work were generally better, with office workers, teachers and health workers enjoying more social security protection than did the manual working class as a whole. Finally, this was the class most dependent on state employment, and which represented most social mobility opportunities for women – female office workers earned significantly higher salaries than did females in the manual wage-earning categories – domestic and other personal services. By the 1970s this class was likely to have amounted to about 16 per cent of the total urban population.[80]

The transformation of the occupational structure of Latin America had contradictory consequences for income distribution, and for the share of

informal proletariat: 'Economía informal en el Gran San Salvador', in Menjívar and Pérez Sainz, *Informalidad Urbana,* pp. 91–148. Portes estimates the informal petty bourgeoisie in 1970 as 10 per cent, the formal proletariat as 22 per cent, and the informal proletariat (which includes the peasant population) as 60 per cent: 'Latin American Class Structures', table 2. Telles' study of occupations, earning and stratification in the six major metropolitan areas of Brazil in 1980, cited above, indicates that the formal proletariat averages just under a third of the economically active population of these cities, and the informal proletariat about the same proportion.

77 But see Portes' reasons for *not* distinguishing between non-manual and manual workers: 'Latin American class structures', p. 13.

78 For comparisons between the wages of a secretary, bookkeeper, cashier, accountant and a mechanic see J. Reyes Heroles, *Política Macroeconómica y Bienestar en México* (Mexico, D. F., 1983), table II.21.

79 Telles provides a complete list of mean occupation income and occupational prestige scores of urban occupations: 'The consequences of employment structure in Brazil', Appendix B., pp. 173–81.

80 This estimate is based on subtracting Portes' figures of 8% for the combined dominant/bureaucratic class from the total percent in Table 5.2 for higher non-manual and office categories. See Portes, 'Latin American Class Structures'.

the different urban classes in that distribution. In general, in the period up to the mid-1970s, there was a rise in real incomes for all strata of the urban populations – a general trend interrupted in some cases by economic cycles and by political conjunctures. During this same period, however, income concentration increased in Latin America. The top 10 per cent of households by income receive a greater share in 1975 than they had in 1960.[81]

The social strata that have been described above were likely to be differentiated by sources of income and by the amounts they receive. The highest income levels corresponded to the dominant and bureaucratic-technical class. The upper middle income levels were made up of aspiring members of those classes, just beginning their careers in government or in the private sector, some small-scale entrepreneurs in industry and the services, and, in some countries, skilled workers of key industries, such as petroleum or, in this period, the car industry. The intermediate levels of income in this period included the lower middle class – teachers, ancillary personnel in the health and welfare services, bank clerks, and office workers in private and public sectors – and the less successful members of the informal bourgeoisie, the more successful among the self-employed, and skilled workers in industry, transport and communications. The lower middle levels of income included the bottom end of the lower middle class – sales clerks and non-specialized office workers – skilled workers in basic goods industries, in construction, and in the services, and the self-employed in industry and certain of the services. The bottom income levels included semi- and unskilled formally employed workers in industry, construction and the services, together with most self-employed workers and informally employed workers. The self-employed, and skilled informally employed workers, were, in this period, likely to be in the upper end of these strata, especially craft-workers, while those in personal services, were at the bottom end.

Combining evidence from Mexico and Brazil with that from other countries of Latin America suggests that by the mid-seventies, urban income distribution, while demonstrating sharp inequalities, also evidenced the consolidation of these various strata.[82] The bureaucratic-

[81] See Portes, 'Latin American Class Structures', table 3.

[82] Ibid.; Enrique Iglesias, 'La crisis económica internacional y las perspectivas de América Latina', in *América Latina y la Crisis Internacional* (Montevideo, 1983); Fernando Cortes, and Rosa María Rubalcava, *Autoexplotación Forzada y Equidad por Empobrecimiento* (Mexico, D. F., 1991); Charles H. Wood and José de Carvalho, *The Demography of Inequality in Brazil* (Cambridge, 1988) table 3.5; Agustín Escobar and Bryan R. Roberts, 'Urban Stratification, the Middle Classes, and Economic

dominant group – who are likely to be synonymous with the richest 10 per cent of households in income – had clearly benefited from the rise in real salaries and in profits. In the period from 1960 to 1975, they probably increased their share of household income slightly from 46.6 per cent to 47.3 per cent.[83] However, the informal bourgeoisie, the lower middle class, and the formal proletariat had also increased both their real wages and, probably, with the exception of Brazil, their share of income.[84]

These gains reflected a series of factors in the pattern of economic development since the 1960s: the dominant groups and the informal bourgeoisie benefited from the general dynamism of the economies of the region and the entrepreneurial opportunities they generated; the lower middle class from the growth of state employment and the benefits given to state employees; and the formal proletariat gained from the power of organized labour to extract wage concessions. While the unskilled and informal workers appear to have decreased their share of total income, thus creating a certain polarization in the class structure, this was offset by a rise in real incomes even among these strata.

The discussion of class structure and income inequality is further complicated by needing to take account of the household in determining patterns of stratification. By the mid-1970s, most urban households in Latin America had more than one member who was economically active. Female participation rates had risen sharply, as we have seen, and it was increasingly common for wives, and not just adult children to work for a wage or help with the family business. The distribution of extra wage-earners was not, however, even across the class strata, both for economic and demographic reasons. Overall, households in the highest strata had, by the 1970s, smaller families and fewer members in the labour market, and the lowest urban strata, larger families and most members in the labour market.[85] The higher participation of very poor households was also the case even controlling for the number of available workers in the household.[86] In the higher

change in Mexico', in Mercedes González de la Rocha and Agustín Secobar Latapi (eds), *Social Responses to Mexico's Economic Crisis of the 1980s* (San Diego, 1991).

83 Portes, 'Latin American Class Structures', table 3.

84 Wood and Carvalho's (*Demography of Inequality in Brazil*) figures for Brazil show a decline in the share of income of the intermediate and lower-middle urban strata, which contrasts with the increasing share of these strata in Portes' ('Latin American Class Structures', table 3) data.

85 Mexican data show this clearly. See Henry Selby, Arthur D. Murphy and Stephen A. Lorenzer, *The Mexican Urban Household Organizing for Self-Defense* (Austin, Tex., 1990).

86 See Brigida García, Humberto Muñoz and Orlandina de Oliveira, 'Migration, Family Context and Labour-force Participation in Mexico, D.F.', in Jorge Balán, (ed.), *Why People Move* (Paris, 1981), pp. 217–18.

strata, the income of the head of household was usually sufficient to maintain the family at its expected level of subsistence, and other members worked to pursue a professional career and/or to increase the level of consumption which, at times, resulted in higher rates of female economic participation.[87] In the bottom deciles of income, the salaries of the head of household were often insufficient to make ends meet or were close to the margin of subsistence. In these cases, supplementary incomes earned by other family members were an essential means of household survival.

The bottom income strata, and the classes associated with them, can, thus, be identified not simply by occupational titles or by whether the job was formal or informal, but by the overall household strategy for obtaining an income. These were the urban poor for whom income pooling, and sharing housing, food and other resources, were essential means of urban survival. Family and friendship networks were also crucial to urban subsistence strategies by providing help with housing, food and finding work.[88] Poor households might contain formally or informally employed workers, the self-employed or domestic servants. They were less likely to have the spare resources to keep a child out of the labour market, or a mother to devote herself solely to bringing up children and keeping up the household. Thus was added to income inequality that arising from poorer standards of nutrition, health and general welfare.

Poor households were not homogeneous in their social and economic characteristics. The greater use of available labour among households whose heads had low incomes led to considerable occupational heterogeneity among the poor. It was common for workers of different types to be present in the same household: workers in the manufacturing sector, service workers, white collar and blue workers, workers in the formal and informal sectors and so on. Studies in Mexico City and Guadalajara indicated that in households headed by manual workers, the sons were usually also manual workers, whereas the daughters and wives – when they

[87] The relative participation rates of the different urban strata show that women from 'middle class' (non-manual) households are more likely to be economically active than women from working-class households. Women with higher levels of education can earn enough to substitute their own domestic labour with paid domestic services. See Brigida García, Humberto Muñoz and Orlandina de Oliveira, *Hogares y Trabajadores en la Ciudad de México* (Mexico, D. F., 1982), table V.1.

[88] See Balán et al., *Men in a Developing Society,* for Monterrey, Mexico; Roberts, *Organizing Strangers,* for Guatemala City; M. Margulis, *Migración y marginalidad en la sociedad argentina* (Buenos Aires, 1970) for Buenos Aires; and Butterworth and Chance, *Latin American Urbanization,* for other Latin American cities. In the case of Mexico, D.F., 90 per cent of individual migrants were preceded or followed by a family member. See Brigida García, Humberto Muñoz and Orlandina de Oliveira, 'Migración, familia y fuerza de trabajo en la Ciudad de México; *Cuadernos del CES* 26 (Mexico, D.F. 1979).

worked for a wage – worked in a variety of occupations, contributing to the heterogeneity mentioned above.[89] Furthermore, households included both migrants and natives. For example, in Mexico City in 1970, the urban labour force was mainly made up of migrant heads of families and their native children, and, in 1980, in Reynosa – one of the northern border cities of Mexico – migrants and natives were members of the same family and shared the same household.[90]

Migration needs also to be considered as a factor adding to inequality by the 1970s, though its impact was heterogeneous, varied between cities and differed depending on whether the migrant was male or female. There is evidence for some cities that migrant selectivity declined after the 1960s, with those arriving in the cities possessing less education and skills relative to their populations of origin than had previous migrants. Migrants who arrived in the 1950s and 1960s in Monterrey – an industrial city to the north of Mexico – were less skilled and were more likely to fill manual job positions than previous migrants.[91] Likewise, from the 1960s there was an increasing migration of unskilled rural workers to Mexico City who take-up unskilled urban positions.[92]

Usually, rural migrants were disproportionately found in unskilled manual jobs in construction, manufacturing and services, whereas non-manual jobs, created by the rise of the modern services and which demanded relatively high levels of education, fell to those born in the city or in other cities with good educational facilities. The city-born and those urban migrants with at least primary education worked, in general, in skilled and semi-skilled work in manufacturing, in service firms or in family workshops.[93]

Casual labour in personal services, in construction and in manufacturing was often provided by temporary rural-urban migration, so that in

89 García, Muñoz and Oliveira, 'Migración'; Mercedes González de la Rocha, *Los Recursos de la Pobreza: Familias de Bajos Ingresos en Guadalajara* (Mexico, D.F., 1986).

90 For Mexico, D.F., see García, Muñoz and Oliveira, 'Migración'; for Reynosa, see M. Margulis and R Tuirán, *El mercado de trabajo en el capitalismo periférico: el caso de Reynosa* (Mexico, D.F., 1986).

91 See Balán et al., *Men in a Developing Society*, pp. 146–7.

92 For Mexico, D.F., see Orlandina de Oliveira, 'Industrialization, Migration and Entry Labor Force Changes in Mexico, D.F., 1930–1970', unpublished Ph.D. dissertation (Univeristy of Texas, Austin, 1975). In Buenos Aires, migrants, both male and female, were as likely to be found working in manufacturing and construction as those born in the city. And in Mexico, D.F., migrants played an important part in the expansion of the industrial labor force and of non-manual jobs. See A. Marshall, *El mercado de trabajo en el capitalismo periférico: el caso de Argentina* (Santiago, 1978); Orlandina de Oliveira and Brigida García, 'Migración a grandes ciudades del Tercer Mundo: algunos implicaciones sociodemográficas', *Estudios Sociológicos*, Mexico, D. F., 2/4 (1984).

93 See Agustín Escobar, *Con el sudor de tu frente* (Guadalajara, 1986).

certain countries informal workers often appeared ethnically distinct from those formally employed.[94] Where, as in Argentina, there was no peasant economy to provide temporary migrants, the unskilled migrants to Buenos Aires came from neighbouring countries, and these fulfilled similar functions to the temporary flows in Mexico.[95]

Though rural migrants did not, as we have seen, suffer substantial disadvantage when compared with the urban born, this was not the case of those migrants who came from ethnic minorities that were clearly distinct from the bulk of the population. The *cabecitas negras* from the northern provinces of Argentina were looked down upon by European migrants and the city born. Paraguayan and Bolivian migrants had by the 1970s become a distinct underclass in Buenos Aires. In Brazil, despite its reputation for harmonious race relations, Blacks became the most disadvantaged sector of the urban population. Taking account both of levels of education, rural or urban origins, and region of the country, Blacks were paid less than Whites, lived in the worst housing conditions, and suffered the worst health. The available evidence suggests a similar conclusion for the Indian groups that migrated to Latin American cities. In Guatemala, Indians were disadvantaged in all areas of urban stratification – income, housing, education, health – when compared to Whites. In Lima, Aymara- and Quechua-speaking migrants were among the poorest in the city.[96]

Gender remained a contributing factor to inequality in the 1970s. Female-headed households had increasing numerical importance in the region, and represented the most impoverished group of households. In Mexico City and Buenos Aires, the proportion of households with female heads was around 17 per cent; in Recife (in the northeast of Brazil) this figure rose to 22 per cent; and in Santiago, Chile, it was 20 per cent. These households were, on average, smaller than those with males heads, and the female head combined the tasks of earning a living with domestic

[94] See for example, Peruvian highland villagers picking strawberries and selling fruit in Lima, and Mazua women in Mexico, D.F.

[95] See Jorge Balán, 'Estructuras agrarias y migración en una perspectiva histórica: estudios de casos latinoamericanos', *Revista Mexicana de Sociologia,* XLII/1, (1981) and *International Migration in the Southern Cone* (Buenos Aires, 1985). International migration – from Bolivia and Paraguay to Argentina, from Colombia to Venezuela – has created enclaves of poor and ethnically distinct migrants in several Latin American cities.

[96] For Guatemala City, see J. P. Pérez Sainz, *Ciudad Subsistencia e Informalidad: Tres Estudios sobre el Area Metropolitana en Guatemala* (Guatemala City, 1990). T. Altamirano shows both the poverty of highland indian migrants in Lima, but also their capacity for organization in face of difficult material circumstances: *Presencia Andina en Lima Metropolitana* (Lima, 1984), and *Cultura Andina y Pobreza Urbana* (Lima, 1988).

duties and had also to maintain the networks that brought in non-monetary resources. Almost 45 per cent of female headed households in Belo Horizonte, Brazil, were below the poverty line, whereas the equivalent figure for two-parent households was approximately 28 per cent.[97]

In a comparative study of two Brazilian cities (Recife and São José dos Campos), it was found that both men and women worked more when they belonged to a female-headed household. Since women earned, on average, lower incomes than men, the low income of the female head made more necessary the earnings of male and female children.[98] The fact that female-headed households needed to use all their available resources to survive meant that they had less flexibility in face of the worsening economic crisis.[99]

Urbanization, the changes in urban occupational structure, and the relative decline of agriculture as a source of livelihood had resulted in considerable social mobility in the period from the 1940s to the 1970s.[100] The various patterns of social mobility in the region crystallize the differences and divergences in the social and occupational transformations that have been reviewed. In general, the four decades from 1940 to 1980 were years of a high degree of social mobility because of the massive transfer of labour from agriculture to urban jobs. The countries that had the highest rates of total structural mobility (defined as the sum of the proportionate increase in non-manual jobs and the proportionate decline in agricultural employment in the period) were those with the highest rates of urbanization – in our examples, Brazil and Mexico. Those countries which experienced urbanization earlier – for example, Argentina – showed less structural mobility, both because they had less agricultural workers at the beginning of the period, and because, at that time, they also had high levels of non-

[97] For Mexico, see García, Muñoz and Oliveira, *Hogares;* for Argentina, Zulma Recchini de Lattes, 'Empleo feminino y desarrollo económico: algunos tendencias', *Desarrollo Economico,* 17, 66(1977): 301–17.; for Chile, Edith Pantelides, *Estudios de la población feminina económicamente activa en América Latina, 1950–1970* (Santiago, 1976); for Recife, Brigida Garcia, Humberto Munoz and Orlandina de Oliveira, *Familia y Mercado de Trabajo. Un estudio de dos ciudades brasileñas* (Mexico, D. F., 1983).; for Belo Horizonte, T. W. Merrick and M. Schmink, 'Female Headed Households and Urban Poverty in Brazil', paper presented to workshop on 'Mujeres en la pobreza: qué sabemos?' Belmont Conference Centre (1978). See also Elizabeth Jelin, *La Mujer y el Mercado de Trabajo Urbano* (Buenos Aires, 1978).

[98] García, Muñoz and Oliveira, (1983), op. cit.

[99] See Mercedes González de la Rocha's longitudinal study of household coping strategies in Guadalajara, Mexico: 'Economic Crisis, Domestic Reorganization and Women's Work in Guadalajara, Mexico', *Bulletin of Latin American Research,* 7, 2 (1988): 207–23.

[100] The following analysis relies heavily on Durston in 'Transición estructural'.

manual jobs.[101] The contrasts between Chile and Peru were also indicative of differences in the pace and nature of economic modernization. Chile had the higher level of structural mobility between 1960 and 1980, as a result of a sharp drop in the agricultural population and a large increase in lower non-manual jobs. However, if the high levels of unemployment in 1980 and the low levels in 1960 were taken into account, structural mobility in Chile would be low or non-existent. The drop in the proportion of the agricultural population was less rapid in Peru, and one of the lowest in the region, and structural mobility was concentrated in the lower non-manual strata with little increase in the non-agricultural manual strata.

The experience of social mobility was different according to gender and age. For men, the major form of mobility in the period up to 1980 was through the increase in the higher non-manual strata. For women, the traditional form of mobility – from the countryside to urban domestic service – was replaced, in this period, by entry into the lower non-manual strata, such as shop assistants and clerks, but with lower incomes than those in skilled manual jobs that were still dominated by males.

Most mobility occurred between generations, with the twenty-five to thirty-four year-old age cohort being substantially more likely to have non-manual jobs than their counterparts twenty years earlier. There was, however, some evidence of mobility within a generation since the twenty-five to thirty-four year age cohorts of 1960 were more likely to have non-manual jobs, and less likely to have agricultural jobs in 1980 when they were aged forty-five to fifty-four years old.[102]

A major reason for the high rates of social mobility among the young age cohorts were the rising levels of education in the region which benefitted the younger age cohorts most. The increasing demand for non-manual workers in the 1960s and 1970s discussed above was met by an increase in the supply of people with the requisite levels of education, particularly the urban-born. Education became a more important avenue to occupational mobility than it had been in the previous period. The changes in educational levels between 1950 and 1970s were dramatic, with each of the six countries reducing illiteracy by more than 50 per cent (see Table 5.3). Despite these gains, the educational levels of the economically active population remained low in several countries (see Table 5.4). The excep-

[101] For a calculation of the differences in total structural mobility between the ten countries considered as ranging between the lowest of minus 1.1 per cent in Uruguay and 9.2 per cent in Argentina, and the highest of 41 per cent in Honduras, 37.5 per cent in Bolivia, and 36.1 per cent in Brazil in a twenty-year period up to 1980, see CEPAL, *Transformación* tables 1–6.

[102] Ibid., tables 1–9.

Table 5.3. *Illiteracy in six Latin American countries: 1960–85 (population of fifteen years and older, %)*

Country	1950	1960	1970	1980	1985[a]
Argentina	13.6[b]	8.6	7.4	6.1	4.5
Brazil	50.6	39.7	33.8	25.5	22.3
Colombia	37.7[c]	27.1	19.2	12.2[d]	17.7[e]
Chile	19.8[f]	16.4	11.0	8.9	5.6
Mexico	43.2	34.5	25.8	16.0	9.7
Peru	–	38.9	27.5	18.1	15.2

Notes: [a] UNESCO estimate.
[b] Population of fourteen years of age and higher.
[c] 1951 figures.
[d] Population of ten years of age and higher.
[e] Excludes Indian population of tropical lowlands.
[f] 1952 figures.
Sources: UNESCO, *Statistical Yearbook, 1963;* ECLA, *Statistical Yearbook for Latin America, 1980.*

tions were Argentina and Chile, with less than 30 per cent of their economically active population with three or fewer years of education in 1980. The equivalent figure for Brazil was 51.9 per cent. In contrast, in Peru the economically active population was 'over-educated' for the available non-manual jobs. Rapid increase in educational levels between 1970 and 1980 resulted in almost 26 per cent of the Peruvian economically active in 1980 having completed secondary education, most of whom would be young entrants to the labour market facing, as we have seen, little increase between 1972 and 1982 in higher non-manual jobs.

A distinctive characteristic of educational levels in Latin America has been their polarization. Alongside a persistently large percentage of those failing to finish primary school, there are growing numbers with secondary and university education. Though the trend is obscured, to some extent, by the lack of comparable classifications between the censuses, the increase of those with seven or more years of education shown in Table 5.4, is marked.[103] Both the rapid increase in non-manual jobs and in

[103] This is the case in the figures for Argentina and Colombia. The 1980 figures for Mexico are only available for total population, and not for the economically active population. This difference is likely to produce a slight upward bias by including those still in high school and beyond, but this is likely to be compensated by the downward bias of including those adults who are not part of the economically active population. The educational levels of this segment are, in the Mexican case,

Table 5.4. *Educational levels of economically active population six Latin American countries, 1960, 1970, 1980 (%)*

Country	Census year	None	1–3	4–6	7–9	10–12	13+	No info.
			Number of years of study					
Argentina	1960[a]	6.9	24.4	45.8	4.7	9.6	4.4	4.2
	1970[b]	0.0	15.8	20.3	36.7	13.1	5.9	8.2
	1980[c]	–	29.4[d]	48.4[e]	16.9[f]	–	5.3[g]	–
Brazil	1960[b]	41.6	30.6	19.2	1.9	3.0	3.2	0.5
	1970	36.0	27.6	22.9	6.1	4.9	2.3	0.1
	1980[b]	27.2[i]	24.7	28.1	10.1	6.8	3.1	0.1
Colombia	1960	–	–	–	–	–	–	–
	1970[j]	21.6	31.1	27.8	10.0	5.6	2.8	1.1
	1980[k]	11.5	49.2[l]	–	29.8[m]	–	7.7[b]	1.8
Chile	1960[j]	14.1	21.3	35.2	12.3	10.0	2.3	4.8
	1970[j]	8.2	15.4	31.6	13.0	13.5	4.0	14.3
	1980[o]	4.9	11.3	25.9	14.9[p]	33.3[q]	9.7	–
Mexico	1960[j]	35.4	32.0	24.3	4.6	2.1	1.6	0.0
	1970[j]	27.1	30.3	29.7	5.9	3.7	3.3	0.0
	1980[y]	16.2	22.1	34.7	16.2	4.6	6.2	–
Peru	1960[r]	32.8	– 52.2 –		– 11.6 –		2.5[r]	0.9
	1970[o]	19.3	27.3	28.1	7.9	9.4	4.8	3.2
	1980[o]	12.4	24.2[l]	18.4[u]	13.1[v]	13.8[w]	12.1[x]	6.0

Notes: [a] Economically active population (EAP) fourteen years and older; [b] EAP, ten years and older; [c] EAP, fourteen years and older; [d] EAP without any year of schooling and incomplete primary; [e] EAP with complete primary and incomplete secondary; [f] EAP with complete secondary and incomplete higher; [g] EAP with complete higher; [h] EAP ten years and older; [i] Includes EAP with less than one year of studies; [j] EAP of twelve years and older; [k] Employed population of twelve years and older; [l] EAP with some primary; [m] EAP with some secondary; [n] EAP with some higher; [o] EAP, fifteen years and older; [p] EAP with seven or eight years of study; [q] EAP with a minimum of nine and a maximum of twelve years education; [r] EAP, six years and older; [s] University education; [t] EAP, with incomplete primary; [u] EAP, with complete primary; [v] EAP, with incomplete secondary; [w] EAP, with complete secondary; [x] EAP, with higher education; [y] Total population of twelve years and older less those from twelve to fourteen years attending primary school.
Sources: UNESCO, United Nations, *Statistical Yearbook for Latin America and the Caribbean, 1989*. For Mexico, 1980: *X Censo General de Población y Vivienda, 1980*, Resumen General Vol I, Cuadros 11–15, INEGI, 1986.

people with primary and higher levels of education meant a certain depreciation of these jobs and of educational qualifications. The increase in non-

slightly lower than of those in the labour market. CEPAL, *Transformación*, (tables 1–2) provides figures for the changes in educational levels of the population of fifteen to twenty-four years of age between 1960 and 1980 for Chile, Brazil, Panama, Peru, Ecuador, and Uruguay. This young population also shows substantial increases in the proportions with secondary and higher levels of education in all six countries.

manual workers in Mexico meant a relative decline in their salaries with respect skilled manual workers. Whereas literacy was a sufficient qualification for most skilled manual jobs in the 1960s, primary education became essential by the 1970s, and similar increases in required educational qualifications occurred for non-manual jobs. Though part of the demand for higher qualifications arose from the requirements of new jobs based on advanced technology in the services or industry, even the same jobs in 1980 required higher levels of education than in 1960.[104]

Studies of occupational mobility that obtained life-time and intergenerational mobility data enable us to give a more detailed account of the nature and extent of mobility than is possible using census data only.[105] They show that rates of social mobility have indeed been high in Latin America, and comparable to those reported for the United States and West European countries in the post Second World War period. The analysis of life histories showed that migrants to the large cities competed reasonably successfully with urban natives to obtain the better jobs, particularly after a few years of urban residence. Their relative success, however, was, in part, based on the fact that the migrants of the 1940s and 1950s were quite selective when compared to their populations of origin. These migrants often came from the provincial middle classes, and had relatively high levels of education enabling them to take up the clerical and professional jobs that were opening up in the cities. Likewise, the emigration of craft-workers from villages and small towns provided a skilled working class for the cities.

While family status continued to be a significant factor in children's occupational attainment, its impact occurred mainly through its effect on childrens' education. As a determinant of childrens' educational attainment, the socio-economic status of the family was more important than place of origin (whether born in rural or urban areas), and continued to influence attainment even with the rapid expansion of educational opportunities in the 1960s.

[104] CEPAL, *Transformación,* pp. 38–41. On the issue of the link between education and occupational mobility in this period, see Jorge Balán, 'Migrant native socioeconomic differences in Latin American cities. a structural analysis', *Latin American Research Review,* 4, 1 (1969): 3–29, and Bryan Roberts, 'Education, urbanization and social change', in R. Brown (ed.), *Knowledge, Education and Cultural Change* (London, 1973), pp. 141–62.

[105] Examples are Balán, Browning and Jelin's study of geographic and social mobility in Monterrey, Mexico, *Men in a Developing Society* (1973) and Muñoz, Oliveira and Stern's study of Mexico City, *Migración y desigualdad social en la ciudad de México* (1977). The CEPAL method of calculating structural mobility consists in comparing equivalent cohorts taken from national censuses at different time periods. There is no guarantee, however, that a cohort identified in the first census will consist of the same people as its counterpart in the next census, and parents and childrens' occupations cannot be linked.

There were, in fact, indications that the increase in private (usually religious) education at primary and secondary levels, in the 1960s and later, reflected the importance placed on education by middle-class parents, and their dissatisfaction with overcrowded urban public schools. The 1960s and 1970s saw also an expansion of private universities, both religious and secular, catering for the increased demand for higher education and providing a more privileged educational environment for those with money than did the mass public universities. By 1980, education had become the single most important factor in obtaining higher status and better paid occupations.

SOCIAL INEQUALITY IN THE 1980S

During the 1970s and 1980s, the demand for workers in urban areas was negatively affected by technological changes that saved on labour and by the decline in the regional economy. The result was the persistence of unpaid family workers and the self-employed, and, by 1990, the increasing importance throughout the region of these categories of urban employment. When added to changes in the pattern of migration and a substantial increase in female participation rates, the increasing differentiation of the structure of urban employment created a heterogeneous and polarized urban social structure. There was a sharp reduction in social mobility because of the declining importance of rural-urban migration, of the stagnation of the region's economies, and of policies aimed at reducing public expenditures that cut non-manual bureaucratic employment. The mobility opportunities for the younger generation were, consequently, much less than for their parents. This greater rigidity in the social structure operated differently, as we will see, according to country and city.

In the 1970s, there were clear signs that the long secular trend of rising real urban wages was coming to an end.[106] In Mexico, the over-expansion of government expenditures and increases in inflation resulted in adjustment policies which reduced government expenditures and wages from 1979 onwards. Urban minimum salaries were the most affected, and declined by 8.4 per cent between 1978 and 1981. In contrast to Mexico, Brazil had a high dependence on oil imports, and increased its external debt after the first oil crisis (1973–4) as a means of offsetting the negative shift in the terms of trade. From 1978, however, the continuing worsening of the terms of trade resulted in a marked drop in the rate of increase of the Brazilian real

[106] The following data on wages in the six countries are taken from PREALC, *Empleo y salarios* (Santiago, 1983).

minimum wage – general, in industry and in construction. In Argentina and Chile, economic policy in the 1970s was directed towards controlling salaries as a means of stabilization and of improving international competitiveness. Wage policy was used as a means of controlling the labour force, and was accompanied by a breaking-up of the trade union structure to lessen organized opposition to the anti-industrial and anti-employment policies that were followed. In Argentina, the reduction in real salaries from 1975 to 1978 was of the order of 50.4, 54.9 and 55.9 per cent for the urban minimum wage, the industrial minimum wage and the construction minimum respectively. In Chile, the sharp decreases took place between 1970 and 1975 when the urban minimum salaries dropped by 41.1 per cent, industrial minimum by 41.8 and construction by 18.3 per cent. In Peru, real wages also dropped markedly between 1975 and 1978.

In the 1980s, the decline in real wages was more general and consistent throughout the region: Between 1980 and 1987, the real minimum wage declined by 13.6 per cent in Latin America, though with some recuperation between 1985–7.[107] The decline appears to have been most severe in public sector wages which declined by 17.1 per cent, and least severe in manufacturing which declined by 9.9 per cent. This overall trend concealed important variations by country and city. The declines were most severe in Peru and Mexico, while in Colombia, real wages appear to have increased. Of the six countries, Colombia was the only one to carry out an economic policy that permitted the expansion of the volume of exports, the neutralization of the effects of the drop in international prices, and an increase in real wages from the 1970s up to 1987.

The impact of the crisis on labor markets varied between the Latin American countries. For example, the unemployment rate in Chile increased dramatically from 8.3 per cent in 1974 to 18.6 per cent ten years later. In Peru, the increase was less marked in the same period, and in Argentina, Brazil, Colombia and Mexico, change was minimal. In terms of levels of poverty, the Chilean data indicate that the proportion of homes below the poverty line (with incomes insufficient to meet minimal nutritional levels) increased from 11.7 per cent in 1979 to 23.0 per cent in 1984. In Peru, the equivalent figures indicate an increase from 8 to 21.2 per cent between 1970 and 1982.[108]

For the urban poor, economic crisis made it even more necessary to use

107 For this and the following statistics, see PREALC, 'La evolución del mercado laboral entre 1980 y 1987', Work Document series, No. 328 (Santiago, 1988).

108 PREALC, 'Pobreza y mercado de trabajo en cuatro países: Costa Rica, Venezuela, Chile y Perú', Documento de trabajo (Santiago, 1987).

various monetary and non-monetary resources to make ends meet. A single salary became increasingly inadequate to maintain a family in face of the decline in real wages. Even the low salaries of the young and women became necessary to sustain the household, along with increased domestic work. This has been the major factor increasing female labour force participation in the poorest households.

In the metropolises of Latin America, women's paid work had become an essential part of the domestic budget by 1980. There are no detailed studies of the changes in the female labor market from 1980 to 1990 in the six countries, but data from Mexico and Brazil can be used to illustrate the trends. In Mexico there was a marked expansion in female employment during the 1980s, with an increase of 6.5 per cent per year in the participation rate of economically active women between 1979 and 1987 (compared with 3.5 per cent annually between 1970 and 1979.)[109] The trend in Brazil was similar with an increase of 7.6 per cent in female participation between 1980 and 1985 (compared with 4.6 per cent between 1970 and 1980).[110]

Economic recession in the 1980s led in Mexico to the mobilization of a potential supply of labour mainly made up by adult women (thirty-five to forty-nine years) of low levels of education, married and with young children. In contrast, young, single women (twenty to thirty-four), with middling or high levels of education showed a relative decrease in their participation in the labour market. This contrast was likely to have been produced by the contraction in non-manual employment opportunities, and the increase in informal employment.[111] The Brazilian data indicate a similar tendency in terms of educational levels and age of the female labour force. Women with low levels of education increased their participation rates by 56.3 per cent between 1980 and 1985, whereas women with five or more years of study showed more modest increases. Women between thirty and forty-nine had higher increases in participation in the same period than younger women.[112]

The changes in the characteristics of women entering the labour market

[109] Orlandina de Oliveira and Brígida García, 'Cambios en fecundidad, trabajo y condición feminina en México', Paper presented at XXII World Congress of Sociology (Madrid, 1990); Mercedes Pedrero Nieto, 'Evolución de la participación económica feminina en los ochenta,' *Revista Mexicana de Sociologia,* LII, 1 (1990): 133–49.

[110] See C. Bruschini, *Tendências da Força de Trabalho Feminina Brasileira nos Anos Setenta a Oitenta: Algumas Comparações Regionais* (São Paulo, 1989).

[111] Oliveira and García, 'Cambios en fecundidad'.

[112] Bruschini, *Tendências.*

occurred in conjunction with transformations in the form of their insertion. In Mexico, the percentage of non-manual workers (professionals, technicians and clerical workers) in the female economically active population decreased significantly, and only the most qualified workers succeeded in obtaining the few non-manual jobs that were created.[113] The female economically active population with low levels of education showed a clear drop in their participation in manual wage work, but those with middle levels of education increased their presence. Both these trends indicate stricter requirements for contracting labour in periods of recession.

Domestic servants became a significantly smaller proportion of the female economically active population, as did manufacturing workers. Only manual wage workers in the service industries increased their share of female wage work. The female self-employed increased their share of employment, especially those with the low levels of education, living in common-law unions and with young children. The increase in self-employment occurred not only in the tertiary sector – the sector with the most female employment – but in manufacturing. This expansion of self-employment was not only due to survival strategies on the part of poor families, but to the restructuring of manufacturing activity through the use of sub-contracting to workshops and to domestic workers.[114]

The decline in real wages had important implications for the class structure, especially since it occurred in the context of a cut-back in state expenditures and employment. In the 1980s, the Latin American economies increasingly adopted free market policies aimed at stimulating the private sector and reducing state intervention in the economy. Dramatic consequences were probably felt by the urban middle and working classes, especially the group we have labelled lower middle class, and formal and informal proletariat. The incomes of intermediate and lower level state employees, including teachers and health personnel, appear to have

[113] The following data, from Oliveira and García, 'Cambios en fecundidad', is based on a national sample of women between 20 and 49 years of age for the years 1982 and 1987.

[114] Escobar, *Con el sudor;* Víctor Tokman, 'El sector informal: quince años despues,' *El Trimestre Económico,* 215 (1987), 513–36.; Marta Roldan and Lourdes Benería, *The Crossroads of Class and Gender* (Chicago, Ill., 1987); Roberts, 'Employment structure, life cycle and life chances: formal and informal sectors in Guadalajara,'; A. Marshall, 'Non-standard Employment Practices in Latin America', in Discussion Paper OP/06/1987, (Geneva, 1987); P. Arias, 'La pequeña empresa en el occidente rural', *Estudios Sociologicos,* 6, 17 (Mexico, D.F., 1988); Brígida García, *Desarrollo Económico y Absorción de Fuerza de Trabajo en México: 1950–1980* (Mexico, D.F., 1988); Alejandro Portes, Manuel Castells and Lauren A. Benton (eds) *The Informal Economy: Studies in Advanced and Less Developed Countries* (Baltimore, Md., 1989).

dropped sharply in these years, so that public sector workers in Uruguay, for example, earned 56 per cent of their 1975 wage by 1985.[115] In Mexico, the decile of household incomes that mainly included the lower middle class became differentiated from the one above, and, in terms of income and sources of income, became more similar to those below.[116] Between 1980 and 1988, growth of state employment was low or non-existent in most countries of the region.

These white-collar workers also depended on the state for social services since their low incomes entailed that various members of the family were at work, and that services, whether of education, health or domestic help, could not easily be purchased on the market. The interests and preoccupations of this lower middle class were likely to have become closer to those of manual workers in the 1980s. Furthermore, the problems of daily urban life (light, water and so on) increasingly became shared by the different social sectors, resulting, frequently, in a common opposition to the state as a result of its failure to provide basic services. An increasing social heterogenity of residential areas was reported for various cities, a result of middle and working classes invading each other's space to find cheap accommodation.

The relative decline in incomes at the top of the income distribution was also sharp, but here there were signs of differentiation between the entrepreneurial section and high level administrators and professionals. The income from profits rose during the years of crisis, while salaries dropped substantially. However, for the upper urban classes incomes were still substantially above those of other classes, and though consumption may have diminished in these years, income remained adequate for a comfortable life style.[117]

The bottom end of the urban class structure appears to have suffered also in relative terms from the crisis, despite beginning with very low levels of income. The formal proletariat saw reductions in their incomes that were not offset by the increasing importance of non-wage benefits and by other sources of income, including remittances from abroad. Furthermore, the formal proletariat lost relative importance as part of the Latin

115 International Labour Office, *World Labour Report, 1989* (Geneva, 1989), p. 5.

116 Fernando Cortés and Rosa María Rubalcava, *Autoexplotación Forzada y Equidad por Empobrecimiento* (Mexico, D.F., 1991).

117 For an indication of some of the monetary and non-monetary benefits that these upper strata continued to receive – company cars, productivity-linked bonuses, school fees, free travel, and so on, see Agustín Escobar and Bryan R. Roberts, 'Urban Stratification, the Middle Classes, and Economic Change in Mexico'.

American working classes in the 1980s, as the informal proletariat grew substantially both in numbers and as a proportion of the urban labour force. Official figures suggest that in the region as a whole urban informal employment grew by 56.1 per cent between 1980 and 1987, an annual rate of 6.6 per cent, with the most substantial increases occurring in Mexico and Brazil.[118] The same sources indicated that private sector employment grew at 2.3 per cent annually, substantially below the growth rate – 3.7 per cent – of the non-agricultural economically active population, with large-scale enterprises having little or no growth. Public sector employment grew at 4.1 per cent annually, though with substantial variation between countries. By 1987, informal employment was estimated to make up 28.9 per cent of total urban employment in the region, compared with 23.9 per cent in 1980.

Data from Mexico and Central America provide a more detailed picture of these trends. In the three major metropolitan areas of Mexico, there was an increase in employment in small-scale enterprises, in self-employment and in unpaid family employment, and this was particularly marked in the repair services and in commerce.[119] Informal employment (including domestic service) was estimated at 33 per cent of the urban labour force in 1987. The self-employed and workers in small enterprises appear to have suffered a drop in real incomes, and the informal sector had by 1989 become synonymous with bare subsistence. Only the owners of small-scale enterprises and informal workers with skills in demand earned significantly more than the minimum wage, but their enterprises were, in general, poorly equipped, and showed little sign of capital accumulation.

By 1989, the urban labour markets of most Central American countries were highly informalized. In Managua, suffering the effects of the economic blockade, the war in the countryside, and with a weak industrial base, the informally employed were 48 per cent of the urban labour force,

[118] PREALC, 'La evolución del mercado laboral entre 1980 y 1987.' Work document series, No. 328, (Santiago, 1988), Cuadro 1; ECLAC, *Statistical Yearbook for Latin America and the Caribbean, 1989* (Santiago, 1989), table 3. Informal employment was defined as the sum of self-employment, unremunerated family employment, and employment in enterprises of less than five workers (thus including domestic service).

[119] INEGI, "Encuesta nacional de Empleo Urbana: Indicadores Trimestrales de Empleo', (Aquascalientes, 1988), SPP, *La Ocupación Informal en Areas Urbanas* (Mexico, D.F., 1979). See also Agustín Escobar, 'The Rise and Fall of an Urban Labor Market: economic crisis and the fate of small-scale workshops in Guadalajara, Mexico', *Bulletin of Latin American Research*, 7, 2, (1988), González de la Rocha, 'Economic Crisis, Domestic Reorganization and Women's Work in Guadalajara, Mexico', Roberts, 'The Changing Nature of Informal Employment.'

not counting domestic servants.[120] In other Central American capitals, the equivalent percentages were 33 per cent in Guatemala City, 29.9 per cent in Tegucigalpa, 28 per cent in San Salvador, and 23 per cent in San José.[121] Costa Rica, whose economy had been less affected than most Latin American economies by the recession of the 1980s, was the only one of the Central American countries not to have experienced increasing informalization in the 1980s.

Informal workers in the Central American cities were disproportionately drawn from the younger and older age groups, from migrants, from women, and from those with low levels of education. Informal employment was mainly in commerce, though about a quarter of the informally employed were in the industrial sector. In all the cities, the informal sector was socially and economically heterogeneous with large differences in income between the owners of small-scale enterprise, their employees and the self-employed. Case studies of samples of the self-employed and small-scale enterprises in these cities indicated that informality for the self-employed was basically a household survival strategy in face of unemployment and declining real wages. Only the small-scale entrepreneurs earned a wage significantly above the minimum, and, as in Mexico, even this sector showed little economic dynamism.

Because informal employment provided relatively easy access to incomes that could supplement household incomes, it facilitated a household strategy of placing more members on the labour market as a means of off-setting the declines in real wages. Households containing members of the informal proletariat were likely, as a consequence, to have experienced a smaller reduction in overall income than other working-class families. Evidence from Mexico suggests that this was the case, with non-wage sources of income, such as remittances and self-provisioning, also having become more important.[122] The result of these various tendencies was a

120 See Amália Chamorro, Mario Chávez, and Marcos Membreño, 'El sector informal en Nicaragua', in J.P. Pérez Sainz and Rafael Menjívar (eds), *Informalidad Urbana en Centroamerica: Entre la Acumulación y la Subsistencia* (San Jose, 1991), pp. 217–58. In Managua, the informal sector was already large by the time of the 1979 revolution, expanding rapidly after the earthquake of 1972. From 1979 onwards, the informal sector was alternatively encouraged and discouraged by the Sandinista regime, though by 1989, it was viewed as providing essential services within the war-torn economy.

121 Estimates based on household surveys in the various cities. See Pérez Sainz and Menjívar (eds), for detailed results. The informally employed were defined as the self-employed, unpaid, and workers and owners of firms with less than five workers.

122 Evidence for the increase in the numbers of household members in paid work among the poorest strata is provided by Mercedes González de la Rocha, 'De por qué las mujeres aguantan golpes y cuernos: un análysis de hogares sin varón en Guadalajara,' in Luisa Gabayet et al., *Mujeres y Sociedad:*

continuing polarization of incomes in Mexico despite a slight decline in income inequality.

One of the most important aspects of urban life in the late 1980s and early 1990s was the pressure on households and on the residential community as they became the essential means of survival, particularly for low-income families and for those who had recently migrated to the city. Complementing low incomes and sharing housing, whether among the *allegados* of Santiago, the poor of Lima or migrants to the city of Mexico, was crucial for the survival of the poor. At the same time, mutual help among neighbours and collective strategies of survival, such as communal kitchens, were equally important. Both households and community survival strategies generated tensions which led to household break-up and community fragmentation.[123] The pressure on family relationships was considerable, particularly on women. Women, as mothers and housewives, carried a double responsibility: they had to look after the house and care for other household members, and seek out income sources through domestic out-work or employment outside the home. Male heads, though unable to maintain the household on their low salaries, often remained resistent to their wives working outside the home and were reluctant to contribute their entire income to the family budget, increasing the potential for family conflicts. Fathers expected both their sons and daughters to contribute to the family pot, while they, in turn, wished to use their earning for individual needs. The gender and generational conflicts that arose within households had become a marked characteristic of urban life in Latin America.

The changes in the labour market tended to weaken the job as the central factor structuring daily life, redefining the bases for social stratification. The intensification of sub-contracting by large-scale enterprises to domestic outworkers or workshops, the increase in unemployment, the casualization of much of the labour force and the increase in labour-force turnover pro-

Salario, Hogar y Acción Social en el Occidente de México (Guadalajara, 1988), Henry A. Selby, et al., *The Mexican Urban Household,* and Oliveira, 'La participación femenina en los mercados de trabajo urbanos en México: 1970–1980,' Cortes and Rubalcava, *Autoexplotación,* cit. demonstrate the change in sources of incomes among the lowest income deciles, and that these strata of households show the least reduction of all the Mexican strata in overall income between 1977 and 1984.

123 See Guillermo de la Peña, Juan Manuel Duran, Agustín Escobar and Javier García de Alba, *Crisis, Conflicto y Sobrevivencia: Estudios Sobre la Sociedad Urbana en Mexico* (Guadalajara, 1990), and, particularly, the essay by Mercedes González de la Rocha, Agustín Escobar and Maria de la O. Martínez Castellanos, 'Estrategias versus conflicto: reflexiones para el estudio del grupo domestico en epoca de crisis', for analysis of the collective strategies of survival among poor households and neighbourhoods, and the conflicts that arose because of the unequal burden such strategies imposed on different categories of household members.

duced greater instability in employment. These processes worked against the consolidation of the urban social classes in Latin America. An individual's occupation became a less useful indicator than in the past of social and class position. This was especially true for the working class, for whom employment was decreasingly linked to particular skills and to a stable work career, and for whom the individual salary was usually insufficient to maintain a household. The importance of occupation in defining life changes and social position was replaced by that of position within the household structure and by stage in household cycle – heads of nuclear or extended households, with small children or not, with or without spouse, and so on – and access to community and family help and information networks. Stable occupational careers (characterized by remaining in the same enterprise, obtaining skills and promotion, benefiting from seniority and social security) became rare, and the increase in inter-urban mobility was one indication of frequent changes of job. This residential mobility also implied that neighbourhoods became less stable than in previous decades, as did the neighbourhood basis for social solidarity.

CONCLUSION

Patterns of urbanization and transformations in urban social structure in Latin America after 1930 were closely related to developments in the industrial sector that were linked to changes in the international division of labour. Before the 1940s, the various countries of Latin America were primarily exporters of primary products and had a weak development of the internal market. They were mainly rural countries. Non-agricultural employment was, above all, in commerce and in the crafts. Women had a very low participation in urban labor markets. From the 1940s, import-substitution policies, first in basic goods, and then, in consumer durable, intermediate and capital goods, resulted in a dramatic transformation in social stratification.

This transformation was based as much on demographic as on economic factors. Rural-urban migration was intense and the cities grew rapidly. The dynamism of manufacturing industry made possible the absorption of the increasing supply of workers, which, in the early period, did not grow as fast as it would in subsequent years when women began to enter the urban labour market in increasing numbers, and the new cohorts of workers were swollen by the delayed impact of population growth. This early absorption made possible the consolidation of a working class – at times with a strong rural migrant component – and the possibility of social mobility into non-manual work for those urban sectors that had higher levels of education. Despite the evident problems of social marginality these years constituted a period in which the working classes shared, to a certain extent, in the benefits of development. At this time, there was also signs of the emergence of a welfare-orientated state, as the social bases for populist governments were created. Elites seeking to promote industrial development needed political support from the urban social classes, not least the industrial working class, against entrenched commercial and agrarian interests.

In the later stages of import substitution, however, the basis for even this limited working-class participation in politics broke down. This was the period, the 1960s and 1970s, of what has been called the politics of exclusion in Latin America. Military governments came to power espousing developmentalist (in the sense of top down, state directed development) and nationalist ideologies of rapid economic growth and seeking to curtail the demands for better wage and living conditions by both working and middle classes. Yet these classes consolidated in this period, leading to increased demands on the state – demands that were the more pressing because they were often made in the capital. At the same time urban economies had become more complex, increasingly crucial parts of national economies due to the growth of the internal market. The rapid, unplanned growth of the cities and their poverty was fertile ground for neighbourhood-based social movements, such as those of squatters seeking to defend and enhance their settlements. Often, industrial workers and their unions took a lead in these struggles since they mainly lived in unplanned and poorly serviced settlements. Also, the new middle classes, especially government employees such as teachers, became increasingly effective in demanding higher wages and improved benefits as they became more numerous and better organized.

In the 1970s, a new set of factors began to produce considerable diversification based on the fragmentation and polarization of the different social sectors. The supply of workers increased rapidly – as a result of migration, natural increase and higher female participation – while the manufacturing sector lost its capacity to absorb labour both as a result of technological change and because of the downturn in the Latin American economies. At the same time, there was a weakening in the developmentalist and welfare orientation of the state. This period was characterized by increased concentration of population in urban areas and a reduction in the possibilities of social mobility.

The changes in occupational structures meant, at one and the same time, modernization, greater diversity and social inequality. Modernization was clear in the expansion of new middle classes – professionals, managers, technicians and office workers. These sectors provided the labour needed for an industrialization based on advanced technology and transnational capital with its attendant services, for the expansion of social services, and for a range of personal services connected with the entertainment and tourist industry.

This modernization of the class structure created the appearance of uniformity among the countries of Latin America, and a relative convergence with the class structure of advanced industrial countries. Though the Latin American middle classes represented a smaller proportion of the labour force than in the industrialized world, they shared the perceptions, aspirations and demands of their counterparts in Europe and the United States: consumerism, education as a means of social mobility, low taxes and a preference for greater economic liberalism.

But, if by 'middle classes' we refer to groups with higher levels of education and job and income security, then the situation in Latin America was very different from that of the industrialized countries. In Latin America, the social and economic bases of the middle classes were weaker than in the industrialized world because of their shallow historical roots and internal heterogeneity. The greater part of the Latin American middle classes were formed by occupations that had only recently been created, and which used a considerable amount of female labour, with low levels of education and low incomes – schoolteaching, banking and office work. Likewise, a part of these non-manual workers came from working-class families, and were in the labour market to obtain incomes that would allow their families to maintain minimum levels of welfare.

The economic crisis of the 1980s, with its high levels of inflation and sharp drop in real wages, contributed to the relative impoverishment of the middle classes. For these classes, modernization was halted and social mobility became less possible. The impoverishment of the middle classes led them, at times, to seek to lower their expenditures by seeking cheaper housing in working-class areas. The consequence was a greater social diversification at the neighbourhood level, diminishing, in some cities, spatial segregation. There were important differences in these respects between countries: relative middle-class decline was more accentuated in Argentina, for example, than in Mexico or Brazil.

The working class of Latin America was never homogeneous and large-scale industry played only a relatively minor role in its formation. In this respect, there was no repetition of the historical experience that formed a working-class in Britain and Germany during the nineteenth and the beginning of the twentieth centuries. In Latin America between 1930 and 1990 the working class was constituted by service and construction workers as much as by workers in manufacturing industry. Furthermore, the increase in the proportion of wage labour had ended by 1980, and was replaced by an increase in the proportions of the self-employed and non-waged workers.

This tendency led some commentators to emphasize the rise of an 'informal' economy in the region. Informal workers were not, however, a homogeneous sector since they included the very poor for whom self-employment was their only means of subsistence, small-scale entrepreneurs and disguised wage workers who worked at home or in a small workshop, but who were sub-contracted by large national and multinational firms. Also, there were blurred boundaries between 'independent' workers and the casual workers who moved in and out of large-scale firms. Informalization was part of a secular change in the way in which labour was used and in the organization of labour markets. As was the case in some advanced industrial countries, there was a move in Latin America towards more flexible forms of contract and more flexible use of labour, that resulted, at times, in greater instability, more part-time work, and fewer labour rights. This tendency was based on the pressures to make use of labour in ways compatible with technological change in a highly integrated international market. In this situation, even informal employment had limited possibilities of expansion as was shown by increasing levels of open unemployment in several countries.

A further factor in the heterogeneity of the working classes was the centrality of the family for daily survival. The worsening in salaries made it necessary for several members of the household to enter the labour market. The ever greater presence of households with several workers resulted in a greater occupational diversity within families. The job of the male head of household lost importance as a source of family income and as a source of identity for the members of the family. There were few examples in Latin America of the types of working-class community that were common in nineteenth- and early twentieth-century Europe in which popular culture was shaped by one predominant type of work. These processes resulted in apparently contradictory tendencies in class formation. There was an increasing fragmentation of the working classes as fewer workers shared a similar position in the labour market, and common work experience was less likely to be the key factor in social (and political) identity. Yet, family and community solidarity was more important in times of crisis, and generated needs and interests that were common to broad sectors of the population.

By 1990 different patterns of national and regional development and differences in urban context were probably more important than in previous periods in shaping classes and relations between classes. The heterogeneity of urban social structure and of social mobility in Latin America meant that there was no single pattern of social stratification in the region.

Appendix 1. *Urban growth in six countries, 1940–80*

Urban size	1940	1980	Annual Rates of Growth (%) 1940–50	1950–60	1960–70	1970–80
ARGENTINA						
Urban	61.2	82.1	2.6	3.0	2.0	2.2
in urban places:						
Up to 100,000	35.9	30.3	1.6	2.4	1.3	2.9
100,000 to Metro	18.7	26.3	3.5	4.5	3.0	2.2
Metropolis	45.4	43.4	2.9	2.8	2.0	1.7
Population	(14.2)	(28.2)	1.9	1.8	1.5	1.6
BRAZIL						
Urban	31.0	67.6	3.9	5.5	4.8	4.1
in urban places:						
Up to 100,000	61.3	36.8	2.8	5.0	3.0	2.4
100,000 to Metro	5.6	23.1	5.6	8.5	9.7	8.7
Metropolis	33.1	40.1	5.4	5.6	5.5	3.7
Population	(41.5)	(121.3)	2.5	3.1	2.8	2.2
CHILE						
Urban	52.0	81.3	3.0	3.7	3.1	2.5
in urban places:						
Up to 100,000	55.9	37.2	2.3	3.6	1.6	0.7
100,000 to Metro	8.0	20.3	5.2	4.1	6.6	5.8
Metropolis	36.1	42.5	3.5	3.7	3.9	2.9
Population	(5.1)	(11.1)	1.8	2.2	2.2	1.6
COLOMBIA						
Urban	30.4	64.2	4.8	4.8	4.4	3.0
in urban places:						
Up to 100,000	69.0	31.5	1.7	4.8	2.0	1.2
100,000 to Metro	18.1	46.9	11.2	3.8	5.5	4.7
Metropolis	12.9	21.6	4.8	7.3	7.5	2.5
Population	(9.1)	(25.8)	2.4	2.9	2.9	2.2
MEXICO						
Urban	35.1	68.9	5.3	4.8	4.7	4.2
In urban places:						
Up to 100,000	48.3	30.2	5.1	3.9	2.4	2.8
100,000 to Metro	15.9	30.3	6.0	5.9	7.9	5.7
Metropolis	35.8	39.5	5.2	5.3	5.2	4.3
Population	(19.7)	(69.4)	3.3	3.0	3.2	2.7

cont.

Appendix 1. *(cont.)*

Urban size	1940	1980	Annual Rates of Growth (%) 1940–50	1950–60	1960–70	1970–80
PERU						
Urban	35.4	62.3	2.7	3.7	5.0	3.5
In urban places:						
Up to 100,000	71.8	36.0	0.5	2.5	3.2	0.7
100,000 to Metro	0.0	21.4	–	9.6	11.4	7.7
Metropolis	28.2	42.6	5.7	5.2	5.1	4.5
Population	(6.2)	(17.3)	2.1	2.6	2.8	2.7

Source: United Nations, *Demographic Yearbooks, 1948 and 1984,* table 8. United Nations, *Patterns of Urban and Rural Population Growth,* table 48, New York, 1980. For Colombia, 1950–1980, Departamento Administrativo Nacional de Estadistica (DANE), *Avance de Resultados Preliminares, Censo 85* (Bogotá, 1986) and *XV Censo Nacional de Población y IV de Vivienda, Colombia,* Vol. I (Bogotá, 1986). (1986a, pp. 116–22; 1986b). For Peru in 1980, Instituto Nacional de Estadistica (1981, Cuadro 14).

Appendix 2. *Occupational stratification in Argentina, 1917–80*

	1914	1947	1960	1970	1980
Higher non-manual strata					
Employers, independent professionals	6.5	8.9	3.3	3.1	3.2
Managers, employed professionals & technical personnel	2.6	1.9	8.4	8.2	11.6
Total	9.1	10.8	11.7	11.3	14.8
Lower non-manual strata					
Office workers	9.3	15.2	15.0	14.2	16.2
Sales clerks	11.3	6.2	5.0	6.8	6.7
Total	20.6	21.4	20.0	21.0	22.9
Small-scale entrepreneurs					
Commerce	0.0	5.1	4.7	2.3	2.5
Other (manufacturing services)		.0	3.3	.8	2.4
Total	0.0	5.1	8.0	3.1	4.9
Self-employed					
Commerce	4.5	2.6	3.3	6.0	6.5
Other	13.1	5.3	7.8	11.2	11.3
Total	17.6	7.9	11.1	17.2	17.8
Wage Workers					
Transport	4.7	5.5	2.1	3.8	2.8
Construction	5.2	6.1	5.8	7.1	6.1
Industry	25.5	22.8	21.9	17.1	15.2
Services	5.2	11.6	12.4	12.0	8.7
Total	40.6	46.0	42.2	41.0	32.8
Domestic servants	12.1	8.8	7.0	7.4	6.8
TOTAL	100.0	100.0	100.0	100.0	100.0
Agriculture (% of the active population)	31.0	25.2	20.6	16.0	13.1

Source: Calculations based on the national censuses of 1914, 1947, 1960, 1970 and 1980.

Appendix 3. *Occupational stratification in Brazil, 1940–80*

	1940		1950		1960		1970		1980	
Higher non-manual strata										
Employers, independent	3.2		3.9		1.1		1.2		1.6	
Managers, employed professionals & technical personel	2.3		4.6		8.3		11.6		15.7	
Total		5.5		8.5		9.4		12.8		17.3
Lower non-manual strata										
Office workers	8.5		7.5		8.8		9.5		10.3	
Sales clerks	8.1		7.9		6.3		8.4		6.1	
Total		16.6		15.4		15.1		17.9		16.4
Small-scale entrepreneurs										
Commerce	1.2		1.9		.9		.5		.9	
Other (manufacturing, services)					.4		.2		.7	
Total		1.2		1.9		1.3		.7		1.6
Self-employed										
Commerce	7.2		6.1		6.7		5.8		4.4	
Other	19.8		13.7		17.4		9.8		13.6	
Total		27.0		19.8		24.1		15.6		18.0
Wage workers										
Transport	7.9		3.7		6.6		4.2		2.7	
Construction	5.7		9.1		8.2		9.3		7.3	
Industry	20.1		19.3		17.5		16.0		18.4	
Services	1.9		11.5		8.1		12.1		9.6	
Total		35.6		43.6		40.4		41.6		38.0
Domestic servants	14.1		10.8		9.7		11.4		8.7	
TOTAL	100.0		100.0		100.0		100.0		100.0	
Agriculture (% active population)	65.5		59.8		52.1		44.9		31.2	

Source: Calculations based on the national censuses of 1940, 1950, 1960, 1970 and 1980.

Appendix 4. *Occupational stratification in Chile, 1940–82*

	1940		1952		1960		1970		1982	
Higher non-manual strata										
Employers, independent professionals	3.7		4.0		3.3		3.2		3.7	
Managers, employed professionals & technical personnel	2.9		6.3		7.4		10.4		10.4	
Total		6.6		10.3		10.7		13.6		14.1
Lower non-manual strata										
Office workers	7.5		8.6		10.3		12.7		15.8	
Sales clerks	3.3		7.2		3.4		3.8		5.2	
Total		10.8		15.8		13.7		16.5		21.0
Small-scale entrepreneurs										
Commerce	0.0		.7		.1		.1		.3	
Other (manufacturing, services)	0.0		.5		.5		.6		.3	
Total		0.0		1.2		.6		.7		.6
Self-employed										
Commerce	10.5		7.7		7.9		7.1		6.4	
Other	12.2		12.9		10.3		11.5		8.5	
Total		22.7		20.6		18.2		18.6		14.9
Wage workers										
Transport	7.0		1.4		3.4		2.7		3.9	
Construction	5.9		5.9		7.7		7.9		6.7	
Industry	25.1		19.3		20.1		18.5		14.4	
Services	9.3		11.7		12.3		12.4		15.7	
Total		49.2		38.3		43.5		41.5		40.7
Domestic servants	12.6		13.8		13.3		9.1		8.7	
TOTAL	100.0		100.0		100.0		100.0		100.0	
Agriculture (% active population)	46.0		34.3		30.0		23.2		16.5	

Source: Calculations based on the national censuses of 1940, 1952, 1960, 1970, 1982.

Appendix 5. *Occupational stratification in Colombia, 1938–73*

	1938		1951		1964		1973	
Higher non-manual								
Employers, independent professionals	6.3		6.6		2.7		2.3	
Managers, employed professionals & technical personnel	12.3		5.3		8.3		8.8	
Total		8.6		11.9		11.0		11.1
Lower non-manual strata								
Office workers	8.1		5.5		9.5		12.3	
Sales clerks	2.2		4.6		5.4		6.7	
Total		10.3		10.1		14.9		19.0
Small-scale entrepreneurs								
Commerce	0.0		.8		.8		2.8	
Other (manufacturing, services)	0.0		1.4		2.2		2.1	
Total		0.0		2.2		3.0		4.9
Self-Employed								
Commerce	12.3		6.2		8.0		6.6	
Other	27.4		16.8		14.5		10.4	
Total		39.7		23.0		22.5		17.0
Wage workers								
Transport	3.5		2.7		3.1		2.8	
Construction	7.4		6.8		6.7		6.9	
Industry	13.0		16.2		16.3		13.8	
Services	3.9		7.3		8.4		13.0	
Total		27.8		33.0		34.5		36.5
Domestic servants	13.6		19.8		14.1		11.5	
TOTAL	100.0		100.0		100.0		100.0	
Agriculture (% active population)	64.8		57.2		50.2		39.3	

Source: Calculations based on national censuses of 1938, 1951, 1964 and the preliminary sample of the 1973 census.

Appendix 6. *Occupational stratification in Mexico, 1940–80*

	1940		1950		1960		1970		1980	
Higher non-manual strata										
Employers, independent professionals	3.3		2.3		1.4		5.1		3.5	
Managers, employed professionals & technical personnel	1.2		5.3		8.0		9.0		9.9	
Total		4.5		7.6		9.4		14.1		13.4
Lower non-manual strata										
Office workers	8.5		11.3		12.9		13.4		16.7	
Sales clerks	5.6		4.0		7.3		4.5		4.9	
Total		14.1		15.3		20.2		17.9		21.6
Small-scale entrepreneurs										
Commerce	0.0		0.8		.5		1.7		1.8	
Other	0.0		0.0		0.0		3.8		2.8	
Total		0.0		.8		.5		5.5		4.6
Self-employed										
Commerce	20.8		14.5		11.8		7.5		6.7	
Other	17.1		13.7		8.7		10.6		11.9	
Total		37.9		28.2		20.5		18.1		18.6
Wage workers										
Transport	4.7		4.2		4.8		2.9		2.5	
Construction	3.3		5.4		6.4		5.8		8.3	
Industry	19.5		17.7		21.6		17.9		14.5	
Services	5.3		13.1		9.1		10.1		11.2	
Total		32.8		40.4		41.9		36.7		36.5
Domestic Servants	10.7		7.7		7.5		7.7		5.3	
TOTAL	100.0		100.0		100.0		100.0		100.0	
Agriculture (% active population)	65.2		58.1		49.4		40.3		29.5	

Source: Calculations based on national censuses of 1940, 1950, 1960, 1970 and 1980. The 1960 figure for agriculture is taken from Garcia (1988: table IV-1).

Appendix 7. *Occupational stratification in Peru, 1940–81*

	1940	1950	1961	1972	1981
Higher non-manual strata					
Employers, independent professionals	7.8	5.2	2.0	1.7	2.0
Managers, employed professionals technical personnel	2.1	4.7	7.9	12.6	12.7
Total	9.9	9.9	9.9	14.3	14.7
Lower non-manual strata					
Office workers	7.3	8.0	8.9	11.3	18.3
Sales clerks	2.0	2.7	3.5	4.6	4.5
Total	9.3	10.7	12.4	15.9	22.8
Small-scale entrepreneurs					
Commerce	3.8	2.2	.4	.2	.5
Other (manufacturing, services)	0.0	0.0	.5	.2	.5
Total	3.8	2.2	.9	.4	1.0
Self-employed					
Commerce	5.1	8.3	12.1	11.7	14.2
Other	28.4	23.9	18.0	17.2	14.0
Total	33.5	32.2	30.1	28.9	28.2
Wage workers					
Transport	3.3	2.6	1.8	4.0	2.8
Construction	4.8	5.1	5.4	6.0	4.3
Industry	13.5	13.9	14.1	11.9	10.4
Services	7.7	10.1	13.0	11.1	9.3
Total	29.3	31.7	34.3	33.0	26.8
Domestic servants	14.0	13.3	12.4	7.5	6.7
TOTAL	100.0	100.0	100.0	100.0	100.0
Agriculture (% active population)	64.3	57.7	52.3	47.1	40.1

Note: a. The figures for 1950 are estimated as the mid-point between the censuses of 1940 and 1961.
Source: Calculations based on the national censuses of 1940, 1961, 1972 and 1981.

6

THE AGRARIAN STRUCTURES OF LATIN AMERICA, 1930–1990

The period from the 1930s to the 1980s was marked by far-reaching changes in agrarian structures throughout Latin America. Indeed, it could be argued that the magnitude of change was greater during this half century than in the preceding four centuries. Agricultural production increased dramatically but, by 1990, in almost all Latin American countries, agriculture had become a less important contributor to the gross national product than industry. The social and political significance of agriculture altered sharply. In the 1930s most people in Latin America made their living from the land. Land ownership was still the key to political and economic power at the regional and national level. Many presidents and key political figures were members of the landed elite. By the 1980s those working directly in agriculture were only a quarter of the total labour force. Urban interests and occupations based on industry and services (which included a wide range of financial and administrative services) had become politically dominant.

Crucial changes in the process of agricultural production accompanied this shift in the economic, political and social significance of agriculture and landholding. In the 1930s agricultural production, though usually market-orientated, was largely decentralized. Cropping practices and the organization of agricultural inputs varied from region to region, depending upon ecology, the availability of labour and the nature of the market. This had given rise to a diversity of agrarian structures that generated distinctive regional identities. By the early 1980s agricultural production had become increasingly centralized through the state or large-scale agribusinesses, usually linked to international marketing and financial institutions. This led to a greater homogenization of farming practices with most types of agriculture increasingly subordinated to industrial imperatives and to international consumption requirements. The result was the erosion of distinctive regional systems of production.

These transformations were produced by a set of interrelated processes. First, there was a change in Latin America's relationship to the international economy, both in terms of the nature and intensity of the exchanges. In the perriod after 1930, the Latin American economies added to 'traditional' exports, such as sugar and coffee, new agricultural export products and manufactured goods. At the same time, the agricultural sector imported an increasing range of domestic and foreign commodities, such as fertilizers, agricultural machinery and basic consumer goods, integrating closely the urban and rural economies.

The pace of change was not the same throughout the period. During the 1930s, in the aftermath of the Depression of 1929 and the crisis in the export sector, export agriculture resumed its traditional role as the motor of economic growth. From the 1930s to the 1960s, and especially during the 1950s, Latin America countries adopted import-substitution industrialization policies and in these agriculture was assigned a subordinate role – that of supplying cheap foodstuffs and labour to the expanding urban-industrial sector. Then, in the 1970s, as the Latin American economies became once again more closely integrated into the international economy, agriculture came under pressure to modernize both for exports and as part of the industrial economy, supplying the inputs for a variety of agro-industries. The peasant sector survived, but was reshaped as part of it became a reserve of labour for large-scale commercial production and as another part accommodated to the increased urban demand for foodstuffs by specializing in producing specific crops for the market.

These economic trends were accompanied by important demographic developments. Throughout this period population growth was an independent factor creating pressure for change. In 1930, the Latin American population was a little over 100 million. By 1990 it had grown to approximately 450 million.[1] Though much of this population growth was absorbed by the fast-growing cities of Latin America, particularly from the 1940s onwards, the numbers of people working in agriculture increased constantly. From an estimated 21 million in 1930, those working in agriculture increased to 39 million in 1980 (see Table 6.1). Rapid urban growth – by 1990, half the Latin American population was living in places of more than 50,000 people – created a higher demand for agricul-

[1] On population change in the period 1930–90, see chapter by Thomas Merrick in this volume.

tural products. At the same time, the continuing growth of the rural population meant that the man/land ratio deteriorated sharply. This further reinforced the pressure towards the modernization of agriculture.

This was also the period in which the state played an increased role in agriculture, as it did in other sectors of the economy. Throughout Latin America, State intervention through bureaucratic agencies and programmes of extension, inputs and marketing became a regular feature of the agrarian economy. This extension of State control became a major factor in the consolidation of centralized government until the 1980s, when economic and political constraints led to a certain shrinkage in the State's role in promoting economic development. The increasing internationalization of Latin America's agricultural economy, and the proliferation of international development agencies, working directly with local non-government organizations, led to a marked privatization of agrarian development by 1990. These processes were met by a variety of individual and collective responses on the part of the rural population which, in turn, further limited the effectiveness of State planning and control of the agrarian sector.

The chapter begins by examining the major trends in the period 1930 to 1990. It goes on to explore what these changes meant for the rural household and for the work roles of its members. We then subdivide the period in order to identify the most salient characteristics of each subperiod and to provide more detail on regional variation. The periodization is, inevitably, untidy. Because of differences in economic and social development, the rhythm of change varied within Latin America; some countries, for example, experimented with agrarian reform long after it was a dead issue elsewhere. Furthermore, there were no marked watersheds, and change occurred gradually, though unevenly, throughout the period.

GENERAL TRENDS

The major force accelerating change from the 1930s was the industrialization of the Latin American economies, which gathered strength in the decades following the ending of the Second World War. Whereas in 1930, there was not a single Latin American economy whose industrial product was greater than its agricultural product, by 1990, the industrial product of every Latin American country, with the exception of El Salvador, was at least equal to and in most cases considerably larger than its agricultural product.

Industrialization set in train a process of urbanization that interlinked rural and urban areas through an increasing flow of commodities and people. The timing and pace of change were different in the various countries. These differences demonstrate the variations in the dynamic of growth of the Latin American economies and, as we will see, in the role of commercial agriculture. Industrialization was already well under way in Argentina by 1930. In contrast, Ecuador and the Central American Republics began to industrialize rapidly only in the 1960s, while even by 1990 Haiti had barely begun to modernize its economy. These contrasts mean that the significance of agriculture as a social issue, in terms of rural welfare and outmigration or in terms of agrarian reform, varied through time, and in its salience for each country. This diversity can be seen in Table 6.1, which indicates the proportions of the labour force working in agriculture at different times in all twenty Latin American republics.

By 1930, the Southern Cone countries (Argentina, Uruguay and Chile) had only a minority of their labour force working in agriculture. These were countries with flourishing urban economies based on manufacturing and services, and in which there was little peasant, subsistence-orientated agriculture. These low proportions working in agriculture were not matched by the other Latin American countries until the 1980s. For most Latin American countries, the most rapid period of change in the structure of employment came after 1960. In that year agriculture still provided the bulk of employment in fifteen of the twenty countries. By 1970 only nine countries, mainly in Central America and the Caribbean, had most of their labour-force working in agriculture.

It should be noted, however, that the pace of change was not consistent between countries. Bolivia showed little change in the importance of agricultural employment, though, in part, this was due to the drop in the numbers of non-agricultural *rural* employment opportunities. Early in the century, the Bolivian census reported large numbers of rural women working as spinners, complementing the pastoral economy. In the course of the century these jobs were displaced by competition from factory products. Some countries, such as Peru, showed a relatively slow and even decline in the proportions working in agriculture; while for others, such as Brazil and Mexico, the fall sharply accelerated after 1960. The 1990 Mexican population census reported just 22 per cent of the economically active population working in agriculture and related activities.

In the 1930s and 1940s, most farming households of peasant smallhold-

Table 6.1 *Labour force in agriculture: 1930–80*

	% of Labour Force Working in Agriculture					
	c. 1930	1940	1950	1960	1970	1980
Argentina	24.0	24.5	25.1	20.6	16.0	13.0
Bolivia	50.3		61.3	56.2	52.1	46.4
Brazil	68.7	67.4	59.8	52.0	44.9	31.1
Colombia	73.6	72.7	57.2	50.1	39.3	34.2
Costa Rica	62.6		57.5	51.2	42.6	30.8
Cuba	52.8	41.4	42.7	36.7	30.2	23.8
Chile	37.5	35.6	34.2	30.0	23.2	16.4
Dominican Republic	76.7		72.7	63.7	54.7	45.7
Ecuador			65.3	58.8	50.6	38.5
El Salvador	75.3		65.3	61.5	56.7	43.2
Guatemala		71.1	68.4	66.6	61.3	56.8
Haiti		85.6	79.9	74.3	70.0	
Honduras	89.4		72.3	70.4	64.9	60.5
Mexico	67.3	64.9	60.4	55.1	44.1	36.6
Nicaragua		73.1	67.9	61.8	51.6	46.5
Panama		52.6	56.4	51.0	41.6	31.8
Paraguay			55.4	54.7	51.0	33.3
Peru		62.5	57.7	52.3	47.1	40.0
Uruguay			24.3	21.3	18.6	15.7
Venezuela	55.5	51.2	42.8	33.3	25.9	16.0
Total	74.4	66.1	53.2	47.4	39.7	28.9
Nos (000) in Agriculture[a]	21,200	25,900	30,907	33,931	36,827	39,263

Notes: [a] These estimates are based on the available national censuses for the period up to 1940. The figures for 1950–80 are taken from International Labour Office (ILO), *Economically Active Population: 1950–2025* (Geneva, 1986), Vol. III, table 3, pp. 119–30.

ers, tenants and sharecroppers were organized in terms of a maximum utilization of family labour. In part, this was necessary because of the temporary labour migration of males to centres of work in many parts of Latin America. Also, non-mechanized agriculture demanded a range of labour inputs throughout the year that could be divided among household members from the youngest to the oldest. Women played a crucial role in agriculture and in handicrafts. When the male head of household was absent, they had a special responsibility for maintaining subsistence production on the smallholding as a necessary supplement to the cash earned externally.

Inter-household relationships within the community were reinforced through reciprocal exchanges to compensate for labour shortages. Households with a temporary or permanent deficiency of labour sought help from those which had a labour surplus. The external wages were just sufficient to meet the basic cash requirements of households, but left little surplus for the purchase of industrialized foodstuffs and consumer goods. Consequently, a great deal of family labour was used to substitute such goods through laborious food processing and through other forms of domestic self-provisioning of items such as clothing, domestic utensils, production equipment and housing.[2]

In this period, land was the major, steady source of livelihood for the rural population of Latin America. Temporary work, both within agriculture and outside it, was a common phenomenon, but only in a minority of cases did it become a permanent way of life. In Chile, for example, the temporary workers on the *haciendas* were usually the children of the permanent workers. Temporary work was usually associated with a stage in the life cycle, when young single men migrated away to work before inheriting land and establishing their own household. Most rural people expected to spend the major proportion of their adult lives in stable relation to land.

The major change affecting rural households from the 1950s onwards was the rapid urbanization of Latin America. One of the most significant consequences of this urbanization was the intensification of rural-urban linkages, both in terms of social relationships and in terms of political and economic organization. From the 1950s onwards, the infrastructure of the agrarian sector was considerably improved and extended to stimulate the development of export crops and domestic food production. Road networks interconnected regions to an extent that rail, orientated simply to moving primary goods to the coastal ports, had not achieved. In some cases, this brought hitherto virgin areas, such as the Amazonian basin, into the national economy, while giving even remote, village subsistence cultivators easy access to markets. Electricity, health and educational facili-

[2] As we show in a later section, this general view of farming households in the 1930s and 1940s needs to be qualified to take account of the types of family farms that were more orientated to the market. See, for Peru, H. Castro Pozo, 'Social and Economic-political Evolution of the Communities of Central Peru', in J. Steward (ed.), *Handbook of South American Indians,* Vol. II (Washington, D.C., 1946) and H. Tschopik, *Highland Communities of Central Peru* (Washington, D.C., 1947); for Mexico, Elsie Parsons, *Mitla* (Chicago, Ill., 1936), R. R. Redfield, *The Folk Culture of the Yucatan* (Chicago, Ill., 1941), C. Hewitt de Alcántara, *Anthropological Perspectives on Rural Mexico* (London, 1984); for Argentina, C. C. Taylor, *Rural Life in Argentina* (Baton Rouge, La. 1948); and for Chile, G. M. McBride, *Chile: Land and Society* (New York, 1936).

ties for villages followed, though their spread was uneven and the timing of their introduction varied between regions.

This integration provided new cash-earning opportunities for local farmers, while at the same time remittances from labour migration increased the circulation of cash in the rural sector. Even peasant farmers had a greater incentive to produce a surplus for sale, often through specializing in new crops such as vegetables for the urban market. Some of these crop innovations were to be the direct consequence of urban migration. Two examples will suffice. Potato farming in a previously subsistence village economy of the state of Mexico was begun, in the early 1960s, by three migrants who had contacted, in their travels, wholesalers in the city of Mexico. The wholesalers, looking for new sources of supply, provided credit and introduced new strains of potato developed in one of the research centers sponsored by the United States and the Mexican government as part of the Green Revolution.[3] Similarly, in the 1950s migrants from the central Peruvian highland village of Pucará worked as agricultural labourers, on market gardens run by Chinese entrepreneurs on the outskirts of the city of Lima. They returned to their village and began the extensive vegetable production that dominated the village's economy in the 1970s and 1980s.[4]

Urbanization increased cash circulation, and this, combined with the rising supply of nationally produced cheap industrialized goods, led the household to depend increasingly on goods bought in local shops. This extended to the purchase of processed foodstuffs. By the late 1970s, about half the food consumption of peasants, surveyed in eight remote villages of highland Peru, was bought from shops.[5] The food included industrialized products such as vegetable oils, sugar, salt, flour and noodles. The families also purchased a wide range of non-durables, such as clothing and shoes.

Despite a substantial exodus from the rural areas, it was not sufficient,

[3] The Green Revolution refers to a technological package consisting of improved seeds, fertilizer and other chemical inputs. Much of the early work was sponsored by the Rockefeller Foundation in the 1950s and led to the setting up in Mexico of the international agricultural research centre CIMMYT (the centre for research and improvement of maize and wheat), specializing in developing new varieties of high yielding hybrids. For a case study of the implementation of the Green Revolution in a Mexican village, see Laurentino Luna, 'Development of Capitalist Agriculture in a Peasant Area of Mexico', unpublished Ph.D. dissertation, University of Manchester, 1982.

[4] J. Solano Sáez, 'From Cooperative to Hacienda: the Case of the Agrarian Society of Pucara', in N. Long and B. Roberts (eds), *Peasant Cooperation and Capitalist Expansion in Central Peru* (Austin, Tex., 1978), p. 192.

[5] A. Figueroa, *Capitalist Development and Peasant Economy in Peru* (Cambridge, 1984), pp. 50–1. W. P. Mitchell reaches similar conclusions in his study of the Peruvian village of Quinua: *Peasants on the Edge: Crops, Cult, and Crisis in the Andes* (Austin, Tex., 1991).

except in a few cases such as that of Argentina, to lead to an absolute decline in agricultural population.[6] Rates of natural increase in the rural areas rose steadily through the 1970s, reaching a rate of over 3 per cent in many areas. An analysis of demographic change in a highland village of Peru – the Ayacucho community of Quinua – showed the difference between births and deaths to result in a 1.2 per cent annual growth rate in 1960, and 2.8 per cent in 1980.[7]

The increase in the rural population was not fully absorbed by agriculture. The trend among large-scale commercial farming operations was for the demand for permanent labour to decrease. Also the dense concentrations of rural population were in poor, dry-farming zones where there were little or no opportunities for expanding employment opportunities in agriculture.[8] Rural population increase was, under these conditions, absorbed by households relying more than previously on combining small-scale farming with a variety of other activites – temporary wage-labour, trading, service and craft activities. The average size of units of less than 20 hectares decreased in Latin America from 4.9 hectares in 1960 to 4.7 hectares in 1970.[9] In Brazil, the number of units of less than 1 hectare multiplied tenfold between 1940 and 1970, and those between 1 and 10 hectares increased four times.[10]

The impact of these economic changes on household organization and the household division of labour was considerable. One trend was towards forms of farming, both on smallholdings and on larger farms, that were less suited to the use of all of a household's labour resources. Mechanization marginalized the contribution of women and children by replacing labour-intensive tasks such as sowing and by specializing in one main marketed crop, thereby reducing the diversity of tasks that provided work for household members. In some areas, labour-replacing trends in the

[6] The rural population – which includes those working in non-agricultural activities – continued to increase in most countries of Latin America. It was 122 million in 1975 and was projected to rise to 141 million by the year 2000. See Centro Latino Americano de Demografia (CELADE), *Boletín Demográfico,* No. 23 (Santiago, 1979). It is estimated that the rural areas of Latin America lost 37 per cent of their natural increase through out-migration between 1940 and 1950, 49 per cent between 1950 and 1960, and 58 per cent between 1960 and 1970.

[7] See Mitchell, *Peasants on the Edge.*

[8] For an analysis of the rural areas in the west of Mexico which 'expelled' population, see: Alejandro J. Arroyo, *El Abandono rural: un modelo explicativo de la emigración de trabajadores en el occidente de México* (Guadalajara, 1989), pp. 167–89.

[9] E. Ortega, 'La agricultura campesina en América Latina', *Revista de la CEPAL* No. 16, (Santiago, 1982), Table 9, p. 98.

[10] Ibid., Table 8, p. 97. Much of this increase was due to colonization. Small landholdings also prolifereated in areas of established farming, such as the northeast.

rural economy converged. At the same time as women ceased to provide non-wage agricultural labour, processed foodstuffs and modern utensils made of plastic or metal decreased the hours required for household tasks. Home-based crafts, such as traditional healing practices and brewing, tended to disappear.[11] Under these conditions, the intensive and diverse utilization of unpaid household labour – the basic survival strategy of peasants in the 1930s – became less appropriate to the rural situation.

The diversity of agrarian structures, and differences in the pace of economic change, meant that there was no uniform trend in the use of household labour.[12] Studies in Chile and Colombia show that, under certain conditions, women's agricultural work increased as farming became more commercialized.[13] In areas of small-scale farming, where households had enough land for subsistence but profit margins were low, the non-paid labour of female household members increased, lowering production costs by diminishing the need for hired labour. Furthermore, in many peasant areas, women continued to diversify their economic activities to supplement the income derived from the farm.

Women, or even children, took up temporary wage labour outside the household and engaged in a series of cash-generating, non-farming activities ranging from trade to outwork for urban manufacturers and traders.[14] Women's entrepreneurial activities led, in some cases, to a less patriarchical way of managing the family budget than existed before. Such women were less likely to consult their husbands over using their earnings to further childrens' education or to improve household amenities. Young dependent members of the household became more likely to save their

[11] Lourdes Arizpe, 'Relay Migration and the Survival of the Peasant Household', in Helen Safa (ed.), *Toward a Political Economy of Urbanization in Third World Countries* (Oxford, 1982).

[12] For a contrast between farming practices, household strategies and migration in two villages of central Mexico, see L. Arizpe, *Campesinado y migración* (Mexico, D. F., 1985).

[13] P. Campaña, 'Rural Women in Three Contrasting Situations of Capitalist Development in Chile and Peru', unpublished Ph.D. dissertation, University of Durham, 1985, contrasts women's work in peasant households in two different areas of the Central valley of Chile: an area of mixed farming and a fruit-growing area. Women took on more agricultural tasks on their own farms when they had sufficient land for subsistence, since the poor returns in the mixed farming area made it unprofitable to hire in labour. On the other hand, women undertook non-farm economic activities where the land was insufficient or too poor for subsistence. Magdalena León de Leal, *Debate sobre la mujer en América Latina y el Caribe: discución acerca de la unidad producción-reproducción* (Bogotá, 1982), shows how the extent of women's agricultural work varied according to region and type of farming.

[14] See F. E. Babb, 'Producers and Reproducers: Andean marketwomen in the economy', in J. Nash and H. Safa (eds), *Women and Change in Latin America* (South Hadley, Mass., 1985); C. Deere and M. León de Leal, *Women in Andean Agriculture: Peasant Production and Rural Wage Employment in Colombia and Peru* (Washington, D.C., 1982); S. C. Bourque and K. B. Warren, *Women of the Andes: Patriarchy and Social Change in Two Peruvian Villages* (Ann Arbor, Mich., 1981).

earnings and, when opportunities arose, migrate away. In other cases, women remained excluded from crucial resources, and, in some situations, the out-migration of males led to an increase in the number of impoverished female-headed households, dependent on other households for their survival.[15]

As migration became a permanent feature of rural life, household and community organization was restructured, though to different degrees depending upon the intensity of national economic changes and on social class position. Out-migration, by removing permanently whole households or members of households, usually young adult males and females seeking education or work in the urban centres, restructured inter- and intra-household co-operation. The households that remained, while more likely to contain male and female heads permanently committed to the local economy, were less likely to have additional labour resources. Though the locality might contain more households than previously, each rural household had by the 1980s a smaller number of members. This both reduced the possibilities of inter-household co-operation and increased the need for those households with more land to employ wage labour. The farming strategy of such households was inevitably geared to maximizing the profits to be gained from farming and associated activities. Also, the hunger for cash and outmigration severely reduced the amount of able-bodied labour available to the subsistence economy.[16] The combination of all these factors resulted in a process of social differentiation in the rural sector based on the increasing specialization and commoditization of the household.[17]

The impact of these changes was generational. As each generation reached adulthood, its pattern of agricultural work was shaped by the opportunities available at the time. It was the children of the generation of the 1930s and 1940s, not their parents, who felt the full brunt of the break-down of family-based agriculture, where that had occurred. They were a transitional generation for whom temporary work opportunities,

[15] See Nash and Safa, *Women and Change*.

[16] In a long-term study of back and forth migration between a Peruvian highland village and a coffee colonization area, J. Collins, *Unseasonal Migrations: the Effects of Rural Labour Scarcity in Peru* (Princeton, N.J., 1988) shows that migrants became more firmly embedded in the cash economy of the coffee area, resulting in them increasingly withdrawing labour from the agricultural and craft activities of the home village. Hence, the highland village economy was starved of labour, and was sustained, with difficulty, mainly by older people.

[17] For an account of this process for women working in the coffee producing areas of Brazil, see: V. Stolcke, *Coffee Planters, Workers, and Wives: Class Conflict and Gender Relations on São Paulo Plantations, 1850–1980* (Oxford, 1988).

either in agriculture or outside of it, became a permanent way of life in many parts of Latin America. They remained in the rural areas because their parents still worked there while they, unlike the subsequent generation, had not been fully caught up in the increasing flow of cityward migration. The temporary work opportunities taken-up in early adulthood were not replaced by a stable attachment to land, either as a smallholder peasant or as a permanent worker. In the subsequent generation, work opportunities in agriculture, for those few children who remained, were more stable, even though they were as likely to be wage workers as smallholders.[18]

Industrialization directly and indirectly created pressures to modernize and restructure agricultural production.[19] Revenues from traditional exports were always a crucial means of paying for the expansion of industry. The ending of the first stage of import substitution industrialization (ISI) in the 1960s meant that governments had to pay renewed attention to agriculture as a source of export revenue to finance intermediate and capital goods industries. The growth in population, and the urban population in particular, created an increasing demand for marketed foodstuffs. New opportunities were seized by some classes of farmer to supply the urban foodstuff market with products such as rice and beef, which had not, in most cases, been peasant products. Cattle and dairy production stimulated the production of fodder crops such as alfalfa and sorghum. Also, new cash crops such as fruit, vegetables and soya beans emerged catering both for the export and high-income internal markets.

The period from the late 1940s to the 1980s witnessed a substantial increase in overall agricultural production in Latin America, which more than doubled in volume (see Table 6.2). However, in most cases the increase in production of food crops for the internal market did not keep pace with growing domestic demand consequent upon population increase and urbanization.[20] One result of this was an increase in the imports of

18 For a description of this generational change in the nature of work opportunities for the fruit-growing area of the central valley of Chile, see Sylvia Vanegas, 'Family Reproduction in Rural Chile: a Socio-demographic Study of Agrarian Change in the Aconcagua Valley, 1930–1986', unpublished Ph.D. thesis, University of Texas, Austin, 1987. She shows a substantial increase in temporary work among the transitional generation (those reaching adulthood in the 1950s), but the predominance of permanent wage work among the modern generation of males. A significant factor in this trend is declining fertility, entailing that recent generations, unlike their predecessors, have fewer children seeking work.

19 For a summary of how these pressures operated, see A. de Janvry, *The Agrarian Question and Reformism in Latin America* (Baltimore, Md., 1981), pp. 65–81.

20 See United Nations, *Statistical Yearbook for Latin America* (1984); de Janvry, *The Agrarian Question*, pp. 69–72.

Table 6.2. *Indices of agricultural production Latin America: selected products (1975 = 100)*

Product	1934–6	1945	1950	1955	1960	1965	1970	1975	1981	1987
Wheat	58	39	55	64	63	68	71	100	101	154
Maize	48	37	34	50	57	81	100	100	148	148
Potato	35	45	61	71	77	97	105	100	132	134
Rice	92	189	97	119	118	136	97	100	103	120
Vegetables							51	100	122	146
Fruit-							83	100	110	126
Cotton	57	57	70	107	103	148	128	100	110	93
Sugar	17	21	29	36	57	78	87	100	117	157
Coffee	120	86	141	153	211	94	116	100	188	189
Soya[a]								100	177	226
Meat	31		35	45	35	66	83	100	127	139

Notes: [a] Soybeans only begin to be produced in appreciable quantities in 1970 when 10 million metric tonnes are produced, and Latin America becomes the second largest producer in the world, after the United States.
Source: FAO, *Production Yearbooks,* 1946–87.

basic grains throughout the period, especially marked in the case of wheat which, by 1980, had affected even Mexico, one of the most successful countries in improving grain production.[21] Chile, which had in the 1930s been a net grain exporter, was, by 1980, importing about one-third of national grain needs.[22]

The years from the 1930s to the late 1950s witnessed, in general, stagnation in the production of grains and other basic foodstuffs. Export crops, particularly sugar, showed some increase in production, but in general the growth of export agriculture was slow and fluctuating – in contrast to the situation of the early part of the century when the rapid growth of a few export crops had transformed the agrarian structures of Latin America. This picture, however, needs to be qualified for individual countries. For example, Mexico's agricultural production recovered in the 1940s, surpassing the levels attained before the Revolution.[23] In Peru, the

[21] FAO, *Yearbook,* Vol. 37, (1983), table 155. Mexico's recorded yields in wheat production rose from 760 kg per hectare in the 1930s to 3,700 kgs per hectare by the 1980s. These yields were mainly obtained by extensive irrigation and highly commercial farming. See also M. R. Redclift, *Development and the Environmental Crisis: Red or Green Alternatives?* (London, 1984), p. 85, Table 3.

[22] This estimate is based on the production and trade figures given in the FAO yearbook for 1988.

[23] For an account of the role of Mexican agriculture as an 'engine of growth' from the 1940s to the 1970s, see S. E. Sanderson, *The Transformation of Mexican Agriculture: International Structure and the Politics of Rural Change* (Princeton, N.J., 1986), pp. 36–7.

1940s and 1950s was a period of mixed, but, on the whole, successful export agriculture.[24]

Up to the late 1950s, neither governments nor farmers in Latin America made substantial efforts to increase agricultural productivity by new investment and technological innovation. In Argentina, for example, which in 1930 had the most advanced farming in Latin America, the years until 1960 were marked by decreasing yields for grains and cotton and failure to keep up with improvements in agricultural productivity in the United States.[25] In general, export agriculture was taxed to finance urban and industrial expansion. Over-valued currencies protected domestic industry, but reduced the returns to export agriculture. Non-export agriculture also suffered as governments sought to keep down food costs in the cities by fixing the price of food staples. In addition, international price trends in these years were generally unfavourable to agricultural commodities.

The reasons for the relative lack of interest in improving agricultural productivity were as much political and social as they were economic. Agriculture was marginalized politically as priority was given to industrialization. In most countries, this resulted in a policy of leaving alone existing systems of land tenure and local power. This, after all, was an inexpensive and easy option for governments intent on marshalling resources to promote industry and faced with the new political and social challenges brought by rapid urban growth. An example of this was the tacit alliance whereby Getúlio Vargas in Brazil (1930–45) did not interfere with the local power of landowners, concentrating instead on regulating and promoting industrial growth through a favourable tariff and taxation policy, and building-up political support through government controlled trade unions. In Mexico, with the exception of the administration of Lázaro Cárdenas (1934–40), governments did little until the 1960s to advance the agrarian reform initiated in the aftermath of the Revolution of 1910. In Argentina, Perón (1946–55) intervened to favour rural workers and tenants, promoting union organization among the former and regulating rents for the latter. Even in this case, however, little was changed since landowners opted for

[24] R. Thorp and G. Bertram, *Peru 1890–1977: Growth and Policy in an Open Economy* (London, 1978), pp. 2–6.

[25] C. F. Díaz-Alejandro points out that only a small part of the spectacular advances in rural technology since the 1930s found their way to Argentina: *Essays on the Economic History of the Argentine Republic* (New Haven, Conn., 1970), p. 145. Again, Mexico was a partial exception since there was considerable public investment in large-scale irrigation projects in the 1950s and 1960s. These benefited primarily the commercial farmers of the northwest, a zone with close export links to the United States.

short-term leases and, where appropriate, moved into less labour intensive forms of farming, such as cattle raising.

Various factors combined in the period 1930 to 1960 to create an uncertain economic climate in which market-orientated farmers were unlikely to invest in improving productivity. Instead, they spread risks, if they were large-scale landowners, by continuing existing practices of sharecropping, short-term tenancies and using seasonal labour from peasant villages. On the other hand, the peasant farmer diversified his economy, complementing agriculture with labour migration, trade and craft work. The rising demand for foodstuffs for the urban population was met in many countries, such as Peru, by increasing food imports. In Brazil, agricultural production was expanded by bringing vast new areas of land into cultivation, both for export and domestic food crops. However, the yields obtained from crops hardly increased, and many crops showed decreasing yields.[26] As we will see later, it was in this period that agrarian reform became an important political issue in Latin America.

The most far-reaching changes occurred in the years after 1960 when, as Table 6.2 shows, there was a substantial increase in the production of foodstuffs – meat, vegetables, fruit, and cereals and pulses used by food-processing industries – for the 'new' urban market both at home and abroad. This improvement in productivity was generated by public investments in agricultural infrastructure such as irrigation systems, by the dissemination of new technology, particularly high yielding seed varieties and the use of fertilizer and insecticides, and, to a lesser extent, by mechanization. Agricultural production became increasingly geared to the consumption patterns of high-income urban dwellers at home and abroad, encouraging, as we argue in a later section, the internationalization of Latin American agriculture, and the integration of the producer, whether small- or large-scale, into extensive credit, marketing, and food-processing networks.

The structure of agricultural exports and imports after 1966 can be seen in Table 6.3. The real dollar value of Latin America's export trade in agricultural products doubled from 1966 to 1988. Traditional exports, such as coffee, sugar and cotton (classified under textile fibres) played the major part in this growth, and continued to be the dominant exports. They were complemented by 'new' export crops such as vegetable oils, fish, fruit and vegetables. By 1981, tomatoes accounted for half of Mex-

[26] United Nations, *Statistical Yearbook* (1984), pp. 300–8. Mexico is an exception to this trend because of dramatic increases in the yields of wheat, mainly occurring from the 1950s onwards.

Table 6.3. *The structure of agricultural exports and imports by commodity: Latin America, 1966–88 (three year moving averages, %)*[a]

Commodity	1966–8		1971–3		1976–8		1981–3		1986–8	
	Import	Export	Import	Export	Import	Export	Import	Export	Import	Export
Meat & animals	7.8	13.4	7.9	15.6	6.8	7.6	6.1	8.4	10.2	7.0
Cereals	35.8	11.6	34.5	8.4	35.2	8.3	42.9	10.0	32.2	4.1
Fruit & vegetables	11.1	10.1	10.6	10.5	10.0	9.4	9.8	10.9	8.0	16.1
Sugar and coffee	7.2	41.6	6.7	41.8	6.7	52.5	9.3	45.3	5.2	49.8
Feedstuffs	2.1	5.7	2.0	5.0	2.7	7.3	3.8	8.9	5.7	6.0
Textile fibres	6.9	12.6	4.0	3.9	2.5	6.1	2.2	4.3	4.9	2.4
Fixed veg. oils	4.8	2.1	4.7	2.5	6.3	3.6	5.7	3.8	6.3	3.7
Fish and fishery	3.2	2.2	3.9	6.4	3.1	4.1	2.1	7.1	3.8	9.8
Fertilizer	10.3	.6	12.4	.6	14.6	.5	10.1	.5	15.9	.4
Agricultural machinery	10.7	.1	13.3	.3	12.1	.6	8.1	.7	7.9	.7
TOTAL	100.0	100.0	100.0	100.0	100.0	100.0	100.0	100.0	100.0	100.0
Total US$ (billions) in 1982 prices[b]	3,545	14,050	5,260	18,684	9,104	30,040	9,762	28,655	7,600	27,014

Notes: [a] The countries included are Argentina, Bolivia (not included in 1971–3), Brazil, Chile, Colombia, Ecuador, Peru, Uruguay (not included in 1966–8, 1971–3), Venezuela, Mexico, Costa Rica, El Salvador, Guatemala, Honduras, Nicaragua, Panama, Cuba (not included 1966–68, 1971–3), and the Dominican Republic.

[b] The dollar amounts for each period are adjusted to the purchasing power of the dollar of 1982 in producer prices. U.S. Bureau of the Census, *Statistical Abstract of the United States* (Washington, D.C., 1990), table 756.

Source: FAO, *Trade Yearbooks*, vol. 23 (1969), table III, vol. 28 (1974), table IV, vol. 31 (1977), table IV, vol. 37 (1983), table IV, vol. 42, table IV.

ico's considerable export earnings in the category of fruits and vegetables.[27] Though by 1988 export earnings on agricultural commodities still exceeded outgoings on imports, the favourable balance had narrowed somewhat. In these years, the amounts spent outside of Latin America on basic foodstuffs, and especially on cereals, increased considerably, averaging about one-third of the total import bill. This constant high need to import basic foodstuffs occurred despite the improvements in yields and production levels noted above.

The impact of these trends on the Latin American countries varied significantly. Some managed to increase their export revenues more dramatically than others. Brazil showed the highest growth rate in this period, while Peru had one of the lowest. The growth in non-traditional agricultural exports, such as vegetable oils, animals feeds or table vegetables occurred mainly in Brazil and Mexico, while other countries, such as the Central American Republics, increased their earnings through traditional export staples such as coffee or bananas. However, even in these cases, there was a greater diversification of exports, as in the case of coffee exports in Honduras, a country previously dependent on the export of bananas. In the late 1980s, Guatemala became an important exporter of broccoli, artichokes and Chinese cabbages to the North American markets. Underlying this diversity, however, was a consistent pattern: the intensification throughout Latin America of production for export.

The modernization of agriculture in the 1960s and 1970s through mechanization, hybrids and other industrial inputs created a market for industry. Agro-industries, such as those processing foodstuffs, showed rapid growth. And the change in economic climate was accompanied by a change in political climate. Agriculture became an important political issue, with powerful urban economic interests, such as financiers, industrialists, and traders, lending their support to the call for agrarian modernization.

1930S TO 1950S

Before 1930 many rural areas in Latin America had been fully integrated into the international economy through the export of cash-crops, livestock

[27] Many of these crops had been exported in the period previous to the Second World War. What is new is the volume of exports and their value. For example, between 1934–8 and 1981, Chile increased the volume of its exports of grapes by a factor of seventy, of apples by twenty, and had become a substantial exporter of pears and peaches. See FAO, *Production Yearbook,* Vol. II (1949), pp. 71–89 and FAO, *Production Yearbook,* (1983), pp. 144–68.

products and minerals. Even those areas not directly involved in export-production had been economically stimulated by the growth of internal trade and the emergence of new urban markets. Most regions, with the exception of the Amazon, had acquired the patterns of farming, of land tenure and of local power which characterized them until the 1960s when agricultural modernization, and economic and political centralization, began to affect even the least commercial farming areas.

Agricultural production in Latin America had long been shaped by the demands of European and North American markets for specific commodities. This demand created entirely new farming regions, settling populations where none had existed before, and dislocating indigenous types of production. Agriculture also became linked to non-agricultural forms of production such as mining and urban-based food processing industries. None of these processes were self-generating since they required political and economic intervention to establish *ab initio* large-scale plantation or mining enterprises and to ensure that labour was made available where indigenous populations were either reluctant to abandon their own farming or where there was none, or little, locally resident population.

A distinctive feature of Latin America's historical development was that the agrarian structures of its various regions had been assembled by the early twentieth century, mainly as a result of external economic interests which, in alliance with regionally dominant classes, sought different primary products for the needs of the industrialized world, and consequently became involved in the recruitment and control of labour and the provision of necessary infrastructure. These structures were based on a dominant type of agriculture, together with its associated crops and livestock, forms of land tenure and technology. However, an agrarian structure goes beyond this set of technical, natural resource and production factors, usually called 'the farming system'.[28] It embraces, in addition, the legal and political institutions supporting this system, rural-urban relationships, marketing structures, the social classes present in the rural area, traders, crafts-people and different classes of cultivators and the wider economic system stretching in some cases as far as the world economy.

A variety of agrarian structures can be identified to take account of the diversity of ways in which Latin American regions and sub-regions developed. Substantial differences existed between areas dominated by planta-

[28] On this point, see E. Clayton, *Agrarian Development in Peasant Economies* (Oxford, 1964), pp. 137–60; Norman Long and Bryan Roberts, *Miners, Peasants and Entrepreneurs: Regional Development in the Central Highlands of Peru* (Cambridge, 1984), pp. 240–2.

tion agriculture, by livestock-raising, by commercial foodstuff farming for the national market or by small-scale peasant farming. These differences appeared not only in the way in which agriculture was practiced – the techniques that were used – but in density of population, its settlement pattern, and in the social structure and institutions of communities. They entailed differences in class and power structures. They were also associated with distinctive styles of life and culture which, in turn, shaped individual and household economic strategies.

By 1930 export agriculture and mining had left a clear imprint on the agrarian structures of Latin America. The pampas of Argentina had become one of the world's major exporters of cereals and meat. Coffee in both Brazil and Colombia had helped create thriving regional economies. Chile was one of the world's major sources of copper and nitrates. Though the mining areas were too barren to support a thriving local economy, they were the basis for the prosperity of, and population concentration in, Santiago and its port of Valparaiso which stimulated the agriculture of the central valley. In Peru, sugar on the northern coast, cotton on the central coast, mining in the central highlands and wool in the southern highlands had all generated distinctive regional agrarian structures. Mexico also had distinctive export-orientated regional economies: cotton in the La Laguna region of the North; mining and export agriculture in Sonora; henequen in the Yucatan. Tropical fruits had turned much of Central America into a vast North American-owned plantation, whereas Cuba and other Carribbean islands had become the leading international suppliers of sugar. Integration into the world economy through exports had, in fact, diversified the agrarian structure of Latin America. Despite the high level of commoditization in all these regional economies, there was no uniformity in labour processes, property relations, mechanisms of surplus extraction or in the organization of the household economy.

What, then, was the range of regional agrarian structures to be found at the beginning of our period? We will outline four main types – large-scale commercial farming, enclave production, small-scale farming, and subsistence farming – in order to identify the contrasts arising from the geographically specific impact of export production, and from the diversity of labour and property relations in the countryside. The various types of agrarian regional structure often co-existed spatially. Certainly, the geographical boundaries of these regions were not clear-cut. For example, some indigenous communities close to the Bolivian mines were completely separate from the mining economy, whereas the more distant villages of the Cochabamba valley were an integral part of that economy, supplying both labour and foodstuffs.

At first sight, a European or North American observer might have been more impressed by the similarities, rather than the contrasts, in the living and working situation of Latin American countryfolk. Everywhere, most rural people lived at the margins of subsistence. Farming was carried out mainly by hand and by animal-driven ploughs.[29] Most labour was family-based. Even in the case of wage labourers on large farms or plantations, unpaid family labour was a crucial part of their subsistence, helping at peak times in the agricultural cycle and cultivating a kitchen garden and rearing animals. Also, the different agrarian classes were found throughout Latin America: the estate owner, the small proprietor cultivating for the market, the peasant farming mainly for subsistence, the tenant or sharecropper and the landless labourer. All these rural societies were part-societies, inextricably linked to wider economies and polities, but the market opportunities open to the farmer, the importance of local community organization to farming strategies and the power holders on whom the farmer depended varied, significantly, between the four types.[30]

The first type of agrarian structure – large-scale commercial production – was found mainly in the countries of the Southern Cone and in southern Brazil. It was based on the massive immigration of Europeans at the end of the nineteenth and beginning of the twentieth centuries. They provided a readily available labour force to develop the fertile virgin lands. Like their counterparts in the United States, they came to America in the expectation of being able, eventually, to set up independently and make a good living from the soil. But in contrast to the farmer of the mid-west of the United States, their possibilities of progress were severely limited by the direct control that established elites retained over the land, relegating most immigrants to the status of landless labourer or tenant.

Cereal and cattle production in the pampas of Argentina and coffee production in the state of São Paulo in Brazil were highly commercialized

[29] Argentina was an exception. Mechanization was well advanced in the La Pampa region by the 1930s, although ploughs were mainly horse drawn. Harvesting machines, planters and drills were also common in this area. Argentina had become a major importer of U.S. agricultural machinery. See Taylor, *Rural Life in Argentina*, pp. 146–7.

[30] For the concept of part-society, see A. Kroeber, *Anthropology* (New York, 1948). For an outline of the types of relations that link local peasant communities in Latin America to powerful outsiders, see E. Wolf, 'Aspects of Group Relations in a Complex Society: Mexico', *American Anthropologist*, 58, 6 (1956).

and geared to the demands of the international market. Farmers neither did, nor could, plan their cultivation primarily to meet their subsistence needs and, consequently, were especially exposed to fluctuations in the world market. The units of production varied in size, with the cattle estates and large coffee plantations covering thousands of acres, while cereal farms were usually between two to three hundred acres. Though coffee dominated rural production in São Paulo until 1930, foodstuffs for the urban market were also cultivated, often intermixed with coffee. The coffee estates, especially in the frontier areas of São Paulo, were at times no more than a hundred acres and could be cultivated mainly by family labour. These various types of farming unit supported a large, but frequently transient population, of permanent and temporary labourers, tenants and small proprietors.

In his travels through Argentina in the early 1940s, Taylor reported the poor living conditions of the tenant farmers of the pampas whose homes usually had hard dirt floors and few amenities. Contracts were usually for a five-year period and landowners sought to shorten the contract in order to profit from rising rents and land values. The insecurity of tenure discouraged tenants from investing in infrastructure, and they moved so frequently that observers likened them to nomads. In a representative sample of cereal and cattle belts, Taylor reported that approximately 70 per cent of farmers were tenants and that these belts also had between a third and a half of the farmers with less than five years residence.[31]

In São Paulo, immigrants worked as *colonos* on the coffee plantations. They were paid a wage based on the number of trees they cared for and given a small amount of land on which to cultivate subsistence crops. Conditions of living were poor and in the early years of the twentieth century, there was a high degree of labour mobility from the countryside towards the major urban centers of São Paulo. By 1930, however, immigrants owned a substantial share of the coffee properties, especially in the west of the state. This social mobility was probably due to the greater bargaining power of labour under the conditions of Paulista as against pampas agriculture, enabling households with several adult labourers to make savings from their paid work and the sale of crops from their subsistence plots. Coffee required year round care and labor instability may have been more costly to the Paulista landlord, leading to the offer of incentives to workers, than to his Argentine counterpart whose labour

[31] Taylor, *Rural Life in Argentina*, pp. 195–200.

needs were more seasonal. With the expansion westward, and the pressures on landowners resulting from the cyclical crises in coffee, opportunities arose for immigrants to buy land. The 'new' west of São Paulo was not controlled, as was the 'old' west by large landowners – the *coroneis* – in alliance with the exporting houses of the port of Santos. But the new marketing structures, based on local intermediaries and São Paulo trading houses were as effective as those of the old coffee regions in channelling resources out of the rural area and did little to develop local infrastructure.[32]

The salient point is that this type of agrarian structure facilitated rapid economic growth. The country folk in these agricultural frontiers of Brazil and Argentina were, from the beginning, dependent upon the market and had little alternative other than to specialize in cash crops. The pioneer, whether labourer, tenant or small proprietor, needed credit to buy basic necessities and to tide the family over from one harvest to the next. Italian immigrant households in Argentina were reported to be concentrating their labour on cash crop activities, to the neglect of subsistence production. Cheese and butter-making, animal raising and bread-making were substituted by products from the local store and diet also changed to include meat and other purchased foodstuffs.[33]

Credit, short-term tenancies and the lack of an established community infrastructure were powerful instruments subordinating the rural labourer and small-scale farmer to large landowners and urban traders. Politically powerful landowners monopolized the best land in the pampas and in the first coffee-producing areas of São Paulo, often controlling trade and credit. The geographical isolation of the small farmer and the large distances to the major urban centres put intermediaries, as well, in a powerful position. Local storekeepers, agents of the trading houses of the major urban centres, and owners of milling and husking machines could sell goods at an artificially high price and pay artificially low prices for the crops.

The opening-up of these areas generated, by 1930, immense, but inequitably distributed, wealth and economic opportunities. Yet the structure of marketing and of land tenure channelled the profits of agriculture outside the rural area. In this type of agrarian structure, there was little

[32] See W. Dean, *Rio Claro: a Brazilian Plantation System, 1820–1920* (Stanford, Cal., 1976); T. H. Holloway, *Immigrants on the Land: Coffee and Society in São Paulo* (Chapel Hill, N.C., 1980).

[33] E. Scarzanella, ' "Corn Fever": Italian tenant farming families in Argentina (1895–1912)', *Bulletin of Latin American Research*, 3, 1 (1984): 1–23.

rural development in terms of higher standards of living for the rural worker, in terms of farming unions and co-operatives or through a flourishing network of local urban centres that provided services for the farming population. The poor working conditions of the rural population gave rise to organized protests and strikes, such as the 1912 *Grito de Alcorta* in the Pampas region of Argentina. In general, however, the rural population was politically unorganized. For many people, in both Brazil and Argentina, insecure opportunities farming as *colonos,* tenants or small proprietors were an acceptable means of making a living. Good years on the fertile lands of the pampas or of São Paulo brought profits beyond what immigrants could expect in Europe. Some returned to Europe with their savings, others moved on to the cities of Argentina and southern Brazil, and others accumulated capital in machinery and bought land.

By the 1930s, Mexico also had a region of highly commercialized agriculture: the northwestern states of Sonora and Sinaloa. These had become prosperous farming regions in the last decades of the nineteenth century after the elimination of the local Yacqui Indian population. North American companies had invested in agriculture and a substantial part of the production was exported to the United States. Here farming was based on migrants from other parts of Mexico seeking land on what was then Mexico's agricultural frontier.

The exploitation of all these regions was based on speculation and individual entrepreneurship. No single enterprise monopolized resources or had the responsibility for organizing the opening-up of the agricultural frontier. This responsibility was left, in great part, to the State, both local and national, which subsidized railroads, built roads and power generators or helped with large-scale irrigation. In addition, it was the state in Argentina and Brazil, which organized the recruitment of labour, especially from abroad, and provided the police force to control it.

This type of agrarian structure was characterized by a highly commercial agriculture, a geographically mobile rural population and an underdeveloped social infrastructure, in terms of education, welfare services and housing. One consequence in some regions was the concentration, by the 1930s, of economic power and population in a large city, such as Buenos Aires or São Paulo. These cities industrialized early, on the basis both of the reinvestment of the profits of the export sector and of the existence of an internal market for basic consumer goods provided by proletarianized labour in the countryside and city. Furthermore, the pace of economic development, and the class conflicts associated with it, had contributed to the emergence of a more powerful government apparatus than was the case in nations in which other types of agrarian structure predominated. The fortunes of everyone in these rural areas were closely tied both to fluctuations in the international market and to central government decisions about food prices, rural credit and tariff policies.

This characterization needs modification to take account of the generative effects that accompanied cash-crop production. Despite the surpluses extracted from the rural areas of the pampas region of Argentina, enough remained to stimulate a variegated pattern of small-scale enterprise and, in certain areas, a network of flourishing small towns. Not all small farmers in the pampas region were tenants. Taylor emphasizes the prosperity of towns, such as Esperanza in the Argentine province of Santa Fe, which were centres of mixed and dairy farming, colonized first by Swiss and German immigrants who owned the land and who formed farmers' co-operatives.[34]

The second type of agrarian structure – the economic enclave – was also based on export production, but, in this case, a large-scale economic 'enclave' predominated, constituted by plantation or mining enterprises. The contrast with the first type partly lay in the scale of production of the dominant enterprises. They covered vast areas, required large amounts of wage labour and substantial capital investment. In the case of sugar plantations and mines, production involved elaborate on-the-spot processing. Their infrastructure was usually built and maintained by the company or entrepreneur. This scale of investment meant that plantations and mines were often owned by large-scale foreign companies. Examples for this period were banana and sugar plantations in Central America, the Caribbean, the Morelos region of Mexico, northern Peru and northwest Argentina, and mining enterprises in highland Peru and Bolivia.[35] A further contrast was that control of production was highly

[34] Taylor, *Rural Life in Argentina*, pp. 11–13. Ezquiel Gallo points out that smallholder farming, based on immigrants dependent on the market for their inputs and supplies, stimulated a diversified economic structure in Santa Fe: *'Boom' cerealero y cambios en la estructura socio-política de Santa Fe (1870–1895)* (Buenos Aires, 1974). See also E. Archetti and K. A. Stølen, *Explotación familiar y acumulación de capital en el campo argentino* (Buenos Aires, 1975).

[35] The organization of the Peruvian sugar enclave is described in P. F. Klarén, *Modernization, Dislocation and Aprismo: Origins of the Peruvian Aprista Party 1879–1932* (Austin, Tex., 1973). Other accounts of this type of enterprise and agrarian structure associated with them for the mining enterprises of the central highlands of Peru are A. J. Laite, *Industrial Development and Migrant Labour* (Manchester, 1981) and A. W. De Wind, 'Peasants become Miners: the Evolution of Industrial mining systems in Peru', unpublished Ph.D. thesis, Columbia University, 1977. For the sugar plantations of Salta and Jujuy in Argentina, see S. Whiteford, *Migration, Ethnicity, and Adaptation: Bolivian Migrant Workers in Northwest Argentina* (Austin, Tex., 1975).

centralized, leaving labour less say and less opportunity for individual gain than tenants or *colonos*. Workers were also less dependent on the market than those of the southern cone. Food and other necessities were often obtained from company stores. Much of the labour on plantations was seasonal and provided by peasants tied to village subsistence-based economies. Even mine labour was mainly drawn from peasant villages and it was common for miners to leave their families in the village but to return frequently – the phenomenon of the peasant-miner.

The enclaves had an impact on regional development, but a limited one. Though they developed their own infrastructure for processing and shipping the product and for housing and provisioning their workers, labour and commercial linkages existed with nearby rural areas. One consequence was that the peasant communities became economically diversified, but on the basis of considerable land fragmentation. Population pressure on existing resources was, by the 1930s, one reason for the labour migration of peasants to mines and plantations. The income they so derived enabled them and their families to retain a base in the village, despite the increasing difficulty of obtaining a living from plots too small for subsistence. Migration and the money flows it generated also provided small-scale entrepreneurial opportunities in trade and transport.

The village economies subsidized the plantation and mining enterprises by providing their labour with a temporary or more permanent subsistence in times of recession or seasonal inactivity. For example, the small village of Muquiyauyo in the central highlands of Peru received a considerable influx of returning miners laid-off, in 1930, due to the impact of the 1929 Depression on Cerro de Pasco corporation's operations.[36] In La Laguna, in Mexico, also, the impact of the Depression of the 1930s was disastrous since the United States was the principal purchaser of the cotton.[37] Maize and wheat were sown on lands previously given over to cotton. The cotton workers survived through returning to their villages of origin in central Mexico or subsisting on smallholdings which were often rented from the former cotton estates.

There was little possibility of any class of peasant in enclave regions accumulating sufficient land to develop into capitalist farmers.[38] The process

[36] See M. Grondin, *Comunidad andina: explotación calculada* (Santo Domingo, 1978).

[37] C. Hewitt de Alcántara, *The Modernization of Mexican Agriculture: Socioeconomic Implications of Technological Change 1940–1970* (Geneva, 1976).

[38] On peasant differentiation, and the relationship between the peasant and the mining enclave, see Long and Roberts, (eds), *Peasant Cooperation and Capitalist Expansion*, pp. 315–21, and Long and

of differentiation at the village level had become relatively frozen in regions such as the Mantaro valley of Peru and the Cochabamba valley of Bolivia by the 1930s: the village economies were highly monetized by the links with the enclave, but without any substantial opportunities for local capital accumulation. The Peruvian village of Muquiyauyo is illustrative of this process.[39] By 1930, it had a substantial national reputation as a 'progressive' village which had installed its own electricity generators which supplied even the neighbouring town of Jauja. Almost all of the adult males had worked, at one time or another, in the mining economy, and most village households had absent males. The wages of the miners helped to improve the town, but mainly through better housing, educational facilities and other public buildings. There had been almost no new investment in agriculture. Agricultural productivity was low. Women had a major responsibility for it in the absence of males and very few households survived from agriculture alone. Muquiyauyo's economy was heavily dependent on remittances, trade and crafts; agriculture was almost a secondary occupation.

Even at the level of the major urban centres of these regions, there were difficulties in accumulating capital through trade and industry. The enclaves so monopolized the major economic flows that they left relatively few resources for local or regionally based elites. The major cities of the region were, at best, 'entrepot' towns helping to service the enclaves and the import-export economy on which they were based. By the 1930s, for example, the Peruvian central highlands town of Huancayo was the location of branches of many foreign import-export houses and of mining agencies. It did not, however, have an indigenous entrepreneurial class based on land-ownership or industry.[40] Control over the enclaves was often in foreign hands, but even when it was based on national capital, as in the

Roberts, *Miners, Peasants and Entrepreneurs,* pp. 246–8. Brooke Larson describes a similar process, over a longer historical period, for the Cochabamba valley in Bolivia: *Colonialism and Agrarian Transformation in Bolivia, Cochabamba, 1550–1900* (Princeton, N.J. 1988).

[39] A detailed account of Muquiyauyo in the 1950s is given in R. N. Adams, *A Community in the Andes: Problems and Progress in Muquiyauyo* (Seattle, Wash., 1959). In 1950, 60 per cent of the economically active population either did not work in agriculture or only worked part-time. The subsequent restudy by Girondin confirms the main lines of Adams' analysis and provides further data on the impact of the mining economy on the village. Grondon characterizes the period 1930–50 as the period of *least* innovation in agricultural production, compared with the nineteenth and early twentieth century and the post-1950s: Grondin, *Comunidad andina,* p. 136.

[40] See Long and Roberts, *Miners, Peasants and Entrepreneurs,* pp. 71–87. Large-scale textile production began in Huancayo after the 1940s in response to the opportunities for selling woollen clothing to the mining population and the local availability of wool. This industry had collapsed by the 1960s, with its Lima-based owners moving plant and machinery to the capital.

case of the northern sugar plantations of Peru, this class lived in the capital, Lima, and their monopolization of the region's resources contributed to the stagnation of the regional centre of Trujillo. Merida in the Yucatan province of Mexico had a similar role in the development of the henequen plantations.[41]

This type of regional agrarian structure included areas of widely differing levels of economic activity. Plantations had a seasonal rhythm that was considerably more marked than that of mines, due to the cropping cycles. Thus, Salta, the dominant town of the sugar plantation area of Northwest Argentina, was a major international trade centre during the colonial period, but by the 1930s it had not industrialized and served mainly as the place of residence for the plantation owners and as a center of local commerce.[42] Its level of economic activity changed sharply with the seasons: during the harvesting of cane it was a bustling centre of activity which after the harvest lost both population and economic functions. In contrast, Huancayo was economically active the year round and the servicing of the mining economy of the Peruvian central highlands led it to have the appearance of a 'boom' town with fast growing, but small-scale commercial, transport and industrial enterprises.

Enclave production did not promote strong national government. The scale and profitability of the enterprises enabled them to provide their own infrastructure and policing. Government intervention through taxation or regulation was unwelcome. There were even cases of plantation and mine labour recruiters who came into conflict with government officials seeking conscripts for military service and public works. The effects of the export economy were to create agrarian structures which were centrifugal in their economic and power relationships: a peasant economy with little capacity to accumulate and not open to national market pressures, but closely tied to the fortunes of enterprises which were totally dependent on the international market. In this type of agrarian structure, national government was a distant and unfamiliar master for the rural population. They laboured to provide subsistence goods for themselves and to produce the raw materials for alien cultures.

The extreme case was where the plantation totally dominated the economy; indeed whole countries became organized around it. Beckford talks of the 'plantation economies' of tropical America in which the plantation

[41] See G. Joseph, *Revolution from Without: Yucatan, Mexico and the United States, 1880–1924* (Cambridge, 1982).

[42] See Whiteford, *Migration, Ethnicity and Adaptation*, p. 14.

was the dominant economic, social and political institution.[43] He identifies eighteen such economies in the Caribbean and Latin America, mainly island societies. He spells out the implications of plantation production for society. First, the export orientation of most plantation agriculture created a series of direct external linkages to foreign markets and finance institutions that played a central role in determining the levels of production, investment, and types of technology used. This created a high level of external dependency which was both economic and political.

Second, the plantation was fundamentally a social institution that closely regulated, like a 'total institution', the lives of all those who lived within its bounds. This social control function was, in part, necessitated by the fact that labour was frequently recruited from groups different in ethnic origin from that of the owners and supervisory staff. From this followed two other characteristics of plantation economies, namely, that they were 'plural' societies in which ethnic groups co-existed but where they were held together by the political power and economic monopoly exercised by the dominant group. This also meant that there was a sharp difference between the 'metropolitan' culture and orientation of the dominant group and the life styles of the plantation workers. Being isolated and subordinated within the plantation system, social mobility for subordinated groups became identified with the adoption of the values and styles of life of the dominant group. Though because of racial discrimination full social mobility was impossible, Beckford stresses how the values of the white, traditionally dominant, ethnic group formed the basis for social integration and set the main criteria for social stratification.

The third type of agrarian structure that can be identified in the 1930s was present in those areas in which agricultural commodities were mainly produced and controlled by smallholders, largely on the basis of family labour. Examples are the Antioqueño region of Colombia, the Mendoza region of Argentina, parts of Rio Grande do Sul, Santa Catarina and Paraná in southern Brazil, and the western area of Mexico, including parts of the states of Michoacan, Jalisco, Leon and Guanajuato. The Otavallo valley of Ecuador demonstrates this structure on a smaller scale.[44]

[43] G.L. Beckford, *Persistent Poverty: Underdevelopment in Plantation Economies of the Third World* (New York, 1972).

[44] On the economy and cultures of small-scale farming areas, see, for Antioquia, M. Palacios, *Coffee in Colombia 1850–1970: an Economic, Social and Political History* (Cambridge, 1980); for Mendoza and Tucuman, J. Balán, 'Una cuestion regional en la Argentina: burguesias provinciales y el mercado nacional en el desarrollo argoexportador', *Desarrollo Económico*, 18, 69 (1978); for southern Brazil,

These were regions in which farming was market-orientated, but served regional or national markets that were less lucrative than the international ones. The small-scale level of production coupled with low yields were further factors reducing the profitability of agriculture. Cereal and livestock production on soils of relatively low fertility were, by the 1930s, unattractive to large landowners who concentrated their direct farming in the fertile valley beds and on irrigated land. Independent smallholders, sharecroppers and tenants, mainly using family labour and diversifying their economies, did, however, make a precarious and frugal living. Coffee, tobacco and cotton, though export commodities, were also suited to this production system.

The small-scale farmer retained a high degree of control over production and marketing. One consequence was the emergence of marketing networks, often based on small towns, which concentrated the surplus for processing and shipment to national and, in the case of export crops, international markets. The urban structure was a more balanced one than in the first and second types of agrarian structure and did not display population concentration in a single city. Village and town-based artisans and traders were important elements of the regional economy. The agrarian structure was thus socially heterogeneous, but less socially and economically polarized than in the first and second types. There were a greater number of opportunities for social mobility and for small-scale entrepreneurship in trade, transport and petty manufacturing. On the other hand, the degree of commercialization and market competition impeded the development of strong community organization, based on reciprocal exchange, and resulted in a significant degree of social and economic differentiation.

The town of San José de Gracia in Michoacan was the home of many small-scale ranchers by the 1930s. Their economy was a market one, producing milk and cheese for the towns and also trading in pigs. The standard of town housing was reasonable: sewing machines and brass beds were reported for this period. Newspapers reached the town, were

Joseph L. Love, *Rio Grande do Sul and Brazilian Regionalism, 1882–1930* (Stanford, Cal., 1971) and *São Paulo in the Brazilian Federation, 1889–1937* (Stanford, Cal., 1980); for Mexico, J. A. Meyer, *The Cristero Rebellion: the Mexican People between Church and State, 1926–1929* (Cambridge, 1976), pp. 85–94, L. Gonzalez, *San José de Gracia: Mexican Village in Transition* (Austin, Tex., 1974), and F. Schryer, *Rancheros of Pisaflores: the History of a Peasant Bourgeoisie in Twentieth-century Mexico* (Toronto, 1980); and for the Otavallo valley of Ecuador, P. Meier, 'Peasants and Petty Commodity Producers in the Otovallo Valley of Ecuador', unpublished Ph.D. dissertation, University of Toronto, 1982.

avidly read and educational facilities, both state and church, were relatively good. The Mexican Revolution and the Cristero rebellion, in which many from the town participated, had impoverished the economy, but its main characteristics remained. It was dominated by the 200 or so families who owned property. Some owned more than others, though this differentiation was less important than the fact of land ownership. Local people identified only two honest and morally right ways to acquire property: by purchase or by inheritance. The majority of families were landless, working in urban occupations or, when there was work, for the ranchers. The town had a reputation for being highly religious. This religion was not the folk religion of peasant communities, but one closely tied to the Catholic Church and the priest. There were festivals, though the popular dances of the region and other folk customs had been purged from them. The property owners expected the Church to defend their independence and to be opposed to the land reforms that, in the 1930s, appeared to be giving land away free to the 'improvident' and 'incapable'.[45]

The independence of the small-scale farmer was limited by the control of credit and marketing on the part of urban-based intermediaries and by the control of the best land by large landowners. In Colombia, the Antioqueño ideology of a 'middle-class' entrepreneurial society had to be set against considerable income polarization between the smallholder colonizers and the urban elites. In the case of the Medellin elites, this led to a process of industrialization similar to that of São Paulo and Buenos Aires, though on a smaller scale. The level of living and community organization of the independent farmer was often not very different from that of peasants, especially those who traded with and produced for mining and plantation enterprises. A prosperous village of the Mantaro valley in Peru, such as Muquiyauyo, would have been similar in appearance and amenities, in the 1930s, to San José de Gracia. Both towns were populated by farmers, traders and craftsmen, used to travelling to distant markets. But the inhabitants of San José would have appeared more formally devout in their Catholicism and more recalcitrant in their suspicion of central government. Conversely, community festivals would have appeared more elabo-

[45] L. Gonzalez, *San José de Gracia,* emphasizes that the agrarian struggle was not as bloody in San Jose as in other towns of the region. Ties of kinship bound property owner and propertyless. Most of them had recently fought side by side against the central government in the Cristero rebellion. Also, the large landowners, who suffered expropriation, often did not live in San José and were not liked by the local small landowners.

rate and ostentatious in Muquiyauyo, based in part on the money spent by miners returning for the holiday.

Large areas of Latin America were not directly involved in the export economy and their level of market activity was less than that of the small-scale farmer. By the 1930s, there still remained substantial areas of subsistence farming, interspersed with estates of low productivity, whose economies were based on supplying low value products to local, regional and national markets. These were rarer in the Southern Cone countries which had only recently been settled by European immigrants brought in to work on the export staples. They were, however, common in Chile whose estate system in the 1930s was notorious for its inefficiency and low productivity.[46] They were frequently encountered moving northwards through the areas of pre-Hispanic settlement in Bolivia, Peru and Ecuador. Also, they were to be found in the northern areas of Brazil where the decline of the sugar economy had resulted in the predominance of subsistence farming even on large estates. In Central America and Mexico, a variety of indigenous cultures and estates farmed by tenants and sharecroppers survived mainly in temperate highland areas geographically distant from the zones of export production.

The estate (*hacienda* or, in Brazil, *fazenda*) often controlled vast tracts of relatively infertile land whose production was of low market value and was normally obtained through non-wage forms of labour, such as sharecropping or labour service. A crucial feature of the estate was that it usually operated a decentralized form of production. The property was divided into two types of landholding – the demesne land directly controlled by the owner and that of the tenants or sharecroppers who were given plots in return for various forms of rent (in labour, produce or cash). The proportions allocated to these two types of landholding varied according to ecology, types of crop or livestock and, crucially, market fluctuations.

Two principal patterns can be distinguished: one in which the landlord leased out most of the estate to peasants who thus account for most of the production, and the other in which the landlord directly cultivated most of the land, using some wage labour, and leased the remainder to tenants in order to obtain cheap additional labour. In the first pattern, the peasant might, in part, produce directly for the landowner as when in arable farming peasants often held tenancies in return for a stipulated proportion

[46] See McBride, *Chile: Land and Society*.

of the harvest. Likewise, a shepherd might care for *hacienda* animals, receiving a share of the offspring and the right to graze his or her own animals on estate land. The difference with the second pattern rests, therefore, on the degree of control exercised by landlords over productive resources. Whereas direct control over production was likely to be advantageous to the landlord in terms of maximizing returns on production, this strategy was risky because of its higher cash outlays on labour and other production inputs in the face of possible harvest failures, market difficulties and labour shortages. However, the alternative strategy of relying on peasant production made it difficult for the landowner to ensure a good return since he or she could not easily control the level or quality of production, take advantage of improved market conditions, or ensure, in sharecropping, that the peasant was providing the agreed proportion of the product.

By the 1930s, the *hacienda* system was a fertile source of conflict between landlord and peasant and within the peasantry itself. Individual peasants and whole communities competed to obtain favours from the landlord. Landlords sought to intensify their control over production at favourable market conjunctures, exacting more labour from tenants and taking more land into their direct control. Likewise, peasants encroached on demesne land and resisted attempts to dislodge them from tenancies or to diminish their rights to water, woods and pastures.[47] These conflicts were an integral part of agrarian development in Latin America, reflecting the shifting fortunes of the landlord and peasant economy at different historical periods.[48]

These *hacienda*-community regions were characterized by decentralized power systems. The economy of the landowner depended on a local power base which gave them the capacity to obtain non-wage labour and tribute. Peasants were expected to labour on the estate in return for access to land for their own subsistence. There was the long-established practice in southern Peru of *hacienda*-based peasants being rented out to other *haciendas,* receiving a subsistence payment while their 'owner' received the legal

[47] Peasants were often the aggressors as well as the victims in land conflicts. For accounts of peasant strategies against the estate, see C. Samaniego, 'Peasant movements at the turn of the century and the rise of the independent farmer', in Long and Roberts (eds), *Peasant Cooperation;* G. A. Smith and H. P. Cano, 'Some Factors Contributing to Peasant Land Occupations in Peru: the Example of Huasicancha, 1963–1968', in Long and Roberts (eds), *Peasant Cooperation;* G. A. Smith, *Livelihood and Resistance: Peasants and the Politics of Land in Peru* (Berkeley, Cal., 1989).

[48] Smith, *Livelihood and Resistance,* provides a detailed historical and anthropological study of the struggles between the peasant community of Huasicancha and neighbouring haciendas in highland Peru covering the period 1850 until the early 1980s.

wage.[49] These estate owners were frequently resident in nearby provincial towns and were linked to a network of social and political ties binding together a regional elite which also included merchants and other businessmen. In many areas of Latin America, the power of the landlord was more effective and apparent than that of central government. In Brazil, this phenomenon was known as *coronelismo:* the landowner maintained a band of followers to enforce his wishes and acted as the sole intermediary between the peasants of the area, which he controlled, and government. The *coronel* gave favours in return for loyal support, especially in elections. He also often monopolized marketing. In Spanish America, these local bosses were termed *gamonales* or *caciques*. They lived close to their domains and their dress and style of life was often little different from that of the local peasantry. The pre-agrarian reform *hacienda* of highland Peru has been likened to a 'triangle without a base', that is, a peasant workforce tied to an apex of economic and political power and lacking strong horizontal ties of solidarity.[50]

Yet, the difficulties that landlords had in actually achieving this degree of control underlines an essential weakness in their structural position. They could not easily monopolize the agricultural surplus since a substantial part remained in peasant hands. There were regional exceptions, particularly in Mexico, based on particularly profitable crops or livestock. On the whole, however, the *hacienda* provided a relatively modest profit for its owner, usually insufficient or too uncertain to enable the landowner to engage in substantial projects of modernization or, for that matter, to employ more staff or wage workers to control or replace the peasantry.

The counterpart to the estate, both in terms of geographical proximity and economic interdependence, was the peasant community. One crucial distinction between types of peasant community is their responsiveness to externally initiated change. One such contrast is between the 'closed' corporate community and the 'open' community.[51] As an ideal type, the closed community represents a self-contained ethnic group, often based on a communal pattern of landholding, in which activity is regulated by strong community norms implemented through a distinctive politico-

[49] Oscar Núñez del Prado, *Kuyo Chico: Applied Anthropology in an Indian Community* (Chicago, Ill., 1973), p. 3.

[50] See J. Cotler, 'The Mechanics of Internal Domination and Social Change in Peru', *Studies in Comparative International Development*, 3, 12 (1967–8).

[51] See Wolf, 'Aspects of Group Relations in a Complex Society: Mexico'.

religious system. Agricultural and craft production in such communities was less orientated to the market economy and the population was economically relatively homogeneous. Economic, social and ritual relations reinforced each other, acting as a block on community differentiation and on political and economic integration into the wider society.[52]

In contrast, the 'open' community was strongly peasant in character, having close links with the wider economy through the marketing of agricultural and craft goods or through the sale of its labour in external centres of work. Landholding was based upon smallholder ownership or control of land and was associated with a more marked pattern of socio-economic differentiation. The dominant cultural idiom was mestizo rather than Indian, with consumption patterns similar to urban centres.

Even in the 1930s, however, it would be a mistake to make too sharp a distinction either between closed and open peasant communities or between modern and traditional estates. Even in areas not directly involved in the export economy, there was an important cash element in all estate and household economies, introduced through marketing and labour migration. Robert Redfield's description of the Mexican village of Tepoztlán, in the 1930s, illustrates this ambiguity.[53] His account is of a relatively homogeneous community in which the level of living of almost all the inhabitants was similar and basic, and in which communal institutions, such as the communal lands, unified the village. Most villagers slept on mats (*petates*). Their staple diet consisted primarily of corn and beans. Ritual events, based on *barrios* with distinct social and cultural identities, punctuated the yearly cycle, each month being associated with celebrations that required widespread participation. These rituals followed the agricultural calendar, involving both Christian and pre-Hispanic beliefs and festivals. In his restudy of Tepoztlán, Oscar Lewis demonstrated that

[52] The best-known examples are the Mexican communities studied by Redfield, *Folk culture,* E. Vogt, *Zinacantan: a Maya Community in the Highlands of Chiapas* (Cambridge, 1969), G. Foster, *Tzintzuntzan* (Boston, Mass., 1967), F. Cancian, *Economics and Prestige in a Mayan Community: the Religious Cargo System of Zinacantan* (Stanford, Cal., 1965); and the Peruvian communities studied by Nuñez del Prado, *Kuyo Chico,* Castro Pozo, 'Social and economic-political evolution', and the Cornell team of applied anthropologists: H. Dobyns, P. L. Doughty and H. D. Lasswell (eds), *Peasants, Power and Applied Social Change: Vicos as a Model* (Beverly Hills, Cal., 1971). A recent analysis of the ways in which a community reproduces itself culturally and materially mainly outside the commodity economy and without internal economic differentiation is provided in a study of the Laymi people of highland Bolivia: Olivia Harris, 'Labour and Produce in an Ethnic Economy, Northern Potosi, Bolivia', in D. Lehmann (ed.), *Ecology and Exchange in the Andes* (Cambridge, 1982).

[53] Redfield's emphasis is on culture and social integration. His monograph *Tepotzlán, a Mexican Village* (Chicago, Ill., 1930) contains little economic data.

Redfield's emphasis on the relative homogeneity of the village and on its social integration obscured internal conflict, poverty and economic hardship.[54] He calculated that in 1944, some thirty years after Zapata had led some of these same peasants to victory in the Mexican Revolution, 81 per cent of the villagers had a level of wealth below that needed for subsistence. The inhabitants of Tepoztlán had, before the Revolution, survived by cultivating subsistence crops and by working for local landowners or on the nearby sugar *haciendas* for part of the year. The mountainous land controlled by the peasants was too poor to allow them to subsist completely, let alone to accumulate. Caciques dominated the town, nominating the municipal authorities, controlling access to the communal land, thereby ensuring that they had an available supply of cheap local labour to farm their own private holdings. Their houses were the only ones built of stone or brick and adorned with windows. A study of Mitla, in southern Mexico, in the 1930s, showed essentially the same picture. There was little accumulation in the village and agriculture alone did not allow most people to subsist. The people of Mitla were inveterate traders, travelling long distances and absent for long periods, but with a low turnover and small profits on each item. A hacienda dominated the valley of Mitla and its owner was a familiar and powerful local figure. The *hacienda* had over 200 tenants and was, along with a medium-sized estate, a major source of local employment. The owner of the medium-sized estate also owned the largest store and grain mill in the town. Only in the houses of the two *caciques* were there iron bedsteads with mattresses.[55]

These so-called 'traditional' communities were often socially differentiated internally. Such differentiation was, in part, a consequence of the type of political and economic incorporation into the wider economy. The form taken by so-called traditional institutions was shaped by the changing pressures of the external environment.[56] Even these localized economies, then, were a part, even if a less well-articulated one, of the dynamic of the export-oriented agrarian structures of Latin America in the 1930s. Most were not, in the 1930s, self-contained cultural and economic units,

[54] In contrast to Redfield's earlier study, Oscar Lewis, *Life in a Mexican Village: Tepoztlán* (Urbana, Ill., 1951) gives detailed information on land tenure, agriculture and standards of living. He stresses, and documents, the historical changes in Tepotzlán; also, in opposition to Redfield, he emphasizes the individualism of peasant social life.

[55] See E. Parsons, *Mitla* (Chicago, Ill., 1936).

[56] Apparently 'traditional' institutions, such as the fiesta and the community itself, can be revitalized or 'invented' as a result of economic growth. See, for example, F. Mallon, *The Defence of Community in Peru's Central Highlands: Peasant Struggle and Capitalist Transition, 1860–1940* (Princeton, N.J., 1983) and Long and Roberts (eds), *Peasant Cooperation*, pp. 297–328.

but rather social and economic peripheries generated by the capitalist penetration of the Latin American economies.

Finally, the economic and social processes embodied in the four types of agrarian structure in Latin America from the 1930s to the 1950s, described above, must be placed within the context of a constant process of land colonization on the frontier, which characterized Latin America from colonial times.

During the 1930s, colonization in, for example, the Amazon area often took the 'predatory' pattern.[57] Settlements sprung up on the Amazon frontier for the specific purpose of extracting forest products such as rubber for sale in outside markets, rather than opening up new zones for agricultural production. Basic food such as manioc floor, beans, rice, coffee and canned goods, as well as manufactured products ranging from matches and needles to machinery, were all imported. Although transportation costs were high and the journey into the area was arduous, thereby inflating the price of all imported articles, local merchants made a handsome profit at the expense of local collectors who, particularly during periods of low prices for the exported raw materials, were never far from poverty.

Although in the 1930s colonization of new areas was often predatory and still very incomplete, with large areas of the continent remaining outside the commodity economy, the moving frontier continued to be the main means by which export farming, such as coffee in Brazil and Colombia, or livestock in Mexico, expanded production. The frontier also attracted independent colonists who settled to produce food for the work force of the new enterprises, or, as in the case of northern Mexico, to consolidate control over national territory in the face of external threat. Settlement was also often followed by the later abandonment of farming enterprise: for example, many areas which had originally been opened-up for large-scale production later reverted to subsistence-orientated peasant cultivation. This was, for example, the situation of the *caipira* peasants of the Cuñha region of São Paulo.[58] The salient feature of these colonization areas was their general economic and political instability and lack of

[57] See C. Wagley, *Amazon Town: a Study of Man in the Tropics* (New York, 1953) for a historical account of the opening up of the Amazonian region which he develops through a detailed account of the social and economic life of a small town in the Lower Amazon.

[58] See R. W. Shirley, *The End of a Tradition: Culture Change and Development in the Municipio of Cunha, São Paulo, Brazil* (New York, 1971), pp. 34–47.

established institutionalized forms of control characteristic of the older settled areas. As we shall see, the extension of state control over areas of new colonization gradually formed part of a planned strategy of agricultural development based on 'extraction at the frontier and accumulation at the centre'.[59]

THE 1960S AND 1970S

Despite the continuing diversity in agrarian structures the outstanding trend from the beginning of the 1960s to the 1980s was for the agrarian structures of Latin America to look more alike. Large and medium-scale capitalist farming played an increasingly dominant role throughout the continent, while, in contrast, peasant forms of production contributed less to national agricultural production. In the mid-1970s, 44 per cent of farming units in Brazil, over two million peasant-type establishments, accounted for a mere 4 per cent of total agricultural production with each one having an output below the value of the minimum wage.[60] Peasants became fully or, more often, partially proletarianized, indicating the insufficiency of land resources to provide a subsistence living for a growing rural population. In these processes agrarian reform played a critical role. In this section, we will first examine the nature of that reform. Subsequently, we take up the more general issues of the extension of state control and the development of capitalist farming.

We have noted above how urban growth and industrialization placed agrarian reform on the political agenda in many Latin American countries. By the 1950s, population pressure on inadequate land resources was a further factor making reform an urgent issue in densely populated regions, such as the highlands of Bolivia and Peru. Reform had come earlier in Mexico, as a result of the Revolution of 1910. By the 1930s, Mexico had

[59] The expression is from J. Foweraker, *The Struggle for Land: a Political Economy of the Pioneer Frontier in Brazil from 1930 to the Present Day* (Cambridge, 1981).

[60] The vast majority of these small farms were essentially consumption units. This conclusion is at odds with earlier studies that depicted peasant producers as significant suppliers of 'cheap' urban food supplies. For Brazil, see J. Graziano da Silva, 'Estructura tenencial y relaciones de producción en el campo brasileño', *Estudios Rurales Latinoamericanos* (Bogotá) 5, 2, (1982) and Juarez Brandão Lopes, 'Capitalist development and agrarian structure in Brazil', *International Journal of Urban and Regional Research*, 2, 1 (1978); and for the importance of peasant production in various Latin American countries, Ortega, 'La agricultura campesina en América Latina'. There are inherent difficulties in measuring the importance of peasant agriculture, partly because a considerable part of peasant output is consumed on the farm and partly because the criterion often used to identify the peasant sector (that is, units of less than twenty hectares) includes highly capitalized family farms.

embarked on an ambitious program of land redistribution, confiscating estates and forming *ejidos* among landless or smallholder peasants.[61] Some of the estates confiscated, such as the cotton estates of La Laguna and some of those in Sonora, were formed into collective farms, worked by members of the *ejidos.* On other *ejidos,* farming was carried out on an individual household basis, but members were not allowed to sell the land. Though there were some attempts at limited land reform elsewhere in Latin America, the next major redistribution of land did not occur until the Bolivian land reform of 1953, which was more limited than that of Mexico. Whereas 13 per cent of Mexico's land surface had been cumulatively distributed by the end of the Cardenas administration in 1940, only 5.4 per cent of Bolivia's land surface was affected by 1964 after more than ten years of Revolution.[62]

The 1960s brought major efforts at land reform in Latin America.[63] Twelve countries enacted land reform measures in that decade, in response to the anxieties aroused by the Cuban Revolution of 1959 and following the 1961 Charter of Punta del Este which embodied the Kennedy administration's view that 'progressive' reforms would be needed to avert further revolutions in Latin America. The redistributive effects of these land reforms were relatively minor. By 1969, Mexico, Bolivia and Venezuela had distributed more land to more peasants than had all the other countries put together.[64] Agrarian reform in Latin America was substantially advanced by the Peruvian reform of 1969 and the Chilean reform begun under Frei in 1967. By 1973, at the end of Allende's administration just over 40 per cent of agricultural land in Chile was in the reformed sector; but even here beneficiaries were only a small fraction of the rural farming population, numbering just over one-third of the total permanent workers on large farms prior to the reform.[65]

In all cases, agrarian reform included two fundamental measures. First, large estates which were underexploited and not directly farmed by their owners were expropriated and expropriated land was redistributed to

[61] For an analysis of the administrative and political processes involved in the struggle for *ejido* land in the pre-Cárdenas and Cárdenas periods in Mexico, see H. W. Tobler, 'Peasants and the Shaping of the Revolutionary State, 1910–1940', in F. Katz (ed.), *Riot, Rebellion, and Revolution: Rural Social Conflict in Mexico* (Princeton, N.J., 1988).

[62] J. W. Wilkie, *Statistical Abstract of Latin America,* vol. 15, (Los Angeles, Cal., 1974), p. 55.

[63] For a typology of Latin American land reforms, stressing their functions in furthering capitalist development in agriculture, see De Janvry *The Agrarian Question,* pp. 203–7.

[64] Ibid., table 1.

[65] See the calculations in L. Castillo and D. Lehmann, 'Chile's Three Land Reforms: the inheritors', *Bulletin of Latin American Research,* 1, 2 (1982), 35–7.

small-scale farmers. Second, small-scale farmers were encouraged to produce more efficiently by being grouped into co-operatives of various types. The justification governments used to undertake reform was twofold: the urgent need to alleviate poverty in the countryside and the benefits that could be gained through increased agricultural efficiency. Thus reform had a double purpose – not only to reduce and control emergent class conflict in the countryside but also to promote the modernization of agriculture, increasing export earnings and food production for the urban centers.

Agrarian reforms throughout Latin America were imposed from above. They were rarely initiated as a direct response to the demands of rural protest movements. Rural unions or peasant leagues had little say in the implementation of agrarian reform. Not all Latin American governments carried out agrarian reforms, and those that did varied considerably in the extent to which they restructured land tenure and production. The diversity of agrarian structures in Latin America meant that agrarian reform had different implications in different countries, and in different regions of the same country. In regions dominated by the decentralized estate, the problems facing farmers were insecure tenure or lack of land; while in zones of small-scale farming, they were lack of infrastructure and the need for government support for the small farmer; and in areas dominated by commercial estates or plantations, they were mainly wage levels and conditions of work. Furthermore, attempts to promote co-operatives inevitably clashed with entrenched household-based farming practices and existing patterns of differentiation among the peasantry itself.

Despite these limitations, agrarian reform produced substantial changes in agrarian structures. It put an end to the underexploited, decentralized estate, and, inadvertently, fostered the development of the middle-sized, privately-owned farm. To understand these trends, we will review some cases of agrarian reform, and contrast them with Brazil where the modernization of agriculture was carried out without any serious government attempt to break-up the large, privately-owned estate.

In Bolivia, redistribution was particularly effective in improving the social and economic situation of the peasant since land had been highly concentrated in large landholdings farmed through labour-rent systems.[66]

[66] The *arrendero* was given a plot of land or access to pasture in return for a specified number of days of labor a year. In addition, the *arrendero* might be obliged to give part of his own production to the landowner. Landowners farmed an average of 25 per cent of their land directly, and the remainder was farmed by the tenants. See D. Heath, C. J. Erasmus, H. C. Buechler, *Land Reform and Social Revolution in Bolivia* (New York, 1969).

The increased freedom of the peasant to market his or her produce resulted in the flourishing of local market places after the reform, and in better standards of living and the prevalence of consumer goods such as bicycles, radios and accordions. The reform had little success in promoting co-operative farming. Peasants were distrustful of their complex organization and, in any event, preferred to farm and market individually.

The 1969 Agrarian Reform of Peru expropriated all estates above a certain size which varied according to zone and irrigation, but which was usually less than 100 hectares. These estates were transformed into production co-operatives and not subdivided. The structure of agricultural production was affected less than in the case of the Bolivian reform. Most Peruvian peasants were independent smallholders before the reform, and they continued to farm their land individually afterwards. The nominal beneficiaries of expropriations were workers on the estates and the independent peasants of the communities surrounding the estates, but they did not gain greater control over production.[67] The limited impact of agrarian reform in Peru was, in part, due to the decision of the government to control production levels on the large commercial estates and to keep them intact as production units. Consequently, the powers of co-operative members over production decisions were restricted. In part, the reform's impact was also limited by its concentration on improving large-scale agricultural production, rather than on stimulating various types of rural farm and non-farm economic activity. This concentration on large-scale livestock co-operatives (SAIS) or large cash-crop co-operatives (CAPS) had little relevance to the livelihood strategies of most of Peru's rural population who, by this date, depended on multiple sources of farm and non-farm income, often based on rural-urban migration and on economic linkages between town and village.[68]

Agrarian reform often accentuated differentiation among the rural population. Beneficiaries of reform were usually those who had a long-standing relationship with the expropriated estate. Tenants and permanent workers

[67] See, for the Peruvian agrarian reform, A. Lowenthal (ed.), *The Peruvian Experiment* (Princeton, N.J., 1975); C. McClintock, *Peasant Cooperatives and Political Change in Peru* (Princeton, N.J. 1981); D. Horton, *Land Reform and Reform Enterprises in Peru*, Vols. I and II (Madison, 1974), and Cristóbal Kay, 'Achievements and Contradictions of the Peruvian Agrarian Reform', *Journal of Development Studies*, 18 2 (1982): 141–70.

[68] Many of the highland villagers who became part-owners of the large pastoral estates had long since ceased to derive their main income from livestock farming. See B. Roberts and C. Samaniego, 'The Evolution of Pastoral Villages and the Significance of Agrarian Reform in the Highlands of Central Peru', in Long and Roberts (eds), *Peasant Cooperation*, and R. Rivera and P. Campaña, 'Highland *puna* Communities and the Impact of the Mining Economy', in Long and Roberts, *Miners, Peasants and Entrepreneurs*.

were favoured, but not the temporary workers who came to work seasonally. Initially, in Peru, the workers in the sugar mills and permanent workers on the livestock estates bettered their situation in comparison with the pre-reform period.[69] However, the seasonal workers on the sugar estates and the peasant communities who became the nominal owners of the livestock estates gained few direct benefits. In the Chilean agrarian reform of 1967, any rural property of over eighty standardized hectares could be expropriated and used to establish *asentamientos,* self-managing co-operatives. Throughout the reform period, members tended to give higher priority to their individual landholdings, than to farming the collective lands. A further source of differentiation was the fact that, especially under the Frei administration, the permanent workers (*inquilinos*) on expropriated estates often benefited at the expense of temporary workers (*afuerinos*). The Állende government attempted to redress these inequalities of redistribution, but neither temporary workers nor independent smallholders benefited much from the reform.[70]

The preoccupation with export earnings and with the food supply for urban centres entailed that, in most agrarian reforms, governments attempted to safeguard agricultural production by keeping intact highly productive estates, even when these were expropriated and passed into the reformed sector. This was the case, as we have seen, in Peru. A similar preoccupation influenced the course of agrarian reform in Nicaragua following the revolution of 1979.[71] A first concern of the Sandinista government was to preserve production levels on the estates expropriated from the Somoza group and to preserve an alliance with large-scale commercial farmers, a policy dictated both by economic and political considerations. State farms, not worker-owned production co-operatives, were established on the expropriated land. The lands of other large landowners were left untouched, but workers' unions were fostered on both state and private sector farms. Such a policy did little, however, to improve the lot of those landless workers who did not have permanent jobs on the large estates, nor that of peasants without sufficient land for subsistence.

[69] Cynthia McClintock, 'Reform Governments and Policy Implementation: Lessons from Peru', in M. S. Grindle (ed.), *The Politics and Policy of Implementation* (Princeton, N.J., 1980), pp. 90–1.

[70] Smallholders were given improved credit facilities, but the opportunities for off-farm employment declined as estates modernized and reduced their labour requirements and as the reformed sector (*asentamientos*) used permanent labor in preference to temporary labour. See Castillo and Lehmann, 'Chile's Three Land Reforms', and C. Kay, *Chile: an Appraisal of Popular Unity's Agrarian Reform,* Occasional Paper no. 13, Institute of Latin American Studies, Glasgow, 1974.

[71] See Carmen D. Deere, R. Marchetti, and N. Reinhardt, 'The Peasantry and the Development of Sandinista Agrarian Policy. 1979–1984', *Latin American Research Review,* 20, 3 (1985): 75–109.

The need to boost domestic foodstuff production meant that help had to be given to peasant production. The extension of credit was the major means, in the first years, of helping this sector. The organization of peasants into co-operatives, mainly into credit and service ones, was a second plank of the policy. The handling of the peasant sector proved a difficult one for state agencies: credit policy was inadequate due to a lack of knowledge of peasant farming, and little technical or marketing help was given. Moreover, fears of jeopardizing the alliance with medium and large landowners meant that government did not tackle directly the question of land shortage through substantial further expropriations.

With the increasing political isolation of Nicaragua and the break-down of the alliance with the propertied classes the Sandinista government's agrarian reform became more extensive. Two aspects of Sandinista policy deserve comment. First, there was a sustained attempt to improve the prices paid for farm products and to subsidize the farm sector through credit and infrastructural services. In fact, both consumer and producer food prices were subsidized, showing both sensitivity to the situation of the peasant producer and to the situation of the urban poor. Second, the peasant sector was given increasing help. Land was expropriated in greater quantities as a result of the 1981 Agrarian Reform Law so that, by July 1984, 45,000 households or some 32 per cent of rural Nicaraguan households had directly benefited from land redistribution. Though production co-operatives, and the various forms of mixed and pre-co-operatives, gained most expropriated land, the government's actions had, by the mid-1980s, become more clearly pro-peasant than at the beginning of the revolution.[72] Individual peasants received expropriated land, and, though collective projects were encouraged, a variety of co-operatives benefitting individual farmers were supported. The peasant's organization (Unión Nacional de Agricultores y Ganaderos, UNAG) gained in strength and membership rivalling the rural worker's association (Asociación de Trabajadores del Campo, ATC).

Despite the greater sensitivity to peasant needs on the part of the Sandinista government, peasant suspicion of, and resistance to, agrarian reform continued in many parts of the country. Peasant producers wanted to market directly to urban markets and not through established state channels, a strategy that was eventually accepted by the Sandinista government in its last two years of office (1988–90). A significant, and special,

[72] L. Enriquez, *Harvesting Change: Labor and Agrarian Reform in Nicaragua 1979–1990* (Chapel Hill, N.C., 1991) documents the evolution of this policy until 1990, indicating the problem of sustaining export production in face of labour shortages produced by the Contra war and by pro-peasant policies on the part of the government.

set of factors in the Nicaraguan case was that peasant recalcitrance was aggravated by the devastating impact on the economy of U.S. economic sanctions and of the U.S.-supported Contra guerrilla movement.

The course of Nicaragua's agrarian reform until 1990 indicated similarities, however, to earlier Latin American reforms, both in the problems faced and the solutions proposed. It shared with other agrarian reforms the difficulties of imposing a centrally organized reform on peasants accustomed to using diverse and flexible livelihood strategies. Like the other reforms, its room for manoeuvre was limited by the need to maintain production levels and to achieve greater technical efficiency, while restructuring the rural sector to obtain greater equity. These similarities between land reform policies that occurred in different political circumstances arose from a common history of insertion into the world economy as producers of primary goods, resulting in a dualistic structure of commercial export agriculture and peasant farming of low productivity.[73]

The clearest beneficiaries of most Latin American agrarian reforms were the 'middling' stratum of farmers. This stratum gained its strength from two converging processes. First, there were the pressures to modernize estates which resulted in more intensively farmed and smaller units of production. Second, expropriation and measures to promote more efficient small-scale farming helped create, directly and indirectly, a land market which allowed small-scale farmers to consolidate holdings and increase their market production. In Mexico, this led in 1982 to an important modification of the agrarian reform law which made it legally possible for *ejido* land to be rented privately. The extension of credit and measures to promote increased commercial production inevitably accelerated change in the agrarian structure, exposing large numbers of farmers to the opportunities and risks of the market.

It was the middling stratum of farmers that were best able to seize these opportunities and overcome the risks. They bought-out the small-scale farmers who failed, or purchased from estate owners who subdivided their land under the pressures of agrarian reform. Even before the 1967 agrarian reform in Chile, there were signs that estates were increasingly being farmed directly and intensively. The reform encouraged the subdivision of estates and spawned large numbers of intensively cultivated medium-sized farms. With the reversal of the Chilean reform after the military coup of 1973, these trends were accentuated, with increased opportunities to buy

[73] This is the central point of de Janvry, *The Agrarian Question*, on land reforms and other rural development strategies in Latin America.

land from the peasant beneficiaries of the reform. Those expropriated lands, which were reassigned, went to fewer beneficiaries and in larger family units. By 1977, the large estate had practically disappeared in Chile, and its place was taken by landholdings of between five and eighty hectares.[74]

Brazil was unusual in Latin America in avoiding any semblance of agrarian reform in the 1960s and 1970s. Only one set of measures, the Rural Labor Statute and related legislation in 1962–3, sought to strengthen the position of the rural poor against the landowner. Instead, agrarian policy in Brazil sought to foster rapid growth in agriculture through market mechanisms, trusting to the expansion of opportunities, in both town and countryside, to alleviate rural discontent and reduce population pressure on the land. From 1966, the military government encouraged investment in the Amazon and increasingly centralized control over Amazonian development.[75] The most dramatic example of this policy was the promotion of colonization in the Amazon, chiefly through the National Institute of Colonization and Agrarian Reform (INCRA).[76] Here the state encouraged the migration of peasants from areas of high population density. This colonization was closely managed by state agencies which provided the infrastructure and credit, and which controlled production and marketing. State control transformed the colonist from a subsistence-orientated farmer into a petty commodity producer dependent on the market for consumption and agricultural inputs. The state delegated some of its functions to large-scale private colonization ventures. The private companies received land in large blocks and then sold it in small lots to small producers, but maintained control over commerce and services. Large-scale ranching companies also benefited from the colonization of the Amazon. The Polamazonian programme of 1974 granted large tracts of land for cattle raising and for mineral extraction. The ranchers used the labour of the colonist to clear the land and to plant it with pasture. Considerable violence marked these relationships, resulting, in 1980–1, in many deaths, including those of fifteen union leaders and activists.[77]

74 See Castillo and Lehmann, 'Chile's Three Land Reforms', table 8. Venegas, 'Family Reproduction in Rural Chile', shows that this process was particularly accentuated in the fruit-growing regions of the Aconagua valley where, however, it antedated agrarian reform.

75 See Marianne Schmink and Charles H. Wood, *Contested Frontiers in Amazonia* (New York, 1992), ch. 3, 'Militarizing Amazonia, 1964–1985'.

76 On the different facets of planned colonization in the Amazonian basin, covering Brazil, Peru, Ecuador, Bolivia and Venezuela, see J. Hemming (ed.), *The Frontier After a Decade of Colonization* (Manchester, 1985).

77 A detailed account of the struggles between colonists and ranchers in Acre, southwest Amazonia, and the role of SUDAM and INCRA in promoting large-scale farming, is given by Keith Bakx,

The Brazilian government promoted the modernization of agriculture mainly through fiscal policies to encourage increased private investment in agriculture and the use of modern technology, such as preferential exchange rates, tariff exceptions, fiscal incentives and rural credit at low interest. These policies depended on the market for their efficacy, and encouraged investment in export farming. Far fewer resources were spent in helping subsistence farmers to join together in co-operatives to modernize their farming. The combined result of extending cultivation in both new and established areas, and intensifying production in export crops, enabled Brazil, with some lapses, to increase export earnings and avoid bottlenecks in the supply of urban foodstuffs, thus diminishing one source of pressure for agrarian reform. Furthermore, massive migration to the city, as well as to the frontier, acted as a safety valve for rural discontent.

As we have seen, in the 1930s Latin American countries exhibited a marked pattern of regional differentiation which was often accompanied by a high degree of political fragmentation. Local and regional *caciques* controlled municipal and provincial governments in countries such as Mexico, Colombia and Peru. In Brazil, *coroneis* dominated the political process and federal government policy resulted from an ordered negotiation between different regional factions. Political centralization was the key process in the decades that followed. Since decentralization was based, to a considerable extent, on the diversity of agrarian structures, state intervention in agriculture through tariff and pricing policies and investment in infrastructure became a means of extending central control throughout the national territory.

A very early example of this was the Mexican case during the Cárdenas administration (1934–40). Cárdenas expropriated various foreign assets, including oil, railroads and land. The largest cotton estate of La Laguna, which had been foreign owned, was transformed into a collective farm which became increasingly controlled by government bureaucrats and technicians. In the following years, the La Laguna region became economically and politically dependent on the center, replacing the earlier situation in which it had formed a power base for foreign and regionally-based economic interests.[78] In general, the *ejido* programme under Cárdenas

'Peasant Formation and Capitalist Development: the Case of Acre, Southwest Amazonia', unpublished Ph.D. dissertation, University of Liverpool, 1986.

[78] See T. Martínez Saldaña, *El costo social de un exito politico: la politica expansionista del estado Mexicano en el agro lagunero* (Chapingo, Mexico, 1980).

created direct links between small cultivators and the state through government regulated access to land and through the provision of various services. This programme undermined the power of landed elites in many parts of the country. It served to provide a popular base for the government at a time when it was engaged in a radical programme to limit foreign influence and to sponsor nationally-based industrialization.

Economic and technological factors were also important in promoting state intervention. Industrialization, as we have noted, created an increasing need to promote agricultural productivity both for export and for the internal market. From the 1940s to the 1960s, attempts to increase productivity mainly concentrated on extending the agricultural land base. This was done through promoting the colonization of virgin lands, irrigation schemes, road programmes and mechanization. These policies involved large-scale expenditures which had to be provided by the state, though often assisted by international development agencies. Particularly important was the development of credit facilities to finance agriculture, leading in many Latin American countries to the setting-up of government agricultural banks.

Towards the end of the 1960s, emphasis increasingly shifted to attempts to intensify agricultural production through the introduction of new crops, hybrid seeds, fertilizer and insecticides. This was part of the Green Revolution package which was developed in experimental stations in Mexico from the 1940s, and spread throughout Latin America by the 1960s. Intensification of agriculture entailed increasing state intervention. The new inputs were expensive and had to be financed on a yearly basis. Making efficient use of the new techniques required special instruction and supervision. Both to administer credit and to promote the new farming methods involved a rapid expansion in state bureaucracy. Agricultural extension workers, based in regional and local centres, were needed to promote the new policies.[79] In turn, the credit agencies, both public and private, established a network of local branches. Under these conditions, agricultural decision-making became increasingly removed from the control of the farmer and concentrated in the hands of central government agencies.

By the 1970s, many countries had elaborate programmes of regional agricultural development organized and implemented by state agencies.

[79] T. Martínez Saldaña, 'Los campesinos y el estado en México', unpublished Ph.D. dissertation, Universidad Iberoamericana, Mexico, D.F., 1983, p. 109, documents the growth of the extension service in Mexico from 375 employees in 1967 to 9,000 in 1979, and to 30,000 in 1982.

In Brazil, for example, the Superintendência do Desenvolvimento do Nordeste (SUDENE) and the Superintendência do Desenvolvimento da Região Amazônica (SUDAM), agencies directly responsible to the Presidency, controlled farming and related services over vast areas. The river basin projects in Mexico, such as that of the Paploapan basin, had a similar structure.[80] Even where no large-scale regional development projects were implemented, the State extended its control over agriculture through forms of directive change which created production, marketing and servicing co-operatives and which organized the pooling of machinery and the storage of products. Also, national agricultural plans often placed legal requirements on the growing of crops, such as sugar, in order to ensure supplies for industrial processing. Though governments frequently stressed the participatory element in agricultural development programmes, the reality was more central State control through credit, through pricing policies concerning inputs and products, and through national production targets. Jobs in state agricultural agencies became a massive source of national and local employment.

Agricultural development programmes concentrated on promoting exports through irrigation, credit schemes and infrastructure. Though export crops were produced on smallholdings, as well on large estates, government programmes generally benefited the larger producers who had the resources to adopt new technology. The peasant sector, in contrast, mainly produced basic food staples, but received little state aid and was often disadvantaged by state policies to cheapen food prices. By the 1970s, most Latin American countries were importing basic foodstuffs, such as wheat and corn, on a massive scale and at prices below those at which local producers could profitably operate, given the poor quality of the soil and the small size of the peasant landholding. Demographic pressures exacerbated the difficulties facing the peasant, leading to further fragmentation of holdings and the increasing need to find off-farm work. A substantial labour reserve was created for seasonal work on the larger farms, contributed to urban migration movements, and provided the impetus for colonization.

With the advent of intensive cultivation techniques and high-yielding varieties of crops, such as wheat and maize, production for the internal market became an attractive investment, but the opportunities were

[80] D. Barkin and T. King, *Regional Economic Development: the River Basin Approach in Mexico* (Cambridge, 1970).

mainly seized by the capitalized farmer. The costs of the inputs, combined with credit policies that favoured the larger operator, made it difficult for the smallholder peasant to make a success of this new agriculture. Some of those that tried succeeded, but many because indebted and had to sell or rent out their land. Hence, the smallholder peasant ceased to be primarily a producer of foodstuffs for the market. Instead, the peasant plot served to meet basic subsistence requirements, while the bulk of necessary cash income was derived from wage work or petty commodity activities.

This process is illustrated by a case study of the marginalization of peasant production in the south of the Cauca valley in Colombia.[81] Here the dominant tendency was the development of capitalist agriculture in sugar and cacao, which co-existed with peasant farms that provided temporary labour to the estates. At an earlier period, peasant farms were relatively self-sufficient, producing for the market a skilful combination of labour-intensive cash and subsistence crops. Peasant farming became increasingly differentiated, however, between those who had sufficient land and capital to produce cash crops for market and those whose land resources were no longer sufficient for subsistence. The diminution of land resources among the peasant sector was a direct result of the expansion of the estates, often by violent means. Differentiation was also accentuated by state policies encouraging the adoption of new cash crops among small farmers, such as soya, which required a more intensive form of farming in terms of labour and other inputs. The costs of these forced many peasants to sell-up, while those who survived often did so through credit links with urban merchants and agro-industries. Both in the earlier and later periods, peasant production was shown to have been more efficient in terms of profitability and in providing income to farm workers than were the estates. Indeed, since the estates used land extensively and inefficiently in terms of return on capital invested, their profitability depended on being able to draw upon labour cheapened by the persistence of its subsistence base. These processes were reinforced by the political structure of the region in which the dominant regional elites, resident in Cali, were committed to foreign and national investment to modernize agriculture, but within the existing structure of land tenure.

Governments and international agencies, such as the World Bank, be-

[81] See M. T. Taussig, 'Peasant economies and capitalist development of agriculture in the Cauca Valley, Colombia', in J. Harriss (ed.), *Rural Development: Theories of Peasant Economies and Agrarian Change* (London, 1982).

came concerned about these marginalization trends.[82] They designed intervention strategies to reach small producers and to raise their productivity and incomes. However, such rural development projects also tended to benefit the richer peasant stratum, since they were the only group to possess sufficient resources to take advantage of the new technology and to protect themselves from the risks of crop failure and indebtedness.[83] The constant failure of official projects to help the smallholder peasant has led some commentators to liken them to a conspiracy against the peasant that favoured capitalist farming. In his review of rural development projects in Mexico, Peru and Colombia, de Janvry argued that these projects reproduced the objective basis of what he calls functional dualism.[84] They provided basic public amenities and allowed smallholders to survive on a deteriorating resource base. In the three project areas, most of the peasant households did not have enough land to provide adequately for their subsistence and earned most of their income from non-farm activities, such as wage labour, craft work, commerce and remittances from absent kinsmen. In contrast, the richer peasants raised their incomes and productivity, and were able to take advantage of the labour of their poorer neighbours. They dominated local co-operatives or farmers' organizations and developed social networks with urban merchants, bureaucrats and politicians, acting, at one and the same time, as clients of powerful outsiders and patrons of the poorer peasantry.

Despite a rhetoric which, throughout Latin America, emphasized the importance of promoting small-scale farming, government bureaucracies, in practice, undermined the independence and viability of small-scale production. Various studies in Mexico, for example, show that state intervention to promote agriculture has subordinated the small producer, irrespective of whether cultivators were organized in terms of collective farming units or worked on an individual household basis.[85]

In the Plan Chontalpa in Tabasco nearly seven thousand small producers were concentrated into a number of collectively organized ejidos for the production of sugar. Decisions concerning production became the responsibility of state officials and the whole project, instead of creating

[82] See, for example, World Bank, *Rural Development* (Washington, D.C., 1975), pp. 3–5.

[83] Redclift, *Development and the Environmental Crisis,* pp. 94–8 reviews a number of such projects.

[84] De Janvry, *The Agrarian Question,* pp. 231–54. By functional dualism, de Janvry means a situation in which capitalist agriculture benefits from the existence and maintenance of an impoverished peasantry, mainly as a source of cheap labour.

[85] See D. Barkin, *Desarrollo regional y reorganización campesina: la Chontalpa como reflejo del problema agropecuario Mexicano* (Mexico, D. F., 1978).

employment opportunities, tended to reduce the number of stable jobss in agriculture. In the case of the tobacco growers of Nayarit, *ejidatarios* farmed on an individual household basis, but were dependent financially and technically on the state company, TABAMEX, which had the monopoly of the crop. In contrast, state agencies had less control over large-scale commercial farmers. Both in Mexico and in Brazil, cattle ranchers prospered at the expense of government programmes designed to help small farmers.[86]

Despite the establishment of collective *ejidos* in Mexico, the balance of production remained in the hands of large landowners.[87] These overcame the size limitations imposed on estates by the Agrarian law through registering property in the names of others and through official tolerance. The landowners controlled state political office and were influential in the national governing party. In the 1950s, the landed interests obtained higher guaranteed prices for wheat and began to mechanize and extend production. At the same time, the collective *ejidos* were sabotaged by being starved of credit by both private and government banks, while *ejidatarios* were pressured to farm their lands individually.

With the advent of the new Green Revolution technology, the large farmers profited the most. The new seeds and inputs were not only costly, but required constant updating. The level of state-provided extension services were insufficient in Sonora, for example, to provide adequate services to all farmers and so it was the largest farmers that obtained the best. They partly financed the federal experimental station and hired their own private technical advice. Even when the price of wheat was reduced by the government, the improvements in yields that the larger farmers had obtained still allowed them to make an adequate profit. In contrast, the small farmer was unable to produce enough to meet his subsistence needs, particularly in the face of the high costs of services and commodities in Sonora. By 1971, a considerable number of *ejidatarios* had ceased to farm and had either abandoned their land or were renting it to richer neighbours. In 1960, there were an estimated 77,300 landless labourers in Sonora, which constituted 62 per cent of those employed in agriculture. By 1970, landless labourers had risen to 75 per cent and their figures do

[86] Cases of this inequality of outcome are given for Brazil by Foweraker, *The Struggle for Land*, and for Mexico by E. Feder, *Strawberry Imperialism: an Enquiry into the Mechanisms of Dependency in Mexican Agriculture* (The Hague, 1977).

[87] See the case study by Hewitt de Alcántara, *The Modernization of Mexican Agriculture: Socioeconomic Implications of Technological Change*.

not include the temporary harvest workers who had migrated in from other parts of Mexico.

Despite the forces shaping change in Latin America as a whole, regional diversity in agrarian structures persisted. The large-scale commerical farming areas benefited first, and most, from state policies to stimulate *both* export commodities and the domestic food supply, since, as the major areas of commercial production, they offered the prospect of rapid returns on state investment in agriculture. In Brazil, for example, rural credit in 1975 was heavily concentrated in areas of commercial farming. The southeast and the south had 73 per cent of the total credit distributed equally between them, whereas the north received one percent, the northeast 14 per cent and the central-west 12 percent.[88] The northwest of Mexico became the major source of export crops, such as vegetables for the U.S. market, and of wheat and other grains for the domestic market. This was the area that received most government investment via irrigation.

Improved market opportunities and credit facilities led to more rationalized forms of production, leading to the expulsion of tenant farmers and the reduction in the numbers of permanent workers. Less permanent workers were needed because of mechanization and, often, the introduction of new crops or crop varieties that were suited to more standardized farming. Furthermore, the widespread introduction of irrigation, under appropriate ecological conditions, evened out and simplified the production process. Tenancies, whether labour or sharecropping, were reduced to consolidate landholdings and enable the landowner to take full advantage of the new market opportunities. There was also a tendency for the average size of arable farms to be reduced. The high investment needed for intensive farming made medium-sized units more attractive and manageable than large units.

These processes were found, for example, in parts of Colombia from the 1930s onwards, in parts of the Central valley of Chile in the 1960s and in southern Brazil from the 1940s onwards. Large modernized landholdings required, however, a substantial input of labor at certain periods of the year. Coffee and fruit harvesting are examples of periods when a heavy seasonal labour input was required for harvesting and packaging or processing. In regions of large-scale modernized farming, there was, then, the likelihood that settlements of temporary farm-workers, often clustered

[88] David Goodman and Michael Redclift, *From Peasant to Proletarian* (Oxford, 1981), p. 160.

around small provincial towns, would evolve. In Brazil, these workers were known as *boias frias,* after the prepared lunches which they took from their homes to the fields.[89]

This type of temporary worker was also found in the fruit-growing areas of the central valley of Chile, where the permanent labour force was reduced and the demand for seasonal labour was estimated at 330,000 workers in 1980.[90] The farm workers in the fruit-growing areas were often women, particularly for the specialized jobs in selection and packaging. Their earnings, during the season were considerably more than they could earn, for example, in domestic work for a whole year. The settlements in these commercial farming areas often had a polarized social structure in which a nucleus of well-constructed housing for relatively prosperous farm owners, managers, professionals and traders was surrounded by a belt of shanties in which temporary labour resided.

In thc second type of agrarian structure, characterized by the relationship of economic enclave and peasant community, the development of an internal market for foodstuffs increased the differentiation of the local community. There were, for example, clear signs in the Mantaro valley of Peru of the emergence by 1980 of a small capitalist farming class, mainly producing milk and seed potatoes.[91] Alongside this class, there had developed a peasant smallholder system which included both landless workers and small-scale farmers who diversified their economy to include trade, transport and labour migration to enable them to survive in the village. The capitalist farming class took up the more profitable branches of production such as alfalfa, seed potatoes and milk; whereas the peasant strata were the main producers of the traditional staples of wheat, maize and beans.

However, differentiation was limited because of the difficulty of consolidating landholdings in areas which had high population densities and land scarcity. Most peasants still retained land as an essential and secure compo-

89 D. Goodman and M. Redclift, 'The 'Boias-frias' – Rural Proletarianization and Urban Marginality in Brazil', *International Journal of Urban and Regional Research,* I, 2 (1977).

90 This is an estimate based on field work in 1980 in Aconcagua and Curico provinces of Chile by R. Rivera: *Notas sobre la estructura social agraria en Chile* (Santiago, 1985). Daniel Rodriguez, 'Agricultural Modernization and Labor Market in Latin America: the case of fruit growing in Central Chile', unpublished Ph.D. dissertation, University of Texas, Austin, 1987, provides a systematic analysis of the labour market in the fruit-producing region, emphasizing the urban residence of most of the agricultural workers. Fruit exports to the United States have been the most dynamic part of Chilean agriculture up to 1990. Farming was intensive and closely linked to packaging and shipping operations.

91 Long and Roberts, *Miners, Peasants, and Entrepreneurs,* pp. 176–80; Mallon, *The Defence of Community in Peru.*

nent of their household economy. Even urban migrants kept rights to land in Peru and elsewhere, thereby inhibiting the development of an active land market. The capitalist farmer remained a small minority and had to resort to strategies such as the renting of both private and community land in order to expand production and accumulate capital. The limits this imposed on accumulation encouraged diversification into non-agricultural activities such as transport and commerce. By 1980, these areas had become economically dynamic, but built upon small-scale enterprise and economic diversification. They had not undergone the 'full transition' to commercial farming, but remained important areas of population retention and small-scale capital accumulation. Unlike either the areas of large-scale landholdings or of medium-size capitalist farms, this area was less affected by state intervention and less dependent upon it for economic growth.

In the third type of agrarian structure, that dominated by small-scale farming, the capitalist nature of the independent family farm was intensified. This type of farming was favoured by government credit and mechanization programmes stimulating production of foodstuffs which were suited to this scale of farming. Examples were wheat, soybeans and dairy farming. This process has been labelled, following Lenin, as the 'farmer road of capitalist development', entailing a process of differentiation in which some prospered, while others lost their land and became landless labourers or migrated away.[92] The size of these farms was modest as compared with the landholdings of the first type, averaging around fifty hectares. The farm owner, with the help of a small number of permanent workers, provided almost all the labour required. Farming became highly capital intensive, using modern farm technology. The capitalized family farm depended on bank loans and made use of a range of public and private agricultural services. Farming was, thus, highly market dependent and profit orientated. In many parts of Latin America, it provided a source of investment for professionals and merchants. In the west of Mexico, where we noted the presence of impoverished small-scale farmers, the trend in the 1970s was towards the capitalization of family farms based on milk and small animal production. This type of farming

[92] The farmer road is based on the dominance of small and medium-scale farming, originating in a homesteader type colonization or in the ending of feudal landowning. The development dynamic is provided by competition between these producers which results in the elimination of the inefficient and unlucky. See de Janvry, *The Agrarian Question*, pp. 106–9, for a discussion of the various 'roads' to capitalist development and their applicability to Latin America.

lent itself to domination by agro-industrial capital because of the high costs of production and because of the latter's control of processing and marketing. Large agro-industrial enterprises throughout Latin America contracted the production of small producers in commodities such as wheat, grapes, tobacco, vegetable oils and milk, exercising a close technical control.[93]

Another means by which small producers diminished the risks created by high costs of production and marketing difficulties was through the formation of producers' co-operatives. These did not protect the independence of the family farmer; rather they were the instruments through which the State ensured the modernization of the family farming sector. State agencies responsible for co-operatives in both Brazil and Mexico effectively controlled the production of the small producer through credit policies, technical services and marketing monopolies. Successful small-scale farmers could make a comfortable living, but often at the cost of their independence.

One consequence of these trends was that these areas were unable to sustain their previous populations. They became, in the 1970s, some of the main areas of population expulsion in Latin America. On the one hand, smaller, less efficient farmers were forced out of business. On the other hand, the capital-intensive farms that survived were unable to absorb the displaced labour or that created by population expansion. In these areas, the market for seasonal labour was also weaker than in the first case – that of the commercial estates – and so, the region as a whole, did not retain or attract population. In Brazil, in the 1970s, the main source of peasant colonists for the Mato Grosso area of the Amazonian frontier was the group of small-scale tenant farmers expelled from the centre-south, and not, as previously, the impoverished peasants of the northeast. The relative prosperity of this type of farming, and its dependence on local servicing, meant, however, that a network of moderately prosperous service centres developed.

In our fourth type of agrarian structure, that characterized by the more economically marginalized areas of Latin America, the impact of integration into the national economy led to contradictory tendencies. These were

93 D. Goodman, B. Sorj and J. Wilkinson, 'Agro-industry, State Policy, and Rural Social Structures: recent analyses of proletarianization in Brazilian agriculture', in B. Munslow and H. Finch (eds), *Proletarianization in the Third World* (London, 1984) cite outgrower arrangements between agro-industrial enterprises and small farmers in the south of Brazil in crops such as tobacco and in viticulture. In these cases, the entrepreneurial activities of the owner-operators are severely constrained.

the areas that in the 1950s and 1960s were *least* likely to provide migrants to the urban centres or, in the case of Mexico, international labour flow. The poverty and low levels of education of such areas meant that the relevant urban skills, education and capital that facilitated migration were in short supply. Migration was a selective process since undertaking the journey involved considerable material and psychic costs.

Increasing population pressure on land meant increased rural poverty and this inhibited agricultural modernization among the peasantry. Their situation was made worse by a change in their relation to the large estate. Previously, as we saw above, peasants supplied labour to the estate in return for access to land and, often, a small wage. Though the large estates of the marginalized areas did not modernize as rapidly as their counterparts in the zones of highly commercial agriculture, they were gradually transformed. One of the most widespread transformations was the increase in livestock farming which offered, for a relatively low investment in animals and in improved pasture, the possibility of making a good profit from land which had not been highly productive. Livestock farming required relatively little labor and simplified the task of controlling production on a very large estate. The need for temporary peasant labour was eliminated, as was the possibility of leasing land. This process was widespread in the northeast of Brazil where estates converted cropland to grazing.

The poor, economically more marginal regions of Latin America constituted the labour reserves for the cities and for the more economically dynamic rural areas. In the Mantaro valley of Peru, the landless labour of the villages was provided by migrants from the adjacent, but poorer, highland areas in the Department of Huancavelica. By the 1980s, even migrants from the most remote villages now figured in the populations of Latin America's metropolises, occupying the unskilled, ill-paid positions in construction or the 'informal' economy. In Mexico, highland villages in the state of Oaxaca sent migrants to work temporarily in the United States, as well as to the major Mexican cities.[94] Even in the Amazonian region, small-scale indigenous societies have been incorporated into wider national and international economies through being recruited as labour in the frontier towns and forming part of the chain of illegal cocaine produc-

[94] For an analysis of the implications of the Mixtec migration that began in the 1960s from the western part of the state of Oaxaca, Mexico, to the US and Mexican border cities, see C. Nagengast and M. Kearney, 'Mixtec Ethnicity: social identity, political consciousness, and political activism', *Latin American Research Review*, 25, 2, (1990): 61–91.

tion and distribution.[95] It was in these areas that the disintegrative effects of capitalist penetration were often most evident.

Family-based peasant farming it seemed was, by 1980, in the process of extinction in Latin America as a widespread and viable source of livelihood, to be replaced either by modernized estates or capitalized family farms. An impressive body of evidence has been marshalled to suggest that this was, in fact, the case for Mexico. However, in other areas such as Peru, Bolivia or the northeast of Brazil, peasant farming showed no sign of such an early demise. The key variables explaining this difference are the slower pace of economic modernization in the latter areas, and the considerable risks and uncertainty attending farming with unfavourable ecological and climatic conditions. The small peasant farm was economically efficient because it could adapt its labour resources (both wage and non-wage) to the changing agricultural cycle, using the work of most household members, switching their labour from one form of farm or non-farm labour to another and making multiple uses of the scanty equipment they possessed.[96]

Further, in the marginalized areas, the use of kinship and community ties and resources provided an important strategy for economic survival, enabling local populations to accommodate to market forces, without losing their group identity. They did this in two ways. Traditional ideologies were reinterpreted, helping communities to adjust collectively to the inroads of capitalism. In both Bolivia and Colombia, folk Catholic beliefs were used to explain the new proletarianized work relationships into which peasants were forced, and to account for the social differentiation that resulted from market forces. In other communities, money earned outside, though essential for the purchase of certain basic industrial foodstuffs and used to maintain rituals and customary obligations, was not used to purchase local staples or hire labour on a regular basis. Money remained in a distinct sphere and did not undermine the exchanges of food and labor that maintained community cohesion and inhibited differentiation.[97]

[95] For a case study of these processes among Colombian indigenous groups, see S. Hugh-Jones, 'The Palm and the Pleaides: initiation and cosmology in Northwest Amazonia', in *Cambridge Studies in Social Anthropology*, 24 (1987).

[96] Long and Roberts *Peasant Cooperation*, pp. 306–8, use this argument to explain the vitality of peasant farming in the Mantaro valley of Peru. M. Lipton, 'Family, Fungibility and Formality: rural advantages of informal non-farm enterprise versus the urban-formal state', in S. Amin (ed.), *Human Resources, Employment and Development* (London, 1984) uses the term 'fungibility' to describe these advantages of the peasant enterprise.

[97] The account of Bolivia and Colombia is given by M. Taussig, *The Devil and Commodity Fetishism in South America* (Chapel Hill, N.C., 1980). Several anthropologists have documented the ways in which indigenous cultures have preserved their identity in face of the increased penetration of

THE 1980S

Despite the trends towards political and economic centralization in the 1960s and 1970s that were noted above, the period from the end of the 1970s to 1990 was marked, in general, by reverses in the control exercised over rural population and production both by the dominant classes of the Latin American countries and by the state. Part of the reason was the increasing internationalization of agriculture through agro-industrial activities linked to multinational companies. Though the bureaucratic reach of the state extended enormously in this period, its capacity to implement policy was limited both by the specific interests of its own functionaries, and by an increasingly organized and articulate producer population. At both national and international levels, there was, starting in the 1970s, a greater questioning of large-scale, state-directed agricultural modernization programmes. The World Bank, along with other international institutions, began to shift their preoccupation with problems of economic growth to a broader concern for the eradication of rural poverty and for the development of policies aimed at a more effective redistribution of wealth/income in favour of the poorest groups.[98] The International Labour Office (ILO) widened its emphasis on unemployment to embrace a commitment to fulfill the basic needs of the poor, whether employed or unemployed. Other agencies dedicated themselves to the achievement of 'basic human needs' or 'minimum living standards'.

This reorientation was in part stimulated by the realization that previous attempts at redistribution, such as national land reform programmes, had in many cases led to increased marginalization of the poorest groups and to deteriorating relations between the State and peasantry, the former using these reforms to impose tighter, more centralized control. In simple economic terms, many land reforms had failed to dynamize production and to redress the balance between rural and urban standards of living. Politically, as was the case with Peru and Chile, they generated increased rural unrest as peasants fought to retain some degree of local autonomy vis-à-vis the State.

In this concluding section, we outline the major trends that can be

market forces. See Sarah Lund Skar, 'Interhousehold Cooperation in Peru's Southern Andes: a case of multiple sibling group marriage', in N. Long (ed.), *Family and Work in Rural Societies: Perspectives on Non-Wage Labour* (London, 1984); O. Harris, 'Labour and Produce in an Ethnic Economy'; T. Platt, *Estado boliviano y ayllu andino: tierra y tributo en el norte de Potosi* (Lima, 1982).

98 See, for example, World Bank, *Rural Development* (Washington, D.C., 1975).

identified for the 1980s. Some of these reinforce the tendencies for change in the agrarian structures that we examined in the previous sections, while others modify or run counter to these. More acutely than in the earlier sections, the short historical perspective inhibits both a full analysis of these trends, and requires caution in attributing to them any longer-term significance.

Though the Latin American economies had, as we have seen, a long history of involvement in export agriculture, several commentators have noted important differences between this involvement and the internationalization of agriculture in the 1970s and 1980s. Agricultural production became, in these years, more dependent on external and international considerations and finance, and less on state policy and the decisions of local producers. The consolidation of a world market for foodstuffs accentuated an international division of labour whose consequences for Latin America were increases in food imports in certain basic products, such as maize, beans, rice and potatoes, and specialization in products in demand in the urban markets, both at home and abroad, such as meat, fruit, and vegetables. These products were, by the late 1970s, being produced with the aid of advanced agricultural technology, and to meet fairly uniform standards of quality required by the international market and by middle-class consumers at home.

Because of the costs and sophistication of technology, the complexity of marketing on an international scale and the need for credit, agriculture became increasingly organized as part of agro-industry in which all the steps from the point of production to the final consumer were controlled by large corporations, usually multinationals.[99] Under the typical contracts made between producers and the agro-industrial enterprise, decisions concerning farm management, including inputs such as seeds, fertilizer, and insecticide, were under the control of the company. In contrast to earlier forms of export production, companies usually did not buy land, but preferred to rent or contract out production to small-scale farmers. Examples are the Nestlé company which bought milk for processing from producers in cattle-raising regions of various Latin American countries, or

[99] See E. Feder, 'Agroindustries and rural underdevelopment', in D. A. Preston (ed.), *Environment, Society and Rural Change in Latin America* (London, 1980); C. D. Scott, 'Transnational Corporations and Asymmetries in the Latin American Food System', *Bulletin of Latin American Research*, 3, 1 (1984) pp. 63–80; D. Goodman, B. Sorj and J. Wilkinson, *From Farming to Biotechnology: a Theory of Agroindustrial Development* (Oxford, 1987).

companies such as Pepsi-Cola which contracted out the production of crops such as potatoes and corn for its food-processing operations.[100]

Detailed case studies of the operation of agro-industry modify this picture of top-down control by the large corporations. In Sonora, Mexico, multinational companies, such as Anderson Clayton, were active from the 1950s to the 1970s in purchasing cotton from local farmers, offering credit, providing technical assistance and quality inputs. But local farmers continued to pursue their own farming and livelihood strategies, making use of loans both from the state and from the corporations, to meet household consumption needs and spread their risks, and not simply to fulfil the production goals set by the state and corporations.[101]

Estimates of the value of agricultural production under the agro-industrial system are difficult to obtain, but the growth and importance of agro-industry is evident.[102] The significance of agro-industry was increased by its contribution to industrialization in Latin America. Agro-industrial corporations in foods, drink, and timber were in the forefront of modern manufacturing. By 1970, agroindustry accounted for 42 per cent of Peruvian manufacturing, 30 per cent of Colombian, 20 per cent of Brazilian and 20 per cent of Mexican.[103] These percentages had declined fairly uniformly over Latin America by 1980, as the urban-industrial economies matured through the development of consumer durable goods industries, such as automobiles, electrical and electronic products, or through intermediate and capital goods industries.

In the 1980s, the increasing dominance of agro-industry was tempered by changes in national economies and their relation to the international

[100] CEPAL, 'Los mercados de insumos tecnológicos y su adecuación a las economias campesinas; agroindustrias y agricultura campesina.' *Estudios e Informes* (Santiago, 1984), pp. 107–10, discusses the importance of multinationals in food production, pointing out that the sales of the leading companies, such as Unilever, Nestlé, Swift or Kraft, are often greater in value than that of the GNP of several Latin American countries.

[101] For an analysis of these production strategies in Caborca, Sonora, from the 1950s to the 1970s, see A. E. Zazueta, 'Agricultural policy in Mexico: the limits of a growth model', in B. S. Orlove, M. W. Foley and T. F. Love (eds), *State, Capital, and Rural Society: Anthropological Perspectives on Political Economy in Mexico and the Andes* (Boulder, Colo., 1989). By the 1970s, the multinationals were withdrawing from providing credit and organizing marketing for cotton due to deteriorating prices for cotton in international markets, leaving the state with the task of subsidizing local production strategies. The state responded to the economic difficulties facing farmers by providing credit and by purchasing land at prices favorable to the farmers.

[102] See S. E. Sanderson (ed.), *The Americas in the New International Division of Labor* (New York, 1985), pp. 56–60 and Sanderson, *The Transformation of Mexican Agriculture,* pp. 28–30, where he discusses the importance of industrialized poultry production in Mexico and Brazil, and the integration of such production with other sectors of agriculture, such as sorghum production.

[103] CEPAL, 'Los mercados de insumos tecnológicos', table 2.

economy. As the Latin American economies became more urban-based, investment in agriculture had increasingly to compete with opportunities arising from urban real estate and other service activities, as well as from new branches of manufacturing. Also, it became more attractive for national capital to invest externally. Finally, the debt crisis of the 1980s resulted in a dearth of funds, private and public, for investment, both because of local shortages, and because foreign banks and companies became less inclined to make credit available.

However, this scarcity of national capital strengthened, in some countries, the economic leverage of agro-industry, as multinational corporations became one of the few sources of new investment, thus further weakening the state's capacity to steer and control agricultural development. In 1989, Mexico liberalized its investment requirements both for industry and for agriculture in order to attract new foreign investors, permitting, for example, foreign corporations for the first time to rent land from *ejidos*.

During the 1970s and 1980s, severe limits appeared in the state's capacity to plan and implement agricultural programmes beyond those related to the internationalization of agriculture. As state projects in various countries faced increasing difficulties, problems inherent in the bureaucratic management of development became evident. By 1980, state employment was accounting for a considerable proportion of total employment, often exceeding 10 per cent.[104] Bureaucratic agencies involved in regional or agricultural development programmes proliferated, generating new sources of employment at local, regional and central government levels.[105]

There were several dimensions to this problem. First, because of the scale and complexity of many of these programmes, successful management depended on a detailed knowledge of local conditions and clear strategies for adapting the overall plan to these conditions. This proved impossible on two major counts. The quality of the information available on the characteristics of the rural population, existing farming systems,

[104] On the increase in state employment, see chapter by Orlandina de Oliveira and Bryan Roberts in this volume and chapter by Laurence Whitehead in *CHLA*, VI Part 2.

[105] T. Martínez Saldaña, 'Los campesinos y el estado en Mexico', table 53, lists over ten government agencies involved in providing services to four of the largest collective *ejido* regions in Mexico, generating 23,000 jobs. This compared with 5,250 in 1950. In Brazil, agrarian development agencies such as SUDAM, SUDENE, INCRA, and POLOCENTRO were amongst the largest employers in the de-centralized sector of state employment which generated more than two million jobs by 1980. See A. C. Medeiros, *Politics and Intergovernmental Relations in Brazil: 1964–1982* (New York, 1986).

household economies and ecological conditions was generally poor, and therefore provided no adequate basis for decisions concerning resource allocation and intervention strategy. This was compounded by the sheer diversity of local organizational forms, and the multiplicity of livelihood strategies practiced by small-scale farmers. It was almost impossible for development project personnel to acquire a detailed working knowledge of the everyday practices of so-called 'target populations'. A second factor related to the fact that development agency personnel had been socialized into working with generalized planning models. These were in effect designed to perpetuate 'systematic areas of ignorance' which in fact made it possible for them to muddle through and even to claim success for their efforts, however problematic in outcome. In some cases, even the failure to reach particular project goals could become a justification for trying again, that is for continuing with the programme unaltered.

A second significant dimension relates to the existence of personal and political interests among bureaucrats that ran counter to the objectives of the programme for which they were responsible. This arose because bureaucratic careers characteristically entailed politicking for promotion or competition for access to institutional resources. Also various case studies showed that successful careers in administrative organizations depended on learning particular administrative and political styles of operation, based for example on patron–client relations, old-boy networks and sometimes underhand or 'corrupt' practice. These commitments were often accorded priority over project goals. These processes were brought out graphically by Grindle's study of the Mexican government agency, CONASUPO, in which bureaucratic and personal career interests took precedence over the efficient delivery of services.[106]

A third issue concerns inter-agency competition in the design and implementation of development programmes. The large-scale interventions of the 1970s required co-operation between different government departments and institutions, for example the extension service, the irrigation department, the agricultural credit bank and the several agencies responsible for promoting farmer organization, co-operatives, and so on. Credit agencies were naturally interested in financial soundness and profitability whereas extension services were essentially concerned with reaching as wide a clientele as possible and with transferring knowledge about new

[106] See M. S. Grindle, *Bureaucrats, Politicians, and Peasants in Mexico: a Case Study in Public Policy* (Berkeley, Cal., 1977).

farming techniques. This multiplicity of institutions involved at various levels in the planning and implementation process led to clashes over the priority of specific tasks (e.g., delivering credit, transferring technology, promoting improved farming practice, increasing the claim-making capacity of farmer groups), and also to a scramble for financial and other resources for distribution among their respective administrative and technical personnel.

In this struggle taking place at the point of implementation, agency personnel often aligned themselves with peasant or other local actors in an attempt to advance the specific interests of their agency. This was to be a major problem in the implementation of Peru's 1969 agrarian reform in which organizations such as the community development and mobilization agency, SINAMOS, the Ministry of Agriculture, and the Peasant Community Agency, competed with each other for both local and national political influence.[107] The result was a highly dynamic and conflictive set of relations at the interface of development implementation. The outcomes were highly unpredictable, and, for all intents and purposes, impossible to manage from the top-down, especially in large-scale development interventions such as colonization or resettlement programmes, as was the case in Brazil's Amazonian development projects of the 1970s.[108]

Ambitious state programmes of rural development met their nemesis in the late 1970s and 1980s with the generalized economic recession that resulted in sharp cut-backs in state expenditure. Though the recession had a negative impact on agricultural production and worsened rural poverty, it also underscored the need for local producers and households to solve their own livelihood problems. This was to strengthen existing patterns of small-scale informal and diversified activities. It also led to new forms of farmer and community organization. These were increasingly supported by various national or international non-government organizations.

In the 1970s and particularly in the 1980s, the employment situation in most Latin American countries deteriorated sharply. As we have seen, the

[107] See P. Cleaves and M. Scurrah, *Agriculture, Bureaucracy, and Military Government in Peru* (Ithaca, N.Y., 1982), and C. McClintock, *Peasant Cooperatives and Political Change in Peru*.

[108] S. G. Bunker, *Underdeveloping the Amazon: Extraction, Unequal Exchange, and the Failure of the Modern State* (Urbana, Ill., 1985) provides a detailed analysis of inter-agency conflict in the Amazon. He argues that these processes have the effect of seriously distorting the state's declared aims of establishing long-term, self-sustaining production systems which would primarily be orientated to the welfare of the peasant population. Moreover, under pressure from various capitalist interests many agencies finished up promoting the interests of the dominant classes of the region.

modernization of agriculture and high birth-rates had for many years created a surplus rural population. In the 1980s, urban migration became a less viable solution to rural un- and under-employment. Rates of open unemployment rose sharply in most Latin American cities, and informal employment, often synonymous with underemployment, increased markedly.[109] There is evidence of an increase in return migration from urban to rural areas for several Latin American countries during this period. Preliminary estimates of the growth of the population employed in agriculture indicated a marked increase to an annual growth rate of 1.7 per cent between 1980 and 1987, compared with 0.3 per cent for the decade 1970–80.[110] Keeping people occupied on the land became a political priority. In Brazil, for example, social security was extended to the rural areas and peasant farmers became entitled to pensions. Some areas of Brazil, such as the state of Piaui, derived a considerable amount of revenue from federal welfare payments and these complemented local peasant economies.[111]

In some countries, international migration had, by the late 1970s and during the 1980s, become a major source of income for rural households. In Mexico and the Central American countries such as Guatemala, Nicaragua and El Salvador, migration to the United States intensified during these years. Though increasing numbers of these migrants remained for long periods in the United States, most of them regularly sent remittances back to their families at home. These remittances were not a solution to rural poverty, but they did provide a source of livelihood independent of state development programmes and of local wage opportunities. In some cases, migrant earnings had the effect of turning on its head the usual pattern of rural stratification, since migrant labour households received a higher cash income than did local farmers.[112]

In other countries of Latin America, international migration also provided wage-earning opportunities for an impoverished rural population. There were movements of population from Bolivia and Paraguay to Argentina, and from Colombia to Venezuela. Elsewhere the relative decline of urban income opportunities appears to have intensified the colonization of

[109] See chapter by Oliveira and Roberts in this volume. CEPAL, *Transformación ocupacional y crisis social en América Latina* (Santiago, 1989) provides estimates of the rise in urban unemployment for Latin America, and for the growth of urban informal employment.

[110] Ibid., table 2. This increase in employment was not matched by the growth of the agricultural product, which was substantially lower between 1980–87 than in previous years.

[111] See Lopes, 'Capitalist Development and Agrarian Structure in Brazil'.

[112] I. Adelman et al., 'Life in a Mexican Village: a SAM perspective', *Journal of Development Studies*, 25 (1988) pp. 5–24 shows this pattern for a Mexican village.

frontier regions. This was especially the case for Peru and Brazil. Even though the state fostered and attempted to organize colonization in Brazil, the evidence points to mismanagement and ineffectiveness on the part of state planning institutions, which, depending upon the area, created room for poor migrants and small-scale entrepreneurs, as well as large-scale corporations, to pursue their own strategies in relatively uncontrolled and conflictive ways. This had the effect of undermining the legitimacy of state-planned development.

The major new Latin America export of the 1980s – cocaine – was inherently subversive of state planning and centralized control, and relied to a considerable extent on the individual strategies of peasant farmers.[113] By 1990, coca had become the most important crop of Peru's colonization areas, replacing crops that were officially promoted by government and international development agencies. State control in these areas, whether directly through local authorities such as the police or indirectly through credit provision and agricultural extension services, became irrelevant in the face of the illegally organized drug economy.

From time immemorial, coca had been produced on a small scale and its link now to the illegal drug trade ensured, in the 1980s, that it remained an agricultural production activity for peasant farmers. In Bolivia and Peru, and to a lesser extent in other Latin American countries, it became practically the only viable cash crop for small farmers. The success of the coca crop in the 1980s attracted migrants from other rural and urban areas to work on its production, and created a network of processing, trading and transport enterprise in which many small-scale entrepreneurs played a role. Latin American governments, using U.S. and other international aid, attempted to eradicate coca cultivation through crop eradication programmes aimed at promoting alternative crops. By 1990, there was, however, no evidence of any substantial success in this endeavour, since the level of resources committed to providing attractive alternatives to farmers was far below that estimated to be necessary to promote alternative cash crops.

Within an economic and political climate of considerable uncertainty, space was created for local producers to develop their own forms of local level

[113] See E. Morales, *Cocaine: White Gold Rush in Peru* (Tucson, Ariz. 1989), L. Gill, *Peasants, Entrepreneurs, and Social Change: Frontier Development in Lowland Bolivia* (Boulder, Colo., 1987), P. T. Parkerson, 'Neither "green gold" nor "the devil's leaf": coca farming in Bolivia', in Orlove, Foley and Love (eds), *State, Capital and Rural Society,* and C. Sage, 'Petty Producers, Potatoes, and Land: a Case Study of Agrarian Change in the Cochabamba Serranía, Bolivia', unpublished Ph.D. dissertation, University of Durham, 1990.

organization. The current political trend in Latin America towards democratization altered the balance of political power, creating opportunities for smallholders or farm-labourers to organize and bargain with new and old political groupings. In Mexico, for example, the 1970s and 1980s saw a proliferation of peasant actions that broke with the dominant corporatist style of politics and rural development. Land invasions were common, as were non-land struggles over such issues as municipal democratization, fairer producer and input prices, and, from the mid-1980s, environmental issues concerning control over natural resources and against industrial pollution. These grass-roots movements were focussed on locally specific concerns, and did not result in national level mobilization. They were independent of state agencies and of government-controlled peasant federations. What was new about many of these organizations was their declared apolitical stance, being ready to negotiate with, and make temporary alliances with, the agencies and political parties that offered the most favorable terms. Examples of such organizations were producer co-operatives, unions of farmworkers, small-farmer associations, regional consumer organizations, and credit unions aimed at countering the ending of government subsidized loans.

Support for local level organization among the rural population often came from non-government organizations committed to 'bottom-up' participatory forms of development. These non-government organizations had various origins and sources of funding. Many were church inspired, such as the Catholic or Protestant community welfare and development organizations. Others were international humanitarian or environmental organizations, and others were locally formed groups usually deriving funding from international agencies, and charities. The number of non-government organizations working in the various countries of Latin America increased exponentially in the 1980s, so that in some countries the number of their personnel and the size of their budgets rivalled that of the state agencies working in agrarian development.

In Mexico, there were at least 600 formally registered NGOs working in the agrarian sector. In Peru, the number of nationally registered non-government bodies concerned with development rose from sixty in 1979 to 148 in 1981.[114] In Guatemala, there were several hundred NGOs working in development projects in the late 1980s, when over fifty new development associations were being registered each year. Guatemala pro-

[114] M. Padron, *Las organizaciones no gubernamentales de desarrollo en el Perú* (Lima, 1988), p. 100.

vided an interesting case of the way in which non-governmental organizations came to replace State-directed development initiatives.[115] The Christian Democrat government of 1986 to 1990 sought to increase local participation in the development process, assigning 8 per cent of State revenues to municipalities, and encouraging local groups to devise and implement projects. The economic difficulties of the government, and its need to retrench on public spending, led, however, to an increasing privatization of the development effort. International aid was the equivalent of 10 per cent of government revenue, and though this aid effort was co-ordinated with the government, funds were mainly channelled through local non-government organizations. The Guatemalan private sector, stressing the need to reduce dependence on the state, also sponsored non-government organizations to provide technical assistance and credit to small enterprises in both the agricultural and non-agricultural sectors. Secular and religious charitable organizations worked directly with their national counterparts or directly with producer and consumer groups. By 1990, the rural population of Guatemala was highly connected externally, but with little co-ordination at either regional or national level, through a wide range of non-government organizations which were distrustful of central government control.

Although the growth of non-governmental organizations meant the development of an 'alternative network or structure' of development, it did not, in many cases, significantly replace the state. Many of the personnel who worked in these non-government organizations had previously worked for government and maintained their ties with persons still in government service.

The explosion of non-government organizations was, then, many-sided. In certain contexts it represented a challenge to existing development thinking and to the state itself, but in others it was no more than an extension of the 'development effort' and one that was less costly than if the state were to do it all itself. Yet the fact that many of these alternative approaches were built upon the notion of grassroots participatory development provided a political dynamic that was at times considered a threat by the state and by the dominant classes.

By the end of the 1980s, there was, therefore, a build-up of apparently contradictory processes, on the one hand strengthening the centralization

[115] AVANSCO/IDESAC, *ONGS, Sociedad Civil y Estado en Guatemala: elementos para el debate* (Guatemala City, 1990).

of agricultural production through international capital, and, on the other, supporting the capacity of local groups to initiate their own development projects and thus gain more political space. The clear loser in these struggles was the state, particularly in its administration and control over resources and population. By 1990, the uncertainties surrounding agrarian development in Latin America had multiplied. National and international forces threw up a series of ambiguous messages – as for example in the development of Amazonia. Throughout the continent there was a renewed emphasis on privatizing development initiatives, leading in Mexico to the effective dissolution of the *ejido* sector. However, the lack of state resources to improve infrastructure, coupled with the limited interest of private capital in agricultural investment, somewhat paradoxically created spaces for grass-roots action and pressures from peasant and worker unions and non-government sponsored forms of co-operative farming. This trend was reinforced by the international concern for sustainable development and conservation of primary national resources.[116]

[116] An account of environmental issues and their social implications for the Latin American rural sector is given in D. Goodman and M. Redclift, *Environment and Development in Latin America* (Manchester, 1991).

Part Four

ECONOMIC IDEAS

7

ECONOMIC IDEAS AND IDEOLOGIES IN LATIN AMERICA SINCE 1930

The history of ideas in Latin America is typically confined to the description of regional adaptations of European ideas. However, in the field of economic ideas in the period from the Depression of the 1930s to the debt and growth crises of the 1980s, first 'structuralism,' associated with the U.N. Economic Commission for Latin America (ECLA, or in Spanish, CEPAL), and subsequently 'dependency theory' were notably autochthonous, distinctly Latin American contributions to development theory. Moreover, they were widely embraced by theorists and policy-makers in the Third World at large. Although Marxism is treated and corporatism is discussed in brief compass, it is to the development of structuralism and dependency – arguably the most influential ideas ever to appear in Latin America – that this essay is principally devoted.[1] It deals with the diffusion of ideas, the formation of new ideas, and, necessarily, the independent rediscovery of ideas already developed elsewhere. Because they are sometimes inseparable in the Latin American context, it also occasionally treats policy as well as theory. The project is inherently a comparative one, since only by comparison can originality or distinctiveness be assessed. Genetic connections between ideas in Latin America and elsewhere will be indicated, as well as the independent rediscovery of identical or closely analo-

[1] Neo-classical and Keynesian ideas are not formally considered, except as necessary elements in the story of the advances and checks of structuralism and dependency – not because they are unimportant, but because there is little uniquely 'Latin American' about them. Also not treated is the contribution of the English-speaking Caribbean, where a related school of dependency developed in a slightly later period. There the issues were somewhat different (for example, greater population pressure on fewer resources); and problems of scale (and hence the urgency of integration) played a larger role. There also the debt to the neoclassical school was relatively greater. In the Caribbean the work of W. Arthur Lewis played a role similar to that of Raúl Prebisch in Latin America. On these matters, see Norman Girvan, 'The development of dependency economics in the Caribbean and Latin America: Review and Comparison', *Social and Economic Studies,* 22, 1 (March, 1973): 1–33.

gous propositions.[2] Finally, in social thought, it seems obvious that theory, if its tenets are assumed to be true and are not subject to empirical verification, slips easily into ideology, a set of propositions which implicitly justifies social values or social configurations. Both theory and ideology are part of the story.[3]

The central issue that economic theory and ideology addressed in Latin America in the period after 1930 was industrialization, both as fact (at first a consequence of the decline of export-led growth) and as desideratum (for ECLA, at least at the outset, a 'solution' to the problem of economic underdevelopment). In the early years, before 1949, with some notable exceptions, the process of industrialization was defended without the benefit of economic theory and a counterpart coherent ideology. The arguments were often limited in scope to special circumstances, sometimes inconsistent, and frequently apologetic. This was because, in part, they 'contradicted' neo-classical theory. In particular, they ran afoul of the Ricardian model of the international division of labour, still very much alive in the early years of the Depression of the 1930s, despite a surge of protectionism around the world in the previous decade.

In the 1930s the proponents of industrialization were almost exclusively the industrialists themselves, though by the Second World War they were joined by government spokesmen, at least in the four most industrialized countries – Argentina, Brazil, Mexico and Chile. ECLA, whose analyses legitimized and prescribed industrialization, reached the apogee of its influence in the decade after 1949. The defence of industrialization was now much more coherent and aggressive. But in the 1960s came the unpredicted failure of the industrialization process to maintain its momentum relative to population growth, and a failure of Latin American politi-

[2] I have avoided the temptation to set the problem in the framework of Thomas Kuhn's 'paradigms' or Imre Lakatos's 'scientific research programs', because the disputes over the applicability of the Kuhn and Lakatos models to the history of economic ideas would seem to make such an effort at the world-region level gratuitously problematic and polemical. See Thomas S. Kuhn, *The Structure of Scientific Revolutions*, 2nd edn (Chicago, Ill., 1970); Mark Blaug, *The Methodology of Economics: Or How Economists Explain* (Cambridge, 1980). One need not assert for economic thought, as Robert Merton has claimed for the natural sciences, that multiple independent discoveries are more the rule than the exception. Yet it is hardly surprising that such things happen: consider the contemporaneous and independent formulation of the theory of marginal utility in the 1870s by Karl Menger, Léon Walras, and Stanley Jevons. Inevitably, as Merton has noted, the *prioritätstreit* characterizes the social as well as the natural sciences. See Robert K. Merton, *The Sociology of Science: Theoretical and Empirical Investigation* (Chicago, Ill., 1973), pp. 289, 343–70, 394–5.

[3] Though many economic theorists have argued that the scientific project of economic analysis can be successfully separated from ideology, Ronald Meek is persuasively sceptical. See his *Economics and Ideology and Other Essays* (London, 1967), esp. pp. 196–224.

cal regimes to bring about the social changes advocated by ECLA. These facts put the agency's theses in jeopardy. The theory was reworked, and new consequences flowed from it: a school of dependency analysis, whose proponents had lost faith in the ability of the industrial bourgeoisies of Latin America to develop the region along Western lines, emerged from structuralism.

EARLY ADVOCATES OF INDUSTRIALIZATION

Industrialization in Latin America was fact before it was policy, and policy before it was theory. In the half-century preceding 1930, there seemed to be a rough correspondence between the fact of high-performance, export-led growth and the theory of comparative advantage, which 'justified' Latin America's specialization in raw materials production. This theory, originated by David Ricardo (1817), and elaborated by John Stuart Mill (1848), Alfred Marshall (1879), and others later, can be summarized as follows: (a) Given an absence of commerce between two countries, if the relative prices of two commodities differ between them, both can profit by trading such commodities at an intermediate price ratio (that is to say, both can gain even if one country produces both traded goods more efficiently than the other); (b) countries export commodities whose production requires relatively intensive use of factors found in relative abundance within their boundaries; (c) commodity trade reduces, if it does not eliminate, international differences in wages, rents, and other returns to factors of production; (d) among other things, the theory assumes the absence of monopoly power and the spread of the benefits of technological progress across the whole trading system.

In Latin America, an explicit articulation of the advantages of specialization in trade for the independent states could be heard over the course of the nineteenth century. Yet the refrain was repeated much more frequently in the decades after 1880, corresponding to the beginning of a half-century of unprecedented production of agricultural and mineral goods, to be exchanged on the world market for manufactures.[4]

A corollary, derivable from Ricardo, was that there are 'natural' and

[4] See, for example, Vicente Reyes Gómez, 'Si la depreciación del papel moneda en Chile debe considerarse como una causa o un efecto de la baja del cambio', *Revista Económica* (Chile), año 3, 14 (June, 1888), pp. 86, 88; Joaquim Murtinho, *Relatório apresentado ao Presidente da República dos Estados Unidos de Brasil no ano de 1899* (Rio de Janeiro, n.d.), p. xiii; V[ictorino] de la Plaza, *Estudio sobre la situación política, económica, y constitucional de la República Argentina* (Buenos Aires, 1903), pp. 49–50, 68–9. La Plaza served as president of Argentina, 1914–16.

'artificial' economic activities based on a country's factor endowments, and that 'artificial' industries should be discouraged because they result in misallocation of resources. In Brazil, for example, Joaquim Murtinho, the Brazilian Minister of Finance, would do nothing for 'artificial' industries in the financial crisis of 1901–2. Such was the policy that governments of the region generally followed until the latter years of the Depression of the 1930s, or even later. It was not a laissez-faire policy, however, since such regimes provided direct and indirect support (e.g., through artificially low exchange rates or through exchange rate deterioration) for their export industries and the interests behind them. Paying their costs in local currency and receiving 'hard' currencies for their exports, such groups profited by obtaining more local currency as its exchange value fell.

Nevertheless, in Chile, export-led growth, focussing on the nitrate boom before and after the War of the Pacific (1879–83), laid a foundation for a manufacturing sector, and a Chilean industrialists' association (SOFOFA) appeared as early as 1883. This fact was less unusual than that some Chileans favouring industrialization discovered and propagated the ideas of Friedrich List, the founder of the German historical school of economics. List found his Chilean paladin between 1880 and the First World War in the person of Malaquías Concha, who popularized List's argument that infant industries would eventually become competitive, as internal economies of scale and economies external to the firm developed over time.[5] At all events, Chile probably industrialized more fully in terms of structural change than any other Latin American country before the Second World War.[6]

List seems to have had little influence elsewhere, and before 1945 Latin American proponents of manufacturing tended to be apologetic, timid, and accommodationist; they sought a place in the sun *alongside* the traditional export industries. This was true, for example, of Alejandro Bunge and Luis Colombo in Argentina; of Roberto Simonsen, Alexandre Siciliano, Jr., and Octávio Pupo Nogueira in Brazil.[7] There were aggressive

[5] Malaquías Concha, 'Balanza de comercio', *Revista Económica* año II, 23 (March, 1889), pp. 327–8; Concha, *La lucha económica* (Santiago, 1910), pp. 25–7. List was also cited in the Argentine tariff debate of the 1870s and championed by Luís Vieira Souto in Brazil at the turn of the century.

[6] By the mid-1930s domestic suppliers produced 90 per cent of all manufactured goods consumed in Chile, and over 70 per cent of the durable consumer and capital goods. José Gabriel Palma, 'Growth and Structure of Chilean Manufacturing Industry from 1830 to 1935' (unpublished Ph.D. thesis, Oxford University, 1979), pp. 344–5.

[7] On the complementarity between industry and agriculture and the general defensiveness of industrialists, see Alejandro Bunge, *La economía argentina,* 4 v. (Buenos Aires, 1928–30); Luis Colombo (in note 15); Roberto Simonsen, *Crises, Finances and Industry* (São Paulo, n.d.), p. 6; Octávio Pupo

sallies, nevertheless; Brazilian industrialists tried to counter the charge of 'artificiality' by pointing to the apparent legitimacy of the coffee-roasting industry in the United States and the sugar-refining industry in England, for which domestic raw materials did not exist.[8]

By the 1930s, however, the Brazilians had discovered a theorist who, in their view, provided a scientific basis for industrialization. This was Mihail Manoilescu, the Rumanian economist, politician, and ideologue of corporatism, who recommended industrialization *à outrance* for agricultural-exporting countries. In his major economic study, *Théorie du protectionnisme* (1929) and in *Le siècle du corporatisme* (1934), Manoilescu made a frontal attack on the existing international division of labour, and argued that labour productivity in 'agricultural' countries was intrinsically and measurably inferior to that in 'industrial' countries – so categorized by the composition of their exports. Manoilescu did not hesitate to call agricultural countries 'backward', contending that surplus labour in agriculture in such nations should be transferred to industrial activities.[9] He denounced the international division of labour and the classical theories of trade which recommended to agricultural nations that they continue to channel their labour force into areas of what he considered inherently inferior productivity. New industries should be introduced as long as their labour productivity was higher than the national average. In a vulgarized version of his argument in *Le siècle du corporatisme,* Manoilescu asserted that the average industrial worker produces ten times the value of an agricultural worker, and that agricultural countries 'are poor and stay poor' as long as they do not industrialize. Thus the international division of labour was basically a swindle: classical international trade theory 'justified' the exploitation of one people by another.[10]

In São Paulo, officials of the Centre of Industries corresponded with Manoilescu, and published *Théorie du protectionnisme* in Portuguese in 1931. In the early thirties three important industrial spokesmen – Simonsen,

Nogueira, *Em torno da tarifa aduaneira* (São Paulo, 1931), pp. 91–112, Alexandre Siciliano, Jr., *Agricultura, comércio e industria no Brasil* (São Paulo, 1931), p. 18; *Revista de Industria* (Mexico, D. F.), 1, 1 (November 1937): 3; *Revista de Economía* (Mexico, D. F.), 8, 10 (October, 1945): 6. Less defensive is Oscar Alvarez Andrews, *Historia del desarrollo industrial de Chile* (Santiago, 1936), perhaps because of the Listian heritage and Chile's relative success in industrializing by the mid-1930s.

8 Pupo Nogueira, *Em torno,* p. 136; Siciliano, *Agricultura,* pp. 27–28; Simonsen, *Crises,* p. 88. In 1903 Serzedelo Correia had pointed to the 'artificiality' of the British cotton textile industry. Correia, 'As indústrias nacionais', in Edgard Carone (ed.), *O pensamento industrial no Brasil (1880–1945)* (São Paulo, 1971), pp. 42–3.

9 Mihail Manoilescu, *Théorie du protectionnisme et de l'échange international* (Paris, 1929), pp. 61, 65, 184; *Le siècle du corporatisme: Doctrine du corporatisme intégral et pur* (Paris, 1934), p. 28.

10 Manoilescu, *Théorie,* p. 184; *Le siècle,* pp. 28–30.

Siciliano Jr. and Pupo Nogueira – took Manoilescu's work to be proof of the legitimacy of their interests. Adding a touch of racism, Siciliano neatly adapted Manoilescu's theory by contending in 1931 that Brazil could not continue to rely on traditional exports, because of the lower wages that Africans and Asians would accept in competing agricultural activities, implicitly raising their labour productivities; thus agriculture in Brazil did not possess any intrinsic superiority to industry.[11] Manoilescu's theory as a 'scientific' rationale for Brazilian industrialization did not, however, survive the 1930s – chiefly because of the attacks by Jacob Viner and other neo-classical theorists on his work, and also perhaps because of his open adherence to fascism in the late thirties and his support for Germany in the Second World War. Manoilescu's ideas were slowly abandoned for more practical and circumstantial arguments. Simonsen, who frequently cited Manoilescu in the early 1930s, has ceased referring to the master by the time of the war.[12] Meanwhile, in 1944, Simonsen presided at an industrialists' congress which called for the 'harmonious' development of agriculture and industry, and even championed government aid to agriculture.[13]

The general absence of theoretical foundations for industrial development notwithstanding, Argentina, Brazil, and Chile had made rapid industrial advances in the 1920s. But after 1929 they faced a sustained crisis in export markets (the dollar value of Argentina's exports in 1933, for example, was one-third the 1929 figure); and despite the importance of industrialization in the 1920s, the following decade can still be understood as a period of significant structural and institutional change. In Argentina, Brazil, Chile and Mexico, convertibility and the gold standard were abandoned early in the Depression. The rise in prices of importables, because of a fall in the terms of trade and exchange devaluation, encouraged the substitution of domestic manufactures for imported goods, as did expansionary fiscal and monetary policies. By 1935 a North American economist would hazard that 'There is probably no major section of the world in which there is a greater industrial activity relative to pre-depression years than in temperate South America', that

[11] Siciliano, cited in Pupo Nogueira, *Em torno,* pp. 133; 3, 131 (on Manoilescu); Siciliano, *Agricultura,* pp. 12, 62; Simonsen, *Crises,* p. 58.

[12] In the debate between Simonsen and Eugênio Gudin on planning in 1945, it was Gudin, not Simonsen, who referred to Manoilescu, viewing him as a discredited charlatan. Roberto Simonsen and Eugênio Gudin, *A controvérsia do planejamento na economia brasileira* (Rio de Janeiro, 1977), pp. 108–9.

[13] Congresso Brasileiro de Indústria, *Anais* (São Paulo, 1945), I, pp. 225–6. What the Brazilian industrialist expected and received from Vargas was government control of the labour movement, in exchange for their acceptance of welfare legislation for workers.

is, Argentina, southern Brazil, and Chile.[14] When war came in 1939, manufactures in international trade became scarce again, permitting futher industrialization to the extent that capital goods, fuel, and raw materials were available.

During the 1930s spokesmen for industry probably grew bolder, except perhaps those Brazilians who had initially followed Manoilescu. Note, for example, the themes chosen by Luis Colombo, the president of the Unión Industrial Argentina. In 1931, he supported a moderate and 'rational' protectionism, and defended the manufacturers against the charge of promoting policies inimical to the interests of Argentine consumers; in 1933, he even-handedly justified protection for both industry and agriculture; and by 1940 he was attacking the industrial countries as having themselves violated the rules of the international division of labour by developing large agricultural establishments, only choosing to buy abroad when convenient.[15] Industrialists pointed to the vulnerability of export-economies, which they more frequently dubbed 'colonial' than before. Gathering war clouds in Europe added another argument: domestic industries were necessary for an adequate national defence.[16] A basic characteristic of the period 1930–45 was an intensification of state intervention in the economy, in Latin America as elsewhere, and industrialists like other economic groups sought state assistance; they asked for subsidies, credits, and increased tariff protection. The state should, they argued, aid in 'economic rationalization', that is, cartelization, a theme of European industrialists in the thirties.[17]

In Argentina, Brazil, Chile, and Mexico, governments began to heed the importuning of manufacturers. State aid to industry in the form of development loans tended to converge in the early years of the war. The establishment of industrial development banks was an important symbolic act, as we shall see, but changes in tariff structures, which have not so far been thoroughly analysed, may have been more important for growth. The

14 D. M. Phelps, 'Industrial Expansion in Temperate South America', *American Economic Review,* 25 (1935): 281.

15 See Colombo's speeches in *Anales de la Unión Industrial Argentina,* año 44 (December, 1931), pp. 25, 27; ibid., año 46 (July, 1993), p. 37; *Argentina Fabril,* año 53 (Jan., 1940), p. 3.

16 Unión Industrial Argentina, *Revista,* año 57 [sic] (May, 1946), p. 9. Alvarez Andrews, *Historia,* pp. 6, 328, 348; 'Necesitamos una política económica de industrialización' [editorial], *Revista de Economía y Finanzas* (Peru), 16, 92 (August, 1940), p. 128.

17 Alvarez Andrews, *Historia,* pp. 327–8, 385; Pupo Nogueira, 'A propósito da modernização de uma grande indústria', *Revista Industrial de São Paulo,* año 1,6 (May, 1945), p. 18; 'Industrialización', [editorial], *Revista Económica* (Mexico, D. F.), 8, 10 (October, 1945), p. 6. In 1942, Enrique Zañartu Prieto defended 'autarky' in Chile, but in vague terms. See his *Tratado de economía política,* 2nd edn, (Santiago, 1946), p. 243.

reasons for such a shift by governments are clear in retrospect: a decade of wrestling with the intractable problem of reviving traditional export markets; the relative unavailability of foreign industrial goods over virtually a fifteen-year period (1930–45); and the fact that states (and particularly the officer corps) as well as industrialists began to consider the relation between manufacturing and national defence – a process that had already begun in Chile in the late twenties.

Governments, however, moved hesitantly and inconsistently toward addressing the problems of industry. In Argentina, Luis Duhau, the Minister of Agriculture, in 1933 proclaimed the necessity of producing industrial goods that could no longer be imported (for lack of foreign exchange), and he pledged his government's support for the process.[18] But in the same month the Argentine government supported the U.S. initiative for general tariff reductions at the Pan American Union Conference in Montevideo. Earlier that year Argentina had yielded to British pressure in the Roca-Runciman pact, a trade agreement favouring British manufactures in the Argentine market in exchange for a share of the British beef market for Argentina. As late as 1940, Finance Minister Pinedo's plan for the economic development of Argentina still distinguished between 'natural' and 'artificial' industries, implying that industrial development would occur in concert with the needs of the agricultural and pastoral sectors. By the time of the colonels' coup in June 1943, intervention for industrial development had become state policy, and an industrial development bank was created in 1944. Yet even at that point support for manufacturing was far from unrestrained: the ministry of agriculture still housed the department of industry, and the minister assured Argentinians that the development of manufacturing would not threaten, but would contribute to the growth of the country's 'mother industries', stockraising and agriculture.[19] In the next few years, however, the Perón government would demonstrably put the interests of industrialists above those of ranchers and farmers.

In Brazil, Getúlio Vargas favoured industry – was he not the friend of all established economic interests? – but he had opposed 'artificial' industries (that is, manufacturing) in his presidential campaign in 1930. Government loans to 'artificial' industries were still prohibited in 1937. Osvaldo Aranha, Vargas's Minister of Finance in 1933, even termed industries

[18] 'The Argentine Industrial Exhibition', *Review of the River Plate*, 22 (December, 1933), pp. 11, 13, 15.

[19] Diego Masón, Introduction to Mariano Abarca, *La industrialización de la Argentina* (Buenos Aires, 1944), p. 5.

'fictitious' if they did not use at least 70 per cent domestic raw materials.[20] Vargas only became committed to rapid industrial expansion during his Estado Novo dictatorship (1937–45). Although he said in 1939 that he could not accept the idea of Brazil's remaining a 'semi-colonial' economy, as late as 1940, when the coffee market was still depressed after a decade of attempts to revive it, Vargas wanted to 'balance' industrial and agricultural growth. In 1941 a division for industrial development of the Bank of Brazil began to make significant loans, but from 1941 through 1945 the Bank only disbursed an annual average of 17.5 per cent of its private sector loans to manufacturing concerns.[21] In Mexico, industrialization in the 1930s made impressive advances even while agrarian reform was at the top of Lázaro Cárdenas' agenda. It was not, however, the result of government policy. Nacional Financiera, a partly government-owned development bank, had been established in 1934, but only became seriously committed to manufacturing after its reorganization at the end of 1940, when the new pro-industry administration of Avila Camacho took office. During the Second World War, the pace quickened.[22] In Chile, nominal government support for industrial development began with the creation of an Institute of Industrial Credit in 1928. Ten years later the Popular Front government of Pedro Aguirre Cerda established Corporación de Fomento de la Producción, the government development corporation. But in 1940 the sum budgeted for the development of manufacturing was less than each of those for agriculture, mining, energy and public housing.[23]

All the same, government attitudes were changing, as were the views of economists both inside and outside Latin America. Even the economists of the League of Nations, champions of free trade in the twenties and thirties, had begun to doubt the advisability of full agricultural specialization

[20] Getúlio Vargas, *A nova política do Brasil,* I (Rio de Janeiro, 1938), pp. 26–7; *O Estado de São Paulo,* 8 March 1933.

[21] Getúlio Vargas, *A nova política,* VI (Rio de Janeiro, 1940), p. 91; VIII (Rio de Janeiro, 1941), p. 179; Annibal Villela and Wilson Suzigan, *Política do governo e crescimento da economia brasileira: 1889–1945* (Rio de Janeiro, 1973), p. 352.

[22] Stephen Haber, *Industrialization and Underdevelopment: The Industrialization of Mexico, 1890–1940* (Stanford, Cal., 1989), pp. 176–7; René Villareal, *El desequilibrio externo en la industrialización de México (1929–75): um enfoque estructuralista* (Mexico, D.F. 1976), pp. 43–5; Calvin S. Blair, 'Nacional Financiera: Entrepreneurship in a Mixed Economy', in Raymond Vernon (ed.) *Public Policy and Private Enterprise in Mexico* (Cambridge, Mass., 1964), pp. 210, 213; Rafael Izquierdo, 'Protectionism in Mexico', in ibid., p. 243; Alfredo Navarrete R., 'The Financing of Economic Development', in Enrique Pérez López et al., *Mexico's Recent Economic Growth: The Mexican View,* trans. Marjory Urquidi (Austin, Tex., 1967), p. 119.

[23] Presidente de la República [de Chile, Pedro Aguirre Cerda], *Mensaje . . . en la apertura . . . del Congreso Nacional 21 de Mayo de 1940* (Santiago, 1940), pp. 21–2, 95.

for the world's poorer countries. As early as 1937, the League's economic section stated a preference for a modicum of industrialization for agricultural countries, on the practical ground that factor flows remained substantially blocked, seven years after the onset of depression. A League study at the end of the War argued that the poorer agricultural countries had to industrialize to some degree, because of their lack of sufficient agricultural surpluses 'to ensure them a plentiful supply of imported manufactures'.[24]

In 1943 Paul Rosenstein-Rodan, in a article often considered the point of departure for modern development theory, called for the industrialization of agrarian countries, as did the trade theorist Charles Kindleberger. At a policy level, the Hot Springs conference of the Allied Nations the same year favoured a degree of industrialization for the 'backward' countries. More boldly, the economist Colin Clark had written in 1942 that future equilibrium in world trade depended on the willingness of Europe and the United States 'to accept a large flow of . . . exports of manufactured goods' from India and China.[25]

The somewhat 'unintended' industrialization of the larger Latin American countries and a partial acceptance of it by United States government was reflected at the Chapultepec conference of the Pan American Union (1945). The meeting's resolutions gave a qualified benediction to the industrialization process in Latin America.[26] At the end of war, therefore, it was clear that industrialization had greatly advanced in Latin America; the process was characteristically import-substitution industrialization (ISI) – the replacement of imported goods with domestic manufactures, based on existing patterns of demand. Economists in several countries were noting the trend and searching for a theory to legitimate it.[27] That theory – and concomitant policies – would be provided by the United Nation's Economic Commission for Latin America in the years immediately after the Second World War.

[24] S[ergei] Prokopovicz, *L'industrialisation des pays agricoles et la structure de l'économie mondiale après la guerre,* trans. N. Nicolsky (Neuchatel, 1946), p. 276; League of Nations: Economic, Financial and Transit Department, *Industrialization and Foreign Trade* (N.p., 1945), p. 34.

[25] Paul Rosenstein-Rodan, 'Problems of Industrialization of Eastern and Southeastern Europe', in A. N. Agarwala and S. P. Singh (eds) *The Economics of Underdevelopment* (London, 1958 [orig., 1943]) pp. 246, 253–4; Charles Kindleberger, 'Planning for foreign investment', *American Economic Review,* 33, 1 (March, 1943), Supplement: 347–54; Prokopovicz, *L'industrialisation,* 278–9; Colin Clark, *The Economics of 1960* (London, 1942), p. 114.

[26] *Revista Económica* (Mexico, D. F.), 8, 1–2 (28 February 1945): 30.

[27] Sergio Bagú, '¿Y mañana, Qué?', *Revista de Economía* (Mexico, D. F.), 7, 5–6 (30 June 1944): 37; Heitor Ferreira Lima, "Evolução industrial de São Paulo', *Revista Industrial de São Paulo,* ano 1, 7 (June, 1945), p. 17; 'Monetary Developments in Latin America', *Federal Reserve Bulletin,* 31, 6 (June, 1945), p. 523; Gonzalo Robles, 'Sudamérica y el fomento industrial', *Trimestre Económico,* 14, 1 (April–June, 1947), p. 1.

PREBISCH AND CENTRE-PERIPHERY

The Economic Commission for Latin America was dominated in its early years by the ideas, personality, and programmes of Raúl Prebisch. We must therefore consider Prebisch's early career and formative experiences during the Depression of the 1930s and war years to learn how the ECLA theses of 1949 crystallized, for much of Prebisch's reasoning was apparently based on empirical observation and learning from failed policies.

Born in the city of Tucumán in 1901, Prebisch studied at the University of Buenos Aires, whose Department (Facultad) of Economics at the time was probably the best school for economic theory in Latin America.[28] Prebisch gave early promise of a distinguished career within Argentina's economic establishment. At the age of twenty he published his first professional study in economics. In 1923, upon completing a master's degree in that discipline, he was asked to join the staff at the University.[29] Although Prebisch the student was an assistant of Alejandro Bunge, the foremost promoter of Argentine industrialization in his day, the young man's career followed the more direct route of success, in an early and intimate association with the leaders of the pastoral industry. In 1922, that is, before Prebisch's graduation, Enrique Uriburu, on behalf of the elite Sociedad Rural Argentina, the powerful stockbreeders' association, appointed the young man director of the Sociedad Rural's statistical office. Two years later the Sociedad Rural sent Prebisch to Australia, where he studied statistical methods related to stockraising, and where, presumably, he also obtained a broader perspective on Argentina's position in the international economy.[30] By 1925 he was both a teacher at the University and an official in the Argentine government's Department of Statistics. In 1927 he published a Sociedad Rural-sponsored study that became the basis for government action on behalf of stockbreeders in the foreign meat market.[31]

Leaders of the Sociedad Rural were apparently impressed by the need for

28 In 1918, Luis Gondra introduced South America's first course in mathematical economics at the University of Buenos Aires. Luis Gondra et al., *El pensamiento económico latinoamericano* (México, D. F., 1945), p. 32.

29 Raúl Prebisch, 'Planes para estabilizar el poder adquisitivo de la moneda', Universidad Nacional de Buenos Aires: Facultad de Ciencias Económicas (hereafter UBA: FCE), *Investigaciones de Seminario,* II (Buenos Aires, 1921), pp. 459–513; interview of Prebisch by author, Washington, D.C., 10 July 1978.

30 Prebisch, 'Planes', p. 459 (on Bunge); Prebisch, *Anotaciones demográficas a propósito de los movimientos de la población* (Buenos Aires, 1926), p. 3.

31 Prebisch's study offered statistical proof that the meat pool's interference in the market had been beneficial for the British packing-houses, but not for the Argentine cattlemen. See Raúl Prebisch, 'El régimen de pool en el comercio de carnes', *Revista de Ciencias Económicas* (hereafter RCE) 15 (December, 1927): 1302–21.

good statistical data, by the need for economic analysis, and by Prebisch. In 1928 he was again working part time for the Sociedad Rural, compiling a statistical yearbook for the organization. Thus, from the outset of his career, Prebisch was interested in policy issues, set in the context of the international trading system. In 1928 he launched the publication of the *Revista Económica,* the organ of the government-directed Banco de la Nación Argentina, for which Prebisch established a research division.[32] The journal was concerned not only with pressing monetary matters, but also with the problems of stockraising, agriculture, and international trade – not with theoretical issues in economics.

In the early 1930s Prebisch served as an economic advisor to the Argentine government's ministries of finance and agriculture, and proposed the creation of a central bank (with powers to control interest rates and the money supply) to the government of General José Uriburu, who had seized power in 1930. After several years of study and parliamentary debate, in 1935 the Banco Central became the nation's first true central bank, and from its inception until 1943, Prebisch served as its Director-General. In addition, the Bank functioned as the government's economic 'brain trust', as a member of Prebisch's group put it.[33] In many respects, Prebisch and his colleagues in the 1930s were treading in theoretical terra incognita. Before the Depression of the 1930s it was considered axiomatic that Argentina had prospered according to the theory of comparative advantage. The benefits of export-led growth, based on an international division of labour, made comparative advantage a near-sacrosant doctrine.

The twenties were a period of disequilibrium as well as expansion in world trade, and though Argentina prospered, the country experienced the same problems as a number of other primary-producing nations in the final years before the October 1929 crash – namely, falling export prices, rising stocks, and debt-payment difficulties. Argentina and Uruguay were, in fact, the first nations in the world to abandon the gold standard in the Depression – before the end of 1929. Following Britain's departure

[32] Banco de la Nación Argentina, *Economic Review,* 1, 1 (August, 1928): 2. Duhau, the president of the Sociedad Rural, had a hand in these events as a member of the Bank's governing board: Interview of Ernesto Malaccorto by Leandro Gutiérrez, Buenos Aires, Aug. 1971 (Inst. Torcuato di Tella), p. 7 [copy at Columbia University, Oral History Collection].

[33] *Who's Who in the United Nations and Related Agencies* (New York, 1975), pp. 455–56; Raúl Prebisch, "Versión taquigráfica de la conferencia de prensa . . . 15 de noviembre de 1955', pp. 23–4 (Prebisch file, Economic Commission for Latin America (hereafter ECLA), Santiago, Chile); Carlos F. Díaz-Alejandro, *Essays on the Economic History of the Argentine Republic* (New Haven, Conn., 1970), p. 97; Banco Central de la República Argentina, *La creación del Banco Central y la experiencia monetaria argentina entre los años 1935–1943* (Buenos Aires, 1972), 1: 267 *et seq.;* Malaccorto interview, p. 40 ('brain trust').

from the gold standard, in October 1931 Argentine authorities introduced exchange controls to try to stem the outflow of capital and facilitate the repayment of loans negotiated in hard currencies. Prebisch later wrote that 'Exchange control was not the result of a theory but was imposed by circumstances'.[34] The Depression thus brought the abandonment of many hallowed economic doctrines and practices.

In the crisis, Great Britain exploited her monopsonistic position against her many suppliers. As a rule she attempted to purchase less abroad, and thereby got her imports cheaper. In the case of Argentina, Britain's trading power was magnified by the South American nation's loss of dollar investments. The United States had become a major supplier to Argentina in the mid-1920s, but Argentina had chronic difficulties in paying directly for U.S. imports with her own non-complementary exports. Therefore Argentina had depended on U.S. capital exports, but during the Depression, North American lenders disinvested in Argentina. Excluded from the U.S. market by high tariffs and other regulations, and cut off from continental markets as well in the early thirties, Argentina feared above all the loss of British market; indeed, it was already partly closed by the Ottawa Conference agreement (1932) among Great Britain and her dominions, several of which were Argentina's export competitors. Britain's trading power was further enhanced by the fact that in these years she bought much more from Argentina than she sold to that country. In the four years 1930–33, Britain took over 40 per cent of Argentina's exports, but supplied only about 20 per cent of Argentina's imports.

Consequently, Argentine statesmen and government economists – among them Raúl Prebisch – were willing to enter into the Roca–Runciman Pact of 1933, an arrangement more to Britain's advantage than Argentina's, whereby the United Kingdom agreed to keep up a certain level of meat purchases in exchange for regular debt service payments and tariff reductions for British manufactures. Thus beef exports, the traditional preserve of the Argentine oligarchy, were favoured over wheat. A bilateral agreement in 1936 was even more favourable to British interests. After war broke out in 1939, the British government played its monopsonistic position to yet greater advantage, in negotiations between the Bank of England and Argentina's Central Bank, led by Raúl Prebisch. One can easily surmise that Argentina's protracted and notorious dependency on her major trading

[34] ECLA, *The Economic Development of Latin America and its Principal Problems* (Lake Success, N.Y., 1950), p. 29.

partner left a lasting impression on Prebisch. Furthermore, the Argentine government made great sacrifices to retain its credit rating by paying its debts; perhaps Argentine statesmen were overly influenced by the manifest success, before the Depression, of export-driven growth.[35]

The Depression of the 1930s not only brought about bilateral negotiations, but a series of international economic meetings as well. In 1933 Prebisch, as an invitee of the Council of the League of Nations, attended a gathering of the Preparatory Committee of the Second International Monetary Conference in Geneva. From Switzerland Prebisch reported to the *Revista Económica* that the assembled monetary experts believed that one basic blockage in the international economic system derived from the facts that the United States had replaced Great Britain as the world's chief creditor country, and that high American tariff schedules (especially the Smoot-Hawley Act of 1930) did not permit other countries to repay U.S. loans with exports. Consequently, the rest of the world tended to send gold to the United States, and the bullion was not recirculated in the international monetary system.[36] Prebisch soon went to London to help negotiate the Roca–Runciman Pact as a technical advisor. Later in 1933, he attended the World Monetary Conference in the same city. But the Conference broke up in failure, and the tendency toward bilateralism in world trade continued.

In Argentina, Prebisch sought to understand another vexing problem wrought by Depression – declining terms of trade. In 1934 he published an article pointing out that 'agricultural prices have fallen more profoundly than those of manufactured goods', and that in 1933 Argentina had to sell 73 per cent more than before the Depression to obtain the same quantity of (manufactured) imports. In the same article Prebisch attacked as 'scholastic' the orthodox equilibrium theories of his senior colleague at the University of Buenos Aires, Professor Luis Gondra, because such doctrines ignored the stubborn fact of sustained depression.[37]

[35] On the Argentine economy in the 1930s, see Javier Villanueva, 'Economic Development', in Mark Falcoff and Ronald H. Dolkart (eds), *Prologue to Perón: Argentina in Depression and War: 1930–1943* (Berkeley, Cal., 1975), pp. 57–82; Jorge Fodor and Arturo A. O'Connell, 'La Argentina y la economía atlántica en la primera mitad del siglo XX', *Desarrollo Económico,* 13, 9 (April–June, 1973); Vicente Vásquez-Presedo, *Crisis y retraso: Argentina y la economía internacional entre las dos guerras* (Buenos Aires, 1978).

[36] Prebisch, "La conferencia económica y la crisis mundial, in [Banco de la Nación Argentina], *Revista Económica* 6, 1 (January, 1933), pp. 1, 3. Another reason for U.S. absorption of the world's gold supply was the overvaluation of the pound sterling, when Britain returned to the gold standard in 1925.

[37] Prebisch, 'La inflación escolástica y la moneda argentina', *Revista de Economía Argentina,* año 17, 193 (July 1934), pp. 11–12; 194 (August, 1934), p. 60. Later it was discovered that the purchasing

Prebisch was a member of an economic 'team' groping with the crisis, and recent research has emphasized that the policies of Federico Pinedo (Finance Minister, 1933–5 and 1940–1) and his collaborators, including Prebisch, involved extensive governmental intervention in the economy; such innovation occurred despite the oligarchic political cast of the regime from 1930 to 1943 (the 'infamous decade' of political history).[38] Not only did the state reform the monetary and banking system through the creation of a central bank and the introduction of exchange controls, but it also intervened in the processing and marketing of Argentina's main exports, that is, beef and grain. This novel and vigorous activity by the state may have had corporatist sources of inspiration or not, but in the endeavour Argentina was clearly in step with her neo-protectionist trading partner, Great Britain.

The return of severe depression in 1937–8, a problem originating in the United States, had its major spread effects in the less developed agricultural- and mineral-exporting areas of the world, because Europe and Japan were 'pump priming' through their armaments programmes. Wheat was one of the commodities for which prices fell sharply in 1937.[39] As other countries introduced new trade controls, so did Argentina, in 1938, in the form of quantitative restrictions on imports. In the next two years, Argentina's banking officials, among them Raúl Prebisch, were trying to keep international credits and debts in balance 'in the strictest short-run sense'. Thus trade policy was not yet consciously used to foster industrialization.[40]

Yet manufacturing in Argentina grew impressively in the 1930s and early 1940s, a fact which was recognized by contemporaries at home and abroad. In particular, the Central Bank's *Revista Económica* noted an increase in output of 85 per cent (by value) between the industrial census of 1913 and that of 1934–5.[41] In its annual report for 1942 (published in 1943), the Bank followed through on its changing economic emphases by

power of Argentina's exports fell by about 40 per cent between 1925–9 and 1930–4. Between these two periods the capital flow was also temporarily reversed, so in 1930–4 Argentina's capacity to import fell to 46 per cent of what it had been in the preceding five years. Aldo Ferrer, *The Argentine Economy,* trans Marjory M. Urquidi (Berkeley, Cal., 1967), p. 162.

38 On Raúl Prebisch's role, see interview of Federico Pinedo by Luis Alberto Romero, Buenos Aires, June 1971 (Inst. Torcuato di Tella), esp. pp. 64–7 [copy at Columbia University, Oral History Collection].

39 Charles P. Kindleberger, *The World Depression: 1929–1939* (London, 1973), pp. 278–9.

40 Walter Beveraggi-Allende, 'Argentine foreign trade under exchange control' (Ph.D thesis, Harvard University, 1952), p. 219 (quotation), p. 246; Malaccorto interview, p. 64.

41 Phelps, 'Industrial Expansion', p. 274; *Economic Review* [Eng. tr. of *Revista Económica*], series 2, 1, no. 1 (1937): 69.

championing industrialization. The report, reflecting Prebisch's views, argued that exports and industrial development were by no means incompatible; rather, the issue was to change the composition of imports from consumer to capital goods.[42]

Prebisch the policy-maker interests us less than Prebisch the emerging economic theorist, though the two can hardly be separated. In the latter capacity he was beginning to formulate a theory of unequal exchange by 1937. In that year the *Revista Económica* noted that agricultural production was inelastic compared to industrial output, and that its products' prices tended to rise and fall faster than industrial prices in the trade cycle. The *Revista* also noted the related problem of the lack of organization of agricultural producers, and concluded: 'In the last depression these differences manifested themselves in a sharp fall in agricultural prices and in a much smaller decline in the prices of manufactured articles. The agrarian countries lost part of their purchasing power, with the resultant effect on the balance of payments and on the volume of their imports.'[43] The emphasis was thus on the elasticity of supply of industrial production, and implicitly on monopoly, and not on wage contracts in the industrial countries, which was later to be a focal point of Prebisch's analysis.

In the same comment the *Revista* noted that Argentina's industrial complex made its greatest gains in two periods, the First World War, and during 'the world wide recrudescensce of the policy of economic self-sufficiency during the years 1929–1936'.[44] Thus Prebisch seemed to be considering the possibility that export-led growth was no longer a viable path to economic development.

Prebisch was also intensely interested in the trade cycle in Argentina. The Central Bank began its effort to conduct counter-cyclical monetary policy in 1937, by decreasing the public's purchasing power through the sale of bonds in that boom year; in the following period of contraction, it would attempt to expand purchasing power by lowering the rediscount rate.[45] In 1939, in its annual report for the previous year, the Central Bank – representing Prebisch's thinking on the matter – argued that the nation's trade cycles were primarily a reflection of those of its principal (industrialized) trading partners. It held that Argentina's internal credit expansion began with an export surplus, which led to additional demand for foreign goods, because of exporters' high propensities to import; when

42 Banco Central de la República Argentina, *Memoria . . . 1942* (Buenos Aires, 1943), pp. 30–31.
43 *Economic Review*, series 2, 1, 1 (1937): 26–7.
44 Ibid., p. 69.
45 Rafael Olarra Jiménez, *Evolución monetaria argentina* (Buenos Aires, 1968), p. 13.

combined with heavy import requirements, the process repeatedly produced a balance-of-payments crisis in the national business cycle.[46]

After his dismissal from the Central Bank in 1943, apparently because the coup makers associated him with the ranching oligarchy, Prebisch began to read widely in the recent economic literature.[47] Returning for the moment to teaching, he prepared a series of lectures in 1944 in which he referred, for the first time, to 'Centre' and 'Periphery', terms he would later make famous.

Prebisch developed a historical argument, with Britain as the nineteenth-century 'Centre' of the trading and monetary systems based on the gold standard. (Clearly, this was a better model for the first half of the century than the second half, but Britain as Centre for the whole period fit Argentina's situation well enough.) Under Britain's leadership as the cycle-generating Centre, Prebisch argued, the world's economic system had equilibrated gold flows and the balance of payments over the course of the cycle for both Centre and Periphery. 'Gold tended to leave Great Britain, the Center of the system, and to enter countries of the Periphery in the upswing of the cycle'. Then it returned in the downswing. A problem for peripheral countries was that when gold departed in the downswing, 'there was no way to diminish the gold flow except by contracting credit . . . No one could conceive of . . . the possibility of raising the rediscount rate in competition with the monetary Center in London'. Thus overall monetary stability was only maintained at the cost of economic contraction of the 'Periphery'. 'The gold standard was therefore an automatic system for the countries of the Periphery, but not for the Center', where the rediscount rate could be adjusted for domestic needs. In the Periphery, the gold standard had the effect of exaggerating rather than offsetting the cycle.[48]

Passing on to the post-First World years, Prebisch concluded that New York bankers in the 1920s and 1930s did not have the knowledge or experience of the 'British financial oligarchy', though of course the world situation was dramatically different after the War. By 1930 the United States had sucked up the world's gold. Consequently, 'the rest of the world, including our country, [is] forced to seek a means of inward-directed development (*crecer hacia adentro*)'[49] – a phrase that ECLA would later make famous.

[46] Banco Central, *Memoria . . . 1938* (Buenos Aires, 1939), pp. 5–8; Prebisch to author, Washington, D.C., 9 November 1977.

[47] Prebisch interview.

[48] Prebisch, 'La moneda y los ciclos económicos en la Argentina' [class notes by assistant, approved by Prebisch], 1944, pp. 61–5, mimeo. [Located at UBA: FCE.]

[49] Ibid., p. 65.

The Argentine business cycle, Prebisch continued, had depended on exogenous factors operating through the balance of payments. In the upswing, exports and foreign investment produced an influx of gold and exchange credits, creating new money and therefore imports. Such changes also expanded credit to agricultural industries; but because of inelastic supply, during the downswing, credit was immobilized in the rural sector. Additional imports were paid for with reserves, producing a monetary crisis.[50]

In seeking a solution to Argentina's problems, Prebisch began to think in more general terms about Latin America and its relation with the United States; his first concern in that area had involved the previously mentioned plan in 1940 – probably drafted by Prebisch, but presented to Congress by Finance Minister Pinedo – to link the Argentine economy to the United States and to expanding Latin American markets, in part by exporting manufactures.[51]

Freed from his duties at the Central Bank, Prebisch was twice in Mexico during the mid-forties at the invitation of Mexico's central bank (Banco de México). On both occasions he participated in international meetings: once in 1944 at a gathering of intellectuals from Latin America at the Colegio de México on problems the region would face in the post-war era,[52] and again in Mexico City at an inter-American meeting of central bankers in 1946.

Prebisch's interest in industrialization as a solution to Latin America's economic problems originally arose from the desire, shared by many Argentine contemporaries, to make Argentina less economically 'vulnerable', a vulnerability painfully evident for the whole period 1930–45. As noted above, the Argentine Central Bank, under Prebisch's leadership, had begun to advocate industrialization in its 1942 report. By implication Prebisch was recommending similar policies to other Latin American governments in his Colegio de México lecture of 1944.[53] In his 'Conversations' at the Banco de México in the same year, Prebisch again noted that the period of greatest industrial development in Argentina had been the

[50] Summary of 'La moneda', in Olarra Jiménez, *Evolución,* p. 76.

[51] See Javier Villanueva, 'Economic Development', in Falcoff and Dolkart, (eds), *Prologue to Perón,* p. 78. On Prebisch as probable author of the Pinedo plan, see Díaz-Alejandro, *Essays,* p. 105, note 37.

[52] At the same time Prebisch gave a series of lectures at the Banco de México on 'the Argentine monetary experience (1935–1943)', that is, covering the period in which he was the Director-General of the Central Bank. See Banco Central, *La creación,* 1:249–588; 2:599–623.

[53] Raúl Prebisch, 'El patrón oro y la vulnerabilidad económica de nuestros países' [a lecture at the Colegio de México], *Revista de Ciencias Económicas,* año 32, serie 2, no.272 (March, 1944), p. 234; Banco Central, *Memoria . . . 1942,* p. 30.

Great Depression and the times of war, periods in which the nation had to produce for itself what it could not import.[54] Later, ECLA theorists would explore the implications of this observation, as they elaborated the concept of 'inward-directed development'.

In a 1944 article in Mexico's *Trimestre Económico,* Prebisch noted that the United States, unlike Argentina, had a low propensity to import (defined as the change in the value of imports generated by a given change in the national product). Since other countries, he implied, had high propensities to import, and the U.S. had replaced Britain as the chief industrial trading partner of the Latin American states, Prebisch expanded on the League experts' argument in 1933, and warned that the postwar international trading system faced the danger of permanent disequilibrium.[55]

Prebisch first used the terminology 'Center-Periphery' in print in 1946, at the second meeting mentioned above, that of the hemisphere's central bankers, who convened at the invitation of the Banco de México. Prebisch now identified the United States as the 'cyclical Center' and Latin America as the 'Periphery of the economic system'. The emphasis, as indicated, was on the trade cycle, whose rhythms the U.S. economy set for the whole international system. Fiscal and monetary authorities in the United States could pursue a policy of full employment without producing monetary instability, Prebisch argued; furthermore, such authorities did not need to be especially concerned about the impact of full employment policies on the exchange rate of the dollar in other currencies. By contrast, Prebisch asserted, the nations of the Periphery could not apply the same monetary tools as the Centre did. Extrapolating from his 1944 argument with reference to Argentina, Prebisch contended that the money supply in peripheral countries not be expanded in pursuit of full employment, because, with a high propensity to import, any expansion of income would quickly exhaust foreign exchange, assuming devaluation.

This 1946 statement and previous writings of Prebisch implied that peripheral countries faced three options, all with undesirable consequences; they could have strong currencies and maintain high levels of imports at the cost of high unemployment; they could fight unemployment with an expansionary monetary policy, but would thereby create

[54] Raúl Prebisch, 'Análisis de la experiencia monetaria argentina (1935–1943)', in Banco Central, *La creación,* 1, p. 407. See the similar judgements by Adolfo Dorfman, *Evolución industrial argentina* (Buenos Aires, 1942), p. 74 (on First World War and Great Depression); Heitor Ferreira Lima, 'Evolução industrial', p. 17 (on São Paulo, Second World War).

[55] Raúl Prebisch, 'Observaciones sobre los planes monetarios internacionales', *Trimestre Económico,* 11, 2 (July–September, 1944), pp. 188, 192–3.

inflation and put pressure on the exchange rate, thus raising the cost of repaying foreign debts; or, if they used monetary policy to maintain high levels of employment, but failed to devalue, their reserves would disappear. When prices of the Periphery's products fell during the downswing of the cycle, furthermore, governments of peripheral countries, at least in isolation, could not affect world prices for their goods as the Centre could for its goods. Thus equilibrium theories in international trade were not acceptable.[56] This was an assault on the policy prescriptions of neo-classical economics. Prebisch's message in Mexico City was in tune with the pessimism then prevailing in Latin America regarding international trade as a long-term engine of growth. Even the improving terms of trade of the early post-war years was widely viewed as transient.

In the classroom in Buenos Aires in 1948, Prebisch specifically attacked the theory of comparative advantage, and noted that its precepts were repeatedly violated by the industrialized nations, whose economists none the less used neo-classical trade theory as an ideological weapon. He also implied that industrial countries acted as monopolists against agricultural countries in the trading process. Prebisch then asserted that historically, in both the United States and Britain, technological progress did not result in a decrease in prices, but in an increase in wages. 'The fruit of technical progress tended to remain in Great Britain' in the nineteenth century; yet because Britain had sacrificed its agriculture, part of the benefits of technological progress had been transferred to the 'new countries' in the form of higher land values. Britain's nineteenth-century import co-efficient (defined as the value of imports divided by real income) was estimated by Prebisch as 30–35 per cent, whereas that of the United States in the 1930s was only about 5 per cent. All of this implied a blockage to growth for the agricultural-exporting Periphery under the new largely self-sufficient Centre.[57]

This Centre-Periphery framework implied a single system, hegemonically organized.[58] To appreciate the significance of the concept, we should

[56] Raúl Prebisch, 'Panorama general de los problemas de regulación monetaria y crediticia en el continente americano: A. América Latina', in Banco de México, *Memoria: Primera reunión de técnicos sobre problemas de banca central del continente americano* (Mexico, D. F., 1946), pp. 25–8; 'Observaciones', p. 199.

[57] Raúl Prebisch, 'Apuntes de economía política (Dinámica económica)' [class notes], 1948, pp. 88–97 (quotation on 97), mimeo. [Located at UBA: FCE]

[58] Though the term 'hegemony' did not appear in this early use of Centre-Periphery terminology, Prebisch himself, years later, would specifically employ the word to characterize relations between the two elements of the world economy. Prebisch, 'A Critique of Peripheral Capitalism,' *CEPAL Review*, January–June 1976, p. 60.

bear in mind that the idea that there was something fundamentally different about the economies of the underdeveloped areas was still novel in the 1940s. The concept of 'underdevelopment' as a syndrome was only elaborated in that decade, chiefly after the creation of specialized United Nations agencies in 1947–48. The euphemisms 'developing countries' and 'less developed countries' were still in the future.[59] While a few Marxists and others preferred to employ 'backward' rather than 'underdeveloped', even 'backward' among these non-Centre-Periphery terms did not in itself imply hegemony; nor did 'backward' necessarily put the central emphasis on the international capitalist system. Rather, such a term could imply that the problem was largely one of the leads and lags – the modernization thesis in its ahistorical setting.

Despite the fact that some of the key ideas of Prebisch's later analysis were set forth in international meetings in 1944 and 1946, there were no discussions on these occasions of an Economic Commission for Latin America, the U.N. agency that was subsequently to be Prebisch's principal theoretical and ideological vehicle. Rather, it resulted from a Chilean initiative in 1947 at U.N. headquarters in Lake Success, New York. The agency was approved by the U.N. Economic and Social Council in February 1948, and ECLA held its first meeting in Santiago, Chile, in June of that year. Alberto Baltra Cortés, the Chilean Minister of the Economy, presided at the occasion. At the opening session Baltra, who was familiar with Prebisch's ideas, stressed Latin America's need to industrialize, an attitude to which representatives of the United States and the European colonial powers professed not to object. For the future of ECLA, or at least its most famous thesis, the chief outcome of the meeting was a resolution calling for a study of Latin America's terms of trade.[60]

Without Prebisch's leadership, ECLA was not yet ECLA. His personality, theses, and programmes so dominated the agency in its formative phase that it stood in sharp relief to the Economic Commission for Asia and the Far East (established in 1947) and the Economic Commission for Africa (1958), agencies with more purely technical orientations. The year of ECLA's founding, 1948, seemed propitious for obtaining Prebisch's services: in Juan Perón's Argentina he was excluded from official posts,

[59] See Gunnar Myrdal, 'Diplomacy by Terminology', in *An Approach to the Asian Drama: Methodological and Theoretical* (New York, 1970), pp. 35–6.

[60] UN ECOSOC E/CN.12/17 (7 June 1948), p. 2; E/CN.12/28 (11 June 1948), p. 6; E/CN.12/71 (24 June 1948).

perhaps because of his long and close association with the nation's traditional economic elite. Meanwhile, his reputation as an economist in Latin America had been enhanced by the publication in Mexico of his *Introducción a Keynes* (1947).

Prebisch in fact turned down the first offer to direct the Santiago-based ECLA in 1948, because he feared an international organization like the U.N. would not permit underdeveloped countries to analyse economic problems from their own perspectives; in this regard, he had in mind the League of Nations' lack of interest in underdeveloped areas.[61] Meanwhile, this concern was apparently justified by the failure of the U.S. Congress to take action on a U.N.-sponsored International Trade Organization (ITO), proposed in 1948 as a third leg – along with the World Bank and the International Monetary Fund (IMF) – of an international economic system. The ITO was to have dealt with an issue of great concern to the Latin Americans, commodity price stabilization.

In any event Prebisch was again invited to go to Santiago to work on special assignment as editor and author of the introduction to an economic report on Latin America, authorized at the initial ECLA meeting. In Santiago he elaborated his thesis on the deterioration of the terms of trade in *El desarrollo económico de América Latina y sus principales problemas,* published in May 1949 (English translation: *The Economic Development of Latin America and its Principal Problems,* 1950), an essay termed the 'ECLA Manifesto' by Albert Hirschman.[62] Prebisch had already formed his opinions about the direction of Latin America's long-range terms of trade, since he had argued in the classroom in 1948 that the benefits of technological progress were absorbed by the Centre. Now, a new study, *Relative Prices of Exports and Imports of Underdeveloped Countries,* by Hans Singer of the U.N. Department of Economic Affairs, provided an empirical foundation for Prebisch's thesis. This work was an examination of long-term trends in relative prices in the goods traded by industrialized and raw materials-producing countries, and concluded that the terms of trade from the late nineteenth century till the eve of the Second World War had been moving against the exporters of agricultural goods and in favour of the exporters of industrial products: 'On the average, a given quantity of primary exports would pay, at the end of this period, for only 60% of the

[61] Prebisch interview. For support on the League's lack of interest in underdeveloped areas, see H. W. Arndt, *Economic Development: the History of an Idea* (Chicago, 1987), p. 18.

[62] Albert O. Hirschman, 'Ideologies of Economic Development in Latin America', in Albert O. Hirschman (ed.), *Latin American Issues: Essays and Comments* (New York, 1961), p. 13.

quantity of manufactured goods which it could buy at the beginning of the period'.[63]

ECLA explained this finding in part by arguing that gains in productivity over the period in question were greater in industrial than in primary products, thus challenging basic assumptions of the theory of comparative advantage. If prices of industrial goods had fallen, this development would have spread the effects of technical progress over the entire Centre-Periphery system, and the terms of trade of agricultural goods would have been expected to have improved. They did not do so; and the significance of this fact had to be understood in terms of trade cycles. During the upswing, the prices of primary goods rise more sharply than those of industrial goods, but they fall more steeply during the downswing. In the upswing the working class of the Centre absorbs real economic gains, but wages do not fall proportionately during the downswing. Because workers are not well organized in the Periphery (least of all in agriculture), the Periphery absorbs more of the system's income contraction than does the Centre.[64] Thus in current jargon, Prebisch focussed on the 'double factorial terms of trade' – domestic labour's compensation vs. that of its foreign counterpart.

In the *Economic Survey of Latin America: 1949* (Spanish edition, 1950; English edition, 1951), Prebisch expanded on these arguments. He held that there were two distinct sources of the potential deterioration of the terms of trade, namely, those from technological productivity gains in the Centre, and those in the Periphery. He assumed the Centre's gains would be greater, and if the system worked normally, these would, to some extent, spread to the Periphery. In that case, over the long run the Centre's terms of trade would deteriorate, and the periphery's would improve. If the Periphery's terms deteriorated, such fact would indicate that it was not only failing to share in the Centre's presumably larger gains, but was transferring some of its *own* productivity gains to the Centre.[65] Since *Relative Prices* had established a deterioration in the Periphery's terms, protection for industry was a sine qua non to arrest the concentration of the fruits of technological progress in the Centre.

The basic cause of the deterioration was the surplus labour supply and

[63] United Nations: Department of Economic Affairs, *Relative Prices of Exports and Imports of Under-Developed Countries: A Study of Postwar Terms of Trade between Under-Developed and Industrialised Nations* (Lake Success, N.Y., 1949), p. 7.

[64] ECLA, *Economic Development*, pp. 8–14.

[65] ECLA, *Economic Survey of Latin America: 1949* (New York, 1951), p. 47.

the underlying population pressure in the precapitalist, largely agricultural, sector of the Periphery's economy. As modern agricultural technique penetrates and reduces the size of the precapitalist sector, the *Survey* stated, a labour surplus develops. It then adduced historical data to show that the export sector in Latin America could not absorb this surplus. Industrialization, in part to absorb the labour surplus, was the centrepiece of a policy of economic development, the *Survey* contended. Even when protection was needed, industries were 'economical in so far as they represent a net addition to real income'. National income could be increased by selectively lowering components of the import coefficient.[66]

Another initial ECLA argument grew out of Prebisch's observations on Argentina's import problems in the 1930s. The United States, the principal cyclical Centre, had a much lower import co-efficient than export co-efficient, and the former was also much lower than those of the Latin American countries. The U.S. tended to sell more to Latin America than it bought from the region, exhausting Latin American reserves, and creating a tendency toward permanent disequilibrium. Such a tendency had not existed, ECLA averred, during the time in which import-hungry Great Britain had been the principal Centre.[67] The U.S. economy even grew by closing: ECLA produced statistics showing that the United States' import co-efficient had fallen from the 1920s to the late 1940s. The explanation was that technological progress in some industries was much greater than on average; this allowed such industries to pay much higher wages, driving up wages in general, and in some other industries, above productivity gains. Therefore rising costs led to greater average protectionism and a 'closing' of the Centre.[68]

But Prebisch and the ECLA team he organized were also interested in another dimension of the problem – monopolistic pricing at the Centre. The original analysis in 1949–50 laid much more emphasis on the rigidity of wages in the downward phase of the cycle than on monopolistic pricing as such, but the latter argument was there.[69] In any event, both wage rigidities and monopoly were assumed to be non-existent in neo-classical

[66] Ibid., p. 78 (quotation), 79. At that time Prebisch believed that by changing the composition of imports from consumer to capital goods, Latin American countries could reduce their import coefficients. ECLA, *Economic Development*, pp. 44–5.

[67] ECLA, *Economic Development*, pp. 15–16; ECLA, *Economic Survey 1949*, pp. 20, 35–8.

[68] *Economic Survey 1949*, pp. 35, 75.

[69] Ibid., p. 59. More ambiguously, *Economic Development* stated that 'the income of entrepreneurs and of productive factors' in the Centre increased faster than did productivity in the Centre from the 1870s to the 1930s; but in another passage the document placed exclusive emphasis on the role of wages in the Centre (pp. 10, 14).

trade theory. Peripheral countries did not have monopolies on the goods they offered in the world market, with rare and temporary exceptions, just as they lacked well-organized rural labour forces that would resist the fall in wages during the downswing of the cycle.

The preceding analysis, taken as a whole, pointed to negative features in the Periphery's economy: structural unemployment, external disequilibrium, and deteriorating terms of trade – all of which a properly implemented policy of industrialization could help eliminate.

In 1950, the year after the appearance of the original Spanish version of the 'ECLA manifesto', another United Nations economist independently made a case related to the ECLA theses. Hans W. Singer, who had directed the U.N. study *Relative Prices* – the data base for ECLA's terms-of-trade argument – alleged that technological progress in manufacturing was shown in a rise in incomes in developed countries, while that in the production of food and raw materials in under-developed countries was expressed in a fall in prices. He explained the differential effects of technological progress in terms of different income elasticities of demand for primary and industrial goods – an extrapolation of Ernst Engel's law that the proportion of income spent on food falls as income rises – and in terms of the 'absence of pressure of producers for higher incomes' in underdeveloped countries. Since consumers of manufactured goods in world trade tended to live in underdeveloped countries, and the contrary was true for consumers of raw materials, Singer continued, the latter group had the best of both worlds while the former had the worst.[70] This idea was linked to Prebisch's, and quickly termed the Prebisch–Singer thesis, though both economists later stated that there was no direct exchange of views at the time the related sets of propositions, based on the same U.N. data, were developed.[71] (Prebisch was then in Santiago, and Singer in New York.)

In fact Prebisch had made *two* arguments, of which one was better stated by Singer. (Singer in turn had touched on Prebisch's theme of contrasting degrees of labour organization in Centre and Periphery.) Prebisch's central argument related to differential productivities in Centre and Periphery. His other argument dealing with disparities in import

70 H[ans] W. Singer, 'The distribution of gains between investing and borrowing countries', *American Economic Review: Papers and Proceedings*, 40, 2 (May 1950): 473–85 (quotation on 479). Income elasticity of demand for a good refers to the relative response of demand to a small percentage change in income, $\Delta q/q / \Delta y/y$, where q is the quantity demanded, and y is disposable income).

71 Prebisch to author, 29 June 1977; Singer to author, Brighton, England, 21 August 1979.

coefficients was rougly analogous to Singer's more elegant argument on differential income elasticities. Since Prebisch's *Economic Development,* ECLA's 'manifesto', appeared in print in May 1949, more than six months before Singer presented his paper to the American Economic Association (published in the *American Economic Review* in May 1950), Prebisch seems to have reached his position earlier than Singer; in fact, Singer's *Relative Prices* simply bolstered conclusions he had already drawn.

By 1951, the year that ECLA became a permanent organ of the United Nations, the agency was referring less to import coefficients than to disparities in income elasticities of demand at the Centre for primary products, and those at the Periphery for industrial goods.[72] This adoption of Singer's terms was significant, because it dealt with the Centre countries as a group and not just the United States, which had unusually low import requirements because of its tremendous agricultural output. Though ECLA first emphasized differential productivities, by the late fifties it was tending to emphasize differential income elasticities of demand, possibly as a result of perceived export stagnation in Argentina and Chile.[73]

Such were the main lines of Prebisch's and ECLA's early development. Yet it seems useful to digress briefly on other possible, and sometimes specifically alleged, influences on Prebisch. If these were not genetically related, comparing such propositions and theories with ECLA's will serve to highlight the distinctive features of the ECLA model.

One obvious possibility is the work of Alejandro Bunge, Argentina's leading advocate of industrialization in the 1920s, and Prebisch's former teacher at the University of Buenos Aires. Like *ancien régime* mercantilists, Bunge defended industrialization not in theoretical but in policy terms, and saw it as a means of reducing imports to relieve pressure on the balance of payments; yet he viewed industrialization as a complement to export-driven growth more than a substitute for it.[74]

A Latin American who anticipated a more important element in the Prebisch model was Víctor Emilio Estrada, the director of Ecuador's central bank in the 1920s. In 1922 he wrote that his country's terms of trade for its traditional exports would deteriorate indefinitely. Estrada attrib-

[72] E/CN.12/221 (18 May 1951), p. 30.

[73] For example, see Raúl Prebisch, 'Commercial policy in the underdeveloped countries', *American Economic Review: Papers and Proceedings,* 49, 2 (May, 1959): 251–73.

[74] Alejandro E. Bunge, *La economía argentina* (Buenos Aires), 2 (1928), pp. 229–31; 4 (1930), p. 131. Also see Tulio Halperín Donghi, 'Argentina: ensayo de interpretación' in Roberto Cortés Conde and Stanley J. Stein (eds), *Latin America: A Guide to Economic History, 1830–1930* (Berkeley, Cal., 1977), pp. 67, 115.

uted the price-scissors problem principally to rising labour costs in manufacturing in the United States, Ecuador's chief trading partner; this fact owed to trade-union activity, a pressure which was lacking in the price-formation of Ecuadorian exports. But Estrada did not generalize beyond his own country, nor associate his idea with the trade cycle; he was only groping for measures to offset the falling prices of cacao, Ecuador's leading export at the time.[75]

Another possible influence is Werner Sombart, whose *Der moderne Kapitalismus* was the first work to distinguish between Centre and Periphery in the world economic system. Specifically, Sombart wrote, 'We must . . . distinguish a capitalist Center – the central capitalist nations – from a mass of peripheral countries viewed from that Center; the former are active and directing, the latter, passive and serving. England constituted the capitalist Center in the first half of the nineteenth century; later, in the longer period of High Capitalism, Western Europe [joined England] . . . Finally, in the last generation, the eastern part of the United States has moved up [to the Center]'. Sombart also wrote of the 'dependency' of peripheral countries, and even of the servitude of the peasantry of the Periphery, in part caused by western European capitalism.[76] But he did not provide any theory of relations between Centre and Periphery; in particular, he offered no analysis of the relation between business cycles and the international distribution of income. Later Prebisch did not recollect acquaintance with Sombart's passage at the time of his initial use of the terms 'Centre' and 'Periphery', but even if he was inspired indirectly, Prebisch would owe little more than an arresting phrase, since Sombart only used 'Centre' and 'Periphery' in a few scattered paragraphs.[77]

More plausible as a theoretical influence than the writings of Bunge or Sombart, however, is the work of the aforementioned Rumanian, Mihail Manoilescu. The Canadian-American trade theorist Jacob Viner linked the

[75] Víctor Emilio Estrada, *Ensayo sobre la balanza económica del Ecuador* (Guayaquil, 1922), p. 77. (I am grateful to Paul Drake for bringing this work to my attention.)

[76] Werner Sombart, *Der moderne Kapitalismus* (München, 1928), III [2 vols. bound as 1], Vol. 1, pp. xiv–xv (quotation), 64; Vol. 2, p. 1019.

[77] Prebisch to author, Washington, D.C., 26 June 1979. Still another possible source of inspiration for the Centre-Periphery terminology was the work of Ernst Wagemann, the German economist born in Chile. In *Struktur und Rhythmus der Weltwirtschaft* (Berlin, 1931), Wagemann, a specialist in business cycles, used 'central cycle' [*zentrische Konjunktur*] to designate money income movements *within* a given country, and 'peripheral cycle' [*periphere Konjunktur*] to designate capital movements at the international level (pp. 70–1). Thus Wagemann employed a Centre-Periphery scheme in connection with a cyclical movement, but not in the sense which Prebisch shared with Sombart. In 1977 Prebisch did not recall how he came to use the terms 'Centre' and 'Periphery.' Prebisch to author, 29 June 1977.

theses of Manoilescu with those of ECLA as early as 1950.[78] Over the next twenty years, others in Latin America, the United States and Rumania would concur in Viner's judgement.

During the thirties and forties, Manoilescu was in fact well known in certain parts of the Iberian world: several of his economic and political works had been published in those years in Spain, Portugal, Brazil and Chile. The most likely sources of inspiration were two articles appearing in Chile, one about Manoilescu and the other by him, in 1945 and 1947, respectively. They were published in *Economía,* the economics journal of the University of Chile, later to be edited by Aníbal Pinto Santa Cruz, one of ECLA's leading figures. In Argentina, however, Manoilescu seems to have had less influence than in Chile and Brazil.[79] Clearly, there were broad similarities between the two theories of unequal exchange which converged in the same policy prescription of industrialization. It is notable that Prebisch's focus on productivities within Centre and Periphery paralleled Manoilescu's. And both shared a common theoretical perspective: the separation of the critique of imperialism from that of captialism.[80]

Prebisch was probably not directly influenced by Manoilescu, and there are no references to the Rumanian economist's works in Prebisch's early writings. Prebisch in 1977 confirmed the absence of such an influence, though he may have been familiar with Manoilescu from the brief discussions the latter's ideas received in the *Revista de Ciencias Económicas* in the late thirties. Nevertheless, Manoilescu's ideas – in the Latin American circles where they were known – probably helped pave the way for the acceptance of ECLA doctrines when they appeared in 1949.

Another source of possible inspiration for Prebisch in the latter forties was François Perroux's theory of the 'dominant economy' (1948).[81] His analysis focused on different elasticities of demand of the United States and 'the rest of the world', a perspective similar to one Prebisch was employing in the mid-1940s. Perroux was principally interested in 'dominated' econo-

[78] Jacob Viner, *International Trade and Economic Development* (Glencoe, Ill., 1952) [lectures delivered in 1950], pp. 61–4.

[79] See Edgar Mahn Hecker, 'Sobre los argumentos proteccionistas de List y Manoilesco' [sic], *Economía* (Chile), no. 17 (December, 1945): 59–70, Mihail Manoilesco, 'Productividad del trabajo y comercio exterior', *Economía,* no. 22–3 (September, 1947): 50–77. In the late 1930s Manoilescu's works had been discussed in the *Revista de Ciencias Económicas,* the journal of the UBA: FCE, where Prebisch had been a professor.

[80] Moreover, Manoilescu in 1940 and the structuralists Hans Singer and Celso Furtado in the 1950s independently worked out models of what is now called 'internal colonialism'. See Joseph L. Love, 'Modeling internal colonialism: history and prospect', *World Development,* 17, 6 (1989): 905–22.

[81] François Perroux, 'Esquisse d'une théorie de l'économie dominante', *Economie Appliquée,* 2–3 (August–September, 1948): 243–300.

mies of pre-Marshall Plan Europe, but he also argued that agricultual exporters had deteriorating terms of trade, owing to the import patterns of the dominant economy.[82] It seems unlikely that any genetic connection exists between Perroux and Prebisch, and it is notable that Perroux's emphasis on differential elasticities of demand is closer to Singer than Prebisch. Perroux in the 1930s, like Manoilescu, had explicitly espoused corporatism, and we may note that both share with ECLA a focus on monopoly relations (e.g., in labour and capital markets). But Manoilescu believed there was no necessary connection between his economic and political theories, and it seems inappropriate to label ECLA's economics 'neo-corporatist'.[83]

In fact, Prebisch's sources of inspiration were eclectic, as shown by his debt to the American neo-classical trade theorist Charles Kindleberger. In 1943 Kindleberger had published two articles calling for the industrialization of agricultural and raw material producers on the basis of long-term deterioration of the terms of trade, and Prebisch was familiar with at least one of them.[84] In 'International Monetary Stabilization', Kindleberger argued that the terms of trade moved against agricultural products 'because of the institutional organization of production' in industry, a references to internal and external economies and possibly to monopoly elements, and also because of differences in the elasticity of demand for agricultural and industrial products.[85]

Kindleberger pointed out that an agricultural country's increased productivity in primary activities under these conditions could only raise real income if the labour freed from agriculture were permitted to emigrate or found employment in industry – a proposition he borrowed from Colin Clark.[86] Otherwise, the terms of trade would move against the country, and it would have realized no benefit from the increased output of primary

82 Ibid., p. 297.

83 François Perroux, *Capitalisme et communauté de travail* (Paris, [1938]); Mihail Manoilescu, 'Doctrinele şi teoriile noastre in lumina criticei (răspuns D-lui Prof. Gh. Tasca)' *Anale Economice şi Statistice*, 20, 3–5 (March–May, 1937): 27. On ECLA's doctrines as neo-corporatism, see Charles W. Bergquist (ed.), *Alternative Approaches to the Problem of Development: A Selected and Annotated Bibliography* (Durham, N.C., 1979), p. xiii.

84 Kindleberger, 'Planning for foreign investment', *American Economic Review*, 33, 1 (March, 1943), Supplement: 347–54; and 'International monetary stabilization', in Seymour E. Harris (ed.), *Postwar Economic Problems* (London, 1943), pp. 375–95. Prebisch cited the latter article in 'Observaciones sobre los planes monetarios internacionales', *Trimestre Económico*, 11, 2 (July–September, 1944): 195–6, though he did so in order to contest the American's references to the behaviour of the Argentine economy.

85 Kindleberger, 'International monetary stabilization', p. 378.

86 Ibid., p. 377, citing Clark, *The Economics of 1960* (1942).

goods. But domestic industry need not be as efficient as that abroad: an agricultural country's real income would be increased if, 'at some level of costs, labor displaced from agriculture can produce industrial products previously imported to enable part of the proceeds of an unchanged volume of exports to be spent upon other types of imports', Kindleberger wrote, thereby endorsing import-substitution industrialization.[87]

Looking ahead to the post-war era, Kindleberger foresaw disequilibria in the international trading system. A specific instance was the case of two countries with differing marginal propensities to import. For the country heavily dependent on exports and having a high propensity to import, a rise in exports could eventually produce an unfavourable balance of trade. 'It may be suggested that the United States has a comparatively low propensity to import and a low ratio of exports to national income, whereas the rest of the world has a relatively high elasticity of demand for United States exports of manufactured goods and a relatively high ratio of exports to income'.[88] One may infer the external imbalance was, potentially at least, a structural problem. In fact, at Prebisch's seminar on central banking in Mexico in 1944, he cited Kindleberger's thesis that the U.S. would have a persistent trade imbalance with the rest of the world because of disparities in demand elasticities. At the time, Prebisch was not certain the thesis was valid,[89] but later decided it was. Kindleberger's contribution to Prebisch's original structuralism thus seems large.

In any case, ECLA's theses, from their initial appearance in 1949, were hotly contested by neo-classical trade theorists, such as Viner. The economics profession in 1948–9 had just been treated to a formal demonstration by Paul Samuelson that, under certain conventional (but unrealistic) assumptions, trade could serve as a complete substitute for the movement of factors of production from one country to another, indicating that international trade could potentially equalize incomes among nations. Thus the less rigorous, but much more realistic, arguments of Prebisch and Singer burst upon the scene just after Samuelson had raised neoclassical trade theory to new heights of elegance, and against this theory the new ideas would have to struggle.[90] In particular, the terms-of-trade thesis came

[87] Kindleberger, 'International Monetary Stabilization', pp. 378–9.

[88] Ibid., p. 381. The writer was referring both to income- and price-elasticity (p. 380).

[89] Prebisch, in Banco Central, *La creación,* I, pp. 530–1.

[90] Albert O. Hirschman, 'A Generalized Linkage Approach to Development, with Special Reference to Staples', *Economic Development and Cultural Change* 25, 1977 supplement, p. 68. Samuelson's articles were 'International Trade and the Equalisation of Factor Prices', *Economic Journal,* 58 (June, 1948): 163–84 and 'International Factor-price Equalisation once again', in ibid., 59 (June, 1949): 181–97.

under severe attack, as the validity of the data was challenged on a variety of grounds.[91]

ECLA: THE HALCYON YEARS

Despite the disputations that ensued, the terms-of-trade argument was a point of departure for a structuralist school which would seek to restrict the applicability of neo-classical economics to Latin America, and by extension to all underdeveloped countries. In this endeavour Prebisch was able to attract to, or retain in, his agency a pleiad of talented economists in the early years, including Aníbal Pinto, Jorge Ahumada, and Pedro Vuscovic, all of Chile; Aldo Ferrer of Argentina; Juan Noyola Vázquez and Víctor Urquidi of Mexico; and Celso Furtado of Brazil. These men were entering economics just as the field was becoming a profession in a number of Latin American countries.

Furtado, who joined the ECLA staff shortly before Prebisch officially took over, quickly drew further conclusions from Prebisch's analysis of the business cycle and high import co-efficients. Arguing that income tended to concentrate in Brazil during the upswing of the cycle, owing to a highly elastic labour supply, he then hypothesized that much of the effect of the Keynesian multiplier 'leaked' abroad, owing to the high propensity to import. Furtado anticipated, by four years, W. Arthur Lewis's famous analysis of an infinitely elastic labour supply as the source of wage 'stickiness' in underdeveloped countries. Such analysis, of course, pointed again to the importance of an industrialization policy.[92]

According to a study of ECLA's theoretical innovations by Octavio Rodrí-

[91] The principal arguments and sources in this long debate have been summarized and evaluated by John Spraos, who concludes that Prebisch was right about long-term deterioration of net barter terms of trade for 1870–1939, but that the trend was weaker than Prebisch thought. Furthermore, for 1900–75, Spraos concludes the data were trendless. Yet Prebisch would still argue, one assumes, that anything less than a *favourable* trend for primary products would show that the Centre was benefiting more than the Periphery in the trading process (assuming greater technological productivity gains in the centre). See Spraos, 'The statistical debate on the net barter terms of trade between primary commodities and manufactures', *Economic Journal*, 90 (March, 1980): 107–28, esp. p. 126. More recent studies of long-term data have tended to support Prebisch and Singer. For an extensive review of the literature, generally supporting Spraos's findings, see Dimitris Diakosavvas and Pasquale L. Scandizzo, 'Trends in the terms of trade of primary commodities, 1900–1982: the controversy and its origins', *Economic Development and Cultural Change*, 39, 2 (January, 1991), p. 237 (on Spraos).

[92] Celso Furtado, 'Características gerais da economia brasileira', *Revista Brasileira de Economia*, 4, 1 (March, 1950), p. 11; W. Arthur Lewis, 'Economic Development with Unlimited Supplies of Labour', *Manchester School*, 22 (May, 1954): 132–91. ECLA was also referring to highly-elastic labour supplies in 1950, and it is not clear whether Furtado introduced this concept.

guez, a former staff economist, its major theoretical contributions, beyond its analysis of the terms of trade, have fallen in the areas of problems of industrialization; the analysis of structural obstacles to development; and the related problem of the causes of inflation. Rodríguez further argues, in a work which is far from uncritical, that ECLA's period of greatest originality was from 1949 through the latter sixties, after which few new theses were presented.[93] Other contributions cited in ECLA publications were the promotion of Latin American economic integration, implicit in the agenda of the 1949 'manifesto'; 'programming' or planning economic development; and helping to create the Inter-American Development Bank (IDB) and the U.N. Conference on Trade and Development (UNCTAD).[94] Although some governments in the 1950s, notably Brazil's, openly acknowledged ECLA as a source of their developmentalist policies, Argentina's *desarrollistas* were quick to distance themselves from ECLA, possibly because of Prebisch's previous activity in national policy formation.[95] In any event, such activities of ECLA were in applied fields, not theory, and many policy prescriptions had little success, as noted below, when implemented by Latin American governments. Yet regional integration, part of ECLA's strategy from 1958, began to produce complementary industrial structures by the late 1960s. Intra-regional trade, and that in manufactures in particular, grew faster than extra-regional trade overall and that in manufactures between 1965 and 1979.[96]

Of the theoretical endeavours, the 'structuralist' explanation of inflation, a challenge to 'monetarism', is sometimes viewed as only second in importance to the terms-of-trade thesis.[97] Despite the fact that a number of ECLA economists helped develop it, it was never accorded recognition from ECLA as part of its official doctrine, though at times Prebisch himself endorsed it in the agency's publications.[98]

[93] Octavio Rodríguez, 'On the Conception of the Center Periphery System', *CEPAL Review*, January–June 1977, p. 196; Rodríguez, *La teoría del subdesarrollo de la CEPAL* (Mexico, D.F., 1980), p. 297. More strictly, Rodríguez believes ECLA's best years for theory ended with the 1950s: *La Teoría*, p. 15.

[94] CEPAL, *El aporte de las ideas-fuerza* (Santiago, 1978); CEPAL, *XXV años de la CEPAL* (Santiago, 1973), p. 34.

[95] For an instructive comparison of Argentine *desarrollismo* and Brazilian *desenvolvimentismo* in the 1950s and 1960s, analysing the greater success of the latter, see Kathryn A. Sikkink, *Ideas and Institutions: Developmentalism in Brazil and Argentina* (Ithaca, N.Y., 1991).

[96] Werner Baer, 'Import Substitution and Industrialization in Latin America: experiences and interpretations', *Latin American Research Review*, 7, 1 (1972) p. 104; Inter-American Development Bank, *Economic and Social Progress in Latin America: Economic Integration. 1984 Report* (Washington, D.C., n.d.), p. 98.

[97] For example, Ignacy Sachs, *The Discovery of the Third World* (Cambridge, Mass., 1976), p. 137.

[98] Raúl Prebisch, 'Economic Development or Monetary Stability: the false dilemma', *Economic Bulletin*

Inflation was more rampant in Latin America during most of the post-war decades than in all other areas of the world. The basic structuralist proposition was that *underlying* inflationary pressures derive from bottlenecks produced by retarded sectors, especially agriculture, whose backward state yields an inelastic supply, in the face of rapidly rising demand by the burgeoning urban masses. In Chile, where the analysis was first applied, the stagnation of the export sector was also recognized as a structural cause. Repeated devaluations to raise export earnings automatically boosted the price of imports. A related cause in this view was deteriorating terms of trade, fuelled by a demand for imports that rose faster than the demand for exports. Also associated with the foreign trade problem was a shift in the fiscal system: as exports stagnated, the relative weight of revenues provided by regressive domestic taxes tended to rise, allowing more income for the already import-orientated upper classes. To a lesser degree the ECLA economists noted as a cause of inflation national industrial monopolies and oligopolies, shielded by high tariffs, which could raise prices quickly.[99]

The several 'structural' features of inflation were distinguished from 'exogenous' or adventitious causes (for example, natural disasters, changes in the international market), and 'cumulative' causes (action by government and private groups to raise wages and prices in a climate of inflationary expectations). It is important to recognize that the thesis did not deny that orthodox 'monetarist' explanations of inflation had some validity – for example, that some supply inelasticities were caused by distortions in exchange rates and prices, following an inflationary spiral.

In a broad sense, 'structuralism', which received its name in the context of the analysis of inflation, owed something to the 'doctrine of market failure' that led to Keynesianism in Britain in the 1930s. More directly, Michál Kalecki, who had been at Oxford in the thirties and forties, published a seminal article on inflation in Mexico's *Trimestre Económico* in 1954; its influence on the structuralist school was acknowledged by Juan Noyola and the Chilean economist Osvaldo Sunkel.

for Latin America, 6, 1 (March, 1961): 1–25, esp. 3, where agriculture is cited as a structural cause of inflation (because of antiquated land-tenure systems). Rodríguez stresses personal, rather than official, contributions of *cepalistas* in *La Teoría del subdesarrollo,* pp. 4, 190. ECLA's *Aportes* and *XXV años* do not mention any contribution by ECLA as such on inflation.

99 See Juan Noyola Vázquez, 'El desarrollo económico y la inflación en México y otros países latinoamericanos', *Investigaciones Económicas,* 16, 4 (1956): 603–18; Osvaldo Sunkel, 'Inflation in Chile: an unorthodox approach', *International Economic Papers,* no. 10 (1960): 107–31 [orig. in *Trimestre Económico* (1958)]; Rodríguez, *Teoría,* chapter 6.

Kalecki emphasized the 'inelasticity of agricultural supply and monopolistic tendencies in industry' in inflationary patterns in underdeveloped countries. Since inflation was due to 'basic disproportions in productive relations', it could not 'be prevented by purely financial [monetary] devices'.[100]

For the Latin Americans, this was not the whole story, for among other things the fact that Chile experienced major inflationary pressures while Mexico did not, had to be explained. Part of the answer for Noyola was that Mexico's agrarian reform had produced a more elastic supply of farm goods than latifundia-dominated Chile, but Noyola also emphasized that Chile had 'propagating mechanisms', while Mexico lacked them. The latter country had a large labour surplus which tended to depress the wage level, whereas Chile had a well-organized working class which sought to protect its share of national income.[101] Finally, one might argue that the structuralist interpretation of inflation was implicit in Prebisch's early observation that a given rise in income produced a more than proportional rise in imports, since imports were identified as a source of inflationary pressure, assuming, as ECLA did, that Latin America's terms of trade tend to deteriorate.

A number of ECLA economists, especially those concerned while Chile, developed the structuralist interpretation of inflation in the mid- and late fifties. The contributors were so numerous and the contributions so nearly simultaneous that attribution is difficult; but the Mexican Juan Noyola may have been the first in print to emphasize the role of the backward agrarian sector. He and the Chilean Aníbal Pinto in 1956 were the first to distinguish between 'structural' causes and 'propagating mechanisms' – fiscal policies, credit, and the wage-price spiral.[102]

The inherent weakness of the structuralist thesis on inflation as a policy guide is that any increase in economic efficiency – even if agriculture is the most notorious offender – will diminish 'basic' inflationary processes; 'it is therefore always possible to claim that inflation is due to the failure to carry out one particular improvement', and it can be associated with a

[100] Michál Kalecki, *Essays on Developing Economies* (Atlantic Highlands, N. J., 1976 [orig. Spanish edn, 1954]), pp. 50, 62.

[101] Noyola, 'El desarrollo', pp. 605, 608–612.

[102] Noyola, 'El desarrollo'; Aníbal Pinto in *La intervención del Estado* . . . (Santiago, 1956). On their priority, see Rodríguez, *Teoría,* p. 190. Furtado puts Noyola first in his memoir *A fantasia organisada* (Rio de Janeiro, 1985), p. 185. Other contributors include Osvaldo Sunkel, Jorge Ahumada, Jaime Barros, and Luis Escobar, all from Chile. Hirschman independently developed an analogous approach. See Albert O. Hirschman, 'Inflation in Chile', in his *Journeys toward Progress: Studies of Economic Policy-Making in Latin America* (New York, 1963), p. 213, note 1.

variety of social problems.[103] Therefore, the emphasis on 'underlying' or 'structural' causes could be interpreted in different ways: it could be used as a rationale either for government-sponsored reform, or, in the absence of reform, to explain government powerlessness to stem an inflationary tide. Structuralism became the dominant interpretation of inflation – and a stimulus for reform – in two Latin American administrations in the 1960s – those of João Goulart in Brazil (1961–4) and Eduardo Frei in Chile (in his first eighteen months of office, 1964–6). Though the structuralist view of inflation has seen its heyday, economists are still debating its merits, and econometric testing is cited for and against it, as in the case of the terms-of-trade thesis.[104] Structuralists seemed to have lost their influence on the inflation issue because of their relative neglect of monetarist measures necessary in times of hyperinflation.[105]

The reformist views implicit in structuralism were part of an increasing concern with social issues by the ECLA staff, a concern that quickened with the growing radicalism of the Cuban Revolution after 1959. More dramatic than ECLA's contribution to the Alliance for Progress (for which it helped win acceptance for the goals of agrarian reform, commodity price stabilization, and economic integration) was Prebisch's call for social reform in his 1963 essay, *Toward a Dynamic Development Policy for Latin America*. Here he appealed for specific reforms in agrarian structure, income distribution, and education.[106] Beyond this, he wrote that Latin American industrialization was based on the technology appropriate to the labour-saving needs of the developed countries, and that the consumption patterns of Latin America's upper strata exacerbated the problem through their preferences for capital-intensive consumer goods. It was 'absolutely necessary [*ineludible*] for the state to deliberately compress the consumption of the upper strata'. Given the sharply skewed pattern of income

[103] Hirschman, 'Inflation in Chile', p. 216.

[104] See, for example, Susan M. Wachter, 'Structuralism vs. Monetarism: Inflation in Chile', in Jere Behrman and James Hanson (eds), *Short-term Macroeconomic Policy in Latin America* (Cambridge, Mass., 1979), pp. 227–55, esp. 247 (qualified support for structuralism); Raouf Kahil, *Inflation and Economic Development in Brazil: 1946–1963* (Oxford, 1973), p. 330 (against structuralism). Luis Cáceres and F. J. Jiménez have concluded that two structuralist variables, the dynamism of investment and the elasticity of agricultural supply, are basic causes of Latin American inflation. Cáceres and Jiménez, 'Estructuralismo, monetarismo e inflación en Latinoamerica', *Trimestre Económico* (May–June, 1983): 151–68.

[105] See Albert O. Hirschman, 'The Social and Political Matrix of Inflation: Elaboration of the Latin American Experience', in Albert O. Hirschman, *Essays in Trespassing: Economics to Politics and Beyond* (Cambridge, 1981), p. 183.

[106] Raúl Prebisch, *Hacia una dinámica del desarrollo latinoamericano* (Montevideo, 1967 [orig., 1963]), pp. 41, 52.

distribution and the upper classes' high propensity to consume, deteriorating domestic terms of trade between agriculture and industry had their explanation 'in the insufficient dynamism of development, which does not facilitate the absorption of the labor force [because such absorption is] not required by the slow growth of demand [for agricultural products] and the increase of productivity in primary activities. This insufficient dynamism prevents a rise of wages in agriculture parallel to the increase in productivity, and . . . [thus] primary production loses in part or in whole the gains from its technological progress'. Prebisch further denounced the actual pattern of industrialization in Latin America, pointing out that the exaggerated pattern of protection had allowed grossly inefficient industries to arise. Latin America had, on average, the highest tariffs in the world, depriving it of economies of scale and opportunities to specialize for export.[107] In retrospect this 1963 statement anticipates the somber Prebisch of *Capitalismo periférico* (1981).

In the same period Prebisch acknowledged that 'social' as well as economic forces had to be 'influenced' if reforms were to be achieved.[108] To this end, in 1962 ECLA established an annex called the Latin American Institute for Economic and Social Planning (ILPES). Meanwhile, ECLA's long-standing proposals for restructuring the international trading system were largely shifted in 1963 to a new U.N. agency, UNCTAD, which, under Prebisch's leadership as its first executive secretary, was clearly the international body most appropriate for such efforts.

ECLA's reformism had definite limits, however, since it was an international agency whose constituent members were western hemisphere states and disengaging European colonial powers. At a theoretical level, it always assumed that the state was an exogenous factor in the economic and social system. In the latter 1960s its reformist efforts were still focussed on pressuring governments of developed countries to liberalize their trade policies, thus assisting the new UNCTAD, and persuading Latin American states to accept a greater degree of regional integration. Furthermore, ECLA had always welcomed foreign investment in Latin America, under certain conditions, and this attitude patently ruled out a number of radical strategies.[109]

The reformism of the sixties was conditioned by, and for an increasing

[107] Ibid., pp. 21, 41, 90, 99.

[108] Prebisch, 'Economic Development or Monetary Stability', p. 24.

[109] Girvan, 'Development of Dependency Economics', p. 8; ECLA, *International Cooperation in a Latin American Development Policy* (New York, 1954), p. 15.

number of structuralists, made irrelevant by, a long evolution of ECLA's views on its initial key policy recommendation – import-substitution industrialization (ISI). An ISI policy had seemed a brilliant success, especially in Brazil in Mexico, during the 1950s, but success owed in part to unusually high commodity prices during the Korean War. In the latter fifties, ECLA began to consider the complexities of ISI. By 1957 the organization had distinguished between two types, which in the 1960s would be seen as phases, of import substitution. The first involved the relatively easy substitution of simple domestically produced consumer goods for previously imported items. The second, more difficult, type involved the production of intermediate goods and consumer durables, a shift from 'horizontal' to 'vertical' ISI – so denominated because of the substitution of simple goods on a broad front in the first phase, and in the second, an integrated line of production of fewer final goods and their inputs. A third phase, the production of capital goods, would ensue at a later date.[110]

In 1956 ECLA had still assumed the existence of a threshold in structural changes in the economy, beyond which 'dependence on external contingencies' would diminish. Yet the following year the agency first suggested that dependence on 'events overseas' might even increase as ISI advanced; all the same, it still held that 'import substitution' consisted of lowering 'the import content of supplies for the home market'.[111]

Argentina was Latin America's most industrialized country, and despite its unique political phenomenon of *peronismo,* ECLA tended to view it in 1957 as a trendsetter for other Latin American nations. Argentina, ECLA noted, had reduced its imports of finished goods to one-third the total dollar amount. Yet its declining capacity to import had meant that reducing the importation of consumer goods was not sufficient to contain balance-of-payment difficulties; capital goods and fuels also had to be reduced, and this fact was reducing the rate of growth. Chile was seen as facing similar though less dire problems. ECLA seemed to wonder aloud whether the Argentine experience was the future of Latin America. Two conclusions followed: that primary exports and food production for domestic consumption had to be increased (the latter to relieve pressure on

[110] ECLA, *Economic Survey of Latin America: 1956* (New York, 1957), p. 116; ECLA, *The Process of Industrial Development in Latin America* (New York, 1966), pp. 19–20; Rodríguez, *Teoría,* pp. 202–3.

[111] 'The Situation in Argentina and the New Economic Policy', *Economic Bulletin,* 1, 1 (January, 1956): 30; ECLA, 'Preliminary Study of the Effects of Postwar Industrialisation on Import Structures and External Vulnerability in Latin America', in *Economic Survey 1956*, p. 115.

imports), and that a region-wide common market must be developed to assure the future development of efficient manufacturing industries.[112]

Why should industrialization bring rising import requirements in its train? Using a simple two-sector model, Furtado in 1958 explained the problem as one in which, by assumption, the advanced sector, A, had a larger import coefficient than the backward sector, B. As the economy developed, A's co-efficient grew ever larger as a share of the whole economy's coefficient, and *pari passu* the average import co-efficient tended to rise.[113] If the terms of trade were deteriorating, the pressures on the balance of payments became even more acute.

Thus, for ECLA economists in the mid- and late fifties, the import requirements in the later stages of ISI, unless offset by capital inflows or rising exports, could cause 'strangulation' – a favourite ECLA metaphor for stagnation caused by insufficient imports of capital goods and other industrial inputs. As a partial solution to stuttering ISI, ECLA in 1957–8 formally appealed to its sponsoring states for a Latin American common market, which, ECLA held, would provide incentives (through economies of scale) for the production of capital and intermediate goods.[114]

Yet in its early years the Latin American Free Trade Area, established in 1960, was only an expression of hope for alleviating the ills associated with ISI. Already in 1959 Prebisch had observed that the more economically advanced Latin American countries were becoming increasingly the hostages of external events, because they had compressed their imports to the absolute essentials for the maintenance of growth. Two years later he wrote, 'It remains a paradox that industrialization, instead of helping greatly to soften the internal impact of external fluctuations, is bringing us a new and unknown type of external vulnerability.'[115]

The agonizing reappraisal of ISI came in 1964. In that year an ECLA study, though blaming Latin America's declining rates of growth on deteriorating terms of trade in the 1950s, also noted that 80 per cent of regional imports now consisted of fuels, intermediate goods, and capital equipment. Consequently, there was little left to 'squeeze' in the

112 ECLA, 'Preliminary Study', pp. 128, 150, 151.

113 Celso Furtado, 'The External Disequilibrium in the Underdeveloped Economies', *Indian Journal of Economics* 38, 151 (April, 1958), p. 406.

114 'Bases for the Formation of the Latin American Regional Market', *Economic Bulletin*, 3, 1 (March, 1958): 4. The seventh session of ECLA in 1957 adopted a resolution calling for steps toward the creation of a region-wide common market.

115 Prebisch, 'Commercial Policy', p. 268; Prebisch, 'Economic Development or Monetary Stability', p. 5.

region's import profile to favour manufacturing.[116] Meanwhile, two monographs highly critical of ISI appeared in the agency's *Economic Bulletin* – one on the Brazilian experience in particular, and the other on Latin America in general.[117] These articles pointed to problems that by the 1960s were beginning to affect other parts of the Third World as well.

Examining the Brazilian case in the fifties and early sixties, Maria da Conceição Tavares argued that ISI had failed because of the lack of dynamism of the export sector, coupled with the fact that ISI had not diminished capital and fuel import requirements. Other problems were the apparent ceilings on the domestic market, owing in part to highly-skewed income distribution, which also determined the structure of demand; the constellation of productive resources – for example, the lack of skilled labour; and the capital-intensive nature of industrialization in more advanced phases of ISI, which implied little labour absorption. In the advanced stages of ISI, Tavares contended, the low labour absorption of manufacturing tended to exaggerate rather than to terminate the dualism of Brazil's economy. Among other things, she argued that bottlenecks in the food supply, partly due to the antiquated agrarian structure, put unsustainable pressures on the import bill. Tavares recommended agrarian reform as a partial solution.[118]

In the same number of the *Bulletin,* Santiago Macario wrote a blistering critique of the way in which ISI had actually been practised in Latin America, following up Prebisch's observation the previous year, 1963, that the region had the highest tariffs in the world. Macario observed that the governments of the four most industrialized countries – Argentina, Brazil, Mexico and Chile – had used ISI as a deliberate strategy to counteract a persistent lack of foreign exchange, and to create employment for expanding populations. But in those four countries, and in most of the others of the region, protectionism, primarily in the form of tariff and exchange policies, had been irrational, in that there was no consistent policy to develop the most viable and efficient manufacturing industries. On the contrary, the most inefficient industries had received the greatest protection; there had been over-diversification of manufacturing in small

[116] ECLA, *The Economic Development of Latin America in the Postwar Period* (New York, 1964), pp. 14, 21.

[117] Maria da Conceição Tavares, 'The Growth and Decline of Import Substitution in Brazil', and Santiago Macario, 'Protectionism and Industrialization in Latin America', in *Economic Bulletin for Latin America,* 9 (1964): 1–59, and 61–101, respectively.

[118] Tavares, 'Growth and Decline', pp. 7–8, 11, 12, 55.

markets in the 'horizontal' phase; and these factors had contributed, in some instances, to real dissavings.[119]

Nor did Latin American manufactures hold their own in international markets, continued Macario, at a time when exchange earnings had become critical for the future of industrialization. On the positive side, there were tendencies in the early sixties to abolish exchange controls, quantitative restrictions, and multiple exchange rates, and a related tendency to begin tariff reduction; yet Macario asserted that Latin American tariffs were still being built on a makeshift basis, resulting in a gross misallocation of scarce resources.[120]

Rational criteria were needed to develop industries – such as the use of factors in greatest abundance (e.g. labour), or the promotion of industries that could earn foreign exchange. Equally important, thought Macario, was the establishment for each country of a 'uniform level of net protection'. Overall, his thesis was less that ECLA's policy prescriptions had initially been wrong – which Tavares's analysis in some ways showed – than that the region's governments had flagrantly ignored ECLA's technical advice, pursuing, in Macario's words, 'import substitution at any cost'.[121] Though Hirschman suggested four years later that Tavares and Macario had issued the death certificate of ISI somewhat prematurely, other scholars soon added new charges, such as ISI's having increased the concentration of income with regard both to social class and to region (within countries).[122]

FROM STRUCTURALISM TO DEPENDENCY

ECLA had voiced its first doubts in 1956 whether industry, in the world region with the fastest growing population, could absorb surplus labour from agriculture; nine years later its survey of ISI showed that non-agricultural employment in Latin America had increased from 13 to 36 million persons between 1925 and 1960, but that only five of the 23

[119] Macario, 'Protectionism', pp. 65–7, 77, 81.

[120] Ibid., pp. 67, 78, 81.

[121] Ibid., pp. 67 (quotation), 84 (formula for 'uniform level of net protection'), 87.

[122] *Inter alia,* Hirschman argued that the failure of ISI was not inevitable, but depended on the interaction of social and political factors with economic elements. See his 'The Political Economy of Import-substituting Industrialization in Latin America' [orig., 1968] in Albert O. Hirschman, *A Bias for Hope* (New Haven, Conn., 1971), pp. 85–123, esp. 103. On ISI failures, see the discussion of Sunkel and Furtado in the following section, and the literature surveyed in Baer, 'Import Substitution', pp. 95–122, esp. 107.

million additional employees were absorbed in industrial activities.[123] Furtado, writing over his own signature, contemporaneously noted that while Latin America's industrial output in the 1950s had risen 6.2 per cent a year, industrial employment had risen only 1.6 per cent annually, about half Latin America's average population growth rate. The problem in part was the labour-saving technology which the Periphery had imported from the Centre.[124]

Furtado explained that ISI was fundamentally different from European industrialization in the eighteenth and nineteenth centuries. In the classic phase, technology continually cheapened the relative cost of capital goods, creating the possibility of solutions to social problems. In twentieth-century Latin America, unlike nineteenth-century Europe, technology was exogenous to the regional economy, and was specifically designed for the requirements of the developed countries. Factor absorption, therefore, did not depend on the relative availability of factors, but on the type of technology used, and over this matter Latin Americans could exercise little choice.[125] Among other things, they had to complete in their own national markets with high-technology, multinational corporations.

This tendency by the mid-sixties to take the longer view and seek lessons in history was partly the result of the fact that, from ECLA's perspective, Latin America now had thirty-five years of import-substituting experience; but it was also due in part to the inclination to take a long-term perspective that was part of ECLA's original style. Prebisch's 1949 *Survey* had tried to view the sweep of economic history from the 1880s to the mid-twentieth century for the region, and in more detail for the four most industrialized nations. In some ways this volume was a model for country case studies to be carried out between 1959 and 1963 – Furtado on Brazil, Pinto on Chile, Aldo Ferrer on Argentina, and later, Osvaldo Sunkel and Pedro Paz on the whole region.[126] Furtado's study, however, derived principally from his pre-

[123] ECLA, 'The Situation in Argentina', p. 42; ECLA, *The Process of Industrial Development* (New York, 1966 [Sp. orig., 1965]), p. 38.

[124] Celso Furtado, *Subdesenvolvimento e estagnação na América Latina* 2nd edn (Rio de Janeiro, 1968) [orig., 1966]), pp. 9–10. As noted above, Prebisch had previously made this point in *Hacia una dinámica,* p. 38.

[125] Ibid., pp. 9–11. A later perspective permits a slightly more sanguine view of industrial employment than that ECLA and Furtado faced in the mid-sixties: Although industry in Argentina and Chile absorbed a smaller percentage of the labour force in 1981 than in 1965, in 1981 it employed a larger share in Brazil, Mexico, Colombia and Venezuela. But in no Latin American country in 1981 did industry account for as much as a third of the labour force. International Bank for Reconstruction and Development, *World Development Report: 1985* (New York, 1985), pp. 214–15.

[126] Celso Furtado, *Formação econômica do Brasil* (Rio de Janeiro, 1959); Aníbal Pinto Santa Cruz, *Chile, un caso de desarrollo frustrado* (Santiago, 1959); Aldo Ferrer, *La economía argentina: las etapas de su*

ECLA interests in the defining features of colonial Brazil. In fact, more than anyone else at ECLA, Furtado was responsible for 'historicizing' structuralist analysis, and departing from cyclical concerns.[127]

Explicit in the 1949 *Survey* was the thesis that industrialization in Latin America had historically occurred in periods of world crisis; that is, ECLA viewed development as occurring through the agency of 'external shocks', in Celso Furtado's phrase.[128] For the Brazilian case, Furtado pointed to rapid industrial growth in the Depression, partly due to 'the socialization of losses' through exchange devaluation, which none the less helped maintain domestic demand.[129] In Brazil, Furtado viewed expansionary fiscal and monetary policies during the Depression of the 1930s as a form of unwitting Keynesianism. His views on Brazilian industrialization touched off a long debate. Yet it now seems clear for Brazil, as for the other most-industrialized countries, that the two world wars and the Depression were less important in producing 'inward-directed growth' than was believed by some contemporaries to these events, and by ECLA economists later. A now widely held view is that investment in industry (capacity) grew in line with export earnings for the period 1900–45, while output (but not capacity) tended to rise during the 'shocks', when imports had to be curtailed. Capacity could not grow appreciably during the Depression for lack of exchange credits to buy capital goods and inputs, nor during the world wars because of the unavailability of capital goods and fuels from the belligerent powers.

Thus the perceived failure of ISI as a historical process – and perhaps the growing suspicion that industrial growth had varied directly and not inversely with export earnings – was a leading cause of pessimism among structuralists in the mid- and late sixties. There were reasons for pessi-

desarrollo y problemas actuales (Mexico, D. F., 1963); Osvaldo Sunkel and Pedro Paz, *El subdesarrollo latinoamericano y la teoría del desarrollo* (Mexico, D. F., 1970). Later a more specialized structuralist work appeared on Mexico: Villareal's *El desequilibrio externo,* in note 22. Villareal argues, however, that structuralism accounts more adequately for Mexico's external disequilibrium in the period 1939–58 than in 1959–70.

127 Furtado's pre-ECLA dissertation does not contain much formal economic analysis of any kind. Celso Furtado, 'L'économie coloniale brésilienne (XVIe et XVIIe siècles): Eléments d'histoire economique appliqués' (Ph.D. thesis, Faculté de Droit, U. de Paris, 1948); but *A economia brasileira* (Rio de Janeiro, 1954) offers a structuralist analysis of Brazil's economic history.

128 See ECLA, *Economic Survey 1949* (Sp. orig., 1950), p. 97, citing the case of Argentina; Furtado, 'Características gerais', p. 28.

129 See Furtado, 'Características gerais'. For a similar thesis about the socialization of losses through exchange depreciation and government maintenance of aggregate demand, see ECLA, *Economic Survey 1949*, pp. 60, 171–72. For a summary of Furtado's arguments, best developed in *Formação econômica do Brasil,* and the subsequent debate, see Wilson Suzigan, *Indústria brasileira: origem e desenvolvimento* (São Paulo, 1986), pp. 21–73.

mism as well in a variety of other areas, both immediate and long-term. ECLA's efforts at 'programming' – calculating required savings and inputs to meet government-specified development targets – had had some success in the 1950s (notably in Brazil during the presidency of Juscelino Kubitschek, 1956–61), but were increasingly seen as futile exercises in the 1960s. ECLA publications were now criticizing the agency's own earlier efforts in the field for failing to take into account 'social and political viability' as an essential criterion in the attempt to set and meet realistic development targets. Another problem, perceived in 1966 and having an obvious social dimension, was the rising degree of income inequality among social classes in Argentina, usually viewed as the pacesetter.[130] The problem of increasing income concentration was already observable in Mexico, and would be so in Brazil after the census of 1970.

Meanwhile Sunkel, writing in his own name in 1966, revealed a new pessimism characteristic of structuralist thinking in the mid-sixties.[131] Among the problems he identified as without apparent solution were the decline in the (perceived) rate of growth of Latin America's domestic product from 1950 to 1965; the persistent, rather than diminishing, dependency on the foreign sector, with its deteriorating terms of trade, as the key to growth; the concentration of income in the upper income brackets; and the falling share of industry in non-agricultural employment, as population climbed higher. The last observation seemed to show the failure of the structuralist programme of industrialization as the cornerstone of development. Sunkel wrote that 'the record of development policy in Latin America with respect to the area of employment opportunities is very poor indeed, and the long-term prospect is frightening'.[132]

Other structuralist criticisms of the Latin American economies in the latter sixties included the perception of a sustained balance-of-payments disequilibrium and a 'debt spiral' for the most industrialized countries, and of high rates of inflation, with consequent social tensions and political instability. For ECLA, these problems were chiefly structural problems – the agrarian pattern of latifundium and minifundium; industrial structure

130 Rodríguez, *Teoría,* p. 223 (on planning); 'Income Distribution in Argentina', *Economic Bulletin for Latin America,* 11, 1 (1966): 106–31.

131 Sunkel, 'The Structural Background of Development Problems in Latin America' in Charles T. Nisbet (ed.), *Latin America: Problems in Economic Development* (New York, 1969 [Sp. orig., 1966]), pp. 3–37. For an indication of a more generalized pessimism at the time, see the essays by Aníbal Pinto, Víctor Urquidi, Celso Furtado, Hélio Jaguaribe, Osvaldo Sunkel, and Jacques Chonchol, in Claudio Véliz (ed.), *Obstacles to Change in Latin America* (London, 1965).

132 Sunkel, 'Structural Background', pp. 7, 11, 13, 23.

(indivisibilities of scale, tending to produce under-utilization of capital, and high capital density, with the implication of low labour absorption); the rigidly stratified social structure; and the consequent maldistribution of income.[133]

On the political front, another source of pessimism was the end of the 'developmentalist' experiment in Brazil, where the populist regime of Goulart was ousted by military coup in 1964; two years later, a coup in Argentina installed a conservative and authoritarian government. Though less dramatic, the inability of the Frei government in Chile to carry through major economic and social reforms was likewise a disappointment. Furthermore, the diminished interest of the United States under Lyndon Johnson in the reform and development goals of the Alliance for Progress, coupled with the U.S. invasion of the Dominican Republic in 1965 – the first such action in Latin America since the twenties – was a blow to reformism.

More broadly, the intellectual and political climate in which dependency analysis would be received was radicalized by the international resistance to the U.S. war in Vietnam, of which the Dominican intervention was a consequence – to prevent a 'second Cuba' and the danger of two simultaneous long-term military engagements. Resistance to the Viet Nam War interacted with anti-establishment protest in a variety of countries, often led by students, and reached a peak in the demonstrations and repressions of 1968–70.

Yet there was a tendency, if not yet a dominant one, for official economic policy in Latin America to move in a contrary direction from the radicalism of the streets. Anti-ECLA orthodoxy made its reappearance during the mid-1960s in the programmes of 'monetarists' who set policy in the anti-populist, anti-inflationary, and authoritarian regimes of Generals Humberto Castelo Branco in Brazil and Juan Carlos Onganía in Argentina. In Brazil, at the end of the decade, it was a professedly neo-classical economist – though hardly an orthodox one, because of his use of state intervention – Antônio Delfim Neto, who implemented ECLA's earlier calls for the export of manufactures.[134] Liberal orthodoxy would assume the dominant position at the policy level under most military regimes in the 1970s, though in Brazil the state's role in the economy expanded. The

133 Rodríguez, *Teoría,* pp. 187–88, 214–17.

134 In 1957 ECLA had still denied that Latin America could compete in manufactured exports on the world market, but in the 1960s the agency viewed the export of manufactures as a requirement for continued development. ECLA, *Economic Survey 1956,* p. 151; Rodríguez, *Teoria,* p. 222.

rising star of neo-classical orthodoxy and associated policies in the late 1960s, even if less distant from structuralist policy in practice, as in the Brazilian case, probably contributed to a frustration in intellectual circles which prepared the way for the acceptance of dependency analysis.

In this regard, Chile's experience under its first Christian Democratic administration was probably even more important than that of Brazil, though Chile's military coup was still several years away. The host country for ECLA, Chile was the site of a major reformist experiment under the administration of Eduardo Frei for the six years beginning in November, 1964. Jorge Ahumada, Frei's chief economic advisor and a former ECLA analyst, in the economic plan of 1965 wanted concurrently to achieve faster growth, a redistribution of income (in part through agrarian reform), and the elimination of the structural causes of inflation. After an initial success in stimulating economic growth through expansionary policies, the Frei government saw the growth rate fall from an average of 6.0 per cent in 1965–6 to 3.2 per cent in 1967–70. The rate of investment also dipped in the Frei years, as employers became wary of the government's social experiments, and unemployment rose. To contain inflation, from late 1966 Frei cut government expenditures, but without notable success: the rate of inflation, held to 17.0 per cent in 1966, averaged 28.5 per cent in 1967–70. The foreign sector, so important in structuralist analysis, was not responsible for these difficulties, as copper prices remained high, along with exports and imports in general.[135] Consequently, the Frei experience revealed the enormous political difficulties of implementing ECLA-inspired reforms as envisioned in Prebisch's *Toward a Dynamic Development Policy* and other structuralist writings of the 1960s.

Ironically, in the retrospect of the 1990s, a rather favourable economic climate in Latin America can be seen in the 1960s, the years in which dependency analysis emerged. The rate of population growth in Latin America, highest among the world's major regions, had peaked in the early 1960s, and had begun a long-term decline – something Sunkel could not have known in the middle of the decade. The international economy was more dynamic in the period 1960–73 (ending with the OPEC oil price shock) than in any other period in the post-war era,

[135] Sergio Bitar, *Transição, socialismo e democracia: Chile com Allende*, trans. by Rita Braga (São Paulo, 1980), pp. 49–50; Aníbal Pinto, 'Desarrollo económico y relaciones sociales', in Aníbal Pinto, Sergio Aranda and Alberto Martínez, *Chile, hoy* (Mexico, D. F., 1970), p. 47; Enrique Sierra, *Tres ensayos de estabilización en Chile: Las políticas aplicadas en el decenio 1956–1966* (Santiago, 1970), pp. 91–4, 183–5.

permitting diversification of Latin American exports, including manufactures. Perhaps most ironical was the fact that the post-war economic growth rate for the region reached a peak in 1965–73, and in the same years, industrial output in the region averaged 8.0 per cent annually, a higher rate than in any other period before or since.[136] But analysts of the mid-sixties, in the midst or on the cusp of these developments, had no way of knowing Latin America was beginning its most successful period of economic growth and diversification.

At all events ECLA's theories and policy prescriptions were not only challenged by the neo-classical right, but also by a heterodox left, some of whose members had been leading figures in ECLA itself, notably Furtado and Sunkel. This new left would quickly make 'dependency theory' famous. Although ECLA itself had produced nothing if not a kind of dependency analysis, the new variety was set off by its more clear-cut 'historicizing' and 'sociologizing' tendencies in both its reformist and radical versions.

Not only had Furtado and Sunkel in the mid-sixties adopted an explicitly historical view of development, noted above, but Furtado now elaborated on an earlier contention that development and underdevelopment were linked. As early as 1959 he had written that there was a 'tendency for industrial economies, as a result of their form of growth, to inhibit the growth of primary economies', and he expanded on the idea in *Development and Underdevelopment* two years later. In 1966 he argued that because the two processes were historically associated, underdevelopment could not be a phase in the passage to development.[137]

[136] See chapter by Ricardo Ffrench-Davis, Oscar Muñoz and José Gabriel Palma, 'The Latin American economies, 1950–1990', in this volume

[137] Celso Furtado, *A operação Nordeste* (Rio de Janeiro, 1959), p. 13; Furtado, *Desenvolvimento e subdesenvolvimento* (Rio de Janeiro, 1961), p. 180 and passim; Furtado, *Subdesenvolvimento*, pp. 3–4. These statements lend credence to a claim of priority for Furtado as the first theorist of dependency, but I believe H. W. Arndt has exaggerated in tracing Furtado's dependency position back to *The Economic Growth of Brazil* (Berkeley, Cal., 1963 [Portuguese orig., 1959]), which in my view is more correctly described as the full historicization of structuralism. (See Arndt, *Economic Development*, p. 120.) In any event, in a recent retrospective Furtado dates his major contributions to dependency analysis in books and articles published between 1970 and 1978. In these works, Furtado views as a central feature of underdevelopment the adoption of the consumption patterns of the developed West by the upper strata of underdeveloped areas, as these regions entered the international division of labour. This process was the 'result of the surplus generated through static comparative advantages in foreign trade. It is the highly dynamic nature of the modernized component of consumption that brings dependence into the technological realm and makes it part of the production structure'. Novel items of consumption require increasingly sophisticated techniques and increasing amounts of capital. But capital accumulation is associated with income concentration, so industrialization 'advances simultaneously with the concentration of income'. Celso Furtado, 'Underdevelopment: to conform or reform', in Gerald Meier (ed.), *Pioneers in*

In his analysis of economic history, Furtado also introduced the element of social class. He argued in 1964 that class struggle had historically been the engine of economic growth in the west: workers 'attack' through organization in order to raise their share of the national product and capitalists 'counterattack' by introducing labour-saving technology. Since labour is unorganized in the Periphery, above all in the rural sector, he asserted, the process fails to work there. These *marxisant* propositions are perhaps less surprising than they appear at first glance, since they are an extrapolation of Prebisch's initial explanation of declining terms of trade.[138] Furtado's several essays in the latter sixties, written largely in exile in Paris, pointed to the need for an analysis of the whole capitalist system, Centre and Periphery together.

Another Brazilian, Fernando Henrique Cardoso, played a major role in moving the dependency perspective toward an analysis of social relations during his association with ECLA (through its sociological annex, ILPES) in the latter sixties. Indeed, Santiago, with its various research institutions through which structuralists and their leftist critics moved, was the crucible of dependency analysis.[139] Independently of ECLA, Cardoso had arrived at a pessimistic view of the 'national bourgeoisie' through his empirical studies of industrialists in Brazil and Argentina; and his view that Latin America lacked what Charles Morazé has called a 'conquering bourgeoisie' was shared by other sociologists who had studied the matter.[140] Cardoso had reached his position before the presence of multinational corporations became so prominent, and native industrialists less conspicuous, in the more open economies of the Argentine and Brazilian dictatorships of the latter 1960s.

Development, second series (New York, 1987), pp. 210–211. A full statement of Furtado's mature views on dependency is *Accumulation and Development: The Logic of Industrial Civilization,* trans. by Suzette Macedo (Oxford, 1983 [Port. orig., 1978]), in which he relates accumulation to power and social stratification. Thus the evolution of Furtado's thought on this matter was similar to Prebisch's between *Hacia una dinámica* (1963) and *Capitalismo periférico* (1981).

138 Furtado, *Subdesenvolvimento,* p. 7; Furtado, *Diagnosis of the Brazilian Crisis,* trans. by Suzette Macedo (Berkeley, Cal., 1965 [Port. orig., 1964]), pp. 48–51.

139 For example, note the Brazilian contributors to dependency who were in Santiago in the years following the 1964 coup in their country: Furtado, Fernando Henrique Cardoso, Theôtonio dos Santos, Rui Mauro Marini, and José Serra (still a student).

140 See Fernando Henrique Cardoso, *Empresário industrial e desenvolvimento econômico no Brasil,* (São Paulo, 1964); Cardoso, 'The Entrepreneurial Elites of Latin America', *Studies in Comparative International Development,* 2 (1966): 147; Cardoso, *Ideologías de la burguesía industrial en sociedades dependientes (Argentina y Brasil)* (Mexico, D. F., 1971) [data collected in 1963, 1965–6], pp. 1, 103, 146, 158, 215; Dardo Cuneo, *Comportimiento y crisis de la clase empresarial* (Buenos Aires, 1967), pp. 129, 172, 192; and Claudio Véliz, 'Introduction', in Véliz (ed.), *Obstacles to Change in Latin America,* pp. 2, 7–8.

While Sunkel spoke of the international capitalist system as 'a determining influence on local processes', and one which was 'internal' to the Periphery's own structure, Cardoso and his Chilean collaborator, Enzo Faletto, preferred to speak of two sub-systems, the internal and the external, and emphasized that the international capitalist system was not solely determining. There was a complex internal dynamic to the system, they asserted.[141]

Beyond this, Cardoso and Faletto stressed the mutual interests among social classes *across* the Centre-Periphery system. The interests of the bourgeoisie of the Centre, and by implication, those of its proletariat, overlapped those of the bourgeoisie of the Periphery; these links became all the more intimate as multinational corporations loomed ever larger in Latin America.[142] Cardoso and Faletto analysed the development of the 'populist' coalition of national and foreign capital with the working class, corresponding to the successful phase of ISI, and linked the failure of import substitution with the demise of the populist political style. In the current phase of capital accumulation, they believed, authoritarian regimes were needed to assure a political demobilization of the masses.[143]

Their treatment of dependency, despite its early appearance, was more nuanced than others, emphasizing contradiction, shifting alliances, and a range of historical possibility. Cardoso and Faletto distinguished between simple enclave economies and those controlled by local bourgeoisies. For the latter, they entertained the possibility of significant manufacturing sectors. In a scheme they called 'associated development' or 'development with marginalization [*marginalidad*]' and which Cardoso would later term 'associated-dependent' development, they noted that contemporary foreign capital was focusing its investment in manufacturing operations. Furthermore, the public sector, multinational capital, and the 'national' capitalist sector were joining hands under authoritarian rule. Like Furtado, Cardoso and Faletto pointed to the international system as a whole as the proper unit of analysis; and like Furtado, they saw development and underdevelopment not as stages, but as locations within the international

141 Osvaldo Sunkel, "The Pattern of Latin American Dependence', in Victor L. Urquidi and Rosemary Thorp (eds), *Latin America in the International Economy* (London, 1973), p. 6; Fernando Henrique Cardoso and Enzo Faletto, *Dependencia y desarrollo en América Latina: Ensayo de interpretación sociológica* (Mexico, D. F., 1969), pp. 17, 28, 38.

142 In 1965 Hélio Jaguaribe had already specified a 'consular' bourgeoisie, with distinct interests from the 'national' or 'industrial' variety: 'The Dynamics of Brazilian Nationalism', in Véliz (ed.), *Obstacles*, p. 182.

143 Cardoso and Faletto, *Dependencia*, pp. 27, 143, 154, 155.

economic system, for which they offered a schematic historical analysis of the Periphery's class dynamics.[144]

Concurrent with the efforts of Cardoso and Faletto, another researcher in Santiago was producing a radical version of dependency that was almost as widely, and perhaps more hotly, debated. This was the German-born, U.S.-educated André Gunder Frank, whose *Capitalism and Underdevelopment in Latin America* has sold 100,000 copies in nine languages, compared to an equal number in the Spanish edition alone by Cardoso and Faletto.[145] Because Frank borrowed from a Marxist tradition – probably without being decisively influenced by it – it is necessary to consider the history of Latin American Marxism, which, like structuralism, was undergoing a fundamental reassessment in the 1960s.

The crisis of Marxism in Latin America in the 1960s revolved around one of the issues that had most troubled structuralists, namely, the role of the local or national bourgeoisies. Since the twenties, the Communist parties of Latin America had vacillated – in truth, oscillated – between the view that the local bourgeoisie was progressive, and the view that it was reactionary, depending largely on the varying position of the Communist International (Comintern) and the Soviet Union. In 1929 the Peruvian José Carlos Mariátegui, usually regarded as the most original Latin American Marxist writing before the Second World War, had argued that capitalism had reached Latin America too late for the local bourgeoisies to emulate the historic role of their European forbears.[146] Yet the prevailing doctrine in most Latin American Communist Parties, from the Popular Front period, beginning in 1934, until the early sixties, was that the local bourgeoisie was a progressive force: contending that their continent had large feudal residues, Party spokesmen argued that proletarians and bour-

144 Cardoso and Faletto, *Dependencia,* pp. 28, 32–3, 135 (quotation), 142, 147, 155. For Cardoso's views on dependency in the early 1970s, see his 'Associated-dependent Development: theoretical and practical implications', in Alfred Stepan (ed.), *Authoritarian Brazil: Origins, Policies and Future* (New Haven, Conn., 1973), pp. 142–78. This feature of Cardoso's dependency analysis, emphasizing the possibilities of growth, against the theses of Furtado, Frank, and Marini, became more prominent in the midst of the 'Brazilian miracle'. The role of the multinationals became the subject of a major research agenda in the 1970s for students of dependency and for ECLA as such; in the absence of a 'European' bourgeoisie, the multinational corporations would dominate the new phase of industrialization in Latin America.

145 Andre Gunder Frank, 'The Underdevelopment of Development' [a memoir], *Scandinavian Journal of Development Alternatives* 10, 3 (September, 1991), p. 35; interview with F. H. Cardoso by author, São Paulo, 8 June 1990.

146 José Carlos Mariátegui, 'Point de vue anti-imperialiste' [1929] in Michael Lowy, *Le marxisme en Amérique latine de 1909 à nos jours: Anthologie* (Paris, 1980), p. 113.

geois must struggle in concert, at the present phase of history, to eliminate feudal residues and to contain imperialist penetration. They agreed with Mariátegui that capitalism was relatively recent in Latin America; it had made its first appearance there in the nineteenth century.[147] But unlike Mariátegui, they concluded that capitalism could and must, by grim necessity, be developed in the region.

Support for the national bourgeoisie and capitalist industrialization was the position, for example, of the Communist Party of Brazil, an organization effectively part of Brazil's 'developmentalist' and populist coalition for much of the period 1945–64. In Cuba, as late as August 1960, just two months before Castro's sweeping nationalization of the economy, the Communist leader Blas Roca announced that the Cuban Revolution was not socialist, but 'bourgeois-democratic'.[148] Yet the issue that the Cuban Revolution posed after October 1960 was the viability of 'the uninterrupted path to socialism', a thesis long defended by Latin American Trotskyists, but more audibly proclaimed as viable policy by Ernesto 'Che' Guevara the same year. After Fidel Castro's public adherence to Marxist-Leninism in December, 1961, the thesis that contemporary Latin America could only sustain bourgeois-democratic regimes would have to be reappraised.[149]

A pre-existing historiography was now discovered – beginning with Sergio Bagú's *Economía de la sociedad colonial* in 1949, an essay which argued that Latin America had never had a feudal past at all, but in broad outline had evinced fundamental features of capitalism since the sixteenth century. The Spanish and Portuguese empires in the New World, Bagú and others alleged, were basically commercial enterprises, for which 'feudal' titles and trappings were but a veil.[150] This school, composed chiefly of non-conformist Marxists, would oppose Communist orthodoxy on the role of the bourgeoisie *not* by asserting that capitalism had arrived too late

[147] For example, V[olodia] Teitelboim, 'El desarrollo del capitalismo en Chile', in Alexei Rumiantsev (ed.), *El movimiento contemporaneo de liberación y la burguesía nacional* (Prague, 1961), p. 156. On feudal residues in contemporary Latin America, see Rodney Arismendi, 'Acerca del papel de la burguesía nacional en la lucha anti-imperialista', in ibid., pp. 134, 136.

[148] Lowy, *Le marxisme*, pp. 223–6 (Brazil), 47 (Cuba).

[149] [Ernesto] Che Guevara, *Guerrilla Warfare* (New York, 1961 [Sp. orig., 1960]), p. 15; Lowy, *Le marxisme*, p. 269.

[150] Sergio Bagú, *La economía de la sociedad colonial: Ensayo de la historia comparada de América Latina* (Buenos Aires, 1949). Bagú's work was not explicitly Marxist, unlike those of four other contributors to this thesis: Marcelo Segall and Luis Vitale of Chile, Milcíades Peña of Argentina, and Caio Prado, Jr. of Brazil, whose writings on this matter are anthologized in Lowy, *Le marxisme*, pp. 243–53, 413–22. From a non-Marxist perspective, Roberto Simonsen had denied that Brazil had known anything other than capitalism in its colonial history, well before the Marxist debate. Simonsen, *História econômica do Brasil (1500–1820)*, 4th edn (São Paulo, 1962 [orig. 1937]), pp. 80–3.

in Latin America, as Mariátegui had contended, but that, on the contrary, capitalism had already prevailed too long in the region; consequently there was nothing to hope from the local bourgeoisie. This class, rather than overseas imperialists, would constitute the 'immediate enemy', as Frank put it, for Cuba-inspired groups.

In Brazil, for instance, between 1960 and 1966 Caio Prado Jr. elaborated the argument that from the outset his country's agriculture had been capitalist in its essential features, that is, that the Portuguese colony was a mercantile enterprise in which there existed (at a theoretical level), legal equality among the settlers. In *A revolução brasileira* (1966), a work which influenced a generation of urban guerrillas and was the unstated reason for his incarceration in 1969, Prado reviewed the course of Brazilian history to show that his country, as fully 'capitalist', was ripe for revolution, contrary to the official position of the nation's Communist Party, of which he had long been a member. Prado's thesis seems to have had a major influence on Andre Gunder Frank, who expanded Prado's argument on capitalism in Brazilian agriculture in Prado's journal, *Revista Brasiliense,* in 1964.[151]

Frank's work forms the most obvious point of contact between the revisionist Marxists who emphasized relations of exchange and the structuralists. In the mid-sixties he would in fact rework ECLA's theses to yield a radical conclusion.[152] Frank was explicit about at least some of his sources: from Sergio Bagú – whose work was not cast in Marxist terms – he borrowed the proposition that Latin America's economy had been essentially capitalist from the colonial era. From the economist Paul Baran, a Russian-born U.S. Marxist, Frank took the proposition that capitalism simultaneously produces underdevelopment in some areas as its produces development in others.[153] Frank briefly worked on commission for ECLA,

[151] Caio Prado, Jr., *A revolução brasileira* (São Paulo, 1966). Prado's articles of the early 1960s are collected in his *A questão agrária* (São Paulo, 1979). Andre Gunder Frank's essay reflecting Prado's influence was 'A agricultura brasileira: capitalismo e o mito do feudalismo', in *Revista Brasiliense,* 51 (January–February, 1964), published in English in Frank, *Capitalism,* pp. 219–77. Frank acknowledges Prado's influence in 'Underdevelopment of Development', p. 26. Fernando Henrique Cardoso in 1977 viewed Prado as one of a group of Brazilian scholars trying to identify a colonial mode of production. See Cardoso, 'The Consumption of Dependency Theory in the United States', *Latin American Research Review,* 12, 3 (1977), pp. 11–12. I do not believe Prado saw the problem in that way in the early 1960s: his category was capitalism.

[152] Frank's model has the force and crudity of W. W. Rostow's 'stages of growth' model, to which it has been compared. See Aidan Foster-Carter, 'From Rostow to Gunder Frank: conflicting paradigms in the analysis of development', *World Development,* 4, 3 (1976): 167–80, esp. 175.

[153] Despite Frank's attribution of Baran, H. W. Arndt has pointed out that Frank went beyond Baran, who had held that capitalism was an obstacle to the underdeveloped world's progress, to argue that underdevelopment was *caused by* capitalism: *Economic Development,* p. 127.

from which he presumably took his thesis of deteriorating terms of trade, though he was to emphasize monopoly elements in the process much more than ECLA had. Frank's antinomy 'metropolis-satellite' is surely derived from 'Centre-Periphery', and his notion of 'involution' – the development of the satellite in periods of crisis in the metropolis – is directly analogous to ECLA's historical analysis of 'inward-directed' growth.

From the Mexican political scientist Pablo González Casanova, Frank borrowed the thesis of 'internal colonialism', whereby industrial and political centres within the satellite exploit their dependent regions through fiscal and exchange policies, and by draining off capital and talent.[154] Frank linked transnational exploitation with internal colonialism, hypothesizing a concatenation of metropolis-satellite relations from Wall Street down to the smallest Latin American village, in which only the end points of the continuum would not stand in both relationships.[155]

Frank, perhaps more than any other writer except the Mexican sociologist Rodolfo Stavenhagen,[156] hammered away at the theme that dualism did not exist in Latin America: all areas were linked by an unequal exchange of goods and services, consequent to underdeveloped capitalism. Thus Frank attacked the traditional Communist positions on 'feudal residues' and non-Marxist dualism as well.[157] Frank's polemical essay paralleled the simultaneous but less didactic and less explicit efforts of Furtado and Sunkel to find causal links between development and underdevelopment.

Frank the synthesizer was also an effective wordsmith, and he termed the plight of Latin America and, by extension, that of the Third World, the 'development of underdevelopment'. For Frank, Latin America had been 'underdeveloping' for more than four centuries, a process which he divided into four phases, each defined by the principal form of monopoly

[154] Andre Gunder Frank, *On Capitalist Underdevelopment* (Bombay, 1975), p. 11 (on Prebisch), 26 (on Bagú), 68 (terms of trade), 73 (González Casanova); Frank, *Capitalism and Underdevelopment in Latin America* (New York, 1967), pp. xi, xviii (on Baran), xii (association with ECLA). On Frank's professional development, see his memoir, 'Underdevelopment of Development'.

[155] This was an independent 'rediscovery', I believe, of a model Manoilescu had developed a generation earlier, and one Singer and Furtado had worked out in a structuralist framework in the 1950s. (See note 80 above.)

[156] Rodolfo Stavenhagen, 'Seven Fallacies about Latin America', in James Petras and Maurice Zeitlin, (eds), *Latin America: Reform or Revolution?: A Reader* (Greenwich, Conn., 1968 [Sp. orig., 1965]), pp. 15–18.

[157] The non-Marxist dualism Frank and Stavenhagen attacked was less that of ECLA than that of the Dutch colonial economist J. H. Boeke, who had first developed the concept of virtually unrelated modern and peasant subsistence sectors in the Indonesian economy. Although ECLA had hypothesized the existence of a dual economy in the 1949 *Survey*, in its model the surplus labour force passed from subsistence to modern sectors, assuming a highly wage-elastic labour supply. ECLA in any event preferred the term 'heterogeneous' to 'dualist'.

exercised from the metropolis: commercial monopoly, in the age of mercantilism; industrial monopoly, during the age of classical liberalism; monopoly of capital goods, 1900–50; and monopoly of technological innovation, 1950 to the present.[158]

It is notable that the stages developed by Frank, the Brazilian Theotônio dos Santos, and the Norwegian Johan Galtung (who had extensive contacts in Santiago)[159] were stages in the development of the entire capitalist system, not stages in the sense of W. W. Rostow, in which the underdeveloped countries would repeat the unilinear trajectory of the advanced capitalist nations.[160] A similar emphasis on the development of the whole system was also implicit in the work of Furtado, and Cardoso and Faletto.

For Frank, exit from the system in a revolutionary struggle, following the Cuban example, was the path to development. Only in that manner could 'involution', a partial and temporary exit, be transformed into continuous development. There was an urgency in Frank's voluntarist view that the continued underdevelopment inherent in capitalism would make the breakthrough all the more difficult.[161] He argued that the gap between metropolis – the United States – and satellite – Chile, a case study – was widening 'in power, wealth, and income'; and that the 'relative and absolute' income of the poorest classes in Chile was decreasing.[162] Frank agreed with Cardoso and other dependency writers on the existence of a single Centre-Periphery system, developing historically; on the consequent error of a Boekean dualist approach (see note 157); on the failure of national bourgeoisies to provide leadership in capitalist development; and on the existence of unequal exchange. But he differed with Cardoso on the political inferences to be drawn, and on the extent of unequal exchange, interpreting it in 'drain' terms rather than as unequal gains between Centre and Periph-

[158] Frank, *Capitalism,* p. 211.

[159] Galtung was in Santiago in 1962–63, and maintained contact with Santiago-based personnel later. His model of imperialism cites the dependency literature, and Sunkel criticized the essay in manuscript. See Johan Galtung, 'A Structural Theory of Imperialism', *Journal of Peace Research,* 2 (1971): 81–117.

[160] Theotônio dos Santos, 'The Structure of Dependence', *American Economic Review: Papers and Proceedings,* 60, 2 (May, 1970), pp. 231–36, esp. 232; Johan Galtung, in preceding note; W. W. Rostow, *The Stages of Economic Growth: A Non-Communist Manifesto* (Cambridge, 1960).

[161] Revolution would be more costly in human terms because of the strengthening of capitalist institutions in the development-underdevelopment process. Frank, *On Capitalist Underdevelopment,* p. 110.

[162] Frank, *Capitalism,* pp. 47–8. A writer who took a similar position on the 'superexploitation' of workers in dependent countries was Rui Mauro Marini, in *Dialéctica de la dependencia* (Mexico, D.F. 1973). In 1974 F. H. Cardoso argued that Frank and Marini were repeating an error of the *narodniki* in denying the possibility of capitalist development in the Periphery. Cardoso, *Autoritarismo e democratização* (Rio de Janeiro, 1975 [orig., 1974]), pp. 27–30.

ery. Frank clearly disagreed with Marx and Prebisch, who, holding that rising productivity was the essence of capitalist development, did not believe that the development of the Centre had to be *primarily* at the expense of the Periphery.[163]

Just as we examined the roots of Prebisch's Centre-Periphery model, so it is necessary to ask about the origins of the dependency school. This is important, since Marxist roots have been ascribed to dependency analysis by one of its best students, José Gabriel Palma, and by the man with one of the best claims to be the school's founder, Fernando Henrique Cardoso. Many other contributors to, and students of, dependency have agreed with its derivation from a Marxist or Leninist tradition.[164] This interpretation has been reinforced by the English edition of *Dependency and Development* (1979) by Cardoso and Faletto, in which preface, postscript, and parts of the text show a strong Marxist orientation. By contrast, the first Spanish edition (1969) is far less obviously influenced by Marxism, and the original draft (1965) is recognizably an ECLA product. In this first version the authors challenge the Parsonian categories of modernization theory, and they are pessimistic about the reformism of local bourgeoisies, but from an eclectic perspective. No Marxist studies were cited in the draft, and Marxist categories are almost completely lacking. The theme receiving most attention in the 1965 version was the inadequacy of the bourgeois-directed project of development, partly resulting from increasing market domination by multinational corporations.[165]

The issue is clouded, however, by elements in Cardoso's 1964 study of

163 Frank's use of Marxist analysis was quickly challenged. Ruggiero Romano and Ernesto Laclau charged him with 'circulationism' – putting primary emphasis on relations of exchange rather than relations of production, whereas for Marx, as Laclau emphasized, capitalism was defined by a (free) wage labour market: Only when labour power had become a commodity could relative surplus value be maximized, and this process occurred in the Centre long before it appeared in the Periphery. Romano, review of *Capitalism and Underdevelopment* in *Desarrollo Económico,* 10, 38 (July–September, 1970), p. 287; Laclau, 'Feudalismo y capitalismo en América Latina' [orig., 1971], in Carlos Sempat Assadourian, (ed.), *Modos de producción en América Latina* (Mexico, D.F. 1973), pp. 28–37, 43.

164 José Gabriel Palma, 'Dependency: a formal theory of underdevelopment or a methodology for the analysis of concrete situations of underdevelopment?', *World Development,* 6, 7–8 (1978), p. 882 (while Palma acknowledges ECLA as a contributor to dependency analysis, he gives far more attention to Marxism); Cardoso, 'Consumption', pp. 10, 14; Heraldo Muñoz, 'Cambio y continuidad en el debate sobre la dependencia y el imperialismo', *Estudios Internacionales,* 11, 44 (October–December, 1978): 104; Sheldon B. Liss, *Marxist Thought in Latin America* (Berkeley, Cal., 1984), p. 25; José Aricó, *La cola del diablo: itinerario de Gramsci en América Latina* (Buenos Aires, 1988), p. 106.

165 See Cardoso and Faletto, *Dependencia y desarrollo* (1969); and the original draft, 'Estancamiento y desarrollo económico en América Latina: Condiciones sociales y políticas (Consideraciones para un programa de estudio)', mimeo., late 1965, located in ILPES files, at the Santiago headquarters of the U.N.

Brazilian entrepreneurs. That work adumbrates one of his most important contributions to the dependency tradition – namely, his denial of the adequacy of the modernization paradigm, although in the limited context of the role of entrepreneurs.[166] In that work, Cardoso, though eclectic in methodology, cast his major conclusions within a Marxist paradigm.[167] Thus the sources of Cardoso's contribution were various, and a safe conclusion would seem to be that he could make his statement in either a structuralist or a Marxist idiom. Yet it was initially made in the former, as dependency emerged in Santiago.

As the decade of the sixties developed, many writers on dependency adopted an exclusively Marxist perspective, and dependency analysis matured as a 'region' of Marxism: It offered a perspective on imperialism which the classical Marxist theorists of the subject had ignored, namely, the view from the Periphery.[168] A respectable Marxist pedigree was apparently required to validate the dependency perspective after its radicalization, and after it was challenged by those claiming to represent an orthodox Marxist tradition. Yet most of the dependency propositions were initially derived from structuralism, rather than Marxism, even when compatible with the latter school.[169] In any event, dependency became influential outside Latin America in the 1970s. The best-known historical model of world capitalism developing the implications of dependency was Immanuel Wallerstein's *Modern World System.* As Wallerstein had a major impact on Anglophone scholars, so Samir Amin extended dependency perspectives in Francophone areas, and to Africa more broadly.[170]

While 'orthodox' Marxists attacked dependency for focussing on relations in the international market and neglecting class analysis – a charge only partly justified in the case of Cardoso – the dependency school was attacked by non-Marxist social scientists, especially in North America, for

166 Cardoso denied that the roles played by Europe's historical bourgeoisies in economic development could be replicated by Brazilian entrepreneurs in the 1960s. Cardoso, *Empresário,* pp. 41, 44, 183.

167 Ibid., pp. 181–7.

168 Though a critic of the dependency literature, one of the few writers on dependency who worked within a framework of formal Marxist economics, as opposed to historical materialism, was the Colombian Salomón Kalmanovitz. He sketched a theory of dependent reproduction, accounting for the incomplete accumulation process in the Periphery. See his *El desarrollo tardío del capitalismo: Un enfoque crítico de la teoría de la dependencia* (Bogotá, 1983).

169 Cf. a fuller argument in Joseph L. Love, 'The Origins of Dependency Analysis', *Journal of Latin American Studies,* 22, 1 (1990): 143–68.

170 Wallerstein's main project, *The Modern World System,* a history of capitalism from the late middle ages to modern times, has yielded three volumes to date (New York, 1974, 1980, 1989). Amin's major works were *Accumulation on a World Scale,* 2 vols (1974 [Fr. orig., 1970]) and *Unequal Development* (1976 [Fr. orig., 1973]), both published in New York and translated by Brian Pearce.

its vagueness, inconsistencies, and alleged inability to generate propositions which could be falsified (in Karl Popper's sense). Cardoso's affirmation that the school did not offer a body of theory, but a perspective for contextual and historical analysis, was seen as elusive. Its inability to provide unambiguous solutions or programmes, in the Cardoso version, also weakened its appeal.

THE MODES OF PRODUCTION DEBATE

For economic policy in the late 1960s and 1970s, neo-classical orthodoxy, not structuralism nor dependency, provided the signposts for most of Latin America. The neo-classical counter-attack dismissed dependency and challenged structuralist interpretations of the capital-intensive bias in Latin American industry. Orthodox economists argued that the *actual* cost of labour was greater than that of capital (relative to respective shadow prices). Capital costs in Latin America were kept artificially low by liberal depreciation allowances, low or even negative real interest rates (in periods of inflation), low tariffs on capital imports, overvalued exchange rates, and institutionally induced high wages. Therefore, according to this reasoning, choices of labour-saving techniques had been rational, in the face of distortions of relative prices. Furthermore, the neo-classical school argued that low productivity in agriculture was not necessarily caused by a lack of rural entrepreneurship – as a result, for example, of a traditional *latifundista* mentality – but derived in great measure from government programmes of import-substitution. By this analysis, ISI, resulting in high-cost manufactured goods, had turned the domestic terms of trade against agriculture. Furthermore, exchange policies designed to assist industrialization had given agricultural exporters less than the full value of their foreign sales, and thereby discouraged production.

Economic orthodoxy was frequently introduced by repressive regimes, if for no other reason than to reduce wages in an effort to restore profits after ISI had faltered, and to control inflation. Four counties in which the military held power for long periods – Brazil, Argentina, Chile, and Uruguay – were particularly influenced by the monetarist economics of the Chicago school.[171] It was in this economic climate – and in a political context of repression and the failure of urban guerrilla movements in the

[171] See Alejandro Foxley, *Latin American Experiments in Neo-Conservative Economics* (Berkeley, Cal., 1983), esp. on Chile, where monetarism was applied most rigorously. Juan Gabriel Valdés offers a scholarly but equally unsympathetic study in *La escuela de Chicago: Operación Chile* (Buenos Aires, 1989).

late sixties and early seventies – that Marxist intellectuals in Latin America began to move in more abstract and theoretical directions, and to experience the impact of the modes of production debate in France, particularly concerning an 'African' mode.

For the historical development of the West, Marx had defined five 'modes of production', which were complex assemblages of the relations of production between producer and non-producer, and of the forces of production. These were the primitive collective, slave, feudal, capitalist, and socialist modes, which corresponded to past, present, and future of the west. He had also written of an Asiatic mode, in which a despot skimmed all but a negligible surplus. Therefore, this mode included no investment nor technological change; it was cyclical and history-less. Stalin directed Soviet ideologues to strike the Asiatic mode from the catalogue in 1931, and proclaimed the inevitability of the sequence of the five others in the 1930s. All existing societies were reinterpreted by Communist theorists as falling into the western stages, even though it was obvious to specialists that such sequential 'stages' for many societies were inadequate. The Comintern's linear view of national histories was, in fact, a counterpart to modernization theory. Thus the rehabilitation of the Asiatic mode in the 1950s was an element in the revitalization of Marxist research in Europe. It was in this context that Marxist students of Africa in France, influenced by the recent translation and diffusion of Marx's *Grundrisse,* began to search for modes of production unknown, and unknowable, to Marx and Engels.[172]

The modes-of-production debate in Latin America was conditioned not only by French writings specifically directed to the issue, but by the broader current of structuralist Marxism associated with the work of Louis Althusser and Etienne Balibar. On the modes problem, Balibar had written in *Reading Capital* (1965) that two or more modes could be articulated in a single 'simultaneity', during a period of transition from one mode to another, provided that one was dominant.[173] Althusser's rereading of *Capital* and his defense of the mature 'Leninist' Marx against the young 'humanist' Marx inspired seminars on Marx's magnum opus in several Latin American cities during the mid-sixties. The most important of these

[172] Maurice Godelier, Jean Suret-Canale, and Catherine Coquery-Vidrovich were the principal participants in the debate, which took place in the Marxist journal *La Pensée* over the decade of the 1960s.

[173] Etienne Balibar, 'Elements for a Theory of Transition', in Louis Althusser and Balibar, *Reading Capital,* trans. by Ben Brewster (London, 1970 [French orig., 1965]), p. 307. A Spanish edition of Althusser's *Pour Marx* was published in Mexico in 1967.

was held in Santiago, already mentioned as the locus of the dependency school; many of this group participated in the *Capital* seminar.[174] Also among the participants was Marta Harnecker, who probably did more than anyone else in Latin America to diffuse the work of Althusser, with whom she had studied in Paris. Harnecker's Althusserian primer, *Los conceptos elementales del materialismo histórico,* was first published in 1969 and had reached its thirty-fifth edition eight years later.[175] Many other Latin Americans, of course, were in direct contact with French Marxist ideas through study in Paris or acquaintance with *La Pensée* and other French Marxist publications.

Yet for Latin Americans, French Marxism was not the only source; indigenous forces were also at work. In some respects the modes of production debate was a response to the dependency school, in that it questioned the uses to which Marxist theory was put. Viewed from a different perspective, the 'modes' debate was an extension of an increasingly formally Marxist dependency literature. It dealt with the same basic problem, namely, how 'backward' structures are related to an advancing capitalist order.

Dependency might even be seen as the opening phase of the modes-of-production debate, since the conventional thesis of 'feudal residues' was challenged by Frank in his polemic in 1965 with Rodolfo Puiggrós, a former leader of the Argentine Communist Party. Among other things, Frank argued that Latin America's so-called feudal estates were not related to a subsistence economy, but were the decadent result of a previous phase of capitalist expansion. The exchange resonated especially in Argentina and Mexico.[176]

The issue was reframed when the Argentinian Ernesto Laclau attacked Frank in two articles in 1969 and 1971. Laclau, who had read the debate on the 'African' mode in *La Pensée,*[177] argued that students of the Latin American economy, a congeries of disparate elements, did not have to choose between capitalism and feudalism: The region could have more than one mode of production, as long as a dominant, structuring mode –

174 Interview with Theotônio dos Santos by author, Rio de Janeiro, 22 July 1985.

175 Marta Harnecker, *Los conceptos elementales del materialismo histórico* (Mexico, D. F., 35th rev. edn, 1977 [orig. 1969]).

176 The debate, originally in *El Gallo Ilustrado,* a Sunday supplement of the Mexican daily *El Día,* was twice published in both Mexico, D.F. and Buenos Aires. Puiggrós's essay was 'Los modos de producción en Iberoamérica', and Frank's counterthesis, '¿Con qué modo de producción convierte la gallina maíz en huevos de oro?' See *El Gallo Ilustrado* (no. 173 of 17 October 1965).

177 Interview of Ernesto Laclau by author, Urbana, Ill., 12 November 1984.

capitalism – established the laws of motion for the whole system. Feudal elements were intensified, or even invented, by the international market, but were subordinated to it.[178]

In 1973 a collection of studies by Carlos Sempat Assadourian and others, *Modos de producción en América Latina,* reflected the influence of French Marxism and revealed that Latin America, like Africa, offered fertile ground for theorizing. Laclau's essay, 'Feudalism and Capitalism', was republished there. The introductory essay by Juan Carlos Garavaglia, another Argentinian, argued that Latin America had experienced several analytically distinguishable modes of production in the colonial era. Ciro F. S. Cardoso, a Brazilian, called for an effort, to which he contributed, to build a theory of a slave-based 'colonial' mode. Other contributors to the collection identified highly specific modes, such as Garavaglia's 'despotic village' mode in the Jesuit missions of Paraguay. Yet in the view of the contributors, the proliferation of types did not pose the danger of historicism – the view that all historical patterns are unique – because, as Garavaglia put it, the main proposition of the group was that the dominant mode, capitalism, was exterior to the 'dominated space' of colonial Latin America. Or, as Ciro F. S. Cardoso formulated the proposition more in accord with French thinking, dominant and dominated modes coexisted in the same 'social formation'.[179] The latter term was understood as a concrete historical whole, defined by specific economic, political, ideological, and theoretical processes of production. Yet as more and more researchers 'discovered' new modes of production, the prospect loomed that every case study would produce its own mode; where, then, was Marxist science, if every instance was unique?

In 1973 a seminal article appeared in *La Pensée,* in which Balibar revised his views on conceptualizing modes of production. The philosopher now argued that 'mode of production' was necessarily an ahistorical abstraction, and that class struggle determined the mode. Since class struggle only occurred in a given social formation, the latter, in effect, determined the mode, not vice-versa, as the contributors to the Sempat Assadourian volume had posited.[180]

178 Ernesto Laclau, 'Modos de producción, sistemas económicos y población excedente: Aproximación a los casos argentino y chileno', *Revista Latinoamericana de Sociología,* 5, 2 (1969), pp. 305–11; 'Feudalismo y capitalismo'.

179 Carlos Sempat Assadourian et al., *Modos de producción en América Latina,* pp. 14, 94, 161, 212.

180 Etienne Balibar, 'Sur la dialectique historique: Quelques remarques critiques a propos de *Lire le Capital*', *La Pensée* (August, 1973), p. 47. Also see Enrique Tandater, 'Sobre el análisis de la dominación colonial', *Desarrollo Económico,* 16, 61 (April–June 1976), p. 154.

This reformulation apparently affected the thinking of participants at an international symposium on modes of production held the following year in Mexico City, which now replaced Santiago as the chief venue of radical intellectual exchange.[181] One participant was the Ecuadorian Agustín Cueva, who contended that there could be no colonial mode, because colonialism and 'mode of production' were concepts at different levels of abstraction. In other words, a concept at the level of theory, mode of production, was being fused with an empirical category, colonialism. The symposium revealed a growing dissensus on the utility and proper use of the concept of precapitalist modes.[182] Other problems with any sort of colonial mode are the issues of who constitutes the ruling class – local or overseas groups – and how class struggle under such conditions can be specified.

A more fruitful form, perhaps, of theorizing about articulated modes concerned contemporary urban underemployment, for which the category 'marginality' was the subject of academic debate among students of dependency in the decade after 1965. Francisco de Oliveira, Lúcio Kowarick, Paul Singer, as well as Fernando Henrique Cardoso – all researchers at the Centro Brasileiro de Planejamento e Análise (CEBRAP) in São Paulo during the early 1970s – took issue with Aníbal Quijano of Peru and José Nun of Argentina, who had worked at CEPAL and other Santiago-based institutions. Quijano and Nun viewed marginality, in the sense of huge numbers of urban un- and under-employed, as a specific deformity of dependent capitalism, something distinct from Marx's 'industrial reserve army', the unemployed workers who served the purpose of holding down wages. Nun held that marginality as a Latin American social phenomenon exceeded the dimensions of a reserve army, in an age of monopoly capitalism and labour-saving technology. Though some marginals directly con-

181 General Augusto Pinochet's coup in September 1973 prompted Marxists to flee Chile, and Mexico, D.F. became the home of many exiles. The Puiggrós-Frank polemic had occurred in the Mexican capital in 1965, and the new journal *Historia y Sociedad* published the modes-of-production papers of the 1974 Congress of Americanists, as well as later contributions on the problem. For the development of Latin American Marxism in general, the prominence of Mexico, D.F. owed significantly to the writing, editing, and publishing José Aricó, an Argentine national and Latin America's leading scholar of Marxism. He transferred his Pasado y Presente operations, which had first published the Sempat collection on modes of production, from Argentina to Mexico, D.F. in the mid-1970s.

182 Roger Bartra et al., *Modos de producción en América Latina* (Lima, 1976); in particular, see Cueva, 'El uso del concepto de modo de producción en América Latina: Algunos problemas teóricos', p. 28. José Roberto do Amaral Lapa provides a list of sixty works on modes of production in Brazil, divided into four types of interpretation – feudal, capitalist, uniquely Brazilian modes, and works revising the others, in his introduction to *Modos de produção e realidade brasileira* (Petrópolis, 1980), pp. 29–33.

tributed to capitalist accumulation, for example, in the construction industry, Nun's 'marginal mass' was partly dysfunctional for the capitalist system because of its overwhelming strain on urban services.[183]

The CEBRAP group denied that marginality constituted a social problem for which classical Marxian categories were inadequate.[184] Accusing Nun and Quijano of introducing a new dualism, CEBRAP researchers saw marginality as a phenomenon which was linked to dependent capitalist accumulation through the articulation of capitalist and precapitalist modes, or the precapitalist relations of production derived from them; this articulation was dominated by the logic of the former system, locating the precapitalist elements largely in the service sector.[185] Not only did newly urbanized peasants hold down the wage level as an 'unlimited supply of labour',[186] but poorly paid hawkers helped realize profits on industrial goods with their intensive sales techniques; moreover, urban services such as car-washing, or, one could add, even shoe-shining, indirectly contributed to the realization of surplus value in the industrial sector by distributing and maintaining its products at low cost. Workers furthermore diminished the cost of wage goods for employers by constructing their own housing.[187] Thus CEBRAP analysts tended to identify marginality with the economic contributions of the informally employed or underemployed, whereas Quijano and Nun had a less sanguine view of their productivity, and emphasized the precarious nature of marginal employment. Whether influenced by the articulation approach of otherwise, the issue of marginality generated a variety of empirical and theoretical studies of the informal sector, contributions which questioned the adequacy of the concept of underemployment in Third World countries.[188]

But this was the only avenue of the modes debate that seemed to open new doors. In Brazil and elsewhere, although participants in the debate frequently appealed to the authority of Marx, the issue was vexed by the lack of a general definition of 'mode of production' in Marx's own writ-

183 For a summary of Quijano's and Nun's positions and a critique, see Cristóbal Kay, *Latin American Theories of Development and Underdevelopment* (London, 1989), pp. 100–24. Kay also discusses the CEBRAP group in this context, and I draw upon his work.

184 Fernando Henrique Cardoso, 'Participação e marginalidade', in *O modelo político brasileiro e outros ensaios* (São Paulo, 1972), p. 184.

185 Lúcio Kowarick, 'Capitalismo, dependência e marginalidade urbana na América Latina: Uma contribuição teórica', *Estudos CEBRAP* 8 (April–June, 1974), pp. 79–80; Francisco de Oliveira, 'A economia brasileira: Crítica a razão dualista', *Estudos CEBRAP* 2 (October, 1972), p. 27.

186 In W. Arthur Lewis's sense. Kowarick, 'Capitalismo, dependência e marginalidade', pp. 92, 96.

187 Oliveira, 'A economia brasileira', pp. 29, 31.

188 See Kay, *Latin American Theories*, ch. 4.

ings, and by his use of 'society' and 'social formation' interchangeably.[189] An indication of the general barrenness of the modes-of-production controversy in Latin America was that most of the early enthusiasts, at least those who contributed to the Sempat Assadourian volume, simply dropped the issue – overarching as it was – in their later monographic studies, though subsequently the theoretical effort probably helped produce some major economic studies of the colonial period, focussing on relations of production, the production process, and the circulation of commodities.[190] One of the few general results was the modest conclusion that precapitalist relations of production after the Conquest gained their significance from their *relation* to capitalism, not from any inherent 'feudalism'; another was the refutation of the thesis of an omnipresent and sempiternal capitalism. A final contribution was the CEBRAP group's work on marginality, but researchers outside the modes-of-production debate were also beginning to study the 'informal sector'.

STRUCTURALIST REPRISE

As we have seen, ECLA's theories and policy recommendations were out of favour with most of the governments of Latin America throughout the 1970s; meanwhile ECLA marshalled persuasive arguments that industrialization was still critical for social reasons. In 1979 ECLA's demographic annex had calculated that in 1990 Latin America would need 37 million more jobs than in 1980, the vast majority of them urban. In this situation, industry, broadly interpreted, was far from an unambiguous failure, in the opinion of ECLA economist Aníbal Pinto: in 1980 27 per cent of Latin America's economically active population was involved in manufacturing, power, construction, and transport; manufacturing employment alone grew faster than the region's general population growth rate from 1950 to 1980. Thus, implied Pinto, Prebisch's call for industrialization in the forties was still relevant in the eighties.[191] Furthermore, Víctor Tokman, an economist at an ECLA-associated agency, demonstrated that, compared to the historical experience of the developed countries, the

189 Harnecker, *Conceptos elementales*, p. 137; Tom Bottomore, 'social formation', in Bottomore (ed.), *A Dictionary of Marxist Thought* (Cambridge, Mass., 1983), p. 444.

190 For example, Sempat's own *El sistema de la economía colonial: El mercado interior, regiones y espacio económico* (Mexico, D. F., 1983); and Garavaglia, *Mercado interno y economía colonial* (Mexico, D. F., 1983).

191 Aníbal Pinto, 'Centro-periferia e industrialización: Vigencia y cambios en el pensamiento de la CEPAL', *Trimestre Económico*, 50, 2 (April–June, 1983), pp. 1063–4.

problem of insufficient employment opportunities in Latin America owed less to excessive population growth and a low rate of expansion in industry than to a failure of the service sector to absorb the 'informally' employed into activities of higher productivity.[192]

Nor had the terms-of-trade thesis disappeared from the scene. The British economist John Spraos revived Prebisch's argument in a more sophisticated form. The net barter terms of trade used by Prebisch is 'one-dimensional concept' for Spraos, because a policy that resulted in deterioration of net barter terms of trade might nevertheless have merit if offsetting gains in employment and labour productivity occurred. Thus Spraos proposed a measure which takes into account (net barter) terms of trade, employment, and productivity – the 'employment-corrected double factorial terms of trade'. Applying econometric tests to world trade data for 1960 – 77, he found substance in the arguments that disparities exist in elasticities of both income and supply between agricultural commodities and manufactures, coupled with pressure for increasing the supply of commodities, owing to the excess supply of labour in agriculture.[193] The Prebisch–Singer thesis of unequal exchange, thus transformed, survived into the 1990s. Furthermore, although Prebisch received not a little blame for the excesses of Third World industrialization, it may be argued that, *without* significant industrialization, terms of trade would have deteriorated much more than they actually did for primary-exporting countries.

Prebisch's own activity as economic theorist and policy advisor continued until his death at eighty-five in 1986. Though he did not associate himself directly with the dependency school, his book *Capitalismo periférico,* written in his final years, shows strong affinities with the dependency tradition, and incorporates social and political elements into his economic analysis. It dealt by implication with Brazil and Southern Cone, where military regimes were in power as the seventies ended, though the problems he treated were Latin America-wide in most respects.

The capitalism of the Periphery, Prebisch contended, was structurally different from that in the central industrialized countries, in that it was insufficiently dynamic. Prebisch focussed on the 'surplus', a concept pre-

192 Víctor Tokman, 'Unequal Development and the Absorption of Labour: Latin America 1950–1980', *CEPAL Review,* 17 (August, 1982), p. 126.

193 John Spraos, *Inequalising Trade* (Oxford, 1983), pp. 15, 33, 113, 118. Though the term did not yet exist, Prebisch was interested in the double factorial terms of trade from his earliest concern with labour costs in the industrial and agricultural trading nations, and Singer was implicitly so.

sumably inspired by classical economics: the surplus was 'the productivity increment, which, not being transferred to the labor force . . . is appropriated by the owners of the means of production.' Prebisch's surplus differed from Marx's surplus value in that it excluded compensation of entrepreneurial and managerial services.[194] The owners of the means of production appropriated productivity gains such that labour got less than a proportional share, according to Prebisch, but much of the surplus was wasted in unwarranted consumption rather than being applied to productive investment. The upper classes' interests, as well as their tastes and life styles, were closely bound up with those of the Centre. Though the Centre itself, because of its technological and economic superiority, helped generate increasing productivity in the Periphery, it also siphoned off part of these productivity gains through the activities of multinational corporations and through market and extra-market 'power relations': the Centre was 'hegemonic' for Prebisch.[195]

In peripheral capitalism new production techniques, always more capital-intensive, replaced older ones before the latter were fully amortized, because the newer ones produced the goods demanded by the Periphery's 'privileged consumer society'. Thus there was a conflict between the rationality of the firm, especially of the multinational, which would replace physical capital through amortization funds and reduce the labour force to increase efficiency, and 'collective rationality, which would choose to prolong the working life of physical capital and use the amortization funds for new investment that would provide more employment'.[196]

In the course of the struggle within the Periphery for the benefits of technological progress, there was a conflict between democratization of polity and economy and the 'serious socioeconomic bias of the mechanism for income distribution and capital accumulation in favor of the higher social strata'.[197] Conflicts between the two tended to result in the emergence of authoritarian regimes in order to restore the threatened system of income distribution and accumulation, while the population excluded from the privileged consumer society was continually increasing. Prebisch re-

[194] Raúl Prebisch, 'Power Relations and Market Laws', Working Paper no. 35, Kellogg Institute (University of Notre Dame, 1984), p. 22; also see Prebisch, *Capitalismo periférico: Crisis y transformación* (Mexico, D.F. 1981), p. 40.

[195] Prebisch, *Capitalismo periférico,* pp. 203–10.

[196] Raúl Prebisch, 'A Critique of Peripheral Capitalism', *CEPAL Review,* January–June 1976, p. 30.

[197] Raúl Prebisch, 'Five Stages in my Thinking on Development', in Gerald M. Meier and Dudley Seers (eds), *Pioneers in Development* (New York, 1984), p. 189. For a summary of Prebisch's views on 'peripheral capitalism', see pp. 183–92.

tained his faith in the state as an exogenous actor to bring about the socio-economic changes he though imperative: 'The state must regulate the social use of the surplus, to increase the rhythm of accumulation and progressively to correct the distributive disparities of a structural character'.[198]

This theoretical *envoi* was not regarded as sacrosanct by ECLA and other U.N. agencies in Santiago, where Tokman's finding of parallel experiences between the history of developed countries and the contemporary Latin American experience in industrial employment – published a year after *Capitalismo periférico* – clearly implied an excessive pessimism by Prebisch on the secondary sector.

The wave of dictatorships in the 1970s, government rejection of structuralist policies, and the expanded dependence of foreign borrowing no doubt made Prebisch and others more pessimistic about development within democratic contexts, but the economies of Latin America were still growing. From 1950 to 1981 per capita income in the region grew, in constant 1970 dollars, from US$420 to 960. The eighties, however, were the 'lost decade' for Latin American growth: of the years through 1990, per capita income for the region never attained the level of 1980, and a net outflow of capital occurred, as Latin American nations sacrificed investment to repay foreign debt. The degree to which monetarist-inspired policies can be blamed for this failure is debatable, but the 'lost decade' and the collapse of the Soviet model in 1989–91 seemed to open new vistas for the debate on development.

Structuralism during the eighties yielded to 'neo-structuralism'. The new version would avoid the mistakes of ISI and incorporate lessons from neoliberalism, seeking, for example, export opportunities, in a flexible policy to develop both internal and external markets: 'inward-directed development' would be replaced by 'development *from* within'. The state would remain interventionist, seeking to collaborate with the private sector, but would concern itself as well with social development, equity issues, and environmental problems.[199] A counter-trend emphasizing privatization, focussed on the waste of 'rent-seeking' behaviour within state bureaucracies and supported by such powerful ideological statements as the Peruvian Hernando de Soto's *El otro sendero*,[200] proved the stronger force.

198 Raúl Prebisch, 'Centro y periferia según Prebisch', *Revista Idea* año 7, no. 71 (November, 1983), p. 22. For the similar evolution of Furtado's views on dependency, see note 137.

199 See the essays in Osvaldo Sunkel (ed.) *El desarrollo desde dentro: Un enfoque neoestructuralista para la América Latina* (Mexico, D. F., 1991).

200 Hernando de Soto, *El otro sendero: La revolución informal* ([Lima], 1986). Published in English as *The Other Path: the Invisible Revolution in the Third World* (London, 1989).

CONCLUSION

The preceding pages have traced the development of economic ideas and ideologies, and especially those concerning industrialization, from a largely pre-theoretical phase in the 1930s through the rise and fall of structuralism and dependency analysis to the dominance of neo-liberalism in the 1980s. In essence, there were two phases in this story, corresponding to perceived failures in economic performance, which both implied inadequacy in analysis. The first was the failure of export-led growth, giving rise to the Prebisch–Singer thesis, which is still the subject of debate more than forty years later. The second was the failure of import-substitution industrialization, begetting in succession a dependency school on the fringes of the ECLA camp, and a Marxist riposte to dependency, a modes-of-production literature. A broader attack on the perceived failures of structuralism by neo-classical theorists, contemporaneous with that of dependency, resulted in the wave of privatization that coincided with, and was reinforced by, the failure of socialism in the Soviet Union and Eastern Europe.

In the earlier phase, Prebisch formulated his thesis of unequal exchange between Centre and Periphery over the course of two decades of direct involvment in economic and financial policy. He came to reject the thesis of comparative advantage via his partial rejection, in the context of peripheral economies, of the monetary and banking policies of Keynes. Prebisch was an eclectic, however, and also drew on the writings of Kindleberger and others. He had formulated the elements of his thesis before the appearance, in 1949, of the empirical base on which the thesis would rest in its first published form – Singer's U.N. study, *Relative Prices*. 'Structuralism' had been present in embryonic form in Prebisch's institutional arguments as to why neo-classical economics did not apply to the Periphery without modification. The analysis contained some historical elements from the outset (e.g. the decisive shift, in Prebisch's view, of the principal centre after the First World War), and a young group of ECLA economists subsequently employed structural analysis in formal historical studies.

Structuralism, in tune with international trends after 1930, gave the state a key role in the development process, in contrast with the dependency school, whose members viewed the state as less autonomous of social forces and more bound to particular class interests. In its assumption of government action as an independent variable, ECLA had perhaps approached a Hegelian position wherein the state, possessing a monopoly on objective consciousness, was the demiurge of development and the protagonist of the historical process.[201] At all events, structuralism distinguished itself from neo-classical analysis in its emphasis on macroeconomics, institutions, and interdisciplinary approaches to economic issues, as well as in treating long-term (trans-cyclical) changes.[202]

'Dependency' as a body of doctrine grew out of the perceived inability of the Latin American states to surmount the difficulties ECLA had identified – above all, the alleged dead-end of ISI, but also inflation and other problems rooted in institutional rigidities. Much of the contribution of ECLA, and its theorists writing in their own names, in this period was 'negative'. Explanations of the failure to transform the Latin American economy provided material for dependency analysts, who widened their focus from the historical development of the economy to embrace society and politics as well. Furtado and Sunkel bridged the gap between structuralism and dependency, because their examination of Latin American issues was based on a critique of international capitalism. Furtado had first raised the issue of the relation between development and underdevelopment in his study of internal colonialism, using a model derived from structuralism.

Prebisch's terms-of-trade thesis and other pro-industrialization arguments had initially provided ideological support – intentionally or not – for Latin America's national bourgeoisies.[203] Yet by the latter 1960s it was

201 Guido Mantega, *A economia política brasileira* (São Paulo, 1984), p. 43.

202 The relationship between French structuralism, which ranged across a wide spectrum of disciplines in the post-war era, and the structuralism of ECLA economists was in part coincidental. To some degree, however, the French school did have an impact on the ECLA economists, largely through the work of François Perroux, whose work on the 'dominant economy' paralleled Prebisch's, and whose subsequent work on growth poles did influence Latin American structuralism. Of the early ECLA group, Furtado, having trained in Paris, was closest to the French tradition, which defined wholeness, transformation, and self-regulation as basic features of social structures. French structuralism informed the Marxism of the Althusserians as well, leading to a possible terminological confusion for the uninitiated: one writer calls the followers of Althusser 'the Latin American structuralists'. See Richard Harris, 'Structuralism in Latin America', *The Insurgent Sociologist,* 9, 1 (Summer, 1979): 62–73.

203 There can be little doubt that early ECLA writings did define a project for the national bourgeoisies of Latin America. Yet ECLA's 'representation' of these groups was necessarily indirect, since it was an agency answerable to member states, not to social classes or corporate groups. The degree to which the several national bourgeoisies 'embraced' ECLA's theses is a much more difficult issue, since many businessmen were not versed in economic analysis and were often unsympathetic toward state planners' designs for development. A look at the business journals in the period under examination offers some clues. But the issue is clouded by the fact that there was as yet little distinction between 'business' and 'economics' periodicals. It was perhaps to be expected that such economics journals as *Trimestre Económico* (Mexico), *Revista de Economía* (Mexico), *Revista Brasileira de Economia,* and *Economía* (Chile) – all 'academic' publications – would give ECLA a favourable hearing. Yet it is interesting to note that some journals with a substantial readership of industrialists and other businessmen also occasionally or frequently published ECLA materials or com-

questionable whether that class could achieve the historical project which Prebisch had envisioned. Frank attempted to expose the exploitative nature of the national bourgeoisies, while Fernando Henrique Cardoso emphasized their diminished relevance.

Before the sixties had ended, Frank's version of dependency was challenged by claimants to a Marxist orthodoxy, theorists who saw themselves restoring relations of production to their rightful primacy. Yet the modes-of-production controversy which ensued was European-derived and scholastic, though it had Latin American features, since it began, in part, as a critique of dependency. For example, the anti-dualism of the dependency school almost necessitated an 'articulation' explanation of local relations of production. The repercussions of the Latin American modes-of-production debate were far weaker than those of structuralism and dependency, which in the late work of Prebisch tended to converge. Whether neo-structuralism is merely an epigonal phenomenon remains to be seen, but the tradition of state intervention in the economies and societies of Latin America – and therefore of an interventionist doctrine of some sort – is not likely to disappear quickly.

mented favourably on them, for example, *Revista de Economía Argentina, Economía y Finanzas* (Chile), *Industria* (Chile), *Industria Peruana, Estudos Econômicos* (Brazil), and *Desenvolvimento e Conjuntura* (Brazil). Some other businessmen's journals, however, tended to ignore ECLA, and the issue of how widely and in what ways Latin American industrialists supported the agency awaits further research. (For Brazil, in any event, Kathryn Sikkink notes that 'industrial leaders in Rio de Janeiro and São Paulo already had adopted CEPAL terminology in their speeches by the early 1950s'. Sikkink, *Ideas and Institutions,* p. 155.)

Part Five

SCIENCE AND SOCIETY

8

SCIENCE AND SOCIETY IN TWENTIETH-CENTURY LATIN AMERICA

INTRODUCTION

The development of science as an organized activity in Latin America has rarely been smooth or lineal. Rather it has been replete with false starts, with periods of consolidation followed by periods of fragmentation and reverse, often for political reasons.[1] Moreover, the considerable national variation both in the organization of science and the level of achievement of different disciplines makes any homogeneous synthesis problematical at best. This chapter treats the history of selected scientific disciplines – biology, biomedicine, psychoanalysis, physical and exact sciences, and geology – in Latin America in the twentieth century. Because of substantial gaps in the secondary literature coverage must necessarily be incomplete. The chapter focusses on the formative years of these sciences, primarily before the Second World War but with some attention of developments during the two decades after the war. Science in the second half of the twentieth century is then treated in a more general sociological mode, reflecting the bias of the secondary literature, which is supplemented by materials from the author's own collection of internal documentation of scientific institutions. Here we will follow the institutionalization of science, the emergence of a scientific ethos and changing relationships between scientists, government and society. If this leaves us with an imperfect view, we are content at least to advance some working hypotheses and provide an armature for future research.

[1] For example, on the trauma of independence which ruined the hopes and confirmed the anxieties of those, especially the naturalists, who at the end of the eighteenth century were beginning to conceptualize a science that was distinctly American and that could mature without a constant infusion of energy, materiel and information from European expeditionaries, see Thomas F. Glick, 'Science and Independence in Latin America', *Hispanic American Historical Review,* 71,2 (1991): 307–34.

An important chronological break came in 1939 when Spanish refugee scientists, joining other specific, mainly Jewish, refugees from Nazism, began acting as catalysts of an institutional transformation whose first phase was completed in the 1950s when substantial numbers of young scientists trained mainly in the United States began to make their presence felt. This transformation had both institutional and cognitive foci and was accompanied by a value change involving the implantation – socially selective and politically incomplete – of a scientific ethos.

At the beginning of the Civil War in July 1936 Spain was more advanced scientifically and producing scientific research at a higher level than any Latin American nation, although Argentina's science establishment was perhaps marginally larger. Spain's success was mainly due to the ability of her scientists to mobilize government support for science in the wake of neurohistologist Santiago Ramón y Cajal's winning the Nobel Prize for medicine in 1906. Cajal headed the Junta para Ampliación de Estudios, founded soon after, an institution which provided scholarships for study abroad and established laboratories in the most promising biomedical fields, including neurohistology and physiology. In the 1920s, attracted by the Junta's programme and congruent value structure the Rockefeller Foundation made substantial investments in Spanish medicine and physics. The Spanish Junta itself became a model that was explicitly emulated by more than a few countries of Latin America as they attempted to expand their scientific capabilities in the 1920s and after.[2]

Spanish scientists left the country in great numbers after the Republic's defeat in 1939. Five hundred medical doctors went to Mexico alone where they constituted 10 per cent of that country's medical community. But many Latin American countries that received far fewer refugees were the beneficiaries of a scientific stimulus not measurable in numbers alone. They arrived there just as their Latin American colleagues were gaining self-awareness of their collective professional and social roles as scientists.

The implantation of a scientific ethos in Latin America was strongly conditioned by attitudes laid down by the positivists of the nineteenth century. Arturo Ardao has argued that European positivism appeared as the culmination of one hundred years or more of scientific revolution, but

[2] See J. M. Sánchez Ron (ed.), *La Junta para Ampliación de Estudios e Investigaciones Científicas: 80 años después*, 2 vols (Madrid, 1988).

that in Latin America the relationship was more nearly the inverse: there 'positivism anticipated and precipitated scientific culture, instead of resulting from scientific thought as in Europe'.[3] In Latin America, scientific positivism did not have its origins in science but rather in the political philosophy and educational programmes – national 'diagrams' – of leading positivists.[4] In the nineteenth century, as put into practice by positivist political leaders like Domingo Sarmiento, in Argentina the scientific programme of positivism centered on the description of natural resources with an eye towards their exploitation in the interest of modernization. But the rest of the diagram(s) related to science materialized only at the rhetorical level in the nineteenth century and emerged in a programmatic way in the twentieth as, for example, in the creation of scientific institutions in the wake of the Mexican Revolution, or in the scientific programmes of specific ministries, such as the Brazilian Ministry of Agriculture, both a hotbed of positivism and a fecund generator of scientific projects in the first four decades of the century.

If positivism preceded rather than followed the development of science in Latin America, the same is true of science policy and the discussion and evaluation of the place of science in society. Different groups formed attitudes about science prior to the inception of national scientific institutions, producing in the process a very interesting body of discussion of the role of science in society. Concomitant with the inception of modern scientific institutions the ethos informing modern science had also to take root. These two processes took place in politically charged atmospheres, such as the continuing institutionalization of the Mexican revolution under Cárdenas in the late 1930s or the transition from the Pérez Jiménez dictatorship to democracy in Venezuela of the late 1950s. As a result the social and political study of science has both an immediacy and a sensitivity to social and cultural issues that it lacks in the developed countries. There is greater attention to the 'high tradition' in the sociology of science in Latin America than we are accustomed to in the Anglo-American academic world, as sociologists of science, observing scientific culture in the act of creation, routinely work through the great themes of science/society interaction as defined by Robert Merton, Derek Price, Thomas Kuhn and others.

[3] Arturo Ardao, 'Assimilation and Transformation of Positivism in Latin America', *Journal of the History of Ideas*, 24 (1963), p. 517.

[4] The notion of positivist diagrams is that of Oscar Terán, *Positivismo y nación en la Argentina* (Buenos Aires, 1987), p. 12.

Two considerations of a theoretical nature underlie the discussion that follows. The first is that in general science has been generated from the metropoli – that is Europe and the United States – by a process of diffusion (a cognitive process) that has a number of concomitant components. Diffusion curves show that ideas spread by contagion and that the process is self-generating, once initiated. But reception is shaped by a specific context, that of peripherality, with respect to the 'mainstream' science of the metropolis, which produces characteristic reactions. The parameters of such reaction to scientific ideas can be grouped under two modal types, called active and passive.[5] Passive receptions are limited to assimilation of scientific ideas with ability to further diffuse them but without the ability to add creatively to the set of ideas in question. Active reception involves the capacity to carry the paradigm further in original research programmes. Although both modes assume dependence, the dependent variables of each also reflect the differential ability of recipient groups to generate original responses to the stimulus diffused. Clearly, such modes reflect different institutional features prevailing in the disciplinary groups in the recipient societies that receive and rework the ideas. Groups that have achieved a 'critical mass' of highly trained personnel have the ability to carry new paradigms further. Both the training of such personnel and their ability to assimilate new ideas critically depends in turn on issues of cultural congruence and a variety of educational and communication factors.

The implantation of institutional models also can be described in terms of the metropolitan experience and the specific contours of the recipient society. The Pasteur Institute provided a universal model for the implantation of microbiology, both pure and applied. Its success or failure relates to the conditions prevailing in local settings. Finally, although many modern scientific disciplines were born in Latin American countries under situations of 'scientific imperialism' with mentors sent out, rather like apostles, from the scientifically developed countries, the motives of those missionaries, as Lewis Pyenson shows, were frequently far from imperialistic or self-seeking.[6] Many of the foreign scientists who played such a large role in the institutionalization of science in twentieth-century Latin Amer-

[5] See Thomas F. Glick, 'La transferencia de las revoluciones científicas a través de las fronteras culturales,' *Ciencia y Desarrollo* (Mexico, D.F.), 12, no. 72 (1987), pp. 77–89.

[6] Lewis Pyenson, 'Functionaries and Seekers in Latin America; missionary diffusion of the exact sciences, 1850–1930,' *Quipu,* 2 (1985): 387–420. See also Thomas F. Glick, 'Crítica a N. Stepan y L. Pyenson,' ibid., pp. 437–42.

ica had no metropolitan connections whatever when they arrived (e.g., Spanish republicans and Jewish refugees from Nazism). How then can they be portrayed as serving imperialist interests? Actors must be accorded some autonomy. To insist on arguing that such persons were acting as mere unconscious agents of imperialism is either to miss the point of their personal career patterns and objectives or else to reduce an intellectual process to a purely transactional one in a wider and impersonal movement of power politics. The two interpretations are not mutually exclusive by any means, but generalization runs the risk of misreading as political, scientific processes that had in themselves little or no political content or, at worst, converts the antimony of international science/local interests into an exercise in special pleading. *Mutatis mutandis,* phenomena with overtly economic overtones, such as invasion of mining countries by legions of U. S. Geological Service geologists, may well have had politically neutral outcomes, such as the generation of university instruction in such fields.

BIOLOGY

Darwinism

The reception of Darwinism, which put an end to the old Natural History and created modern biology, was, in most Latin American countries, a phenomenon of the 1880s. However that reception was characterized by a debate among positivist lawyers, doctors and social thinkers; only in Argentina were there any researchers actively engaged in biological research programmes that could directly incorporate the orientation of evolutionary biology, although in other countries evolutionary perspectives were assimilated in some medical school theses. In Brazil the preeminence of philosophers among historians of ideas has led to the exaggeration of the impact of Comtean positivists and the neglect of Spencerians and Darwinians whose impact was just as great.[7] Darwinists were particularly powerful in the Bahia Medical School and in the Recife Law School. Medical doctors were characteristically Darwinian in science and republican in politics. In Chile, there was a kind of mute assimilation of Darwinian ideas, especially in applied areas such as agronomy and field geology,

[7] On Brazilian Spencerianism, see Richard Graham, *Britain and the Onset of Modernization in Brazil, 1850–1914* (Cambridge, 1958), ch. 9; on Darwinism, Therezinha Alves Ferreira Collichio, *Miranda de Azevedo e o darwinismo no Brasil* (São Paulo, 1988).

no doubt because of the pre-eminence of Comteans in the academic world.[8] The reception of Darwinism in Cuba was marked by the variegated philosophical discussion accompanying it. Not only was there a Spencerian contingent composed mainly of medical doctors (the Spencerianism of doctors was marked throughout Latin America), but also the group of neo-Hegelian lawyers who wrote in the *Revista de Cuba,* also staunchly Darwinian.[9] In Mexico, Justo Sierra introduced Darwin's ideas in 1875 and by the end of the decade they had entered official curricula. But the leading Mexican positivist, the French-trained Comtean Gabino Barreda was a Lamarckian and followed the French line on Darwin, whose frequently metaphorical language seemed at odds with the canons of positivist science.[10]

In Uruguay, positivists – as much Darwinian as they were Spencerian – controlled the educational system in the 1870s and 1880s and Darwinian professors controlled both the faculties of medicine and law. Catholics took their futile complaints of a 'positivist dictatorship' to the floor of the congress. But even before the positivist/Catholic debate, Darwin's ideas had already been debated by cattlemen, perhaps as early as the mid-1860s. In the polemic over how best to upgrade the herds of creole cattle, some *estancieros* asserted that natural selection had already acted upon native herds to adapt them to local conditions of pasture and climate; they argued against crossing with imported Durham bulls on the grounds that Darwin did not believe that such admixtures would be permanent.[11]

In Argentina, Darwinism was well entrenched by 1875 when Eduardo Holmberg began teaching evolutionary theory in the Escuela Normal de Maestras; two years later the English naturalist was elected to membership in the Argentine Scientific Society.[12] Argentina produced the only 'classical' evolutionist in Latin America, the paleontologist Florentino Ameghino (1854–1911). A prodigious field worker, Ameghino discovered more than 6,000 species of fossil mammals. He accepted 'the laws of

[8] Bernardo Márquez Bretón, *Orígenes del darwinismo en Chile* (Santiago, 1982).

[9] Pedro M. Pruna and Armando García González, *Darwinismo y sociedad en Cuba: Siglo XIX* (Madrid, 1989).

[10] Roberto Moreno, *La polémica del darwinismo en México: Siglo XIX* (Mexico, D.F., 1984); Rosaura Ruiz Gutiérrez, *Positivismo y evolución: Introducción del darwinismo en México* (Mexico, D.F., 1987); Charles A. Hale, *The Transformation of Liberalism in Late Nineteenth-Century Mexico* (Princeton, N.J., 1989), pp. 206–10.

[11] Thomas F. Glick, *Darwin y darwinismo en el Uruguay y en América latina* (Montevideo, 1989), chs 5 and 6.

[12] Marcelo Montserrat, 'La mentalidad evolucionista: Una ideología del progreso', in Ezequiel Gallo and Gustavo Ferrera (eds), *La Argentina del Ochenta al Centenario* (Buenos Aires, 1980), pp. 785–818.

evolution' as undisputed principles and devised a natural classification system in his *Filogenia* (1884) based on morphological features. His achievement was vitiated by his obsession with proving the American origin of man, a fallacy resulting from his misdating of South American strata. He was a rhetorical Darwinian, his notions of the mechanisms of evolution being closer to those of the neo-Lamarckians he had met in France. In the early decades of the twentieth century, Ameghino became a political symbol, defended by the left and opposed by the Jesuit biologists who led the Catholic crusade against Darwin.[13]

By the turn of the century the controversy had died down in most places, but in Venezuela it erupted anew, revealing the unresolved antagonism between evolutionary biology and traditional Catholicism. There, the comparative anatomist and evolutionist Luis Razetti, while acknowledging that evolution, either in its neo-Lamarckian or Darwinian form, was established officially in Venezuelan education, still sought to have the Academy of Medicine of Caracas, the nation's highest scientific authority, proclaim it to be the basis of scientific biology. In order to accomplish this, he proposed in 1904 that the Academy adopt three conclusions: that life has its origin in inorganic matter; that present-day organisms derive by descent from that primitive living matter; and that man is one organism more, subject to the same natural laws as the others. By a deft parliamentary manoeuvre Razetti further insisted that the Academy had to accept his conclusions if members were unable to prove their falsity without straying from the bounds of experimental science; those who voted against did so at the risk of exposing themselves as retrograde ideologues. The Academy accepted Razetti's proposals, but not before bowing to pressure from the archbishop of Caracas who insisted on the insertion of a qualifying phrase. The promotion of Darwinism, thus became a matter for political action. In 1906 Razetti's materialist book, *What is Life?* was published with a government subvention: it was in the interest of the positivist dictator Cipriano Castro to promote evolution, inasmuch as his political enemies, the traditionalist 'Goths' were as much opposed to him as to Darwin.[14]

[13] Julio Orione, 'Florentino Ameghino y la influencia de Lamarck en la paleontologia argentina del siglo XIX,' *Quipu,* 4 (1987): 447–71; Justo Garate, 'Florentino Ameghino', *Dictionary of Scientific Biography,* I, 129–32; 'Hablan los hombres de ciencia del país sobre las asendereadas teorías de Ameghino', *Estudios,* 22 (1922): 428–45.

[14] For an account of the Razetti polemic, see Thomas F. Glick, 'Perspectivas sobre la recepción del darwinismo en el mundo hispano', in *Actas, II Congreso de la Sociedad Española de Historia de las Ciencias,* 3 vols (Zaragoza, 1984), I: 49–64, on pp. 53–7.

Around the turn of the century, the leading Mexican biologist was Alfonso L. Herrera (1868–1942). The rubrics of his *Recueil de lois de la Biologie Générale* (Paris, 1897) are Darwinian (e.g., differentiation, variation, adaptation, selection, distribution, struggle for life, evolution). Two years later in *La vie sur les hauts plateaux* (Mexico, D. F., 1899) he argued that flora and fauna alike adapt to the harsh conditions of high altitude and that certain mechanisms of adaptation are most likely hereditary. Herrera was such a materialist and evolutionist that he proposed an experimental crossing of a human and an ape to demonstrate the animal nature of man.[15] Herrera was best known for his pioneering speculations on the origins of life. In 1942 he explicated his concept of 'sulphobes', microstructures within cells which he claimed to have replicated chemically. Herrera's work was significant because he explained the origin of organisms by alluding to inorganic polymers, whereas contemporary origin theorists focused on organic macromolecules.[16]

Social Darwinism

Social Darwinism in general is better called Social Spencerism, because it stressed the struggle for life (a term Darwin picked up from Spencer) and competition, rather than attempting to extend the Darwinian sense of selection into the social sphere. In Latin America, much of the writing in this vein had to do with distinctions between Europeans, Blacks and Indians.

Brazilians, in particular, were much concerned with what was perceived as biological differentiation between various racial and ethnic groups. An extreme social Spencerian was Euclides da Cunha. This is apparent in the sociological sections of his great book *Os Sertões* (1902) (translated into English as *Rebellion in the Backlands*) which is an account of a revolt of mestizo *sertanejos,* brutally put down by the government in 1897. Mestizos were racially degenerate, a 'hyphen' (he says) between three races, the Indo-European, the Negro and Indian which 'represent evolutionary stages in confrontation'. 'According to the conclusion of the evolutionist,' da Cunha asserted, 'even when the influence of a superior race has reacted

[15] Alfonso L. Herrera, *El híbrido del hombre y el mono* (Valencia, 1933). Herrera was prescient on the closeness of apes and humans; see 'Redrawing the Ancestral Tree: genetics changes traditional ideas about chimpanzees and gorillas', *Harvard Alumni Gazette,* (February 1990): 17–18.

[16] See Sidney W. Fox and Klaus Dose, *Molecular Evolution and the Origin of Life* (San Francisco, Cal., 1972), pp. 6–8.

upon the offspring, the latter show vivid traces of the inferior one. Miscegenation carried to an extreme means retrogression.'[17] The result of this hereditary degeneration, though not an evolutionary result in itself, has evolutionary consequences, because such groups are disadvantaged in the struggle for existence: 'The fact is that in the marvelous competition of peoples, all of them evolving in a struggle that knows no truce, with selection capitalizing those attributes which heredity preserves, the mestizo is an intruder. He does not struggle.'[18]

The mestizo thereby violates the laws of nature. Although the genetic tendency is regression towards the primitive race (the Negro in this case), mestizos despise Negroes and avoid mating with them. They seek intermarriages, by force, with whites who will extinguish the despised traits: 'This [social] tendency is significant. In a manner of speaking it picks up the thread of evolution which miscegenation has severed.' The superior race becomes the biological objective and in seeking it the mestizos are obeying the instinct of self-preservation, an instinct with evolutionary implications. 'The laws of the evolution of species are inviolable ones.' The missionaries proved unable to civilize the Indians, who will nevertheless civilize themselves through miscegenation.

Not all social Darwinians, however, reached the conclusion that Indians were evolutionarily or biologically degenerate. The exact opposite conclusion, in fact, was reached by Vicente Riva Palacio (1832–96), a Mexican politician and amateur naturalist. In 1884 he asserted in a history of colonial Mexico that if the Indians were judged from a evolutionist perspective, it would have to be concluded that they were superior to all other known races. For example, Mexican Indians lacked body hair; they also lacked wisdom teeth and had an extra molar in place of the rudimentary canine tooth that Europeans have. Such traits indicated that they were more highly evolved than Europeans.[19] Riva Palacios' theory was picked up by Andrés Molina Enríquez in his great social critique of 1909, *Los grandes problemas nacionales,* a work which had a tremendous influence on the Mexican revolutionary generation. Molina quotes Riva Palacios at length and then adds a long 'scientific note' on selection, comparing its action upon individuals with that upon groups.[20] He distinguishes be-

[17] Euclides de Cunha, *Os Sertões;* Eng trans, *Rebellion in the Backlands* (Chicago, Ill., 1964), pp. 84–85.

[18] Ibid., p. 86.

[19] Roberto Moreno, 'Mexico', in Thomas F. Glick (ed.), *The Comparative Reception of Darwinism,* 2nd edn (Chicago, Ill., 1988), pp. 366–68.

[20] Andrés Molina Enriquez, *Los grandes problemas nacionales* [1909] (Mexico, D.F., 1978), pp. 346–8.

tween groups in more densely settled areas who, because of constant conflict, have evolved a kind of collective strength, and those from less densely settled areas upon whom selection acts at the individual level. For this reason, the indigenous peoples of America had a number of highly evolved individual traits but could not stand up collectively to the Europeans. Social evolution, therefore, is portrayed as a biological process.

Social Darwinism continued well into the twentieth century as a force to be reckoned with in Latin American social science. A representative figure is the Cuban anthropologist Fernando Ortiz who, in the early part of his career, was a biological determinist and social Darwinist, who viewed Blacks as primitive and lustful. In 1914 he wrote that 'Evolutionism is today the law of life in all of its manifestations . . . Perhaps our national future could in the end be nothing more than a complex problem of ethnic selection. [Humanity] continues abandoned to the most elementary socio-physical laws, struggling against the general biological promiscuity of inferior species.'[21]

Genetics

The rediscovery of Mendel was appreciated early in Argentina where, in 1908, the biologist Angel Gallardo published a short book on modern research on heredity in biology, whose bibliography demonstrates his acquaintance with European genetics. Articles followed on practical applications of Mendel's law to agriculture and cattle breeding and on the polemic between Mendelians and Galtonian biometricians, a topic of interest in Argentina where Galton's work had been followed in the 1880s. Teaching of genetics was introduced by Miguel Fernández, trained in Germany, at the University of La Plata in 1915. Fernández was the teacher of Salomón Horovitz and Francisco Alberto Sáez who built a tradition in genetics in Argentina. Horovitz's early research, on chromosomes in plant meiosis, appeared in 1927, antedating his doctoral dissertation at Cornell on segmented interchange in plants. His research, as professor of genetics at the Faculty of Agronomy in La Plata (1938–47) was mainly on applied problems. An opponent of Perón's dictatorship, he emigrated to Venezuela in 1947. Sáez (1898–1976), Uruguayan by birth, directed the cytology laboratory in the same faculty from 1938 to 1947, when he also

[21] Cited by Roberto González Echevaría, *Alejo Carpentier: The Pilgrim at Home* (Ithaca, N.Y., 1977), p. 47 n. 26.

departed to join the Institute of Biological Research in Montevideo. Sáez introduced cytogenetics in Latin America in 1925. A pronounced evolutionist, he asserted in a 1929 article the value of cytology and genetics for the future of systematics, which should be based on the behavior of chromosomes from a phylogenetic perspective. When Clarence McClung visited Argentina in 1930, he stimulated Sáez's future research both in sex chromosomes and in the genetics of grasshoppers. In 1935 Sáez and his student Eduardo De Robertis made the striking discovery that amphibians have no morphologically differentiated sex chromosomes. In 1946 Sáez and de Robertis published the first edition of their influential textbook on general cytology. In the late 1940s and 1950s a number of Argentinians went to Berkeley to study with G. Ledyard Stebbins. One of Stebbins' disciples, Juan Hunziker, performed research on the evolution of the karyotype in various genera of gymnosperms with large chromosomes.[22]

Drosophila research was introduced by Arturo Burkart in his Buenos Aires thesis of 1931. Burkart had studied in Germany with Curt Stern and his account of the methodology of fruit-fly research was influential in Argentinian biology. Nevertheless, fruit flies were used primarily for instruction. Systematic research did not begin until 1957 when two disciples of Herman Muller, Juan I. Valencia and his wife Ruby Allen returned from Indiana (Valencia to the University of Buenos Aires, Allen to the genetics laboratory of the Nuclear Energy Commission). Their work on the genetic effects of ionizing radiation led to the International Symposium of Genes and Chromosomes, held in Buenos Aires in 1964 under the aegis of the American Atomic energy Commission and the Oak Ridge Laboratory. In 1966 the Valencias returned to the United States.[23]

Mendelism was introduced in Brazil through the agricultural schools. Carlos Texeira Mendes, professor at Piracicaba, is generally regarded as the first Brazilian Mendelian for the treatment of genetics in his 1917 book on improvement of agricultural varieties.[24] Texeira Mendes began teaching genetics and evolution there in 1918. A real research effort, however, was

[22] Luis B. Mazoti and Juan H. Hunziker, 'Los precursores de la genética en la Argentina', in Mazoti and Hunziker (eds), *Evolución de las ciencias en la República Argentina, 1923–1972: Genética* (Buenos Aires, 1976), pp. 5–12; and Hunziker and Francisco A. Sáez, 'Citogenética y genética evolutiva vegetal y animal', ibid., pp. 33–75.

[23] Beatriz Mazar Barnett, 'Genética de Drosophila', in Luis B. Mazoti and Juan H., Hunziker (eds), *Evolucíon de la ciencias en la República Argentina, 1923–1972: Genética* (Buenos Aires, 1976), pp. 219–27.

[24] Thomas F. Glick, 'Establishing Scientific Disciplines in Latin America: genetics in Brazil, 1943–1960', in A. Lafuente, A. Elena and M. L. Ortega (eds), *Mundialización de la ciencia y cultural nacional* (Aranjuez, 1993), pp. 364–5.

not mounted until the arrival of the German Friedrich Brieger as professor of cytology and genetics in 1936. Brieger built an important research programme in plant genetics with Rockefeller Foundation aid and a programme of interchange with foreign scholars. Brieger himself wrote important studies on the origins of corn. He also worked on the evolution of plants in the tropics, a major theme of genetics in Brazil, showing the Orchids to be in a phase of explosive evolution. Genetics at the Campinas agricultural school was of a more applied nature, centring on diseases of coffee and other cultigens.[25]

A critical moment for Brazilian genetics came in 1943 when Theodosius Dobzhansky arrived at André Dreyfus's genetics department at the University of São Paulo for the first of a number of visits. Dobzhansky had just concluded a series of studies on the genetics of natural populations, in which he had studied the distribution of native populations of *Drosophila* in temperate zones; now he wanted to extend his research programme by comparing temperate to tropical populations. The research he conducted over a fifteen-year period with Brazilian colleagues and disciples revealed the greater genetic variety and plasticity of tropical species and had important implications for evolutionary biology. From the Drosophilists trained by Dobzhansky came the future leaders of Brazilian genetics. The success of Brazilian genetics was due in large part to the Rockefeller Foundation, which consistently supported the entire Drosophila programme, enabled numerous Brazilians to study in Dobzhansky's laboratory at Columbia University, and which then broadened its support to encompass human genetics in the 1950s.[26]

In the 1970s the Multinational genetics Project of the Organization of American States facilitated research in human genetics in a number of countries by standardizing biochemical techniques important in medical genetic research. This was the origin of the biochemical genetics programme in the Institute of Human Genetics (founded 1972) of the University of San Andrés medical school in Bolivia.[27]

[25] Ernesto Paterniani, 'Genética vegetal', in Mario Guimaraes Ferro and Shozo Motoyama (eds), *História das ciências no Brasil,* 3 vols (São Paulo, 1979), I: 219–40.

[26] Glick, 'Establishing Scientific Disciplines in Latin America', pp. 365–75; A. Brito da Cunha, 'The Seventy Years of Life of C. Pavan and Science', *Revista Brasileira de Genética,* 12 (1989), pp. 691–9; C. Pavan et al., 'Departamento de Biologia Geral da Faculdade de Filosofia, Ciências e Letras da Universidade de São Paulo', *Atas do Primeiro Simpósio Sul-Americano de Genética* (São Paulo, 1961), pp. 61–95; Simon Schwartzman, *Formaçao da comunidade científica no Brasil* (São Paulo, 1979), pp. 274–80; and the symposium, 'A genética no Brasil: passado e futuro', *Ciência e Cultura,* 41 (1989). 439–66.

[27] Universidad Mayor de San Andrés, Facultad de Medicina, Instituto de Genética Humana, 'Breve reseña histórica del Instituto de Genética Humana' (typescript).

Eugenics

Eugenics, a socially constructed application of genetics, was, in part, the application of social Darwinian constructs in an attempt to preserve the predominance and 'racial purity' of whites, in countries where miscegenation was in evidence, and to encourage the immigration of socially favoured groups in predominantly European countries. As in Europe, eugenics was an attempt to biologize social problems and propose 'scientific' solutions for them.[28]

In Europe eugenics found its scientific roots in Mendelian genetics informed by a harsh selectionism inherited from social Darwinism. The congenitally infirm, the psychopath and other 'unfit' elements were to be selected out of the body politic, using sterilization as the instrument of eugenic policy. The Nazi racial programme was, of course, the apotheosis of selectionist eugenics, whose terrible implementation had the effect of discrediting the scientific pretensions of eugenics.

Latin American eugenics in general was not selectionist, since its base in biological theory was neo-Lamarckian, rather than Darwinian and Mendelian, and, in its public health aspect was pro-natalist rather than Malthusian (promoting the medicalization of pregnancy and birth rather than birth control). Inasmuch as the Church opposed (and in the encyclical *Casti Connubi* of 1930) officially banned eugenics as a challenge to the Church's authority in matrimonial and sexual matters, attempts to promote sterilization of the undesirable were muted in Latin America. Emphasis was laid on 'puericulture', the hygienic treatment of infants and on maternal health care. Alcoholism, criminality, tuberculosis and other conditions thought to be inheritable were viewed, under the ethos of neo-Lamarckian meliorism, to be responsive to public health measures, the improvements being passed on to succeeding generations.

It is in the area of race, however, that Latin American eugenics most reflected ideological influence. As Nancy Stepan has demonstrated, all Latin American eugenics movements were, to a greater or lesser degree, about race.[29] In Argentina, eugenics became intertwined in the discussion of national identity and post First World War agitation to limit immigration in order to exclude Jews, Arabs and other peoples whose ability to assimilate was questioned. Victor Delfino, founder of the Argentine Eu-

[28] Nancy Stepan, *The Hour of Eugenics: Race, Gender and Nation in Latin America* (Ithaca, N.Y., 1991), pp. 1–14.

[29] Ibid., ch. 5: 'National Identities and Racial Transformations', pp. 135–70.

genics Society, argued for control of immigration and against racial crossing. In accord with the norms of 'biotypology', race as well as family history entered into the biological monitoring of society.[30] The Argentine Association of Biotypology and Eugenics, whose intellectual roots originated in Italian Fascism, was able to associate Latin civilization with eugenic superiority and in that way create a different criterion for assessing races than that associated with German or English eugenics. Argentinian eugenists fretted that Argentinian society was still too racially heterogeneous to establish strong institutions.

Brazilian social Darwinians, like Francisco José de Oliveira Vianna, proposed to solve the racial problem by 'aryanizing' or whitening the racially inferior groups by encouraging their intermarriage with Europeans – immigrants to be imported for that purpose.[31] Further north, 'whitening', retread to eugenic specifications, came up again in Guatemala, in an unlikely source: Miguel Angel Asturias's law thesis of 1925. According to Asturias the Indians had fallen into 'physiological decadence' to which there was but one solution, a biological one: 'only inheritance is strong enough to combat inheritance.' Social palliatives such as converting Indians into small landholders didn't work. The Indians needed new blood; European immigrants must come and biologically mix with the indigenous population. 'The laws of society,' Asturias concluded, 'resolve themselves inexorably; mortally wounded organisms, like our population, are destined to disappear.'[32]

In Mexico, as already indicated with respect to social Darwinism, racial eugenics was given a progressive twist. There miscegenation was viewed positively, as the origin of a distinctively Mexican race – a 'cosmic race' in José Vasconcelos' term – the biological underpinning of political and intellectual *indigenismo* in the 1920s. It is also true, however, that to identify Mexican nationality with the *mestizo* was to depreciate the worth of the Indian as a race.[33]

The 'soft' nature of eugenics in Latin America, in contrast to the hard selectionism of Germanic and English versions, calls into question what is

[30] Biotypology had been introduced in Argentina by Nicolo Pende in a 1930 visit. Its central concept was that human populations could be broken down into analytical types based on characteristic illnesses, personality and racial origin. The inventory of biotypes was a prerequisite to rational organization of the biological resources of the state (ibid., p. 65).

[31] On whitening in Brazilian sociology, see the discussion by Oracy Nogueira, 'A sociologia no Brasil', in Guimaraes and Motoyama (eds), *História das ciências no Brasil,* III: 181–234, on pp. 191–2.

[32] Jesús J. Amurrio, *El positivismo en Guatemala* (Guatemala City, 1966), pp. 80–87 (mimeo).

[33] Ibid., p. 256.

normative in science. In general the original version of any scientific idea or tradition is taken as normative and departures from the norm are measured against it. Comparative study reveals patterns of reception – such as that of eugenics in the Latin world – which display pervasive systemic differences from the original cognitive system (in this case Galtonian selectionism) to a degree where the relationship of the transferred idea with its 'hearth' loses much of its significance.

BIOMEDICINE

The new microbiology that resulted from the discoveries of Pasteur and Koch transformed medical research and public health everywhere from the 1880s. Latin Americans went to the Pasteur Institute in Paris soon after its founding (1885) to master the new techniques and theories. Among the first was the Brazilian Augusto Ferreira dos Santos who studied there in 1886 and inaugurated a Pasteur-style institute to treat rabies in Rio de Janeiro soon after. In São Paulo, the Frenchman Félix Le Dantec arrived to found a Pasteur Institute in 1892 but left the country precipitously and the facility, the first modern research laboratory in Brazil, was directed by Adolfo Lutz, highly regarded for his research on cholera and yellow fever.[34] In Venezuela a Pasteur Institute was founded in 1895 by Santos Aníbal Dominici; it closed in 1902 when Dominici ran afoul of the dictator Cipriano Castro. Another Pasteur Institute was established in Maracaibo in 1897.[35] In Paraguay, Miguel Elmassian, an Armenian graduate of the Pasteur Institute, was from 1900–5 first director of the National Institute of Bacteriology. With his disciple and successor Luis E. Migone, he produced important research on equine flagellosis and various amoebic diseases.[36]

At the turn of the century, yellow fever was the burning issue in what had come to be called 'tropical medicine'. Since its cause turned out to be a virus, Koch's bacteriological methodology only occasioned repeated false starts in identifying the pathogen. But, as early as 1881 the Cuban Carlos

[34] On bacteriology in Brazil, see Nancy Stepan, *Beginnings of Brazilian Science: Oswaldo Cruz, Medical Research and Policy, 1890–1920* (New York, 1976). Lutz's Bacteriological Institute was the antecedent of Butantan Institute, established by Lutz with Vital Brasil as director in 1899; see Jandira Lopes de Oliveira, 'Cronologia do Instituto Butantan (1888–1981), Vol. 1: 1888–1945', *Memorias do Instituto Butantan*, 44/45 (1980–81): 11–79.

[35] Marcel Roche, *Rafael Rangel: Ciencia política en la Venezuela de principios de siglo* (Caracas, 1978), p. 43.

[36] Arquimedes Canese, 'La microbiología y parasitología en el Paraguay,' *Anales de la Facultad de Ciencias Médicas de la Universidad Nacional de Asunción*, 15 (1983): 395–7.

Finlay had correctly identified the vector of the disease, the mosquito eventually named *Aedes aegypti*. Finlay's discovery, however, had no impact until after the War of 1898 when Reed Board in the United States performed further experiments, along lines laid out by Finlay, and quickly confirmed his hypothesis.[37] The U.S. Army's public health effort, led by General William Gorgas, quickly wiped out yellow fever first in Cuba and, later in Panama. Then in 1914 the recently-founded Rockefeller Foundation decided to make a major effort to locate endemic foci of yellow fever and destroy the mosquitos. It established a commission to identify such foci in Ecuador, Peru, Colombia, Venezuela and Brazil. The Commission had only one Hispanic member, Juan Guiteras, a Cuban who, like Finlay, had served as a doctor in the U.S. Army during the Cuban war of independence against Spain, and indeed the Foundation's efforts in Ecuador and Peru, although successful in conquering yellow fever, made no contribution to national medical science.[38] The most glaring case was Peru where Henry Hanson, a member of the Rockefeller Foundation's Yellow Fever Commission, was actually named the country's Director of Public Health in 1919–22. Hanson wiped out yellow fever by placing fish in home cisterns to eat mosquito larvae. The Rockefeller's take-over of Peruvian public health resulted in the virtual cessation of local bacteriological research.[39]

The Serum Therapy Institute founded at Manguinhos near Rio de Janeiro in 1900, was also in the Pasteurian mold, particularly after Oswaldo Cruz, himself trained in Paris, became director in 1903. In a letter to the Brazilian congress the same year, Cruz made clear what kind of establishment he had in mind: 'an institute for the study of infectious and tropical diseases, along the lines of the Pasteur Institute of Paris'. The facility was to prepare sera and vaccines, of course, but also would give instruction in bacteriology and parasitology and would, as a result, 'transform itself into a nucleus of experimental studies that would greatly enhance the name of our country abroad'. Cruz rode a yellow fever campaign based on the Finlay Doctrine to success in transforming a serum institute into a great research organism, renamed the Institute of Experimental Pathology in 1906. The original staff was wholly Brazilian, alumni of the Rio de

[37] Nancy Stepan, 'The Interplay between Socio-economic Factors and Medical Science: yellow fever research, Cuba and the United States', *Social Studies of Science*, 8 (1978): 397–423.

[38] See Wilbur A. Sawyer, 'A History of the Activities of the Rockefeller Foundation in the Investigation and Control of Yellow Fever', *American Journal of Tropical Medicine*, 17 (1937): 35–50.

[39] Marcos Cueto, *Excelencia científica en la periferia: Actividades científicas e investigación biomédica en el Perú, 1890–1950*, (Lima, 1989), pp. 144–8.

Janeiro medical school, and included such future leaders of Brazilian medicine as Henrique de Rocha Lima and Artur Neiva; Cruz taught them microbiology in a course patterned after a famous one given in Paris by Emile Roux. As research activities increased medical students in Rio de Janeiro soon became aware that 'a new kind of science' was being practised in Manguinhos.[40] Interestingly, Cruz's 1904 campaign to make smallpox vaccination obligatory was opposed by Brazilian positivists who styled it 'hygienic despotism' while attacking the germ theory as 'fantasy'.[41]

The most famous discovery of the Institute's early years was that of American sleeping sickness (*Trypanosomiasis americana*), or Chagas's Disease, by Carlos Chagas in 1908. Chagas made the discovery serendipitously while on an anti-malaria campaign in Minas Gerais. The disease, which induced multiple symptoms in its victims, had eluded classification before. Once described, a wealth of studies ensued, on the pathology, incidence and geography of the disease, making it one of most closely studied of all human diseases.[42] Many of these studies were published in the *Memorias* do Instituto Oswaldo Cruz, which began publication in 1909.

The initiation of bacteriology in Peru was associated with Carrión's disease, which had long confused researchers because its pathogen causes two discrete illnesses: one is Oroya fever and it usually precedes the second, called *verruga peruana* after the tumour-like skin eruptions that it causes. It receives its name from a medical student named Daniel Carrión who in 1885 inoculated himself with the infection, proved that the two diseases had the same origin, and died. The disease was described in 1898 in a classical clinical monograph by Manuel Odriozola but not until 1909 was the pathogen isolated by Alberto Barton. Barton's discovery stimulated the growth of bacteriology in Peru, including the establishment of a first-rate laboratory at the Municipal Institute of Hygiene in Lima under the direction of the Italian Ugo Biffi and a scholarship programme to send promising researchers to Europe for training.[43]

Between 1916 and the late 1920s the Rockefeller Foundation commissioned a series of reports assessing medical education in virtually all Latin American countries. The reports are remarkable for the uniformity of the pattern revealed throughout the region. In particular, the Rockefeller leg-

[40] Stepan, *Beginnings of Brazilian Science*, ch. 5.

[41] Angela Porto, 'Positivismo e seus dilemas', *Ciência Hoje*, 6, no. 34 (August 1987), 55–61.

[42] Stepan, *Beginnings of Brazilian Science*, pp. 118–19.

[43] Cueto, *Excelencia científica en la periferia*, ch. 4; Myron G. Schultz, 'A History of Bartonellosis (Carrión's Disease)', *American Journal of Tropical Medicine and Hygiene*, 17 (1968): 503–15.

ates were looking for what they termed 'didactic' instruction methods (that is, lectures unaccompanied by demonstrations or laboratory assignments), for a deficient university structure, characterized by semi-autonomous chairs headed by clinical practitioners rather than departments with full-time research professors. And they were looking for talent: scientists in whom they could invest in order to 'make the peaks higher' and who would act like 'young Turks' in promoting institutional reform.

In the University of Bogotá, Alan Gregg found a medical school under the domination of the Catholic Church, whose laboratories were under-equipped (ten microscopes in bacteriology, six in pathological anatomy), or completely lacking (neither internal pathology nor general surgery offered laboratory work), with French textbooks used in all courses. 'A "young Turk" party of graduates who had had experience abroad would in ten years do the most to improve the teaching, the relations and the influence of the medical school of Bogotá,' Gregg concluded.[44]

In Brazil (surveyed first in 1916, and then again on three separate occasions), the Rockefeller assessors found both a defective institutional structure and signs of hope that the 'new science' championed by Oswaldo Cruz was diffusing through the system. In the medical school of Bahia, which had been a bastion of Darwinism in the 1880s, R. A. Lambert found that defective organization was subverting the utilization of the laboratories: only a fraction of the students could work in the laboratory at any one time. The pathological anatomy laboratory had only twelve microscopes, that of histology, fifteen. On the other hand, the total amount of apparatus was quite large. If the current chairs were brought together into eight departments, the number of microscopes would be sufficient. Teaching was found to be 'didactic' and one student reported never having seen an autopsy in the department of pathological anatomy and only occasional slide demonstrations. Research judged worthwhile was found only in parasitology and legal medicine.[45]

In Belo Horizonte, bacteriology was taught in 1916 by Ezequiel Dias of the Cruz Institute. 'His working tables were well outfitted with Zeiss microscopes and practically every useful instrument found in a well-equipped laboratory was on hand.' Chemistry was taught by Alfred Schaeffer, a German, 'and is a fine course . . . His department was the largest and best equipped in the school'.[46] Another Cruz product, Pereira

[44] Stepan, *Beginnings of Brazilian Science*, p. 95.
[45] Rockefeller Archives Center, Record Group 1.1, series 305, folder 15.
[46] Ibid., p. 91.

Filho, had a laboratory in the Pasteur Institute of Porto Alegre which the Rockefeller assessor found to be 'the best of this type we have seen anywhere'.[47] But in 1925 when Lambert visited Dias' laboratory, conditions had already deteriorated: 'it has only seven microscopes and no suitable desks for students. It is my impression that in this department, as in physiology, physics and parasitology, the teaching is largely didactic.' He then counted microscopes ('the common measure of equipment') and found only thirty-eight in the entire faculty.[48] Later, in Paraná Lambert found only a half dozen microscopes, all for histology.[49] Two years later, Lambert reported from the medical school in Rio that the situation in pathological anatomy illustrates 'the present hopeless inadequacy of space and other shortcomings'. Only nine microscopes could be found, including one in the professor's office, with six students at each table sharing a microscope in an overcrowded class of 500. Carlos Chagas's son, referring to this school as it was in the 1930s, described it as 'a cemetery of scientific vocations (cemitério dc vocações científicas)'.[50]

Richard M. Pearce filed a gloomy assessment of laboratories at the University of Buenos Aires in 1916: physiology had but seven tables; anatomy had eighty, but the class size was eight hundred. The situation in the analytical chemistry and pharmacology laboratories was even worse, 'while that devoted to physiological chemistry has such poor equipment that our guide apologized for it on the ground that the essential practical work in biological chemistry was given in connection with the various clinical courses. Still, he ranked laboratory instruction as superior to that in Brazil. Instruction in anatomy, bacteriology and pathology approached that of United States medical schools but was far inferior in physiology or chemistry. Entire systematic courses in physiology, chemistry and embryology were lacking. 'As in Brazil, the fault lies with the system which permits the appointment of clinicians as heads of laboratory departments and denies the advantage of full-time men to encourage teaching and research in the laboratory branches.[51]

In 1925, R. A. Lambert received a negative impression of Houssay's physiology laboratory (where work that would bring Houssay the Nobel

[47] Ibid., p. 276.

[48] Ibid., p. 123. Twenty of the microscopes were in the pathology laboratory, eight in bacteriology, six in natural history and parasitology and four in the clinical labs of the hospital.

[49] Ibid., p. 146.

[50] Ibid., p. 252; Maria Clara Mariani, 'O Instituto de Biofísica da UFRJ,' in Simon Schartzman (ed.), *Universidades e instituicoes científicas no Rio de Janeiro* (Brasilia, 1982), pp. 199–208, on p. 200.

[51] Rockefeller Archives Center, Record Group 1.1, Series 301, Box 2, folder 18, pp. 135–7.

Prize was already underway): 'I got the impression that the disorder was probably chronic and that B. H. [sic] is one of those laboratory workers to whom housekeeping is a bore. The departmental library showed the lack of method evident elsewhere.'

Interpretation of the Rockefeller reports raises the issue of conflicting scientific cultures. The North Americans were unused to the economy of scarcity and deprivation that reigned throughout Latin American laboratories. There, researchers were accustomed to make the best with what they had; resourcefulness in designing experiments was perhaps the key to the best Latin American science of the period. Still, one must give the Foundation's men credit for identifying scientists of talent. Houssay, of course, was the prime example.

Born in 1887, Bernardo Houssay earned degrees in pharmacy and medicine and by 1912 was professor of physiology at the University of Buenos Aires Veterinary School.[52] There he developed a method for removing the pituitary gland from experimental animals in order to study that organ's function. In the 1920s, as professor of physiology in the medical school and director of its Institute of Physiology he performed a series of experiments to test the effects of injections of insulin (recently discovered) on animals from whom various glands had been removed. One series of experiments produced the astounding finding that the anterior lobe of the pituitary inhibited the utilization of glucose, implicating the pituitary in the etiology of human diabetes. Related research, on the role of the pituitary in the metabolism of carbohydrates, won him the Nobel Prize in 1947.

The Rockefeller Foundation began backing Houssay's research in 1929. By 1941, when the foundation established a regional office in Buenos Aires, Houssay's laboratory was already a world-class institution and was training physiologists from other Latin American countries. Then in 1943, he was dismissed from the University along with other academics following the military coup that eventually brought Péron to power. The dismissal forced Houssay to create a private research institute, the Institute of Biology and Experimental Medicine, free from governmental interference. The Institute opened in March 1944, staffed mainly by others who had been dismissed

[52] On Houssay, see Frank Young and Virgilio G. Foglia, 'Bernardo Alberto Houssay (1887–1971)', *Biographical Memoirs of Fellows of the Royal Society*, 20 (1974): 247–70; Foglia, 'The History of Bernardo A. Houssay's Research Laboratory, Instituto de Biología y Medicina Experimental: the first twenty years, 1944–1963', *Journal of the History of Medicine and Allied Sciences*, 35 (1980): 380–96; Foglia and Venancio Deulofeu, (eds) *Bernardo A. Houssay, su vida y su obra, 1887–1971* (Buenos Aires, 1981); and Marcos Cueto, 'La política médica de la Fundación Rockefeller y la investigación científica latinoamericana: El caso de la fisiología', in *Anais do Segundo Congresso Latino-Americano de História da Ciência e da Tecnologia* (São Paulo, 1989), pp. 366–75.

(Juan T. Lewis, Oscar Orias) or who had resigned in protest (Eduardo Braun Menéndez, Virgilio Foglia). Such an Institute fulfilled two of the Rockefeller Foundation's desiderata: its researchers held full-time appointments and the Institute was free of traditional university bureaucratic structures. A stream of young researchers was sent abroad, many on Rockefeller fellowships, and the result was research on a high level: Braun Menéndez on renin; Luis Leloir on the biochemistry of carbohydrates (which won him Latin America's second Nobel in 1970).[53] Houssay's Institute produced three related laboratories, an index of its success: Lewis's Institute of Medical Research in Rosario, Orias's laboratory in Córdoba, and Leloir's Institute of Biochemical Research (the Campomar Foundation).

Houssay's laboratory was part of a international physiology network whose nerve centre was Walter Cannon's laboratory in Boston and whose research programmes (hormonal action) and methodologies (piqûre, organ extirpation) were closely linked. Others in this network were Arturo Rosenblueth and José Joaquín Izquierdo in Mexico, Franklin Augusto de Moura Campos in Brazil, Joaquín V. Luco and Fernando Huidobro in Chile, and, after 1940, Rossend Carrasco Formiguera in Venezuela, all trained by Cannon, and others influenced but not trained directly by Cannon: August Pi-Sunyer in Venezuela, his son Jaume and Alexander Lipshutz in Chile.[54]

This network was the one Houssay and Braun Menéndez relied on to organize a journal, *Acta Physiologica Latinoamericana* which began publishing in 1950 to diffuse the results of Latin American physiology. From its inception the journal published mainly in English (never less than 69 per cent of its articles, reaching 100 per cent in 1971), with Argentinian authors predominating. The journal illustrates the difficulty that high-quality Latin American researchers had (and have) in diffusing their results: the leading figures in physiology chose mainly to publish in mainstream journals, leaving the *Acta*'s author pool skewed towards Argentinians and second-line researchers.[55]

Rosenblueth, returning to Mexico in 1944 after fourteen years with Cannon to head the physiology laboratory in the Cardiology Institute (a

[53] On Leloir, see César Lorenzano, 'La ciencia paradigmática de Luis Leloir', in *Anais do Sequndo Congresso Latino-Americano da História da Ciência e da Tecnología* (São Paulo, 1989), pp. 164–72, and bibliography cited.

[54] See Cueto, 'Política médica de la Fundación Rockefeller', p. 372. Cueto sees this network as a medium for the diffusion of Argentinian influence in Latin American physiology.

[55] Hebe Vessuri, 'Una estrategia de publicación científica para la fisiología latinoamericana: *Acta Physiologica Latinoamericano,* 1950–1971', *Anais do Segundo Congresso Latino-Americano de História de Ciência e da Tecnologia* (São Paulo, 1989), 232–40.

new institution, outside of the university structure, heavily funded by the Rockefeller Foundation), had performed a classic series of experiments with Cannon, extirpating the sympathetic nerve chains of cats in order to demonstrate the regulatory function of the autonomic nerve system. This research drew Rosenblueth into collaboration with Norbert Wiener on the functional analysis of the nervous system, whose results were crucial in the foundation of cybernetics.[56]

One other group of physiologists, not in the Cannon-Houssay network, also performed high-quality research in the 1930s and 1940s. This was a distinctive group of high-altitude or environmental physiologists working in the Institute Andean Biology founded by Carlos Monge in 1934. Monge had previously described a kind of chronic mountain sickness now known as Monge's Disease. The Rockefeller Foundation (and later the United States Air Force) provided laboratory equipment and fellowships for study abroad. Monge's later research was related to the acclimatization of cattle at high altitudes, while his colleague and successor Alberto Hurtado studied pulmonary edema and other problems of human physiology in the mining districts of the high Andes.[57]

The work of Monge and Hurtado provided a model for centres of Andean biology and medicine established later, for example, the Institute of High-Altitude Pathology (Clínica IPPA), in La Paz, Bolivia (founded 1970) and the Veterinary Institute of Tropical and High-Altitude Research of the University of San Marcos (Lima), founded in 1985, which has a unique Information Centre on South American Camelidae.

Historians of Mexican medicine all stress the role of Spanish republican researchers in training students and founding distinctive research 'schools' in various specialties. Four figures were of particular significance. Isaac Costero, trained in neurohistology by Pío del Río-Hortega joined the Institute of Cardiology where he developed a distinctive approach to pathological anatomy; he is recognized as the founder of the Mexican school of pathology. Rafael Mendez, a pharmacologist, who before arriving in Mexico was chairman of pharmacology at the University of Chicago, was head of the pharmacology department of the Institute of Cardiology where he developed a working group in cardiovascular pharmacology. Dionisio Nieto, a German-trained psychiatrist, led the department of neuroanatomy and neuropathology at the Laboratory (later Institute) of

[56] See A. M. Monnier, 'Arturo Rosenblueth', *Dictionary of Scientific Biography,* 16 vols (New York, 1970–80), 11: 545–7.

[57] On high altitude physiology in Peru, see Cueto, *Excelencia científica en la periferia,* ch. 5, and *idem,* 'Andean Biology in Peru: scientific styles on the periphery', *Isis,* 80 (1989): 640–58.

Biomedical Research (a unit established at The Universidad Nacional Autónoma de México (UNAM) by the Rockefeller Foundation to provide a research facility for exiled Spaniards[58]) as well as the department of neurobiology at UNAM where he strove to create a Mexican neurological school in the mold of that of Cajal. José Puche continued in Mexico the root concerns of August Pi-Sunyer's Catalan school of physiology, in research on trophic sensitivity, physiological correlation, and an inventive programme in the metabolism of crustaceans.[59]

Among other Spaniards who contributed to Mexican medical research was the gynaecologist Alejandro Otero who stimulated gynaecological research in the Laboratory of Medical Research of the General Hospital in Mexico, D.F. and was instrumental in the formation of the Medical Association for Sterility Studies.[60] Spanish physicians also revitalized provincial medicine in Mexico. Two founded provincial medical journals: Luis Fumagallo (*Monterrey Médico*) and Antonio Aparicio Sánchez Covisa (*Acta Médica Hidalguense*).[61]

Spanish exiles also played a significant role in Mexican biology. In entomology were Cándido Bolívar (who became president of the Mexican Society of Natural History), Gonzalo Halffter Salas (who became director of the Museum of Natural History), and Federico Bonet. In oceanography came the de Buen family: the aged Odón, a pioneer Spanish Darwinian, and his sons Rafael, who held posts at UNAM and at the University of Michoacán, and Fernando, appointed to the limnological station at Pátzcuaro (he subsequently left the country to become director of fisheries in Uruguay); Enrique Rioja; and Bibiano Osorio Tafall. Among botanists was Faustino Miranda, founder of UNAM's botanical garden.[62]

Although the density of republican scientists was considerably less marked in other countries, it is worth reviewing some representative figures and contributions. In Cuba, the parasitologist Gustavo Pittaluga

58 Larissa Lomnitz, 'Hierarchy and Peripherality: the organization of a Mexican Research Institute', *Minerva*, 17 (1979): 527–48.

59 José Cueli, 'Ciencias médicas y biológicas', in *El exilio español en México, 1939–1982* (Mexico D.F., 1982), pp. 495–528, especially pp. 503–8; Augusto Fernández Guardiola, 'Semblanza de cuatro médicos españoles', in María Luisa Capella, (ed.) *El exilio español y la UNAM (coloquio)* (Mexico D.F., 1987), pp. 43–48; Rafael Mendez, *Caminos inversos: Vivencias de ciencia y guerra* (Mexico, D.F., 1987); José Luis Barona Vilar and María Fernández Mancebo, *José Puche Alvarez (1896–1979). Historia de un compromiso* (Valencia, 1989), pp. 57–73, 95–111,

60 José Fernández Castro, *Alejandro Otero, el médico y el político* (Barcelona, 1981), p. 204.

61 *Exilio español*, p. 514. See also Germán Somolinos d'Ardois, *25 años de medicina española en México* (Mexico D.F., 1966), p. 20 (for republican doctors in Matehuala, Culiacán, Ciudad Valles, Veracruz and Jalapa); and Patricia W. Fagen, *Exiles and Citizens: Spanish Republicans in Mexico* (Austin, Tex., 1973), pp. 70–4.

62 *Exilio español*, pp. 526–8.

(Spain's leading malariologist), became head of the Department of Experimental and Clinical Hydrology in the Ministry of Health. There he trained a distinctive Cuban school of epidemiology.[63] In Venezuela, August Pi-Sunyer transferred from Barcelona his distinctive approach to experimental physiology in the Institute of Experimental Medicine at the Central University. There, along with Rossend Carrasco Formiguera, a Catalan colleague who had performed with Walter Cannon the crucial experiment establishing Cannon's 'emergency theory' of adrenaline, he not only trained a group of Venezuelan physiologists but participated in a broader movement of scientific professionalization.

PSYCHOANALYSIS

The reception of psychoanalysis in Latin America makes an interesting comparison with that of relativity (see below). Popular and intellectual diffusion was a certainty due to the notoriety of Freud and Einstein. But more profound reception depended on the presence of professional groups with appropriate training. Both psychologists and physicists were in short supply in Latin American countries in the 1920s. Thus the reception of psychoanalysis by psychiatrists is in some sense parallel to that of relativity by engineers. Psychiatrists in the Latin world, although trained in a wholly somatic approach to mental illness, had traditionally adopted a eclectic stance with regard to medical theory and this pronounced eclecticism strongly coloured the reception of Freud in the period before the establishment of 'orthodox' psychoanalytical groups in the 1940s and 1950s. Inasmuch as most 'histories' of psychoanalysis are written from within the movement, the 'prehistory' has been derogated, when not ignored completely, resulting in a deformed picture of Freud's impact on Latin American culture.[64] Yet Freud's influence was already enormous in the 1920s, when his collected works, in Luis López Ballesteros' Spanish translation, were read in all the capitals of the region.[65]

[63] Leonard Jan Bruce-Chwatt and Julian de Zulueta, *The Rise and Fall of Malaria in Europe* (Oxford, 1980), p. 126; Victor Santamaria, 'El Prof. Gustavo Pittaluga', *Archivos Médicos de Cuba,* 7 (1926): 221–27; Concepción Carles Genovés and Thomas F. Glick, 'Gustavo Pittaluga Fatorini', in J. M López Piñero (ed.), *Diccionario Histórico de la Ciencia Moderna en España,* 2 vols (Barcelona, 1983), II: 187–7.

[64] The terms 'psychoanalysis' and 'Freudian psychology' are used interchangeably. The second term avoids the bounded cognitive and professional structures that the first implies, particularly for its practitioners. With respect to the reception of Freudian psychology, the fidelity of the receivers to orthodox canons is not the most significant aspect.

[65] For the history of the Spanish translation of Freud's works, see Thomas F. Glick, 'The Naked Science: psychoanalysis in Spain, 1914–1948', *Comparative Studies in Society and History,* 24 (1982): 533–71.

The first sustained interest in psychoanalysis in Latin America dates from Honorio Delgado's first writings on the subject in 1915. Delgado, a Peruvian psychiatrist was, as a young man, very enthusiastic about the therapeutic possibilities of psychoanalysis although from the outset he had reservations regarding its theoretical underpinnings, in particular the concept of libido. His 1919 volume *El psicoanálisis* was the first volume in Spanish on the subject and the beginning of his correspondence with Freud himself which led to Delgado's becoming the institutional representative of psychoanalysis in Latin America. In 1922, he attended the psychoanalytic congress in Berlin, meeting Freud and his lieutenants in person, and an intellectual biography of Freud followed in 1926. Delgado's objective, however, was not to become a psychoanalyst but simply to assimilate Freudian therapeutic methods in his clinical practice. His psychological ideas were, in fact, an amalgam (rather typical in the world of Latin psychiatry), of Freud, Jung and Adler, a theoretical promiscuity which brough Delgado a mild rebuke from Freud. Even in his therapy, however, Delgado's methods were quite unique: he claimed to have cured psychotic patients simply by having them attend seminars he organized for them on the Freudian explanation of their symptoms. By 1927, when he attended the Innsbruck psychoanalytical congress his enthusiasm had cooled, and over the next decade his position moved from sceptical to overtly antagonistic.[66]

After 1929 Delgado used his chair of psychiatry to oppose Freud in Peru, thereby retarding the emergence of professional analytic groups. But his activity in the 1920s had been influential in the diffusion of Freudian ideas. It was through him that Peruvian intellectuals like José Carlos Mariátegui learned of Freud. (Mariátegui, however, noted in 1927 that 'the Latin spirit seems the least apt to understand and accept psychoanalytic theories which French and Italian critics reproach for their Nordic and Teutonic content, when not for their Jewish origins'.) In Ecuador Julio Endara based his understanding of personality in part on Freudian ideas gleaned from Delgado's early articles. The emergence of orthodox psychoanalysis in Peru is associated with Carlos A. Seguín, who had undergone analysis at the New York Psychoanalytic Institute in the 1940s

66 Alvaro Rey de Castro, 'Freud y Honorio Delgado. Crónica de un desencuentro', *Hueso Humero* (Lima), nos. 15–16 (1983): 5–76; José Carlos Mariátegui, "El 'freudismo' en la literatura contemporánea," *Sagitario* (La Plata), 2 (1927): 205–210, on p. 209; Julio Endara, 'Notas acerca de la evolución de la personalidad' (1922), Leopoldo Zea (ed.), *Pensamiento positivista latinoamericano* (Caracas, 1980), pp. 529–58. See also Javier Mariátegui's edition of Delgado, *Freud y el psicoanálisis: Escritos y testimonios* (Lima, 1984).

and returned to Peru to practice psychosomatic medicine. The first group of orthodox analysts were his students. The Peruvian Society of Psychoanalysis was founded in 1980.[67]

The first Brazilian, probably the first Latin American, to speak publicly of Freud was Juliano Moreira in his chair of psychiatry in Bahia in 1899. Later, when he was director of the psychiatric hospital in Rio de Janeiro he supported the establishment there by Carneiro Ayrosa of a laboratory of psychoanalytic diagnosis in 1929. From as early as 1914 the psychiatrist Henrique Roxo was recommending psychoanalysis as a diagnostic method and this approach to Freud was characteristic of his reception. There were also examples of self-taught analysts in the 1920s, such as Júlio Porto-Carrero in Rio de Janeiro and Durval Marcondes in São Paulo. (Marcondes provided the link between the early reception and introduction of normative psychoanalytic methods, when he recruited the Jewish refugee Adelheid Koch to begin orthodox training in 1937.) At the end of the 1920s Marcondes and Francisco Franco de Rocha (who had been lecturing on Freud in the medical school since 1918) in São Paulo together with Porto-Carrero and Moreira in Rio founded a short-lived Brazilian Psychoanalytical Society, not as a professional association but rather to diffuse the ideas of Freud among the Brazilian elite. In the wake of the Revolution of 1930, many of Freud's supporters (including Ayrosa, Porto-Carrero, Inaldo Neves-Manta and Arthur Ramos) weighed in with books addressing the relevance of psychoanalysis to Brazilian culture and society generally, an indication of the successful diffusion of Freudian ideas among the intellectual class.[68]

In Argentina, there was ample commentary on Freud in the 1920s, especially in academic journals. A series of lectures on the theory and methods of psychoanalysis by Spanish psychiatrist Gonzalo R. Lafora in 1923 was influential in establishing the significance of Freudian ideas among the medical community of Buenos Aires.[69] Medical students who

[67] Alvaro Rey de Castro, 'El psicoanálisis en el Perú: Notas marginales', *Debates en Sociología,* 11 (1986): 229–310, on p. 236.

[68] On the early reception of Freud in Brazil, see Silvia Alexim Nunes, 'Da medicina social à psicanálise', in Joel Birman (ed.), *Percursores na história da psicanálise* (Rio de Janeiro, 1988), pp. 61–122; Marialzira Perestrello, 'Primeros encontros com a psicanálise. Os precursores no Brasil (1899–1937)', in Sérvulo Figueira (ed.) *Efeito PSI: A influência da psicanálise* (Rio de Janeiro, 1988), pp. 151–181; Gilberto S. Rocha, *Introduçao ao nascimento da psicanálise no Brasil* (Rio de Janeiro, 1989); and Roberto Sagawa, 'A psicanálise pionera e os pioneiros da psicanálise em São Paulo', in Figueira, ed., *Cultura de psicanálise* (São Paulo, 1985), pp. 15–34.

[69] Gonzalo R. Lafora, 'La teoria y los métodos del psicoanálisis', *Revista de Criminología, Psiquiatria y Medicina Legal* (Buenos Aires), 10 (1923): 385–408.

read Freud's works in López Ballesteros' translation in the 1920s wrote extensively on psychoanalytic theory and therapy in medical journals in the 1930s as they integrated them into their clinical practice. Gregorio Bermann said that he had practiced psychoanalysis in the 1920s (such reminiscences are a leitmotiv in autobiographies of psychiatrists), meaning most likely that dream interpretation, free association and other Freudian techniques were worked into his clinical practice. Others who wrote about Freud in this period were Gonzalo Bosch, Jorge Thenón, Emilio Pizarro Crespo and two future analysts Federico Aberastury and Enrique Pichón-Riviere.[70]

The 'official' history of Argentinian psychoanalysis begins in 1942 with the foundation of the Argentinian Psychoanalytical Association by the Spanish refugee Angel Garma, Celes Cárcamo, Arnaldo Rascovsky and Pichón-Riviere. Garma, trained in Berlin and a specialist in psychosomatic medicine, had been the first practicing psychoanalyst in Spain. Cárcamo had read Freud in the late 1920s and practised psychotherapy, as a doctor, in the 1930s. Rascovsky had discovered Freud around 1935, when he began clinical research on the psychosomatic background of endocrinological problems like obesity. He convened a Freudian discussion group in his house from 1937 and, when Garma arrived, underwent a didactic analysis with him. In the same period Pichón-Riviere was conducting classes of psychoanalytic psychiatry in the Hospicio de las Mercedes; he also was analysed by Garma.[71] Also involved in the early APA was Marie Langer, an Austrian Jewish refugee analyst.

The APA shortly began to offer professional seminars through its teaching arm, the Institute of Psychoanalysis, organized along German lines, although contact was lost with the German-speaking analysts. The APA analysts read Freud in English, or in the López Ballesteros version, corrected against James Strachey's standard English translation.[72] The early interests of Pichón in the psychoanalytic theory of psychosis and of

[70] Jorge Balán, *Profesión e identidad en una sociedad dividida: La medicina y el origen del psicoanálisis en la Argentina* (Buenos Aires, 1988; Documento Cedes, 7), pp. 11–16.

[71] Arminda Aberastury, Fidias R. Cesio, Marcelo Aberastury, *Historia, enseñanza y ejercicio legal del psicoanálisis* (Buenos Aires, 1967), pp. 24–45. This is very much the officialist APA view of the introduction of psychoanalysis in Argentina. An entertaining, but equally myopic, Lacanian view of the same events is Germán L. Garciía, *La entrada del psicoanálisis en la Argentina* (Buenos Aires, 1978). See also Antonio Cucurullo, Haydée Faimberg and Leonardo Wender, 'La psychanalyse en Argentine', in Roland Jaccard (ed.), *Histoire de la psychanalyse,* 2 vols (Paris, 1982), pp. 453–511. The national studies in the Jaccard volumes are narrowly focussed studies by movement insiders, largely bereft of sociological and cultural perspective.

[72] According to Garma (personal communication, 1979).

Aberastury in the psychology of children shaped the future involvement of psychoanalysis in public health.[73] The first thirteen years of the APA, until the fall of Perón in 1955, were a period of hibernation. In the intellectual effervescence following Perón's fall the first Argentinian intellectuals underwent psychoanalysis, initiating a boom in the field's popularity. Also in 1956, Garma and Rascovsky organized the Second Iberoamerican Congress of Medical Psychology in which Argentinian analysts displayed their Freudian wares. Foreign students, notably from Brazil and Mexico, came to Argentina for training and didactic analysis.[74] Inasmuch as there had been practically no clinical psychology at all in the country, 'this empty space was filled by psychoanalysts' trained by the APA. As psychology was added to university curriculum, its first teachers were psychoanalysts. This led to a real boom in psychoanalysis in the 1960s, coinciding with the graduation of the first university-trained psychologists. The psychoanalysts rode out the coup of 1966 and the ensuing university crisis by retreating to their private practices. Then in the 1970s there was a new expansion. At the same time the APA lost its monopoly over accreditation and numerous new analysts emerged. The coup of 1976, however, brought on a severe repression of Freudian psychology, now portrayed by the regime as anti-Christian, and there was a mass migration of Freudians to other Latin American countries (Marie Langer for example, went to Mexico) and Spain.

In Colombia, Freud appeared in medical theses as early as 1922 and J. B. Montoya lectured on Freud's concept of hysteria in Medellín in 1923. Analytic therapy did not begin until 1948 and the Colombian Psychoanalytical Society was not founded until 1961.[75] The early reception of Freud in Mexico has not been studied. His work was amply diffused there in the 1920s and 1930s. And in 1938 there was a movement – originating in Yucatan – to offer Freud a refuge in Mexico. This idea was backed by five influential labour unions, suggesting that Freud's ideas had diffused well beyond the 'groves of academe' and the medical community.[76] At the end

[73] The following section is based on Emiliano Galende's lucid contribution to 'El psicoanálisis argentino: Un cuestionamiento', *Vuelta 16*, II, 16 (1987): 25–40, 32–6.

[74] Marie Langer, Jaime del Palacio y Enrique Guinsberg, *Memoria, historia, y diálogo psicoanalitico* (Mexico, D.F., 1981), p. 89, where Langer also gives an interesting account of the sociology of the early analysands.

[75] Humberto Roselli, 'Evolución de la psiquiatría en Colombia', in Fondo Colombiano de Investigaciones Científicas, *Apuntes para la historia de la ciencia en Colombia*, I (Bogotá, 1971), pp. 69–100, on p. 98.

[76] Archivo Histórico Genaro Estrada, Secretaria de Relaciones Exteriores, Mexico, D.F., III-423-3, III-425-4.

of the 1940s the first Mexicans professionally interested in psychoanalysis went abroad to study. When they returned in the early 1950s they were already affiliated with the international analytic movement and in 1955 a Mexican group was accepted in the International Association under the supervision of the Argentinian APA.[77]

In Brazil, the Spanish psychiatrist Enrique Mira y López was the founding father of applied psychology as director of the Institute of Testing and Professional Orientation of the Vargas Foundation from 1947 until his death in 1964. Mira, who had introduced the Rorschach test in Spain and given the first course there on psychoanalysis, brought to Brazil psychodiagnostic tests and methods of his own invention (the myokinetic test), founding the Brazilian Psychotechnic Association and editing its *Arquivos Brasileiros de Psicotécnica.* Mira trained an entire generation of Brazilian psychologists at his institute,[78] another example of a Spaniard filling an empty professional niche and creating a new national disciplinary group. But Mira also travelled widely and was influential in the modernization of psychology in Argentina and Uruguay, here he lived briefly, and in Venezuela.[79]

In Mexico, the Spanish neurologist Gonzalo R. Lafora joined Dionisio Nieto at Laboratory of Medical Research where he continued his research on neuropathology. In 1942 Lafora wrote a series of articles examining the case of a serial murderer, Gregorio Cárdenas, based on interviews with the killer, which included free association and Rorschach tests, on the basis of which Lafora rejected a psychogenic etiology of the criminal's actions in favour of a neurological one (epilepsy). Lafora was subsequently accused by the criminal's family of having revealed privileged information publicly and the affair was debated in the Mexican Neurological Society. The public furor was a measure of Lafora's great prestige in the Mexican psychiatric community.[80]

77 Ramón Parrés and Santiago Ramírez, 'Historia del movimiento psicoanalítico en México', *Cuadernos de Psicoanálisis* (Mexico, D.F.), 2 (1966): 19–29.

78 Franco LoPresti Seminério, 'Emilio Mira y López e a psicologia contemporanea – uma interpretaçao', *Arquivos Brasileiros de Psicologia Aplicada,* 30 (1978): 21–36; Alice Madeleine Galland de Mira, *PMK: Psicodiagnóstico miocinético* (São Paulo, 1987), pp. 9–12; Thomas F. Glick, 'Emilio Mira y López', in López Piñero, (ed.), *Diccionario Histórico de la Ciencia Moderna en Espana,* II: 63–4.

79 On the influence of Mira in Latin America, see Gregorio Bermann, 'In Memorian: Dr. Emilio Mira y López', *Acta Psiquiatrica y Psicológica de América Latina* (Buenos Aires), 10, 1 (March 1964): vi–xi; articles by and about Mira in *Revista de Psiquiatria del Uruguay,* no. 28 (July–August 1940); and J. F. Reyes Baena, *Emilio Mira y López: Ensayo biográfico* (Caracas, 1975).

80 Raquel Alvarez Peláez and Rafael Huertas García-Alejo, *¿Criminales o locos? Dos peritajes psiquiátricos del Dr. Gonzalo R. Lafora* (Madrid, 1987), pp. 225–311; 145–60.

PHYSICAL AND EXACT SCIENCES

Physics

In Latin America there was virtually no independent discipline of physics until the twentieth century. The subject matter of theoretical physics was traditionally the province of mathematics. Mechanics was taught in departments of mathematics until well into the twentieth century. Nor was it uncommon for astronomers to teach physics. Until the emergence in this century of modern faculties of science, the experimental side of physics, on the other hand, was domiciled in the special schools, especially those of engineering and mining. (Indeed, military engineers were the carriers of the high tradition in mathematics and physics from colonial times through to the end of the nineteenth century.)

In Argentina, Maxwellian physics was introduced only in 1892, by the engineer Jorge Duclout.[81] Substantial change did not come until the University of La Plata was reorganized in 1904 by Joaquín V. González, who was determined to introduce modern physical sciences in the country. This he did by contracting with the German physical chemist, Emil Bose, who arrived to assume the directorship of the Institute of Physics at the end of 1909.[82] Bose was soon able to attract two first-rate colleagues, Jakob Laub, a pioneer in the theory of relativity as Einstein's first collaborator, for the chair of geophysics, and, as head of electrical engineering, Konrad Simons. Bose quickly built the best physics library in Latin America, using his personal collection as the core, and the government came through with promised funds for laboratory equipment. A visiting U.S. physicist remarked that he had never seen 'so much apparatus together in one place'. When Bose died in 1911 he was replaced by Richard Gans who became the dominant figure in Argentinian physics during the first quarter of the century.

La Plata was the first university in Argentina with authority to grant doctorates in physics and astronomy. Students were quickly recruited, the number of those in degree programmes rising from 67 in 1911 to 126 in 1914. Most of these students, however, were candidates for engineering degrees; only a handful were physicists. Instruction was of the highest calibre: Walter Nernst gave a short course on thermodynamics in 1914,

[81] Ramón G. Loyarte, *La evolución de la física* (Buenos Aires, 1924), p. 64.

[82] The story of the implantation of German physics in Argentina is told by Lewis Pyenson, *Cultural Imperialism and Exact Science: German Expansion Overseas, 1900–1930* (New York, 1985), ch. 3.

Laub's lectures on relativity were surely the first on the subject in the New World, and Simons' electrical engineering textbook 'defined a discipline in Ibero-American cultures'.[83] Argentinian physicists trained at La Plata included Teófilo Isnardi, who worked with Nernst in Berlin and produced some important research in atomic theory and Ramón Loyarte, Gans' successor as director of the Institute.

No episode marked the coming of age of Argentinian physics, while at the same time demonstrating both its strengths and its limitations, than Albert Einstein's visit to Argentina in 1925. As did Einstein's trips to other countries, the visit stimulated an avalanche of popular books and articles on the theory of relativity as well as the realization that such high interest was in part a reflection of the general level of scientific activity in the country. 'It is clear,' *La Prensa* commented, 'that had there not existed a scientific sentiment, Einstein would not not have awakened intense and strongly felt interest in so great a mass of people.'[84] Much was made in the press of the capacity shown by Argentinian scientists by their very ability to direct questions at the visiting physicist in a public meeting at the Academy of Sciences: 'If half the population of Argentina finds itself disorientated and trying only to gain an approximate idea of the theory of relativity, a group of Argentinian professors has demonstrated its profound knowledge of it.'[85] Einstein, unfortunately, was not as impressed, noting in his travel diary: 'Was asked a lot of stupid scientific questions so that it was difficult to keep a straight face.'[86] Einstein's reservations notwithstanding, the reception of relativity in Argentina was notable for the lack of conflict it generated; since Maxwellian physics had been incompletely assimilated, there was no entrenched group of physicists wedded to mechanistic principles to oppose relativity on physical grounds.

Einstein's theory was widely commented upon in Argentina: by Georg Friedrich Nicolai (a German physiologist at the University of Córdoba and the only German professor other than Einstein who had refused to sign the notorious Manifesto of German professors supporting the Kaiser's war aims), by engineers like Enrique Butty and José Galli, and by the physicists Loyarte and Isnardi.[87] In Uruguay, where Einstein made a short visit,

83 Ibid., p. 206.

84 *La Prensa*, 31 March 1925.

85 *La Prensa*, 17 April 1925; Einstein was questioned by Loyarte, Isnardi and others. See also a transcription of a private exchange between Isnardi and Einstein, *La Prensa*, 20 April.

86 Einstein Travel Diary, 1925, Einstein Papers, Princeton Duplicate Archive.

87 Jorge F. Nicolai, 'La base biológica del relativismo científico y sus complementos absolutos', *Revista de la Universidad Nacional de Córdoba*, 12 (1925): 1–378; José Galli, *Einstein explicado* (Buenos Aires,

relativity was likewise explained in popularizations addressed by engineers to engineers. There too he met with the philosopher Carlos Vaz Ferreira, probably the first Latin American to lecture on relativity.[88]

In all the countries which Einstein visited (Brazil, Argentina and Uruguay, in Latin America) he and his ideas were heralded as symbols of modernization, and the mastery of his ideas as indicative of the will to modernize. In all these countries where the scientific community was thinly populated, engineers, standing in for non-existent physicists, were eager to associate themselves with this particularly abstract idea. Among engineers (and it is well to recall that the leading Brazilian mathematicians during Einstein's visit to Rio de Janeiro, were professors at the Escola Politécnica), the capacity (either individually or in a collective sense) to understand relativity stood for the capacity to do modern science. Note that this is the same class of people who in Europe and the United States opposed relativity as excessively abstract and scientifically regressive! Engineers, typically a conservative group in Latin countries, by associating themselves with relativity were able to contest leadership of the professions with medical doctors, traditionally liberal. This was a standard pattern in the reception of relativity in Latin countries (including Spain and Italy): relativity is mainstream, it is practical, engineers should at least understand the special theory, and one cannot expect to implant modern science in a country whose mathematicians are incapable of teaching it.

Scientific and academic politics aside, relativity, because of its connotations of philosophical relativism, was commonly appropriated for direct application to politics. Spanish anarchists, for example, were quick to point out that they espoused economic relativism and the relativity of political institutions, just as Einstein espoused the relativism of time and space. It is hardly surprising that Latin America, that laboratory of politics, should have produced perhaps the most original political embroidery of relativity: *El espacio-tiempo histórico* of Víctor Raúl Haya de la Torre. Haya was almost certainly informed of the relativity revolution from

1925); Ramón G. Loyarte, 'La obra de Einstein', *Revista de Filosofía,* 21 (1925): 475–8; Teófilo Isnardi, 'En torno a la relatividad', *La Nación,* 20 April 1925. On Einstein's visit to Córdoba and his pallid reaction to Nicolai's treatise, see Wolf Zuelzer, *The Nicolai Case* (Detroit, Mich., 1982), pp. 379–82.

[88] A. Geille Castro, 'La teoría de la relatividad', *Revista de la Asociación Politécnica del Uruguay,* 18 (1924): 132–43 and following; José Llambias de Olivar, 'Consideraciones sobre la teoría de Einstein', 19 (1925): 177–88 and following. On Vaz Ferreira and Einstein, Sara Vaz Ferreira de Echevarria, 'Carlos Vaz Ferreira con Alberto Einstein' (Montevideo, 1965), typescript.

around 1923 and between 1935 and 1945 elaborated a coherent *americanista* political philosophy for APRA (Alianza Popular Revolucionaria Americana) using Einsteinian relativity as a convenient source of political analogies.

According to Haya, the Hegelian and Marxian dialectic suffered the handicap of having been elaborated under the constraints of pre-Einsteinian physics characterized by Newtonian absolutes and a circumscribed (Galilean) concept of relativity. Hegelian and Marxian views of the new world are hopelessly Eurocentric, but in post-Einsteinian history there can be no privileged observers. Because of the immobility of the observer, Marxism is dogmatic, and dogmatism is anti-dialectical. Marxism, in Haya's view, cannot be held to be a fixed and absolute entity and there can be no standard evolutionary cycle that all societies pass through, as Marx had posited. There is no absolute parallelism in the vastness of historical space-time, just as there is none in the Einsteinian universe. Each historical society constitutes its own distinctive space-time and proceeds according to its own rhythms, not strictly comparable with those of any other society. Capitalism may be a late form of economic organization in European societies, not necessarily elsewhere.[89]

Two promising theoretical physicists trained at La Plata, Enrique Gaviola and the Uruguayan Enrique Loedel, emerged in the 1920s. Loedel's specialty was general relativity (he was the only Argentinian scientist able to pose an interesting question to Einstein during his visit). Gaviola published research on the atomic spectrum of mercury (with R. W. Wood) and then, in 1931, an important paper on wave-particle duality. Indeed, in the 1920s Gaviola was the only Argentinian physicist (besides Gans, of course) who attained 'citation visibility' in Europe (in German publications above all). Argentina was the only Latin American nation whose production in physics registers in the Citation Index for this period.[90]

Although the accomplishments of the Institute of Physics were considerable, in the long run the effort was a failure. The German professors were unable to establish a local research market or to transplant the research ethic so closely identified with German excellence in physics. Pyenson suggests that Argentinian students may well have had difficulty identifying with the authoritarian disciplinary style of German physicists and

[89] V. R. Haya de la Torre, *El espacio-tiempo histórico* (Lima, 1986).

[90] Pyenson, *Cultural Imperialism and Exact Science*, pp. 237–8 (Loedel), 240–6 (Gaviola); Pyenson and M. Singh, 'Physics on the Periphery: A world survey, 1920–1929', *Scientometrics*, 6 (1984): 301.

their upper class manners. European chemistry, more democratically organized, won more adherents.[91]

Other countries were considerably less fortunate in physics in the 1920s than was Argentina. In Cuba, for example, Manuel Gran, professor of physics at the University of La Habana from 1923 until he was named ambassador to France in 1960, left an evocative memoir of the desolate state of Cuban physics in the 1920s when university instruction in the subject was inferior to that imparted in the better secondary schools. The laboratory had not been restored to use after its destruction in the cyclone of 1906 and the apparatus was broken or dispersed. The mathematics education of the students was so deficient that 'it was necessary first to explain a point of higher mathematics before getting to the physics topic that depended on it'.[92] In Venezuela, there were virtually no physicists before the 1950s. Relativity, for example, was received and commented on by a fine mathematician, Francisco J. Duarte.[93]

In Brazil, systematic instruction in physics dates from the creation of the Escola Politécnica in 1893, and instruction mainly in applied physics by Francisco Ferreira Ramos (who demonstrated x-rays in his laboratory in 1896, within a year of their discovery) and, later, by Luiz Adolfo Wanderly.[94] At the time of Einstein's visit there in 1925, however, only astronomers, mathematicians and engineers could comment on his theory. Of the astronomers Henrique Morize, director of the Brazilian National Observatory, had planned the English expedition to view the solar eclipse at Sobral in 1919, when the general theory was confirmed. He and Lélio Gama, a member of the Sobral commission, wrote popularizing articles in the press during Einstein's visit.

Among Brazilian mathematicians Einstein's visit drew attention to a deep division in their ranks between entrenched Comtean positivists (Licinio Cardoso was the leading figure) and a younger generation more attuned to European mathematics and mathematical physics. The Com-

[91] Lewis Pyenson, 'The Incomplete Transmission of a European Image: physics at Greater Buenos Aires and Montreal, 1890–1920', *Proceedings of the American Philosophical Society,* 122 (1978): 114.

[92] Luis Felipe LeRoy y Gálvez, *Profesores de física de la Universidad de la Habana desde su secularización en 1842 hasta Manuel F. Gran* (Havana, 1979), pp. 24–33.

[93] Luis Urbina Luigi, 'Reseña histórica y bibliográfica de la ciencias físicas y matemáticas en Venezuela', in IVIC, *La ciencia, base de nuestro progreso* (Caracas, 1965), pp. 93–103. See also *Hemenaje al Dr. Francisco J. Duarte, 1883–1972: Personalidad y correspondencia* (Caracas, 1974).

[94] For general accounts of the history of modern physics in Brazil, see José Goldemberg, *100 años de física* (Rio de Janeiro, Centro Brasileiro de Pesquisas Físicas, 1973; Ciência e sociedad, vol.2, no. 2); Shozo Motoyama, 'A física no Brasil', in Guimaraes and Motoyama (eds), *História das ciências no Brasil,* I: 61–91; and J. Costa Ribeiro, 'A física no Brasil', in Fernando de Azevedo (ed., *As ciências no Brasil,* 2 vols (São Paulo, n.d.), I, pp. 163–202.

teans clung dogmatically to regressive ideas long ago promoted by Comte which impeded the reception of both non-Euclidean geometry and the Maxwellian concept of fields, both decried as metaphysical abstractions. Accordingly, Einstein's appearance in Rio de Janeiro precipitated a fierce debate in the Brazilian Academy of Sciences in which a group of relativists led by the mathematician Manoel Amoroso Costa and the engineer Roberto Marinho were able successfully to discredit Cardoso and the old-line Comtean positivists in noisy sessions held on 10 June and 8 July, 1925.[95] Once the Comteans were defeated, there were none to oppose Einstein's theories and opposition was notably weak. Einstein flattered his Brazilian hosts by noting 'The problem conceived in my head had to be solved by the luminous sky of Brazil.'[96] In his diary, Einstein was less than charitable: of his lecture on relativity at the Engineering Club he noted 'Little understanding for science. To them, I am a kind of white elephant, and for me they are fools.'[97]

Even in the provinces, Einstein was a beacon of modern science. In Recife, Luiz de Barro Freire explained Einstein's theory and defended it against a well-known traditionalist attack by Henri Bouasse. Freire, engineer, mathematician and physicist, was largely self-taught in contemporary science. He imparted his enthusiasm to a gifted generation of students, including physicists Mario Schenberg and José Leite Lopes and mathematician Leopoldo Nachbin.[98]

Profound understanding of theoretical physics had to wait until the 1930s when two important research groups were founded, each by an European immigrant. In Rio de Janeiro, the German Jewish physicist Bernard Gross performed a series of important experiments in 1934–7 at the Instituto Nacional Tecnológico measuring the intensity of cosmic rays in an ionization chamber.[99] Gross trained J. Costa Ribeiro who discovered the thermodialectric effect in 1944. At the University of São Paulo the Russian-born Gleb Wataghin, who arrived from Turin in 1934, was also

95 Antonio Paim, 'O neopositivismo no Brasil. Período de formação da corrente', in M. Amoroso Costa, *As idéias fundamentais da matemática e outros ensaios,* 3rd edn (São Paulo, 1981), pp. 41–63, p. 58. Some short articles on relativity by Amoroso Costa are reproduced in the same volume, pp. 101–19. See also, Paim, 'Indicadores do término do ciclo positivista,' *Revista Brasileira de Filosofía,* 30 (1980): 335–49.

96 For a chronicle of Einstein's trip to Brazil, see Roberto Vergara Caffarelli, 'Einstein e o Brasil,' *Ciência e cultura,* 31 (1979), 1437–55.

97 Einstein Travel Diary, 6 May 1925. Einstein Papers, Princeton Duplicate Archive.

98 Ivone Freire de Mota e Albuquerque and Amélia Império Hamburger, 'Retratos de Luiz de Barros Freire como pioneiro da ciência no Brasil', *Ciência e Cultura,* 40 (1988): 875–81.

99 L. Jánossy, *Cosmic Rays,* 2nd edn (Oxford, 1950), p. 139.

interested in cosmic rays. This proved to be an appropriate field on which to found Brazilian experimental physics in view of the low cost of experiments. It also had the advantage of stimulating a number of interconnected fields such as astrophysics, nuclear physics and the physics of elementary particles. In the late 1930s, Wataghin's group, joined by the Italian Giuseppe Occhialini, performed experiments on cosmic ray showers, with two young Brazilians, Marcello Damy de Souza and Paulus Aulus Pompéia, discovering the penetrating or 'hard' component of cosmic radiation. This research programme was consolidated by the International Conference on Cosmic Rays, held in Rio de Janeiro in 1941. Another disciple of Wataghin, Mario Shenberg, collaborated with George Gamow in 1941 on the neutrino theory of stellar collapse, a phenomenon associated with the tremendous production of light associated with novae and supernovae. The following year, Shenberg co-authored an important paper with Subrahmanyan Chandresakhar on the growth of helium nuclei in the evolution of stars.

In the mid-1940s Occhialini and a Brazilian student César Lattes joined in collaborative research with Cecil Powell of the University of Bristol in England who had developed a method of detecting elementary particles by exposing photosensitive plates to cosmic radiation at mountain altitudes. The Brazilians induced Bolivian colleagues to refit a meteorological observatory high in the Bolivian Andes at Chacaltaya for cosmic ray research. There in 1947 they discovered the pi meson, or pion (a highly unstable particle which decays forming a muon and a neutrino) whose existence had been predicted by H. Yukawa. The following year, Lattes and E. Gardner, produced an artificial pi meson in the cyclotron of the Berkeley Radiation Laboratory.[100] The discovery of the pi meson was the starting point of modern elementary particle physics. In the next step of meson research, the Brazilian Jayme Tiomno and J. L. Wheeler of Princeton, in a famous paper delivered at the AAAS meeting in 1948, explained the one-half spin of muons in terms of a weak 'Fermi' interaction.[101]

The institutional fall-out from pi meson research was of considerable

[100] On pi meson research, see Alfredo Marques, *24 años da descoberta do meson*, 2nd edn (Rio de Janeiro, CBPF, 1985; Ciência e sociedade, vol. I, no. 12), and Bruno Rossi, *Cosmic Rays* (New York, 1964), pp. 133–6. This research brought Powell the Nobel Prize in 1950.

[101] José Leite Lopes, 'Point-counterpoint in Physics: theoretical prediction and experimental discovery of elementary particles', *Fundamenta Scientiae*, 6 (1984): 165–77. On Tiomno, see A. Luciano L. Videira, *Da relatividade as particulas (ida-e-volta): Cuarenta anos de física de Jayme Tiomno* (Rio de Janeiro, CBPF, 1980, mimeo) and José Maria Filardo Bassalo, *Jayme Tiomno, os mésons e a física paraense* (Rio de Janeiro, CBPF, 1987, mimeo).

significance for the future of Latin American physics: first, Chacaltaya was developed into an outstanding research facility, the Laboratory of Cosmic Physics of San Andrés University. Under its first director, the Spaniard Ismael Escobar, and later, Gastón R. Mejía, the range of research was broadened to include meteorology, solar radiation, the ionosphere, glaciology, and so forth. The success of the Laboratory was reflected in other sections of the university, stimulating, for example, the foundation of the University Computing Centre, directed by a member of the Laboratory, where Bolivia's first computer was installed in 1965.[102] Secondly, the success of the pi meson research programme led directly to the establishment of the Centro Brasileira de Pesquisas Físicas (CBPF), in Rio, which became the nerve center of Brazilian physics.

The Rockefeller Foundation had backed the physics effort at the University of São Paulo, allowing it to produce world-class research in the 1940s. But the department at the Universidade do Brasil in Rio de Janeiro could not attain the same grant level because there were no full-time research positions (a key Rockefeller requirement) in that university. Therefore, the CBPF was conceived as a private institute, with some links to the university, where original research in physics would proceed under the direction of José Leite Lopes in theoretical and Lattes in experimental physics.[103]

After the Second World War a school of nuclear physics built upon the prior accomplishments in theoretical and particle physics. In São Paulo experimental nuclear physics began when Damy de Souza acquired a Betatron (a kind of particle accelerator) in 1951 and Oscar Sala, an electrostatic generator in 1954, giving the São Paulo group two different ways of bombarding atomic nuclei. Pompéia and others worked on the detection of elementary particles and Sala, in the United States, investigated nuclear reactions induced by neutrons. In theoretical physics Schenberg ranged over a host of topics from general field theory and electrodynamics to the theory of elementary particles and astrophysics. The Brazilian school never lost its interest in elementary particles. In 1949, Richard Feynman, then working on meson theory, began a long relationship with Brazilian physicists which took him to Brazil frequently over the next fifteen years. He and José Leite Lopes collaborated on studies of weak particle interactions,

[102] Ismael Escobar, *Anteproyecto para el Observatorio de Física Cósmica en Chacaltaya* (La Paz, 1950); Gastón R. Mejia, *El rol del Laboratorio de Física Cósmica en el desarrollo de la ciencia y tecnologia boliviana* (La Paz, 1969).

[103] José Leite Lopes, 'A física nuclear no Brasil', *Ciência e Cultura,* 8 (1956), 14–21 and *idem,* 'Trinta años de física no Brazil: Evocações', *Revista Brasileira de Tecnología,* 16 (1985): 25–33.

publishing a joint paper on weak pseudoscalar coupling in 1952. A few years later, Leite, stimulated by Feynman and Gell-Mann's research, predicted the existence of another elementary particle, the neutral vector boson (z_o) which was subsequently discovered experimentally in 1983.[104]

The phenomenal growth of Brazilian physics from its formative period in the 1930s (when virtually all of the future leaders of the discipline were recruited from the engineering schools) is attributable to the success of the cosmic radiation research programme. By 1960 there were approximately one hundred Brazilian research physicists, a number which grew to eight hundred by 1977.

Cosmic radiation research was introduced in Argentina by a number of the leading figures in physics: Gaviola, Guido Beck, Isnardi. The lead institution was the Jesuit Observatory of San Miguel, established in 1935 under the direction of the Catalan Ignasi Puig (1887–1961). Puig was succeeded in 1943 by Juan Bussolini who inaugurated a department of solar physics. In 1968–9 the observatory was reorganized and its director Mariano Castex became president of the National Geoheliophysical Research Commission, established to coordinate solar research in Argentina, including the solar observatory of La Rioja and the Patagonian Centre of Geoheliophysics. It was also in the mid-1940s that cosmic physics was established at the Laboratory of Cosmic Radiation of the University of Buenos Aires. In 1952 this group moved to the Atomic Energy Commission (DNEA, later CNEA) which sent the future director of its cosmic radiation laboratory, Juan Roederer, to finish his doctorate at Gottingen. The DNEA, which tended to absorb all nuclear-related research-front physics during this period, also sponsored a new cosmic studies center at the University of Tucumán (1961). In 1964, Roederer was named director of the National Center of Cosmic Radiation which installed neutron supermonitors in Buenos Aires and Antarctica. Argentine research in cosmic radiation has been more observational than theoretical in focus.[105]

In Mexico, modern physics dates to the career of Manuel Sandoval Vallarta.[106] Sandoval was trained at MIT (1917–29) where he was a profes-

[104] Leite Lopes, 'Point-counterpoint in Physics', pp. 176–7, and *idem, Richard Feynman in Brazil: Recollections* (Rio de Janeiro, 1988).

[105] José Federico Westerkamp, *Evolución de las ciencias en la República Argentina, 1923–1932: Física* (Buenos Aires, 1975), pp. 161–70; Otto Schneider, *Evolución de las ciencias en la República Argentina, 1923–1972: Geofísica y geodesia* (Buenos Aires, 1980), pp. 36–9. On Puig, see *Escriptors jesuïtes catalans. Bibliografia 1931–1976* (Barcelona, 1977), pp. 233–49.

[106] The following section is based on Regis Cabral, 'Sandoval Vallarta, as condições de validade da macromecânica, e a estructura conceitual de mecânica', *Quipu,* 5 (1988), 327–37; Héctor Cruz Manjarrez, 'Reseña histórica del Instituto de Física, Primer etapa 1938–1953' (Mexico, D.F.,

sor from 1926 (teaching the first course there on electromagnetic theory) until he returned to Mexico in 1949. His early research interest in relativity and quantum mechanics (in particular the application of relativity to atomic models) yielded, from 1932 on, to a dedication to cosmic rays (the nature of the particles forming them and the effect of the earth's magnetic field upon them). He was an influential pedagogue: the American Nobel laureate Richard Feynman and the Mexicans Carlos Graeff and Luis Enrique Erro were among his students.

Here too, the Spanish republicans made a mark. Mexico welcomed Spain's leading physicist, Blas Cabrera, the only Spanish member of the Solvay Institute, and the astronomer, Pedro Carrasco, both nearing the end of their careers. Cabrera installed a machine shop in his Laboratory of Precision Electrical Measurement at the Institute of Physics (UNAM) for use in his own magnetism research and to build instruments, not only for the Institute, but for the rest of the University.[107] Cabrera must have modelled his shop after Leonardo Torres Quevedo's famous automation laboratory in Madrid which supplied Cabrera's Institute there with instruments and built equipment for all scientific disciplines in the 1920s. The many exiled Spanish mathematicians made their mark primarily in secondary schools, particularly by writing text books, thereby influencing future generations of Mexican mathematicians.[108] Prior to 1930 there had been practically no organized higher mathematics in Mexico; therefore the Spaniards filled a particularly useful niche.

In the late 1940s Mexican theoreticians elaborated upon aspects of George Birkhoff's theory of gravitation in flat space-time, a model consistent with Einstein's special relativity but which avoided the general theory's curvilineal coordinates, which Birkhoff 'always considered to be unnecessary and difficult to interpret experimentally'.[109] Indeed, Birkhoff had expounded his idea in a 1944 lecture in Mexico, D.F.,[110] and a group of Mexican physicists were working on Birkhoffian relativity or on comparisons between Einstein's and Birkhoff's cosmologies, including Jaime Lifshitz (Birkhoff's student), Fernando Alba Andrade, Graeff and Sandoval.

1975) and 'Reseña histórica del Instituto de Física, Segunda etapa 1953–1970' (Mexico, D.F., 1976) (mimeo); and Juan Manual Lozano et al., 'Historia de la Sociedad Mexicana de Física', *Revista Mexicana de Física,* 3 (1982): 277–93.

107 Cruz Manjarrez, 'Reseña histórica del Instituo de Física. Primera etapa 1938–1953,' pp. 24–5.

108 José Cueli, 'Matemáticas, física y química', in *Exilio español,* pp. 531–43, on pp. 532–3.

109 Marston Morse, 'George David Birkhoff', *Dictionary of Scientifc Biography,* II: 143–6.

110 George D. Birkhoff, 'El concepto matemático de tiempo y la gravitación', *Boletín de la Sociedad Matemática Mexicana,* 1 (1944): 1–24.

By 1950 the Mexican physics community consisted of three Ph.Ds, one M.S. and a licenciate. Still, two years later there was enough interest to found the Mexican Physics Society, with Graeff as president, which by 1982 had grown to 1400 members. This exponential growth is in part explained by the dynamism that nuclear physics imparted to the discipline beginning with the acquisition of a Van de Graaf accelerator in 1950–52. Three young physicists sent to MIT to learn how to use it became the nucleus of an experimental physics research group. Virtually all physics research in Mexico has concentrated in the National University (UNAM) and it has been difficult to establish viable centres elsewhere in the country.

After the Second World War physics research in Argentina, Brazil, Chile and Mexico became increasingly focussed on atomic physics. In Argentina, there was a politically charged debate among physicists as to the degree to which research in physics should be linked to the armed forces. Enrique Gaviola argued that the hierarchical and disciplinary structure of the military was at odds with the keystones of scientific training which were 'intellectual rebelliousness, dissatisfaction with existing theories and methods and a rejection of hierarchical authority in science and technology'.[111] Gaviola's argument was found persuasive by the Argentinian Senate which, in November of 1946, was considering a draft law establishing the Institute of Physical and Chemical Research.

In 1949 Perón hired a refugee German physical chemist named Ronald Richter to direct an ambitious project of nuclear science. Richter convinced Perón that he could produce controlled nuclear fusion with cheap materials in a process that could underwrite a vast expansion of the nation's industrial capacity by supplying cheap energy in huge quantities. Perón's reasons for backing Richter were wholly in line with the ideology of modernization that informed his concept of the 'New Argentina'; he had no interest in the military uses of atomic energy but saw it as a way to expand iron and steel production quickly and cheaply. In February 1951 Richter made the sensational announcement that he had achieved controlled nuclear fusion under laboratory conditions (a claim ultimately proven false; Richter was charlatan who had simply exploded hydrogen in a voltaic arc). Even so, the announcement had important, though unforeseen

[111] From a letter from Gaviola to General Savio, 28 September 1946), cited by Mario Mariscotti, *El secreto atómico de Huemul* (Buenos Aires, 1985), p. 63. The following section is based on Mariscotti's fascinating account. See also, Regis Cabral, 'The Perón-Richter fusion program, 1948–1953', in Juan José Saldaña (ed.), *Cross-Cultural Diffusion of Science; Latin America* (Mexico, D.F., 1987; Cuadernos de Quipu, 2), pp. 77–106.

consequences: the news from Argentina stimulated the United States to begin a fusion programme and, at the same time, the Argentinian government purchased a syncho-cyclotron from the Netherlands. Not long after Richter had been exposed (by a series of committees that included Richard Gans and José Antonio Balseiro) the cyclotron became the central element in training a distinguished generation of Argentine nuclear scientists who early on produced internationally recognized results in the field of radioisotopes. The Dirección Nacional de Energía Atómica (DNEA) became the focus of a rapid institutionalization of physics around 1953 (the multiplication of sub-specialties, large expenditures on instrumentation, grants established to send young scientists abroad, were some of the signs). In 1950, the year of DNEA's founding, the Dirección Nacional de Investigaciones Técnicas (DNIT – antecedent of CONICYT) was also established. Hence, atomic research was the stimulus that led to the crystallization of a general scientific research structure. Balseiro had been a disciple of Guido Beck, an Austrian emigré quantum physicist whom Gaviola had hired at the Córdoba Observatory.[112] With Beck, Balseiro cut his teeth as a theoretical physicist in research on the quantum structure of magnetic fields. After study abroad (in Liverpool), Balseiro returned to Argentina to head the theoretical section of the Atomic Energy Commission. Then in 1950, he was named director of the Bariloche laboratory which he promptly removed from politics, recruiting the best Argentinian talent (Gaviola organized a high-temperature laboratory there in 1953) for faculty and sixty students in its initial class.[113] The depoliticization of nuclear physics promoted its rapid institutionalization in the 1950s: subdisciplinary groups multiplied and ample funds were spent both on the purchase of instruments and on fellowships for foreign study. The success of the DNEA had no precedent in Argentina; its budget under Enrique P. González exceeded that of any other Argentinian university or institute scientific programme.

Numerous other atomic physics centres were established in Latin America. In 1954, for example, a Nuclear Physics Group was established in the Physics Department of the University of Chile; the group acquired a Dutch particle accelerator and Chileans were trained by a team of Dutch physi-

[112] According to Gaviola, Beck's stimulus was crucial for the program of Argentine physics. The year after Beck's arrival in 1943, Gaviola and others at Córdoba founded the Asociación Física Argentina (Gaviola, 'La Asociación Física Argentina: su historia hasta', 1965) (mimeo). See also H. M. Nussenzveig, *Guido Beck: 1903–1988* (Rio de Janeiro, 1989).

[113] On Beck and Balseiro, see Alberto Maiztegui, 'Un investigador que actuó en una época tan difícil como la de hoy,' *La Voz del Interior,* 16 June 1985; Guido Beck, 'José Antonio Balseiro (1919–1962), *Ciencia e Investigación,* 18 (1962), 145–9.

cists.[114] In 1956 an Atomic Energy Commission was established in Guatemala, which developed a sizeable atomic physics research establishment (the National Institute of Nuclear Energy, founded 1970, and the Dirección General de Energía Nuclear, a bureau of the Ministry of Energy and Mines). Mexican nuclear physics expanded rapidly with the acquisition of four reactors between 1960–70. A dynamitron accelerator and financial support from the Rockefeller Foundation and other U.S. bodies underlay the growth of research beginning around 1965. The Mexican National Institute of Nuclear Research, like the Guatemalan effort, is highly applied in nature, focussing on agriculture, medicine and metallurgy.

Astronomy, Astrophysics and Geophysics

The status of astronomy in Latin America at the beginning of the century can be appreciated from the composition of the astronomical commissions witnessing the solar eclipse of 10 October 1912, which was visible only in Brazil. The Chilean and two Argentinian delegations were led by foreign astronomers: the German F. W. Ristenpart and the North Americans William Joseph Hussey and Charles D. Perrine, directors of the observatories of Santiago, La Plata and Córdoba respectively. Only the two Brazilian commissions led by Henrique Morize and composed mainly of Brazilian personnel were Latin American in the true sense.[115]

Latin American astronomy throughout the century, but particularly in the first half, was closely tied to European and U.S. astronomy as a source both of technical know-how and of research programmes. The most advanced countries like Argentina, Mexico and Brazil developed dual observatory structures, with the older, more urban observatories performing the tasks of classical astronomy (charting the stars of the southern hemisphere and measuring their magnitudes) and newer, usually more outlying, dependencies initiating the study of astrophysics (cosmology, spectroscopy, galactic astronomy).

In Mexico the National Observatory of Tacubaya in Mexico City, founded in 1878, devoted much of its labors to the unification of time, the country being a hodge-podge of different time zones (which interfered, logically, with the efficient functioning of the incipient railroad system). The staff was duly concerned with the elaboration of the Mexican zone of the celestial map and photographic star catalogue as well as other classical

[114] J. Mir Dupont, *Evolución de la energia nuclear en Chile* (Santiago, 1985), p. 2.
[115] Roberto Vergara Caffarelli, 'O eclipse solar de 1912', *Ciência e Cultura*, 32 (1980): 561–73.

endeavours such as the observation of solar eclipses.[116] A Mexican team had gone to Spain in 1905 to view the solar eclipse there. The solar eclipse of 1923 was visible in Mexico, and mindful of the ambiguous results of the 1919 Sobral eclipse, the Mexican government had invited Einstein himself to direct the eclipse observations.[117]

In 1942 the Astrophysical Observatory of Tonantzintla (Puebla) was inaugurated under the direction of Luis Enrique Erro. Its Schmidt telescope was one of the largest of the period and similar to Harvard Observatory's where its mechanical parts were made. Erro was in close contact with Harvard astronomers, notably Leon Campbell and his American Association of Variable Star Observers, and the observatory's early research programme was just a descriptive hand-me-down from Harvard. MIT-trained Carlos Graeff was the theoretical physicist on Erro's team; he gave an early seminar on quantum mechanics and wrote on Birkhoff's relativistic cosmology while Paris Pismis conducted original research on galactic cinematics. A fresh round of original research ensued when Guillermo Haro returned from Harvard to take up the direction of both Tacubaya and Tonantzintla. Under his direction, theoretical work was concentrated at Tacubaya and observational work, including his own research on nebulae in Andromeda, at Tonantzintla, air pollution having made the older facility almost useless for observation.[118] As pollution worsened Tacubaya was closed as its equipment moved to Tonantzintla whose own utility was increasingly jeopardized by deteriorating air quality. The observatory was integrated into an Institute of Astronomy established at the National University in 1967 even as the search was underway for a site for a new national observatory. In 1970 construction began on a facility in Baja California in close collaboration with the University of Arizona. The new national observatory, used mainly for photometric observation, became the axis of a new scientific research centre (CICESE) designed to complement its own activities.[119]

[116] On the history of modern classical astronomy in Mexico, see Marco Arturo Moreno Coral, 'El origen de la investigación astronómica en México,' *Actas de las Sociedad Mexicana de Historia de la Ciencia y de la Tecnología,* 1 (1989), 79–94, and *idem,* 'El Observatorio Astronómico Nacional y el desarrollo de la ciencia en México (1878–1910)', *Quipu,* 5 (1988), 59–67, and Joaquín Gallo Sarlat, 'Entre eclipses y cometas: Reminiscencias de la vida de Joaquín Gallo,' in Moreno Corral (ed.), *Historia de la astronomía en México* (Ensenada, 1983), pp. 245–66.

[117] *New York Times,* 9 June 1923.

[118] Bart J. Bok, 'Astronomía mexicana, 1930–1950', in Moreno Corral, *Historia de la astronomía en México,* pp. 267–80; Paris Pismis, 'El amanecer de la astrofísica en Mexico,' ibid., pp. 281–97.

[119] Manuel Alvarez and Eduardo López, 'Los últimos diez años del Observatorio Astrónomico Nacional', in *Historia de la astronomía en México,* pp. 311–36.

In Argentina the two major observatories were founded in the late nineteenth century – Córdoba in 1871, La Plata in 1882. The North American Benjamin Gould, the first of a succession of foreign directors at Córdoba, published a number of important star catalogues beginning with the famous *Uranometría Argentina* in 1879.[120] Córdoba continued this work under two more North American directors, John M. Thome who replaced Gould in 1885 and Charles D. Perrine who replaced Thome in 1909 and served until 1936. By the end of Perrine's term the effort of Córdoba was widely viewed as out of touch with the ambient culture. As an investigation of 1927 noted, 'After more than a half century's existence, the Observatory still preserves its basic original character as a foreign mission in Argentina. With its foreign personnel, its total disconnectedness with the technical and cultural problems of our country, this National Observatory remains alien to the life of the nation.'[121] In particular it was perceived as playing no role in the training of Argentinian scientists. Although astrophysics had begun under Perrine, its real impulse resulted from the transition to Argentinian leadership, under the directorships of Juan José Nissen (1937–40) and Enrique Gaviola (1940–47), the founding of an astrophysical station at Bosque Alegre, and the melding of astronomical research interests with those of theoretical physics under the leadership of Gaviola and Guido Beck, as already described. The research programme at Bosque Alegre included stellar spectography (e.g., Jorge Sahade's research on spectroscopic binaries) and direct photography.

The La Plata Observatory had a more varied programme. It owned a geodesic station at Oncativo where important studies on the variation of latitude in the southern hemisphere were conducted in the nineteenth century. Systematic astronomy (in the form of star catalogue work) began only under the North American director William J. Hussey (who served 1911–15). Hussey brought two other North Americans with him: Bernhard Dawson, who discovered numerous double stars in collaboration with Hussey and later became director and Paul Delavan, who in 1913 rediscovered Westphal's comet (which since has borne his name). Astrophysics began in earnest in the 1930s with the arrival as refugees from Germany of Alexander Wilkens, former director of the Breslau observatory with re-

[120] For exhaustive descriptions of the southern star catalogues produced at the Córdoba Observatory, see Enrique Chaudet, *La evolución de la astronomía durante los últimos cincuenta años (1862–1922)* (Buenos Aires, 1926).

[121] Félix Aguilar and Norberto B. Cobos, 'Informe sobre el Observatorio Nacional de Córdoba', in Simón Gershanik and Luis A. Milone (eds), *Evolución de las ciencias en la República Argentina, 1923–1972: Astronomia* (Buenos Aires, 1979), pp. 173–6 (Appendix 3).

search on the spectroscopic temperatures of double stars, and his son Herbert.[122]

The National Observatory of Brazil in Rio de Janeiro, under the long directorship of Henrique Morize was another Observatory of the old school with a classical metrological function and descriptive research programme. Perhaps its great accomplishment was directing the logistics of the 1919 expedition to view the solar eclipse at Sobral, confirming the theory of general relativity. Around the same time Amoroso Costa, the astronomer-mathematician who was Einstein's leading supporter in the Brazilian scientific community, was investigating double stars and worked out the evolution of a binary system following a theory of George Darwin on the formation of the earth/moon system. Like its counterpart at La Plata, the Brazilian Observatory maintained a geodesic station at Vassouras for the study of terrestrial magnetism. There were also observatories at São Paulo (the Observatorio da Avenida, founded in 1903, which moved, because of air pollution, to a park south of the city in 1941 and later became the Astronomical and Geophysical Institute of the University of São Paulo) and Porto Alegre (1908).

Theoretical astrophysics, as we have noted above, was another result of Wataghin's efforts in physics; Schenberg's collaborations of the 1940s with Gamow and Chandrasekhar represented a new direction in Brazilian theoretical astronomy. Modernization in observational astronomy and geodesy dates to the appointment of Lélio Gama as director of the National Observatory in 1951. A new geomagnetic observatory was established near the magnetic equator. In the 1970s a new astrophysical observatory as established at Brasópolis (Minas Gerais) and the National Center of Radio Astronomy and Astrophysics was founded in São Paulo.[123]

In Peru, efforts in astronomy were subordinated to geophysics. For some years early in the century, Harvard ran an observatory there, called Boyden Station, for photographing variable stars. Later on the Carnegie Institution built (between 1919–22) a magnetic observatory at Huancayo, a site determined to be equidistant between the Córdoba Observatory and a U.S. facility in Panama. The research programme at Huancayo was to measure the magnetic field and to make meteorological observations. In

[122] On the La Plata Observatory, see Pyenson, *Cultural Imperialism and Exact Sciences,* pp. 185–205, and Simón Gershanik, 'El Observatorio Astronómico de La Plata', in *Evolución de las Ciencias . . . Astronomia,* pp. 5–122.

[123] For surveys of astronomy in Brazil, see Abraão de Morais, 'A astronomía no Brasil', in Azevedo (ed.), *As ciências no Brasil,* I: 81–161, and Ronaldo Rogério de Freitas Mourão, 'A astronomía no Brasil', in Guimarães and Motoyama (eds), *Historia das ciências no Brasil,* II: 409–41.

1932 a seismograph was installed and, the following year, a spectrohelioscope was contributed by the Mount Wilson Observatory. As a result the research programme was broadened to include cosmic radiation and observation of the ionosphere. The Huancayo facility was transferred to the government of Peru in 1947 and was renamed the Geophysical Institute of Peru in 1962. During the 1960s a number of dependent stations were founded, including a radio observatory at Jicamarca (established under contract with the U.S. National Bureau of Standards for ionospheric studies), an ionospheric station at Talosa, and seismological station at Ñaño. Finally, in the 1970s the Cosmos Station, an installation purely for monitoring solar activity, was built at Huancayo by Kyoto University. It is interesting to note that although the Geophysical Institute has become one of the major physical science units in Latin America, contacts with foreign institutions have been crucial and the financial contribution of the Peruvian government minimal.[124]

The San Calixto Seismographic Observatory in La Paz, Bolivia, is an example of an institution with scant funding and inadequate instrumentation which preserved and made a significant contribution.[125] The observatory was founded in 1911 by Esteban Tortosa, a Spanish Jesuit who had worked at the Observatory of Cartuja in Granada, Spain, with Manuel Navarro Neumann. The director, who arrived in 1912, was the French Jesuit, Pierre M. Descotes. In May 1913 he began publishing as bulletin of seismic data which has continued uninterrupted to this day. The instruments, patterned after those in Granada, were home made in a rudimentary shop. Nevertheless, the data was so good that a standard American seismological text stated that 'La Paz at once became, and still remains, the most important single seismological station of the world. This is a consequence of its isolated location, the sensitive instruments, and the great care with which records were interpreted and reports issued under the direction of Father Descotes.' With the passage of time an astronomical section was added and the Bolivian government awarded Descotes a salary (which the Jesuit applied to new instrumentation). In 1960, when Descotes retired, the observatory joined an a program directed by the Department of Terrestrial Magnetism of the Carnegie Institution. Under the new director, Ra-

[124] Gustavo Estremadoyro, 'Historia de la astronomía en el Perú', in Ernesto Yepes (ed.), *Estudios de historia de la ciencia en el Perú,* 2 vols (Lima, 1986), I: 37–62, and Alberto Gisecke Matto, 'El desarrollo de la geofísica', ibid., I: 115–26.

[125] Pierre M. Descotes, S. J., *Le nouvel observatoire sismologique de la Compagnie de Jésus a La Paz, Bolivie* (La Paz, 1913); Ramón Cabré, S. J., 'Datos históricos del Observatorio San Calixto, en La Paz, Bolivia' (typescript).

món Cabré five subsidiary stations were installed, all communicating data to La Paz electronically. A variety of geophysical phenomena were studied, including anomalies of gravity and electric conductivity.[126]

Another Jesuit seismology station is the Geophysical Institute of the Colombian Andes, in Bogotá. Seismology in Colombia dates to 1923 when Simón Sarasola, the Spanish director of the National Meteorological Observatory, introduced the nation's first seismograph. At the same time, Enrique Pérez Arbeláez and Carlos Ortiz Restrepo were trained in seismology in Spain by Navarro Neumann, ordering for Bogotá a seismographic of his design constructed in Automotation Laboratory of the great inventor Leonardo Torres Quevedo. Finally, a new geophysical observatory was established in 1941 with Sarasola in charge of meteorology and seismology under the direction of Emilio Ramirez who had just completed graduate work in the seismology programme of the University of St. Louis. In 1945 an accelerograph was obtained from the U.S. Coast and Geodetic Service in whose observational network the Institute participated.[127]

In 1966 a regional centre for the study of seismic phenomena (CERESIS) was established with Ramon Cabré as its first president.[128] This is a consortium of nine South American countries operating under UNESCO auspices to exchange technical data and train personnel for seismographic observatories. Among its numerous publications are a multi-volume catalogue of earthquakes, a book on historical earthquakes, studies of economic effects of quakes, and a series of maps. If the origins of CERESIS can be traced to Descotes' modest observatory, then the lesson is that persistence, vision and adeptness at attracting the support of foreign institutions can eventually pay off.

Mathematics

Advanced research in physics and astronomy presupposes a pool of scientists trained in higher mathematics. Although mathematics is the most basic of sciences Latin American dependence upon Europe – particularly Italy – and the United States in this field well into the second half of the present century was notable.

[126] Ramón Cabré, S. J., 'Geophysical Studies in the Central Andes', *Geodynamics of the Eastern Pacific Region*, 9 (1983), 73–6.

[127] J. Emilio Ramírez, *Historia del Instituto Geofísica*, 2 fascicles (Bogotá, 1977).

[128] Alberto A. Giesecke, 'Centro Regional de Sismología para America del Sur: CERESIS' (mimeo, 1986).

The Italian Hugo Broggi of the University of La Plata, where he taught between 1912 and 1927, was associated with the modernization of mathematics in Argentina, but the Spaniard Julio Rey Pastor of the Faculty of Sciences in Buenos Aires was more influential, creating a distinctive Argentinian school of mathematical research. The Faculty of Sciences (which early in the century was an engineering school) had a doctoral programme in mathematics and physics but no courses had been given since 1900. From then until Rey Pastor's arrival some improvement had occurred in mathematics instruction for engineers, but higher mathematical study was in full decadence. Operationally, Rey Pastor's task was to convince engineering professors of the utility of any mathematics other than what appeared in elementary textbooks.

In his first course in 1917 Rey Pastor introduced, as he had already in Madrid, Felix Klein's famous 'Erlangen Program', a course of geometry instruction based on the theory of groups, whose method is to establishment the invariants of each one, topology being the most general. His next course, the following year, was a specialized course for engineering students. His impact was immediate and profound, in that among this early group of advanced students were the future leaders of Argentinian mathematics. The topics he covered – e.g. functions of a complex variable, conformal mapping – were standard in Germany and Italy, but completely new in Argentina.[129]

Rey Pastor received a six-year contract (followed by a permanent appointment) and restructured mathematics instruction at the Faculty of Sciences by offering courses on advanced (including non-Euclidean) geometry, mathematical analysis and mathematical methodology. Mathematicians of the old school, whose instruction was based on outmoded French manuals, were incensed at what they regarded as a usurpation by a foreigner.[130] Rey Pastor taught mainly engineering students among whom he recruited prospects for pure mathematics. This implied no contradiction, because he believed both that engineering school mathematics courses, which stressed the techniques of calculation, were good preparation for pure mathematicians and also that pure mathematicians should never lose touch with applications.

[129] Sixto Ríos, Luis A. Santaló and Manuel Balanzat, *Julio Rey Pastor, matemático* (Madrid, 1979), pp. 59–61, 71, 89. On Rey Pastor and the renewal of mathematics in Spain, see Thomas F. Glick, *Einstein in Spain* (Princeton, N.J., 1988), pp. 17–26.

[130] See Claro Cornelio Dassen, *Las matemáticas en la Argentina* (Buenos Aires, 1924), especially the sarcastic comments on pp. 69–70.

After his permanent appointment in 1927, Rey Pastor held two chairs, those of Mathematical Analysis and Higher Geometry, and, in 1928, founded an influential Mathematical Seminar patterned after one he had established in Madrid in the previous decade. Its shortlived *Boletín* published the first modern research in Argentinian mathematics. By the end of the decade, his first disciples were presenting papers in scholarly meetings abroad. As he had in Spain, Rey Pastor brought a succession of important foreign mathematicians to give short courses, including the Italians Federigo Enriques (1925), Francesco Severi (1930) and Tullio Levi-Civita (1937), and the Frenchmen Emile Borel (1928) and Jacques Hadamard (1930).

In the 1940s his best students began to make their mark in international research. Among these were Alberto González Domínguez (who became an important figure in Argentine quantum physics), Alberto Calderón (future chairman of mathematics at the University of Chicago whose specialty was singular integrals), Roque Scarfiello (theory of distributions), Emilio Roxin (control systems and optimal controls) and Misha Cotlar. At the same time, Spanish exiles including Esteban Terradas, Luis Santaló, Manuel Balanzat, and Pedro Pi Calleja, and the Italian Beppo Levi at the Mathematics Institute of Rosario, considerably enhanced the collective teaching capacity of the mathematical community.

By the time Rey Pastor retired in 1952 Argentinian mathematics had been transformed. Virtually every engineering student at the University of Buenos Aires between 1921 and 1952 had studied with him and, in other institutions and through his textbooks, he influenced generations of secondary school teachers as well. He had laid the foundation for the great Argentinian 'Generation of 1961'.

Rey Pastor had not taught the members of the Generation of 1961 (mathematicians born between 1937–40). They were more directly influenced by Mischa Cotlar. Of the ten most important members of this group[131], all studied in the United States and eight earned doctorates there (three at New York University and three at the University of Chicago). Three of this group – Beatriz Margolis (differential equations), Cora Sadowsky (singular integrals) and Víctor Pereyra (numerical analysis) – ended up at the Central University in Caracas in the 1970s where they participated in the modernization of mathematics there.

[131] As listed by Luis A. Santaló, 'La matemática en Buenos Aires y La Plata (Período 1943–1972', in Luis A. Santaló (ed.), *Evolución de las ciencias en la República Argentina, 1923–1972: Matemática* (Buenos Aires, 1972), pp. 54–103, on pp. 85–8.

The Central University's School of Physics and Mathematics had been founded in 1958 with a largely foreign faculty (including five Spanish mathematicians, three Brazilians and a number of Argentinians including Rodolfo Ricabarra who energized students in geometry and topology in the 1960s). Towards the end of the 1960s, Mischa Cotlar and Cora Sadowski arrived to stimulate research in harmonic analysis and integral equations. This was the moment of the awakening of Venezuelan mathematics, associated with the leadership of Luis Baez first at the Central University and then at the Instituto Venezolana de Investigaciones Científicas (IVIC), and was quickly followed by the creation of institutions: the Caracas Mathematical Colloqium (1976), the first Venezuelan Mathematical Congress (1977), the Seminar of Mathematical Logic (1978), and the Foundation of the Venezuela Mathematical Society (1980). The 1970s saw a diversification of topics of research, which had hitherto centred on analysis.[132]

Uruguay developed a fine school of mathematicians in the 1950s and 1960s, also under the stimulation of contact with Argentinian mathematics, and in this case, with Rey Pastor directly. At the end of the 1930s, Rey Pastor began to give regular weekend seminars on general topology in Montevideo to a group which included José Luis Massera, Mischa Cotlar, and Rafael Laguarda. The Institute of Mathematics and Statistics (IME), established in the Engineering School in 1942, became the center of an emergent school of Uruguayan mathematics. The research programmes of both Massera and Laguarda were set in the course of fellowships in the United States, Massera's on differential equations and Laguarda's on integral transformations. By 1960, with the maturation of the 'third generation' of Uruguayan mathematicians, the identity of a distinctive school had emerged and research interests broadened considerably (into probability, differential topology and so forth). Cotlar returned from Argentina after the military coup of 1966 had paralyzed the University of Buenos Aires. The military intervention in Uruguay in 1973 brought, in turn, the ruin of Uruguayan mathematics: Massera was imprisoned, virtually the entire staff of the IME emigrated and, in the early 1980s, twenty-five Uruguayan mathematicians of high quality were employed in other countries.[133]

[132] Carlos A. Di Prisco and Lorenzo Lara, 'Comentarios sobre la investigación matemática en Venezuela,' in Hebe M. C. Vessuri (ed.), *Ciencia académica en la Venezuela moderna* (Caracas, 1984), pp. 237–77.

[133] Rodrigo Arocena and Gonzalo Pérez, 'Matemática', in Ministerio de Educación y Cultura, *Ciencia y tecnología en el Uruguay* (Montevideo, 1986), pp. 71–9, y José Luis Massera, 'Los orígenes y el desarrollo de la escuela uruguaya de matemáticas', *Interciencia,* 13 (1988): 177–82. A memoir of the Institute in the 1950s can be found in Paul R. Halmos, *I Want To Be a Mathematician* (New

In Brazil, Oto de Alencar (1874–1912) was an important precursor of modern mathematics, a student of non-Euclidean geometry who, as professor at the Politécnica of São Paulo introduced Painlevé on differential equations. His student and follower, Manoel de Amoroso Costa (1885–1928) continued to teach modern mathematics which brought him into conflict with positivists of the old school, as we have noted. Another benchmark was the 1918 thesis of Teodoro Ramos (1895–1935) on real variables; he too continued a tenuous modern tradition as professor of rational mechanics at the Politécnica of São Paulo. A relativist, he gave notable courses on vectorial calculus and quantum mechanics. To São Paulo he invited the Italian Luigi Fantappié who introduced functional analysis, a line continued by Omar Catunda and, in some early articles, Mario Schenberg. Lélio Gama was the first great mathematics professor in Rio de Janeiro where visiting Italians (Gabrielle Mammana and Achille Bassi), introduced modern analysis, combinatory topology and similar subjects in the 1940s. The foundation of the Conselho Nacional de Pesquisa (CNPq) in 1951 had a decisive influence on Brazilian mathematics with the establishment in 1952 of the Institute of Pure and Applied Mathematics (IMPA) through which most senior Brazilian mathematicians of the 1970s and 1980s passed in the 1950s and 1960s. IMPA sponsored a biennial Colloquium of Brazilian Mathematics which instilled an unusual cohesiveness in the Brazilian mathematics community. The number of participants in this Colloquium grew dramatically from fifty at the first (1957), to 250 at the sixth (1967), to 700 at the eleventh (1977).[134]

Chemistry

Throughout Latin America chemistry was traditionally associated with pharmacy and the preponderance of chairs were in medical schools well into the present century. At the point at which local chemical industries required a research establishment, institutes and schools were established for that purpose. In many cases the two traditions merged, forming unified departments or faculties of chemistry. In others, pharmacy remained autonomous. The institutional patterning of today's national chemistry

York, 1985), pp. 167–99. Halmos, lecturing to the Institute's 'second generation' in 1950 noted (p. 190) that his audience was 'unfamiliar with the language and attitude of modern mathematics'.

134 F. M. de Oliveira Castro, 'A matemática no Brasil', in Azevedo (ed.) *As ciências no Brasil,* I: 41–77; Chaim S. Hönig and Elza F. Gomide, 'Ciências matemáticas', in Guimaraes and Motoyama (eds), *História das ciências no Brasil,* I, 35–60.

disciplines therefore reflects the previous balance established between pharmaceutical and biochemists, on the one hand, and industrial chemists, on the other.

We can observe this bimodal pattern in Mexico where, during the Revolution, Juan Salvador Agraz, the first Mexican member of the International Commission on Atomic Weights, secured the creation of a National School of Industrial Chemistry in the village of Tacuba near Mexico, D.F.[135] The pharmacists, meanwhile, wanted to leave the Medical School where they felt themselves treated like poor relations, and soon they were folded into the Tacuba school, which continued however to concentrate on chemical engineering. No less than ten of its graduates were sent to Germany (in part, to lessen French influence on Mexican scientific culture) in 1921 for advanced study; when they returned most were employed by the government in various ministerial laboratories, because no one knew what a chemical engineer was supposed to do.

During the directorship of Fernando Orozco, one of the German-trained chemists, the civil engineering component of instruction was reduced and emphasis on biochemistry increased at the same time as Spanish republican refugees were integrated into Mexican chemistry. In 1941 a research unit, the Institute of Chemistry, was founded at the National University with Orozco as director and the Spanish republican Antonio Madinaveitia as director of research. The Institute soon became the centre of chemical research in Mexico, aided by the financial support of the Rockefeller Foundation (which continued to 1963) and the establishment in it of a doctoral programme.[136] Meanwhile, instruction in chemical engineering assimilated the pedagogical model of unitary operations brought from MIT by Estanislao Ramírez. The success of Mexican chemical engineering was proven in the saga of Syntex and the domination of the world market in synthetic steroids by Mexico in the late 1940s and 1950s on the basis of research carried out in Madinaveitia's laboratory at the behest of a company founded by Hungarian and German refugees from Nazism together with the North American Rusell Marker who identified a plant source of progesterone.[137] The Tacuba School was converted into the Autonomous

[135] For the history of the Tacuba School, based on extensive interviews with graduates, see Horacio García Fernández, *Historia de una Facultad: Química, 1916–1983* (Mexico, D.F., 1985).

[136] Pilar Rius, 'Los exiliados españoles y la creación del Instituto de Quimica de la UNAM', in María Luis Capella (ed.), *El exilio español y la UNAM (coloquio)* (Mexico, D.F., 1987), pp. 35–41; Alberto Sandoval L., 'Cinco lustros de existencia', *Boletín del Instituto de Química,* 17 (1965): 83–121.

[137] On Syntex see García Fernández, *Historia de una Facultad,* pp. 186–8; Ingrid Rosenbleuth, 'Dependencia tecnológica e evolución profesional: La industria y la ingenieria química en México',

University's Faculty of Chemistry and moved to the new University City (1957–63). There, chemistry enrolments increased precipitously from 1620 in 1967 to 5420 in 1971 (with 621 professors).

Uruguay presents a similar case of the fusion of industrial and pharmaceutical chemistry.[138] An Institute of Chemistry had been established in Montevideo in the Faculty of Medicine in 1908, housed in a grandiose building modelled after the Chemistry Institute of the University of Berlin and whose first director was the professor of medical chemistry, José Scoseria. He was succeeded by Domingo Giribaldo who struggled to implant modern chemistry against entrenched resistance by old-school pharmacologists. In 1917 he inaugurated a chair of physical chemistry with a course on electrochemistry.

Meanwhile in 1912 an Institute of Industrial Chemistry had been founded under the directorship of the North American Latham Clarke, with the mission of training a small number of industrial chemists. The first members of the staff had been trained in pharmacology or mineralogy. Like Tacuba, the Institute had a production section designed to support the Institute's research and instruction in applied chemistry which commenced in 1915. In 1918 a degree programme in industrial chemistry was instituted; this was precocious in Latin America, inasmuch as chemical engineering had only been created (at MIT) in the first decade of the century. In 1929 a new Faculty of Chemistry and Pharmacy was founded, combining pharmaceutical chemistry with the teaching functions of the Industrial Chemistry Institute. In 1950 the national research effort was restructured in the Laboratory of the Division of Scientific Research of the National Commission of Combustibles, Alcohol and Cement, with five sections (organic, inorganic and physical chemistry, industrial microbiology and experimental biology).

Prior to the establishment of a School of Chemistry at the Central University in the 1940s the only advanced training available in the field in Venezuela was in a small school run since 1912 in the Development Ministry. The new School was initially housed in the Faculty of Pharmacy, then moved to engineering and finally was folded into a faculty of sciences in 1958. The first professors in the 1950s were mainly foreigners, central Europeans and Spanish republicans, who in general were not researchers but who performed the instrumental role of transmitting classical chemis-

Relaciones. Estudios de Historia y Sociedad (Michoacán), 1 (1980): 35–90; and Gary Gereffi, *The Pharmaceutical Industry and Dependency in the Third World* (Princeton, N.J. 1983).

[138] Jorge Grünwaldt Ramasso, *Historia de la química en el Uruguay (1830–1930)* (Montevideo, 1966).

try. In the late 1950s and 1960s several hundred Venezuelans went abroad to study, mainly to the United States but also to England and France and in 1966–70 several dozen Argentinian chemists, including a number of already established working groups, migrated to Venezuela en masse, fleeing military oppression. The Argentinians in general moved on without leaving disciples behind, having perceived Venezuela as infertile ground for chemical research.[139] But here too the growth in chemistry enrolments was astounding, with matriculations in 1955–75 growing at double the rate of the rest of the sciences combined, a phenomenon obviously related to the Venezuelan oil boom.

In Brazil, pharmacology and biochemistry were established in medical schools and institutes. In particular, biochemists of the first half of the century were almost all medical doctors who studied the chemical composition of blood or other tissue. Two biochemists trained by Otto Folin at Harvard rose to distinction in the 1930s: A. A. Cavalcanti (1899–1976) in São Paulo and João Baeta Vianna (1894–1967) in Belo Horizonte. Baeta Vianna worked on the biochemistry of Chagas' Disease. Maurício de Rocha e Silva at the Biological Institute of São Paulo, discovered bradykinin, a pharmacologically important polypeptide. Biochemists at the Oswaldo Cruz Institute worked on vitamins, the action of drugs of enzymes and other topics of medical application in the 1940s and 1950s, while at Butantan Thales Martins (1896–1979) studied the pharmacology of hormones.

Industrial chemistry got under way in 1918 perhaps in response to a famous article, 'Façamos Químicos', written the previous year by José de Freitas Machado, calling for a major school of chemistry modelled on that of Paris. (Freitas Machado organized the first Brazilian Chemistry Congress in 1922 and was the first president of Brazilian Chemistry Society, founded in 1923.) Hence in 1918 the Institute of Agricultural Chemistry was established under the direction of Mário Saraiva. In 1919 the Brazilian Congress established courses of industrial chemistry in eight state capitals, in association with local engineering schools. The Porto Alegre course was taught by Otto Rothe and another German, Erik Schirm, was hired to head a new Institute of Industrial Chemistry. Rothe introduced both

[139] Hebe M. C. Vessuri, 'Scientific immigrants in Venezuela: national identity and international science', in Arnaud F. Marks and Hebe Vessuri (eds), *White Collar Migrants in the Americans and the Caribbean* (Leiden, 1983), pp. 171–97, and Vessuri and Elena Díaz, 'El desarrollo de la química cientifica en Venezuela', in Vessuri (ed.), *Ciencia académica en la Venezuela moderna* (Caracas, 1984), pp. 237–7.

physical chemistry and experimental physics there. The Belo Horizonte course was taught by Alfredo Schaeffer, a German who had directed the State Analysis Laboratory there since 1911. An Institute of Chemistry was likewise organized there in 1921. In its laboratories, Schaeffer introduced 'methods analogous to those used in the majority of advanced European schools'. Schaeffer was followed as director by Rothe. The course in Pará was directed by Paul Le Cointe with an entire teaching staff recruited in France. In 1934 the Ministry of Agriculture, long a backer of positivist projects, organized a National School of Chemistry in Rio de Janeiro at the same time as the first real effort in basic chemistry was begun in the newly inaugurated Faculty of Philosophy and Sciences at São Paulo under the direction of Heinrich Rheinboldt. Rheinboldt had been a chemistry professor in Bonn. His specialties were the chemistry of co-ordination complexes and organic compounds, the latter also the specialty of his assistant Heinrich Hauptmann. Physical chemistry was not introduced until 1946. The major research effort in this area, Hans Stammreich's programme in molecular spectroscopy, was begun in the physics departmental and later incorporated into the Department of Basic Chemistry.[140]

Finally in Argentina, the pharmacy/chemistry split was handled differently in different universities. At the University of Buenos Aires (where a doctorate in pharmacy had been in place since 1875 and in chemistry from 1897) a single curriculum was introduced for basic and industrial chemistry, in the faculty of sciences, while pharmacy was taught in the medical school. La Plata, of more recent foundation, was not bound by the traditional autonomy of pharmacy and offered three parallel programmes (housed in the same building from the 1930s) in pharmacy, basic chemistry and industrial chemistry. The National University of El Litoral had a doctorate in chemical engineering (1919), the first such degree programme in Latin America. In Córdoba, the School of Pharmacy and Biochemistry split from the medical school in 1950 and became the Faculty of Chemical Sciences.[141]

As a result of the precocious establishment of university degree programmes Argentina, in contrast to all other Latin American countries, produced a sizeable number of native chemists. As a result, reliance upon

[140] On chemistry in Brazil, see Heinrich Rheinboldt, 'A química no Brasil', in Azevedo (ed.), *As ciências no Brasil,* II: 9–89; Simao Mathias, 'Evoluçao da química no Brasil', in Guimaraes and Motoyama (eds), *História das ciências no Brasil,* I: 93–110; J. Leal Prado, 'A bioquímica no Brasil', ibid., I, 111–50; and José Ribeiro do Valle, 'A farmacologia no Brasil', ibid., 175–89.

[141] Noemí G. Abiusso (ed.), *Evolución de las ciencias en la República argentina: Química* (Buenos Aires, 1981), 6–18.

foreign chemists was diminished. Chemical activities have been so numerous that it is not feasible to summarize them here. However, one area of development in the field is worthy of comment. As a result of government backing of nuclear research, two important chemistry laboratories were organized within the Atomic Energy Commission in 1951–2.[142] These were the radiochemistry laboratory, who first director Walter Seelmann-Eggebert had been a doctoral student of Otto Hahn, and the general chemistry laboratory under the Argentinian Arturo Cairo. Seelmann worked on radionucleids while Cairo's group began a research programme in inorganic chemistry, centred mainly on uranium. Both laboratories trained many Argentinian chemists. In 1953, Alfred Maddock of Cambridge made the first of a series of visits in order to impart his first-hand knowledge of nuclear chemistry acquired in the atomic projects of the Second World War. That same year the Commission acquired a pilot plant for uranium production to make metallic uranium for reactors. This step led to increased activity in the general chemistry laboratory which by now had several working groups, including a metallurgy group under the physicist Jorge Sábato. At the same time two Phillips particle accelerators stimulated research on artificial radioactivity and chemists discovered fifteen new radionucleids. Finally, so much chemistry activity had been fostered that a Chemistry Department was established within the DNEA in 1954. In 1955, thirty-seven Argentinian papers were presented at the first Conference on the Peaceful Uses of Atomic Energy in Geneva, of which twenty four were by chemists. Among these were reports on the radioactive isotopes of ten different elements, some of them discovered in Argentina. When Argentinian nuclear research burst upon the world after some years of work in secret it caused a sensation internationally, and in the United States in particular, fear of nuclear proliferation.

Geology

Perhaps the most salient element of geological research in those Latin American countries where it was organized early in the century was the influence of the U.S. Geological Survey as an organizational model. In Brazil, the founders of geology were North Americans. The ephemeral Imperial Geological Commission (1875–77) did not survive the death of its

[142] Martín B. Crespo, 'La química en la Comisión Nacional de Energía Atómica en el período 1950–1972', in ibid., pp. 167–72.

founder Charles F. Hartt but nevertheless provided a fecund institutional model for future development. Hartt had recruited three young North Americans, Orville A. Derby, Richard Rathburn and the future president of Stanford University, John C. Branner. Derby (1851–1915), now considered the first Brazilian geologist, was made director of the Geographical and Geological Commission of the State of São Paulo, which he led until resigning in 1906 to lead a geological study of Bahia. In São Paulo, Derby mapped the state on a scale of 1:100,000 using the methodology of the U.S. Coast and Geodetic Survey. The Geological Service of São Paulo was organized along the lines of the U. S. Geological Survey, producing an important series of maps and stimulating a similar effort in Minas Gerais. Then in 1907 Derby became first head of the Brazilian Geological and Mineralogical Service, where he trained the first generation of Brazilian geologists. During the early years of the Service, Derby located huge iron reserves in Minas Gerais while Branner carried out a series of structural and stratigraphic studies which were the basis of the first geological map of Brazil when he published in 1919. He also wrote an elementary geology textbook for Brazilian students (*Geologia elementar,* 1915).

The educational centre of Brazilian geology (as well as physical geography and geomorphology) was the School of Mines at Ouro Preto. (University geology instruction was initiated only in the 1930s.) At Ouro Preto was trained Eusebio Paulo de Oliveira, author of the second geological map of Brazil and a student of the geology and paleontology of Rio Grande do Sul. Another graduate was Djalma Guimarães, named petrographer of the Geological Service in 1923. Guimarães was noted for his theory of hyperstenization which explained the origin of certain rocks by magmatic differentiation.

The 1923 visit of the South African Alex du Toit was important for raising broader issues in geological theory. Du Toit was interested in the geological relationship between Africa and South America and stimulated a discussion of general geological theory among Brazilian naturalists.

Geology in São Paulo, moribund since Derby's departure, was revived by two foreigners. Ettore Onorato, an Italian who had mastered X-ray analysis of crystalline formations in Leipzig and at Sir William Bragg's physics laboratory in Manchester, was chairman of the department of mineralogy and petrography at the University of São Paulo, a model department which trained a new generation of Brazilian researchers. At the same time, the German Viktor Leinz was invited by Guimarães to direct the petrographical laboratory of the National Department of Mineral Production (the successor institution of the Geological and Mineralogical Service). Later he joined the geological division of the National Museum and headed the geology department at the University of São Paulo.[143]

Beginning in 1913 the Geological and Mineralogical Service published the results of paleontological studies by Brazilian, North American, German and English scholars. By the 1940s, however, Brazilians dominated this specialty (e.g, Carlos de Paulo Couto on Cenozoic mammals). In the 1950s, emphasis shifted from fossil mammals and marine life to micropaleontology. The Micropaleontological Laboratory of Petrobrás was the center of paleontological research in the 1960s and 1970s, where paleopalinological methods were used to establish biostratigraphic zones.[144]

Engineering geology, the inception of which is associated with a famous textbook, Ries and Watson's *Engineering Geology* (1914), has a variety of applications from mining geology to soil mechanics and engineering problems related to highway and railway construction. Brazilian soil mechanics date from the 1920s and Alberto Ortenblad's MIT thesis on consolidation mud deposits. In 1947 Karl Terzaghi, one of the pioneers of soil mechanics, came to Brazil to solve a rockslide problem in a hydroelectric project in São Paulo; his lectures in applied geology at the Polytechnic School opened a new era in Brazilian geotechnology.[145]

In Peru the first organized instruction in geology was included in the curriculum of the School of Mines, founded in 1876. At the governmental level, the Development Ministry's corps of mining engineers began publishing a series of bulletins in 1902 which diffused geological research nationally. José Balta, a former director of the corps of mining engineers, became minister in 1904, emphasizing the ministry's close association with mining. The corps, which had been founded in 1902, undertook a series of hydrological surveys lasting until 1920 which were designed in consultation with the U. S. Geological Survey.

A number of foreigners were instrumental in the implantation of modern geology, in particular the German Gustav Steinmann who, in the first

[143] Viktor Leinz, 'A geologia e a paleontologia no Brasil', in Azevedo, ed., *As ciências no Brasil,* I: 243–63; Othon Henry Leonardos, 'A mineralogia e a petrografia no Brasil', ibid., 265–313; José Verissimo de Costa Pereira, 'A geografia no Brasil', *ibid.,* pp. 315–412; Rui Ribeiro Franco, 'A mineralogia e a petrologia no Brasil', in Guimarães and Motoyama (eds), *História das ciências no Brasil,* III: 1–42.

[144] Josué Camargo Mendes, 'A pesquisa paleontológica no Brasil', in Guimarães and Motoyama, *História das ciências no Brasil,* III: 43–71.

[145] Milton Vargas, 'A geotecnologia no Brasil', *Quipu,* 2 (1985): 263–79.

decade of the century, performed the geological and paleontological research that led to his monumental *Geología del Perú*. Another founder, Carlos Lissón, was the author of the country's first geological map. In 1935 he founded the school of geology at the university of San Marcos and was the first Peruvian to teach modern stratigraphy. In the next generation the important figures were Fernando de las Casas, founder of the geology department in the National Engineering University and author of the first metalogenetic map of Peru, and Ulrich Petersen who succeeded H. Mckintry as professor of mining geology at Harvard in 1963. Mckintry had been a geologist with the Cerro del Pasco corporation and was one of a number of U.S. mining geologists who trained Peruvian disciples. George Petersen, Ulrich's father, was a German-born petroleum geologist who spent his entire career in Peru, engaged in research, teaching and applied work. Beginning in the 1950s the U.S. Geological survey sent a series of geologists to collaborate with Peruvian geologists on surveys of mineral deposits, including lead, zinc, iron, mercury and tungsten.[146] Because of the economic importance of mining in Peru, mining engineering was the leading engineering field and the formation of a national school of geologists was closely linked to the international community of mining geology.

As in Peru, geology in Chile was linked to mining as evidenced by the early institutions which cultivate it: the Corps of Mining engineers (1854), the Mining, Geography and Geodesy Service (1888), the Geological and Mining Service (1918), Department of Mines and Petroleum (1930), and so forth. Academic geology in this period was practiced primarily by foreign specialists. In Chile too, the U. S. Geological Survey played an instrumental role in the modernization of geology, particularly in the geological mission of 1954–60 led by George Eriksen, whose systematic mapping led to the Geological Map of Chile. The resulting interchange between U.S. geologists and their Chilean counterparts and geological study in the United States by Chileans transformed Chilean geology and promoted its professionalization. The Institute of Geological Studies was founded in 1957 to co-ordinate the geological map and direct exploration related to the mining sector.[147]

In Venezuela modern geology was linked to petroleum prospecting. In

[146] Pedro Hugo Tumialán, 'El desarrollo de la geología en el Perú', in *Estudios de historia de la ciencia en el Perú*, I: 105–14; Mario Samamé Boggio, 'Historia: Del Cuerpo de Ingenieros de Minas as INGEMMET', *De Re Metallica: Revista del Instituto Geológico Minero y Metalúrgico*, No. 1 (May–June 1984), 25–32.

[147] Servicio de Minas del Estado, 'Los servicios de minas del estado desde su fundación hasta la actualidad' (mimeo); *Instituto de Investigaciones Geológicas* (Santiago, n.d.).

1912 Ralph Arnold led a team of young geologists from Stanford who prepared a geological map in 1914. The first comprehensive geology of the country was published in 1928 by Ralph A. Little, a Standard Oil Company geologist. Ten years later the school of geology, later incorporated into the Central University, was founded.[148]

The Spanish republican geologist José Royo Gómez played a role in two countries. He first became director of the Geological Museum of Bogotá which he fashioned into the best museum of its kind in Latin America. He also played an instrumental role in the execution of the Geological Map of Colombia. In 1951 he moved to Caracas where he founded another geological museum.[149]

SCIENCE AND SOCIETY IN THE SECOND HALF OF THE TWENTIETH CENTURY

In the 1940s, conditions favouring the institutionalization of science occurred simultaneously in several countries of Latin America. At the same time the inaccessibility of European scientific centres in wartime provoked a decisive shift to the United States not only as the pre-eminent provider of scientific education and know-how but also as an increasingly attractive job market for Latin American scientists.

In Brazil, when in 1947 Adhemar de Barros, a populist governor of São Paulo state, pressed the scientific community to produce more applied research, biologists – the largest basic research group – moved to organize scientists to protect their own interests. A meeting held of the São Paulo Medical Association in July 1948 led to the founding of the Brazilian Association for the Progress of Science (SBPC), whose leading spirit was the pharmacologist Mauricio Rocha e Silva.[150] In common with its European and North American prototypes, the SBPC saw science as the basis of social progress[151] and sought to diffuse the scientific ethos and promote solidarity among scientists through a journal – *Ciência e Cultura* – and through annual meetings. The Brazilian Association, perhaps more than most, viewed

[148] Pedro I. Aguerrevere, 'Historia de la investigación geológica en Venezuela', in IVIC, *La ciencia base de nuestro progreso* (Caracas, 1968), pp. 104–10.

[149] Thomas F. Glick, 'José Royo Gómez', in López Piñero (ed.), *Diccionario de Historia de la Ciencia Moderna en España,* II: 267–8.

[150] Antonio José J. Botelho, 'The Professionalization of Brazilian Scientists, the Brazilian Society for the Progress of Science (SBPC), and the State, 1948–60, *Social Studies of Science,* 20 (1990): 473–502.

[151] According to Rocha e Silva himself, 'Vinte años de SBPC', *Ciência e Cultura,* 20 (1968): 581–5, on p. 581.

its role as pre-eminently political and did not hesitate to bring pressure upon different levels of government to respond to its demands.

Although the Brazilian Academy of Science had recommended the establishment of a national research council as early as 1931, no such entity was formed until 1951 when the government, responding to pressure from scientists and from the technical sector of the military interested in developing atomic energy, established the Conselho Nacional de Pesquisa [CNPq], whose first members were predominantly military men and engineers centred mainly in Rio de Janeiro.[152] The initial action of CNPq in the early 1950s was to back nuclear physics (and physics in general) and atomic energy projects. We have already observed some of the projects undertaken by experimental physicists in this period. In its first four years nearly ninety travel grants were given in physics. There were many more in biology, reflecting that field's deeper institutionalization, but the two fields were nearly equal in the total amount of money awarded. After 1955, CNPq's influence diminished: in a time of budgetary retrenchment technical research was favoured over pure science and awards were made more with the objective of training personnel rapidly than with developing the country's research capability. And in the early 1960s, with a political shift to the left, scientists were increasingly called upon to justify themselves in terms of their contribution to the social welfare of the nation.[153]

The relationship between organized scientists and governmental science planning was similar in Venezuela. There, Marta Ardila associates the *prise de conscience* of scientists with the assimilation of European norms instilled in the early 1940s by three European refugees: August Pi Sunyer, founder of the Institute of Experimental Medicine, Martin Meyer, in the Institute of Tropical Pathology, and Rudolph Jaffe in his department of pathological anatomy. Together the three 'established discipline in research and a mystique with respect to the practice of science which they transmitted to their students', the future leaders of the Venezuelan scientific establishment.[154] A student of Pi Sunyer, Francisco de Venanzi, conceived the idea for a scientific association in 1949, having identified about eighty scientists in various fields (no more than ten of whom were full-time research-

152 Jacqueline Pitangui Romani, 'O Conselho Nacional de Pesquisa e institucionalizaçao de pesquisa científica no Brasil', in Simon Scwartzman (ed.), *Universidades e instituições científicas no Rio de Janeiro* (Brasilia, 1982), pp. 137–67, and Botelho, op. cit.

153 Botelho, 'The Brazilian Society for the progress of Science,' p. 27.

154 Marta Ardila, 'Origen y evolución histórica de la Asociación Venezolana para el Avance de la Ciencia,' undergraduate thesis (Caracas, 1981), p. 117.

ers). Accordingly, he convened a meeting in Pi Sunyer's Institute in August 1949. This was the origin of the Venezuelan Association for the Progress of Science [AsoVAC], founded with 150 members in 1950. AsoVAC, in its journal, *Acta Cientifica Venezolana* and in its annual meetings, laboured insistently to diffuse scientific norms and values and to instill a sense of solidarity among scientists, stressing the importance of free scientific research and of the publication of results. In its editorials the journal pictured science as the key to modernization. The leadership of AsoVAC included the organizers of the Venezuelan Institute of Scientific Research (IVIC), established in 1959 on the campus of an institute established under the patronage of the dictator Pérez Jiménez which had oddly conjoined neurology with atomic science (again, an important motor of government interest). At the same time AsoVAC campaigned for the establishment of a national research council run by scientists. In 1962 the Association's leaders occupied key positions in Venezuelan science and met at IVIC to formulate plans for the council, which was not however established until 1969. In the 1970s, CONICIT replaced AsoVAC as the chief institutional spokesman for science and scientists (its leaders were the former activists of AsoVAC including the council's first president, Marcel Roche). With the oil boom of the 1970s, science policy became increasingly orientated to technology, providing AsoVAC an opportunity to reassert its role as promoter of basic science. By 1980 AsoVAC's membership had reached 3,000.

In both Brazil and Venezuela the science associations were instrumental in organizing political support for research efforts at the national level. Once the science councils were established, the associations were either weakened or forced into an adversarial role as state planners stressed practical results. Nevertheless, and in spite of the pure versus applied science debates, the research councils inevitably had a positive effect on the scientific research base.

Scientific research councils were established in virtually all the other Latin American countries between the late fifties and the late seventies, e.g., Argentina (CONICET, 1958), Uruguay (CONICYT, 1961), Chile (CONICYT, 1967), Colombia (CONCYT, COLCIENCIAS, 1968), Peru (CONCYTEC, 1968), Mexico (CONACYT, 1970, although its antecedent organization was founded in 1942), Costa Rica (CONICIT, 1972), Ecuador (CONACYT, 1979).[155] All these organisms were similar in objectives and

[155] *Normas orgánicas del CONCYT y COLCIENCIAS* (Bogotá, 1986); *EL CONACYT hoy* (Mexico, D.F. 1984); *CONICIT in Science and Technology* (San José, Costa Rica, 1983); Guillermo Ramírez and

structure and most had co-ordinate semi-autonomous Foundations which dispersed funds. In addition, various regional and supraregional organizations became significant in science policy co-ordination, for example, the Andean Science and Technology Council (1983) of the Junta del Acuerdo de Cartagena, and the Interamerican Development Bank (which has supplied infrastructural aid to the Scientific Research Councils.[156]

Studies of published output of scientific research in Latin America in the 1970s and 1980s have shown remarkable consistency. Over those two decades, five countries (Argentina, Brazil, Mexico, Chile and Venezuela) have accounted for most of the region's publications; by the mid 1980s, Brazil had replaced Argentina as the top producer, with Argentina falling to second place and no change in the rest of the top five.[157] The percentage of Latin American contributions to mainstream publications was quite low (1.1 per cent in 1973–5), with a marked emphasis on clinical medicine (Latin American publications in this area were 21 per cent above the world norm in the 1970s while, by comparison, production in physics was 29 per cent below it).[158] In terms of citations of Latin American articles in mainstream publications, the most favored fields are geosciences, psychology and biology (in that order).[159]

The Brain Drain

The 'brain drain', that is, the flight of scientific researchers from their country of origin, has been studied primarily with respect to Argentina, the country in which the phenomenon was most marked. Argentina was an exporter of professionals from the beginning of the twentieth century. The migration of scientific and technical professionals became noteworthy in the early 1950s when groups of engineers migrated to the United States. In 1966 the Ongania coup and subsequent 'intervention' in the University of Buenos Aires provoked mass resignations of faculty. Particularly hard hit was the Faculty of Exact Sciences, which lost 215 faculty (71.4 per cent of all the

Alfredo Recalde, 'Institucionalización de la política de desarrollo científico y tecnológico en el país,' in *Preinversión y desarrollo* (Quito, n.d.; Cuadernos de Fonapre, 6), pp. 20–5; *¿Qué es el Concytec?* (Lima, n.d.).

[156] See in particular, 'Enfoque y contribuciones del Banco Interamericano de Desarrollo (BID) en ciencia y tecnología' (Washington, D.C., 1985), mimeo.

[157] Patricia McLauhlan de Arregui, *Indicadores comparativos de los resultados de la investigación científica y tecnológica en América Latina* (Lima, 1988).

[158] J. Davidson Frame, 'Mainstream Research in Latin America and the Caribbean,' *Interciencia,* 2 (1977), p. 144.

[159] McLauchlan de Arregui, *Indicadores comparativos,* p. 27.

University's emigrants and 55 per cent of the total of resignées). These scientists were anti-Peronist, members of the generation of 1955, who subscribed to the general notion of scientific ethos and basic science that we have been discussing. Of the 215 who resigned in 1966, seventy-three (including many physicists and chemists) went to Chile (where the Ford Foundation helped the University of Chile pay their salaries), forty-four to Venezuela (mainly biologists and mathematicians), seven to Uruguay and sixty-four to the United States. In the Faculty of Sciences, the physics, inorganic chemistry and mathematics departments were devastated, and only two departments had no emigrants. Interestingly, a younger, more militantly leftist generation of scientists opposed resignation as a tactical error.[160] The emigration of 1966 was one largely of intellectuals, with scientists forming a particularly prominent contingent. The emigration of the mid-1970s covered a broader social spectrum but also included many scientists; psychoanalysts were especially prominent. One newspaper headlined in 1978 'Nos quedamos sin científicos' [We are being left without scientists].[161]

Among those countries in Latin America which welcomed Argentinian scientists, Mexico stands out. Moreover, Mexico lost relatively few of its own scientists to the brain drain of the 1960s because of the capacity of its National University (UNAM) to absorb large numbers of them.[162] Venezuela, as noted above, received a contingent of Argentinian chemists in the 1970s, including entire working groups, but seemed unable to hold them there. Engineers, however, moved there in large numbers (318 counted in 1981).[163]

Although the absolute number of scientists emigrating from Latin America as a whole has been small, they represent a substantial portion of the region's scientific manpower pool.

The Debate Over Science

The model of excellence in basic science promoted by the Rockefeller Foundation and by Latin American scientists of the generations of Houssay

[160] On the brain drain in Latin American science, see H., Moysés Nussenzveig, 'Migration of Scientists from Latin America', *Science,* 165 (1969): 1328–1332. On the Argentinian brain drain see, Nilda Sito and Luis Stulhman, *La emigración de científicos de la Argentina* (San Carlos de Bariloche, 1970); Marta Slemenson, et al., *Emigración de científicos argentinos: Organización de un éxodo a América Latina* (Buenos Aires, 1970); and Alfredo E. Lattes and Enrique Oteiza (eds), *The Dynamics of Argentine Migration (1955–1984)* (Geneva, 1987).

[161] Lattes and Oteiza, *Dynamics of Argentine Migration,* p. 127.

[162] Romeo Flores Caballero, 'Cerebros, talentos y subdesarrollo en México', *Diálogos,* 5, no. 5 (Sept.–Oct., 1969), 21–4.

[163] Lattes and Oteiza, *Dynamics of Argentine Migration,* p. 100, table 36.

and the leaders of AsoVAC was related to the general theory of modernization which held that cultural factors and values determined social change. Such a conceptualization fits perfectly with the campaign to implant the scientific ethos, which was the specific ideology promoted by scientists during the key phase of professionalization extending from 1940 into the early 1970s. The fact that the newly founded CONICTs and supraregional science organizations were called upon less to co-ordinate pre-existent scientific capacity than to create and foster such capacity had the effect of focussing attention on the role of science in Latin American society. This produced in the late 1960s and 1970s an interesting body of sociological literature centering not on the content of science policy but on its objectives and on the capacity of societies to operationalize them.[164]

A key document in this debate was an article written by Amílcar Herrera in 1972 which drew a distinction between 'explicit' and 'implicit' science policies.[165] The central notion, which subsequently became a reiterated theme of dependency theory comment on science, is that scientific research in Latin America has been unconnected to the organization of the societies in which it is carried out and lacks social relevance. More is invested on basic research than on applied, reversing the pattern of industrialized countries, an investment that has failed to produce any substantial economic or social dividends.[166] The reason is that investment in research is made not on the basis of explicit science policy, as expressed in official documents of science planning agencies, but rather on implicit policies that embody the social objectives of elites, which are to maintain themselves in power. On this view, explicit science policy is only a brilliant façade.

What does this imply for the practice of science? If elites are content to practice import substitution using imported technology, then obviously there will be no interest in supporting either basic or applied research. 'If society, and in particular its productive system, is a dependent structure merely copying other societies', wrote Osvaldo Sunkel, 'scientific research is unnecessary, dysfunctional and without practical utility'. University efforts in promoting scientific research are, in this view, doomed to isolation and unable to ensure their own continuity: 'No disciples are left, as

[164] See Hebe M. C. Vessuri, 'The Social Study of Science in Latin America', *Social Studies of Science*, 17 (1987): 519–54.

[165] Amilcar Herrera, 'Social Determinants of Science Policy in Latin America', *Journal of Development Studies*, 9, (1972–73): 19–36. See also his influential book, *Ciencia y política en América Latina*, 9th edn (Mexico, D.F., 1985).

[166] *Ibid.*, pp. 21–2.

they must go abroad at some stage of their training; if they return, they are either persecuted and expelled by the government or emigrate soon afterwards, when they realize the futility of their isolated efforts.'[167]

To Sunkel and other commentators of the period the perceived failure of science was the inevitable result of a deficient social structure. In a scheme popularized by Jorge Sábato, science and technology were pictured as a part of a triangular model in which the points corresponded to (1) the state, (2) the productive or industrial structure and (3) science and technology research capability. The triangular model provided a context for analysing the relationships in each vertex as well as those among all three (in other work-ups, a fourth point representing the financial sector was added).[168] The assertion by Herrera, Sunkel and others that the industrial sector had been particularly remiss in its backing of scientific and technical research was soon corroborated empirically by statistical studies showing that Latin American countries place less emphasis than the world norm on basic research bearing on industrialization.[169]

The heart of the *dependentista* thesis as it relates to science is that, given the unequal power relation between developed and developing countries, implanted or transferred science becomes a means of cultural domination and causes the disappearance of local knowledge as a possible alternative construction. This critique was popular in Venezuela in the mid-1970s when the scientific generation that founded CONICIT was displaced by a new group of bureaucrats, mainly leftist social scientists, who questioned the social utility of basic, as opposed to applied, research. At the same time, an analogous critique of the academic model of science which dominated the main Venezuela research institution, IVIC, produced a hegira of applied scientists who founded their own research institute, INTEVEP.[170] The problem with the applied science critique of pure science is that it failed to recognize that scientists were not passive actors in the transfer of

[167] Osvaldo Sunkel, 'Underdevelopment, the Transfer of Science and Technology, and the Latin American University,' *Human Relations,* 24 (1970): 1–18.

[168] Sábato's model was first presented at the The World Order Models Conference held in Bellagio, Italy, in September 1968, and widely published thereafter, e.g. Jorge Sábato and Natalio Botana, *La ciencia y la tecnología en el desarrollo futuro de América Latina* (Lima, 1970; Instituto de Estudios Peruanos, Documentos teóricos, 11). Sábato reworked the model on numerous subsequent occasions, e.g., in 'Situación actual del desarrollo científico y tecnológico: Implicaciones al nivel de política y de estrategia' (Washington, D.C., CECIC, 1969; mimeo), a paper presented to an OAS meeting on strategy for technical development held at Viña del Mar, Chile in May 1969.

[169] See Frame, 'Mainstream Research in Latin America', pp. 143–7.

[170] Yajaira Freites, 'La institucionalización del *ethos* de la ciencia: el caso de IVIC,' in Vessuri (ed.), *Ciencia académica en la Venezuela moderna,* pp. 351–86, on pp. 375–6.

mainstream science from Europe or the United States, but in fact participated actively in the process, on the basis of ideological motives associated with both the scientific ethos and that of development and modernization. As Hebe Vessuri has observed, in developing countries the flow of scientific information tends to become hopelessly entangled with economic and power relations, all of which are conflated and confused by contemporary analysts.[171]

The social relevance critiques of the 1970s fell wide of the mark because they failed to realize that national science could not function except as part of an international network. The attack on basic science was misplaced: the applied scientists who left IVIC soon had to apply to their former teachers for the solutions to basic research problems; mathematicians who had stressed applied fields like statistics soon saw that problems in hydrology or petroleum engineering required differential geometry for their solution, and so forth.[172]

Finally let us return to a *leitmotiv* of the history of science in recent Latin America: the constant intrusion by political elites in the institutionalization of science. We have noted repeated repression of scientists to the detriment of their institutions (although in some cases, the same repression stimulated the foundation of institutions designed to be autonomous and thereby somewhat protected from arbitrary interference): for example, Cipriano Castro and the closure of the Pasteur Institute in Caracas, Perón and Argentinian physiology, Pérez Jiménez and Venezuelan bio-medicine.

These intrusions are the consequences of a built-in relationship between the practice of science and the objectives of national elites. As Amílcar Herrera expressed it at the beginning of the 1970s: 'The objective of the ruling classes is not to create R. & D. systems which will make the countries scientifically autonomous . . . Their objectives are mainly to create a scientific and technological system which will help to solve minor problems without putting the system itself in question. It has become apparent, however, that it is extremely difficult to circumscribe scientific activity in this very rigid manner. The more or less autonomous scientific centres, particularly in universities, tend to become discussion centres where the fundamental values of the prevailing order are questioned. The political leadership does not realize that this critical or 'subversive'

[171] Hebe Vessuri, 'Introducción: La formación de la comunidad científica en Venezuela', in Vessuri (ed.), *Ciencia académica en la Venezuela moderna* (Caracas, 1984), p. 33.

[172] Carlos A. Di Prisco and Lorenzo Lara, 'Comentarios sobre la investigación matemática en Venezuela', in Vessuri (ed.), *Ciencia académica en la Venezuela moderna*, pp. 237–77, pp. 269 and 272.

attitude – to use the stereotyped official terminology – has its origins in free discussion of ideas in an atmosphere of scientific objectivity. They become alarmed because they cannot tolerate serious analysis of the system. Consequently they try to neutralize criticism by repressing free expression, by ideological persecution, by selecting scholars for their ideology rather from their intellectual ability, and so on. The result is that the scientific structure, submitted to a régime which is incompatible with genuine intellectual creation, is degraded, until it becomes incapable of satisfying even the limited demand of an essentially static system which only aspires to maintain itself'.[173]

The modernizing rhetoric promoted by scientists in the 1940s and 1950s praising the scientific ethos and basic research had the effect of creating cohesive scientific groups with enough atonomy to launch an effective critique of the societies that refused to back their efforts or which only gave them lip service. Part of this ethos is that science is (in Robert Merton's phrase) 'organized scepticism' and that civil, non-ideologized discourse is required for its advancement (hence, the association, among modernizing scientists, of science, democracy and academic freedom). But scepticism, organized or not, is not a value likely to win praise from authoritarian elites and thus civil discourse may become impossible, polarization inevitable. This is the ultimate dilemma of science in modernizing countries.

Not unexpectedly, scientists in Latin America ran afoul of military regimes in the 1960s and 1970s. An example is the fate of research at the Oswaldo Cruz Institute at Manguinhos in Rio de Janeiro under the directorship of a mediocre doctor, Francisco de Paula Rocha Lagoa, appointed by the Castelo Branco regime that came to power in April 1964. The Health Minister Raymundo de Britto immediately announced that 'exotic ideas that infiltrated Manguinhos would be banned'. Accordingly, Rocha Lagoa began to threaten his enemies and in January 1966 had sixteen scientists investigated for 'conspiring in their laboratories'. One of the accusations was that all favoured the creation of a Science Ministry. Rocha Lagoa systematically ruined the laboratory of Walter O. Cruz, Oswaldo Cruz's son, diverting from him and others monies they had won from U.S. foundations and giving the proceeds to his supporters. Finally in 1970 ten researchers were fired, having their civil rights suspended for ten years. The so-called 'Manguinhos Massacre' summarily extinguished the research programme of those cashiered, virtually shut down all collaborative re-

[173] Herrera, 'Social Determinants of Science Policy', p. 33.

search of the Institute with foreign and Brazilian institutions, and resulted in capricious depredation such as the dispersal or liquidation of important insect collections deemed not of medical interest.[174]

An extreme case of the entanglement of pure science and political ideology is afforded by the infamous vector affair, in Córdoba, Argentina, in 1978. This was a period of great repression when, for example, all fifty psychoanalysts practicing in that city were dismissed from their public posts at once. (The ideological vulnerability of Freudian psychology under traditional authoritarian rule is obvious.) The provincial authorities outlawed the 'new math' on the grounds that, 'Modern mathematics introduces procedures different from those taught by Aristotle . . . This makes doubts arise on this [Aristotelian] logic and promotes lack of confidence in our guiding and traditional figures, and therefore encourages and gives comfort to subversion . . . Some themes of mathematics use words such as vector and matrix, which are typical of a Marxist or typically subversive vocabulary. The same happens with set theory which evidently tends to massify [*masificar*] and to evolve multitudes.'[175]

Like their anti-Darwinian forbears who held that under a Christian system of values, science must produce certainty, the critics of the new math held that mathematics must produce palpable, easily recognizable truth or else it was subversive. This kind of attack on mathematical abstraction in Argentina can be linked to the attacks on Einstein from various members of the military hierarchy, including the later jailed Admiral Massera who in a 1977 speech observed that 'in 1905 Einstein enunciated his Theory of Relativity in which he threw into crisis the inert and static condition of matter, as if something more were needed to confuse a system which was protected by the immutable solidity of its values'. Others alleged that Einstein had destroyed the 'Christian concepts of space and time'.[176]

CONCLUSION: PERIPHERAL SCIENCE

Peripherality in science has been described with respect to a number of distinct parameters: (1) difficulty of insertion in networks of scientific communication, which causes problems of accessibility to research-front

[174] See the chronicle of the affair by one of those affected, zoologist Herman Lent, *O massacre de Manguinhos* (Rio de Janeiro, 1978).

[175] Mauricio Schiojet, 'Who's Afraid of a Vector', *Bulletin of the Atomic Scientists*, June 1980, pp. 60–2, on p. 61. See also anon., 'Polémica con Euclides', *Confirmado*, 30 November 1978, p. 11, and 'Matemática sin polémica', ibid., 21 December pp. 8–10.

[176] Quoted by Anthony Lewis, *New York Times Book Review*, 10 May 1981.

science; (2) smallness of the scientific community, which has both cognitive (lack of inter-criticism) and institutional effects; (3) lack of resources, related to the country's level of economic development: to which is appended in the Latin American discussion, a lack of fit between the 'scientific ethos' and local needs. One problem with the conceptualization of peripherality is that it cannot explain how pockets of 'central' science emerge on the periphery. Cueto's studies of Andean high-altitude biology have shown how in spite of problems of communication, smallness and lack of resources a research-front scientific group emerged nevertheless.[177]

Communication factors are crucial. In Latin America this has meant difficulty of access (whether physical, cognitive or linguistic) to scientific publications and to mainstream science centres. Lack of English skills in part explains the low incidence of Latin American publications in world science statistics, and Derek Price has made the point that there has been a tendency 'for Spanish-speaking countries to be low in science perhaps because of the inadequacy of international scientific literature in what is nevertheless a major world language'.[178]

Smallness conveys another set of problems. With few institutions in place, it is difficult to establish the characteristic structure of modern science with sufficient institutional differentiation to permit career mobility (including positions for young scientists), a viable peer review system, or to accommodate the establishment of new specialties. As Richard Feynman observed of Brazilian science in 1956, 'There are not enough people involved or rather [not enough] separate institutions involved [so] that the thing is stable against statistical fluctuation. You can't go off and get a job at another Centro if the one you are working at is unsatisfactory.'[179]

Looking at discipline formation the large number of what might be termed *unipersonal disciplines* is striking, that is to say, disciplines formed by only one person which then grow as the founder's disciples mature and join him. Carlos Chagas's son's biophysics group in Rio de Janeiro has been described as a family, with researchers 'raised' by him.[180] These disciples typically appear as co-authors of papers with the founder or with each other and they go off to other universities or institutions to found

[177] On peripherality in Latin American science, see Elena Diaz, Yolanda Texera, and Hebe Vessuri, *La ciencia periférica: Ciencia y sociedad en Venezuela* (Caracas, 1983), and comment by Marcos Cueto, 'Andean Biology in Peru', p. 658.

[178] Derek J. de Solla Price, *Little Science, Big Science . . . and Beyond* (New York, 1986), p. 192.

[179] Feynman to Leite Lopes, February 15, 1956, in Leite, *Richard Feynman in Brazil,* p. 25.

[180] Maria Clara Mariani, 'O Instituto de Biofísica da UFRJ', p. 208.

satellite disciplinary groups.[181] Such patterns are typical of small countries. Founders, moreover, are frequently viewed as *isolated geniuses.* Isolated genius myths are typically autogenerated and reflect the difficulty of the scientist (characteristically a founder of a specialty) in establishing a research programme in the absence of any national tradition in his field.

The presence of foreigners in the formation of disciplines has been a trademark of modern science in Latin America, as has the practice of sending students abroad.[182] In general, both processes are patterned: scientific traditions of specific countries are preferred. Thus, Brazilian engineering students throughout the nineteenth century and well into this century were partial to study in Belgium,[183] as Mexican chemists were to Germany. France played a formative role in the conceptualization of science in Brazil,[184] Italy and France in Argentina.[185] Julio Rey Pastor had a practical rationale for sending his Argentinian disciples to Italy: 'It would be desirable,' he wrote in 1927, 'for Argentinian students, for whom Paris is Europe, to share their preferences with Italian universities, where the most intimate contact with professors makes the work more positive.'[186] For Rey Pastor, there was an implicit comparison to be made with the generous and open pedagogical style of Italian mathematicians and the authoritarian and distant styles of German and French professors. Certain national disciplines became so linked to foreign institutions that those planning to enter the field did so with the presumption of completing their doctorate there, and only there: in contemporary Mexican mathematics, for example, this is the 'Princeton o nada' – 'Princeton or nothing' – syndrome.[187] The perception of cultural congruity has clearly been a major factor informing such patterns of cultural influence. Such attachments may be dysfunctional: Schwartzman points out that the structure of French professions

181 Cf. Thomas F. Glick, 'On the Diffusion of a New Specialty: Marañón and the "crisis" of endocrinology in Spain', *Journal of the History of Biology,* 9 (1976): 287–300.

182 An excellent study of the phenomenon in one country is Humberto Ruiz Calderón, 'Una vieja historia: Los becarios de Venezuela en el exterior (1900–1954)', *Interciencia,* 15 (1990): 8–14.

183 Eddy Stols, 'Les étudiants brésiliens en Belgique (1817–1914), *Revista de Historia* (São Paulo), 50 (1974): 653–91, on p. 662.

184 Michel Paty and Patrick Petitjean, 'Sur l'influence scientifique française au Brésil aux XIXe et XXe siècles,' *Cahiers des Ameriques Latines,* new series, 4 (1985), 31–47.

185 Marcelo Montserrat, 'La influencia italiana en la actividad científica argentina del siglo XIX,' in Francis Korn (ed.), *Los italianos en la Argentina* (Buenos Aires, n.d.), pp. 105–23; Miguel J. C. de Asúa, 'Influencia de la Facultad de Medicina de Paris sobre la de Buenos Aires', *Quipu,* 3 (1986): 79–89.

186 Quoted by Thomas F. Glick, 'Einstein, Rey Pastor y la promoción de la ciencia en España,' in *Actas, I Simposio sobre Julio Rey Pastor,* (Logroño, 1985), pp. 79–90, p. 82.

187 See Gilberto Calvillo Vives and Diego Bricio Hernández, 'La actividad matemática en México', mimeo, p. 92.

was too rigid and did not generate first-rate research facilities like the Cavendish Laboratory.[188] European models had to be reinvented at home.

When scientists return home from abroad, having experienced mainstream science first-hand, many find it difficult to adjust. Yajaira Freites found that in spite of many positive achievements in building an infrastructure for science in Venezuela in the 1970s, scientists persisted in viewing the country as possessing an unfavourable environment for science. There is a lack of fit between the reality of scientific activity and scientists' expectations, a result of the general phenomenon of the implantation of the *style* of big science in peripheral countries independent of whether such countries may have the infrastructure to sustain that syle of science.[189] Larissa Lomnitz found the same phenomenon in Mexico, 'a subtle, pervasive feeling that it is futile to do scientific research in Mexico under these general conditions'.[190] Gómezgil, surveying the image of scientists held by Mexican teenagers, found that the adolescents knew who Pasteur, Einstein and Newton were but could not name any Mexican scientists.[191] Both stereotypical images of the scientist and scientific ethos and a negative conclusion regarding the capacity of Mexicans to perform science had been transmitted.

One of the values that Latin American scientists seem to have acquired is to associate high prestige with publication in 'mainstream' journals, to the detriment of regional scientific publications. Indeed the struggle to have a journal recognized as 'mainstream' (by virtue of inclusion in the *Science Citation Index*) is a phenomenon of international politics that impacts upon Latin American science.[192] Nevertheless, the rage for international publication conceals local networks of scientific communication, more informal (e.g., circulation of preprints), in part oral, which represents a higher degree of institutionalization than perhaps has been suspected.[193]

188 Schwartzman, *Formaçao da comunidade científica no Brasil,* pp. 213–14.

189 Yajaira Freites, '¿Es la sociedad venezolana un ambiente favorable a la investigación?' (typescript).

190 Larissa Lomnitz, 'Hierarchy and Peripherality: the organisation of a Mexican Research Institute,' *Minerva,* 17 (1979): 527–8, p. 540. Entrepreneurial scientists, like Carlos Chagas (son), explicitly set out to dispel this kind of myth as they form working groups (Mariani, 'O Instituto de Biofisica da UFRJ,' p. 200).

191 Maria Luisa Rodríguez Sala de Gómezgil, *El científico en México: su imagen entre los estudiantes de enseñanza media* (Mexico, D.F., 1977), pp. 166–73; and summary, 'Mexican Adolescents' Image of the Scientist', *Social Studies of Science,* 5 (1975): 355–61.

192 Vessuri recounts the political play over the de-listing of *Acta Científica Venezolana* from SCI; 'La revista científica periférica: El caso de *Acta Científica Venezolana,*' *Interciencia,* 12 (1987), 124–34. Some twenty Latin American science journals are listed in SCI; see the list provided by Marcel Roche and Yajaira Freites, 'Producción y flujo de información científica en un país periférico americano (Venezuela)', *Interciencia,* 7 (1982): 279–90, on p. 286.

193 Ibid., p. 283, and McLauchlan de Arregui, *Indicadores comparativos,* p. 15.

Regarding the cognitive nature of science on the periphery, Alfonso L. Herrera noted in 1911 that 'we are relatively distant from foreign scientific centres, from official science and from the somnolent and orthodox academies, for which reason we think with absolute freedom, inasmuch as we have been educated in isolation and do not carry stereotyped in our brain certain maxims repectfully gathered from the lips of some dogmatic professors, who have imposed themselves as advisors to humanity and who deftly insinuate their dogmas and errors in foreign academies'.[194] Such a conclusion may have some truth, though it is contrary to the common wisdom that lack of critical mass in a given discipline makes it difficult for peripheral scientists to assess the value of specific research. Isolation more normally causes defensiveness, though in some, like Herrera and Alberto Monge, it may produce an exuberant sense of discovery. Herrera's conclusion was attacked some years later by Eliseo Ramírez, referring to Herrera's theory of plasmogeny: 'In our rachitic environment lack of education is conjoined, as a consequence of it, with confusion between true scientific work and pseudo-work, as a series of provincial disquisitions demonstrate their protection by official elements but which are nothing more than dissimulation in scientific research.'[195]

Herrera clearly viewed his origin of life theory as an ingenious concept that cut through a dogmatic received view, whereas Ramírez viewed it as contrary to scientific common sense as expressed by a majority of scientists. The polemic highlights the fact that what is normative in mainstream science may not necessarily be so perceived on the periphery. To accept mainstream views is safe but not necessarily relevant to one's cognitive or social environment; to reject them is to run the risk of exaggerated isolation.

Finally, there appears to be, in Latin America as in most developing regions, a structurally based lack of fit between the ideology of science as it appears within the subculture of national scientific communities, and the various political ideologies which share a high value for economic development. The latter will portray those involved in basic science as shirking the needs of the society, while the former assert that basic science is a prerequisite for competent application.

194 Alfonso L. Herrera, 'Una ciencia nueva: la plasmogenia,' *Boletín de Ciencias Médicas* (Mexico, D.F.), 1 (1910–11): 309–22, 360–73.

195 Eliseo Ramírez, 'La simulación en la investigación biológica', cited by Fernando Ocaranza, *La tragedia de un vector,* (Mexico, D.F., 1943), pp. 91–2. I am indebted to Adolfo Olea for this reference, as well as that to Herrera in note 194 above.

BIBLIOGRAPHICAL ESSAYS*

1. THE POPULATION OF LATIN AMERICA, 1930–1990

Nicolás Sánchez-Albornoz, *The Population of Latin America. A History* (Berkeley and Los Angeles, Cal., 1974) provides a general overview of population in Latin America; chapters 6–8 cover trends in the twentieth century. A second Spanish edition, *La población de América latina. Desde los tiempos precolombinos al año 2000* (Madrid, 1977) includes revisions and an extensive bibliography. Another, more recent overview is in Carmen A. Miró, 'América Latina: transición demográfica y crisis económica, social y política', in *Memorias del Congresso Latinoamericano de Población y Desarrollo*, Vol. 1 (Mexico D.F., 1984), 65–114. In preparation for the 1974 World Population Conference, the Comité Internacional de Coordinación de Investigaciones Nacionales en Demografía (CICRED) sponsored a series of national monographs in collaboration with Latin American demographic research centres. This series includes *La población de Argentina* (Buenos Aires, 1975); *La population du Brésil* (Paris, 1974); *La población de Chile* (Paris, 1974); *La población de Colombia* (Bogotá, 1974); *La población de Costa Rica* (San José, 1976); *La población de Cuba* (La Habana, 1976); *La población de Guatemala* (Guatemala City, 1976); *La población de México* (Mexico, D.F., 1976); *La población del Peru* (Lima, 1974); and *La población de Venezuela* (Caracas, n.d.). Other general country studies include Thomas W. Merrick and Douglas H. Graham, *Population and Economic Development in Brazil: 1800 to the present* (Baltimore, Md., 1979); Francisco Alba, *The Population of Mexico. Trends, Issues, and Policies* (New Brunswick, N.J., 1982). A useful, but now dated, bibliography is Robert N. Thomas, *Population Dynamics of Latin America. A Review and Bibliography* (East Lansing, 1973). A review of

*Bibliographical essays have been written by the authors of the relevant chapters except essay 4 (by José Gabriel Palma alone).

the coverage and quality of basic demographic data can be found in Valdecir F. Lopes, 'The Traditional Sources of Demographic Data in Latin America', in International Union for the Study of Population, *Proceedings. International Population Conference,* Vol. 2 (Liege, 1973), pp. 355–66. In 1940, representatives of government statistical offices in the region formed the Inter-American Statistical Institute (IASI), and its journal *Estadística* provides information on the planning and implementation of statistical programmes. Summary descriptions of the contents of Latin American censuses have been published in Doreen. S. Goyer and Eliane Domschke, *The Handbook of National Population Censuses. Latin America and the Caribbean, North America, and Oceania* (Westport, Conn., 1983). See also Doreen S. Goyer, *International Population Census Bibliography. Revision and Update, 1945–77* (New York, 1980) and Carole Travis (ed.), *A Guide to Latin American and Caribbean Census Material: a Bibliography and Union List* (London, 1990).

Given the variability in timing and reliability of official reports, many demographers rely on compilations of data by the Centro Latinoamericano de Demografía, CELADE, whose *Boletín Demográfico* provides periodic summaries of important demographic indicators. CELADE adjusts for differences in time references as well as reporting errors. CELADE data are available in machine-readable form as described in its *Boletín de Banco de Datos.* CELADE compilations are also included in United Nations publications, for example United Nations, Department of International Economic and Social Affairs, *World Population Prospects. Estimates and Projections as Assessed in 1982* (New York, 1985).

Mortality patterns in Latin America and their implications are mapped in Eduardo E. Arriaga, *New Life Tables for Latin American Populations in the Nineteenth and Twentieth Centuries* (Berkeley, Cal., 1968) and *Mortality Decline and its Demographic Effects in Latin America* (Berkeley, Cal., 1970) as well as Eduardo E. Arriaga and Kingsley Davis, 'The Pattern of Mortality Decline in Latin America', *Demography,* 6 (1969): 223–42; and in Jorge L. Somoza, 'The Trend of Mortality and the Expectation of Life in Latin America', *Milbank Memorial Fund Quarterly,* 43 (1965): 219–33. Shifts in causes of death are further outlined in Alberto Palloni, 'Mortality in Latin America: emerging patterns', *Population and Development Review,* 7 (1981): 623–49, and Alberto Palloni and Randy Wyrick, 'Mortality Decline in Latin America: changes in the structure of causes of death,' *Social Biology,* 29 (1981): 187–236. A comparison of Latin America and other regions is made in George J. Stolnitz, 'Recent Mortality Trends in Latin America, Asia, and Africa', *Population Studies,* 19 (1965): 111–38. General discussion of the causes of the mortality transition can be found in Thomas McKeown, *The Modern Rise of Population* (New York, 1976), and Samuel H. Preston, *Mortality Decline in National Populations* (New York, 1976) and 'Causes and Consequences of Mortality Decline in Less Developed Countries During the Twentieth Century', in Richard A. Easterlin (ed.), *Population and Economic Changes in Developing Countries* (Chicago, Ill., 1980), pp. 289–360. The topic of natural immunity is addressed in William H. McNeill, *Plagues and Peoples* (New York, 1976). The issue of social class differences in mortality is discussed in Ruth R. Puffer and Wynne G. Griffith, 'The Inter-American Investigation of Mortality', in United Nations, *World Population Conference 1965*, Vol. 2 (New York, 1967), 426–32; Hugo Behm, 'Socio-economic Determinants of Mortality in Latin America', *Population Bulletin of the United Nations*, 13 (1980): 1–15; and Charles H. Wood and José A. Magno de Carvalho, 'Mortality, Income Distribution, and Rural-urban Residence in Brazil', *Population and Development Review*, 4 (1978): 405–20. Further information on mortality trends can be found in Mark Farren, *Infant Mortality and Health in Latin America: an Annotated Bibliography* (Ottawa, 1984).

Data on birth rates in Latin America are assessed in Andrew Collver, *Birth Rates in Latin America: New Estimates of Historical Trends and Fluctuations* (Berkeley, Cal., 1965). The Committee on Population and Demography of the U.S. National Research Council reviewed fertility and mortality trends in a number of Latin American countries. Their reports include: *Fertility and Mortality Changes in Honduras* (Washington, D.C., 1980); *Levels and Recent Trends in Fertility and Mortality in Colombia* (Washington, D.C., 1982); *Levels and Recent Trends in Fertility and Mortality in Brazil* (Washington, D.C., 1983); and *Fertility and Mortality in Bolivia and Guatemala* (Washington, D.C., 1985).

Fertility determinants and their implications are traced by Arthur M. Conning, 'Latin American Fertility Trends and Influencing Factors', in International Union for the Scientific Study of Population, *International Population Conference*, Vol. 2 (Liege, 1973), pp. 125–47, and in Eduardo E. Arriaga, 'The Nature and Effects of Latin America's Non-western Trends in Fertility', *Demography* 7 (1970): 483–501. Alternative views of the comparability of Latin American fertility patterns to those of industrialized countries are found in Steven E. Beaver, *Demographic Transition Theory Reinterpreted: an Application to Recent Natality Trends in Latin America* (Lexington, Mass., 1975) and Frank W. Oechsli and Dudley Kirk, 'Modernization and the Demographic Transition in Latin America and the Caribbean', *Economic Development and Cultural Change*, 23/3 (1975): 391–419.

On intermediate variables affecting fertility, see Kingsley Davis and Judith Blake, 'Social Structure and Fertility: an analytical framework', *Economic Development and Cultural Change,* 4 (1956): 211–35, and John Bongaarts, 'Intermediate Variables and Marital Fertility', *Population Studies,* 30 (1976): 227–41. Calculations of the contribution of each proximate determinant to fertility decline in several Latin American countries are found in John Bongaarts and Robert G. Potter, *Fertility, Biology and Behavior: an Analysis of the Proximate Determinants* (New York, 1980). Survey data on fertility trends in the region are summarized in Robert Lightbourne and Susheela Singh, 'The World Fertility Survey: charting global childbearing', *Population Bulletin,* 37 (1978); Leo Morris et al., 'Contraceptive Prevalence Surveys: a new source of family planning data', *Population Reports,* Series M, No. 5 (1981), and Kathy A. London et al., 'Fertility and Family Planning Surveys: an update', *Population Reports,* Series M, No. 8 (1985). On breastfeeding and fertility in Latin America, see Phyllis T. Piotro et al., 'Breastfeeding, Fertility and Family Planning', *Population Reports,* Series J, No. 24 (1981). Information on abortion is found in Christopher Tietze, *Induced Abortion: a World Review,* 5th edn (New York, 1983) and Santiago Gaslonde Sainz, 'Abortion Research in Latin America', *Studies in Family Planning,* 7 (1976): 211–17.

The literature on recent declines in fertility in Latin America is reviewed in Raúl Urzua, 'Social Science Research on Population and Development in Latin America', *Report of International Review Group on Social Science Research on Population and Development* (Mexico, D.F., 1978), appendix 11. Counttry studies include Thomas W. Merrick and Elza Berquó, *The Determinants of Brazil's Recent Rapid Fertility Decline* (Washington, D.C., 1983); Luis Hernando Ochoa, 'Patterns of fertility decline in Latin America with special reference to Colombia', in International Union for the Scientific Study of Population, *International Population Conference,* Vol. 1 (Manila, 1981), pp. 25–48; Paula E. Hollerbach and Sergio Díaz-Briquets, *Fertility Determinants in Cuba* (Washington, D.C., 1983); and Francisco Alba and Joseph E. Potter, 'Population and Development in Mexico since 1940: an interpretation', *Population and Development Review,* 12 (1986): 415–29.

Data on marriage patterns and their impact on fertility are reported in Ruth B. Dixon et al., 'Age at Marriage and Fertility', *Population Reports,* Series M, No. 4 (1979) and Jane S. Durch, *Nuptiality Patterns in Developing Countries: Implications for Fertility* (Washington, D.C., 1980). The European marriage pattern that Latin American countries follow to a limited extent is described in John Hajnal, 'Age at Marriage and Proportions

Marrying', *Population Studies,* 7 (1953): 111–36. Further discussion of these patterns is found in Zulma C. Camisa, *La nupcialidad de las mujeres solteras en América Latina* (San José, Costa Rica, 1977) and Carmen Arretx, 'Nuptiality in Latin America', in International Union for the Scientific Study of Population, *International Population Conference: London 1969,* Vol. 3 (Liege, 1971), pp. 2127–53. The questions of family structure and kin relationships are examined in Thomas K. Burch and Murray Gendell, 'Extended Family Structure and Fertility: some conceptual and methodological issues', *Journal of Marriage and the Family,* 32 (1970): 227–36 and Francesca M. Cancian, Louis Wolf Goodman, and Peter H. Smith, 'Capitalism, Industrialization, and Kinship in Latin America', *Journal of Family History,* 3 (1978): 319–36. The latter article is an introduction to a special issue of the journal on the family in Latin America.

An international comparison of data on households headed by women is presented in Nadia H. Youssef and Carol Hetler in 'Establishing the Economic Condition of Woman-headed Households in the Third World: a new approach', in Mayra Buvinic, Margaret A. Lycette, and William McGreevey, *Women and Poverty in the Third World* (Baltimore, Md., 1983). The literature on survival strategies in reviewed in Marianne Schmink, 'Household Economic Strategies: review and research agenda', *Latin American Research Review,* 19, 3 (1984): 35–56, with further discussion in Thomas W. Merrick, 'Perspectives on Latin American Population Research', *Items,* 37 (1983): 17–21. Links between reproduction of population and the labour forces are described in Susana Torrado, 'Sobre los conceptos de estrategias familiares de vida y processo de reproducción de la fuerza de trabajo: notas teórico-metodológicas', *Demografía y Economía,* 15 (1981), 204–33. See also Maria Helena Henriques and Nelson do Valle Silva, 'Análise sobre ciclo vital através de parámetros de nupcialidade: estudo do contexto latino-americano', in Associação Brasileira de Estudos Populacionais, *Anais: Segundo Encontro Nacional* (São Paulo, 1980), pp. 667–86; Brigida García, Humberto Muñoz and Orlandina de Oliveira, *Hogares y trabajadores en la Ciudad de México,* (Mexico, D.F., 1982); and Elizabeth Jelín, 'Familia, unidad doméstica y división de trabajo (Qué sabemos? Hacia dónde vamos?)', in *Memorias del Congresso Latinoamericano de Población y Desarrollo,* Vol. 2 (Mexico, D.F., 1983), 645–74. For links between family structure and migration, see Carlos Brambila Paz, *Migración y formación familiar en México* (Mexico, D.F., 1985).

For an introductory discussion on racial differences in Latin America, see the chapter 'The Concept of Social Race in the Americas', in Charles

Wagley, *The Latin American Tradition* (New York, 1968), pp. 155–74. With specific reference to Brazil, see T. Lynn Smith, *Brazil: People and Institutions,* 4th edn (Baton Rouge, 1972). On Guatemala, see John D. Early, *The Demographic Structure and Evolution of a Peasant System: the Guatemalan Population* (Boca Raton, 1982). A synopsis of the data on national origin in the 1950 round of Latin American censuses was prepared by Giorgio Mortara and reported in *Characteristics of the Demographic Structure of the American Countries* (Washington, D.C., 1964). Data on languages spoken by Latin American populations have been compiled in Kenneth Ruddle and Kathleen Barrows, *Statistical Abstract of Latin America 1972* (Los Angeles, Cal., 1974).

Urban population growth trends and definitional differences in measuring urban populations are treated in United Nations, *Growth of the World's Urban and Rural Population 1920–2000* (New York, 1969) and *Patterns of Rural and Urban Population Growth* (New York, 1980); the most recent compilation of urban population for Latin America is available from CELADE through its computerized demographic data base. Denton R. Vaughan provides a useful bibliography in *Urbanization in Twentieth Century Latin America: a Working Bibliography* (Austin, Tex., 1969). Robert Fox has recompiled data on the populations of municípios of metropolitan areas of Latin American countries in *Urban Population Growth Trends in Latin America* (Washington, D.C., 1975) and, with Jerrold W. Huguet, in *Population and Urban Trends in Central America and Panama* (Washington, D.C., 1977). Useful reviews of issues relating to urbanization are found in Richard M. Morse, 'Recent Research on Latin American Urbanization: a selective survey with commentary', *Latin American Research Review,* 1 (1965): 35–74; Douglas Butterworth and John K. Chance, *Latin American Urbanization,* (Cambridge, 1981); John M. Hunter, Robert N. Thomas and Scott Whiteford, *Population Growth and Urbanization in Latin America,* (Cambridge, Mass., 1983); and Ligia Herrera and Waldomiro Pecht, *Crecimiento urbano de América Latina* (Santiago, 1976).

Analyses of the contribution of migration and other demographic and definitional factors to urban growth are presented in John D. Durand and César A. Pelaez, 'Patterns of Urbanization in Latin America', *Milbank Memorial Fund Quarterly,* 43, Part 2 (1965): 168–91; Robert H. Weller, John Macisco, Jr. and George Martine, 'The Relative Importance of the Components of Urban Growth in Latin America', *Demography,* 8 (1971): 225–32; and Eduardo Arriaga, 'Components of City Growth in Selected Latin American Countries', *Milbank Memorial Fund Quarterly,* 46 (1968):

237–52. On the question of primacy, see Harley L. Browning, 'Primacy Variation in Latin America During the Twentieth Century', in Instituto de Estúdios Peruanos, *Urbanización y processo social en América Latina* (Lima, 1972) and Christopher Chase-Dunn, 'The Coming of Urban Primacy in Latin America', *Comparative Urban Research,* 11 (1985): 14–31.

For synopses of research on internal migration in Latin America, see Alan Simmons, Sergio Díaz-Briquets and Aprodicio A. Laquian, *Social Change and International Migration* (Ottawa, 1977); Juan C. Elizaga, *Migraciones a las áreas metropolitanas de América Latina* (Santiago, 1970) and 'International Migration: an overview', *International Migration Review,* 6 (1972): 121–46; Michael P. Todaro, 'Internal Migration in Developing countries', in R. A. Easterlin (ed.), *Population and Economic Change in Developing Countries* (Chicago, Ill., 1989); and Andrei Rogers and Jeffrey G. Williamson, 'Migration, Urbanization, and Third World Development: an overview,' *Economic Development and Cultural Change,* 30 (1982): 463–82. A useful bibliography on migration was prepared under the auspices of the Consejo Latino-americano de Ciéncias Sociales (CLACSO): *Las migraciones en América Latina* (Buenos Aires, 1975).

On factors affecting migration, see Jorge Balán, *Why People Move* (Paris, 1981) and a study of Monterrey, Mexico, Jorge Balán, Harley L. Browning and Elizabeth Jelín, *Men in a Developing Society* (Austin, Tex., 1973); Alan B. Simmons and Ramiro Cardona, 'Rural-urban Migration: who comes, who stays, who returns? The case of Bogotá, Colombia', *International Migration Review,* 6 (1972): 166–81; and M. G. Castro et al., *Migration in Brazil: Approaches to Analysis and Policy Design* (Liege, 1978); and on the consequences of migration, see, Humberto Muñoz, Orlandina de Oliveira and Claudio Stern, *Migración y desigualdad social en la Ciudad de México* (Mexico, D.F., 1977). See also Wayne A. Cornelius, 'The Political Sociology of Cityward Migration in Latin America: toward empirical theory', and Bruce Herrick, 'Urbanization and Urban Migration in Latin America, an economist's view', in Francine F. Rabinovitz and Felicity M. Trueblood, *Latin American Urban Research,* Vol. 1 (Beverly Hills, Cal., 1971), pp. 95–147 and 71–82. On migrant-native differences, see Jorge Balán, 'Migrant-native Socioeconomic Differences in Latin American Cities: a structural analysis', *Latin American Research Review,* 4/1 (1969): 3–29.

For reviews of international migration trends in Latin America, see Mary M. Kritz and Douglas T. Gurak, 'International Migration Trends in Latin America: research and data survey', in *International Migration Review,* 13 (1979): 407–27 and Sergio Díaz-Briquets, *International Migration within*

Latin America, (New York, 1983). The Kritz/Gurak paper introduces a special issue of *International Migration Review* on international migration in Latin America, which includes papers by Susana Torrado, 'International Migration Policies in Latin America', Lelio Mármora, 'Labor Migration Policies in Colombia', Saskia Sassen-Koob, 'Economic Growth and Immigration in Venezuela', Juan M. Carrón, 'Shifting Patterns in Migration from Bordering Countries to Argentina, 1914–70', Adriana Marshall, 'Immigrant Workers in the Buenos Aires Labor Market', Also useful are Mary M. Kritz, 'International Migration Patterns in the Caribbean Basin: an overview,' and Adriana Marshall, 'Structural Trends in International Migration: the southern cone of Latin America', in Mary M. Kritz, Charles B. Keely, and Silvano M. Tomasi, *Global Trends in Migration: Theory and Research on International Population Movements* (New York, 1981).

Latin American immigration to the United States is reviewed in Douglas S. Massey and Kathleen M. Schnabel, 'Recent Trends in Hispanic Immigration to the United States', *International Migration Review,* 17 (1983): 212–44. Estimates of the numbers of illegal immigrants in the United States are assessed in Jacob S. Siegel, Jeffrey S. Passel and J. Gregory Robinson, 'Preliminary Review of Existing Studies on the Number of Illegal Residents in the United States', U.S. Select Committee on Immigration and Refugee Policy *Staff Report* (Appendix E, Washington, D.C., 1981) and Daniel B. Levine, Kenneth Hill, and Robert Warren (eds), *Immigration Statistics: a story of neglect* (Washington, D.C., 1985). On immigrants' impact on the United States, see the essays in George J. Borjas and Marta Tienda (eds), *Hispanics in the U.S. Economy* (Orlando, 1985). See also Barry R. Chiswick, 'Illegal Aliens in the United States Labor Market: analysis of occupational attainment and earnings', *International Migration Review,* 18 (1984): 714–32; Lawrence H. Fuchs, 'Cultural Pluralism and the Future of American Unity: the impact of illegal aliens', *International Migration Review,* 18 (1984), 800–13; Wayne A. Cornelius, A. L. Chavez and J. Castro, *The Mexican Immigrants in Southern California: a Summary of Current Knowledge* (San Diego, 1982); Thomas Muller and Thomas Espenshade, *The Fourth Wave, California's Newest Immigrants* (Washington, D.C., 1985); and Kevin McCarthy and R. Burciaga Valdez, *Current and Future Effects of Mexican Immigration in California* (Santa Monica, Cal., 1986). For an analysis of links between conditions in Mexico and migration to the United States, see Harry Cross and James A. Sandos, *Across the Border* (Berkeley, Cal., 1981).

Latin American labour force participation patterns are compared to other regions in John D. Durand, *The Labor Force in Economic Development* (Princeton, N.J., 1976) and in a recent re-compilation of data by the International Labour Office, *Economically Active Population 1950–2025* (Geneva, 1986). Under-reporting of women's economic activities in Latin America is examined in Catalina H. Wainerman and Zulma Recchini de Lattes, *El Trabajo feminino en banquillo de los acusados: la medición censal en América Latina* (Buenos Aires, 1975). Sectoral shifts are examined in Rubén Katzman, 'Dinámica de la población activa en América Latina', and trends in female pariticpation in Teresita Barbieri, 'Incorporación de la mujer a la economía urbana de América Latina', both in *Memorias del Congresso Latinoamericano de población y desarrollo,* Vol. 1 (Mexico, D.F., 1984), pp. 335–54, and 355–89. Barbieri's article includes an extensive bibliography.

The literature on population and economic development in Latin America is surveyed in Michael Conroy, 'Recent Research in Economic Demography Related to Latin America: a critical survey and an agenda', *Latin American Research Review,* 9/2 (1974): 3–27. The Economic Commission for Latin America (ECLA) published a volume reflecting the perspective of that organization in *Población y desarrollo en América Latina* (Mexico, D.F., 1975). Ansley Coale and Edgar M. Hoover, *Population Growth and Economic Development in Low-income Countries* (Princeton, N.J. 1958) is the classic presentation of the neo-Malthusian position on the question, and includes a case study for Mexico using an economic-demographic model. Coale presents a retrospective assessment of the Mexican case study in 'Population Growth and Economic Development: the case of Mexico', *Foreign Affairs,* 56 (1978): 415–29. Critiques of the neo-Malthusian approach are presented in William W. Murdoch, *The Poverty of Nations: the Political Economy of Hunger and Population* (Baltimore, Md., 1980), chapter 1 and in Angel Fucaraccio, 'Birth Control and the Argument of Savings and Investment', *International Journal of Health Services,* 3 (1973): 133–44. Country cases are presented in Merrick and Graham, *Population and Economic Development in Brazil* and Alba and Potter, 'Population and Development in Mexico since 1940', cited above. For a general review of research on the population and development link, see Thomas W. Merrick, 'World Population in Transition', *Population Bulletin,* 41 (1986): 17–38.

On population policy, Terry L. McCoy (ed.), *The Dynamics of Population in Latin America* (Cambridge, Mass., 1974) provides a useful sampling of views, including J. M. Stycos on 'Politics and Population Control in Latin America,' Thomas Sanders on 'The Relationship between Population Planning and Belief Systems: the Catholic Church in Latin America', and José Conquegra, 'Birth Control as the Weapon of Imperialism', a Marxian view of foreign assistance for family planning programs. Dorothy Nortman, *Population and Family Planning Programs: a Compendium of Data,* 12th edn (New York, 1985) is a basic source of information on policies and programmes. Country-specific bibliographies on policy were prepared by the Programa de Investigaciones Sociales sobre Problemas de Población Relevantes para Políticas de Población en América Latina (PISPAL) in the series *Inventário de investigaciones sociales relevantes para políticas de población,* Vol. 1 *Argentina;* Vol. 2 *Brasil;* Vol. 3 *Colombia;* Vol. 4 *Chile;* Vol. 5 *México* (Santiago, 1975).

Region-wide population projections are compiled periodically by CELADE in its *Boletín demográfico;* they are also maintained in the CELADE data base. CELADE projections are incorporated in the United Nations' *World Population Prospects: Estimates and Projections as Assessed in 1982* (New York, 1985). National statistical offices also prepare and publish projections periodically. See, for example, Instituto Nacional de Estadística, Geografía y Informática/Consejo Nacional de Población, *Proyecciones de la población de México y de las entidades federativas: 1980–2010* (Mexico, D.F., 1985).

2. THE LATIN AMERICAN ECONOMIES, 1929–1939

Economic performance and policy in the 1930s in Latin America has generated a substantial literature as a result of two factors in particular. First, the view put forward after 1950 by the United Nations, Economic Commission for Latin America [and the Caribbean] (ECLA[C]), that the 1930s marked a crucial turning point in the transition from export-led growth to import-substituting industrialization (ISI) (see ECLA, *Economic Survey of Latin America, 1949,* New York, 1951) led to a wave of investigations to test this particular hypothesis. Second, the debt crisis in the 1980s inevitably invited comparisons with the debt crisis in the 1930s with scholars searching for similarities and differences in Latin American responses to the two shocks.

In view of the magnitude of the external shock applied to Latin America at the beginning of the 1930s, it is appropriate in a bibliographical essay to begin by referring to the literature on the international economy between the two world wars. A most important source is Charles Kindleberger, *The World in Depression* (Berkeley, Cal., and London, 1986), which is a revised version of a classic book first published in 1973 and expanded with greater reference to the Latin American experience. There are a number of excellent surveys on world performance and policy including Arthur Lewis, *Economic Survey, 1919–39* (London, 1949) and H. W. Arndt, *The Economic Lessons of the 1930s* (London, 1944). Long-run trends in world trade, including the 1930s, are analysed in Alfred Maizels, *Industrial Growth and World Trade* (Cambridge, 1963) and P. Lamartine Yates, *Forty Years of Foreign Trade* (London, 1959). More specialist works, covering topics essential for a proper understanding of the Latin American economies in the 1930s, are Karl Brunner (ed.), *The Great Depression Revisited* (New York, 1981) and Peter Temin, *Did Monetary Forces Cause the Great Depression?* (New York, 1976). The 1929 stock market crash is the subject of J. Kenneth Galbraith, *The Great Crash, 1929* (Boston, Mass., 1955) and the gold standard is competently described in William Brown, Jr., *The International Gold Standard Reinterpreted: 1914–34* (New York, 1940). There is an excellent study of international capital flows in Royal Institute of International Affairs, *The Problem of International Investment* (Oxford, 1937).

There are a number of good general works on the Latin American economies in the 1930s. These include Carlos Díaz-Alejandro, 'Stories of the 1930s for the 1980s', in Pedro Aspe Armella, Rudiger Dornbusch and Maurice Obstfeld (eds), *Financial Policies and the World Capital Market: the Problem of Latin American Countries* (Chicago, Ill., 1983). A similar comparison, this time involving Asia as well as Latin America, is Angus Maddison, *Two Crises: Latin America and Asia, 1929–38 and 1973–83* (Paris, 1985). There is also an early study by Royal Institute of International Affairs, *The Republics of South America* (Oxford, 1937) which is still very useful on issues of trade, investment and employment. The most comprehensive study is Rosemary Thorp (ed.), *Latin America in the 1930s* (London, 1984) which has overview chapters by Carlos Díaz-Alejandro and Charles Kindleberger as well as case studies on all the major republics and some of the minor ones. Another book worthy of note, although it is primarily concerned with the 1920s, is Paul Drake, *The Money Doctor in the Andes* (Durham, N.C., 1989) which gives an excellent account of the financial reforms carried out in the Andean countries as a result of the missions led by E. W. Kemmerer.

The problems of international capital flows to Latin America in the 1930s are addressed in a number of books. Of particular interest, although covering a longer period, is Barbara Stallings, *Banker to the Third*

World: U.S. Portfolio Investment in Latin America, 1900–1986 (Berkeley, Cal., 1987). There is still much of interest in J. Fred Rippy, *British Investments in Latin America, 1822–1949* (Minneapolis, 1959), although more recent scholarship suggests that some of the statistics should be interpreted with caution. ECLA, *External Financing in Latin America* (New York, 1965) also has illuminating early chapters on the inter-war period. The ECLA thesis on the 1930s as a turning-point is reflected in the relevant chapters of Celso Furtado, *Economic Development of Latin America* (Cambridge, 1970).

The debt problems caused by the defaults of the 1930s have been the subject of several excellent studies. Among these are Barry Eichengreen and Peter Lindert (eds), *The International Debt Crisis in Historical Perspective* (Cambridge, Mass., 1989) which contains an important article by Erika Jorgensen and Jeffrey Sachs entitled 'Default and Renegotiation of Latin American Foreign Bonds in the Interwar Period' as well as case studies of Brazil and Mexico. Historical comparisons are pushed even further back in Albert Fishlow, 'Lessons from the Past: capital markets during the 19th century and the interwar period', *International Organization,* 39/3 (1985) and Carlos Marichal, *A Century of Debt Crises in Latin America: From Independence to the Great Depression, 1820–1930* (Princeton, N.J., 1989). Together with Richard Portes, Barry Eichengreen has written a number of studies on debt defaults in the 1930s which include many examples from Latin America. See, for example, Barry Eichengreen and Richard Portes, 'Debt and Default in the 1930s: causes and consequences', *European Economic Review,* 30 (1986): 599–640. There is also a fine comparative study of debt crises in Latin America by David Felix, 'Alternative Outcomes of the Latin American Debt Crisis: lessons from the past', *Latin American Research Review,* XXII, 2 (1987): 3–46.

Studies on the role of industrialization in the 1930s, and in particular the part played by import substitution, have a long pedigree. In addition to the ECLA study referred to above, a good source is ECLA, *The Process of Industrialization in Latin America* (New York, 1966) which is a classic statement of the argument that the external shock at the beginning of the 1930s induced through import substitution a rapid process of industrialization in the larger countries. As part of its early work, ECLA prepared substantial monographs on many of the Latin American republics which remain an invaluable source on the role of industrialization in the 1930s. See, for example, Comisión Económica para América Latina (CEPAL), *El Desarrollo Económico de la Argentina* (Santiago, 1959) and CEPAL, *El*

Desarrollo Económico del Brasil (Santiago, 1956). There is also a good study of import substitution in the 1930s, stressing the role played by the change in relative prices, in Richard Lynn Ground, 'The Genesis of Import Substitution in Latin America', *Cepal Review*, 36 (1988): 179–203.

Earlier studies on industrialization in the 1930s, although less theoretical, can still be consulted to advantage. See, for example, George Wythe, *Industry in Latin America* (New York, 1945) and Lloyd Hughlett (ed.), *Industrialization of Latin America* (New York, 1946). ECLA has also prepared a number of industry case studies which shed light on the growth of particular manufacturing sectors in the 1930s. See, for example, ECLA, *Labour Productivity of the Cotton Textile Industry in Five Latin American Countries* (New York, 1951). There is also an important early study on foreign investment in Latin American manufacturing, including the first half of the 1930s, in Dudley Phelps, *The Migration of Industry to South America* (New York, 1937).

There are many works on individual republics which are worthy of mention, although most of them are concerned with a period longer than the decade of the 1930s. The outstanding work on Argentina remains the book by Carlos Díaz-Alejandro, *Essays on the Economic History of the Argentina Republic* (New Haven, Conn., 1970) which combines theory, analysis and econometrics in a judicious and effective blend. A less quantitative, but still concise, work is Paul Lewis, *The Crisis of Argentine Capitalism* (Chapel Hill, N.C., 1990). There are several important studies by Argentine economists including Adolfo Dorfman, *Cincuenta años de industrialización en la Argentina, 1930–80: desarrollo y perspectivas* (Buenos Aires, 1983) as well as Guido Di Tella and Manuel Zymelman, *Los Ciclos Económicos Argentinos* (Buenos Aires, 1973). The meat industry has generated a number of good monographs, among which should be mentioned Simon Hanson, *Argentine Meat and the British Market* (Stanford, Cal., 1938) and Peter Smith, *Politics and Beef in Argentina* (New York, 1969). State intervention in foreign trade is discussed in Roger Gravil, 'State Intervention in Argentina's Export Trade between the Wars', *Journal of Latin American Studies*, 2/2 (1970): 147–73 and V. Salera, *Exchange Control and the Argentine Market* (New York, 1941) explores Argentina in the period when peso convertibility began to break down.

Brazil has been particularly well served by works of economic history which include the 1930s. The post-1929 period is singled our for special consideration in Celso Furtado, *The Economic Growth of Brazil* (Berkeley, Cal., 1963). Carlos Manuel Peláez, *História da Industrialização Brasileira*

(Rio de Janeiro, 1972) devotes a great deal of space to Brazil's coffee policies in the 1930s and in doing so takes issue with parts of Furtado's analysis. Pedro S. Malan, Regis Bonelli, Marcelo de P. Abreu and José Eduardo de C. Pereira, *Política Econômica Externa e Industrialização no Brasil, 1939/52* (Rio de Janeiro, 1977) takes up the story at the end of the 1930s, but still has much of interest to say. A. V. Villela and W. Suzigan, *Política do Governo e Crescimento da Economia Brasileira 1889–1945* (Rio de Janeiro, 1973,) is excellent on the question of economic policy in the 1930s. Albert Fishlow, 'Origins and Consequences of Import Substitution in Brazil', in L. E. di Marco (ed.), *International Economics and Development: Essays in Honor of Raúl Prebisch* (New York, 1972) is one of the best sources for Brazilian industrialization in the inter-war period, while Warren Dean, *The Industrialization of São Paulo 1880–1945* (Austin, Tex., 1969) has stood the test of time extremely well. There are also useful chapters on the 1930s in Nathaniel Leff, *Underdevelopment and Development in Brazil. Economic Structure and Change, 1822–1947,* Vol. 1 (London, 1982).

Chilean economic performance in the 1930s has inspired a number of fine monographs. Industrialization is the theme of H. Kirsch, *Industrial Development in a Traditional Society: The Conflict Between Entrepreneurship and Modernization in Chile* (Gainsville, Fl., 1977) as well as of Oscar Muñoz, *Crecimiento Industrial de Chile, 1914–1965* (Santiago, 1968). The same theme is also explored in considerable depth in Gabriel Palma, 'Growth and Structure of Chilean Manufacturing Industry from 1830 to 1935: origins and development of a process of industrialization in an export economy', unpublished Ph.D. dissertation, Oxford University, 1979. More general questions of Chilean structure, performance and policy in the 1930s are examined in Gabriel Palma, 'From an Export-led to an Import-substituting Economy: Chile 1914–39', in Thorp (ed.), *Latin America in the 1930s,* and in Anibal Pinto, *Chile, un Caso de Desarrollo Frustrado* (Santiago, 1959), while the agricultural sector is the subject of Mats Lundahl, 'Agricultural Stagnation in Chile, 1930–55: a result of factor market imperfections?', in Mats Lundahl (ed.), *The Primary Sector in Economic Development* (London, 1985).

Mexico, despite its size and importance, has not attracted as much scholarly attention in this period as one might have expected. This is a consequence of the greater importance attached to the post-1940 period in explaining industrialization and rapid structural change in Mexico. Nevertheless, there is an excellent monograph in the structuralist tradition by René Villarreal, *El Desequilibrio Externo en la Industrialización de México,*

1929–1975 (Mexico, D.F., 1976). The contributions by Enrique Cárdenas, 'The Great Depression and Industrialisation: the case of Mexico', and Valpy Fitzgerald, 'Restructuring through the Depression: the state and capital accumulation in Mexico, 1925–40', in Thorp (ed.), *Latin America in the 1930s,* are particularly illuminating as there are sharp differences between both authors at various points of the analysis. See also Enrique Cárdenas, *La Industrialización Mexicana durante la Gran Depresión* (Mexico, D.F., 1987). Industrialization in Mexico is the subject of Sanford Mosk, *Industrial Revolution in Mexico* (Berkeley, Cal., 1950). It is also explored in Stephen Haber, *Industry and Underdevelopment: the Industrialization of Mexico, 1890–1940* (Stanford, Cal., 1989), a pathbreaking work which uses firm-level data to undermine numerous myths about industrialization in Mexico as well as to develop a number of interesting hypotheses.

The economic performance and policy of some republics in the 1930s has still not received the attention it deserves. Nevertheless, a number of studies are worthy of special mention. In the case of Colombia, scholars are well served by José Antonio Ocampo and Santiago Montenegro, *Crisis Mundial, Protección e Industrialización* (Bogotá, 1984), whose first three chapters are of particular importance for the study of the 1930s. Marco Palacios, *Coffee in Colombia, 1850–1970* (Cambridge, 1980), although devoted to the country's premier product, has much of interest to say on the broader issues of the 1930s. There is a range of excellent articles on the 1930s in *El Banco de la República, Antecedentes, Evolución y Estructura* (Bogotá, 1990) – a work devoted to the central bank's history which in the process illuminates many aspects of economic policy. The Peruvian experience is covered well in Geoffrey Bertram and Rosemary Thorp, *Peru 1890–1977: Growth and Policy in an Open Economy* (London, 1978), while comparative economic policy in Colombia and Peru is the theme of Rosemary Thorp, *Economic Management and Economic Development in Peru and Colombia* (London, 1991).

There are very few studies devoted in whole or even in part to the economics of the Caribbean basin countries in the 1930s. There is an excellent account of Cuban financial problems before the creation of a central bank in Henry Wallich, *Monetary Problems of an Export Economy: The Cuban Experience, 1914–1947* (Cambridge, Mass., 1950). There is a good chapter devoted to Puerto Rico in the 1930s in James Dietz, *Economic History of Puerto Rico* (Princeton, N.J., 1986) and in the case of Haiti Mats Lundahl, *Peasants and Poverty: A Study of Haiti* (London, 1979) can be used to advantage. A rare study of industrialization in the Dominican Republic, although mainly concerned with a later period, is Frank Moya Pons, 'Import-substitution Industrialization Policies in the Dominican Republic, 1925–61', *Hispanic American Historical Review,* 70/4 (1990): 539–77. Economic development in the five Central American republics is addressed in several chapters of Victor Bulmer-Thomas, *The Political Economy of Central America since 1920* (Cambridge, 1987), while the political economy of Venezuela up to the death of Juan Vicente Gómez is the subject of William Sullivan, 'Situación económica y política durante el período de Juan Vicente Gómez', in Fundación John Boulton, *Política y Economía en Venezuela, 1810–1976* (Caracas, 1976).

An important part of the bibliography on the Latin American economies in the 1930s is obtained from studies of particular commodities since a handful of primary product exports continued to exercise an overwhelming influence on the economic life of the region even after the decline of world trade. A number of books, devoted to commodities in general, are still extremely useful. These include J. F. Rowe, *Primary Commodities in International Trade* (Cambridge, 1965) and Joseph Grunwald and Philip Musgrove, *Natural Resources in Latin American Development* (Baltimore, Md., and London, 1970). The classic works on coffee are C. Wickizer, *The World Coffee Economy with Special Reference to Control Schemes* (Stanford, 1943) and Food and Agricultural Organization (FAO), *The World's Coffee* (Rome, 1947). The economics of sugar in the 1930s is explored in B. C. Swerling, *International Control of Sugar, 1918–41* (Stanford, Cal., 1949). Oil, primarily of importance to Venezuela in the 1930s, is the subject of Brian McBeth, *Juan Vicente Gómez and the Oil Companies in Venezuela, 1908–35* (Cambridge, 1983) and tin, of real interest only to Bolivia, is examined in John Hillman, 'Bolivia and British Tin Policy', *Journal of Latin American Studies,* 22/2 (1990): 289–315. The banana trade, of great importance to many Caribbean basin countries, is examined in Thomas Karnes, *Tropical Enterprise: Standard Fruit and Steamship Company in Latin America* (Baton Rouge, La., 1978), while a most unflattering portrait of the United Fruit Company is painted in Charles Kepner and Jay Soothill, *The Banana Empire: a Case Study in Economic Imperialism* (New York, 1935). The tobacco trade, of considerable importance to Cuba in the 1930s, is competently discussed in the first part of Jean Stubbs, *Tobacco on the Periphery* (Cambridge, 1985). The classic work on wheat, a key export for Argentina, remains W. Mandelbaum, *The World Wheat Economy 1855–1939* (Cambridge, Mass., 1953), while Clark Reynolds explores the economics of copper in 'Development Problems of an Export Economy: the case of Chile and copper', in Markos Mamalakis and Clark Reynolds (eds), *Essays on the Chilean Economy* (Homewood, Ill., 1965).

Economic statistics are an important element in the study of the Latin American economies in the 1930s. In addition to country sources, the League of Nations played a useful role in bringing together time-series data for most of the Latin American republics in the inter-war period. The relevant annual publications are League of Nations, *Statistical Yearbook* (Geneva), League of Nations, *International Trade Statistics* (Geneva) and International Institute of Agriculture, *International Yearbook of Agricultural Statistics* (Rome). In addition, the League of Nations published occasional documents providing an invaluable collection of data for Latin America on a comparable basis. See, for example, League of Nations, *Public Finance 1928–37* (Geneva, 1938). ECLAC has also prepared time-series data bringing together its own researches and country sources in a series of helpful publications. See in particular CEPAL, *Series Históricas del Crecimiento de América Latina* (Santiago, 1978) and CEPAL, *América Latina: Relación de Precios del Intercambio* (Santiago, 1976). The occasional reports for each republic by the British Department of Overseas Trade are full of useful statistics as well as being a good contemporary source. The Council of Foreign Bondholders, *Annual Report* (London) brings together in one volume all the statistics for each republic considered most directly relevant to questions of debt repayment. Finally, many time-series data for the 1930s are presented in James W. Wilkie (ed.), *Statistical Abstract of Latin America, 3 Statistics and National Policy* (Los Angeles, Cal., 1974).

3. THE LATIN AMERICAN ECONOMIES, 1939–C.1950

Very little literature on the economic development of Latin America specifically addresses the 1940s. Analyses tend to see the 1929 Depression as initiating the shift to import-substituting industrialization in the form that is recognizable by the 1950s, and give little attention to the precise problematic of the Second World War and its aftermath. The wealth of studies of the 1930s therefore simply find no parallel in the next decade. The international economy is, however, more fully studied, since this was a period of strong institutional innovation. See, for example, S. W. Black, *A Levite among the Priests: Edward M. Bernstein and the Origins of the Bretton Woods System* (Oxford, 1991). Robert A. Pollard, *Economic Security and the Origins of the Cold War, 1945–1950* (New York, 1985) is an important study of the immediate post-war period, especially for our purposes chapter 9: Natural Resources and National Security: U.S. Policy in the Developing World, 1945–50. K. Kock, *International Trade Policy and the GATT, 1947–1967* (Stockholm, 1969) is a useful source on GATT and the role of the United States. Longer-run general studies of the international economy that incorporate this period include: Alfred Maizels, *Industrial Growth and World Trade: An Empirical Study of Trends in Production, Consumption and Trade in Manufactures, 1899–1959* (Cambridge, 1963) and P. Lamartine Yates, *Forty Years of Foreign Trade. A Statistical Handbook with Special Reference to Primary Products and Underdeveloped Countries* (London, 1959). Two works on foreign investment which cover a longer span of Latin American economic history but which are useful for this period are Barbara Stallings, *Bankers to the Third World: U.S. Portfolio Investment in Latin America, 1900–1986* (Berkeley, Cal., 1987) and J. Fred Rippy, *British Investments in Latin America 1822–1949* (Minneapolis, 1959). The latter, however, must be used with care. See also Mira Wilkins, *The Maturing Enterprise: American Business Abroad from 1914 to 1970* (Cambridge, Mass., 1974). On U.S.-Latin American economic relations in the immediate post-war period, see Stephen G. Rabe, 'The Elusive Conference: United States economic relations with Latin America, 1945–1952', *Diplomatic History,* 2, 3 (1978): 279–94. A particularly interesting study of U.S. interests in this period, which explicitly deals with Argentina, is Sylvia Maxfield and James H. Nolt, 'Protectionism and the Internationalization of Capital: U.S. sponsorship of import substitution industrialization in the Philippines, Turkey and Argentina', *International Studies Quarterly,* 34 (1990): 49–81.

On Latin America during the Second World War the outstanding general study is R. A. Humphreys, *Latin America and the Second World War, Vol. 1, 1939–42* (London, 1981), *Vol. 2, 1942–45* (London, 1982). This masterly work has both general sections and extensive country-by-country coverage. For both the war and the post-war period, ECLA (Economic Commission for Latin America) studies provide a wealth of both data and analysis. See ECLA, *The Economic Development of Latin America and its Principal Problems* (Lake Success, N.Y., 1950); *Economic Survey of Latin America, 1949* (New York, 1951); *Foreign Capital in Latin America* (New York, 1955); *Inter-Latin American Trade* (New York, 1957); *External Financing in Latin America* (New York, 1965); and, above all, *The Economic Development of Latin America. The Post-War Period* (New York, 1964). Industrialization is more specifically documented in ECLA, *The Process of Industrialization in Latin America* (New York, 1966) and in the country monographs produced in the 1950s and early 1960s as *El Desarrollo Económico del . . .* There are also some valuable sectoral studies by ECLA: for example, *Labour Productivity of the Cotton Textile Industry in Five Latin American Countries* (New York, 1951). Later works of ECLA which constitute major sources of data are *Series Históricas de Crecimiento en América Latina* (Santiago, 1978) and *América Latina: Relación de Precios del Intercambio* (Santiago, 1976). Apart from ECLA, the principal comparative source of data is James W. Wilkie (ed.), *Statistical Abstract of Latin America, 3 Statistics and National Policy* (Los Angeles, Cal., 1974). For a discussion of ECLA-led ideological developments in the post-war period, see chapter by Joseph L. Love, 'Economic Ideas and Ideologies in Latin America since 1930' in this volume, and E. V. K. Fitzgerald, 'ECLA and the Formation of Latin American Economic Doctrine', in D. Rock (ed.), *Latin America in the 1940s: war and postwar transitions* (Berkeley, Cal., 1994).

Much of the country-specific literature has been cited in the above bibliographical essay on the Latin American economics in the 1930s, since it takes the form of longer-run country studies which yield insights for particular decades, or can be found in the bibliographical essays on individual countries, in *Cambridge History of Latin America* VII (Mexico, Central America and the Caribbean since 1930), 1990, *CHLA* VIII (Spanish South America since 1990), 1991 and *CHLA* IX (Brazil since 1930), forthcoming. The following, however, deserve mention:

On Brazil, see Marcelo de Paiva Abreu, 'Crise, crescimento e modernização autoritária, 1930–1945' and Sérgio Besserman Vianna, 'Política econômica externa e industrialização: 1946–1951', in Abreu (ed.), *A Ordem do Progresso. Cem Anos de Política Econômica Republicana, 1889–1989* (Rio de Janeiro, 1990); Pedro Malan et al., *Política Econômica Externa e Industrialização no Brasil, 1932–52* (Rio de Janeiro, 1977); B. Gupta, 'Import Substitution in Capital Goods: the case of Brazil, 1929–1979', unpublished D.Phil. thesis, Oxford, 1989; M. A. P. Leopoldi, 'Industrial Associations and Politics in Contemporary Brasil', unpublished D.Phil. thesis, Oxford, 1984; and Sonia Draibe, *Rumos e Metamorfoses: estado e industrialização no Brasil: 1930–1960* (Rio de Janeiro, 1985).

On Mexico, see Stephen R. Niblo, *The Impact of War: Mexico and World War II,* La Trobe University, Institute of Latin American Studies, Occasional Paper no. 10 (Melbourne, 1988); René Villarreal, *El Disequilibrio Externo en la Industrialización de México, 1929–1975* (Mexico, D.F., 1976); C. W. Reynolds, *The Mexican Economy, Twentieth Century Structure and Growth* (New Haven, Conn., 1970); L. Solís, *Planes de Desarrollo Económico y social en México* (Mexico, D.F., 1975); S. Mosk, *Industrial Revolution in Mexico* (Berkeley, Cal., 1950); R. J. Shafer, *Mexican Business Organizations. History and Analysis* (Syracuse, 1973) on the role of entrepreneurs; C. Hewitt de Alcántara, *Modernising Mexican Agriculture* (Geneva, 1976) on agriculture; and I. M. de Navarrette, *La Distribución del Ingreso y el Desarrollo en México* (Mexico, D.F., 1960), a unique study for its period on income distribution.

On Argentina, see Carlos F. Díaz-Alejandro, *Essays on the Economic History of the Argentine Republic* (New Haven, Conn., 1970); A. Dorfman, *Cincuenta años de industrialización en la Argentina 1930–80* (Buenos Aires, 1983); G. di Tella and M. Zymelman, *Los ciclos económicos argentinos* (Buenos Aires, 1973); Guido di Tella and D. C. Watt (eds), *Argentina between the Great Powers, 1939–46* (London, 1989); and Carlos Escudé, *Gran Bretaña, los Estados Unidos y la declinación argentina, 1942–1949* (Buenos Aires, 1983).

On Uruguay, see M. H. J. Finch, *A Political Economy of Uruguay since 1870* (London, 1981).

On Chile, see L. Ortega, et al., *CORFO: 50 años de realizaciones, 1939–1989* (Santiago, 1989); Oscar Muñoz, *Crecimiento industrial de Chile, 1914–1965* (Santiago, 1968); and A. Hirschman, *Journeys Toward Progress: Studies of Economic Policy-Making in Latin America* (New York, 1963), ch. 3.

On Peru, see Geoffrey Bertram and Rosemary Thorp, *Peru 1890–1977: Growth and Policy in an Open Economy* (London, 1978).

On Colombia, see José Antonio Ocampo and Santiago Montenegro, *Crisis Mundial, Protección e Industrialización* (Bogotá, 1984).

On Venezuela, see M. Ignacio Purroy, *Estado e Industrialización en Venezuela* (Caracas, 1982).

On Central America, see Victor Bulmer-Thomas, *The Political Economy of Central America since 1920* (Cambridge, 1987).

4. THE LATIN AMERICAN ECONOMIES, 1950–1990

The most methodical attempt to explain the economic history of Developed Market Economies (DMEs) since the Second World War can be found in the work of A. Maddison; see especially *Phases of Capitalist Development* (Oxford, 1982); 'Growth and Slowdown in Advanced Capitalist Economies: techniques of quantitative assessment', *Journal of Economic Literature*, XXV (June 1987): 649–98; 'Growth and Fluctuations in the World Economy, 1870–1960', *Banca Nazionale del Lavoro Quarterly Review*, September 1965; *The World Economy in the 20th Century* (OECD, Paris 1989); and 'A Comparison of the Levels of GDP per capita in Developed and Developing Countries, 1800–1980', *The Journal of Economic History,* XLIII (March 1983): 159–78; See also I. Kravis and R. Lipsey, 'The Diffusion of Economic growth in the World Economy, 1950–80', in J. Kendrick (ed.), *International Comparisons of Productivity and Causes of its Slowdown* (Cambridge, Mass., 1984). Excellent interpretations of the 'Golden Age of capitalism' (1950–73), both in developed and developing economies, and the causes of its decline, can be found in S. Marglin and J. B. Schor (eds), *The Golden Age of Capitalism: Reinterpreting the Postwar Experience* (Oxford, 1990), especially Marglin's, 'Lessons of the Golden Age: an overview', and A. Glyn, A. Hughes, A. Lipietz and A. Singh, 'The Rise and Fall of the Golden Age'. See also the influential book by R. Rowthorn and J. Wells, *De-industrialization and foreign trade* (Cambridge, 1987). On developments in the world economy during the early years of this period, see S. Kuznets, *Economic Growth and Structure* (London, 1966). Statistical information can be found in yearly publications by OECD (Organization for Economic Co-operation and Development) (*Historical Statistics,* and *National Accounts,* Paris); the World Bank (*World Tables* and *World Development Report,* Oxford); and OECD, IMF (International Monetary Fund) and World Bank databases.

Historical statistics and some analysis of the economic development of Third World countries can be found in the work of A. Maddison already cited and in P. Bairoch, *The Economic Development of the Third World since 1900* (London, 1977), and 'The Main Trends in National Economic Disparities since the Industrial Revolution', in P. Bairoch and M. Lévy-Leboyer, *Disparities in Economic Development Since the Industrial Revolution* (London, 1981). The World Bank regularly produces extensive sets of statistics for Less Developed Countries (LDCs); see especially *World Economic Outlook; World Development Report,* and World Bank databases. See also IMF, *International Financial Statistics* and *IFS Database;* UNIDO (United Nations Industrial Development Organization), *Database;* United Nations, *Statistical Yearbook* and *Yearbook of International Trade Statistics,* and *Industry and Development Global Report,* 1987; ILO (International Labour Office), *World Labour Report;* and UNCTAD (United Nations Conference on Trade and Development), *Handbook of International Trade and Development Statistics,* 1984. I. Kravis, A. Heston and R. Summers, *World Product and Income: International Comparisons of Real Gross Product* (Baltimore, Md., 1988) is a useful attempt at producing comparable statistics for LDCs which is being constantly updated. B. R. Mitchell, *International Historical Statistics* (London, 1983) provides a helpful summary of country data.

ECLA is the best source of data on Latin American countries during this period. See the yearly *Economic Surveys of Latin America* and *Statistical Yearbook for Latin America and the Caribbean* (Santiago). It is not possible to mention all the many other relevant works of ECLA here, but publications such as *Dirección y Estructura del Comercio Latinoamericano* (Santiago, 1984) provide useful data and analysis on different aspects of Latin American development. However, there are still some discrepancies between some ECLA and other U.N. sources. For a discussion of this problem, see J. Wells, *Latin America at the Cross-Roads* (Santiago, 1988).

There are relatively few comparative analyses of Latin American performance with that of other regions of the Third World. But see A. Fishlow, 'Some Reflections on Comparative Latin American Economic Performance and Policy', and A. Hughes and A. Singh, 'The World Economic Slowdown and the Asian and Latin American Economies: a comparative analysis of economic structure, policy and performance', in T. Banuri (ed.), *Economic Liberalisation: No Panacea* (Oxford, 1991); K. Suk Kim and M. Roemer, *Growth and Structural Transformation* (Cambridge, Mass., 1981); A. Singh, 'Third World Industrialization and the Structure of the World Economy', in D. Curry (ed.), *Microeconomic Analysis: Essays in Microeconomics and Development* (London, 1981), and 'Third World Competition and De-industrialization in Advanced Countries', in T. Lawson, J. G. Palma and J. Sender (eds), *Kaldor's Political Economy* (London, 1989); J. Sachs, 'External Debt and Macroeconomic Performance in Latin America and East Asia', *Brookings Papers on Economic Activity,* Vol. 2, 1985; and S. Naya, M. Urrutia, S. Mark and A. Fuentes, *Lessons in Development: a Comparative Study of Asia and Latin America* (San Francisco, Cal., 1989). For a comparison of Latin America and the Scandinavian countries, see M. Blomstrom and P. Meller (eds), *Diverging Paths: a Century of Latin American and Scandinavian Economic Development* (Washington, D.C., 1991).

The experience of the NICs (newly industrialized countries), which has become an obligatory point of comparison for any study of recent economic developments in the Third World, is discussed in H-J Chang, *The Political Economy of Industrial Policy: Reflections on the Role of the State Intervention* (Cambridge, 1994). Chang shows how some of the NICs' most ardent enthusiasts – such as I. Little (*Economic Development,* New York, 1982) and D. Lal (*The Poverty of Development Economics,* London, 1983) – have missed the most crucial issue of the post-war economic experience of these countries: namely, their high degree of pragmatism in economic policy-making. See also R. Wade, *Governing the Market: Economic Theory and the Role of Government in East Asian Industrialization* (Princeton, N.J., 1990).

On Latin American economic development during this period, the most influential body of work is obviously that of Raúl Prebisch (see below and bibliographical essay 7 on Latin American economic thought). Besides those of Prebisch, the best known contributions are from A. O. Hirschman (see, for example, *Ensayos sobre Desarrollo y América Latina,* Mexico, D.F., 1981); Carlos Díaz-Alejandro (see his collected essays, edited by Andrés Velasco, *Debt, Stabilization and Development,* Oxford, 1989); F. Fajnzylber (see, for example, *Unavoidable Industrial Restructuring in Latin America,* London, 1990); A. Fishlow, (see particularly his work on Brazil, for instance 'Brazilian Size Distribution of Income', *American Economic Review,* Papers and Proceedings, 62/2 (1972): 391–402); L. Taylor (for instance, *Stabilization and Growth in Developing Countries: a structuralist approach* London, 1989); E. Bacha (see his collected essays *El Milagro y la Crisis: economía brasileña y latinoamericana – ensayos,* Mexico, D.F., 1986); and R. Ffrench-Davis (see *Economia Internacional: teoría y políticas para el desarrollo,* 2nd edn, Mexico, D.F., 1985). ECLA's *Changing Production Patterns with Social Equity* (Santiago, 1990), largely based on F. Fajnzylber's ideas, and *Social Equity and Changing Production Patterns: An Integrated Approach* (Santiago, 1992) have also been very influential.

Other valuable contributions include J. Wells, *Latin America at the Cross-Roads;* R. Ffrench-Davis and E. Tironi (eds), *Latin America and the New International Economic Order* (London, 1982); J. Serra, *Ensayos Críticos sobre el Desarrollo Latinoamericano* (Mexico, D.F., 1983); C. Furtado, *El Subdesarrollo Latinoamericano* (Mexico, D.F., 1987); P. Meller, (ed.), *The Latin American Development Debate. Neostructuralism, Neoconservatism, and Adjustment Processes* (Boulder, Colo., 1991); E. Durán (ed.), *Latin America and the World Recession* (Cambridge, 1985); O. Sunkel (ed.), *El Desarrollo desde Dentro: un enfoque neoestructuralista para América Latina* (Mexico, D.F., 1991; Eng. trans. *Development from Within. Towards a Neo-Structuralist Approach for Latin America,* Boulder, Col., 1993); J. A. Ocampo, 'The Macroeconomic Effects of Import Controls: a Keynesian analysis', *Journal of Development Economics,* 27 (1987). R. E. Feinberg and R. Ffrench-Davis (eds), *Development and External Debt in Latin America* (South Bend, Indiana, 1988; see especially R. Dornbusch, 'World Economic Issues of Interest to Latin America'); and J. G. Palma, 'Dependency: a formal theory of underdevelopment, or a methodology for the analysis of concrete situations of underdevelopment?,'

World Development, 6, 7/8, (1978), republished in G. M. Meier (ed.), *Leading Issues in Economic Development,* 5th edn, (Oxford, 1988).

The role of the external sector in Latin American development has received considerable attention during this period, reflecting its importance in the economic fortunes of the region. The work of Raúl Prebisch and ECLA in general (particularly during its 'classical' period) have been the most influential. For a review of this literature see J. G. Palma, 'Dependencia y desarrollo: una visión crítica', in D. Seers (ed.), *La Teoría de la Dependencia: una revaluación crítica* (Mexico, D.F., 1987): 881–924. See also O. Rodríguez, *La Teoría del Subdesarrollo de la CEPAL* (Mexico, D.F., 1980); ECLA, *El Pensamiento de la CEPAL* (Santiago, 1969); A. Gurrieri, *La Obra de Prebisch en la CEPAL* (Mexico, D.F., 1987); J. Hodara *Prebisch y la CEPAL: sustancia, trayectoria y contexto institucional* (Mexico, D.F., 1987); and J. G. Palma, 'Raúl Prebisch', 'Structuralism' and 'Dependency Theory', in J. Eatwell, M. Millgate and P. Newman (eds), *The New Palgrave: A Dictionary of Economic Theory and Doctrine* (London, 1988). For an analysis of this sector in the 1970s, see R. Ffrench-Davis (ed.), *Intercambio y Desarrollo,* 2 vols (Mexico, D.F., 1981).

The rapid growth of exports of manufactures has been one of the most interesting issues in the recent economic development of the region. See, for example, ECLA's *Analysis and Perspectives of Latin American Industrial Development* (Santiago, 1979); C. Díaz-Alejandro 'Some Characteristics of Recent Export Expansion in Latin America', *Yale Economic Growth Center Papers,* No. 209, 1974; IDB (Inter-American Development Bank), *Economic and Social Progress in Latin America* (Washington, D.C., 1986); and M. Movarec, 'Exports of Manufactured Goods to the Centres: importance and significance', *CEPAL Review,* 17 (1982): 47–77. On the 'maquila' contribution to these exports, see R. Kaztman and C. Reyna (eds), *Fuerza de Trabajo y Movimientos Laborales en América Latina* (Mexico, D.F., 1979), and PREALC, *Más Allá de la Regulación* (Santiago, 1990).

On the effects of trade liberalization and neo-liberal experiments in Latin America in general, see A. Foxley, *Neo-Conservative Experiments in Latin America* (Berkeley, Cal., 1983); J. Ramos, *Neo-conservative Economics in the Southern Cone of Latin America, 1973–1983* (Baltimore, Md., 1986); R. Ffrench-Davis, 'The Monetarist Experiment in Chile: a critical survey; *World Development* (1983): 905–926; R. Cortázar, A. Foxley and V. Tockman, *Legados del Monetarismo* (Buenos Aires, 1984); and S. Edwards and A. Cox-Edwards, *Monetarism and Liberalization: the Chilean experience* (Cambridge, Mass., 1987). See also V. Corbo and P. Meller, 'Alternative

Trade Strategies and Employment Implications: Chile', in A. Krueger et al., *Trade and Employment in Developing Countries* (Washington, D.C., 1979), and R. Ffrench-Davis and M. Marfán, 'Selective Policies Under a Structural Foreign-exchange Shortage', in H. Singer, et al. (eds), *Adjustment and Liberalization in the Third World* (New Delhi, 1991). The monetarist view is put forward by T. G. Congdon, *Economic Liberalism in the Southern Cone of Latin America* (London, 1985).

On the structuralist approach to inflation, see J. Noyola 'El desarrollo económico y la inflación en México y otros países latinoamericanos', *Investigación Económica,* 4th quarter (1956); O. Sunkel, 'Inflation in Chile: an unorthodox approach', in *International Economic Papers,* 10 (1960); A. Pinto, *Ni Estabilidad ni Desarrollo – la politica del FMI* (Santiago, 1958) and *Inflación: raices estructurales* (Mexico, D.F., 1980); and N. Kaldor, 'Economic Problems of Chile', in *Essays on Economic Policy* Vol. II (London, 1964). For an analysis of inflation during the latter part of this period, see for example R. Thorp and L. Whitehead (eds), *Inflation and Stabilization in Latin America* (London, 1979); J. P. Arellano (ed.), *Inflación Rebelde en América Latina* (Santiago, 1990); J. Ros, *On Models of Inertial Inflation* (Helsinki, 1988); and M. Bruno, G. Di Tella, R. Dornbusch and S. Fischer (eds), *Inflation and Stabilization: the experiences of Israel, Argentina, Brazil, Bolivia and Mexico* (Cambridge, Mass., 1988).

On manufacturing industry and ISI the works of Prebisch and ECLA were the most influential until the 1970s (see above). On critical analyses of Latin American ISI the best work is F. Fajnzylber, *La Industrialización Trunca* (Mexico, D.F., 1983). See also F. Fajnzylber (ed.), *Industrialización e internacionalización en la América Latina,* 2 vols (Mexico, D.F., 1982); M. Nolff, *Desarrollo Industrial Latinoamericano* (Mexico, D.F., 1983); and O. Muñoz, 'El proceso de industrialización: teorías, experiencias y politicas', in O. Sunkel (ed.), *El desarrollo desde dentro.* A comprehensive analysis of the capital goods industry in the region can be found in D. Chudnovsky and M. Nagao, *Capital Goods Production in the Third World* (London, 1983). For the capital goods industry in Brazil, see D. Chudnovsky, 'The Entry into the Design and Production of Complex Capital Goods: the experiences of Brazil, India and South Korea', and 'The capital goods industry and the dynamics of economic development in LDCs: the case of Brazil', in M. Fransman (ed.), *Machinery and Economic Development* (London, 1986).

On agrarian issues, see A. Garcia, *Desarrollo Agrario y la América Latina* (Mexico, D.F., 1986); M. Twomey, and A. Helwege (eds), *Modernization and Stagnation: Latin American Agriculture into the 1990s* (Washington,

D.C., 1991); and A. Figueroa, 'Desarrollo agricola en la América Latina', in O. Sunkel (ed.), *El desarrollo desde dentro.* On environmental issues and Latin America, see O. Sunkel and N. Gligo, *Estilos de Desarrollo y Medio Ambiente en la América Latina* (Mexico, D.F., 1986); N. Gligo, 'Medio ambiente y recursos naturales en el desarrollo Latinoamericano', in O. Sunkel (ed.), *El desarrollo desde dentro;* and J. Vial (ed.), *Desarrollo y Medio Ambiente. Hacia un Enfoque Integrador* (Santiago, 1991). On technological issues in the region, see F. R. Sagasti, *Ciencia, Technologia y Desarrollo Latinoamericano* (Mexico, D.F., 1986). On the role of foreign capital in Latin America, see C. Vaitsos, *Inter-country Income Distribution and Transnational Enterprises* (Oxford, 1974); D. Chudnovsky, *Empresas Multinacionales y Ganancias Monopólicas en una Economia Latinoamericana* (Mexico, D.F., 1975); and J. J. Villamil (ed.), *Capitalismo Transnacional y Desarrollo Regional* (Mexico, D.F., 1985). On labour issues the best known work is that of PREALC. See for example *Modelos de Empleo y Politica Económica: una década de experiencias del PREALC* (Santiago, 1987). See also V. E. Tockman, 'Mercados de trabajo y empleo en el pensamiento económico latinoamericano', in O. Sunkel (ed.), *El desarrollo desde dentro.* On gender-based wage differentials, see P. González, 'El diferencial de ingresos entre hombres y mujeres. Teoría, evidencia e implicaciones de política', in *Colección Estudios CIEPLAN,* 34 (1992).

There are many studies on the problems of economic development of specific countries. The best known analysis of Argentina's mounting economic problems is found in C. Díaz-Alejandro, *Essays on the Economic History of the Argentine Republic* (New Haven, Conn., 1970), and *Exchange Rate Devaluation in a semi-industrialized Country: the experience of Argentina 1955–1961* (Cambridge, Mass., 1965). See also G. Di Tella and R. Dornbusch (eds), *The Political Economy of Argentina, 1946–83* (London, 1989); A. Dorfman, *Cincuenta Años de Industrialización en la Argentina, 1930–80: desarrollo y perspectivas* (Buenos Aires, 1983); and R. Mallon and J. V. Sourrouille, *Policy Making in a Conflictive Society* (Cambridge, Mass., 1975).

On Brazil, see M. de Paiva Abreu (ed.), *A Ordem do Progresso: cem anos de política econômica republicana, 1889–1989* (Rio de Janeiro, 1990); W. Baer, *The Brazilian Economy: Growth and Development,* 3rd edn (New York, 1989); and E. Bacha, *El milagro e el crisis.*

On Mexico, see L. Solís, *La Economía Mexicana* (Mexico, D.F., 1985); E. Cárdenas (ed.), *Historia Económica de México,* 4 vols (Mexico, D.F., 1990–); D. S. Brothers and A. E. Wick (eds), *México en Busca de una Nueva Estrategia de Desarrollo* (Mexico, D.F., forthcoming); R. Villarroel,

Industrialización Deuda y Desequilibrio Externo en México: un enfoque neo-estructuralista (Mexico, D.F., 1988); and N. Lustig, *Distribución del Ingreso y Crecimiento en México. Un analisis de las ideas estructuralistas* (Mexico, D.F., 1981). On the Mexican economy during the early years of this period, see also C. W. Reynolds, *The Mexican Economy: Twentieth-century Structure and Growth* (New Haven, Conn., 1970).

On Colombia, see C. Díaz-Alejandro, *Foreign Trade Regimes and Economic Development: Colombia* (New York, 1976); G. Colmenares and J. A. Ocampo, *Historia Económica de Colombia* (Bogotá, 1987); R. Thorp, *Economic Management and Economic Development in Peru and Colombia* (Basingstoke, 1991); and J. A. Ocampo and E. Lora, *Introducción a la Macroeconomia Colombiana* (Bogotá, 1990). On Venezuela, see R. Hausmann, *Shocks Externas y Ajuste Macroeconómico* (Caracas, 1990), and M. I. Purroy, *Estado e Industrialización* (Caracas, 1986). On Peru see Thorp, *Economic Management,* and G. Bertram and R. Thorp, *Peru, 1890–1977* (New York, 1979). On Central America, see V. Bulmer-Thomas, *Studies in the Economies of Central America* (London, 1988) and *The Political Economy of Central America since 1920* (Cambridge, 1987).

The literature on Chile is extensive. For statistical data, see M. Mamalakis, *Historical Statistics of Chile* (Westport, Conn., 1978–). For the earlier years of this period, see O. Muñoz, *Crecimiento Industrial de Chile, 1914–65* (Santiago, 1968); R. Ffrench-Davis, *Políticas Económicas en Chile, 1952–1970* (Santiago, 1973); A. Pinto, *Chile, Una Economía Difícil* (Santiago, 1964); M. Mamalakis, *The Growth and Structure of the Chilean Economy from Independence to Allende* (New Haven, Conn. 1976); and R. Ffrench-Davis and O. Muñoz, 'Economic and Political Instability in Chile' in S. Teitel (ed.), *Towards a New Development Strategy in Latin America* (Washington, D.C., 1992). On the process of industrialization during this period, see O. Muñoz, *Chile y su Industrialización: pasado, crisis y opciones* (Santiago, 1986). For the Popular Unity period the best book is S. Bitar, *Transición, Socialismo y Democracia: la experiencia Chilena* (Mexico, D.F., 1979; Eng. trans. *Chile: Experiment in Democracy* Philadelphia, Pa., 1986). See also J. G. Palma (ed.), *La Via Chilena al Socialismo* (Mexico, D.F., 1973). For the economic consequences of the Pinochet dictatorship, see above, particularly Foxley, *Neo-conservative Experiments,* Ramos, *Neo-conservative economics,* Ffrench-Davis, 'The Monetarist Experiment in Chile', and CIEPLAN, *El Modelo Económico Chileno: Trayectoria de una Crítica* (Santiago, 1982).

The literature on the economics of the Cuban revolution is huge. See for example C. Mesa-Lago (ed.), *Revolutionary Change in Cuba* (Pittsburgh,

Penn., 1971), and *The Economy of Socialist Cuba. A Two-decade Appraisal* (Albuquerque, N. Mex., 1981); Claes Brundenius, *Revolutionary Cuba: The Challenge of Economic Growth and Equity* (Boulder, Col., 1984); F. Pérez-López, *Measuring Cuban Economic Performance* (Austin, Tex., 1987); and Andrew Zimbalist and Claes Brundenius, *The Cuban Economy. Measurement and Analysis of Socialist Performance* (Baltimore, Md., 1989).

On the role of finance in economic development the best book remains C. Kindleberger, *Manias, Panics and Crashes: a History of Financial Crises* (London, 1978). For an analysis of the 1980s debt crisis in an historical perspective, see C. Kindleberger, 'Historical perspective on today's Third World debt problem', in C. Kindleberger, *Keynesianism vs. Monetarism and Other Essays in Financial History* (London, 1985). On the negative consequences for both LDCs *and* DMEs of the large transfer of financial resources from the Third World Keynes' *The Economic Consequences of Peace* (London, 1919) remains indispensable. See also M. Marcel and J. G. Palma, 'Third World Debt and its Effects on the British Economy: a southern view of economic mismanagement in the North', *Cambridge Journal of Economics,* 12, 3 (1988): 341–400. and J. G. Palma, 'UK Lending to the Third World from the 1973 oil shock to the 1980s Debt Crisis: on financial "manias, panics and (near) crashes" ', in P. Arestis and V. Chick, *Financial Development and Structural Change: a Post-Keynesian Perspective* (London, 1994).

Carlos Díaz-Alejandro's analyses of Latin America external finances remain the most influential. See for example, 'Latin American Debt: I don't think we are in Kansas anymore', *Brookings Papers on Economic Activity,* 2 (1984), and 'Some aspects of the development crisis in Latin America', in R. Thorp and L. Whitehead (eds), *Latin American Debt and the Adjustment Crisis* (Oxford, 1987). See also R. Ffrench-Davis and R. Devlin, *Una Breve Historia de la Crisis de la Deuda Latinoamericana* (ECLA, Santiago, 1992) and 'Diez años de crisis de la deuda latinoamericana', *Comercio Exterior* 43 (1993); R. Devlin, 'External Finance and Commercial Banks: the role in Latin America's capacity to import between 1951 and 1975', *Cepal Review,* 5, 1978: 63–97; E. Bacha and C. Díaz-Alejandro, 'Los mercados financieros: una visión desde la semi-periferia', in R. Ffrench-Davis (ed.), *Las Relaciones Financieras Externas: su efecto en la economía latinoamericana* (Mexico, D.F., 1983); C. Díaz-Alejandro, 'International finance: issues of especial interest for developing countries', in R. Ffrench-Davis and E. Tironi (eds), *Latin America and the New International Economic Order;* R. Ffrench-

Davis (ed.), *Relaciones Financieras Externas: su efecto en la economía latinoamericana* (Mexico, 1983); M. Wionczek (eds), *Politics and Economics of the Latin American Debt Crisis* (Boulder, Col., 1985); S. Griffith-Jones, *Managing World Debt,* (New York, 1988); J. Williamson, *Latin American Adjustment: how much has happened* (Washington, D.C., 1990); R. Devlin, *Debt and Crisis in Latin America: the supply side of the story* (Princeton, N.J., 1989).

L. Taylor, in his University of Cambridge 'Marshall Lectures' (*Varieties of Stabilization Experiences,* Oxford, 1989), discusses critically many of the region's stabilization experiences during the 1980s and concludes that '[financial and trade] liberalization and regressive income distribution were not a wise policy mix'. P. Meller, 'Un enfoque analítico-empírico de las causas del actual endeudamiento externo chileno', *Collección Estudios CIEPLAN,* 20 (1988), and R. Ffrench-Davis and J. de Gregorio, 'Orígenes y efectos del endeudamiento externo en Chile', *El Trimestre Económico,* 54 (1987), reach a similar conclusion.

The exception to the 'dance of the millions' during the 1970s is the case of Colombia; see G. Perry, R. Junguito and N. de Junguito, 'Política económica y endeudamiento externo en Colombia', and E. Bacha, 'Apertura financiera y sus efectos en el desarrollo nacional', both in R. Ffrench-Davis (ed.), *Relaciones Financieros Externas.*

On Latin American economic integration the ideas of Prebisch were the most influential during the early part of this period; see *The Latin American Common Market* (New York, 1959). For analysis of ECLA and Prebisch's ideas on the subject, see V. L. Urquidi, *Trayectoria del Mercado Común Latinoamericano* (Mexico, D.F., 1960); O. Rodriquez, *La Teoría del Subdesarrollo de la CEPAL;* J. Hodara, *Prebisch y La Cepal;* and A. Gurrieri, *La Obra de Prebisch en la CEPAL.*

Reviews of the Latin American economic integration experience are contained in INTAL's annual reports on Latin American economic integration; R. Ffrench-Davis, 'Economic integration in Latin America. Failures and successes', in R. Garnaut (ed.), *ASEAN in a Changing Pacific and World Economy* (Canberra, 1980); 'Economic Integration in Latin America', in BID, *Economic and social progress in Latin America;* G. Rosenthal, 'Un examen critico a treinta años de integración en América Latina', ECLA, November 1990; V. Bulmer-Thomas, *Political Economy of Central America since 1920;* and J. M. Salazar, 'Present and Future Integration in Central America', *Cepal Review,* 42 (1991).

On intra-Latin American trade in manufactures, see BID-INTAL, *El Comercio Intra-Latinoamericano en los Años 80* (Washington, D.C., 1987). On tariff preferences, see A. Aninat, R. Ffrench-Davis and P. Leiva, 'La integración andina en el nuevo escenario de los años ochenta', in H. Muñoz and F. Orrego (eds), *La Cooperación Regional en América Latina* (Mexico, D.F., 1987).

On foreign direct investment and transnational corporations in regional integration, see E. Tironi, 'Economic Integration and Foreign Direct Investment Policies: the Andean case', unpublished Ph.D. thesis, MIT, 1976; E. Lahera and F. Sánchez, *Estudio Comparativo de la Decisión 24 en los Paises del Grupo Andino: situación actual y perspectivas* (Santiago, 1985); and E. White, "Las inversiones extranjeras y la crisis económica en América Latina', in R. E. Feinberg and R. Ffrench-Davis (eds), *Debt and Development in Latin America.* On NAFTA (a free trade zone between the United States, Canada and Mexico which would be the largest in the world with a combined GDP in 1990 of US$6.2 trillion and US$720 billion combined exports), see S. Saborio, *The Premise and the Promise: Free Trade in the Americas* (Oxford, 1992). The 'Argentina-Brazil' accord of July 1986 was the most outstanding bilateral agreement of the 1980s, covering issues as varied as the renegotiation of tariff preferences, binational firms, investment funds, biotechnology, economic research and nuclear coordination. See INTAL, 'Nuevos acuerdos para consolidar la integración Argentino-Brasileña', *Integración Latinoamericana,* 129 (1987).

On Latin American income distribution there are very few country or comparative analyses. As is well known, data for income distribution is rather unreliable due to both methodological problems and the fact that it is an extremely sensitive political issue. The best source is ECLA; see especially its publications in the *Serie Distribución del Ingreso* (for example, No. 3, 'Antecedentes estadísticos de la distribución del ingreso en Chile, 1940–82', Santiago, 1987). See also, A. di Filippo, 'Raíces históricas de las estructuras distributivas en América Latina', ECLA, *Serie Monografías* No. 18, 2nd edn (Santiago, 1983); and ECLA, 'Estructura del gasto en consumo de los hogares según finalidad del gasto, por grupos de ingreso', *Cuadernos Estadísticos de la CEPAL,* 8 (Santiago, 1984).

The most interesting and influential work on income distribution within ECLA was done by Fernando Fajnzylber; see especially 'Industrialización en América Latina: de la 'caja negra' al 'casillero vacio', *Cuadernos de la Cepal* 60 (Santiago, 1990), and *Unavoidable Industrial Re-*

structuring in Latin America, cited above. Also, ECLA, *Transformación Productiva con Equidad* (Santiago, 1990), probably the organization's most influential publication since Prebisch's death, was strongly influenced by Fajnzylber's ideas.

Another U.N. organization, PREALC, has done extensive research on income distribution, particularly in its relationship with the labour market. See for example *Buscando la Equidad* (Santiago, 1986), p. 28. See also R. Infante, *Mercado de Trabajo y Deuda Social en los 80* (Santiago, 1991).

The World Bank also publishes data on income distribution for some Latin American countries; see its yearly *World Development Report* (Washington, D.C., various issues). For work on income distribution related to some countries of the region done within the Bank's framework, see G. Psacharopoulos, *Essays on Poverty, Equity and Growth* (New York, 1991).

A. Foxley (ed.) *Distribución del Ingreso* (Mexico, D.F., 1974), and O. Muñoz (ed.), *Distribución del ingreso en América Latina* (Buenos Aires, 1979) are valuable collections of articles on Latin American income distribution. For an excellent analysis of political issues related to distributional conflict, see A. O. Hirschman and M. Rothschild, 'Changing Tolerance for Inequality in Development', *Quarterly Journal of Economics,* 87/4 (1973): 544–66.

On Brazilian income distribution, see A. Fishlow, 'Distribución del ingreso por tramos en Brasil', in A. Foxley, *Distribución del Ingreso,* and 'Brazilian size distribution of income', *American Economic Review* 62 (1972), and C. H. Wood and J. A. Magno de Carvalho, *The Demography of Inequality in Brazil* (Cambridge, 1988). On Chile, see F. J. Labbé and L. Riveros, 'La visión neoclásica y la actual distribución de los ingresos en Chile', Documento de Trabajo No. 33, CED (Santiago, 1987). On Colombia, see ECLA, 'La distribución del ingreso en Colombia. Antecedentes estadisticos y caracteristicas socioeconómicas de los receptores', *Cuadernos Estadísticos de la Cepal* 14, 1988. On Mexico, see N. Lustig, *Mexico: the social impact of adjustment* (Brookings Institution, Washington, D.C., 1991). On Peru, see R. C. Webb, *Government Policy and the Distribution of Income in Peru, 1963–73* (Princeton, N.J., 1972).

On poverty in Latin America, see especially O. Altimir, 'La dimención de la pobreza en América Latina', *Cuadernos de la Cepal,* 27 (1979); and 'The Extent of Poverty in Latin America', *World Bank Staff Working Paper,* 522 (1982). Altimir's definition of the 'poverty line' is country specific and is based on an amount equal to twice the cost of a nutritionally adequate diet. That of the 'indigence line' is an income that would only cover this diet once. See also Sergio Molina, 'Poverty: description and analysis of policies for overcoming it', *Cepal Review,* 18 (1982): 87–110; PREALC, *Deuda Social: qué es?, cuánto es?, cómo se paga?* (Santiago, 1988); CELADE, *Boletín demográfico,* January 1985 and July 1987; and E. Cardoso and A. Helwege, 'Below the Line: poverty in Latin America', *World Development,* 20/1 (January 1992): 19–37.

P. Musgrove, 'Food Needs and Absolute Poverty in urban South America', *Review of Income and Wealth,* 30/1 (March, 1985): 63–83 is a study of nutrition in ten Latin American cities in 1966–9. A. Gilbert and J. Gugler, *Cities, Poverty and Development: Urbanization in the Third World* (Oxford, 1992) includes an examination of the relationship between the hypertrophy of Latin America's service sector, income distribution and poverty. Finally, see ECLA, *Una estimación de la magnitud de la pobreza en Chile, 1987* (Santiago, 1990); *Panorama Social de América Latina* (Santiago, 1991); and *Magnitud de la Pobreza en América Latina en los Años Ochenta* (Santiago, 1991).

5. URBAN GROWTH AND URBAN SOCIAL STRUCTURE IN LATIN AMERICA, 1930–1990

There are few historical accounts that summarize the general processes of urbanization in Latin America or that provide histories of particular Latin American cities for the entire period since 1930. A valuable account of the early (1940s and 1950s) urbanization processes is Philip Hauser (ed.), *Urbanization in Latin America* (New York, 1961), which was published by the United Nations Educational, Scientifice and Cultural Organization (UNESCO), reflecting its new-found preoccupation with urban issues in developing countries. The issues covered were demographic trends, employment, economic development, migration, housing, and planning. Richard Morse, 'Latin American Cities: aspects of function and structure', *Comparative Studies in Society and History,* 16/4 (1961–2): 473–93, reviews research on urbanization in the 1950s and early 1960s, and his two part article, 'Trends and Issues in Latin American Urban Research, 1965–1970,' *Latin American Research Review* 6, 1 and 2 (1971): 3–52 and 19–75, examines trends in the mid- and late-1960s. An important source of information and analysis is the annual series *Latin American Urban Research,* which was published by Sage (Beverly Hills, Cal.) from 1970 to 1976, each year having a different thematic focus, including migration, urban poverty, and metropolitanization.

From a more anthropological perspective Douglas Butterworth and John Chance, *Latin American Urbanization* (Cambridge, 1981) takes account of studies carried out in the 1940s, but concentrates on the 1960s and 1970s. The demographic perspective, analysing the evolution of urban primacy and the preoccupation with rapid population and urban growth in Latin America, is found in Glenn H. Beyer (ed.), *The Urban Explosion in Latin America* (Ithaca, N.Y., 1967). A more recent analysis of trends in city growth and urbanization is Robert W. Fox, *Urban Population Trends in Latin America* (Washington, D.C., 1975). There are a number of overviews of the urbanization process provided by geographers and planners. One of the most complete is Jorge Hardoy's broad survey, *Urbanization in Latin America* (Garden City, N.J., 1975), that includes pre-colonial as well as more contemporary patterns. It provides a model of the stages of change in Latin American urbanization, focussing on the functions of the cities in different periods. Alan Gilbert, Jorge Hardoy and Ronaldo Ramirez, *Urbanization in Contemporary Latin America* (Chichester, 1982), cover political and social trends, but also focus on the physical growth of cities, particularly the development of infrastructure and housing.

In the 1970s, there was an increasing concern with the political economy of urban growth in Latin America, emphasizing the interconnection between politics, economic development and patterns of urbanization. One of the first examples is Paul Singer, *Economia Política da Urbanização* (São Paulo, 1973), which interpreted both the growth and the social problems of the large cities of Latin America as a reflection of the uneven process of capitalist development. A similar perspective is taken by Bryan Roberts, *Cities of Peasants* (London, 1978) which provides an account of urban development in comparative perspective since the 1940s, but concentrates on the 1960s and 1970s. Alejandro Portes and John Walton, *Urban Latin America: the Political Condition from Above and Below* (Austin, Tex., 1976) also provides comparative data on Latin American urbanization and its social consequences, and in a second volume, *Labor, Class and the International System* (New York, 1981), Portes and Walton place the Latin American experience within the context of the development of the world economy.

The major sources of data on the overall pattern of urbanization in Latin America are the population censuses of the different countries of the region. Several Latin American countries have censuses from the end of the nineteenth century, permitting the analysis of long trends. By 1940, most Latin American countries conducted a general population survey. These surveys include data on age and sex distributions of the population, their occupations, and, often, data on migration, ethnicity and religion. Some countries have carried out decennial censuses from that period (Mexico, Brazil and Argentina from 1947), while others have been less regular (Peru, Colombia). In general, the accuracy and comparability of the censuses have increased with time, though the lack of institutional continuity in the offices responsible for the censuses has, at times, resulted in loss of comparability through using different criteria of classification. One of the major factors in improving the censuses has been the influence of the United Nations in persuading governments to use standard classifications for characteristics such as definition of urban, occupation and industry. By 1960, all the major Latin American countries subscribed to the international conventions, and the census data can be compared more easily, though always with caution. A detailed analysis of the changes in classification can be found in Doreen S. Goyer and Eliane Domsdke, *The Handbook of National Population Censuses* (Westport, Conn., 1983).

Another important source of urban data are the household surveys carried out by the statistical offices to monitor changes in fertility, migration and labour force. Because of their smaller size and greater availability in raw data form, these have the advantage over the censuses of enabling researchers to cross-tabulate data at the household as well as individual level, and carry out multivariate analysis. In Mexico, data for the overall urban population and the three major metropolitan areas, was provided from the 1970s by the Encuesta Continua sobre Ocupación (The Ongoing Employment Survey). The Urban Labour Force Survey (ENEU) provides detailed data for specific cities on a quarterly basis, beginning in the 1980s. In Brazil, the PNAD (Pesquisa Nacional por Amostra de Domicilio) has provided similar data, with interruptions, since 1967: see Diana Sawyer (ed.), *PNAD em Foco* (Belo Horizonte, 1988).

Two of the countries that provide the best examples of detailed analyses of urbanization patterns using census data are Argentina and Mexico. Researchers from CENEP (Center for Population Studies), such as Zulma Rechinni and Alfredo Lattes, have carried various analyses through the years of the changing patterns of Argentine urbanization. *La Población de Argentina* (Buenos Aires, 1975) contains detailed analyses up to 1970 of migration (both internal and international), changes in the urban system, urban growth and changes in the labor force. Alfredo Lattes, *Algunas Dimensiones de la Urbanización Reciente y Futura en América Latina* (Buenos Aires, 1984) updates the analysis to the 1980, and places it within the general Latin American picture, providing statistics on changes in labor force, and in city size distributions. In Mexico, perhaps the first systematic analysis was carried out by Harley L. Browning, 'Urbanization in Mexico', (unpublished Ph.D. thesis, Berkeley, Cal., 1962), in his account of the nature of urban primacy, and the changes in the Mexican urban system. The Colegio de México's *La Dinámica de la Población de México* (Mexico, D.F., 1970) provides an analysis comparable to that of *La Población de Argentina*. The most comprehensive analysis remains that of Luis Unikel, Constancio Ruiz and Gustavo Garza, *El Desarrollo Urbano de México* (Mexico, D.F., 1976); the authors combine economic and population censuses to analyse the economic specialization of cities and its relation to population growth and labour force characteristics. For Brazil, Juarez Brandão Lopez, *Desenvolvimento e Mundança Social* (São Paulo, 1976) provides an overview and interpretation of urbanization which also uses available census material. A good example of using partial data to provide an analysis of urbanization in the absence of census data is José Matos Mar, *Las Barriadas de Lima* (Lima, 1957). There were no Peruvian censuses between 1940 and 1961, and Matos Mar brings together survey data on the processes of migration and urban settlement to provide an account of the pattern of population concentration in Lima.

The rapid urban growth of Latin America that began in the 1940s was based, to an important extent, on migration from rural to urban areas. Migration brought to the towns and cities of Latin America a population that, at times, was ethnically distinct, and, often, of lower socio-economic and educational levels in comparison to urban natives. This circumstance created a research agenda that focussed on two main issues: the origins of migrants and the reasons for their migration; and how they fared in the cities compared with native residents. The classic analysis of migration and its consequence for urban social structure can be found in Gino Germani's two major works *Política y Sociedad en una Epoca de Transición* (Buenos Aires, 1968) and *Estructura Social de la Argentina* (1955; Buenos Aires, 1987). His analysis concentrates on the difference between the earlier international migration and the subsequent internal migrations and its consequences for class differences and politics in Buenos Aires.

The migration programme of the Population and Development Commission of CLACSO (Latin American Council of Social Sciences) initiated in the early 1970s studies of the overall patterns of migration in Latin America. This programme also gave rise to theoretical discussions of the economic and social factors affecting rural-urban movements, of which Humberto Muñoz, Orlandina de Oliveira, Paul Singer and Claudio Stern, *Las migraciones internas en América Latina* (Buenos Aires, 1974) was perhaps the most influential on the direction of future research.

An important characteristic of the studies of rural-urban migration and migrant adaptation in specific countries was their use of surveys carried out in places of origin and/or destination, rather than estimates based on censuses. In Jorge Balán, Harley L. Browning and Elizabeth Jelín, *Men in a Developing Society: Geographic and Social Mobility in Monterrey* (Austin, Tex., 1973) the analysis was based both on a survey in Monterrey, and on one carried out in a village, Cedral, from which many Monterrey migrants came. The Monterrey study like the subsequent study of Mexico City by Humberto Muñoz, Orlandina de Oliveira and Claudio Stern, *Migracion y Desigualdad Social en la Ciudad de México* (Mexico, D.F., 1977), analysed the absorption of rural and small town migrants into the urban economic structure. The economic success of migrants was shown, in both studies, to depend more on the job opportunities of the period of their arrival, than on cultural contrasts between migrants and natives. The selectivity of migration – whether migrants came from richer or poorer areas and were better qualified than those that did not move – was shown to be a significant factor in migrant adaption to the city in Colombia (Ramón Cardona, *La Migración Rural-Urbana* (Bogotá, 1978) as well as in Brazil (Douglas Graham, 'Divergent and Convergent Regional Economic Growth and Internal Migration in Brazil, 1940–1960', *Economic Development and Cultural Change,* 18/3(1970): 362–82) and in other countries of the region such as Chile (Juan Elizaga, *Migraciones a las areas metropolitanas de América Latina,* Santiago, 1970).

Adapting to the city is a complex process that is affected not only by selectivity, but by ongoing relations between place of origin and place of destination, and the capacity of migrants to establish their own communities in the place of destination. The pioneer study of these processes is Oscar Lewis, 'Urbanization Without Breakdown: a case study', *Scientific Monthly,* 75, 1 (1952), which looks at how migrants from the village of Tepotzlan, Mexico adapt to the city, while conserving their traditional forms of social organization. A more detailed study of these processes is Lourdes Arizpe, *Migración, etnicismo y cambio económico: un estudio sobre mi-*

grantes campesinos a la ciudad de México (Mexico, D.F., 1978) which shows how migrants from villages with very different economic structures used their networks in Mexico City to occupy particular niches in the city economy, with consequences for the likelihood of return migration. Other examples of studies of migrant adaption, emphasizing social networks and the factors in places of origin and destination affecting these are Robert Kemper's study of Tzintzuntzan migrants in Mexico City, *Migration and Adaptation* (Beverly Hills, Cal., 1977), and Douglas Butterworth's study of Tilantongo migrants to the same city, *Tilantongo, Comunidad Mixteca en Transición* (Mexico, D.F., 1975). Perhaps the most complete study of these processes in Mexico, taking into account rural as well as urban social structure, factors of attraction and repulsion, and the significance of household networks and strategies is Douglas Massey, Rafael Alarcon, Jorge Durand and Hector Gonzalez, *Return to Aztlan* (Berkeley, Cal., 1987). The major city of destination is not, however, Mexico City but Los Angeles. An interesting comparison with Mexican international migration is provided by Sherri Grasmuck and Patricia Pessar in *Between Two Islands* (Berkeley, Cal., 1991) in which they analyse Dominican rural and urban migration to New York.

Many studies of migrant adaption to Latin American cities were carried out, especially in the 1960s and 1970s. Examples from countries other than Mexico are Juarez Brandão's study of rural migrants in São Paulo, 'Aspects of the Adjustments of Rural Migrants to Urban-industrial Conditions', in Hauser (ed.), *Urbanization in Latin America,* Mario Margulis's study on provincial migrants in Buenos Aires, *Migración y Marginalidad en la Sociedad Argentina* (Buenos Aires, 1974), and Teofilo Altamirano's studies of Aymara and Quechua migration to Lima, *Presencia Andina en Lima Metropolitana* (Lima, 1984) and *Cultura Andina y Pobreza Urbana* (Lima, 1988). The concentration of adaption studies in countries such as Mexico and Peru is, to a certain extent, explained by the existence of an important indigenous population affected by the rapid urbanization of the respective countries. Studies of migrant adaption in Bolivia have acquired salience with the rapid growth of La Paz in recent years, though Hans Buechler's article on the role of fiestas in migrant adaptation is an antecedent: 'The Ritual Dimension of Rural-urban Networks: the fiesta system in the Northern Highlands of Bolivia', in William Mangin (ed.), *Peasants in Cities* (Boston, Mass., 1970). An interesting example is Godofredo Sandoval, Xavier Albó, and Tomas Greaves, *Nuevos Lazos con el Campo* (La Paz, 1987) on Aymara identity in La Paz.

Closely linked to the studies of migrant adaptation are those that look at social mobility within the cities of Latin America. Conscious of the rapid changes in the economic structure of Latin American cities from the 1940s onwards, various researchers took up the issues of whether or not a 'new' urban middle class was emerging, and the extent and significance of upward social mobility from manual to non-manual occupations. Since Argentina had the most developed urban economy of the region by the 1940s, the first studies were undertaken there under the direction of Gino Germani. See, besides Germani's own volumes cited above, Torcuato di Tella, *Argentina, Sociedad de Masas* (Buenos Aires, 1974), *Clases Sociales y Estructuras Políticas* (Buenos Aires, 1965), and *Estratificación Social e Inestabilidad Política en Argentina y Chile* (Buenos Aires, 1962), and José Luis Imaz, *La Clase Alta de Buenos Aires* (Buenos Aires, 1962) and *Los que Mandan* (Buenos Aires, 1964) which analyse the changes in the character of the urban middle class, explore the nature of urban upper class, and examine the changing composition of the working class with industrialization.

The intellectual climate within which these studies developed was that of the discussion of modernization as a global though uneven process. Latin American social scientists collaborated with their North American counterparts in exploring the possibilities of achieving a balanced development, and identifying the obstacles to that development. See, for example, Joseph Kahl (ed.), *La Industrialición en América Latina* (Mexico, D.F., 1965), Seymour Martin Lipset and Aldo Solari (eds), *Elites and Development in Latin America* (New York, 1967), and Irving Horowitz (ed.), *Masses in Latin America* (New York, 1968). Other collections were organized under the auspices of United Nations agencies: CEPAL's *El Desarrollo Social de América Latina en la Postguerra* (Santiago, 1966), and UNESCO's *Sociologia del Desarrollo* (Paris, 1970). All these volumes contain empirical analyses of the changing urban class structure in Latin America, and of social mobility, stressing the importance of education and of the rise of a white-collar service sector. The authors stress the differences in class structure between Latin America and the advanced industrial world. They use these differences to show the specificity of the changes in the Latin American occupational structures that result from the pattern of growth of the industrial sectors, such as the early importance of the service sectors and the weakness of manufacturing. In those countries with a more developed industrial structure, such as Argentina and Brazil, attention is given to the emergence of an industrial working class; while in countries such as

Peru, with little large-scale urban industry, emphasis is given, as will be seen in a subsequent section, to urban marginality.

Representative surveys of the economically active population of two Latin American cities permitted a more precise estimate of the extent of social mobility. In their study of Monterrey, *Men in a Developing Society,* Balán, Browning and Jelín used life and work histories to explore the pattern of mobility, both geographical and social, in the 1960s. They found, for instance, that overall levels of social mobility were as high as in the advanced industrial countries, though social origins and education had a different significance in enhancing life chances. Muñoz, Oliveira and Stern's similar study of Mexico City, *Migración y Desigualidad Social* also showed high levels of social mobility resulting from the expansion of non-manual as well as skilled manual jobs. Interestingly, they were able to link position in the occupational structure to the relative expansion of the different sectors of the economy at the moment when new workers entered the Mexico City labour market. Contrary to received opinion, this resulted in rural migrants becoming industrial workers in the manufacturing sector.

In the 1960s, there was already a growing preoccupation with theoretical issues to do with the dependency of Latin America, and its consequences for stifling and distorting development. In the field of urban stratification and mobility this resulted, in the 1970s, in fewer empirical analyses. The predominant analyses of class structure took up conceptual issues, but rarely were these related to empirical studies. Examples are Instituto de Investigaciones Sociales, Mexico, *Las Clases Sociales en América Latina* (Mexico, D.F., 1973) and *Clases Sociales y Crisis Política en América Latina* (Mexico, D.F., 1977), and Fernando Henrique Cardoso (ed.), *Estado y Sociedad en América Latina* (Buenos Aires, 1973).

The empirical tradition did not disappear. The 1970s and 1980s saw an expansion of qualitative analyses of urban social classes, particularly of the urban poor and these will be reviewed in a subsequent section. There were relatively few studies of the industrial working class and its formation. An example from Mexico is Menno Vellinga's study of class formation in Monterrey, *Industrialización, Burguesía y Clase Obrera* (Mexico, D.F., 1979). In *Con el Sudor de tu Frente* (Guadalajara, 1986), Agustín Escobar uses life histories and household data of over a 1000 manufacturing workers in Guadalajara, Mexico in 1982 to examine whether a clearly defined industrial working class was emerging in that city. Studies of the middle and upper classes are less common. John Walton's study of the elites of

Guadalajara and Monterrey in Mexico, and Medellín and Cali in Colombia, *Elites and Economic Development* (Austin, Tex., 1987) provides interesting data on the organization of elites under different economic conditions, on their attitude to the state, and on the economic sectors which they represent. Larissa Lomnitz and Marisol Pérez Lizuar, *A Mexican Elite Family, 1820–1980* (Princeton, N.J., 1986) carried out a case study of a Mexican elite family, analysing the changes in family organization and interests through time, and providing detailed information on the social networks that are used to enhance and consolidate their power. This study is particularly interesting since the family's fortunes have been tied to the evolution of the Mexico City economy, and the family has had to take account of the changing role of government in the economy.

By the late 1970s, there is a return to census based analysis of the evolution of the urban class structure. Some of the articles in Ruben Katzman and José Luis Reyna's *Fuerza de Trabajo y Movimientos Laborales en América Latina* (Mexico, D.F., 1979) use available data to explore the heterogeneity of the tertiary sector – containing 'informal' employment, modern middle-class employment as well as more traditional manual workers – and its link to changes in the class structure. An influential exploration of the heterogeneity of the tertiary sector is Harley Browning's discussion of the tertiarization process: 'Algunos problemas del proceso de terciarización en América Latina', in Jorge Hardoy and Richard Schaedel (eds), *Las Ciudades de América Latina* (Buenos Aires, 1975). Carlos Filgueira and Carlos Geneletti, *Estratificación y movilidad ocupacional en América Latina* (Santiago, 1981) provides an extensive analysis of the patterns of mobility between 1950 and 1980, contrasting the experience of the different Latin American countries. An even more complete analysis is provided by the social affairs division of CEPAL under the direction of John Durston, in *Transformación Ocupacional y Crisis Social en América Latina* (Santiago, 1989) which, among other analyses, looks at the role of education in social mobility from 1950 to 1980, and the changing significance of self-employment. CEPAL has an arrangement with the census authorities in Latin America whereby special tabulations from the Censuses or household surveys are provided on a regular basis. Consequently, CEPAL can carry out more detailed analyses of occupational change and mobility than can those researchers who have to rely only on official tabulations.

By the 1980s, some of the major sources of information on urban class structure were the studies of urban labour markets. These differ from the analyses of occupational mobility not only by having a more specific focus, but by making greater use of survey data and the re-analysis of the raw census data. An early example is by Victor Tokman and Paulo Souza (eds), *El Empleo en América Latina* (Mexico, D.F., 1976), which brings together a series of articles emphasizing the growing heterogeneity of labour markets and occupational structures in Latin America. PREALC's *Mercado de Trabajo en Cifras, 1950–1980* (Santiago, 1982) brings together a comprehensive set of data on labour market trends for the 1980s. The most detailed analysis, though based on one country, of the evolution of labour markets is Brigida García's account of changes in Mexican labour markets, both at the national and regional level: *Desarrollo Económico y Absorción de la Fuerza de Trabajo en México, 1950–1980* (Mexico, D.F., 1988).

New themes emerge such as the increase in female labor force participation. Useful analyses for the whole of Latin America are Edith Pantelides, *Estudio de la Población Feminina Economicamente Activa en América Latina, 1950–1970* (Buenos Aires, 1976) and Elizabeth Jelín, *La Mujer y la Mercado de Trabajo Urbano,* Estudios CEDES, Vol. 1, No. 6 (Buenos Aires, 1979). Good analyses exist of these changes for individual countries such as, for Argentina, Zulma Recchini de Lattes, *Dinámica de la Fuerza de Trabajo Feminino en la Argentina* (Buenos Aires, 1983); for Brazil, Cristina Bruschini, *Tendências da Força de Trabalho Feminina Brasileira nos Anos Setenta e Oitenta* (São Paulo, 1989); and, for Mexico, Orlandina de Oliveira and Brigida García 'Expansión del trabajo feminino y transformación social en México: 1950–87', in *La Sociedad Mexicana en el Umbral del Milenio* (Mexico, D.F., 1990). Accompanying this interest in the general changes in female labour force participation was one in the forms of work that women did. John Humphrey's study of women workers in a Brazilian plant, *Gender and Work in the Third World: Sexual Divisions in Brazilian Industry* (London, 1987), showed both how women were undertaking new types of skilled work, and how the jobs that women did were devalued in comparison to those of men.

An increasing preoccupation in the 1970s and 1980s, particularly of PREALC (the International Labour Office's Latin American branch), is with the so-called informal economy. PREALC's concern has been with the consequences of the growth of micro-enterprise (defined to include the self-employed) for urban poverty in Latin America. PREALC's analyses have tended to rely on census data and urban employment surveys. Consequently, the findings concentrate on the individual characteristics of those in the informal economy, and pay less attention to the organization of enterprises and their linkages with the rest of the economy. Good examples of PREALC's approach and analyses are Victor Tokman, 'El sector informal: quince años después', *El Trimestre Económico,* 215 (1987): 513–36, and the volumes *Urbanización y Sector Informal en América Latina,* 60–80 (Santiago, 1990) and *Empleo en América Latina y la Heterogenidad del Sector Informal* Documentos de Trabajo No. 346 (Santiago, 1990). Case studies of the workings of informal enterprises and of their linkages to the rest of the economy are found in Ray Bromley, *Casual Work and Poverty in Third World Cities* (Chichester, 1979) and in Alejandro Portes, Manuel Castells and Lauren Benton, *The Informal Economy* (Baltimore, Md., 1989). A valuable set of studies comparing the informal sector in five of the Central American countries is Juan-Pablo Pérez Sainz and Rafael Menjivar, *Informalidad Urbana en Centroamérica* (San José, 1991). These studies combine survey data with case material on micro-enterprises to provide an overview of the impact of the economic and political crises of the 1980s on the Central American urban economies.

Since labour markets depend both on the structure of demand and on that of supply, their analysis links research on class structure and social mobility to changes in the organization of industry and the services. Fernando Fajnzylber, *La Industrialización Trunca de América Latina* (Buenos Aires, 1983) points to the changes that followed the ending of the import substitution model of industrialization as some Latin American countries sought to develop export industrialization, while others stagnated as they failed to find a new niche. Since the new industries and the services linked to them have specific labour requirements, and since they often have a pronounced regional location, they are likely to increase the heterogeneity of the class structure, both within countries and between countries.

Though the Latin American cities of the 1930s and 1940s contained considerable numbers of poor people, urban poverty did not become an issue for analysis and policy until the 1950s, and a major issue only in the 1970s and particularly in the 1980s (as a result of the economic crisis). In the earlier period, the major social problems of the cities tended to be seen as resulting from the mass migration of an unacculturated rural population. Indeed, what was to become one of the major influences on poverty research, Oscar Lewis's various studies of poor families In Mexico City and in San Juan (Puerto Rico), originated in a pre-occupation with the adjustment of rural migrants to the city. The 'Culture of Poverty' thesis, as developed in such works as *Children of Sanchez* (New York, 1961) and *La*

Vida (New York, 1966) emphasized the fatalism of the poor and their social and economic marginality. These themes became prominent in the work of Chilean sociologists who described the spatial as well as the social isolation of the poor in Santiago de Chile, living in irregular settlements without urban services or adequate housing. See, for example, Roger Vekemans and Jorge Giusti, 'Marginality and Ideology in Latin American Development', *Studies in Comparative International Development,* 5 (1969/70). These studies of the 1950s and early 1960s tended to emphasize the incapacity of the poor to help themselves. This was challenged by an increasing number of studies in the 1960s that documented the various strategies that poor people used to overcome their poverty. In a series of articles, for example, 'Housing settlement types, arrangements for living, proletarianization and the social structure of the city', in Wayne Cornelius and Felicity Trueblood (eds), *Latin American Urban Research* (Beverly Hills, 1974), Anthony Leeds showed the ways in which the poor helped build the Latin American cities of the 1960s through land invasion, self-constructed housing and small-scale economic enterprise. The theme was elaborated by William Mangin, 'Latin American Squatter Settlements: a problem and a solution', *Latin American Research Review* 2/3 (1967): 65–95 and for Peru by Jose Matos Mar, *Urbanización y Barriadas en América del Sur* (Lima, 1968). In the 1960s, there were a series of city studies of poverty based on intensive case studies of urban neighbourhoods. The titles of these studies are indicative of the emphasis on the active role of people and their networks in coping with urban life: see, for example, Teodor Caplow's and Sheldon Stryker's study of San Juan, Puerto Rico, *The Urban Ambience* (Totowa, N.J., 1964), Lisa Peattie's study of Ciudad Guyana, *The View from the Barrio* (Ann Arbor, Mich., 1968), Bryan Roberts' study of Guatemala City, *Organizing Strangers* (Austin, Tex., 1973), Janice Perlman's study of Rio de Janeiro, *The Myth of Marginality* (Berkeley, Cal., 1976), and Larissa Lomnitz's study of Mexico, D.F., *Networks and Marginality* (New York, 1977).

In the 1970s and 1980s, studies of poverty focussed increasingly on working-class households and their wider relationships. Comparisons with households from other social classes became more common in the 1980s as one means to assess the impact of the economic crisis of these years on the different sectors of the urban population. These studies have often combined survey data with ethnographic materials to explore household organization over the household life cycle. They have focussed on the economic contributions made by different household members and the tensions, as well as solidarities, created by the need to combine forces in face of economic difficulty. A general review is provided by Marianne Schmink, 'Household Economic Strategies: Review and Research Agenda', *Latin American Research Review,* 19, 3 (1984): 87–101. A useful study for Chile is Dagmar Raczynski and Claudía Serrano, *Mujer y Familia en un Sector Popular Urbano* (Santiago, 1984) which looks particularly at strategies in the face of unemployment. Brígida García, Humberto Muñoz and Orlandina de Oliveira compare family strategies in two Brazilian cities, one from the Center-south, São José dos Campos, and one from the Northeast, Recife, in *Familia y Mercado de Trabajo* (Mexico, D.F., 1983). Elisabete Bilac, *Famílias de Trabalhadores* (São Paulo, 1978) looked at the difference between middle- and working-class families in São Paulo. Elizabeth Jelin and Marie Carmen Feijoo, *Trabajo y Familia en el Ciclo de Vida Feminina* (Buenos Aires, 1978) looked at the daily life of working-class families in Buenos Aires and their survival strategies over a period of three years. In Mexico, a series of studies have tried to look at changes over time, whether by re-interviewing the same families at different moments, by taking comparable samples at different times, or by using life histories to reconstruct patterns of change. Mercedes González de la Rocha, *Recursos de la Pobreza* (Guadalajara, 1986) begins the analysis of poor families in Guadalajara, Mexico, at the high point of Mexico's economic boom, and she follows the same families through the crisis years of the 1980s. Henry Selby, Arthur Murphy and Stephen Lorenzen, *The Mexican Urban Household* (Austin, Tex., 1990) provide a view of the household economy in several Mexican cities in the 1970s and look at the situation in one of these cities, Oaxaca, in the 1980s. In a study of Querétaro in 1982 and in 1988 and of Puerto Vallarta and León in 1988, Sylvia Chant, *Women and Survival in Mexican Cities* (Manchester, 1991), compares the family structure and coping strategies of low-income households, examining the ways in which different types of family (single parent, nuclear, extended) make life easier (or otherwise) for the adult woman.

There was an early interest in the urban ecology of Latin America, reflecting in part studies made in the United States. Thus in the 1940s and 1950s there were several studies of the spatial organization of large Latin American cities. See, for example, Teodor Caplow, 'The Social Ecology of Guatemala City', *Social Forces,* 28, 2 (1949) which emphasized the 'traditional' pattern of spatial organization with the major governmental and commercial functions, as well as elite housing, located in the centre of the city. Ruben Reina's *Parana* (Austin, Tex., 1973) followed this emphasis, emphasizing the relatively clear spatial segregation of the different social sectors in Paraná, Argentina.

The studies of the 1970s and 1980s tended to link spatial organization with the peculiar pattern of economic development in the region, emphasizing the over-concentration in the largest cities. John Friedman's studies in Chile and Venezuela, *Regional Development Policy: a Case Study of Venezuela* (Cambridge, Mass., 1966) and *Urban and Regional Development in Chile* (Santiago, 1969), argued for the construction of regional growth poles. In his later studies, such as *Life Space and Economic Space* (New Brunswick, N.J., 1988), Friedman was more pessimistic about regional planning in the face of capitalist development in Latin America. He pointed to the huge imbalances created by the economic growth of the 1970s, and the urgent need to decentralize urban political and economic systems.

The concern with these imbalances led to an interest in the 1970s and 1980s in the phenomenon of intermediate cities. Jorge Hardoy and David Satterthwaite, *Small and Intermediate Urban Centers* (London, 1986) provide data showing the increasing importance of intermediate centres relative to the large metropolises, while Thompson Andrade documents the diversification of the Brazilian urban system in *Sistema urbano e cidades médias no Brasil* (Rio de Janeiro, 1979). Another set of small and intermediate urban centers that have been relatively neglected in research are the cities of the Caribbean and Central America. Useful data on these cities for the period from the 1960s onwards are given in the two volumes edited by Alejandro Portes and Mario Lungo, *Urbanización en Centroamérica* (San José, 1992) and *Urbanización en el Caribe* (San José, 1992).

Although the studies of urban neighbourhoods reviewed in the previous section provide rich ethnographic data on the nature of urban life, they do not give an overall picture of the dynamics of urban spatial organization, and the factors shaping that organization. Alan Gilbert and Peter Ward, *Housing, the State and the Poor* (Cambridge, 1988) provides such a picture for Colombia and Mexico in the 1970s and early 1980s, showing the way that the urban land market brings even squatter settlements into its orbit. Raquel Rolnik, Lúcio Kowarik and Nadia Somekh, *São Paulo: Crise e Mundança* (São Paulo, 1991), brings together an impressive set of data describing the changes in São Paulo's spatial organization in the 1980s, and its implications for the distribution of poverty. A comparative review of urban development and urban poverty is given in Matthew Edel and Ronald Hellman (eds), *Cities in Crisis: the Urban Challenge in the Americas* (New York, 1989).

The social actors responsible for changing urban space – squatters, construction companies, land developers, and the state – feature in Marta Schteingart's analysis of the chaotic construction of Mexico City, *Los Productores del Espacio Habitable* (Mexico, D.F., 1990). The logic that attends this disorder – that of a poorly regulated and uneven capitalist development – is described in Lúcio Kowarik, *A Espoliação Urbana* (Rio de Janeiro, 1980), concentrating mainly on the case of São Paulo.

The importance of the state in regulating – or not regulating – urban development is the theme of several volumes: Gustavo Garza and Marta Schteingart, *La Acción Habitacional del Estado en México* (Mexico, D.F., 1978) reviews housing policies in Mexico since the 1960s; Oscar Yujnovsky provides an overview of Argentine government policies on housing since the 1940s in *Claves Políticas del Problema Habitacional Argentino* (Buenos Aires, 1984); Gil Shidlo, *Social Policy in a Non-Democratic Regime* (Boulder, Col., 1990) concentrates on the various forms of state subsidy for housing in Brazil, and how these subsidies rarely reach the poorest sectors of the urban population. The close relationship between urban spatial organization, poor physical infrastructure, and social deprivation that has emerged as a result of the rapid growth of Latin America's cities is explored in Peter Ward's *Mexico City* (London, 1990). Claude Bataillon and Louis Panabière provide a somewhat different perspective of the same city, exploring urban symbolism, customs and the culture of the different zones in *Mexico Aujourd'hui: La Plus Grande Ville du Monde* (Paris, 1988). One account that combines ethnographic data and other data to provide a general account of a city's development and of its spatial and social organization is Leo Despres, *Manaus* (Albany, 1991).

There have been relatively few studies that focus specifically on the urban politics of Latin America. The studies of Germani, Di Tella, and Imaz, mentioned above, focus on urban politics in Argentina, but their aim is to illuminate the general process of political change. Wayne Cornelius, *Politics and the Migrant Poor in Mexico City* (Stanford, Cal., 1975) was one of the first to use specifically urban variables – in his case, the legality of neighbourhoods – to understand the pattern of urban politics. His emphasis on the vertical relationships of patronage and clientelism that structure urban politics is echoed and extended in David Collier's *Squatters and*

Oligarchs (Baltimore, Md., 1973), which examines the underpinnings of authoritarian rule in Peru. For Mexico, Jorge Alonso brings together a collection of papers on social movements in the metropolitan area of Mexico City, *Los Movimientos Sociales en el Valle de México* (Mexico, D.F., 1985), and Jorge Montaño, *Los Pobres de la Ciudad en los Asentamientos Espontaneos* (Mexico, D.F., 1976) provides an account of urban social movements in Monterrey. Ernesto Pastrana and Monica Threlfall, *Pan, Techo y Poder: El movimiento de pobladores en Chile (1970–1973)* (Buenos Aires, 1974) examines the different strategies used by political parties in Chile to secure the support of low-income urban inhabitants such as clientelism, incorporation, and grass-roots mobilization, and show the limitations of each up to the military coup of 1973. The Chilean urban movements are re-evaluated in Manuel Castells, *The City and the Grassroots* (London, 1983), which provides an overview of what Castells calls the social basis of urban populism, using cases of urban movements of the 1970s in Lima, and Mexico City as well as Santiago de Chile.

6. THE AGRARIAN STRUCTURES OF LATIN AMERICA, 1930–1990

There are few detailed historical studies of changes in the agrarian structure in the period. There are exceptions, but these are cases studies of local-level processes. One of these exceptions is Luis González, *Pueblo en vilo: Microhistoria de San José de Gracia* (Mexico, D.F., 1972); Eng. trans. *San José de Gracia: Mexican village in transition* (Austin, Tex., 1974), a careful reconstruction of social and economic change in the Mexican historian's home town, which is the centre of a mainly ranching economy in the west of Mexico. A useful historical account, written by an anthropologist, again for Mexico and for a ranching economy, is Franz Schryer, *The Rancheros of Pisaflores: the History of a Petty Bourgeosie in Twentieth Century Mexico* (Toronto, 1980), which traces political and social change up to the late 1970s. Gavin Smith, *Livelihood and Resistance: Peasants and the Politics of Land in Peru* (Berkeley, Cal., 1989) is also written by an anthropologist, and provides a detailed historical study of the struggles of one community for land from 1850 to the mid-1970s, showing how changes in livelihood affected political action and consciousness. For Brazil, Verena Stolcke's *Coffee Planters, Workers and Wives* (London, 1988) gives a history of the labour system on the São Paulo coffee plantations from 1850 to 1980, as it passed from slavery to forms of share-cropping to casual wage labour.

Reconstructing the history of rural change in Latin America since 1930 depends on three major sources. First are the population and agricultural censuses for individual countries. These become more generally available from the 1950s onwards, though some countries, such as Brazil, Argentina, and Mexico, have agricultural censuses from the turn of the century. Second are the mainly anthropological studies of local communities in Latin America, of which there are relatively few in the 1930s and 1940s, though increasing rapidly in number from the 1950s onwards. Third are surveys of rural conditions sponsored by government or international agencies which become more frequent as international aid programmes expand, especially in the 1960s.

The anthropological studies of the 1930s and 1940s sought to document the nature of indigenous rural society in Latin America. The anthropologists were mainly North American, and were influenced by the ethnographic and functionalist traditions first developed in studies of Africa and Asia. In Latin America, they adapted their approach to take account of the greater market and urban involvement of rural populations, but still tended to choose field locations in what appeared to be relatively isolated areas with a strong indigenous culture. A classic example is Robert Redfield's study of *Tepotzlán* (Chicago, Ill., 1930) which, in the 1920s, was a village of mainly Nahuatl speaking Indians in the Mexican state of Morelos. *The Handbook of South American Indians,* 7 vols (Smithsonian Institution, Washington, D.C., 1946–59), edited by Julian Steward, documents the diversity of rural cultures through various ethnographic reports.

The 1940s also saw a series of surveys of agriculture and agricultural populations often instigated by US government agencies concerned with hemispheric resources and security. Carl Taylor's survey of rural Argentina, *Rural Life in Argentina* (Baton Rouge, La., 1948), George McBride's studies in Mexico, *The Land Systems of Mexico* (American Geographical Society, New York, 1923), and Chile, *Chile, Land and Society* (American Geographical Society, New York, 1936), and Harry Tschopik's review of highland Peru, *Highland Communities of Central Peru* (Smithsonian Institution, Washington, D.C., 1947) are examples of these studies. The U.S. government also sponsored a series of studies of particular production sectors: for example, Walter McCreery and Mary Bynum, *The Coffee Industry in Brazil,* (U.S. Department of Commerce, 1930). Taylor's *Rural Life in Argentina* is particularly valuable since he describes one of the most advanced agricultural economies of its day. His review of small and large-scale commercial farming enterprises and of the market-town system that serviced them is a useful counterpoint to the studies elsewhere in Latin America of peasant communities and traditional estates.

The 1950s saw an upsurge in community studies that addressed more directly than had been the case for earlier studies the issues of social and economic change brought about by the increasing integration of the peasant community into the national economy and polity. Many of these studies were carried out by North American anthropologists and sociologists, but there is an increasing presence of Latin American social scientists. In Mexico, Gonzalo Aguirre Beltrán explored the dilemmas facing the Indian population in a modernizing economy in *El Proceso de Aculturación* (Mexico, D.F., 1957) and *Regiones de Refugio* (Mexico, D.F., 1967). Oscar Lewis's restudy of Tepotzlán, *Life in a Mexican Village* (Urbana, Ill., 1951) questions Redfield's emphasis on community cohesion and homogeneity through a detailed ethnography of the village economy and its external links. Lewis also uses archival materials to demonstrate the degree of conflict and social division present in the village when Redfield was undertaking his research there. George Foster began, in this period, his long involvement with a Tarascan community in the state of Michoacan, reported in *Tzintzuntzan* (Boston, Mass., 1967), in which he explored the atomism and competitive individualism of peasant society. The presence of a significant Indian population in the Chiapas area of Mexico and in Guatemala ensured that peasant communities in this region were well-documented by anthropologists. Most of these were village community studies, such as Ricardo Pozas's *Chamula* (Mexico, D.F., 1959) or John Gillin's *San Luis Jilotepeque* (Guatemala City, 1958), but they included Manning Nash's study of the impact of industrialization on an Indian village community, *Machine Age Maya* (Menasha, Wis., 1958).

The exploration of the impact of broader social changes on the local community and its relationships is the focus of Rodolfo Stavenhagen, *Social Classes in Agrarian Societies* (Garden City, N.Y., 1975) in which he reports his own studies of ethnic relations in the Chiapas area of Mexico, and reviews the Mesoamerican literature on ethnicity. Race and ethnicity is also an important theme of rural studies in Brazil at this period. Charles Wagley, *Race and Class in Rural Brazil* (Paris, 1952) is one source, as is Marvin Harris, *Patterns of Race in the Americas* (New York, 1964).

In Peru, the focus on community development became paramount. Allan Holmberg and his Cornell collaborators conducted a series of studies in and around the highland settlement of Vicos, documenting the ways in which traditional *haciendas* could be transformed into co-operative peasant enterprises: see *Vicos: Método y Práctica de Antropología Aplicada* (Lima, 1966). This exercise in applied social change was subsequently reviewed by Henry Dobyns, Paul Doughty and Harold Lasswell in *Peasants, Power and Applied Social Change: Vicos as a Model* (New York, 1971) and by George Stein, *Countrymen and Townsmen in the Callejón de Huaylas, Peru* (Buffalo, N.Y., 1974). A similar emphasis on the possibilities of peasant co-operation and modernization in Peru is found in studies of the same period by Richard Adams, *A Community in the Andes* (Seattle, Wash., 1959), José Maria Arguedas, 'Evolución de las comunidades indigenas', *Revista del Museo Nacional* (Lima, 1957), Oscar Núñez del Prado, *Kuyo Chico* (Chicago, Ill., 1973), and Gabriel Escobar, *Sicaya* (Lima: Instituto de Estudios Peruanos, 1973). Other countries of Latin America are less well documented in this period, but there are important exceptions. Orlando Fals-Borda, *Peasant Society in the Colombian Andes* (Gainesville, Fla., 1955) provides an account of the social and economic roots of land conflict in Colombia. In *The People of Puerto Rico* (Urbana, Ill., 1956) Julian Steward, Robert Manners, Eric Wolf, Elena Padilla, Sidney Mintz and Raymon Scheel document the diversity of rural social organization, such as peasant cultivation and plantation agriculture.

In the 1960s, 1970s and 1980s research on rural communities increasingly concentrated on the impact of urbanization and rural-to-urban migration. Population increase, the rapid growth of the cities, and their demand for food and labour drew attention to the diminishing capacity of village agriculture to retain population and to produce for the urban market. Micro-studies of village agriculture were no longer only the domain of anthropologists, but attracted agronomists, economists, geographers and political scientists. Government and international agencies themselves conducted local-level studies.

The community study tradition continued, strengthened by the emergence in several Latin American countries of research institutes committed to the study of rural change. In Peru, the Instituto de Estudios Peruanos carried out a series of village studies whose focus was migration, economic diversification and social mobility: see, for example, Fernando Fuenzalida, J. Villaran, T. Valiente, and J. Golte, *Estructuras Tradicionales y Economia de Mercado. La comunidad de indigenas de Huayopampa* (Lima, 1968), and Giorgio Alberti and Rodrigo Sanchez, *Poder y Conflcto Social en el Valle del Mantaro* (Lima, 1974). In Mexico, the founding of a national research centre for social anthropology (first CISINAH, then CIESAS) under the leadership of Angel Palerm, himself the author of *Agricultura y Sociedad en Meso-America* (Mexico, D.F., 1972), together with the continuing contribution of the Instituto Nacional Indigenista, resulted in numerous studies of village processes throughout the country. See, for example, Arturo Warman, *Y Venimos a Contradecir: Los Campesinos de Morelos y el Estado Nacional* (Mexico, D.F., 1976; Eng. trans., *We came to object: the peasants of Morelos and the national state,* Baltimore, 1980), Guillermo Bonfil *Cholula: la ciudad sagrada en la era industrial* (Mexico, D.F., 1973), and Guillermo de la Peña, *Herederos de Promesas: Agricultura, Política y Ritual en los Altos de Morelos* (Mexico, D.F., 1980; Eng. trans., *A Legacy of Promises: Agriculture, Politics and Ritual in the Morelos Highlands of Mexico,* Austin, Tex., 1981). Similar developments occur elsewhere in Latin America. Thus, the understanding of change in the 1970s and onwards in Chile is aided by the monographic publications of the Grupo de Investigación Agraria, such as Rigoberto Rivera and Maria E. Cruz, *Pobladores Rurales* (Santiago, 1984). In Brazil, the group of researchers based at the Museo Nacional in Rio de Janeiro undertook studies of change among the peasantry and the complex articulations of peasant economies and the wider capitalist economy. An example is Lydia Sigaud, *Os Clandestinos e os Direitos: Estudo sobre trabalhadores da caña de azucar en Pernambuco* (São Paulo, 1979). The founding of the Centro de Estudios de la Realidad Económica y Social (CERES) based in La Paz and Cochabamba, Bolivia, furthered rural research through numerous publications such as *Bolivia: La Fuerza Histórica del Campesinado,* edited by Fernando Calderon and Jorge Dandler (La Paz, 1984).

North American scholars continued to contribute to the community study tradition. See, for example, Evon Vogt, *Zinacantan: a Maya Community in the Highlands of Chiapas* (Cambridge, Mass., 1969), Frank Cancian, *Change and Uncertainty in a Peasant Economy* (Stanford, Cal., 1972), and George Collier, *Fields of the Tzotzli* (Austin, Tex., 1975). Benjamin Orlove and Glynn Custred (eds), *Land and Power in Latin America* (New York, 1980) provides a re-evaluation of the utility of the community/hacienda dichotomy.

There was also a growing interest in regional studies which sought to understand peasant organization and livelihoods in terms of a wider regional economy. For Brazil, Shepard Forman, *The Brazilian Peasantry* (New York, 1975) documented the survival of peasant farming in particular regional contexts, looking at marketing systems and state intervention. An interesting collection of studies with a regional focus is Carol Smith's edited volumes *Regional Analysis, Vols. I & II* (New York, 1976), which discuss several Latin American cases, including Smith's own work on regional marketing in Guatemala and Gordon Appleby's, 'Export Monoculture and Regional Social Structure in Puno, Peru'. This theme is developed by Benjamin Orlove in *Alpacas, Sheep and Men: the wool export economy and regional society in Southern Peru* (New York, 1977), and in Norman Long and Bryan Roberts, *Miners, Peasants and Entrepreneurs: regional development in the central highlands of Peru* (Cambridge, 1984).

An increasingly important theme is how the peasantry survives economically in face of the increasing commercialization of agriculture from the 1960s onwards. Eduardo Archetti and Kristi Anne Stølen, *Explotación Familiar y Acumulación de Capital en el Campo Argentino* (Buenos Aires, 1975), provide a valuable account of what happened in the 1960s to the family farm in Argentina. The transformation of the peasant economy through cash-crop production, in this case coffee, is the central theme of William Roseberry, *Coffee and Capitalism in the Venezuelan Andes* (Austin, Tex., 1983). Likewise, Stephen Gudeman, *The Demise of a Rural Economy* (London, 1978) documents how the involvement of peasant farmers in sugar production in Panama gradually undermined their self-sufficiency. The articulation of the village economy with large-scale commercial production and its negative consequences for the viability of traditional crafts is the theme of Scott Cook, *Zapotec Stoneworkers: the Dynamics of Rural Simple Commodity Production in Modern Mexican Capitalism* (Washington, D.C., 1982), a study of the Oaxaca region of Mexico.

In an interesting study of a Peruvian highland community, spanning a twenty year period, William Mitchell, *Peasants on the Edge* (Austin, Tex., 1991) documents the increasing diversification of the village economy. Out-migration is a fundamental means of livelihood as population increase decreases the amount of arable land while the cost of agricultural inputs rises, and government price controls, aimed at subsidizing urban consumption, further reduced the gains from farming. Diversification and dependence on out-migration is also the theme of Julian Laite, *Industrial Development and Migrant Labour* (Manchester, 1981), a study of the interdependence of the Peruvian highland village economy and the mining sector and its partly negative consequences for agricultural development. Jane Collins, *Unseasonal Migrations: the Effects of Rural Labor Scarcity in Peru* (Princeton, N.J., 1988) further documents the negative effects of temporary migration on food production in the highlands of Peru. In this case, the cash crop, coffee, which is the reason for the migration, offers only limited possibilities due to soil exhaustion and market prices.

The limits on the development of peasant farming, despite the various government and international programmes to foster it from the 1960s onwards, is brought out in two notable studies, both on Peru, by economists using village-level data. José Maria Caballero, *Economía Agraria de la Sierra Peruana* (Lima, 1981) provides an account of the agrarian structures of Peru up to the agrarian reform of 1969. Alberto Figueroa, *Capitalist Development and the Peasant Economy in Peru* (Cambridge, 1984) provides village data on consumption, production and migrant labour for the 1970s, showing the considerable extent to which even remote highland villages were embedded in commodity exchange and the wage economy.

The increasing importance of internal migration is reflected in various studies of the processes which result in people leaving the village, and which tie them permanently or semi-permanently to their urban destinations. For Peru, a general overview of migration is provided by Hector Martínez, *Migraciones Internas en el Perú* (Lima, 1980). David Preston, *Farmers and Towns: Rural-Urban Relations in Highland Bolivia* (Norwich, 1978) has documented the factors influencing rural-urban and rural-rural migration in Bolivia. Robert Kemper, *Campesinos en la Ciudad: Gente de Tzintzuntzan* (Mexico, D.F., 1976) followed migrants from the village studied by George Foster to Mexico City, documenting the types of people who left and the niches they occupied in the Mexico City economy. In Peru, Teófilo Altamirano, *Presencia Andina en Lima Metropolitana* (Lima, 1984) explores the networks between central highland villages and their migrants in Lima, contrasting migrants from a poor ex-*hacienda* zone with migrants from a relatively rich peasant small-holder zone.

The forces leading to internal migration also result in substantial international migration. Scott Whiteford, *Workers from the North: Plantations, Bolivian Labor and the City in North-West Argentina* (Austin, Tex., 1981) describes the migration patterns of Bolivian peasants to the sugar-producing region of Salta in Argentina, and how the migrant household organizes its resources to survive in the slack periods of labour demand. Perhaps the most complete study of the international migration process is Douglas Massey, Rafael Alarcón, Jorge Durand and Hector González, *Return to Aztlan* (Berkeley, Cal., 1987). Four sending communities in Mexico are studied, two urban, two rural, as is one major receiving community, Los Angeles. In the two village communities, access to land is a determining factor in who migrates, but migration has become a permanent feature of life and work careers at the village level. Social networks channel migrants to Los Angeles, and the strength of the links there, over time, result in permanent residence.

In 1930, the agrarian structures of Latin America were still mainly characterized by markedly unequal access to land, and by the use of land monopolies to control labour. In the centuries old struggle between peasants and landlords the peasant sought enough land to avoid dependence on the landlord, and the landlord sought to ensure that dependence by control of land and other resources. This struggle took different forms depending on the particular system of production – for example, *hacienda,* plantation, or tenant farming – and the relative political strength of landowners. See, in particular, Kenneth Duncan and Ian Rutledge (eds), *Land and Labor in Latin America* (Cambridge, 1977), a collection of essays that covers different historical periods, and provides a typology of land-holding systems present in Latin America by the early twentieth century.

Even in Mexico where agrarian reform had been initiated by the Mexican Revolution of 1910, control over land continued to be a major issue in the 1930s. David Ronfeldt, *Atencingo: the Politics of Agrarian Struggle in a Mexican Ejido* (Stanford, Cal., 1973) describes the ways in which the peasants who were given control of sugar cane land as *ejidatorios* in the state of Morelos still remained dependent on the processing monopoly maintained by the privately owned sugar refinery. Agrarian reform was slow in Mexico with substantial delays in the granting of titles as documented in Guillermo de la Peña, *Legacy of Promises* cited above. The *ejido* was usually divided into individual plots that were given in usufruct to households, and were often insufficient in size and soil quality to provide an adequate income. Collective *ejidos* were established, especially under the administration of Cárdenas (1934–40), but they also faced difficulties arising out of insufficient capital, competition from private landholders, and the power exercised by traders and government intermediaries. Their history is documented in Susana Glantz, *El Ejido Colectivo de Nueva Italia* (Mexico, D.F., 1974), Tomás Martínez Saldaña, *El Costo Social de un Exito Político: la Política Expansionista del Estado Mexicano en el Agro Lagunero* (Chapingo, Mexico, 1980), and Cynthia Hewitt de Alcántara, *The Modernization of Mexican Agriculture: Socio-economic implications of technological change, 1940–1970* (Geneva, 1976).

In Peru the polarization between *hacienda* and peasant community was viewed by many in the 1930s as the major obstacle to economic and political progress. The socialist writer José Carlos Mariátegui in his *Siete Ensayos de Interpretación de la Realidad Peruana* (Lima, 1928) argued the case for strengthening community organization as the basis for a collective agriculture to replace the *hacienda* system.

In those parts of Latin America where land was being brought into production for the first time – the typical frontier scenario – the *hacienda*-community conflict was absent. The settlement of the coffee lands of São Paulo attracted large numbers of immigrants from Europe, as described by Warren Dean, *The Industrialization of São Paulo* (Austin, Tex., 1969). A contrast emerged between the 'old' and 'new' West of São Paulo where, as Thomas H. Holloway, *Immigrants on the Land* (Chapel Hill, N.C., 1980) shows, large landowners were unable to exercise a monopoly of resources, permitting a certain degree of economic mobility for immigrant farmers.

The major pressures for land reform in Latin America were felt mainly in those areas where unequal access to land was exacerbated by increasing demographic growth and changes in economic opportunities. This encouraged both landowners and peasants to engage in more intensive forms of cultivation. In the 1950s both the pressures and the opportunities increased. Urbanization created a demand for foodstuffs, while the renewal of world trade following the Second War World continued the demand for export crops. Also in this period there was mounting international pressure on Latin American governments to modernize their economic structures. The generally 'archaic' agrarian structure of Latin America was identified by the Economic Commission for Latin America in *Development Problems in Latin America* (Austin, Tex., 1969) as a major obstacle to economic development. The issue of agrarian reform was made more complex in this period by new technologies that encouraged direct production rather than share-cropping, and favored medium-scale, but intensively farmed enterprises. The central argument of Alain de Janvry, *The Agrarian Question and Reformism in Latin America* (Baltimore, Md., 1981) is that the pace and nature of the agrarian reform process responded to the specific constraints on, and opportunities for, capital accumulation in agriculture in Latin America.

In some countries, such as Brazil, agrarian reform did not take place since capital accumulation could be furthered by geographical expansion rather than structural and technological reform, as Joe Foweraker shows in *The Struggle for Land: a Political Economy of the Pioneer Frontier in Brazil from 1930 to the Present Day* (Cambridge, 1981). In three Latin American countries, however, major agrarian reforms were enacted after 1950 that effectively eliminated the large landed estate. Bolivia was the first to enact agrarian reform in 1952 after armed struggle by peasant groups. This is documented in David Heath, John C. Erasmus and Hans C. Buechler, *Land Reform and Social Revolution in Bolivia* (New York, 1969). In 1969 a reform orientated military government in Peru initiated a far-reaching agrarian reform that transformed the large estates into production co-operatives and encouraged peasant communities to establish co-operative farming. Various commentators have provided a critical appraisal of the reform, indicating its drawbacks for the peasant producer. See, for example, José María Caballero, *Agricultura, Reforma Agraria y Pobreza Campesina* (Lima, 1980), Cynthia McClintock, *Peasant Cooperatives and Political Change in Peru* (Princeton, N.J., 1981), and David Horton, *Land Reform and Reform Enterprises in Peru* (Land Tenure Center, University of Wisconsin, Madison, Wis., 1974). In Chile, the Christian Democrat government of Frei initiated agrarian reform in 1967. This was subsequently extended under the Presidency of Salvador Allende so that at the time of the coup d'état of 1973, 43 per cent of land was in the reform sector. An evaluation of these processes are found in David Lehmann (ed.), *Agrarian Reform and Agrarian Reformism* (London, 1974) and in Cristobal Kay, 'Chilean Agrarian Reform', *América Latina,* 17 (1976). The most recent experiment in agrarian reform is that of Nicaragua following the Revolution of 1979. The evaluations of this reform are as of yet provisional. Carmen Deere, R. Marchetti and N. Reinhardt, 'The peasantry and the development of Sandinista agrarian policy, 1979–1984', *Latin American Research Review,* XX, 3 (1985): 75–109 provide an evaluation up to the mid-1980s, and Laura Enríquez, *Harvesting Change* (Chapel Hill, N.C., 1991), takes the analysis to 1990 and examines the impact of the reform on the export agricultural sector. This sector had, hitherto, relied on a ready supply of cheap peasant labour, which became less readily available, partly because of the *Contra* war, and partly because of the improved opportunities for peasant farming, especially in co-operatives.

There was a substantial foreign presence in agriculture in the 1930s. This mainly took the form of direct investment in export crops, such as sugar, coffee and tropical fruits. An interesting account of this kind of foreign investment and its vicissitudes over time is provided by Phillipe Bourgois in his account of the United Fruit Company, *Ethnicity at Work: Divided Labor on a Central American Banana Plantation* (Baltimore, Md., 1989).

In this early period, the state in Latin America was mainly a bystander in the drive to modernize agriculture. It provided some infrastructure and policing for the export zones, but was not involved directly in promoting agricultural development. This role had changed substantially by the 1960s. International agencies and foreign governments, particularly that of the United States, exerted pressure on Latin American governments to develop their agricultural resources. Financial and technical aid was channelled through Latin American governments, and these, in turn, began to create agricultural development programmes. The development of a state agricultural bureaucracy is illustrated in Merilee S. Grindle (ed.), *The Politics and Policy of Implementation* (Princeton, N.J., 1980) and in a case study by Grindle, *Bureaucrats, Politicians, and Peasants in Mexico* (Berkeley, Cal., 1977), which shows how central control over agricultural production introduced bureaucratic politics into the management of agriculture. This argument is futher developed in Martínez Saldaña, *El Costo Social de un Exito Político,* cited above. The extension of bureaucratic management of agriculture raises the issue of the interface between peasant producers and government agencies. Norman Long (ed.), *Encounters at the Interface: a Perspective on Social Discontinuities in Rural Development* (Wageningen, 1989) explores the difficulties of implementing central policies in face of the resistance both of lower-level bureaucrats and of the various rural interest groups to whom they have to accommodate. The extension of government development agencies has also been considerable in Brazil. Stephen Bunker, *Underdeveloping the Amazon: Extraction, Unequal Exchange and the Failure of the Modern State* (Urbana, Ill., 1985) explores the internal and external conflicts that beset the vast agency, SUDAM, as it seeks to control Amazonian development. Antonio Medeiros documents the massive expansion of state employment in the agricultural bureaucracy between 1964 and 1982 in *Politics and Intergovernmental Relations in Brazil* (New York, 1986).

Foreign investment in agriculture also began to change from the 1960s onwards. Though many of the old export crops remained attractive sources of investment, new opportunities emerged. These were in new export crops such as soya beans or seasonal fruits and vegetables, in the provision of agricultural inputs such as machinery, fertilizer and insecticide, and in the production of industrialized foodstuffs and dairy products for the internal urban market of Latin America. One of the first accounts of the changing international market for foodstuffs and its consequences for local producers in Latin America is Ernest Feder, *Strawberry Imperialism* (The Hague, 1977). A more complete account of the consolidation of a world market for foodstuffs and its implications for Latin America is found in Steven E. Sanderson, *The Transformation of Mexican Agriculture: International Structure and the Politics of Rural Change* (Princeton, N.J., 1986), and Sanderson (ed.), *The Americas in the New International Division of Labor* (New York, 1985).

Though in the 1960s and 1970s, the state played a leading role in providing the institutional means for agricultural development, by the 1980s, fiscal pressures seriously limited the state's capacity to intervene in the agricultural sector. The internationalization of agriculture and its dependence on new investment and technology resulted in direct linkages between foreign and local capital and the producer, marginalizing the state. There was an increasing reliance on market mechanisms for promoting agricultural development, as in the 1991 decree privatizing the key unit of the Mexican agrarian reform – the *ejido*.

By 1990, the major issue promoting state intervention in agriculture was the environmental one. Strong pressures from international agencies, foreign governments, and non-governmental organizations, through such mechanisms as debt swaps, led to a reassertion of the need for government intervention in agriculture. David Goodman and Michael Redclift (eds), *Environment and Development in Latin America: the Politics of Sustainability* (Manchester, 1991) review the increasing ecological vulnerability of Latin America, the erosion of the possibilities of sustainable development, and the need for state intervention. A useful review of the question of sustainable agriculture, and the role of outside agencies in this, is provided by Anthony Bebbington, 'Farmer knowledge, institutional resources and sustainable agricultural strategies', *Bulletin of Latin American Research,* 9, 2 (1990): 203–28.

The number of actors now involved in agricultural development in Latin America had multiplied to include not only national and local actors but a variety of international actors, ranging from multinational corporations to United Nations agencies and non-governmental organizations concerned with ecological issues and with the problem of devising sustainable development strategies. The complex play of forces at work is documented in Marianne Schmink and Charles H. Wood, *Contested Frontiers in Amazonia* (New York, 1992), which depicts a continuing competition for resources among actors of widely different powers and interests: state agencies, ranchers, goldminers, rubber tappers, Indians, small-scale farmers, and large corporations. In this competition, no actor, not even the state, triumphs; even the relatively powerless are able to mobilize sufficient outside help to offset their weaknesses.

Amazonia is exceptional in the amount of outside interest it evokes, with previously ignored groups such as Amazonian Indians becoming the centre of international attention. Nevertheless, the Amazonia case highlights the uncertainties that the changing international context brings to agrarian development in Latin America, as economic growth slows down, 'developmentalist' confidence wanes, and the traditional export crops decrease in importance relative to new ones and to the export of manufactures. Alternative models of development are few, as Philip O'Brien argues in his chapter on 'Debt and Sustainable Development', in Goodman and Redclift (eds), *Environment and Development in Latin America.* But, although the international context, including the indebtedness of Latin American governments, clearly limits centralized development strategies, whether implemented by state or private interests, at the same time it creates space for many small-scale initiatives, as shown in Norman and Ann Long (eds), *Battlefields of Knowledge: the Interlocking of Theory and Practice in Social Research and Development* (London, 1992). These initiatives are not only carried out by small-scale producers, entrepreneurs and local groups but also by frontline development personnel, especially those working for the numerous non-government organizations that have sprung up over the past decade.

7. ECONOMIC IDEAS AND IDEOLOGIES IN LATIN AMERICA SINCE 1930[1]

For general surveys of the development of economic thought in Latin America since the Second World War, see Albert Fishlow, 'The State of Latin American Economics', in Inter-American Development Bank, *Economic and Social Progress in Latin America: 1985 Report* (Washington, D.C., [1986]), pp. 123–48; republished in Christopher Mitchell (ed.), *Changing Perspectives in Latin American Studies: Insights from Six Disciplines* (Stanford, Cal., 1988). Fishlow covers the rise and decline of the several schools of thought, based on their policy outcomes. Also valuable is Cristóbal Kay, *Latin American Theories of Development and Underdevelopment* (London, 1989), which offers a sympathetic but critical review of structuralism and dependency and related works on marginality and internal colonialism. A briefer survey which gives particular attention to policy issues is Felipe Pazos, 'Cincuenta años de pensamiento económico en la América Latina', *Trimestre Económico,* 50, 4 (October–December, 1983): 1915–1948. An old but still useful survey of Latin American adaptations of extra-continental ideas is Juan Noyola Vázquez, 'La evolución del pensamiento económico

1 This brief survey excludes the large North American and European literatures inspired by dependency analysis. It offers English versions of relevant works where they exist. Original versions can be found in the footnotes to the chapter 'Economic Ideas and Ideologies in Latin America since 1930' in this volume, where the reader will also find citations of primary sources. For more on the economic context in which ideas and policies were developed, consult the chapters on the economic history of Latin America since 1930 in this volume.

del último cuarto de siglo y su influencia en la América Latina', *Trimestre Económico,* 23, 3 (July–September, 1956): 269–83.

Three works may serve to indicate the impact of Latin American ideas on development theory at large. H[einz] W. Arndt, *Economic Development: the History of an Idea* (Chicago, Ill., 1987), esp. pp. 119–30, places structuralism and dependency in broad historical context. Björn Hettne, *Development Theory and the Three Worlds* (Harlow, 1990), attempts to address underdevelopment and development in a non-Eurocentric and interdisciplinary framework, and in this context Latin American ideas play a prominent role. Dieter Senghaas, *The European Experience: a Historical Critique of Development Theory* (Dover, N.H., 1985), incorporates structuralist and dependency perspectives in a comparative treatment of European and non-European economic development, emphasizing 'selective de-linking' as a historically proven development strategy.

On the 'pre-theoretical' justifications of industrial development in Latin America, a documentary collection for Brazil, representative in many respects of nations of the Southern Cone, is Edgard Carone (ed.), *O pensamento industrial no Brasil (1880–1945)* (São Paulo, 1971). A debate on the role of industrialization in the development process at the end of that period is Roberto Simonsen and Eugênio Gudin, *A controvérsia do planejamento na economia brasileira* (Rio de Janeiro, 1977).

On the U. N. Economic Commission for Latin America (ECLA, and from 1985, ECLAC, to include the Caribbean), see the agency's anthology, *Development Problems in Latin America: An Analysis by the UN ECLA* (Austin, Tex., 1970). Fundamental structuralist statements include the ECLA documents *The Economic Development of Latin America and Its Principal Problems* (Lake Success, N.Y., 1950) and *Economic Survey of Latin America: 1949* (New York, 1951). Raúl Prebisch was the exclusive author of the first study, and the principal author of the second. Another important work was his *Toward a Dynamic Development Policy for Latin America* (New York, 1963). The classic statement of the structuralist thesis on inflation is Osvaldo Sunkel, 'Inflation in Chile: an unorthodox approach', *International Economic Papers,* No. 10 (1960): 107–31. In *La teoría del subdesarrollo de la CEPAL* [Sp. acronym for ECLA] (Mexico, D.F., 1980), Octavio Rodríguez – a former ECLA economist – surveys, evaluates and critiques the organization's doctrines. Joseph Hodara, *Prebisch y la CEPAL: Sustancia trayectoria y contexto internacional* (Mexico, D.F., 1987), is an exposition of ECLA's doctrines, largely in non-technical terms, combined with an institutional history.

On the European antecedents of structuralism, see H. W. Arndt, 'The Origins of Structuralism', *World Development,* 13, 2 (February, 1985): 151–9. For more on the context of the formulation of Prebisch's first thesis in 1949, see Joseph L. Love, 'Raúl Prebisch and the Origins of the Doctrine of Unequal Exchange', *Latin American Research Review,* 15, 3 (1980): 45–72.

On neostructuralism, a representative collection is Osvaldo Sunkel (ed.), *El desarrollo desde dentro: Un enfoque neoestructuralista para la América Latina* (Mexico, D.F., 1991; Eng. trans. 1993), containing essays by Sunkel, Joseph Ramos, Ricardo Ffrench-Davis, Winston Fritsch, José Antonio Ocampo, Víctor Tokman, Oscar Muñoz, Adolfo Figueroa, and others. A brief introduction to the doctrine, comparing it to neo-liberalism, can be found in Ricardo Ffrench-Davis, 'An Outline of a Neo-structuralist Approach', *CEPAL Review,* no. 34 (April, 1988): 37–44.

Structuralist and neostructuralist thought can be followed not only in *CEPAL Review* (since 1976), and its predecessor, the *Economic Bulletin for Latin America,* but also in *Pensamiento Iberoamericano,* published by ECLA and the Instituto de Cooperación Iberoamericana in Madrid since 1982.

A frequent commentator on Latin American structuralism whose own structuralist writings have often paralleled developments in the Latin American school is Albert O. Hirschman. A survey and critique of ECLA's theses through 1960 is Hirschman, 'Ideologies of Economic Development in Latin America', in Albert O. Hirschman (ed.), *Latin American Issues: Essays and Comments* (New York, 1961), pp. 3–42. On the Structuralist Interpretation of Inflation in Chile, set in a historical context, see 'Inflation in Chile', in Hirschman, *Journeys Toward Progress: Studies of Economic Policy-Making in Latin America* (New York, 1963), pp. 161–223. An explanation of why the structuralist thesis on inflation lost out at the policy level is 'The Social and Political Matrix of Inflation: elaborations of the Latin American experience', in Albert O. Hirschman, *Essays in Trespassing: Economics to Politics and Beyond* (Cambridge, 1981), pp. 177–207. On the crisis of import-substitution industrialization and its implications for structuralism, see 'The Political Economy of Import Substituting Industrialization in Latin America', in Albert O. Hirschman, *A Bias for Hope* (New Haven, Conn., 1971), pp. 85–123; and Werner Baer, 'Import Substitution and Industrialization in Latin America: experiences and interpretations', *Latin American Research Review,* 7, 1 (1972): 95–122.

In the vanguard of the neo-classical counterattack on structuralism and dependency was the Chicago School, which was most influential in Chile.

Juan Gabriel Valdés offers a scholarly but highly critical study of its ideology and practice in *La escuela de Chicago: Operación Chile* (Buenos Aires, 1989). See also Alejandro Foxley, *Latin American experiments in Neo-Conservative Economics* (Berkeley, 1983) which deals principally with Chile.

On 'developmentalism' (*desarrollismo* in Spanish, *desenvolvimentismo* in Portuguese), an ideology and set of policies associated with structuralism in Argentina and Brazil, see Kathryn Sikkink, *Ideas and Institutions: Developmentalism in Brazil and Argentina* (Ithaca, N.Y., 1991). That Argentine *desarrollistas* ignored Prebisch himself, possibly because of his earlier role in forming government policies in Argentina, is shown in Julio G. Nosiglia, *El desarrollismo* (Buenos Aires, 1983). Ricardo Bielschowsky, *Pensamento econômico brasileiro: O ciclo ideológico do desenvolvimentismo* (Rio de Janeiro, 1988) not only considers in detail the relationship between developmentalism and structuralism, but surveys all other major schools of thought in Brazil from the end of the Second World War to the coup d'état of 1964.

A collection of readings of Marxist thought, including contributions by writers who emphasized relations of exchange rather than relations of production and thereby influenced dependency analysis, is Michael Lowy, *Le marxisme en Amérique latine de 1909 à nos jours: Anthologie* (Paris, 1980, Eng. trans. 1992). On Marxism through the 1960s, also see Sheldon B. Liss, *Marxist Thought in Latin America* (Berkeley, Cal., 1984). For the influence of Antonio Gramsci, indirectly important in some versions of dependency through his notion of hegemony, consult José Aricó, *La cola del diablo: itinerario de Gramsci en América Latina* (Buenos Aires, 1988).

A study of dependency analysis should begin with Fernando Henrique Cardoso and Enzo Faletto, *Dependencia y desarrollo en América Latina* (Mexico, D.F., 1969) [the English version, *Dependency and Development in Latin America* (1979), is much revised]; and Andre Gunder Frank, *Capitalism and Underdevelopment in Latin America* (New York, 1967). Later works in the dependency tradition by the evolving structuralists Prebisch and Furtado are important and similar to one another, in their employment of the classical concept of surplus. See Raúl Prebisch, *Capitalismo periférico: Crisis y transformación* (Mexico, 1981) and Celso Furtado, *Accumulation and Development: the Logic of Industrial Civilization,* tr. by Suzette Macedo (Oxford, 1983 [Port. orig., 1978]).

A review of the dependency literature through the mid-1970s can be found in two critical but sympathetic studies: José Gabriel Palma, 'Dependency: a formal theory of underdevelopment or a methodology for the analysis of concrete situations of underdevelopment?', *World Development*, 6, 7–8 (1978): 881–924; and Heraldo Muñoz, 'Cambio y continuidad en el debate sobre la dependencia y el imperialismo', *Estudios Internacionales*, 11, 44 (October-December, 1978): 88–138. For likenesses and differences in Latin American and Caribbean versions of dependency, see Norman Girvan, 'The Development of Dependency Economics in the Caribbean and Latin America: review and comparison', *Social and Economic Studies*, 22, 1 (March, 1973): 1–33. Jorge Larraín offers a defence of dependency as a legitimate Marxist enterprise in *Theories of Development: Capitalism, Colonialism and Dependency* (Cambridge, 1989). On the relationship between Marxism and dependency analysis, also see Ronald H. Chilcote (ed.), *Dependency and Marxism: Toward a Resolution of the Debate* (Boulder, Colo., 1982). For an assessment of the relative importance of Marxism and structuralism, the two traditions from which dependency drew, see Joseph L. Love, 'The Origins of Dependency Analysis', *Journal of Latin American Studies*, 22, 1 (1990): 143–68. Robert A. Packenham, in *The Dependency Movement: Scholarship and Politics in Development Studies* (Cambridge, Mass., 1992), argues that dependency is non-scientific and ideological, including the much-praised work of F. H. Cardoso, though much of his criticism is directed against North American, rather than Latin American, dependency analysts. An extensively annotated bibliography chiefly concerned with dependency is Charles W. Bergquist (ed.), *Alternative Approaches to the Problem of Development: A Selected and Annotated Bibliography* (Durham, N.C., 1979). The volume also deals with structuralism and Third World Marxist contributions.

Though a critic of the dependency literature, one of the few writers on dependency who worked within the tradition of formal Marxist economics, as opposed to historical materialism, is the Colombian Salomón Kalmanovitz, who sketched a theory of dependent reproduction and accounted for the incomplete accumulation process in the Periphery. See Kalmanovitz, *El desarrollo tardío del capitalismo: Un enfoque crítico de la teoría de la dependencia* (Bogotá, 1983).

For the flavour of the modes-of-production debate, see two collections: Carlos Sempat Assadourian (ed.), *Modos de producción en América Latina* (Mexico, D.F., 1973); and Roger Bartra et al., *Modos de producción en América Latina* (Lima, 1976). On the articulation of pre-capitalist relations of production with capitalism in the informal economy, see Lúcio Kowarick, 'Capitalismo, dependência e marginalidade urbana na América

Latina: uma contribuição teórica', *Estudos CEBRAP* 8 (April–June, 1974), pp. 79–96; and Francisco de Oliveira, 'A economia brasileira: Crítica à razão dualista', *Estudos CEBRAP* 2 (October, 1972), pp. 3–82.

On individual writers, including biographical and autobiographical materials, the following may be consulted:

On Prebisch: Comisión Económica para América Latina y el Caribe [CEPAL], *Raúl Prebisch: Un aporte al estudio de su pensamiento* (Santiago, 1987), which contains the Spanish version of his 'Five Stages' (in next item) and an annotated list of 466 of his publications from 1920 to 1986; Gerald M. Meier and Dudley Seers (eds), *Pioneers in Development* (New York, 1984), which includes Prebisch's retrospective, 'Five stages in my thinking on development' (pp. 175–91) and H[ans] W. Singer's 'The terms of trade controversy and the evolution of soft financing: early years in the U. N.' (pp. 275–303); Mateo Magariños, *Diálogos con Raúl Prebisch* (Mexico, D.F., 1991), which offers episodic reminiscences by Prebisch through the 1960s; and a brief survey of Prebisch's career in Joseph L. Love, 'Raúl Prebisch (1901–1986): his life and ideas', in Abraham Lowenthal (ed.), *Latin American and Caribbean Record,* Vol. V: 1985–1986 (New York, 1988), pp. A143–A150. A book-length biography of Prebisch is being prepared by David Pollock, a former ECLA official, and Edgar J. Dosman.

On Furtado: A wide-ranging anthology of his writings with a biographical sketch by the editor is Francisco de Oliveira (ed.), *Celso Furtado: Economia,* (São Paulo, 1983); Furtado's memoirs (still in process) consist of three volumes: *A fantasia organizada* (1985); *A fantasia desfeita* (1989); *Os ares do mundo* (1991), all published in Rio de Janeiro; and a brief autobiographical statement in English, 'Adventures of a Brazilian Economist', in *International Social Science Journal,* 25, 1–2 (1973): 28–38. Furtado's and Singer's work on the implications of structuralism for the domestic economy is examined in Joseph L. Love, 'Modeling Internal Colonialism: history and prospect', *World Development,* 17, 6 (June 1989): 905–22. Other aspects of Furtado's work are considered in Love, *Crafting the Third World: Theorizing Underdevelopment in Rumania and Brazil,* ch. 10 (forthcoming). Two studies that place Furtado's work in the context of postwar Brazilian economic thought are Guido Mantega, *A economia política brasileira* (São Paulo, 1984) and Ricardo Bielschowsky, *Pensamento econômico brasileiro* (above). The former also treats dependency.

On Noyola: Carlos Bazdresch Parada, *El pensamiento de Juan F. Noyola* (México, 1984), which reviews the work of the Mexican economist, one of the earliest structuralist writers, on industrialization, external disequilibrium, and inflation.

On Cardoso: Fernando Henrique Cardoso, 'The consumption of dependency theory in the United States', *Latin American Research Review,* 12, 3 (1977), pp. 7–24, which contains autobiographical elements, and Joseph L. Kahl, 'Fernando Henrique Cardoso', a biographical interview with critical commentary, in Kahl, *Modernization, Exploitation and Dependency in Latin America: Germani, González Casanova and Cardoso* (New Brunswick, N.J., 1976), pp. 129–94.

On Frank: Andre Gunder Frank, 'The Underdevelopment of Development', in the *Scandinavian Journal of Development Alternatives,* 10, 3 (September, 1991): 5–72, an autobiographical statement which treats his intellectual development before, during, and after his dependency period. An appendix contains a complete bibliography of Frank's works, 1955–90 (pp. 133–50).

8. SCIENCE AND SOCIETY IN TWENTIETH-CENTURY LATIN AMERICA

To synthesizc thc history of science in twentieth-century Latin America is to explore a largely uncharted territory. The first great generation of Latin American historians of science, whose representative figures were Juan B. Lastres in Peru, Alfredo Bateman, Enrique Pérez Arbeláez and Guillermo Hernández de Alba in Colombia, Enrique Beltrán and Germán Somolinos in Mexico, worked preeminently on the science of the Enlightenment, when scientific activity in Latin America reached a level of brilliance still unsurpassed. Another group of historians domiciled mainly in Argentina (Aldo Mieli, Cortés Plá, José Babini and Desiderio Papp) wrote on mainstream European science, although Babini provided a useful synthesis of science in Argentina, *Historia de la ciencia en la Argentina* (Buenos Aires, 1949; 1986 edition with a perceptive historiographical introduction by Marcelo Montserrat).

Beside's Babini's primer, there are few other single-country histories of science. Of these, by far the most analytical is Simon Schwartzman, *Formação da comunidade científica no Brasil* (São Paulo, 1979; Eng. trans. *A Space for Science. The Development of the Scientific Community in Brazil,* University Park, PA, 1991). Although the entire twentieth century is covered, the book's strength is its description of the *prise de conscience* by Brazilian scientists of the 1930s through 1950s, based on interviews with sixty-nine scientific leaders; their biographies are given in a satellite volume, *História da ciência no Brasil: Acervo de depoimentos* (Rio de Janeiro, 1984). Marcos Cueto's study of high-altitude physiology in Peru, *Excelencia científica en la periferia: Actividades científicas e investigación biomédica en el Perú, 1890–1950* (Lima, 1989), is also a study of a nascent scientific elite. Much less useful are Ramiro Condarco Morales, *Historia del saber y la ciencia en Bolivia* (La Paz, 1978) which, like too much history of Latin American science, is little more than a list of people and institutions, and Eli de Gortari, *La ciencia en la historia de México,* 2nd edn (Mexico, D.F., 1980) which devotes too much space to a defense of Aztec science and not enough on the achievements of the twentieth century.

In an attempt to cover nineteenth and twentieth century science in Argentina by disciplines, the Sociedad Científica Argentina published two series of studies, one in the 1920s, the other in the 1970s. Although the volumes vary in coverage and style, the earlier series is, on the whole, better. Among the most distinguished and interesting disciplinary histories are those of Ramón G. Loyarte, *La evolución de la física* (Buenos Aires, 1924) and Cristóbal M. Hicken, *Los estudios botánicos* (Buenos Aires, 1923). Less objective is Claro Cornelio Dassen, *Las matemáticas en la Argentina* (Buenos Aires, 1924), which in part is a polemic against modern mathematics. The more recent series consists of multi-authored volumes, in which sub-fields have been delegated to specialists (scientists, not historians) in those areas. As a result most of the volumes are chaotic compilations of names, dates and institutions with scant analysis or synthesis. However, some of the volumes may be mined for their rich lode of information; see, in particular, Luis A. Santaló (ed.), *Matemática* (1972), José Federico Westerkamp, *Física* (1975), Luis B. Mazoti and Juan H. Hunziker, *Genética* (1976), and Noemi G. Abiusso, *Química* (1981). A somewhat parallel treatment can be found for Brazil. First are two volumes published in the 1950s under the editorship of Fernando de Azevedo, *As ciências no Brasil* (São Paulo, 1955), characterized by chapters, again written mainly be scientists who had participated in the institutionalization of their own disciplines, of uniformly high quality. Of particular interest are the chapters on astronomy (Abraão de Morais), physics (J. Costa Ribeiro), geology and paleontology (viktor Leinz) and chemistry (Heinrich Rheinboldt). A more recent work, *História das ciências no Brasil,* Mário Guimarães Ferri and Shozo Motoyama, eds, 3 vols (São Paulo, 1979–81), suffers by comparison. Most of its chapters are unenlightening lists of names and research projects, compiled by scientists in the various disciplines. The same can be said of multi-authored *Estudios de historia de la ciencia en el Perú,* 2 vols (Lima, 1986). Possibly the best collection of disciplinary articles from a single country is Hebe M. C. Vessuri (ed.), *Ciencia académica en la Venezuela moderna* (Caracas, 1984), a collection of mature studies, mainly by social scientists, of discrete disciplines, always within the framework of larger issues of the institutionalization of academic science. In 1993 the Instituto Colombiano para el Desarrollo de la Ciencia (Bogotá) published a nine-volume *Historia Social de la Ciencia en Colombia,* with volumes on Methodology (I), Mathematics, Astronomy and Geology (II), Natural History (III), Engineering and History of Technology (IV–V), Physics and Chemistry (VI), Medicine (VII–VIII), and Social Science (IX).

The Sociedad Latinoamericana de Historia de las Ciencias y la Tecnologia has published since 1984 a distinguished journal, *Quipu* (Mexico, D.F., 1984–), in which appear a variety of studies, by historians, of modern Latin American Science. The Society also publishes an occasional series called *Cuadernos de Quipu,* of which two have appeared, *El perfil de la ciência en América* (1987), and *Cross Cultural Diffusion of Science: Latin America* (1987). The acts of the Society's second congress, with many articles on 20th-century science was published as *Anais do Segundo Congresso Latino-Americano de História da Ciência e da Tecnologia* (São Paulo, 1989).

Few Latin American scientific institutions have had proper histories. For Brazil, Nancy Stepan, *Beginnings of Brazilian Science* (New York, 1976) is a model account of the foundation and early years of the Oswaldo Cruz Institute at Manguinhos, the country's most important bio-medical institution. The more recent history of the Cruz Institute and its political problems under the military dictatorship in the 1960s is chronicled by Herman Lent, *O massacre de Manguinhos* (Rio de Janeiro, 1978). On scientific institutions in Rio de Janeiro, see Simon Schwartzman (ed.), *Universidades e Instituções Científicas no Rio de Janeiro* (Brasília, 1982). On botany, see João Conrado Niemeyer de Lavôr, *História do Jardim Botânico do Rio de Janeiro* (Rio de Janeiro, 1983) and F. C. Hoehne et al., *O Jardim Botânico de São Paulo* (São Paulo, 1941).

For Mexico, Horacio García Fernández's account the Faculty of Chemistry, *Historia de una facultad: Química 1916–1983* (Mexico, D.F., 1985) is a model study of a university science department based in part on interviews with its own alumni. On the related Institute of Chemistry, see Alberto Sandoval L., 'Cinco lustros de existencia', *Boletín del Instituto de Química,*

17 (1965): 83–121. On Mexican physics, there is Héctor Cruz Manjarrez, *Reseña Histórica del Instituto de Física,* 2 vols (mimeo) (Mexico, D.F., 1975–6), and Juan Manuel Lozano, et al., 'Historia de la Sociedad Mexicana de Fisica', *Revista Mexicana de Fisica,* 28 (1982): 277–93. A broader study of university science, for Argentina, is Horacio H. Camacho, *Las ciencias naturales en la Universidad de Buenos Aires* (Buenos Aires, 1971).

Astronomical institutions have fared better than most. For Brazil, Henrique Morize, *Observatório Astronômico: Um século de história (1827–1927),* new edn (Rio de Janeiro, 1987) deals mainly with the nineteenth century; the new edition includes two biographical articles about Morize. For Chile, see Philip C. Keenan et al., *The Chilean National Astronomical Observatory (1852–1965)* (Santiago, 1985). Marco Arturo Moreno Corral, ed. *Historia de la astronomia en México,* (Ensenada, 1983) has an institutional focus.

The few disciplinary histories written tend to be highly institutional in focus; see, for example, Jorge Grünwald Ramasso, *Historia de la Química en el Uruguay (1830–1930)* (Montevideo, 1966). A thrilling institutional and political history of atomic physics in Argentina is Mario Mariscotti, *El secreto atómico de Huemul* (Buenos Aires, 1985).

Hebe Vessuri wrote two pioneering studies of the scientific press: 'La revista cientifica periférica. El caso de *Acta Cientifica Venezolana*', *Interciencia,* 12 (1987): 124–34; and 'Una estrategia de publicación científica para la fisiología latinoamericana: *Acta Physiologica Latinoamericana,* 1950–1971', in *Anais do Segundo Congresso,* pp. 232–40.

There is no tradition of biographical memoirs in Latin American science and, as a result, this kind of literature is scant. Of the great figures in biomedicine, see the commemorative volume *Bernardo A. Houssay, su vida y su obra 1887–1971* (Buenos Aires, 1981), and Ricardo Archila, *Luis Razetti, sintesis biográfica* (Caracas, 1973). For Brazil, see Miguel Osório de Almeida, *Carlos Chagas* (mimeo) (Rio de Janeiro, 1988); Ivone Freire de Mota and Amélia Império Hamburger, 'Retratos de Luiz de Barros Freire como pioneiro da ciência no Brasil', *Ciência e Cultura,* 40 (1988): 875–81, and the biographical essays in M. Amoroso Costa, *As idéias fundamentais da matemática e outros ensaios* (São Paulo, 1981). An unusually informative autobiography is that of the Chilean agronomist Manuel Elgueta Guerin, *Memorias de una vida 1902–1983* (Santiago de Chile, n.d.). See also Enrique Beltrán, *Medio siglo de recuerdos de un biólogo mexicano* (Mexico, D.F., 1977). Interviews are perhaps the most distinctive form of scientific biography in Latin America, especially in Brazil. See, for example, Lourdes Cedran (ed.), *Dialogos com Mário Schenberg* (São Paulo, 1985) and another collection of interviews *about* Schenberg with his students and colleagues in Brazilian physics, Gita K. Guinsburg and José Luiz Goldfarb (eds), *Mário Schenberg: Entre-Vistas* (São Paulo, 1984).

There is a considerable literature of the contributions of foreigners to Latin American science. See, for example, Lewis Pyenson's discussion of the German contribution to physics, physical chemistry and astronomy in Argentina in *Cultural Imperialism and Exact Science: German Expansion Overseas, 1900–1930* (New York, 1985). See also, Marcelo Montserrat, 'La influencia italiana de la actividad científica argentina del siglo XIX', in Francis Korn (ed.), *Los italianos en la Argentina* (Buenos Aires, n.d.), pp. 105–23; H. M. Nussenzveig, *Guido Beck* (mimeo) (Rio de Janeiro, 1989); and J. Leite Lopes, *Richard Feynman in Brazil: Recollections* (mimeo) (Rio de Janeiro, 1988). More analytical is Miguel J. C. de Asua, 'Influencia de la Facultad de Medicina de París sobre la de Buenos Aires', *Quipu,* 3 (1986): 79–89, which raises the issue of European versus American disciplinary and institutional identities. There is a complementary literature on Latin American science students abroad; see, for example, Eddy Stols 'Les étudiants brésiliens en Belgique', *Revista de História* (São Paulo), 50 (1974): 653–91; and Humberto Ruiz Calderón, 'Una vieja historia: Los becarios de Venezuela en el exterior (1900–1954)', *Interciencia,* 15 (1990): 8–14.

There is a considerable literature on Spanish scientific exiles, particularly in Mexico. See two articles by José Cueli in *El exilio español en Mexico 1939–1982* (Mexico, D.F., 1982): 'Ciencias médicas y biológicas' (pp. 495–528) and 'Matemáticas, física y quimica' (pp. 531–43). Biographies of Spanish figures can be culled for the chapters on exile; e.g., José Luis Barona Vilar and María Fernanda Mancebo, *José Puche Alvarez (1896–1979): Historia de un compromiso* (Valencia, 1989) ['El exilio mexicano (1939–1979)', pp. 57–73]; L. Valencia Gayá, *El doctor Lafora y su época* (Madrid, 1977) ['Nueve años de exilio de México', pp. 145–60]. On Lafora and Mexican criminology, see Raquel Alvarez Peláez and Rafael Huertas Garcia-Alejo, *¿Criminales o locos? Dos peritajes psiquiátricas del Dr. Gonzalo R. Lafora* (Madrid, 1987). On Julio Rey Pastor and Latin American mathematics, see Sixto Rios, et al., *Julio Rey Pastor, matemático* (Madrid, 1979) ['Rey Pastor y la matemática en la Argentina', pp. 49–134]; and Mario Otero, 'Las matemáticas uruguayas y Rey Pastor', in Luis Español González (ed.), *Estudios sobre Julio Rey Pastor* (Logroño, 1990), pp. 181–93.

Scientific culture has been thin enough in Latin America to discourage studies of the reception or development of specific ideas there. Those ideas that have had culture-wide repercussions have attracted the most attention. On Darwinism (mainly a nineteenth-century topic, but with tremendous repercussions on popular perceptions of science that extended well into the twentieth century) there are a number of national studies, e.g. Eduardo L. Ortiz, 'La polémica del darwinismo y la inserción del la ciencia en Argentina', in *Actas II Congrso de la Sociedad Española de Historia de la Ciencias,* 3 vols (Zaragoza, 1984), I, pp. 89–108; Marcelo Montserrat, 'La presencia evolucionista en el positivismo argentino', *Quipu,* 3 (1986): 91–101; Terezinha Alves Ferreira Collichio, *Miranda Azevedo e o darwinismo no Brasil* (São Paulo, 1988); Bernardo Marquez Bretón, *Origenes del darwinismo en Chile* (Santiago, 1982); Pedro M. Pruna and Armando Garcia González, *Darwinismo y sociedad en Cuba* (Madrid, 1989); Roberto Moreno, *La polémica del darwinismo en México* (Mexico, D.F., 1984); Rosaura Ruiz Gutiérrez, *Positivismo y evolución: Introducción del darwinismo en México* (Mexico, D.F., 1987); and Thomas F. Glick, *Darwin y el Darwinismo en el Uruguay y en América Latina* (Montevideo, 1989).

On eugenics, see Nancy Stepan, 'Eugenesia, genética y salud pública: el movimiento eugenésico brasileño y mundial', *Quipu,* 2 (1985): 351–84, and the fuller treatment in her book, *The Hour of Eugenics: Latin America and the Movement for Racial Improvement, 1918–1940* (Ithaca, N.Y., 1991).

On the reception of psychoanalysis, the Brazilian case is the best studied. See Gilberto S. Rocha, *Introdução ao nascimento da psicanálise no Brasil* (Rio de Janeiro, 1989); Marialzira Perestrello, 'Primeiros encontros com a psicanálise. Os precursores no Brasil (1899–1937)', in Sérvulo Figueira (ed.), *Efeito Psi: A influência da psicanálise* (Rio de Janeiro, 1988), pp. 151–81; Roberto Yutaka Sagawa, 'A psicanálise pioneira e os pioneiros da psicanálise em São Paulo', in Sérvulo Figueira (ed.), *Cultura da Psicanálise* (São Paulo, 1985), pp. 15–34; and Ana Cristina Figueiredo, 'O movimiento psicoanalítico no Rio de Janeiro na década de 70', in Joel Birman (ed.), *Precursores na história da psicanálise* (Rio de Janeiro, 1988), pp. 123–47. 'Precursors' in this literature refers to early commentators on Freud who were not canonically trained analysts. An important work on Peru is Honorio Delgado, *Freud y el psicoanálisis. Escritos y testimonios,* Javier Mariategui (ed.), (Lima, 1989). Garmán García's *La entrada del psicoanálisis en Argentina* (Buenos Aires, 1978) is a perceptive 'intrahistory' from a Lacanian perspective. More balanced are Jorge Balán's sociologically perceptive *Cuéntame tu vida: Una biografía colectiva del psicoanálisis argentino*

(Buenos Aires, 1991) and Hugo Vezzetti (ed.), *Freud en Buenos Aires* (Buenos Aires, 1989), an anthology of texts.

An excellent introduction to contemporary policy debates can be found in Hebe M. C. Vessuri, 'The social study of science in Latin America', *Social Studies of Science,* 17 (1987): 519–54. Two standard documents are Amílcar O. Herrera, *Ciencia y política en América Latina,* 9th edn (Mexico, D.F., 1985), and J. Leite Lopes, *Ciência e libertação,* 2nd edn (Rio de Janeiro, 1978). On the sociology of science in Mexico, see María Luisa Rodríguez Sala-Gomezgil and Adrián Chavero González, *El científico en México: Su formación en el extranjero, su incorporación y adecuación al sistema ocupacional mexicano* (Mexico, D.F., 1982). For a survey of recent Brazilian science, see the special section on 'Science in Brazil', *Nature,* 342 (1989): 355–74.

INDEX